UMI ANNUAL COMMENTARY

PRECEPTS FOR LIVING®

MISSION STATEMENT

$\mathcal{W}$e are called
of God to create, produce, and distribute
quality Christian education products;
to deliver exemplary customer service;
and to provide quality Christian
educational services, which will empower
God's people, especially within the Black
community, to evangelize, disciple,
and equip people for serving Christ,
His kingdom, and church.

UMI ANNUAL SUNDAY SCHOOL LESSON COMMENTARY
PRECEPTS FOR LIVING® 2020–2021
INTERNATIONAL SUNDAY SCHOOL LESSONS
VOLUME 23
UMI (URBAN MINISTRIES, INC.)

Melvin Banks Sr., LittD, Founder and Chairman

C. Jeffrey Wright, JD, CEO

Cheryl Price, PhD, Vice President of Content

Bible art: Fred Carter

Scripture quotations marked NLT are taken from the Holy Bible, New Living Translation, copyright © 1996, 2004, 2007, 2013, 2015 by Tyndale House Foundation. Used by permission of Tyndale House Publishers, Inc., Carol Stream, Illinois 60188.

Unless otherwise indicated, Scripture references are taken from the King James Version of the Bible.

Item No.: 1-2021. ISBN-13: 978-1-68353-516-4.

PFL Large Print Item No.: 1-2621. ISBN-13:978-1-68353-519-5

Publisher: UMI (Urban Ministries, Inc.), Chicago, IL 60643. To place an order, call us at 1-800-860-8642, or visit our website at www.urbanministries.com.

Get the Precepts for Living® e-book!

Are you among those reading books using a Kindle, iPad, NOOK, or other electronic readers? If so, there's good news for you! UMI (Urban Ministries, Inc.) is keeping up with the latest technology by publishing its annual Sunday School commentary, *Precepts for Living®*, in the leading e-book formats: Kindle (Amazon), NOOK (Barnes & Noble), and iBooks (Apple).

To buy an e-book copy of *Precepts for Living®*, visit our website at urbanministries.com/precepts to find download links and step-by-step instructions.

If you've purchased *Precepts for Living®*, for your e-reader, be sure to leave a rating and a review at the iTunes or Amazon store sites to tell others what you think. Also, spread the word on your favorite social networking sites, and follow *Precepts for Living®* on Facebook @ facebook.com/urbanministriesinc, @umichicago on Twitter, and @UMI on Instagram.

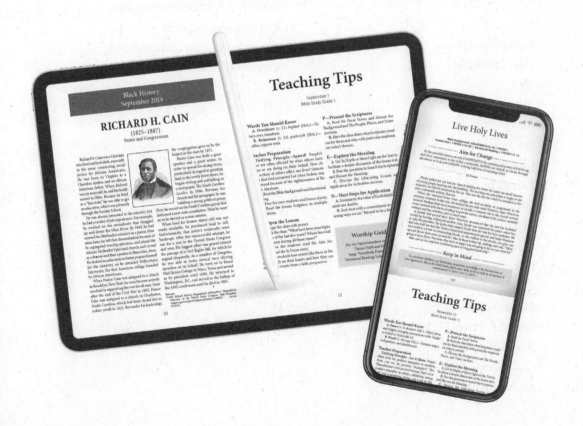

CONTRIBUTORS

Editor

Melvin Banks, Sr. LittD

Developmental Editor/Contributing Writer

Beth Potterveld, MA

Copy Editors

William McGee

Daschell Phillips

Jordan Clayton-Taylor

Cassie M. Chew

Cover Design

David Dawkins

Bible Illustrations

Fred Carter

Contributing Writers

Essays/In Focus Stories

Luvell Anderson, PhD

Kelvin Childs, BA

Dena Dyer

Peter Fenton, BA

Carolyn Greco, BA

Maisie Sparks, MA

Cheryl L. Price, PhD

Rosa Sailes, EdD

Craig Soaries, DMin

Michael Washington, MDiv

Bible Study Guide Writers

Jaimie Crumley, MDiv

Malcolm Foley, MDiv

Kimberly Gillespie, MA

Victoria McAfee, BA

Beverly Moore, MS

Maisie Sparks, MA

More Light on the Text

J. Ayodeji Adewuya, PhD

Norvella Carter, PhD

Moussa et Assita Coulibaly, PhD

Angela Lampkin, PhD

Alajemba Reuben Unaegbu, MA

Jeremy Williams, MDiv

Dear Friend,

It is hard to believe UMI is celebrating its 50th year!

It is commendable since only 30% of all small businesses ever reach this milestone.

UMI is blessed because people like you have believed in us and in the work we do. You have trusted us to remain true to our mission of providing biblical content contextualized for the African American community.

We have sought to remain faithful to the mission God gave us. My life mission was impressed upon me as a boy at twelve years of age while living in Birmingham, Alabama. An old man quoted Hosea 4:6 to me: "My people perish for lack of knowledge." After hearing the man quote that Bible verse, I decided to dedicate my life to studying and sharing God's Word with our people.

Through the years since God has honored this desire so now we can say as Samuel once said, "Up to this point the LORD has helped us!"(1 Samuel 7:12, NLT).

We are immensely grateful for the sustaining grace of God who has guided and provided for us all these 50 years.

But, in truth, our eyes are on the future. We strain our eyes to see what God has in store for us in the coming years.

That's because the world keeps changing in the way we receive and process information. When we began, ink on paper and audio were the main modes of communication. Today, digital content is reaching new heights. We will use this and other methods to keep proclaiming the Good News of God's love and forgiveness. We will keep teaching followers of Christ to fully engage in extending His Kingdom agenda.

Melvin Banks, Sr. LittD

Melvin E. Banks Sr, LittD

Editor, Founder, and Chairman, UMI

Uncovering the Benefits of Precepts

It is a great privilege to participate in Christian education and play a significant role in the spiritual formation of fellow Christians in our churches. *Precepts for Living*® is a resource that is designed to help you lead others toward greater knowledge and practice of following Jesus Christ. To that end, please take full advantage of the substantive offerings provided to you in this year's commentary.

We want the liberating lesson to help you think about collective application and perspective beyond the individual level and the "Application for Activation" to help you think about personal ways to live out the lessons' themes and draw closer to God.

From the standpoint of your vocation as a teacher, it is very important to be aware of the great responsibility that goes along with your position. James 3:1 reminds us that we have such a great opportunity in front of us that we run the risk of greater judgment if we are derelict in our duties. In the Gospels, Jesus is often referred to as "Teacher." Being a teacher means participating in one of the church's greatest tasks, one that the ancient church called "*catechesis*."

This is a strong word that helps us understand the great influence we have when we help our students learn about God's Word. It carries with it the idea of imparting the entirety of the faith to Christians. While many teachers might not be familiar with this word, the truth is that every time we help others learn about God's Word and ways, we are participating in this great task of the church that has been with us from the beginning. Unfortunately, this gets lost amid other concerns. As a teacher, you have an opportunity to energize or revitalize this aspect of your church's ministry. Reflect on how you have prepared for the challenge.

What is the goal when you use *Precepts for Living*® to open up the riches of the Bible to your students? It is beyond the mere acquisition of information. We want students to receive revelation that becomes application. Certainly, we want our students to grow in knowledge, but the knowledge we seek to pass on does not solely comprise Bible facts but includes a larger sense of comprehension where the information and doctrine conveyed is oriented toward a faithful life of discipleship. That is why it is called *Precepts for Living*®, and not Precepts for Knowing.

The "People, Places, and Times," "Background," "In Depth," and "More Light on the Text" sections are there to help you provide insight and understanding of the text. But the sections include more than a simple compilation of information. In each lesson, you will also see "In Focus" stories and "Liberating Lesson" and "Application for Activation" sections serving as catalysts for applying the biblical text to life situations. We as teachers must pass on knowledge that will enable our students to deepen their devotion to God in an upward focus and encourage them to better embody that devotion in a way that makes their lives a living witness to the world. Our hope from every lesson should be to inspire students to become the best living examples of the Scriptures with the understanding that their lives may be the only Bible some people ever read.

To best take advantage of this commentary, utilize the essays to emphasize quarterly themes and enhance the classroom experience.

We believe this commentary is a great tool to help form fully devoted followers of Christ, and we invite you to wholeheartedly partake in all of the resources provided here. May God be glorified as you play your part in this great task of the church!

Creative Teaching

New Features from
Precepts for Living® 2019-2020

Liberating Lesson Section

In each lesson there is a "Liberating Lesson" to replace the "Lesson In Our Society." This section is dedicated to highlighting parallels and or applications to modern life that are reflected in the Bible. This section challenges us to consider how the scriptures relate to our modern society and asks us to respond individually, collectively, and as a community to God's Word. There is a special emphasis on social justice or justice implications in Christian Scripture that the Liberating Lesson brings to the forefront.

Application for Activation Section

In each lesson there is an "Application for Activation" to replace the "Make It Happen." This section provides guidance for practical application the reader or the local church could pursue in response to the lesson to take the lesson from information to living activation.

More Tips for Teachers

• **Energizing the Class.** If the class does not seem as enthusiastic or energy is low, after you open with prayer, have everyone stretch to the sky or outward. Then tell the class to shake off the low energy, and open up their hands to receive the love of God that is right there. You can always have a 30-second meet and greet time. This usually helps to wake people up so you can begin class on a higher energy level.

• **Two Teachers in One Class—Bring Out the Best in Both.** Taking turns works in some classes, but in others, it creates tension and favorites. Encourage teachers to study together, and then divide the segments of the lesson. Perhaps one will teach the introduction while the other teaches a section of the text. Encourage them to also become a true team with each contributing throughout the lesson.

• **Variety.** Everyone cannot read or write at the same level. Use different teaching techniques and styles when teaching. How you learn affects how you teach, so be open and willing to learn and teach through various media.

• **Partner Up.** People often "get it" when they are involved with more than talking about the lesson. Why not allow the class to see the connections themselves? Try using a chart to have adult students work in pairs or groups to compare and contrast Bible people such as David and Solomon or Ruth and Orpah, Naomi's daughters-in-law. To help the students get started, suggest specific categories for comparisons such as lifestyles, families, or public ministry. As class members search the Scriptures, they will learn and remember much more than if you told them about either person individually.

• **Group Studies.** Have the class form groups, and have each group read the Scripture lesson and a section of the Background for the text. Have each group create a two-minute skit about the Scripture to share with the class. Encourage the groups to use their imaginations and energy. You may want to have at least one "leader" in a group if you have more than two or three reserved people in your class.

• **Volunteers.** Many classes begin with reading the lesson. When class members have studied beforehand, this activity is more about bringing minds together than about the actual lesson. Some classes can benefit from dramatic and creative reading of Bible passages at any point in the lesson. As the passage under study lends itself, assign parts to volunteers. This need not be formal—standing up isn't even critical. This strategy works best in passages that have a story such as the conversation between Moses and his father-in-law, Jethro, or Paul confronting the merchants in Thessalonica. Assign one person to each speaking character in the Bible text. Feel free to be creative by giving the class roles as "the crowd." Make sure to assign a narrator who will read the nonspeaking parts. It is fun, it is fast, and it makes for memorable Bible reading.

• **Materials.** You may want to have large sheets of paper, markers, glue or tape, newspapers, and magazines available weekly for the various activities.

• **Themes.** Write the theme on a large poster board or sheet of paper, and ask each person to write a word or draw a picture that best describes the theme. Read the themes aloud, and discuss any of the pictures before you begin your class discussion or activities. If you have a very large class or time is limited, only select a few words or pictures for discussion. You can either lead the discussion or invite members of the class to do so.

• **Websites.** Connect with us by logging onto www.urbanministries.com. Follow us on social media on Facebook at facebook.com/urbanministriesinc, @umichicago on Twitter, and @umi on Instagram.

• **Email us** at precepts@urbanministries.com, and send us some of your favorite Teaching Tips for ages 36 and older that you want to share with others. If yours is selected, we will post them under our Teaching Tips sections for Precepts. If you have ice-breaker activities, please submit them as well.

• **Prayer.** Have a Prayer Request Board for people to write their prayer requests on each Sunday. You may want to make this a weekly activity. Have someone read the prayer request and let the class decide which prayer requests they will pray for during the week. One Sunday School teacher has his class write their prayer requests on sheets of paper and place them in the middle of the floor once a year. He then shares with the class that he will write them all down in a prayer journal that he keeps and prays over them at least once a week. Be creative and create your own prayer journal or prayer tradition(s) within your class.

• **Closing.** At the end of the lesson, give your class the assignment of looking for scenes from films or television, advertisements, or parts of songs that either demonstrate the coming week's "In Focus" story, "Liberating Lesson" section, or "Application for Activation" section. Encourage them to be creative and to come up with an explanation of how their contribution helps make the truth of the lesson come to life.

TABLE OF CONTENTS

Contributors..iv
Letter from the Founder..........................v
Uncovering the Benefits of Precepts......vi
Creative Teaching..................................vii
2016–2022 Scope and Sequence-Cycle Spread.....xi

Fall Quarter 2020

LOVE FOR ONE ANOTHER

September 2020 Quarter At-A-Glance.................1
Engaging the Theme: *God Loves Us*.........................4
Christian Education in Action: *God's Song of Love, Our Song of Praise*.....................................6
Black History: *Gwendolyn Brooks*...........................9

LESSONS
Unit 1: Struggles With Love
SEPTEMBER

6   Issues of Love
    Genesis 37:2-11, 23-24, 28..............................10
13 God Rewards Obedience
    Genesis 41:25-33, 37-40, 50-52.....................21
20 Love Versus Guilt
    Genesis 42:6-25...32
27 God's Plan Revealed
    Genesis 45:1-15...45

Unit 2: What Is Love?
OCTOBER

4   Love and Devotion to Others
    1 Samuel 19:1-7...56
11 Love Your Enemies
    Luke 6:27-36..67
18 Loving Your Neighbor
    Luke 10:25-37..78
25 Love Divine
    1 Corinthians 13..90

Unit 3: Godly Love Among Believers
NOVEMBER

1   Loving by Serving
    John 13:1-15, 34-35.....................................101
8   Abiding Love
    John 15:4-17..112
15 Confident Love
    1 John 3:11-24...123
22 Sharing Love
    Acts 4:32-5:11...134
29 Impartial Love
    James 2:1-13..145

Winter Quarter 2020–2021

CALL IN THE NEW TESTAMENT

December 2020 Quarter-At-A-Glance.............155
Engaging the Theme: *Callings of God*.................157
Christian Education in Action: *Calling, Character, and Compassion*.....................................160
Black History: *William Still*...............................163

LESSONS
Unit 1: The Beginning of a Call
DECEMBER

6   Called through Heritage
    Matthew 1:1-6, 16-17; Hebrews 1:1-5.........165
13 Called Before Birth
    Matthew 1:18-25..177
20 A Regal Response to Holy Light
    Matthew 2:7-15..188
27 Called to Prepare the Way
    Matthew 3:1-12..199

Unit 2: Jesus and Calls in His Ministry
JANUARY

3   Called to Proclaim
    Luke 4:14-22..211
10 Called to Significance
    Luke 5:1-11..222
17 Called to Heal
    Mark 2:1-12..233
24 Called as the Intercessor
    John 17:14-24...244

Unit 3: The Call of Women

31 Prophesying Daughters
    Luke 2:36-38; Acts 2:16-21; 21:8-9..............255

FEBRUARY

7   Called to Evangelize
    John 4:25-42..265
14 Mary Magdalene: A Faithful Disciple
    Luke 8:1-3; Mark 15:40; John 20:10-18.......276
21 Priscilla: Called to Minister
    Acts: 18:1-3, 18-21, 24-26; Romans 16:3-4...288
28 Lydia: Called to Serve
    Acts 16:11-15, 40; 1 Corinthians 1:26-30....300

Spring Quarter 2021

PROPHETS FAITHFUL TO GOD'S COVENANT
March 2021 Quarter At-A-Glance 313
Engaging the Theme: *The Call of God, Part I*.....315
Christian Education in Action: *The Call of God, Part II*......316
Black History: *John Hope Franklin*....................318

LESSONS
Unit 1: Faithful Prophets
MARCH

7   Moses: Prophet of Deliverance
    Deuteronomy 18:15-22 319
14 Joshua: Prophet of Conquest
    Joshua 5:13-6:5, 15-16, 20 329
21 Huldah: Prophet of Wisdom
    2 Kings 22:14-20 340
28 Elijah: Prophet of Courage
    1 Kings 18:5-18 351

Unit 2: Prophets of Restoration
APRIL

4   Salvation is Sealed
    Luke 24:13-16, 22-35 362
11 Ezra: Faith and Action Preacher
    Ezra 10:1-12 374
18 Nehemiah: The Captive Cupbearer
    Rebuilds a Nation
    Nehemiah 2:11-20 386
25 A Plea for Restoration
    Lamentations 5 397

Unit 3: Courageous Prophets of Change
MAY

2   Micaiah: Speaking Truth to Power
    1 Kings 22:15-23, 26-28 409
9   Isaiah: Offering Hope for the Future
    Isaiah 29:13-24.. 420
16 Jeremiah: The Suffering Preacher
    Jeremiah 38:14-23 432
23 Ezekiel: Street Preacher to the Exiles
    Ezekiel 18:1-9, 30-32 443
30 Jonah: Do the Right Thing
    Jonah 3 454

Summer Quarter 2021

CONFIDENT HOPE
June 2021 Quarter At-A-Glance..........................463
Engaging the Theme: *Recipe for Hope*..............465
Christian Education in Action: *Looking for Hope in All the Right Places* 467
Black History: *Paul Cuffe* 470

LESSONS
Unit 1: Jesus Teaches about Faith
JUNE

6   Why Do You Worry?
    Matthew 6:25-34...................................... 472
13 Why Are You Afraid?
    Matthew 8:23-27...................................... 483
20 Healed by Faith
    Matthew 9:18-26...................................... 491
27 Who Do You Doubt?
    Matthew 14:22-33..................................... 501

JULY
4   An Attitude of Gratitude
    Leviticus 13:45-46; Luke 17:11-19............... 512

Unit 2: Faith and Salvation
11 The Power of the Gospel
    Romans 1:8-17.. 522
18 The Faith of Abraham
    Romans 4:1-12.. 533
25 Justification through Faith
    Romans 5:1-11.. 545

AUGUST
1   Salvation for All Who Believe
    Romans 10:5-17....................................... 556

Unit 3: Faith Gives Us Hope
8   Meaning of Faith
    Hebrews 11:1-8, 13-16 567
15 A Persevering Faith
    Hebrews 10:23-36..................................... 579
22 A Conquering Faith
    1 John 4:2-3, 13-17; 5:4-5........................... 591
29 Hope Eternal
    2 Corinthians 4:16-5:10.............................. 601

Glossary...612

2016–2022
SCOPE & SEQUENCE–CYCLE SPREAD

	FALL	WINTER	SPRING	SUMMER
1 YEAR 2016-17	**GOD: SOVEREIGNTY** **Sovereignty of God** Isaiah Matthew Hebrews Revelation	**CREATION** **Creation: A Divine Cycle** Psalms Luke Galatians	**LOVE** **God Loves Us** Psalms Joel Jonah John Romans Ephesians 1 John	**CALL** **God's Urgent Call** Exodus Judges Isaiah Jeremiah Ezekiel Amos Acts
2 YEAR 2017-18	**COVENANT** **Covenant with God** Genesis Exodus Numbers 1 & 2 Samuel Nehemiah Jeremiah Ezekiel 1 Corinthians Hebrews	**FAITH** **Faith in Action** Daniel Matthew Acts Ephesians Colossians 1 Timothy James	**WORSHIP** **Acknowledging God** Genesis Exodus Leviticus 2 Chronicles Psalms Luke John 2 Corinthians Hebrews Revelation	**JUSTICE** **Justice in the New Testament** Matthew Luke Romans 2 Corinthians Colossians
3 YEAR 2018-19	**CREATION** **God's World and God's People** Genesis	**LOVE** **Our Love for God** Exodus Deuteronomy Joshua Psalms Matthew Mark Luke Philippians 2 Thessalonians James 2 John	**CALL** **Discipleship and Mission** Matthew Luke Romans	**COVENANT** **Covenant in God** Ruth 1 Samuel Matthew Luke John Ephesians Hebrews Romans

2016–2022
SCOPE & SEQUENCE–CYCLE SPREAD

	FALL	WINTER	SPRING	SUMMER
4 YEAR 2019-20	**FAITH** **Responding to God's Grace** Genesis Exodus Numbers Deuteronomy 1 Samuel 1 Kings Luke 2 Corinthians 1 Thessalonians 1 & 2 Peter	**WORSHIP** **Honoring God** 1 & 2 Chronicles 1 Kings Ecclesiastes Matthew Luke	**JUSTICE** **Justice and the Prophets** Esther Isaiah Jeremiah Hosea Amos Micah Habakkuk Zephaniah Zachariah Malachi 1 Corinthians	**GOD–WISDOM** **Many Faces of Wisdom** Proverbs Ecclesiastes Matthew Mark Luke John James
5 YEAR 2020-21	**LOVE** **Love for One Another** Genesis 1 & 2 Samuel Luke John Acts 1 Corinthians James 1, 2, & 3 John	**CALL** **Call in the New Testament** Isaiah Matthew Mark Luke John Acts Romans 1 Corinthians Hebrews 2 Timothy	**COVENANT** **Prophets Faithful to God's Covenant** Deuteronomy Joshua 1 & 2 Kings Ezra Nehemiah Isaiah Jeremiah Lamentations Ezekiel Luke	**FAITH** **Confident Hope** Matthew Mark Luke Romans 2 Corinthians Hebrews 1 John
6 YEAR 2021-22	**WORSHIP** **Celebrating God** Exodus 2 Samuel Ecclesiastes Psalms Mark Luke Acts Revelation	**JUSTICE** **Justice, Law, History** Genesis Exodus Deuteronomy 2 Samuel 1 Kings Ezra Job Isaiah Nahum Luke	**GOD–LIBERATION** **God Frees and Redeems** Deuteronomy Ezra Matthew John Romans Galatians	**CREATION** **Partners in a News Creation** Isaiah John Revelation

Love For One Another

God commands us to love one another as God loves us. This quarter begins with a widely known story about Joseph, which deals with love within Jacob's family. From the Joseph story, we proceed with God's laws requiring care and concern for the poor and needy, loving and embracing of the stranger, and the demands of love for one another in the teachings of Jesus in the Gospels. These sessions elaborate on themes of love for one another in the epistles of Paul and James and the expressions of love in the early formations of the church in Acts.

UNIT 1 • Struggles with Love

This unit has four sessions. The lessons reveal aspects of love. Session 1 reveals how a lack of familial love devolves into jealousy and destruction. Session 2 portrays Joseph's commitment to love that refuses to hold on to past wrongs but rather seeks God's path to future success. Sessions 3 and 4 show Joseph's brothers coming to Egypt and reveal how love and reconciliation can prevail in spite of harsh and negative circumstances.

Lesson 1: September 6, 2020
Issues of Love
Genesis 37:2–11, 23–24, 28

Jealousy, hate, and love are emotions that people experience in their families. How do people deal with these emotions? An absence of love for Joseph by his brothers led to envy and finally a plot to kill him.

Lesson 2: September 13, 2020
God Rewards Obedience
Genesis 41:25–33, 37–40, 50–52

It may be difficult to hold on to dreams of future success when faced with extreme hardships. What inner resources are needed to continue one's quest for success? Because Joseph loved and obeyed God, he was able to engage in wise and discerning problem-solving that motivated Pharaoh to appoint him second in command over all of Egypt.

Lesson 3: September 20, 2020
Love versus Guilt
Genesis 42:6–25

Some people allow the guilt of the past to poison their present. Is it ever possible to be free from condemnation for past actions? When Joseph saw and remembered his brothers who sold him into Egyptian slavery, he showed compassion while motivating them to recall and take responsibility for their earlier actions.

Lesson 4: September 27, 2020
God's Plan Revealed
Genesis 45:1–8, 10–15

Sometimes one is overwhelmed by tragic events in his or her life. What can keep hope alive after the struggle ends? Joseph tells his brothers what they meant as the harm was God's plan for saving them, a remnant of God's people.

UNIT 2 • Inclusive Love

This unit has four sessions. The focus of the lessons is on love for the stranger, the poor, and enemies as well as divine love reflected in human life. First Samuel shows David's love for others. Luke explores the teachings of Jesus regarding love for one's enemies and Jesus' parable of the good Samaritan. First Corinthians explores the sermon on love from Paul's writing, which depicts the height of human love coming from divine love.

Lesson 5: October 4, 2020
Love and Devotion to Others
I Samuel 19:1–7

Although families are important, family dysfunction can skew our priorities and lead us to ruin. Is there a greater priority than family? Jonathan opposed the unjust intentions of his father, King Saul, in order to offer support and protection to David.

Lesson 6: October 11, 2020
Love Your Enemies
Luke 6:27–36

We often wonder how we should treat our enemies. How should we respond to them? Jesus taught his disciples to love their enemies by forgiving them, responding to their needs, and by being nonjudgmental.

Lesson 7: October 18, 2020
Loving Your Neighbor
Luke 10:25–37

Selfish desires, self-gratification, and self-interests are highly valued in our time. How can we become better neighbors to one another? Jesus challenges us to address the needs and welfare of everyone, including perceived enemies.

Lesson 8: October 25, 2020
Love Divine
1 Corinthians 13

Special gifts such as knowledge and wisdom can easily make us lose sight of our obligations to others. How can we avoid being pleased with ourselves? Paul suggested that love is the best way to relate to others and forget one's own status.

UNIT 3 • Godly Love Among Believers

This unit contains five sessions. John elaborates on how believers love by serving and portray Jesus' explanation of the intertwining love of God for Jesus and for those who abide in Christ. First John clarifies the abiding love of God through the Holy Spirit, which makes it possible for us to love one another. Acts reveals the expression of the love of God in the formation of the early Christian community by the workings of the Holy Spirit. James tells of the love of neighbor as the fulfillment of the law of God.

Lesson 9: November 1, 2020
Loving By Serving
John 13:1–15, 34–35

Multiple definitions of *love* lead people to be confused about how to love. What is the bottom line ("end") when it comes to love? Jesus taught that our love for one another should be manifested in our service to others.

Lesson 10: November 8, 2020
Abiding Love
John 15:4–17

We try to love, but we feel beaten down by the world's greed and jealousy. How can we love one another in the face of the world's selfishness? Jesus declares that we will be able to love one another if we abide in Him, keep the commandments, and abide in His love as the Holy Spirit abides in us.

Lesson 11: November 15, 2020
Confident Love
I John 3:11-24

Hatred toward others sometimes seems far easier to attain than love. How can we show love for others? The willingness of Jesus to die for us and His command that we live for others brings that confidence.

Lesson 12: November 22, 2020
Sharing Love
Acts 4:32–5:11

In every community, there are people who have less than they need to maintain healthy lives. How can we best meet the needs of everyone in our communities? As the first believers in Jesus shared everything in common, the needs of every one were satisfied.

Lesson 13: November 29, 2020
Impartial Love
James 2:1–13

Favoring one person or group over others is a common occurrence in human relationships. Why is it unacceptable to show partiality to certain people or groups? James reminds us that love requires us to treat everyone equally.

God Loves Us

The most important thing in the world is to know that you are loved by the Creator of the universe. All the riches and wealth of this world cannot buy this love. No one is beautiful enough to attract this love. It is given solely because of God's free will. The question then becomes, how do we know that God loves us? It is easy for us to measure human love. We see how much someone loves us here on earth by the things they do for us. Children know their parents love them by the countless hours they spend training and rearing them. Husbands and wives know whether their spouse loves them by spending quality time together and sacrificing for each other. So how do we know and understand God's love for us when He is invisible?

One of the ways that we know God loves us is the beautiful world He has provided for us. He has given us the sun's dazzling light and the verdant fields and meadows. The spectacular heights of the Himalayas and the crystal blue tropical waters of the Caribbean are gifts from our Creator. Not to mention all of the delicious foods we eat—we get to experience different flavors from mango to barbecue chicken. There is so much God has given us on this earth to explore and enjoy. Just the experience of life is caused to acknowledge that our Creator loves us.

Still, we also have another way to know that God loves us. We can see that God loves us through reading the pages of His love letter, the Bible. There we see a God who walks faithfully with His people even when they do not walk faithfully with Him. Time after time Israel broke their covenant with God and worshiped idols but that did not break God's covenant love for them. God displayed an unfailing covenant love with Israel and no matter how many times they turned their back on Him, He would not turn His back on them.

Not only that, but God promised them a new covenant (Jeremiah 31:31-34). This covenant would wipe away all of their sins and enable Him to write His laws on their hearts. He would give them a new heart and a new spirit. Every covenant is enacted with blood; this covenant would be no different. The only difference is that the blood that enacted this covenant would be His own. He gave His very life to secure a relationship with us. Jesus on the Cross is the sure sign of God's love for us. Every nail and every thorn paid the price for our sins. Every lash of the whip and every bruise was for us.

When we believe in this love, then God sends His Spirit into our hearts and confirms it to be true. God does love us. There is no question of His love when we look at the Cross. It is the ultimate testament of love.

The gift of creation, the pages of the Bible, Jesus' sacrifice on the Cross, and the Spirit living inside of us answer the question of whether God loves us. This is easy to know mentally, though it still may be difficult to experience. Still, we must trust that nothing can separate us from this love (Romans 8:38-39). All of these things are pledges and tokens of God's immeasurable and unfathomable love for us. It is there for us to experience; we must rest in knowing the truth of who God is and the power of His love.

"And may you have the power to understand, as all God's people should, how wide, how long, how high, and how deep his love is" (Ephesians 3:18, NLT).

God's Song of Love, Our Song of Praise

by Michael Washington

Gospel choirs fascinate me. As a singer in my childhood, I remember learning songs, practicing parts, and, of course, singing with others. Along with warm-ups and learning material, watching, submitting to, and obeying the choir director makes music happen. Whether the choir is clapping, swaying, or moaning, attention to a director enables and empowers any choral group. Without the direction of a conductor, the group flounders without vision, motivation, or effectiveness.

Following leaders not only equips choirs for singing but also empowers Christians to live faithfully by God's Word. Once we encounter the life and ministry of Jesus, we are changed, gradually but totally. Where our thoughts and insights were once instruments of God's enemies, they now become tools for God's use and purpose. God's presentation of love in Jesus Christ compels us to respond. As Christian leaders and teachers who respond to God's love, we must also demonstrate ways to represent God's love to others, so that those who follow us are following God too.

Faithfulness remains the goal of Christian leaders, too. Striving to live under the Spirit's direction, leaders watch, submit to, and obey God. Effective leaders live and serve in response to the Gospel's claim on their lives. The Gospel invites and challenges Christians to embody the words and truths in Scripture. It is a starting point for life that empowers leaders to serve the people of God.

God Loves Us

Love reveals itself. Often love changes the complexions of our relationships or it alters the relationship between two people. Love energizes life. Love illuminates people. It challenges our words. In romantic relationships, we may hide love until it seems best to confess it. The lover gathers facts as he or she considers whether their love will be received and reciprocated. Only when a person is comfortable with vulnerability (the inherent risk that comes with devotion) will they reveal their love and the other disclose their care.

However powerful, the love that people have for each other pales in comparison to God's perfect love, a love we know because of Jesus Christ. God shares the love with us in that, when we were farthest from God, Jesus gave the most to us. Because of His love, Jesus affords us communion with God.

The Lord's example is clear in Scripture, giving us the opportunity to have fellowship with God. Jesus prayed, worshiped, and gave of Himself. Jesus sent us the Holy Spirit, and we come to know God as we receive the Holy Spirit. Capturing that great Spirit of Christ happens when we follow Him. Certainly, the only way to discover what it means to follow and be a disciple of Christ is to yield ourselves to His Lordship. Jesus performed acts of service to humankind and we follow after Him when we do the same.

Because of God's radical grace, we can know God in Christ. We look to Him and see the image of God without blemish, sin, or brokenness. In Jesus Christ, we see perfect divinity and impeccable humanity. He discloses who we are and who God is.

Responding to God's Grace

There have always been responses to God's gracious acts of revelation. From the earliest moments when the creative Word brought life from nothing, life has reacted in varied ways. Chief among those reactions is praise to our God and Creator. Creation responds to God in worship. When God spoke and created life out of nothing, creation's response to God's Word was worship. Everything in the created order pleased God by giving its best in praise to the Creator. What God brought forth met its destiny in the worship of God. Humankind included the world and all that dwells therein still meets its destiny when blessing God.

Worship settles the matter of lordship. It redirects the affections of our hearts and reaffirms the sovereignty of God over our lives. In worship, we express our belief that God manages our time and that we live by grace and in God's grace. In moments of reflection, singing, and praying in the church, with prayer partners or during our daily commute, God works His perfect love into our hearts.

A second response to God's actions in our lives is faithful service to God and others. While worship takes different forms, service is always discernible to the eyes. Serving opens itself to the scrutiny and examination of others. Never internal, service moves outward, ensuring that we mirror God's works in our daily lives.

In the early church, the apostles and followers of the Way were devoted to more than worship and teaching. The main concern was the spread of this new message that had at its core the ministry of a Jewish carpenter who died and rose from the dead. Teaching the implications of Jesus' ministry was a concern that the apostles and leaders after them took seriously. Among their other primary concerns, however, were justice in applying doctrines, fairness in acknowledging the gifts of all persons, and equity in the distribution of food and resources to the people. These ethical concerns colored the service of our apostolic fathers and mothers. Still, they continue to reintroduce themselves in the contemporary church.

As in the early apostolic days of Christian history, the Black church in America faces issues of justice, fairness, and equity. Acknowledgment of the contributions of Black people rested at the core of particular leaders' decisions to form separate denominations where Black men and women were welcomed and embraced as the body of Christ. The involvement of women of color in positions of leadership continues to emerge. The willingness and gifts of sisters and the record of their enormous contributions to the development of the church (past and present) during its various embryonic stages remain challenged by many and silently embraced by few. The best thinkers in our wide community continually debate as to whether the structures of our day—the political, social, and economic structures—present Black Christians with similar opportunities as they do other Christians.

All these issues leave us at the door of the church, at the foot of the altar. They provide us with the hunger to pursue justice, peace, and love in tangible ways. Our hunger and thirst for righteousness are not without challenges. In addition to the structural challenges already mentioned, systemic hindrances stop the progress of many individuals in the form of psychological challenges. The greatest of these is fear.

We fear a change in our personal and corporate lives. Therefore, growth approaches impossibility. Fear, then, cancels faith, that necessary element to please God. Without faith, the movement toward God is impossible. Dedicated worship and service remedies fear, granting us a clear vision of Jesus Christ and His love for us. In the words of that gospel hymn, when nothing else can help, His love lifts us.

―――――――――

Michael Washington holds a BS in psychology from the University of Illinois, an MA in theological studies from Wheaton College, an MDiv at Garrett-Evangelical Theological Seminary, and is completeing his doctorate at the same institution.

GWENDOLYN BROOKS

(1917-2000)
Poet and Novelist

Gwendolyn Brooks was born in Topeka, Kansas. Soon afterward her parents, David and Keziah Brooks, moved the family to Chicago. She grew up on the city's South Side in the Hyde Park area. Many of her poems draw from her experiences growing up in Chicago and from the people she knew there.

Brooks was deeply devoted to her family. The strength of her commitment to the family unit derived from her strong, loving relationship with her parents and her brother Raymond, and was evidenced in her own family of her husband, fellow poet Henry Blakely, and their two children Henry, Jr. and Nora. Yet Gwendolyn Brooks' poetry showed that her sense of family did not end at her doorstep. To her, family referred to the overall Black "family" or "community" oneness.

In response to the Black Power Movement of the 1960s, a new element was added to Brooks' poems. She felt especially unified with all of Black America when Dr. Martin Luther King was assassinated in 1968 and when ensuing riots swept across the country. That same year, her book *In the Mecca* detailed the overcrowded, often dangerous conditions of the inner city. The following year, with the release of *Riot Brooks*, she began publishing exclusively with Black-owned presses. She furthered her Black awakening with a pilgrimage to West Africa in 1971.

Gwendolyn Brooks was a participant in the so-called "revolt" of Black intellectuals. Their work ushered in a new self-awareness that resulted in a period of self-naming and self-legitimization. The outcome of this literary movement was a new Black Renaissance that surpassed the "Negro Renaissance" of the 1920s. Other major names of this period included: James Baldwin, Nikki Giovanni, Imamu Baraka, and Lorraine Hansberry.

Brooks' rejection of the clenched fist-militancy of the era resulted in some of her greatest works, like "Beckonings" published in 1975. In the poem "Primer for Blacks", she explains what Blackness is to her: "Blackness is a title/is a preoccupation, is a commitment Blacks/are to comprehend—and in which are to perceive your Glory."

In her 1972 book, *Report From Part One: An Autobiography*, Gwendolyn Brooks explains the change that took place inside her and how it affected her writing: "I—who have 'gone the gamut' … am qualified to enter at least the kindergarten of new consciousness now. New consciousness and trudge toward progress.

"I have hope for myself."

Teaching Tips

Words You Should Know

A. Dream (v. 5) *chalom* (Heb.)—A prophetic or ordinary dream

B. Pit (v. 20) *bor* (Heb.)—A hole used to hold water, a cistern

Teacher Preparation

Unifying Principle—When Love is Lost. Jealousy, hate, and love are emotions that people experience in their families. How do people deal with these emotions? An absence of love for Joseph by his brothers led to envy and finally a plot to kill him.

A. Read the Bible Background and Devotional Reading.

B. Pray for your students and lesson clarity.

C. Read the lesson Scripture in multiple translations.

O—Open the Lesson

A. Begin the class with prayer.

B. Invite participants to share memories of sibling rivalry. Help students compare and contrast the family rivalries of Joseph and his brothers with those of Isaac and Ishmael (Genesis 21:8-9) and Jacob and Esau (Genesis 27).

C. Have the students read the Aim for Change and the In Focus story.

D. Ask students how events like those in the story weigh on their hearts and how they can view these events from a faith perspective.

P—Present the Scriptures

A. Read the Focal Verses and discuss the Background and The People, Places, and Times sections.

B. Have the class share what Scriptures stand out for them and why, with particular emphasis on today's themes.

E—Explore the Meaning

A. Use In Depth or More Light on the Text to facilitate a deeper discussion of the lesson text.

B. Pose the questions in Search the Scriptures and Discuss the Meaning.

C. Discuss the Liberating Lesson and Application for Activation sections.

N—Next Steps for Application

A. Summarize the value of being guided by love rather than jealousy.

B. Challenge the class to find ways to be peacemakers rather than combatants in family disputes.

> ## Worship Guide
>
> For the Superintendent or Teacher
> Theme: Issues of Love
> Song: "Blest Be the Tie That Binds"
> Devotional Reading: Psalm 105:1-6, 16-22

Issues of Love

Bible Background • GENESIS 37
Printed Text • GENESIS 37:2-11, 23-24, 28 | Devotional Reading • PSALM 105:1-6, 16-22

—— Aim for Change ——

By the end of this lesson, we will EXAMINE the circumstances of familial love and hatred between Jacob/Israel's sons, REPENT of times we allowed jealousy and hatred to override a commitment to love, and DEVELOP strategies to allow a commitment to love to override feelings of jealousy and hatred.

—— In Focus ——

Kathy always felt her church could provide greater assistance to locals facing occupational struggles from a lack of education. Her deep passion for this issue led her to approach the church board to ask to start a literacy project for teen moms. Kathy didn't know all of the Board members before she made her presentation, but she went in confident that God had given her a plan that would be of benefit to the church and the community. When the Board members started asking questions, Kathy answered as honestly and humbly as she could. She noticed, however, that one board member seemed to take issue with every point. Something about the woman seemed familiar but Kathy couldn't remember it.

Suddenly it dawned on her. This was Sonya's mother. Kathy and Sonya had been good friends in the early years of grade school, but just before high school, the girls lost touch. Kathy knew that Sonya had some hard times after she had her first child and dropped out of school. That was fifteen years ago and it didn't seem like Sonya's life had gotten easier.

She thought her presentation went well, but Sonya's mother's questions made her wonder if she would get their support. "How did you become an expert in the educational needs of single moms?" This type of questioning was obviously driven by jealousy, but would the other board members recognize that? All Kathy could do was wait and pray.

In today's lesson, we will examine what happens when relationships are not rooted in love, as they should be. What consequences have you seen when you let jealousy and bitterness disturb your relationships?

—— Keep in Mind ——

"And his brethren envied him; but his father observed the saying"
(Genesis 37:11, KJV).

"But while his brothers were jealous of Joseph, his father wondered what the dreams meant" (Genesis 37:11, NLT).

Focal Verses

KJV **Genesis 37:2** These are the generations of Jacob. Joseph, being seventeen years old, was feeding the flock with his brethren; and the lad was with the sons of Bilhah, and with the sons of Zilpah, his father's wives: and Joseph brought unto his father their evil report.

3 Now Israel loved Joseph more than all his children, because he was the son of his old age: and he made him a coat of many colours.

4 And when his brethren saw that their father loved him more than all his brethren, they hated him, and could not speak peaceably unto him.

5 And Joseph dreamed a dream, and he told it his brethren: and they hated him yet the more.

6 And he said unto them, Hear, I pray you, this dream which I have dreamed:

7 For, behold, we were binding sheaves in the field, and, lo, my sheaf arose, and also stood upright; and, behold, your sheaves stood round about, and made obeisance to my sheaf.

8 And his brethren said to him, Shalt thou indeed reign over us? or shalt thou indeed have dominion over us? And they hated him yet the more for his dreams, and for his words.

9 And he dreamed yet another dream, and told it his brethren, and said, Behold, I have dreamed a dream more; and, behold, the sun and the moon and the eleven stars made obeisance to me.

10 And he told it to his father, and to his brethren: and his father rebuked him, and said unto him, What is this dream that thou hast dreamed? Shall I and thy mother and thy brethren indeed come to bow down ourselves to thee to the earth?

11 And his brethren envied him; but his father observed the saying.

23 And it came to pass, when Joseph was come unto his brethren, that they strip Joseph

NLT **Genesis 37:2** This is the account of Jacob and his family. When Joseph was seventeen years old, he often tended his father's flocks. He worked for his half brothers, the sons of his father's wives Bilhah and Zilpah. But Joseph reported to his father some of the bad things his brothers were doing.

3 Jacob loved Joseph more than any of his other children because Joseph had been born to him in his old age. So one day Jacob had a special gift made for Joseph—a beautiful robe.

4 But his brothers hated Joseph because their father loved him more than the rest of them. They couldn't say a kind word to him.

5 One night Joseph had a dream, and when he told his brothers about it, they hated him more than ever.

6 "Listen to this dream," he said.

7 "We were out in the field, tying up bundles of grain. Suddenly my bundle stood up, and your bundles all gathered around and bowed low before mine!"

8 His brothers responded, "So you think you will be our king, do you? Do you actually think you will reign over us?" And they hated him all the more because of his dreams and the way he talked about them.

9 Soon Joseph had another dream, and again he told his brothers about it. "Listen, I have had another dream," he said. "The sun, moon, and eleven stars bowed low before me!"

10 This time he told the dream to his father as well as to his brothers, but his father scolded him. "What kind of dream is that?" he asked. "Will your mother and I and your brothers actually come and bow to the ground before you?"

11 But while his brothers were jealous of Joseph, his father wondered what the dreams meant.

23 So when Joseph arrived, his brothers ripped off the beautiful robe he was wearing.

out of his coat, his coat of many colours that was on him;

24 And they took him, and cast him into a pit: and the pit was empty, there was no water in it.

28 Then there passed by Midianites merchantmen; and they drew and lifted up Joseph out of the pit, and sold Joseph to the Ishmeelites for twenty pieces of silver: and they brought Joseph into Egypt.

24 Then they grabbed him and threw him into the cistern. Now the cistern was empty; there was no water in it.

28 So when the Ishmaelites, who were Midianite traders, came by, Joseph's brothers pulled him out of the cistern and sold him to them for twenty pieces of silver. And the traders took him to Egypt.

The People, Places, and Times

Blended Families. Joseph and his eleven brothers were the sons of Jacob (Israel) but had four different mothers (Leah, Rachel, Zilpah, and Bilhah). While God does not favor polygamy, it was often practiced and resulted in ancient cultures and resulted in complicated family structures. Firstborn sons had prominence because they would inherit the most. However, the father would often adjust the inheritance based on his preference for his sons or their mothers. Reuben was the eldest of all the sons, but Jacob did not favor Reuben's mother, Leah. Joseph was the first born of Jacob's favorite wife, Rachel, but he was the eleventh born of the twelve sons. Sons often jockeyed for position with their father and among themselves.

Cistern. The Hebrew word translated to "a deep hole" (v. 20) describes the place where Joseph was cast by his brothers. It is commonly believed by historians that the "pit" into which Joseph was cast was most probably a cistern. A cistern was a pear-shaped hole in the ground, so the opening at the top was small, but the bottom was significantly larger. Although the cistern was mainly used to store water, when it was not being used for its primary purpose, it served as a dungeon. The shape of these pits made it nearly impossible for a captive to escape without help.

Background

Genesis 29–30 tells the story of Jacob's marriage to both Leah and Rachel. Jacob always declared that he loved Rachel. The competition of the two sisters for the love of this man created a rivalry that was always evident in the home and was passed down to their children. When Rachel was unable to bear sons for Jacob and when Leah thought that her time of childbearing was over, they each gave Jacob a maidservant to bear children for Jacob in their stead. These maidservants were Zilpah and Bilhah. This practice was common and is reminiscent of Sarah giving Hagar to bear a son to Abraham (Genesis 16). That union similarly produced rivalry between the women, between their children, and between the nations that sprang from them for generations to come.

Joseph and his brothers inherited their mothers' rivalry. Israel (Jacob) clearly favored Joseph above the rest, and this provoked the brothers, egged on by Joseph's tattling and bragging about his divinely inspired dreams. Therefore, the brothers seize an opportunity to do away with their younger brother. When Joseph comes to them while they are far from their father's land, they plot to kill him. Reuben convinces them to change their minds and throw him in a cistern instead, thinking he can come back later to save Joseph and win favor with Jacob. While Reuben is gone, however, the brothers change their minds again and sell Joseph into slavery; they are pleased to get rid of the object of their jealousy in any way possible.

At-A-Glance

1. The Provocation (Genesis 37:2–4)
2. Joseph Tells His Dreams (vv. 5–11)
3. Joseph's Brothers Act (vv. 23–24, 28)

In Depth

1. The Provocation (Genesis 37:2–4)

Joseph is seventeen and tending his father's flock with his brothers; however, when they return home, Joseph tells on his brothers for bad behavior. To make it worse, Jacob loves Joseph more than his other children. Our text does not say that Jacob did not love his other children, simply that he loved Joseph more. Jacob was an old man and Joseph the son by Jacob's favorite wife. No doubt these sentiments were behind his partiality. Jacob also makes Joseph a coat. The coat was an ornate garment, likely with long sleeves, which meant the one wearing it was not expected to labor. It was a symbol of Jacob's favoritism and may have indicated Jacob's desire to turn the family birthright over to Joseph.

The brothers, angered by this, do not realize that each person does not always receive the same treatment in relationships. This partiality results in sibling rivalry, provoking the jealousy of Joseph's brothers. Their hatred was so intense they "could not speak peaceably unto him." Jacob's favoritism toward Joseph brings about family conflicts.

How is favoritism shown in modern families?

2. Joseph Tells His Dreams (vv. 5–11)

Joseph shares two dreams with his brothers. The first centers on a farming metaphor. In it, Joseph and his brothers are gathering and bundling the harvest. Suddenly the bundles take on human qualities. Joseph's sheaf rises to a place and position of authority, while the sheaves that represent the brothers bow before Joseph's sheaf. In another dream, Joseph sees the sun, the moon, and eleven stars bow before him. As Jacob states (v. 9), the sun and moon represent Joseph's parents, and the eleven stars are his eleven brothers. For Joseph to even hint that he would receive honor from his brothers and parents is not according to tradition and intensifies their animosity. Joseph's dream is from the Lord. It is prophetic regarding the future of his family; however, because Joseph is already seen as different, his brothers do not see his dreams as signs of providence and blessings. Jacob, however, ponders the dream. Jacob himself was a dreamer (Genesis 28:10-16; 31:8-13). He likely recognized that God was the author of Joseph's dreams.

Was Joseph bragging or just sharing his dream? How did his brothers' personal grievance keep them from recognizing the value in Joseph's words?

3. Joseph's Brothers Act (vv. 23–24, 28)

In verses 12–22, Joseph stays behind while his brothers tend the flock. His father sends him to check on the brothers, but they have gone to another spot. They see Joseph coming before he reaches them and decides to destroy his life and dreams. They originally planned to kill him, but his brother Reuben persuades them not to do that. They fall upon Joseph and remove the coat of many colors. In essence, they strip him of the authority and favor their father had placed in him. They are obviously not thinking of their father and the pain Jacob would suffer.

Eventually, they throw Joseph into an empty, dry hole and leave him starving and open to the elements with no way of escape. After a time, Joseph was pulled from the pit, not because the brothers had a change of heart, but because they seized the opportunity to get rid of Joseph and make money from selling him into slavery. By these actions, we see that the hatred the brothers harbored was only tempered by the greed they possessed.

If Joseph and his brothers had been guided by love instead of hatred, greed, and pride, how do you think this time in their lives would have played out?

Search the Scriptures

1. Compare and contrast the lives of Joseph and his brothers in today's Scriptures.

2. Why did Jacob favor Joseph? (Genesis 37:3)

3. What evidence in the text shows a growing resentment among members of Joseph's family?

4. What is the difference in Jacob's reaction to Joseph's dreams and the reaction of the brothers? (vv. 10-11)

Discuss the Meaning

1. Are we justified when we allow ourselves to become jealous of another person whom God seems to be blessing abundantly? Explain.

2. Some say jealousy is the breeding ground for most violent crimes. Do you agree? Explain.

Liberating Lesson

Our society is fractured into distinct groups that do not trust each other, whether political parties, Christian sects, rival gangs, or just different departments at work. Even though one group may have good ideas to fix problems, other factions do not trust them because they are outside their group. Later Scripture reveals that Joseph's dreams were prophetic, and his ability to interpret dreams will be used in the future to fulfill God's plan to save many lives. However, jealousy between Joseph and his brothers blinds Joseph's family from supporting or even loving Joseph. They do not like what the dreams mean, and they do not like "the way he talked about them" (v. 8, NLT). No one is totally exempt from jealousy and rivalry. What are some messages you struggle to accept because you do not like the messenger or the way they present their message?

Application for Activation

Jealousy is usually the result of our wanting something that someone else has. When we look to the Creator as the supplier of all our needs, however, we realize we never have a reason to be jealous of anyone. The most precious gift God has given is Jesus Christ, a gift available to each of us. Therefore, jealousy has no place in the life of the believer.

There are still numerous reasons people are jealous of others. However, the end result of jealousy is always negative. It has destroyed families, marriages, relationships, and lives. Pledge to notice and rebuke any feelings of jealousy you have in the coming week.

Follow the Spirit

What God wants me to do:

_____

_____

_____

_____

Remember Your Thoughts

Special insights I have learned:

_____

_____

_____

_____

More Light on the Text
Genesis 37:2–11, 23–24, 28

Joseph's story is the next biographical installment in the patriarchal trilogy of faith through the descendants of Abraham, Isaac, and Jacob. In this generational story of call, redemption, and God's grace, God demonstrates how when love is absent or distorted, evil will follow. Divine love is the only way to reconcile and restore a right relationship.

2 These are the generations of Jacob. Joseph, being seventeen years old, was feeding the flock with his brethren; and the lad was with the sons of Bilhah, and with the sons of Zilpah, his father's wives: and Joseph brought unto his father their evil report.

The phrase "these are the generations," notes a move from Jacob (Israel) as the main character to his children being the focus. The next word tells us which son will be the stories' primary focus now: Joseph. Just as Abraham was an odd choice of the main character among any of Shem's other descendants and just as Israel (Jacob) was an odd choice of the main character as Isaac's younger son, Joseph is an odd choice of the main character based on his age and his being Jacob's eleventh son. God often chooses an unexpected person to be the agent for His salvation plan.

Before Joseph dreamed the dream central to this saga, his brothers hated him for his prior indiscretions as a tattletale (Genesis 37:2). As a young lad of seventeen having been his father's favorite son since he was born in Jacob's old age, Joseph misused his favor and did not use discretion or humility in fostering relationships with his brothers. Instead, as he worked with them, Joseph brought his father an "evil report" about them. The Hebrew word *dibbah* (dib-**BAH**), translated "report," is elsewhere-translated "slander." It is usually understood to be bad news. Here, however, the narrator adds the adjective "evil" to make clear the nature of Joseph's summary of his brothers' actions.

3 Now Israel loved Joseph more than all his children, because he was the son of his old age: and he made him a coat of many colours. 4 And when his brethren saw that their father loved him more than all his brethren, they hated him, and could not speak peaceably unto him.

Not only is Jacob (renamed "Israel") guilty of parental preference, but he also demonstrates a lack of discretion when he fuels the feud between the brothers by lavishing a visual reminder of his preference toward Joseph—a special coat.

There is confusion as to what exactly this coat looked like and what exactly it implied because the Hebrew words here are rare. A "coat" (Heb. *kuttonet*, koo-**TOW**-net) can refer to a specifically priestly garment and is often made of fine linen. The adjective "of many colors" (Heb. *pas*, **POSS**) is only used elsewhere in Scripture to describe a special robe worn by virgin princesses (2 Samuel 13:18), perhaps highlighting the garment's connection with royalty. If we look at the word's etymology to help define its meaning, there are still many possibilities. It could imply a garment that has long sleeves reaching to the hands, implying the wearer was not performing manual labor. It could use "hand" as a unit of measure, implying a garment made of many "hand" breadths of fabric. This idea is where the "many colors" interpretation originates, presuming each strip of fabric to be a different color.

Any one of these understandings of the gift would be enough to stoke the brothers' jealousy. Israel might have been labeling Joseph as a priest or as royalty with the coat. If the coat was ornately beautiful with various colors of fine fabric or just long-sleeved, Joseph would not wear it and join his brothers in their hard work sustaining the family. To the brothers, the new coat has a simple, obvious meaning: Israel just loves Joseph "more than all his brethren."

5 And Joseph dreamed a dream, and he told it his brethren: and they hated him yet the more.

Seething with envy, the brothers hated Joseph greatly. Hostility between the brothers was high by the time Joseph had a "dream" (Heb. *chalom*, kha-**LOME**), which can refer to either prophetic or ordinary dreams. The phrasing "dreamed a dream," however, is only used of prophetic dreams. Since such dreams were regarded as a means of divine revelation and taken very seriously, it is not illogical that the brothers' anger increased, knowing that what Joseph dreamed would most likely happen. Whereas maturity and wisdom might have prevented Joseph from telling this particular dream to his brothers, Joseph told them that though they hated him now, they would eventually bow down to him. Note that although Joseph dreamed of his promotion, he had not sensed that he was headed into a series of serious demotions on the journey up. Joseph's brothers hated him "yet the more" (Heb. *yasaph*, yaw-**SAF**, "to add, increase, or do again"), setting the stage for the subsequent events to unfold. This use of *yasaph* is ironic since that is the root word in Joseph's name. He was named Joseph because his mother said, "The LORD shall add to me another son" as a blessing to Israel's family (Genesis 30:24). Here, however, the only thing he is "adding" is more hatred.

6 And he said unto them, Hear, I pray you, this dream which I have dreamed: 7 For, behold, we were binding sheaves in the field, and, lo, my sheaf arose, and also stood upright; and, behold, your sheaves stood round about, and made obeisance to my sheaf. 8 And his brethren said to him, Shalt thou indeed reign over us? or shalt thou indeed have dominion over us? And they hated him yet the more for his dreams, and for his words.

Joseph called his brothers to hear this dream. As the brothers were all binding their sheaves, the inanimate sheaves became animated and represented each brother. Joseph's sheaf "arose," implying a position of authority over the others. Furthermore, that his sheaf also "stood upright" (Heb. *natsab*, naw-**TSAB**, "to be set over or to be appointed") let the brothers know that Joseph would again find favor to be promoted into a position of authority over them. In response to Joseph's sheaf being promoted over the others, the brothers' sheaves came around Joseph's upright sheaf in "obeisance," meaning to bow down before a superior in homage. This position of superiority and subordination angered Joseph's brothers, causing them to make an incredulous, indignant interpretation of Joseph's dream.

9 And he dreamed yet another dream, and told it his brethren, and said, Behold, I have dreamed a dream more; and, behold, the sun and the moon and the eleven stars made obeisance to me. 10 And he told it to his father, and to his brethren: and his father rebuked him, and said unto him, What is this dream that thou hast dreamed? Shall I and thy mother and thy brethren indeed come to bow down ourselves to thee to the earth? 11 And his brethren envied him; but his father observed the saying.

The meaning of Joseph's second dream has as obvious an interpretation as his first had. Here, the sun, moon, and stars represent his parents and brothers as Israel interprets in the next verse.

When Joseph tells this dream to his father in front of his brothers, his father rebukes him sharply. Israel could mean to encourage Joseph to be wise by not further inciting his brothers' obvious anger toward him. Joseph's father also seems mildly offended that his favored son would dream this dream. The posture of bowing down (the same Hebrew word as "obeisance" in vv. 7 and 9) to him in a prostrate position with their faces to the ground would mean total submission. This is not the position a doting father deserves. Perhaps Israel is riled also by the implied disrespect of Joseph's mother, who was his favorite wife.

The family's reaction to Joseph's second dream is mixed. Joseph's brothers "envied" (Heb. *qana'*, kaw-NAW, meaning "to be jealous") him, but his father "observed" (Heb. *shamar*, shaw-MAR, "to give heed") it. The brothers continue with their hatred of their little brother, but Israel (despite his initial outburst against Joseph) paid attention or kept in mind what Joseph said. The Hebrew word *shamar* means not only to listen but also to act accordingly. Israel hears his son's dream and ponders his correct course of action based on it.

23 And it came to pass, when Joseph was come unto his brethren, that they stript Joseph out of his coat, his coat of many colours that was on him; 24 And they took him, and cast him into a pit: and the pit was empty, there was no water in it.

Some time after these dreams, Joseph is sent to track down his brothers, journeying several days away from home to find the flock. The brothers see him coming and plot to kill him. Reuben dissuades them from outright murder and they throw him into a pit (Heb. *bor*, **BORE**, "well, cistern") instead. Reuben was not on good terms with Israel, and he secretly planned to come back and rescue Joseph out of the cistern to get in Israel's good graces again (Genesis 37:21-22).

When Joseph shows up where his brothers are herding their flocks, they strip Joseph out

of his elaborate gift from his father: the coat of many colors. Taking Joseph's coat humiliates and humbles him from walking around so proudly as the favored son and dreamer. Also, the brothers will use the coat as validation of their story that a wild animal ate Joseph (vv. 31-33).

The brothers then throw Joseph into an empty cistern and conspire to leave him there to die alone and helpless. Cisterns are designed to collect rainwater for use during the dry season. It is not uncommon for them to dry up before the rainy season started again, however. The narrator supplies the detail that the cistern was empty at this time, letting the audience know that Joseph was not in danger of drowning, and if left in there would die of dehydration.

28 Then there passed by Midianites merchantmen; and they drew and lifted up Joseph out of the pit, and sold Joseph to the Ishmeelites for twenty pieces of silver: and they brought Joseph into Egypt.

While the brothers sat down to eat, a band of Midianites merchants, bound for Egypt with a cargo of spices and balms, arrive on the horizon (v. 25). Jacob's third son, Judah suggests they take advantage of this opportunity to get rid of Joseph, avoid crime, and make a profit. The brothers sell Joseph to the Ishmaelites (KJV: Ishmeelites), another name for the Midianites. The terms mark the traders as descendants of Abraham (and therefore the brothers' kin) through one of his concubines: Ishmael was Hagar's son (Genesis 16), while Midian was Keturah's son (Genesis 25:1-2). The names are also used interchangeably when the people group fights Gideon's army (Judges 8). Twenty pieces of silver was an amount typical for a slave and the value of about two years of wages. People bought by slave traders seldom saw their home or freedom again and were resold or traded in other areas. The traders eventually bring Joseph to Egypt.

Sources:
Kaplan, Aryeh. *The Living Torah*. New York: Mozniam Publishing, 1981.

Say It Correctly

Midianite. **MID**-ee-ann-ite.
Ishmaelite. **ISH**-mee-ul-ite.
Bilhah. **BILL**-ha.
Zilpah. **ZILL**-pah.

Daily Bible Readings

MONDAY
Rachel, Mother of Joseph and Benjamin
(Genesis 30:22-24; 35:16-20)

TUESDAY
Joseph Checks on Brothers at Dothan
(Genesis 37:12-17)

WEDNESDAY
Jacob Convinced that Joseph Is Dead
(Genesis 37:29-36)

THURSDAY
From Slave to Ruler of Egypt
(Psalm 105:1-6, 16-22)

FRIDAY
Jacob Lives with Joseph in Egypt
(Acts 7:9-15)

SATURDAY
Caution, Disputes May Lead to Violence
(James 4:1-7)

SUNDAY
Jealously Divides Families
(Genesis 37:2-11, 23-24, 28)

Notes

Teaching Tips

Words You Should Know

A. Manasseh (v. 50) *Menashsheh* (Heb.)—Firstborn son of Joseph; the name means "causing to forget"

B. Ephraim (v. 52) *'Ephrayim* (Heb.)—Second son of Joseph; the name means "double fruit"

Teacher Preparation

Unifying Principle—Love Versus Bitterness. It may be difficult to hold on to dreams of future success when faced with extreme hardships. What inner resources are needed to continue one's quest for success? Because Joseph loved and obeyed God, he was able to engage in wise and discerning problem-solving that motivated Pharaoh to appoint him second in command over all of Egypt.

A. Read the Bible Background and Devotional Reading.

B. Pray for your students and lesson clarity.

C. Read the lesson Scripture in multiple translations.

O—Open the Lesson

A. Begin the class with prayer.

B. Encourage class members to graph the ups and downs of the past twenty years or so of their lives. What was their relationship with God like at different points in their lives?

C. Have the students read the Aim for Change and the In Focus story.

D. Ask students how events like those in the story weigh on their hearts and how they can view these events from a faith perspective.

P—Present the Scriptures

A. Read the Focal Verses and discuss the Background and The People, Places, and Times sections.

B. Have the class share what Scriptures stand out for them and why, with particular emphasis on today's themes.

E—Explore the Meaning

A. Use In Depth or More Light on the Text to facilitate a deeper discussion of the lesson text.

B. Pose the questions in Search the Scriptures and Discuss the Meaning.

C. Discuss the Liberating Lesson and Application for Activation sections.

N—Next Steps for Application

A. Summarize the value of offering God's solutions to problems rather than pointing out the problems alone.

B. Ask the class to think this week about when and how God took an injustice they suffered and made it right.

Worship Guide

For the Superintendent or Teacher
Theme: God Rewards Obedience
Song: "His Eye is on the Sparrow"
Devotional Reading: 1 Peter 5:5-11

God Rewards Obedience

Bible Background • GENESIS 41:14–57
Printed Text • GENESIS 41:25–33, 37–40, 50–52 | Devotional Reading • 1 PETER 5:5–11

—————————— Aim for Change ——————————

By the end of this lesson, we will DISCOVER how Joseph's love for God and faithfulness helped him find success in Egypt, ASPIRE to remain steadfast in love and obedience to God when facing extreme hardships, and CELEBRATE God's providential care in times of suffering.

In Focus

Robert had been in his new advertising job for more than six months. He enjoyed the job but didn't really feel like he was making a contribution to his team. All the other team members had talents he could clearly see. Monica was creative; Michelle was a good organizer; Pierce was a good motivator; and Ronald was an excellent long-range planner. Marvin, their team leader, had given each of them the chance to head an important project.

One day his team was discussing the fact that their line of products wasn't being received well in a particular region of the country. The project had been reassigned to Robert's team. What could they do that was different?

"What have they already done?" Robert got up the nerve to ask.

Marvin began to explain some advertising campaigns and slogans the other team had tried. Robert spoke up again. "I think I know what part of the problem may be. I'm from around there and that's just not the way people there make decisions about using a product like ours." He began to explain some of the differences.

"Why don't you head this project then, Robert?" asked Marvin. "You're probably our best hope."

Then and there, Robert said a quick prayer, thanking God for this chance, but also asking God to help him do a good job.

How has God provided places for you to use your gifts and skills? How have you seen Him guiding you through those places?

—————————— Keep in Mind ——————————

> "And Pharaoh said unto Joseph, Forasmuch as God hath shewed thee all this, there is none so discreet and wise as thou art: Thou shalt be over my house, and according unto thy word shall all my people be ruled: only in the throne will I be greater than thou" (Genesis 41:39-40, KJV).

"Then Pharaoh said to Joseph, 'Since God has revealed the meaning of the dreams to you, clearly no one else is as intelligent or wise as you are. You will be in charge of my court, and all my people will take orders from you. Only I, sitting on my throne, will have a rank higher than yours'" (Genesis 41:39-40, NLT).

Focal Verses

KJV **Genesis 41:25** And Joseph said unto Pharaoh, The dream of Pharaoh is one: God hath shewed Pharaoh what he is about to do.

26 The seven good kine are seven years; and the seven good ears are seven years: the dream is one.

27 And the seven thin and ill favoured kine that came up after them are seven years; and the seven empty ears blasted with the east wind shall be seven years of famine.

28 This is the thing which I have spoken unto Pharaoh: What God is about to do he sheweth unto Pharaoh.

29 Behold, there come seven years of great plenty throughout all the land of Egypt:

30 And there shall arise after them seven years of famine; and all the plenty shall be forgotten in the land of Egypt; and the famine shall consume the land;

31 And the plenty shall not be known in the land by reason of that famine following; for it shall be very grievous.

32 And for that the dream was doubled unto Pharaoh twice; it is because the thing is established by God, and God will shortly bring it to pass.

33 Now therefore let Pharaoh look out a man discreet and wise, and set him over the land of Egypt.

37 And the thing was good in the eyes of Pharaoh, and in the eyes of all his servants.

38 And Pharaoh said unto his servants, Can we find such a one as this is, a man in whom the Spirit of God is?

39 And Pharaoh said unto Joseph, Forasmuch as God hath shewed thee all this, there is none so discreet and wise as thou art:

40 Thou shalt be over my house, and according unto thy word shall all my people be ruled: only in the throne will I be greater than thou.

NLT **Genesis 41:25** Joseph responded, "Both of Pharaoh's dreams mean the same thing. God is telling Pharaoh in advance what he is about to do.

26 The seven healthy cows and the seven healthy heads of grain both represent seven years of prosperity.

27 The seven thin, scrawny cows that came up later and the seven thin heads of grain, withered by the east wind, represent seven years of famine.

28 This will happen just as I have described it, for God has revealed to Pharaoh in advance what he is about to do.

29 The next seven years will be a period of great prosperity throughout the land of Egypt.

30 But afterward there will be seven years of famine so great that all the prosperity will be forgotten in Egypt. Famine will destroy the land.

31 This famine will be so severe that even the memory of the good years will be erased.

32 As for having two similar dreams, it means that these events have been decreed by God, and he will soon make them happen.

33 Therefore, Pharaoh should find an intelligent and wise man and put him in charge of the entire land of Egypt."

37 Joseph's suggestions were well received by Pharaoh and his officials.

38 So Pharaoh asked his officials, "Can we find anyone else like this man so obviously filled with the spirit of God?"

39 Then Pharaoh said to Joseph, "Since God has revealed the meaning of the dreams to you, clearly no one else is as intelligent or wise as you are.

40 You will be in charge of my court, and all my people will take orders from you. Only I, sitting on my throne, will have a rank higher than yours."

50 And unto Joseph were born two sons before the years of famine came, which Asenath the daughter of Potipherah priest of On bare unto him.

51 And Joseph called the name of the firstborn Manasseh: For God, said he, hath made me forget all my toil, and all my father's house.

52 And the name of the second called he Ephraim: For God hath caused me to be fruitful in the land of my affliction.

50 During this time, before the first of the famine years, two sons were born to Joseph and his wife, Asenath, the daughter of Potiphera, the priest of On.

51 Joseph named his older son Manasseh, for he said, "God has made me forget all my troubles and everyone in my father's family."

52 Joseph named his second son Ephraim, for he said, "God has made me fruitful in this land of my grief."

The People, Places, and Times

Dreams. In the Old Testament, dreams were very important, though not every dream was thought to be from God. Many divine revelations came through the dreams of various kings, prophets, and ordinary people. God would reveal His plans to those who worshiped Him or to pagans in dreams. In ancient times, the dreams of kings and holy people were considered to have national or international significance. Kings often retained several specialists to interpret their dreams for them, and being able to interpret prophetic dreams was a sought-after skill. While dreams were considered significant, God often warned against relying solely on dreams to know and understand His will (Deuteronomy 13:1-5; Jeremiah 29:8-9; Matthew 16:3; 1 Corinthians 13:9).

Potipherah. Pharaoh gave Joseph Asenath, the daughter of Potipherah priest of On, as his wife (Genesis 41:45, 50). The city On was situated north of Cairo, on the Nile Delta, about 17 miles away from the Pyramids in Cairo. Potipherah is believed to be a high-ranking priest of the Egyptian sun-god Ra, their chief deity. Worship of Ra permeated the city, causing the Greeks to give it the name Heliopolis, "City of the Sun."

What does Joseph's marriage to the daughter of a pagan priest imply about marrying people outside the faith?

Background

While Joseph languishes in prison on false charges, Pharaoh of Egypt has two disturbing dreams. In the first dream, seven healthy cows that come out to the Nile and begin to graze. But then, seven scrawny cows appear and eat the fat ones. In the second dream, seven choice ears of grain grow on one stalk; then seven skinny ears of grain blossom on that stalk and consume the hearty grain. Pharaoh is extremely troubled and beckons experts to give meaning to the dreams, but none of them provide a suitable analysis.

Eventually, these events remind Pharaoh's cupbearer of the time Joseph had rightly interpreted the cupbearer's dream. Pharaoh wastes no time, and Joseph is pulled out of jail to stand before the great ruler! Before Joseph interprets Pharaoh's dreams, he announces that it is not he that provides the interpretation but God. Only God can give the correct answer and assure the Pharaoh of its accuracy. Through this event, God provides an opportunity for Joseph to find favor with Pharaoh and to give God credit for the interpretation.

Does God speak through dreams today? What biblical and experiential evidence to you have for your answer?

At-A-Glance

1. Joseph Interprets the Dream
   (Genesis 41:25-33)
2. Joseph Receives Honor (vv. 37–40)
3. Joseph Establishes Familial Roots
   with the Egyptians (vv. 50-52)

In Depth

1. Joseph Interprets the Dream (Genesis 41:25-33)

God reveals to Joseph that Pharaoh's dreams are a warning to prepare for a famine. Pharaoh had two dreams, but Joseph realizes they were the same and that the repetition addresses the urgency with which Pharaoh should act. The nation of Egypt will have seven years of good crops and plenty, but those will be followed by a seven-year famine of equal proportion. Without this warning, Egypt would have been devastated, and the nation could have dissolved through the death of its people and the vulnerability of its government.

Joseph does not stop at just interpreting the dreams, however, he goes on to apply his gifts of administration to suggest a plan of action. Pharaoh will need a discerning man in charge of the land to put aside extra during the years of plenty so that the nation can survive during the famine.

Like Joseph, when we have been misunderstood and oppressively ostracized, we need to continue cultivating a good relationship with the Lord. It is only through such faithfulness that we will be spiritually ready when God's time comes for our deliverance and vindication. In fact, God will use our spiritual gifts to exalt us into the influential positions in life where He designs for us to be.

2. Joseph Receives Honor (vv. 37–40)

Joseph does not ask to be put in charge. Pharaoh, however, recognizes that Joseph does not rely on his own cleverness and wisdom. Instead, Joseph follows God, who has revealed this great truth. Pharaoh, who neither knows nor serves Joseph's God, concludes that Joseph's ability to interpret his dreams serves as evidence that the hand of God rests upon him. Pharaoh decides to make Joseph the prime minister in charge of the palace and the country (v. 40). By elevating Joseph, Pharaoh acknowledges that God is powerful!

The Lord has the supernatural ability to work in the lives of those inside and outside the faith community. When we are faithful to our Lord, God might elevate us to positions where we have favor even with those who do not know Jesus. In the positions God calls us to serve, we have the ability to make enormous contributions that will impact our society for the good. For God to use us, however, we must commit to acting responsibly. As a result, we also introduce God to others.

When has your faith in Christ drawn others to ask about Him even when you were not "witnessing" aloud?

3. Joseph Establishes Familial Roots with the Egyptians (vv. 50-52)

God not only uses His servants to help people in need, but He enjoys giving personal blessings to those who do His will. Joseph and his Egyptian wife Asenath are blessed with two sons. One is named Manasseh, meaning "forget." Through the blessings of Joseph's elevation, God brought fulfillment to his life, letting him forget the pain of his enslavement and filling the void caused by the distressing experiences of his past (v. 51). The second son is named Ephraim, meaning "doubly fruitful," capturing Joseph's glorious prosperity in Egypt (v. 52).

Through Joseph's marriage and family, God provides for perpetuation of His divine presence with Egypt, and with the Hebrews. The Egyptians were kind and welcoming to Joseph's whole extended family, letting them settle in Goshen, partially because of Joseph's Egyptian family. Joseph's Egyptian sons provide him with a lasting heritage within the nation of Israel. There is no tribe named for Joseph as there is for his brothers, but the tribes of Ephraim and Manasseh, though technically half-tribes, often receive full recognition and blessing comparable to other full tribes, like Levi or Judah.

How have you established roots after a move, whether to a different house, a different job, or a different chapter of life?

Search the Scriptures

1. How does Pharaoh acknowledge God? (vv. 37-39)

2. How is Joseph rewarded for using his gift? (vv. 39-40)

3. What names does Joseph give his children and why (vv. 51–52)?

Discuss the Meaning

1. Why do you think God allows us to endure trials, tribulation, and hardship prior to elevating us?

2. We sometimes underestimate the power of our gifts and miss opportunities to serve God. How does Joseph overcome the urge to underestimate himself?

Liberating Lesson

Each of us faces circumstances that can lead us to doubt our faith and plunge us into despair. It is important that, like Joseph, we find ways to give godly and practical encouragement to others whose situations seem bleak, even if our own circumstance is equally dire.

We would also do well if we, like Joseph, were to see God at work in unlikely places in our own lives. When we seek God's wisdom in solving problems, we should be proactive and prepared for God to act rather than despondent when we face unexpected crises. We should, like Joseph, remain confident that God is working on our behalf as we prepare for His next move in our life.

Application for Activation

During the week, take some time to remember the promises or dreams God has given you, but which have not yet been fulfilled. Have you given up on any of your God-centered dreams? How can you maintain the right kind of attitude that will enable you to be ready if God should suddenly bring your dreams to pass? Share your dreams with trusted friends so you can encourage each other and help each other take steps to see the God-centered dreams come to be.

Follow the Spirit

What God wants me to do:

_____

_____

_____

_____

Remember Your Thoughts

Special insights I have learned:

_____

_____

_____

_____

_____

More Light on the Text
Genesis 41:25-33, 37-40, 50-52

The Pharaoh of Egypt had two dreams that disturbed him for two reasons: (1) the dreams were strange; and (2) there was no one among his wise men to interpret either one. In both Egypt and Babylon, professional dream interpreters were part of the prevailing religious system. In the meantime, Joseph spent more than two years in prison for a crime that he did not commit. But once again, we see the providential hand of God was with him. No one was able to interpret Pharaoh's dreams—until Joseph was allowed access to Pharaoh.

While in prison, Joseph met two of Pharaoh's closest aides, the chief baker and the chief butler, who were also in prison. Each had a dream they did not understand, but God gave Joseph spiritual insight to communicate to both men. The dream told that Pharaoh would restore the cupbearer to a position of honor, while he would hang the chief baker (see Genesis 40).

Pharaoh's counselors and advisors had no idea how to interpret the ruler's dreams. Suddenly, the chief cupbearer remembered his promise to tell Pharaoh of Joseph and his abilities. Pharaoh immediately called for Joseph to come out of prison, and he had his hair cut and clothing changed, to resemble an Egyptian, rather than a Hebrew. Egyptians were clean-shaven.

25 And Joseph said unto Pharaoh, The dream of Pharaoh is one: God hath shewed Pharaoh what he is about to do.

Although there are two different dreams, Joseph tells Pharaoh they have one meaning. The repetition of the dreams serves as emphasis and establishes the truth and surety of what is to happen (v. 32; Deuteronomy 19:15). Joseph once more points Pharaoh toward God, the source of all wisdom and knowledge and the one who rules the universe, and reveals His plan for the future of Egypt's climate and economy. He directs the king to look to God as the author of the events that would take place in Egypt. Here Joseph indirectly denounces all the gods of Egypt before Pharaoh, implying the many gods Egypt worships are nothing and powerless in the face of the God Joseph knows.

Revealing the future to certain people is consistent with God's character. He told Abraham many years before that his offspring would go into a strange land and come out again with great wealth (Genesis 15:12-16), and revealed to Joseph how He would exalt him above his brethren (Genesis 37:5-10). In many instances God makes known His future dealings to pagan rulers whom He uses to carry out the divine plan (Daniel 2:28; 4:25-27; Isaiah 45:1-4). Therefore, Joseph establishes the fact that Pharaoh's dreams are revelations of God's plan. Then he begins to interpret the dreams in detail.

26 The seven good kine are seven years; and the seven good ears are seven years: the dream is one. 27 And the seven thin and ill favoured kine that came up after them are seven years; and the seven empty ears blasted with the east wind shall be seven years of famine. 28 This is the thing which I have spoken unto Pharaoh: What God is about to do he sheweth unto Pharaoh.

Once again, Joseph tells the king that the two dreams are really one. The seven good kine (i.e., cows or cattle, emblems of Egyptian agriculture and prosperity) and the seven good ears (of corn, i.e. grain, rather than the New World plant known today as "corn") both represent seven years of good harvest in Egypt (v. 29). There would be plenty of food on the land for seven years. These would be followed by seven years of famine, which are symbolized by "the seven thin and ill favoured" cattle and "the seven empty ears." Joseph takes care to humbly and responsibly interpret this dream and report it to Pharaoh. Joseph's content and tone tell of the urgency and calamity forthcoming.

29 Behold, there come seven years of great plenty throughout all the land of Egypt: 30 And there shall arise after them seven years of famine; and all the plenty shall be forgotten in the land of Egypt; and the famine shall consume the land; 31 And the plenty shall not be known in the land by reason of that famine following; for it shall be very grievous. 32 And for that the dream was doubled unto Pharaoh twice; it is because the thing is established by God, and God will shortly bring it to pass.

Joseph interpreted the "plenty" as a season of prosperity and abundance throughout the land and for all of Egypt's inhabitants. Conversely, these seven years of plenty would be followed by seven years of famine so severe and devastating that the prosperity would be "forgotten" (Heb. *shakach*, shaw-**KAKH**, "forget, to cease to care"). The people would not care to reminisce about the good old days as the severity of the seven years of famine would indeed "consume" (Heb. *kalah*, kaw-**LAW**, "be complete") or completely destroy life, cattle, and crop.

The repetition of a dream indicated its urgency. Therefore, Pharaoh's dream was "doubled... twice" in a dream sequence that happened over and over, this proved that indeed these were prophetic dreams from God about the things He had established to occur shortly or bring to pass soon. Joseph himself had a doubled dream of ruling over his brothers and family. This showed God would certainly accomplish what the dream foretold.

33 Now therefore let Pharaoh look out a man discreet and wise, and set him over the land of Egypt.

Pharaoh only needed an interpretation of the dreams, but Joseph gives advice on what to do to save the country during the years of famine (vv. 32-33). Pharaoh is to appoint a man full of wisdom and set him over the land of Egypt, Joseph advises.

In preparation for these seasons of feast and famine, the pharaoh is instructed to participate in God's plan for Joseph's liberation and Israel's preservation. Pharaoh must watch for a "discreet" (Heb. *bin*, **BEEN**, understanding), a wise man to set over these affairs during the feast and the famine. Such a man would be one who could see disaster and remedy. Joseph was one such man.

37 And the thing was good in the eyes of Pharaoh, and in the eyes of all of his servants. 38 And Pharaoh said unto his servants, Can we find such a one as this is, a man in whom the Spirit of God is?

As he stood before Pharaoh, the first admonition that Joseph gave him before sharing the dreams' interpretations was that the answer to Pharaoh's dreams was not "in [him]: God shall give Pharaoh an answer of peace" (Genesis 41:16). Following this introduction to Joseph, Pharaoh was given the strategic plan and vision that would save his land and people, and he was impressed with Joseph, using the word "good" to affirm Pharaoh's appreciation (v. 37). The Hebrew word for "good" is *yatab* (yaw-**TAB**), and it means to be pleasing, cheerful, and glad. Pharaoh declared to his royal court that indeed Joseph must be the one because he had the "Spirit of God" (v. 38). Even though Egyptian culture had no knowledge of the Holy Spirit or His work, Pharaoh believed in God's power.

Joseph's advice impressed Pharaoh and his council. The phrase "the thing was good in the eyes" means that Pharaoh was pleased with Joseph's insight and wisdom. The interpretation of the dreams and the advice both sound so good that Pharaoh wastes no time in implementing them. Consulting his council, he asks rhetorically "Can we find such a one as this is?" The answer is obvious since no one was able to give Pharaoh the answer to his dream, let alone follow it up with such wise advice. Pharaoh and his servants realize the power and the wisdom of God. Although they recognize the divine power and wisdom, we have no evidence in Scriptures that they renounced their idolatry to worship the living God Joseph professed before them.

39 And Pharaoh said unto Joseph, Forasmuch as God hath showed thee all this, there is none so discreet and wise as thou art: 40 Thou shalt be over my house, and according unto thy word shall all my people be ruled: only in the throne will I be greater than thou.

Once Joseph had interpreted the dreams and divine plans to Pharaoh, Pharaoh immediately honored the young man with favor. Pharaoh recognized that Joseph's wisdom and understanding came from God (v. 39). Therefore, he avowed that the young Hebrew would be rewarded handsomely for his discernment and wisdom. Joseph's was a unique rags-to-riches story. In a short period of his life, he went from the pit to the palace, from obscurity to influence, all because of the favor and blessings of God. We must keep in mind that we do not need to try to selfishly promote ourselves. Joseph's interpretation was honest and not self-promoting. God is the One who gives us favor with our superiors, relatives, and others. If we are faithful and committed to the Lord, He will bless us as well (see Psalm 75:6–7).

The first area where Joseph would have tremendous influence would be in the house of Pharaoh. Just as he was influential over Potiphar's house (see Genesis 39:4), so, too,

would Joseph reign over Pharaoh's palace (Genesis 41:40). In fact, Pharaoh declared that Joseph's reign and responsibility would be so vast that the only person with greater responsibility and power than Joseph would be Pharaoh himself. All of Pharaoh's people would submit to Joseph's authority and commands. Thus, Joseph becomes the prime minister of Egypt, second in command to his throne.

Pharaoh would serve as the ceremonial president while Joseph is given the charge to run the country. This is made clear in Pharaoh's words "only in the throne will I be greater than thou" (v. 40) and his actions (vv. 41-44). This is the work of God and a fulfillment of God words and revelation to Joseph. It is a true example of how God exalts people from rags to riches, for "by humility and the fear of the LORD are riches, and honour, and life" (Proverbs 22:4). God never fails in His promises. His Word never changes, and His faithfulness is as certain as night and day.

50 And unto Joseph were born two sons before the years of the famine came, which Asenath the daughter of Potipherah priest of On bare unto him. 51 And Joseph called the name of the firstborn Manasseh: For God, said he, hath made me forget all my toil, and all my father's house. 52 And the name of the second called he Ephraim: for God hath caused me to be fruitful in the land of my affliction.

Pharaoh takes care to alter Joseph's Hebrew name, from Joseph to Zaphnath-Paaneah (v. 48). Then Pharaoh gives Joseph an Egyptian wife named Asenath. Her name means "one who belongs to the goddess Neith." The goddess Neith had dominion over war and weaving and is the mother of Ra in some stories. Asenath was the daughter of Potiphera, a priest of On (v. 45). The name Potiphera in Egyptian means "he whom Ra has given."

Potiphera was probably a very important figure in an Egyptian cult. On, which was also called Heliopolis, was one of four great Egyptian cities and was the place where they worshiped the sun god Ra. The priests of On often engaged in widely varied commercial, political, and cultic responsibilities. Thus, Joseph was enveloped in Egyptian culture, but never lost his faith and commitment to Jehovah God.

Joseph is now an "Egyptian" ruler and the prime minister of Pharaoh's entire kingdom. He settles in Egypt and begins a family before the famine engulfed the land. Though thoroughly Egyptian now, Joseph gives his two sons Hebrew names. The first is named Manasseh (Heb. Menashsheh, men-ash-SHEH), which means in Hebrew "cause to forget" or "forgetful." The second son is called Ephraim, which translates to "double fruit" or "very fruitful." Joseph's experience was tragic, from the time he left his father's home, until his ascendancy to the prime minister. From a human perspective, the young man does not want to remember all he endured. His son Manasseh would affirm that Joseph had turned the corner on his oppression and difficulties because he had put his trust in the Lord. Consequently, his son Ephraim would always remind Joseph, that only through God's grace and favor, had Joseph been promoted in Egypt and received increase (was "fruitful") and influence as a result of his faithfulness to the Lord. Even in "the land of [his] affliction," Joseph recognized the centrality of God's compassion and grace. Separation from his father and all that he held dear has not diminished Joseph's perspective that he is still in the hands of God.

Sources:
Butler, Trent. *Holman Bible Dictionary*. Nashville, TN: Broadman & Holman Publishers, 1991.

Say It Correctly

Asenath. **AH**-sen-ath.
Potipherah. **PAH**-teh-**FARE**-uh.
Heliopolis. he-lee-**OH**-poh-liss.
Giza. **GEE**-zah.
Cairo. **KIE**-row.

Daily Bible Readings

MONDAY
Paul and Barnabas
Appointed for Ministry
(Acts 13:1-5)

TUESDAY
Joseph, Chief Interpreter of Dreams
(Genesis 41:9-13)

WEDNESDAY
Dreams of Cows and Corn Explained
(Genesis 41:14-24)

THURSDAY
Preparing for the Expected Famine
(Genesis 41:34-36)

FRIDAY
Storing Grain for the Future
(Genesis 41:41-49)

SATURDAY
Egypt Feeds the Middle East
(Genesis 41:53-57)

SUNDAY
Leadership During Crisis
(Genesis 41:25-33, 37-40, 50-52)

Teaching Tips

Words You Should Know

A. Governor (v. 6) *shallit* (Heb.)—Mighty, one that has power, ruler

B. Bow Down (v. 6) *shachah* (Gk.)—To fall on one's knees in reverence or worship

Teacher Preparation

Unifying Principle—Haunted by Shame. Some people allow the guilt of the past to poison their present. Is it ever possible to be free from condemnation for past actions? When Joseph saw his brothers who sold him into Egyptian slavery, he showed compassion while motivating them to recall and take responsibility for their earlier actions.

A. Read the Bible Background and Devotional Reading.

B. Pray for your students and lesson clarity.

C. Read the lesson Scripture in multiple translations.

O—Open the Lesson

A. Begin the class with prayer.

B. Role-play situations in which someone tries to make another feel guilty and the same situations in which someone tries to assure another that he or she is forgiven.

C. Have the students read the Aim for Change and the In Focus story.

D. Ask students how events like those in the story weigh on their hearts and how they can view these events from a faith perspective.

P—Present the Scriptures

A. Read the Focal Verses and discuss the Background and The People, Places, and Times sections.

B. Have the class share what Scriptures stand out for them and why, with particular emphasis on today's themes.

E—Explore the Meaning

A. Use In Depth or More Light on the Text to facilitate a deeper discussion of the lesson text.

B. Pose the questions in Search the Scriptures and Discuss the Meaning.

C. Discuss the Liberating Lesson and Application for Activation sections.

N—Next Steps for Application

A. Summarize the value of living for the future rather than in the shame of the past.

B. Ask class members to a commitment to pray this week about forgiving someone they felt wronged them.

Worship Guide

For the Superintendent or Teacher
Theme: Love Versus Guilt
Song: "Come Just as You Are"
Devotional Reading: Psalm 51

Love Versus Guilt

Bible Background • GENESIS 42
Printed Text • GENESIS 42:6-25 | Devotional Reading • PSALM 51

Aim for Change

By the end of this lesson, we will EXPLAIN why Joseph's brothers interpreted their misfortune as punishment for their sins, SENSE the need for wholeness in their personal relationships, and IDENTIFY ways to accept God's forgiveness and strive to offer grace to those who mistreat them.

In Focus

Denise was certain that Yuri was the cruelest girl in high school. Almost every day, Yuri would talk about Denise behind her back, spreading mean rumors about who she had a crush on or what she "really" thought about her friends. Even though none of these rumors were true, a few of Denise's friends had believed Yuri's lies and abandoned her. Denise felt alone and hopeless, just wanting this nightmare to be over. All of a sudden, things changed. Yuri stood up in homeroom and said, "My family is moving to Pittsburgh. Today is my last day–just wanted to say goodbye to you all." Denise couldn't believe her ears! Yuri left. In an instant, school became easy for Denise. She graduated high school and went on to cosmetology school, and even opened her own salon.

A few years later, a woman about Denise's age wandered into the salon for her first appointment. Denise gave her usual warm "Hi!" and "Welcome!"–but the other woman froze, and Denise realized why. The woman who came for an appointment was Yuri. The same girl who bullied her so long ago was now coming to Denise to style her hair. Yuri sat silently in the chair, feeling awful for things she had done as a teenager. Denise began the appointment and asked with a smile, "So, how've you been, Yuri?" The two women caught up about their lives. At the end of the appointment, Yuri and Denise each walked away feeling a little better about their past and more importantly, where they will go in the future in their new relationship.

Do you think Yuri apologized? Explain. How have you experienced reconciliation in your life? Describe that experience.

Keep in Mind

"And Reuben answered them, saying, Spake I not unto you, saying, Do not sin against the child; and ye would not hear? therefore, behold, also his blood is required" (Genesis 42:22, KJV).

"'Didn't I tell you not to sin against the boy?' Reuben asked. 'But you wouldn't listen. And now we have to answer for his blood!'" (Genesis 42:22, NLT)

Focal Verses

KJV **Genesis 42:6** And Joseph was the governor over the land, and he it was that sold to all the people of the land: and Joseph's brethren came, and bowed down themselves before him with their faces to the earth.

7 And Joseph saw his brethren, and he knew them, but made himself strange unto them, and spake roughly unto them; and he said unto them, Whence come ye? And they said, From the land of Canaan to buy food.

8 And Joseph knew his brethren, but they knew not him.

9 And Joseph remembered the dreams which he dreamed of them, and said unto them, Ye are spies; to see the nakedness of the land ye are come.

10 And they said unto him, Nay, my lord, but to buy food are thy servants come.

11 We are all one man's sons; we are true men, thy servants are no spies.

12 And he said unto them, Nay, but to see the nakedness of the land ye are come.

13 And they said, Thy servants are twelve brethren, the sons of one man in the land of Canaan; and, behold, the youngest is this day with our father, and one is not.

14 And Joseph said unto them, That is it that I spake unto you, saying, Ye are spies:

15 Hereby ye shall be proved: By the life of Pharaoh ye shall not go forth hence, except your youngest brother come hither.

16 Send one of you, and let him fetch your brother, and ye shall be kept in prison, that your words may be proved, whether there be any truth in you: or else by the life of Pharaoh surely ye are spies.

17 And he put them all together into ward three days.

18 And Joseph said unto them the third day, This do, and live; for I fear God:

NLT **Genesis 42:6** Since Joseph was governor of all Egypt and in charge of selling grain to all the people, it was to him that his brothers came. When they arrived, they bowed before him with their faces to the ground.

7 Joseph recognized his brothers instantly, but he pretended to be a stranger and spoke harshly to them. "Where are you from?" he demanded. "From the land of Canaan," they replied. "We have come to buy food."

8 Although Joseph recognized his brothers, they didn't recognize him.

9 And he remembered the dreams he'd had about them many years before. He said to them, "You are spies! You have come to see how vulnerable our land has become."

10 "No, my lord!" they exclaimed. "Your servants have simply come to buy food.

11 We are all brothers—members of the same family. We are honest men, sir! We are not spies!"

12 "Yes, you are!" Joseph insisted. "You have come to see how vulnerable our land has become."

13 "Sir," they said, "there are actually twelve of us. We, your servants, are all brothers, sons of a man living in the land of Canaan. Our youngest brother is back there with our father right now, and one of our brothers is no longer with us."

14 But Joseph insisted, "As I said, you are spies!

15 This is how I will test your story. I swear by the life of Pharaoh that you will never leave Egypt unless your youngest brother comes here!

16 One of you must go and get your brother. I'll keep the rest of you here in prison. Then we'll find out whether or not your story is true. By the life of Pharaoh, if it turns out that you don't have a younger brother, then I'll know you are spies."

17 So Joseph put them all in prison for three days.

19 If ye be true men, let one of your brethren be bound in the house of your prison: go ye, carry corn for the famine of your houses:

20 But bring your youngest brother unto me; so shall your words be verified, and ye shall not die. And they did so.

21 And they said one to another, We are verily guilty concerning our brother, in that we saw the anguish of his soul, when he besought us, and we would not hear; therefore is this distress come upon us.

22 And Reuben answered them, saying, Spake I not unto you, saying, Do not sin against the child; and ye would not hear? therefore, behold, also his blood is required.

23 And they knew not that Joseph understood them; for he spake unto them by an interpreter.

24 And he turned himself about from them, and wept; and returned to them again, and communed with them, and took from them Simeon, and bound him before their eyes.

25 Then Joseph commanded to fill their sacks with corn, and to restore every man's money into his sack, and to give them provision for the way: and thus did he unto them.

18 On the third day Joseph said to them, "I am a God-fearing man. If you do as I say, you will live.

19 If you really are honest men, choose one of your brothers to remain in prison. The rest of you may go home with grain for your starving families.

20 But you must bring your youngest brother back to me. This will prove that you are telling the truth, and you will not die." To this they agreed.

21 Speaking among themselves, they said, "Clearly we are being punished because of what we did to Joseph long ago. We saw his anguish when he pleaded for his life, but we wouldn't listen. That's why we're in this trouble."

22 "Didn't I tell you not to sin against the boy?" Reuben asked. "But you wouldn't listen. And now we have to answer for his blood!"

23 Of course, they didn't know that Joseph understood them, for he had been speaking to them through an interpreter.

24 Now he turned away from them and began to weep. When he regained his composure, he spoke to them again. Then he chose Simeon from among them and had him tied up right before their eyes.

25 Joseph then ordered his servants to fill the men's sacks with grain, but he also gave secret instructions to return each brother's payment at the top of his sack. He also gave them supplies for their journey home.

The People, Places, and Times

Israel's Sons. Jacob (whom God renamed Israel in Gen 32:28) worked seven years to marry Laban's daughter Rachel. However, on the wedding night, Laban switched Rachel with her older sister Leah. Israel took Leah as his first wife, but Israel married Rachel as well, giving him two wives. A great rivalry grew between the sisters since the younger Rachel was the favorite above Leah, the first wife. Soon after marrying, God blessed Leah with children; she bore Reuben, Simeon, Levi, and Judah. Rachel, who was barren, gave her handmaid Bilhah to Israel to have children by him in her stead. (This was similar to Sarah's actions with Hagar, cf. Genesis 15). Bilhah bore Dan and Naphtali. Leah, believing she could not have more children and fearing she would fall behind in the race to bear sons, gave her handmaid Zilpah to Israel as yet another wife. Zilpah bore Gad and Asher. Then Leah was blessed to have two more sons, Issachar and Zebulun as well as a daughter Dinah. After all this, Rachel finally conceived and bore Joseph, Israel's favorite child. Rachel later gave birth to Benjamin but died shortly after childbirth. These twelve sons of Jacob (Israel) would become the nation of Israel with the generations of each son forming a tribe under that son's name. Joseph is the only exception to this, with his two sons Ephraim and Manasseh each forming a half-tribe in his stead.

Famine. A period of extreme food shortage brought on by drought and excessively dry land. This was the cause of the famine that befell on Egypt during Joseph's time. This was prophesied in Pharaoh's dream of in Genesis 41:6, 23. With ancient agricultural methods providing only enough food for the anticipated population, dying of starvation during a famine was a real and present possibility. A famine could last several years.

Background

Egypt's seven years of agricultural abundance was revealed to Pharaoh in a dream interpreted by Joseph (Genesis 41). Although Pharaoh did not worship the God of Israel, he quickly recognized Joseph's divine connection. God's favor upon Joseph positioned him to receive a life of prominence. As displayed throughout Joseph's life, God also gifted him as a strategic thinker and administrator. Joseph's plan to store grain during the years of plenty prepared Egypt for the coming years of famine. At thirty years old, Joseph became the second most powerful man in the world. He married into one of the leading families of Egypt and was the father of two sons.

The famine hit Canaan where Israel, his sons, and their families lived. Israel heard there was grain in Egypt, and ordered all his sons—except for Benjamin—to travel there to purchase food for their families (Genesis 42:1-4). Benjamin was Israel's remaining son from his beloved wife

Rachel who died giving birth to him (Genesis 35:16-19). Israel was especially afraid to send Benjamin out, after the presumed death of his favorite Joseph. He deeply mourned Joseph (Genesis 37:35) and did not want anything to happen to Benjamin while traveling.

Recount a time when you have seen the goodness of God in the midst of adverse circumstances.

At-A-Glance

1. Confronting Shame (Genesis 42:6-8)
2. Confronting Opportunity (vv. 9-17)
3. Confronting Pain (vv. 18-22)
4. Confronting With Mercy (vv. 23-25)

In Depth

1. Confronting Shame (Genesis 42:6-8)

Over twenty years have passed since the sons of Israel last saw their then-teenage brother Joseph. Now an adult, Joseph is unrecognizable to them. However, Joseph, after many years of pain and separation, immediately recognizes his brothers. He comes face-to-face with the men who turned his world upside down out of vicious envy. As the caravan of brothers approaches Joseph, he sternly asks where they are from, and they respond that they are from Canaan and had come to Egypt to buy food. Joseph's first reaction to seeing his brothers is to treat them as strangers. Because he is in authority and they are in need, he is within his right to treat them harshly. It is a very human response to be curt with someone who caused deep hurt. It is only by recalling God's grace that one can move away from hurtful emotions and respond differently.

As Christians, how can we manage our emotions and maintain godly character?

37

2. Confronting Opportunity (vv. 9-17)

Joseph inwardly recognizes the fulfillment of the prophetic dreams he had as a young man where God revealed how his brothers would bow to him (Genesis 37:5, 9-10). Knowing the brothers' explanation of their motives for traveling to Egypt, Joseph accuses them of being spies. The brothers respond that they are honest men and insist they are sons of one man, who has a total of twelve sons. There are only ten of them present, so the brothers go on to explain how one of the other two is with their father, while the last is deceased. As the highest authority in the room, Joseph refuses to believe their story publicly and continues to accuse the suspicious group of foreign men of being spies. Joseph commands that one of the brothers go back and bring Benjamin to prove their story. Making them experience a little of his pain, Joseph commands the brothers to be locked up for three days.

What would you do if you had the opportunity to pay back someone who hurt you?

3. Confronting Pain (vv. 18-22)

Joseph releases the brothers from prison after three days. He tells them he fears God, and in another test, they must prove they are honest men by leaving one brother behind in prison while the others travel back home with grain to feed their families. If they return with Benjamin, the one in prison will be released and they will all be allowed to live. The brothers talk amongst themselves. The sons of Israel recognize they are being punished for what they did to Joseph whom they believe is deceased. After all the years that passed, the brothers never absolved the guilt of their envious, hate-filled plot to kill their brother and the grief their father experienced. Reuben, Israel's firstborn exclaims how he had warned his brothers, "Do not sin against the child" (from v. 22; cf. Genesis 37:21-22, 29). They all live with considerable regret.

When have you accidentally or purposely inflicted pain on a family member? Were you able to gain forgiveness? Have you forgiven yourself?

4. Confronting With Mercy (vv. 23-25)

Since the sons of Israel believe the man standing before them is Egyptian, the brothers did not realize that Joseph was able to understand every word spoken. Overcome with emotion after hearing the exchange among his siblings, Joseph turns away and weeps. It is too much for him to listen to the brothers take responsibility for what they did to him, and to hear how Reuben defended him against his brothers' plot.

He has Simeon, the second oldest brother, held and the other brothers watch as Simeon is sent back to prison, which places a sense of urgency on their return with Benjamin. Joseph shows mercy to the brothers by sending them back with the grain free of charge, having secretly returned their money to them. Joseph feared God, so seeing his brothers' pain and remorse propels him to give them what they did not give him—a chance to survive.

Recalling God's mercy in your own life, how have you been able to show mercy to others?

Search the Scriptures

1. When Joseph's brothers approached him to buy grain, what was his response (Genesis 42:9, 12, 14)?

2. What do the brothers say in response to Joseph's accusations (v. 10, 13)?

3. Which of the brothers was held in custody? Why (v. 24)?

Discuss the Meaning

1. Do we ever have the right to stay angry? What steps must be taken to mend broken relationships?

2. How can we do a better job at extending grace to others when they fail to meet our expectations or disappoint us?

Liberating Lesson

In a fallen world, we have many occasions to be hurt and mistreated, even by people who are supposed to love us. We also have opportunities to be on the other side as the offender. We have to be prayerful that our actions and reactions are reflective of the love of God in Christ. One of the marks of Christian maturity is the ability to quickly forgive and make amends, which is not an easy task when hurt by someone near your heart. It is the work of the Holy Spirit that brings to remembrance the grace extended to each of us, as we all have been offenders of God. Our lives speak volumes when we can forgive and heal. How can the Church be the agent of change in our world to usher in God's grace, which brings salvation?

Application for Activation

The body of Christ must model before the world the ministry of reconciliation as we to have been blessed to be reconciled to a Holy God. When there is conflict in the church, in our homes, or in our communities, it should acknowledge the validity of those emotions but also never shrink from the hard task of showing humility and forgiveness. We must always engage in a process of mediation that brings forth healing and restoration, not isolation. Jesus gives Christians the model by which to handle conflict (Matthew 18:15-17), and this process with the conviction of the Holy Spirit should bring a loving resolution. Just as God quickly forgives us, we to must be quick to forgive. How can we examine ourselves and our relationships to show the kind of love demonstrated at the Cross?

Follow the Spirit

What God wants me to do:

_____

_____

_____

_____

_____

Remember Your Thoughts

Special insights I have learned:

_____

_____

_____

_____

_____

More Light on the Text

Genesis 42:6-25

Genesis 41 is the story of Joseph's elevation from prison to "prime minister" of Egypt. Joseph had been in an Egyptian prison for two years. But through God's providential plan, he is released to interpret Pharaoh's twofold dreams about Egypt's future economy. He tells Pharaoh that Egypt would experience seven years of bountiful harvest followed by seven years of terrible famine. He advises Pharaoh to appoint "a discreet and wise man" to supervise the preservation of "the fifth part" during the seven good years to be used during the seven bad years of famine (41:33-36). Pharaoh appoints Joseph to the task, placing him in charge of the whole land of Egypt (41:37-44).

39

The seven years of abundance come and go; the seven years of famine begin. The famine has affected everywhere, but there is food in Egypt. All the countries came to Egypt to buy food (Genesis 41:57). Israel (Joseph's father) in Canaan, learning that there is food in Egypt, sends his other ten sons to Egypt to buy food for the family (42:1-5).

6 And Joseph was the governor over the land, and he it was that sold to all the people of the land: and Joseph's brethren came, and bowed down themselves before him with their faces to the earth.

The ten arrive in Egypt and unknowingly meet their brother Joseph who they sold into slavery over 21 years ago (Genesis 37:26-28). He recognizes them, but they do not recognize him. Joseph is the "governor over the land." The Hebrew word translated as "governor" is *shallit* (shal-**LEET**), which means a ruler or person in a position of honor (cf. Genesis 41:40-44). Joseph was in charge of the whole land of Egypt. While Pharaoh is the ceremonial head, Joseph is in charge of the day-to-day administration of the land.

As the ruler over the land, Joseph "sold to all the people of the land." The suggestion here would be that because of the importance of the economy of the land, Joseph takes under his portfolio the ministries of agriculture and commerce for proper accountability and supervision. The phrase does not infer he directly participates in every individual grain transaction or that he deals directly with buyers. There are supervisors who would do that (41:34-36). Moreover, the food supply is stored in different cities around the country (41:46-49). Rather, it is Joseph who gives final approval of all sales. Merchants from all the Middle East and North African world came to Egypt to buy food, including his brothers from Canaan (v. 5). Such foreigners must pass

through Joseph–most likely for security reasons lest there be spies among them (see vv. 9-12).

As his brothers enter Joseph's presence, they bow to him "with their faces on the ground." It is almost universally customary in most African and Arab or ancient Near Eastern countries for people to bow before their superiors–kings, officials, or elders. Joseph's brothers kneel before him just as the dream of his youth said they would (Genesis 37:7).

7 And Joseph saw his brethren, and he knew them, but made himself strange unto them, and spake roughly unto them; and he said unto them, Whence come ye? And they said, From the land of Canaan to buy food. 8 And Joseph knew his brethren, but they knew not him.

As his brothers enter, Joseph recognizes them but hides his identity from them. He "made himself strange unto them" by speaking roughly or harshly to them, camouflaging his identity to make it even more difficult for them to recognize him. Treating them as strangers Joseph asks them where they are from. They answer, "From the land of Canaan to buy food." The repetition in verse 8 that "Joseph knew his brethren, but they knew not him" serves as an emphasis of the fact. They could not have imagined seeing Joseph alive; much less as the man on whom their life literally depends. Joseph was only seventeen years old when they sold them into slavery (37:2); now twenty-one years later he has grown into a young man, his appearance changed. He is now clean-shaven like an Egyptian (41:14), he dresses like an Egyptian, and his language is Egyptian (see Genesis 42:23).

9 And Joseph remembered the dreams which he dreamed of them, and said unto them, Ye are spies; to see the nakedness of the land ye are come. 10 And they said unto him, Nay, my lord, but to buy food are thy

servants come. 11 We are all one man's sons; we are true men, thy servants are no spies.

On seeing his brothers prostrating before him, Joseph remembers the two dreams he had about them many years before. The dreams almost cost him his life, but they caused him to be sold into slavery to Egypt through God's providential grace (37:18ff). He realizes that the faithful God is about to fulfill the promises God made to him through the dreams. He continues the act and intensifies his interrogation. He accuses them of being spies come to "see the nakedness" or vulnerabilities of Egypt. They vehemently deny the accusation and reaffirm their honesty and mission. To further stress their sincerity, his brothers give Joseph details of their family makeup and background. They tell him that they are all siblings, from the same father.

Since the brothers refute the claim of espionage by saying they are brothers, one can assume they guessed Joseph's basis in making his accusation was the improbability of such a number of foreigners traveling together. They are not openly representing a nation, nor are they a whole caravan of traders; they are only ten men. When Moses selects spies to enter the Promised Land, he selects roughly this same number of men (Numbers 13:2-3). The reason for this detail is that it would be irrational for all ten of them from the same parent to engage in spying. Spies would more likely be chosen to represent a wider selection of a population. The brothers respond saying the reason they are a group is not that they are working together on a nefarious plot, but simply that they are brothers.

12 And he said unto them, Nay, but to see the nakedness of the land ye are come. 13 And they said, Thy servants are twelve brethren, the sons of one man in the land of Canaan; and, behold, the youngest is this day with our father, and one is not.

In spite of their denial, Joseph repeats his accusation emphatically. Again unable to convince Joseph of their sincerity, they reveal more about their family. They tell him that they are twelve brothers, "the sons of one man in the land of Canaan." They tell him about their other two siblings too. They tell Joseph that the youngest is left at home with their father, and the other "one is not." Of course, they are referring to Benjamin (Joseph's brother) and Joseph himself whom they presume is dead. Notice they refer themselves twice as "thy servants" (vv. 10 and 13) unwittingly fulfilling Joseph's first dream (37:5-8).

14 And Joseph said unto them, That is it that I spake unto you, saying, Ye are spies: 15 Hereby ye shall be proved: By the life of Pharaoh ye shall not go forth hence, except your youngest brother come hither.

After the brothers' disclosure of their family history, Joseph pretends to be even harder on them. In fact, he is grateful to know that the only brother born of his mother Rachel is alive. As a test, Joseph tells them that they must bring their youngest brother to him. Joseph emphasizes his command by swearing, "By the life of Pharaoh." To swear on the life of a reigning monarch, a deity, or God places great importance to the order or statement (Judges 8:19; 1 Samuel 14:39; 20:3). The Pharaohs of Egypt were regarded as gods, so Joseph continues to play the part of a native Egyptian and swears by one of their gods. His brothers understand the significance of the statement.

16 Send one of you, and let him fetch your brother, and ye shall be kept in prison, that your words may be proved, whether there be any truth in you: or else by the life of Pharaoh surely ye are spies. 17 And he put them all together into ward three days.

To prove their honesty, Joseph suggests that one of them should go home to bring his brother to Egypt, while the rest shall be confined in prison. This would prove "whether there be any truth in you," Joseph says to them. He wants to know if they are really truthful in their dealings or treacherously still the same as they were over twenty-one years ago when they sold him into slavery. The word "truth" (Heb. *emeth*, **EH**-meth) can also mean trustworthiness. Joseph wants to make sure they can be trusted and that there is a genuine change in them. He orders that all ten be kept in prison for three days.

18 And Joseph said unto them the third day, This do, and live; for I fear God: 19 If ye be true men, let one of your brethren be bound in the house of your prison: go ye, carry corn for the famine of your houses: 20 But bring your youngest brother unto me; so shall your words be verified, and ye shall not die. And they did so.

Joseph had suggested that one of them should be sent home to bring their brother (v. 16). But he changes his plan (v. 18). On the third day of their incarceration, Joseph tells them that only one would stay behind bars, while the other nine return home with their purchase. The first reason for changing his plan is spoken directly: It is because of his fear of God. He says, "for I fear God" that is "I revere God." For the first time before his brothers, Joseph mentions "God" (Hebrew, *'elohim*, eh-low-**HEEM**). *'Elohim* is the plural form of the Hebrew *el* (**ELL**) which means "god," and it is widely used of the supreme God. Joseph still worships the true God of Israel, however, the brothers do not know whether to take the comment as a profession of their faith or of faith in general. The translation leans toward "God," but could also mean "gods." The brothers are also hearing Joseph's words through a translator.

The second reason for releasing nine brothers instead of one is implicit. Nine people would carry more food home than one person. Joseph is motivated by his reverence for God and prompted by love and genuine concern for his starving family in Canaan. It appears that the ultimate reason for his change of plan is his love for his younger brother and the desire to see him. Thus the condition is that they must bring him as proof of their truthfulness (v. 20). This is the definitive test of their honesty and holding one back would motivate them to come back with Benjamin.

21 And they said one to another, We are verily guilty concerning our brother, in that we saw the anguish of his soul, when he besought us, and we would not hear; therefore is this distress come upon us. 22 And Reuben answered them, saying, Spake I not unto you, saying, Do not sin against the child; and ye would not hear? therefore, behold, also his blood is required.

This whole experience seems to bring conviction in the brothers' hearts. They realize that they are now reaping what they had sown. Unaware that Joseph understands them, and feeling remorseful, they reminisce how cruel and harshly they treated Joseph a long time ago. They confer among themselves how Joseph's anguish, pleas, and tears never moved them; rather they hardened their hearts and sold him to Egypt. They lament their past actions and their current punishment. Reuben's contribution to the discussion (roughly "I told you so") does not seem to help the situation. Nonetheless, he unconsciously reveals to Joseph his kindness toward him, and the effort he made to rescue him during his time of agony (37:21-22). They however never show genuine repentance for their past wicked conduct. Rather they feel guilty and sorry for themselves, not really remorseful of what they did.

23 And they knew not that Joseph understood them; for he spake unto them by an interpreter. 24 And he turned himself about from them, and wept; and returned to them again, and communed with them, and took from them Simeon, and bound him before their eyes.

As they deliberate, they do not know that Joseph understands all they were saying, for he is speaking to them through an interpreter (v. 23). Up to that point, Joseph has been able to control his emotions. Now on hearing their discussion and the guilt they feel, Joseph can control his feelings no longer. Not yet ready to express his emotions openly though, Joseph withdraws from the room to weep privately. Apart from not wanting to reveal his identity, the (harmful) cultural expectation then and now is that men do not cry. This would be especially true for a person in such a high position of authority. It would be degrading to the office, a show of weakness. Christians know, however, that emotions have no rank when it comes to family and loved ones–particularly in the expression of joy, excitement, and happiness or grief. All people—male and female, powerful and lowly—should be encouraged to exhibit their full range of emotions.

After weeping privately, Joseph returns to the room and resumes his communication with them. Out of the ten, Joseph chooses Simeon, binds him in their presence, and confines him in prison. Why would he choose Simeon the second oldest of the twelve instead of Reuben the firstborn? (29:32-33). It has been suggested that it is because he realized that Reuben showed him kindness and saved his life many years back when the rest had planned to kill him (37:21-22).

25 Then Joseph commanded to fill their sacks with corn, and to restore every man's money into his sack, and to give them provision for the way: and thus did he unto them.

With Simeon in prison, the nine are allowed to go back to their families in Canaan with their purchase. But before their departure, Joseph gives orders to fill their sacks with grain and put each person's money back in his sack. The estimated distance between Canaan and Egypt is about 200 miles; it would take about ten days to make the trip riding donkeys. Probably it would take them more days with the donkeys carrying the heavy sacks of grain and the men trekking on foot. Joseph orders, "to give them provisions for the way," that is, enough food supply to last the nine brothers and their donkeys for the duration of their journey home.

Joseph was generous and kind to his brothers in spite of the harshness of his speech and treatment toward them. Motivated by love and the knowledge that God was in the plan, Joseph forgave them and cared for them. His purpose was to bring them to repentance and reconciliation. That is what genuine love can do, and we can live such lives also.

Sources:

Attridge, Harold, W. *The Harper Collins Study Bible, New Revised Standard Version*. New York, NY: Harper One, 2006. 60-61, 67-69.

Strong, James. *The New Strong's Expanded Exhaustive Concordance of the Bible*. Nashville, TN: Thomas Nelson, 2006.

Wiersbe, Warren W. *The Wiersbe Bible Commentary: Old Testament*. Colorado Springs, CO: David C. Cook, 2007.

Zondervan NIV Study Bible. Grand Rapids, MI: Zondervan, 2008.

Say It Correctly

Reuben. **ROO**-bin.

Canaan. **KAY**-nin.

Daily Bible Readings

MONDAY
Have Mercy on Me, a Sinner
(Psalm 51:1-12)

TUESDAY
Pilate's Judgment of Jesus, "Not Guilty"
(Luke 23:9-15)

WEDNESDAY
Brothers Sent to Egypt to Buy Grain
(Genesis 42:1-5)

THURSDAY
Joseph Returns Money with Grain
(Genesis 42:26-28)

FRIDAY
Joseph Questions Motives of Brothers
(Genesis 42:29-34)

SATURDAY
Jacob Vows Not to Send Benjamin
(Genesis 42:35-38)

SUNDAY
Joseph Confronts
Brothers for Past Behavior
(Genesis 42:6-25)

Notes

_____

_____

_____

_____

Teaching Tips

Words You Should Know

A. Earing (v. 6) *chariysh* (Heb.)—Plowing; plowing time

B. Nourish (vv. 11) *kul* (Heb.)—Feed, attend to, contain, sustain, endure

Teacher Preparation

Unifying Principle—Love Prevails Over All. Sometimes one is overwhelmed by tragic events in his or her life. What can keep hope alive after the struggle ends? Joseph tells his brothers what they meant as harm was God's plan for saving them, a remnant of God's people.

A. Read the Bible Background and Devotional Reading.

B. Pray for your students and lesson clarity.

C. Read the lesson Scripture in multiple translations.

O—Open the Lesson

A. Begin the class with prayer.

B. Divide the class into two groups. Have the first group list reasons people love family reunions and the other group will list reasons people dread family reunions.

C. Have the students read the Aim for Change and the In Focus story.

D. Ask students how events like those in the story weigh on their hearts and how they can view these events from a faith perspective.

P—Present the Scriptures

A. Read the Focal Verses and discuss the Background and The People, Places, and Times sections.

B. Have the class share what Scriptures stand out for them and why, with particular emphasis on today's themes.

E—Explore the Meaning

A. Use In Depth or More Light on the Text to facilitate a deeper discussion of the lesson text.

B. Pose the questions in Search the Scriptures and Discuss the Meaning.

C. Discuss the Liberating Lesson and Application for Activation sections.

N—Next Steps for Application

A. Summarize the value of God's hand in shaping history.

B. Challenge the class to commit to praying this week to know and seek God's will.

Worship Guide

For the Superintendent or Teacher
Theme: God's Plan Revealed
Song: "God Will Take Care of You"
Devotional Reading: John 14:1-14

God's Plan Revealed

Bible Background • GENESIS 43; 45:1–15
Printed Text • GENESIS 45:1–15 | Devotional Reading • JOHN 14:1-14

Aim for Change

By the end of this lesson, we will UNDERSTAND how Joseph viewed his past mistreatment at the hand of his brothers, RECOGNIZE how God is at work in difficult circumstances, and RESPOND to mistreatment not with vengeance but with creative, transforming initiatives.

In Focus

As Melvin sat at his mother's funeral, he couldn't believe she was gone. He deliberately did not sit on the front row with the rest of the family. Many of his relatives were treating him like an outsider—like he had no right to mourn.

He hadn't come to visit after learning the cancer had spread. He didn't want his mother's last memory of him to be as a drug addict.

Other relatives and friends had long abandoned him. Mama had known for years that he abused drugs, but she always held out hope. "Son, I'm praying for you," she would say. "And I know the Lord can hear me." Melvin felt he had let his mother down for not getting clean before she passed.

Melvin began to cry. Never before had he felt so afraid, alone, and unloved. Then, he felt a firm hand on his shoulder. He looked up and saw his younger sister. "Big brother, I've missed you. I'm so glad you came," she whispered. Finally, Melvin looked over his left shoulder. It was the first time he had ever seen his father cry. "Welcome home, son. Welcome home."

The love he felt from his family made Melvin determined to get help immediately.

What is the greatest act of forgiveness you've witnessed? Was all animosity truly forgiven?

Keep in Mind

"Now therefore be not grieved, nor angry with yourselves, that ye sold me hither: for God did send me before you to preserve life" (Genesis 45:5, KJV).

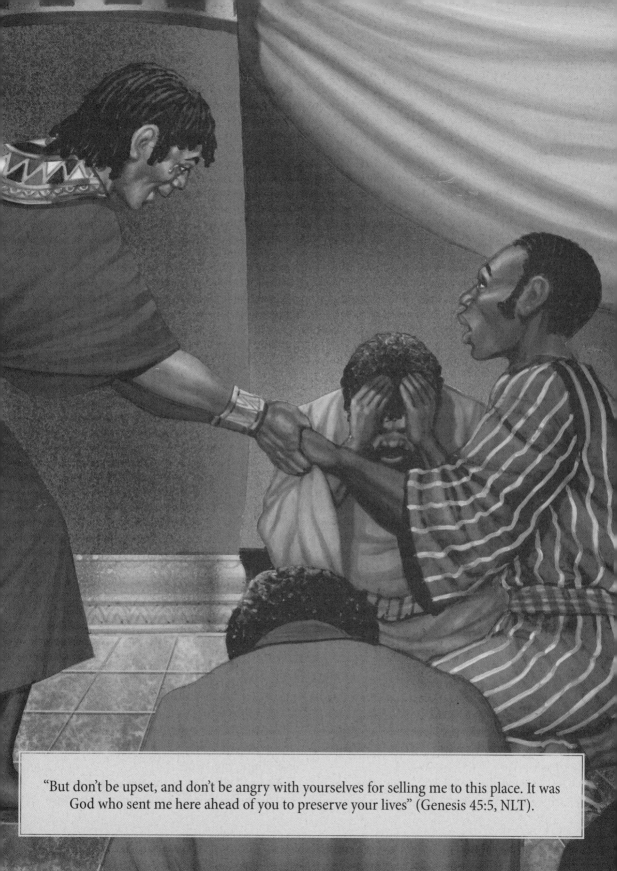

"But don't be upset, and don't be angry with yourselves for selling me to this place. It was God who sent me here ahead of you to preserve your lives" (Genesis 45:5, NLT).

Focal Verses

KJV **Genesis 45:1** Then Joseph could not refrain himself before all them that stood by him; and he cried, Cause every man to go out from me. And there stood no man with him, while Joseph made himself known unto his brethren.

2 And he wept aloud: and the Egyptians and the house of Pharaoh heard.

3 And Joseph said unto his brethren, I am Joseph; doth my father yet live? And his brethren could not answer him; for they were troubled at his presence.

4 And Joseph said unto his brethren, Come near to me, I pray you. And they came near. And he said, I am Joseph your brother, whom ye sold into Egypt.

5 Now therefore be not grieved, nor angry with yourselves, that ye sold me hither: for God did send me before you to preserve life.

6 For these two years hath the famine been in the land: and yet there are five years, in the which there shall neither be earing nor harvest.

7 And God sent me before you to preserve you a posterity in the earth, and to save your lives by a great deliverance.

8 So now it was not you that sent me hither, but God: and he hath made me a father to Pharaoh, and lord of all his house, and a ruler throughout all the land of Egypt.

9 Haste ye, and go up to my father, and say unto him, Thus saith thy son Joseph, God hath made me lord of all Egypt: come down unto me, tarry not:

10 And thou shalt dwell in the land of Goshen, and thou shalt be near unto me, thou, and thy children, and thy children's children, and thy flocks, and thy herds, and all that thou hast:

11 And there will I nourish thee; for yet there are five years of famine; lest thou, and

NLT **Genesis 45:1** Joseph could stand it no longer. There were many people in the room, and he said to his attendants, "Out, all of you!" So he was alone with his brothers when he told them who he was.

2 Then he broke down and wept. He wept so loudly the Egyptians could hear him, and word of it quickly carried to Pharaoh's palace.

3 "I am Joseph!" he said to his brothers. "Is my father still alive?" But his brothers were speechless! They were stunned to realize that Joseph was standing there in front of them.

4 "Please, come closer," he said to them. So they came closer. And he said again, "I am Joseph, your brother, whom you sold into slavery in Egypt.

5 But don't be upset, and don't be angry with yourselves for selling me to this place. It was God who sent me here ahead of you to preserve your lives.

6 This famine that has ravaged the land for two years will last five more years, and there will be neither plowing nor harvesting.

7 God has sent me ahead of you to keep you and your families alive and to preserve many survivors.

8 So it was God who sent me here, not you! And he is the one who made me an adviser to Pharaoh—the manager of his entire palace and the governor of all Egypt.

9 Now hurry back to my father and tell him, 'This is what your son Joseph says: God has made me master over all the land of Egypt. So come down to me immediately!

10 You can live in the region of Goshen, where you can be near me with all your children and grandchildren, your flocks and herds, and everything you own.

11 I will take care of you there, for there are still five years of famine ahead of us. Otherwise thy household, and all that thou hast, come to poverty.

12 And, behold, your eyes see, and the eyes of my brother Benjamin, that it is my mouth that speaketh unto you.

13 And ye shall tell my father of all my glory in Egypt, and of all that ye have seen; and ye shall haste and bring down my father hither.

14 And he fell upon his brother Benjamin's neck, and wept; and Benjamin wept upon his neck.

15 Moreover he kissed all his brethren, and wept upon them: and after that his brethren talked with him.

you, your household, and all your animals will starve.'"

12 Then Joseph added, "Look! You can see for yourselves, and so can my brother Benjamin, that I really am Joseph!

13 Go tell my father of my honored position here in Egypt. Describe for him everything you have seen, and then bring my father here quickly."

14 Weeping with joy, he embraced Benjamin, and Benjamin did the same.

15 Then Joseph kissed each of his brothers and wept over them, and after that they began talking freely with him.

The People, Places, and Times

Joseph. Of Israel's twelve sons, Joseph was his favorite. He was Israel's eleventh son and the first son of his favored wife, Rachel. This designation by his father and Joseph's God-given ability to prophesy caused Joseph's older brothers to hate him. Eventually, Joseph became a vizier, an officer second only to Pharaoh.

Goshen. A fertile river valley in the delta region of Lower Egypt where Israel and his family would live under Joseph's watchful eye. Goshen was fertile because of its proximity to the Nile River and excellent pasturage for herds.

Background

Joseph was a man who honored God in every situation whether it was suffering or success; he honored the one true and living God. Potiphar's wife tried to tempt him, but because Joseph wanted to honor his Master, he would not yield (Genesis 39:9). Although God had given him the ability to interpret dreams, Joseph always gave God the credit for being able to do so (Genesis 40:8). Even when he was before Pharaoh, he honored God. When asked to interpret Pharaoh's dream, Joseph boldly told Pharaoh there would be a specific number of

years of plenty and famine would surely follow (Genesis 41:14–36). When Joseph named his son, Manasseh (which means "to forget"), he was stating that God helped him to forget his sorrow. In today's lesson, Joseph tells his brothers who he is and acknowledges that God is responsible for him being in Egypt. Later after Israel dies, Joseph will reassure his brothers that God had ordered his steps, and God did it for the good of all (Genesis 50:15–21).

In what area of your life do you need to give more honor to God?

At-A-Glance

1. Joseph Makes Himself Known
(Genesis 45:1–8)
2. A Family Reunited (vv. 9–15)

In Depth

1. Joseph Makes Himself Known (Genesis 45:1–8)

After having held back his emotions as best he could for quite a while, Joseph tells his brothers who he really is. His brothers had known him

49

by his Egyptian name, Zaphnath-paaneah, but now he boldly states, "I am Joseph" (v. 3). The brothers are afraid and stand in disbelief or amazement, unable to move or speak. Joseph sees their concern and tries to ease their minds. He calls out to them, beckoning them closer and assuring them they have no reason to fear.

Joseph assures them of God's sovereignty. He understands that whatever they tried to do for evil, God meant for good and a lot of good came out of it. He does not want them to grieve or be angry with themselves for selling him (v. 5). Instead of having a vindictive attitude toward them, he gives recognition to God. God had a perfect plan in mind and was using the brothers' sinful acts to preserve a remnant of His chosen people.

Joseph's statements are not meant to make light of sin or sinners, but rather to illuminate how God does things (vv. 7-8). This was not to give an excuse for sinning, but rather to appreciate and celebrate the almighty power of God in those things we could refer to as "misfortune." God is in divine control.

What can we do to remember, like Joseph, that God is in control even when situations seem evil or chaotic?

2. A Family Reunited (vv. 9–15)

Again, in an effort to make his brothers feel more confident and secure, Joseph promises to take care of his father and all his family during the next years of the famine. He urges his brothers to hurry back to Canaan to get this news to their father Israel and let him know about Joseph's authority in Egypt. Joseph has enough power to help them all. "I will nourish thee," promises Joseph (v. 11). He is delighted to be in the position to help his father and his family. He is excited for his father to know where God has placed him and eager to relieve his father of the stress of the famine.

Joseph's reunion with Benjamin is especially emotional, since Benjamin is his only full brother and since Joseph had missed Benjamin's childhood when his other brothers sold him into slavery. They hugged and began to weep on each other's necks (v. 14). Then Joseph hugs and weeps with all of them, and everyone "talked freely" (v. 15). Joseph's words and actions make his brothers realize that he was not holding a grudge and was genuinely affectionate toward them. Knowing what God has done for all of them and would do in the future; Joseph is compassionate toward the brothers who had hurt him so much. He does not let past experiences with his brothers defeat the purpose of all that the Lord allowed him to go through. Instead, Joseph is warm toward them, and they are able to reciprocate these feelings.

Joseph's reunion with his family was emotional and tearful. How does your family deal with strong emotions?

Search the Scriptures

1. Why did Joseph send everyone outside the room except his brothers? (Genesis 45:1)

2. How did the brothers react when Joseph revealed his identity? (vv. 1-4)

3. Why did God send Joseph to Egypt ahead of his brothers (v. 5)?

Discuss the Meaning

Satan's plan was to use Pontius Pilate, Judas Iscariot, the mob in the streets, and the cruel Roman soldiers to end the plan God had for Jesus Christ. How did these men's actions fulfill God's divine plan of salvation for humankind through His only Son, Jesus Christ? Compare and contrast this example from the New Testament with the actions of Joseph's brothers, before and after they encountered him in Egypt.

Liberating Lesson

Philippians 4:11 tells us that in whatever state we find ourselves, we must be content. In other words, we must accept that the situation will be resolved because God is there and worthy of our praise. He has a plan and a purpose in everything He allows us to go through. Whether we understand His plan or not, we must never forget that God is all we need.

The tragedy is happening all around us. Too many youths are dying and injured due to gangs, gun violence, substance abuse, bullying, and even suicide. Our first instinct is to ask why. While we must be active in our communities to help recognize and combat these issues, we must also realize that God is helping us and speaking even in the midst of these circumstances. It may appear as though the enemy is having his way, but we can be assured that God's plan is being fulfilled for His perfect purpose.

Application for Activation

Joseph's brothers didn't know what to expect after finding out who Joseph was, the position he held, and remembering what they had done to him. Joseph relieved them of their worries by embracing them. As we interact with our families, our brothers and sisters in Christ as well as other people, let us adopt Joseph's attitude, especially with family members. Let us remember to be kind to others always. Our ability to respond to situations as victors, rather than victims, depends on our ability to recognize the hand of God in every situation. We can do this as we incorporate prayer, Bible study and other spiritual disciplines in our lives. This week set aside time each day to spend with God. Thank God for the challenging times you have faced and allowed Him to use you for His glory.

Follow the Spirit

What God wants me to do:

_____

_____

_____

_____

_____

Remember Your Thoughts

Special insights I have learned:

_____

_____

_____

_____

_____

More Light on the Text

Genesis 45:1–15

True to God's word, Egypt knew seven good years of prosperity and plenty (Genesis 41:46ff), just as Joseph had said when he interpreted Pharaoh's dreams. As the good years ended and the seven years of famine began, all of the lands around Egypt experienced the famine, but initially, Egypt did not. When the people began to feel the effects of the famine, they pleaded with the Pharaoh to feed them. He directed them to do whatever Joseph instructed (vv. 53–57). Among the people seeking food from the storehouses under Joseph's rule were ten of his brothers (Genesis 42:1ff). He recognized them, but they did not recognize him. Joseph questions them, imprisoning them, holding one

51

of them for ransom, and secretly returning their payment for the grain. On their second trip to Egypt, they convinced Israel to let Benjamin come, and Joseph treats his brothers to a feast, but interrogates them again, threatening to make Benjamin stay in Egypt as his slave for "stealing" a cup, which he had actually planted in Benjamin's stacks. To stop this from happening, Judah tells Joseph the long story of all Israel's protests to bringing Benjamin to Egypt and how Judah had promised on his own life that Benjamin would return to their old father (Genesis 43:1–44:34).

1 Then Joseph could not refrain himself before all them that stood by him; and he cried, Cause every man to go out from me. And there stood no man with him, while Joseph made himself known unto his brethren. 2 And he wept aloud: and the Egyptians and the house of Pharaoh heard.

Hearing Judah's willingness for self-sacrifice and the precarious age of his father, Joseph can no longer keep up his act. Joseph was unable to restrain his emotions any longer or withhold his identity from his brothers. He cries out to dismiss everyone around, all except his brothers. Joseph likely felt too embarrassed to cry in front of his subordinates, besides wanting to keep this special family reunion private. In this private moment, Joseph wept aloud out of his loving devotion to his brothers despite a dire situation. Joseph wept so uncontrollably that everyone in the building heard their wise, prudent, discerning leader weeping.

3 And Joseph said unto his brethren, I am Joseph; doth my father yet live? And his brethren could not answer him; for they were troubled at his presence.

Upon revealing who he was, Joseph immediately inquires of his father's condition and whether he is still alive. Even though the brothers had told him earlier that his father was indeed alive, they had said this when they knew Joseph as an Egyptian official (Genesis 44:20). Perhaps after hearing Judah's long explanation of how Israel was only one grief away from the grave, Joseph was asking this of them again with a son's emphatic love and longing for his father. Perhaps they had exaggerated the truth when they thought he was only an Egyptian official making polite conversation. Now knowing Israel is his father too, they will tell him the full truth. At first Joseph's brothers could not answer him because they were "troubled" (Heb. *bahal*, baw-**HAL**), meaning "disturbed, alarmed, terrified"—most likely they were shocked by Joseph's "presence" (Heb. *paniym*, paw-**NEEM**), meaning "face" and position. Either understanding of the word is possible here; they could be shocked at the sudden emotion in Joseph's face or shocked at being in the presence of one they thought dead or trouble by knowing the brother they had treated so harshly was now positioned as ruler of a world super-power. They surely remembered the occasion years ago when they had hated Joseph and conspired to kill him.

4 And Joseph said unto his brethren, Come near to me, I pray you. And they came near. And he said, I am Joseph your brother, whom ye sold into Egypt.

But Joseph, overjoyed to see them, calls out to them, "Come near" (Heb. *nagash*, naw-**GASH**), meaning approach him, to get a closer look at the brother they had indeed sold to the Midianites when he was only a teenager. After speaking harshly to them since their first trip to Egypt, Joseph now softens his tone, adding "I pray you" (Heb. *na'*, **NAW**) to his command. The phrase "whom ye sold into Egypt" is not meant to remind them of their foolish and diabolical plot, but rather to impress upon them the truth of his identity. Only Joseph himself would know the brothers had done this.

5 Now therefore be not grieved, nor angry with yourselves, that ye sold me hither: for God did send me before you to preserve life.

In a gracious turn of events, the same Joseph who had been left to die and eventually sold into slavery encourages his brothers not to be "grieved" (Heb. *'atsab*, aw-**TSAB**), meaning "hurt, vexed" by his revelation and not to be "angry" (Heb. *charah*, khaw-**RAH**), meaning "kindled, incensed" against themselves for past actions. One would think that any anger in this situation would be anger on Joseph's part against his brothers, but here he shows great compassion to them, asking them to put away their own anger against themselves. Joseph assured the brothers that God had used those very events to send him ahead of them to Egypt "to preserve life" (Heb. *michyah*, mikh-**YAH**), meaning "provide sustenance" for them now that a famine was upon the region. Although his brothers' actions had not been a dream, Joseph the dreamer was using his interpretive skill to represent God's love and redemptive plan.

6 For these two years hath the famine been in the land: and yet there are five years, in the which there shall neither be earing nor harvest. 7 And God sent me before you to preserve you a posterity in the earth, and to save your lives by a great deliverance. 8 So now it was not you that sent me hither, but God: and he hath made me a father to Pharaoh, and lord of all his house, and a ruler throughout all the land of Egypt.

Knowing these first two years of famine have been harsh for the Canaanites, Joseph tells his brothers the divine revelation that there will yet be five more years of famine. He tells his brothers that the ensuing five years would produce no "earing" (Heb. *chariysh*, khaw- **REESH**), meaning no plowing time (i.e. the time to remove the "ears" of grain) and no harvest. But he also assures them that God, not

their angry jealousy, placed him in position for a "posterity" (Heb. *she'eriyth*, sheh-ay-**REETH**) or portion during the seven good years. Because Joseph had been established as overseer, their lives were going to be preserved. The famine would kill many, but God provided deliverance for the family through Joseph.

Joseph assures his brothers of God's providential hand in the situation. God had established him as "a father" (another title for a viceroy or official spiritual advisor) and a "lord" (Heb. *'adown*, aw-**DONE**), meaning "firm, strong, master" over Pharaoh's immediate household, and "ruler" (Heb. *mashal*, maw-**SHAL**), meaning "someone with dominion" overall inhabitants of the land during the famine. This is an amazing amount of power blessed on a boy who was sold into slavery and imprisoned falsely. Only the living God could have orchestrated that change in his life!

9 Haste ye, and go up to my father, and say unto him, Thus saith thy son Joseph, God hath made me lord of all Egypt: come down unto me, tarry not: 10 And thou shalt dwell in the land of Goshen, and thou shalt be near unto me, thou, and thy children, and thy children's children, and thy flocks, and thy herds, and all that thou hast:

Joseph then charged his brothers to hurry and return to their father with the good news of his life, appointment, and favor. Joseph sends his brothers away with a message of hope and celebration. He invites his brothers and father to come and dwell in the land of Goshen (**GO**-shen), a Hebrew word for a place whose name means "drawing near," a region in northern Egypt east of the lower Nile. It was a fertile area with much access to the riches of trading. There they could be near him and enjoy all the rights, privileges, and protection suitable to his kin. (The Children of Israel lived there from the time of Joseph until the time of Moses.) Joseph's invitation extended to his father, brothers, nieces and nephews; their "flocks" (Heb. *tso'n*, **tsone**), meaning "small cattle and flocks"; their "herds" (Heb. *baqar*, baw-**KAWR**), meaning "large cattle and oxen"; and "all that thou hast," meaning all their possessions. Joseph is not just inviting them to visit or just inviting his father and favorite brothers. He intends to move the entire clan and establish them under the protection of Egypt.

11 And there will I nourish thee; for yet there are five years of famine; lest thou, and thy household, and all that thou hast, come to poverty. 12 And, behold, your eyes see, and the eyes of my brother Benjamin, that it is my mouth that speaketh unto you.

It would be while they were in Goshen—or more importantly, near Joseph—that he would directly "nourish" (Heb. *kul*, **KOOL**), meaning "sustain, maintain, contain" all of his brothers' and father's households, and thereby prevent them from being overcome by "poverty" (Heb. *yarash*, yaw-**RASH**, "impoverished, disinherited"). There is no need for them to continue trekking back and forth between Canaan and Egypt every year. No need for them to buy grain from Egypt with silver. Joseph will gladly use his divinely appointed position in Egypt to take care of his entire extended family. He will keep them from deadly poverty and lack.

Perhaps because the encounter was truly incredible, Joseph appealed to his brothers to verify his identity, especially Benjamin. He and Benjamin barely knew each other, but Joseph knew that Benjamin was his only full brother and thinks of him most dearly. Joseph urgently needs his brothers to understand that it is he, Joseph, who "speaketh" to them (Heb. *dabar*, daw-**BAR**), meaning "declare, promise." His speech has a special weight in Egypt. In spite of how his brothers had treated him and the

poverty they now experienced, Joseph cared for them.

13 And ye shall tell my father of all my glory in Egypt, and of all that ye have seen; and ye shall haste and bring down my father hither. 14 And he fell upon his brother Benjamin's neck, and wept; and Benjamin wept upon his neck. 15 Moreover he kissed all his brethren, and wept upon them: and after that his brethren talked with him.

What concerned Joseph at this point was his father, Israel. Joseph entreated his brothers to inform their father that he (Joseph) was doing incredibly well in Egypt—he was highly esteemed. In order to get Israel to come quickly, Joseph insisted that his brothers tell Israel of all of Joseph's "glory" (Heb. *kabod*, kaw-**BODE**), which refers to abundance, riches, splendor, importance and majesty. In other words, in the midst of a famine, God had seen to it that Joseph was flourishing. God had made the impossible, possible.

Then Joseph could no longer contain himself. He had experienced several encounters in Egypt with his brothers who did not know who they were dealing with while Joseph had known precisely who they were (Genesis 42– 44). Joseph had chosen to reveal the truth of his identity, and then he had graciously offered his forgiveness and his help. He wept with joy and embraced Benjamin. Joseph did not let his honored position hinder his pure tears of joy upon seeing his family again—a family that he probably thought that he would never see again. This was a heart-wrenching moment. Not only did Joseph weep over his baby brother, but also he wept over the brothers who had sold him into slavery and had plotted to kill him. When these brothers saw Joseph's genuine, forgiving spirit was not going to take revenge against them, their guard came down and they began to freely talk to him. Joseph sent his brothers back to Canaan for their father and the whole family so that they could live in Egypt and survive the famine. What Satan had meant for evil, God indeed worked for good. God used Joseph's personal suffering to bless Joseph's family for generations to come. It was a time of healing and restoration that only a loving and merciful God could bring to what had been an extremely dysfunctional family.

Sources:
Henry, Matthew. *Mathew Henry's Concise Commentary on the Whole Bible.* Nashville, TN: Thomas Nelson, 2003.
Life Application Study Bible (New Living Translation). Wheaton, IL: Tyndale House, 1996. 81–82.
Youngblood, Ronald F., ed. *Nelson's New Illustrated Bible Dictionary.* Nashville, TN: Thomas Nelson, 1995. 704–05.

Say It Correctly

Goshen. **GOH**-shun
Manasseh. muh-**NAH**-suh
Zaphnath-paaneah. Zaph-nath-**PA**-a-ne-ah (Joseph's Egyptian name)

Daily Bible Readings

MONDAY
During Trouble, Maintain Hope in God
(Psalm 43)

TUESDAY
Benjamin Sent to Joseph with Gifts
(Genesis 43:1-15)

WEDNESDAY
Stolen Cup Found in Benjamin's Grain
(Genesis 44:1-13)

THURSDAY
Brothers Offer to
Become Slaves to Joseph
(Genesis 44:14-17)

FRIDAY
Judah Pleads with Joseph for Benjamin
(Genesis 44:18-26)

SATURDAY
Jacob Will Die Without Seeing Benjamin
(Genesis 44:27-34)

SUNDAY
Joseph and His Brothers
Reconcile Their Differences
(Genesis 45:1-15)

Notes

Teaching Tips

Words You Should Know

A. Innocent (v. 5) *naqi* (Heb.)—Clean, clear, exempt from obligations

B. Without a cause (v. 5) *chinnam* (Heb.)—Without reason, gratuitously, undeservedly

Teacher Preparation

Unifying Principle—A True Friend Intervenes. Although families are important, family dysfunction can skew our priorities and lead us to ruin. Is there a greater priority than family? Jonathan opposed the unjust intentions of his father, King Saul, in order to offer support and protection to David.

A. Read the Bible Background and Devotional Reading.

B. Pray for your students and lesson clarity.

C. Read the lesson Scripture in multiple translations.

O—Open the Lesson

A. Begin the class with prayer.

B. It is said, "Blood is thicker than water." As a class, discuss if you agree or disagree and why.

C. Have the students read the Aim for Change and the In Focus story.

D. Ask students how events like those in the story weigh on their hearts and how they can view these events from a faith perspective.

P—Present the Scriptures

A. Read the Focal Verses and discuss the Background and The People, Places, and Times sections.

B. Have the class share what Scriptures stand out for them and why, with particular emphasis on today's themes.

E—Explore the Meaning

A. Use In Depth or More Light on the Text to facilitate a deeper discussion of the lesson text.

B. Pose the questions in Search the Scriptures and Discuss the Meaning.

C. Discuss the Liberating Lesson and Application for Activation sections.

N—Next Steps for Application

A. Summarize the value of solving differences by reconciling opposing parties.

B. Have class members consider how they responded when a family relationship was broken. Ask class members to pray this week about how to reconcile a broken relationship.

Worship Guide

For the Superintendent or Teacher
Theme: Love and Devotion to Others
Song: "Stand By Me"
(hymn by Charles A. Tindley)
Devotional Reading: Matthew 5:43-48

Love and Devotion to Others

Bible Background • 1 SAMUEL 19:1-7, 23:1-18; 2 SAMUEL 9
Printed Text • 1 SAMUEL 19:1-7 | Devotional Reading • MATTHEW 5:43-48

Aim for Change

By the end of this lesson, we will EXPLORE the story of Jonathan's defense of David when David was opposed by Saul, LONG for love and justice within the family and beyond, and GROW in love and devotion for justice for others.

In Focus

"Why are you always so much harder on Khai than me?" Dean asked.

John was surprised by the question. He usually prided himself on how he treated the teenage boys equally, even though only Dean was his biological son. He showed up to their games equally; he bought them gifts of equal value; he spent equal time with each of them. But tonight when he talked with the boys about their report cards, his stepson Khai had exploded at him and stormed out.

Dean continued, "You always rag on him for making bad grades, even when my grades are basically the same. He tries really hard in school, even in Advanced Physics, but it's never enough for you."

John was shocked that Dean would speak so bluntly to him. Usually, Dean was the sensible one, unlike Khai who… John realized what he was thinking. Maybe Dean was onto something. John promised Dean he would keep better watch on how he treated them. "I'm sorry Dean," John said. "Please go get Khai so I can apologize to him, too."

It took a minute, but Dean convinced Khai to come back and speak with their dad. John told Khai how Dean had stood up for him.

"Thanks, bro," Khai said. "I'm glad you've got my back."

When have you taken a stand for a friend or family member? How has a particularly deep friendship blessed your life?

Keep in Mind

"And Jonathan spake good of David unto Saul his father, and said unto him, Let not the king sin against his servant, against David; because he hath not sinned against thee, and because his works have been to thee-ward very good." (1 Samuel 19:4, KJV)

"The next morning Jonathan spoke with his father about David, saying many good things about him. 'The king must not sin against his servant David,' Jonathan said. 'He's never done anything to harm you. He has always helped you in any way he could.'" (1 Samuel 19:4, NLT)

Focal Verses

KJV

1 Samuel 19:1 And Saul spake to Jonathan his son, and to all his servants, that they should kill David.

2 But Jonathan Saul's son delighted much in David: and Jonathan told David, saying, Saul my father seeketh to kill thee: now therefore, I pray thee, take heed to thyself until the morning, and abide in a secret place, and hide thyself:

3 And I will go out and stand beside my father in the field where thou art, and I will commune with my father of thee; and what I see, that I will tell thee.

4 And Jonathan spake good of David unto Saul his father, and said unto him, Let not the king sin against his servant, against David; because he hath not sinned against thee, and because his works have been to thee-ward very good:

5 For he did put his life in his hand, and slew the Philistine, and the LORD wrought a great salvation for all Israel: thou sawest it, and didst rejoice: wherefore then wilt thou sin against innocent blood, to slay David without a cause?

6 And Saul hearkened unto the voice of Jonathan: and Saul sware, As the LORD liveth, he shall not be slain.

7 And Jonathan called David, and Jonathan shewed him all those things. And Jonathan brought David to Saul, and he was in his presence, as in times past.

NLT

1 Samuel 19:1 Saul now urged his servants and his son Jonathan to assassinate David. But Jonathan, because of his strong affection for David,

2 told him what his father was planning. "Tomorrow morning," he warned him, "you must find a hiding place out in the fields.

3 I'll ask my father to go out there with me, and I'll talk to him about you. Then I'll tell you everything I can find out."

4 The next morning Jonathan spoke with his father about David, saying many good things about him. "The king must not sin against his servant David," Jonathan said. "He's never done anything to harm you. He has always helped you in any way he could.

5 Have you forgotten about the time he risked his life to kill the Philistine giant and how the LORD brought a great victory to all Israel as a result? You were certainly happy about it then. Why should you murder an innocent man like David? There is no reason for it at all!"

6 So Saul listened to Jonathan and vowed, "As surely as the LORD lives, David will not be killed."

7 Afterward Jonathan called David and told him what had happened. Then he brought David to Saul, and David served in the court as before.

The People, Places, and Times

David. Born in Bethlehem, David as the youngest son of Jesse was a shepherd over his father's flock. As a young man, with one smooth stone David killed Goliath, a much-feared giant Philistine warrior. David was a poet and musician, loyal to King Saul and close friends with Saul's heir Jonathan. God said that David was a man after His own heart (1 Samuel 13:14; Acts 13:22). Ruling according to God's principles, David was the first king to unite in the entire territory of Judah and Israel. God promised David that he would have royalty in his lineage forever. Although David had many accomplishments, he was imperfect; therefore, he stumbled and fell into sin. David recognized his sins and repented; he found forgiveness and restoration through God.

Philistines. Originally these people were seafarers until they were defeated by the

Egyptians. Then they settled along with coastal areas at the southern part of Palestine, where they became the enemy of nearby Israel. The five main Philistine cities were Gaza, Ashdod, Ashkelon, Gath, and Ekron. The Philistines and the Israelites constantly fought over land. On several occasions, God allowed the Israelites to be overtaken by the Philistines as punishment for their disobedience toward Him (cf. Judges 13:1). Once a monarchy was established for Israel with Saul as king, Israel started to prevail over the Philistines, turning the tide of the war by killing the Philistines' champion warrior, Goliath. The giant Goliath was so fierce and famous a warrior that Jonathan refers to him as "the Philistine" (v. 5).

Background

God stripped the kingdom of Israel from Saul because he did not follow God's direct orders and sought to justify his decision with half-hearted obedience (1 Samuel 15). But God is never without or in lack, so He raised and anointed David to succeed Saul as the next king of Israel (1 Samuel 16). David was the least likely among his brothers to be king. Although a young boy, David had a heart for God, and because he was a shepherd, David spent many hours alone with His Creator in intimate fellowship. Also, as a shepherd, he fought to protect his sheep, and God developed his skill as a warrior. David went from fighting animal predators tending his father's flock, to the battlefield as a man of war, fighting most notably the Philistines starting with their nine-foot champion Goliath (1 Samuel 17). As a reward for his brave fight in the name of the Lord, King Saul asked David to live in the palace, where he played the harp for him and served in his army (1 Samuel 18). Feelings of love and honor would soon shift as King Saul exhibited irrational behavior because of David's growing success in battle and fame.

Are you able to celebrate others? How do you handle the success of those around you?

At-A-Glance

1. Love Tested (1 Samuel 19:1-3)
2. Love Intercedes (vv. 4-7)

In Depth

1. Love Tested (1 Samuel 19:1-3)

David became famous throughout Israel for his skill as a warrior and was put in a high position in Saul's house. One of the greatest blessings from David's service to Saul was the friendship he developed with his son Jonathan. The two young men became fast friends and to signify this covenant relationship, Jonathan gave David his royal robe as the son of the king, his military tunic, sword, bow and belt as a commander and leader in the king's army (1 Samuel 18:1-4). Because of his humility, the Spirit of the Lord was with David, and He compelled Jonathan and Saul to acknowledge God's power in him. However, King Saul also grew jealous and more fearful of David's fame. A tormenting spirit drove the king to make multiple attempts on David's life (1 Samuel 18:6-11, 21-25).

King Saul ordered his son Jonathan and all of his servants to kill David. Jonathan recognized his father's erratic behavior. Rather than follow through with his father's plot, Jonathan warned David. He met with David secretly and because of their covenant friendship, he vowed to speak to his father on his behalf. Jonathan knew David was honorable and hoped he could respectfully disagree with his father and bring peace to Saul's soul.

Should you confront someone you love when they are wrong?

2. Love Intercedes (vv. 4-7)

Jonathan met with his father Saul, and as he said he would. He spoke well of David, pleading for his safety. He pointed out that David had in no way wronged the king and that his actions had been nothing but honorable. Jonathan went on to remind the king of all the good David had done for him, and the nation, by risking his life to defeat Goliath. Through David, the Lord had blessed Israel. He reminded his father how he too rejoiced as David triumphed. Jonathan could not understand why his father was so enraged to shed innocent blood for no valid reason. The prince hoped that his bond with his father would be enough to convince him to rethink his actions. Jonathan, for a moment, was successful in reaching his father, and Saul listened to his advice. The king swore to his son before the Lord that he would not have David killed. However, Saul's promise would be short-lived and broken.

Recall a situation where you had to be the peacemaker and settle disputes with a relative or church members. How did you handle it?

Search the Scriptures

1. What did Saul order Jonathan and his servants to do (1 Samuel 19:1)?

2. What did Jonathan say to his father in response to his plans to kill his best friend (vv. 4-5)?

Discuss the Meaning

1. What was the significance of David and Jonathan's relationship? What does it mean to have a friend who sticks closer than a brother?

2. How did Saul's jealousy drive his actions toward David? How did he relate to his own son?

Liberating Lesson

No matter the relationship, as Christians, we must not be silent when someone is wrong, because it affects the whole. We can disagree respectfully, and if the parties are in Christ, there should be avenues to gain quick and peaceful resolution. Paul admonishes the church at Corinth in matters of dispute to forgive and comfort those who have offended as well as to reaffirm love, in this way the devil is not allowed a foothold to cause further damage in relationships or to the whole (2 Corinthians 2:5-11). Those in leadership in the home, church, work, and community should serve as models for reconciling behavior to support the well being of others.

Application for Activation

As believers, our loyalty must align with biblical principles. It is a disservice to the offender not to call attention to the error, but correction must be orderly and respectful, not judgmental and self-righteous. A process is necessary to resolve issues and concerns: hold a meeting, and invite an objective and trusted mediator to help deal with hurt feelings and misunderstood words. Seek to understand each other's perspective; be quick to recognize your role in communication breakdown, and set up some norms for future interaction. The foundation of every relationship should be love for God and each other.

Follow the Spirit

What God wants me to do:

_____

_____

_____

_____

_____

_____

Remember Your Thoughts

Special insights I have learned:

_____

_____

_____

_____

_____

_____

More Light on the Text

1 Samuel 19:1-7

David had become far too popular for Saul's liking. After David killed the great giant Goliath and ended the war with the Philistines, the song sung in the streets was "Saul hath slain his thousands, and David his ten thousands" (1 Samuel 18:7). From that time on, Saul mistrusted David. In a murderous rage, Saul twice tried to spear David as he again took up his post as the court musician. Then Saul sent David out as a commander of the army, hoping the Philistines would kill him. David, however, carried the Lord's blessing and prospered as a military leader, gaining much popular support. Saul feared David would usurp his throne, either from himself or from his son (cf. 1 Samuel 20:30).

Saul's son Jonathan, however, loved David dearly and was happy for David to rule after Saul. Saul had lost the Lord's blessing as king because of disobedience. When the prophet Samuel told Saul of God's decision, Saul accidentally tore Samuel's robe. The prophet explained that the robe (Heb. *me'il*, meh-**EEL**) symbolized Saul's torn kingship (1 Samuel 15:27-28). When David first became well known at court, Jonathan gave him many gifts to symbolize their covenanted

friendship, including his royal robe, *me'il* (1 Samuel 18:4). With that gift, Jonathan has already assured David by action (and later will by word, 1 Samuel 23:17) that David is going to be the next king, and Jonathan looks forward to that divinely appointed reign. Saul is the only one upset by God's guidance of the nation.

1 And Saul spake to Jonathan his son, and to all his servants, that they should kill David.

After failing several times to either kill David himself or send him into danger where he could be killed, Saul tells others about his desire that David should die. Many translations render the Hebrew here along the lines of "they should kill David," implying that Saul is commanding his son and servants to do his dirty work for him. However, the Hebrew is not explicit as to whom Saul intends to do the killing. The verbal form allows a translation of "he spoke to [them] about killing David." He is letting them in on the objective, hoping for their help with the planning and execution.

2 But Jonathan Saul's son delighted much in David: and Jonathan told David, saying, Saul my father seeketh to kill thee: now therefore, I pray thee, take heed to thyself until the morning, and abide in a secret place, and hide thyself: 3 And I will go out and stand beside my father in the field where thou art, and I will commune with my father of thee; and what I see, that I will tell thee.

Jonathan, however, has no interest in killing his best friend. Jonathan reminded the king that he had previously claimed to delight in David's victories against the Philistines (19:5) as Jonathan had (18:22). Jonathan is uniquely qualified to be a mediator between David and Saul since he is close to both of them, one by blood and one by choice. Both men trust Jonathan and Jonathan knows the importance of communication. He begins the mediation by speaking privately with David and sharing his plan to speak privately with Saul.

Jonathan's words show how seriously he takes this situation. He pleads earnestly for his friend to seek safety, adding "I pray thee" to his instructions. In sharing his plan to talk with his father, he emphasizes the personal pronouns: "*I myself* will go out" and "*I myself* will commune (i.e. talk)" with Saul. He will not trust this touchy part of the plan to anyone less knowledgeable of the situation or less ingratiated with both parties. Jonathan himself will look after his friend.

As soon as he hears Saul's desire to murder David, Jonathan comes up with a plan to stop him. Jonathan hopes to talk sense into his father. This is the first time David goes to hide in the field while Jonathan tries to talk Saul out of killing him. This time it works. Next time, David will have to live as an outcast for the rest of Saul's reign (20:5, 42).

Jonathan shows great courage in standing up for David against Saul. Saul has already thrown spears at David (18:11). Saul believes that David opposes his political power. Saul is the king; he is within his legal rights to order a subject's death, even without cause. Further, Saul is Jonathan's father, the patriarch and elder in a society very much still reliant on family ties for strength. It is presumptuous for Jonathan to even think he has a better plan than Saul. To actually follow through and speak against his father's plans is courageous. Jonathan allows his desire for justice to override his social role as a son.

Jonathan's plan is to take Saul out into a field to talk with him about David. He will remove Saul from his court and its distractions. The throne room would physically remind Saul of his recent attempt on David's life and would remind Saul of David's presumed threat to the throne. Most importantly, speaking out

in the field takes Saul away from all his court officials, who expect Saul to lead in a certain way. Jonathan lets Saul have space to change his mind about David privately so the king can save face, making him more likely to agree with Jonathan.

4 And Jonathan spake good of David unto Saul his father, and said unto him, Let not the king sin against his servant, against David; because he hath not sinned against thee, and because his works have been to thee-ward very good: 5 For he did put his life in his hand, and slew the Philistine, and the LORD wrought a great salvation for all Israel: thou sawest it, and didst rejoice: wherefore then wilt thou sin against innocent blood, to slay David without a cause?

Jonathan takes Saul out in private and has the courage to call it like it is, even to his own father, even to his king. He gives his father many reasons for not killing "his servant." Jonathan warns Saul that killing David would be a sin. David is innocent and has in no way earned death (Deuteronomy 19:10, 21:8, 27:25). Jonathan reminds Saul that he has nothing to fault David on, no outright sins and no faulty work in his service. David has shown his usefulness to Saul both with his music, which soothes Saul when he is plagued by an evil spirit and with his sword, which has killed Goliath and many other Philistines.

Just as all Sunday School children know the story of David and Goliath, the story seems to be popular even soon after it first occurred. Significant time has passed since that battle with the Philistines. David has won military honor in many other fights, including killing two hundred Philistines as a bride-price to marry Saul's daughter. Yet, Jonathan speaks of how David "slew *the* Philistine," meaning Goliath. Even without the other military exploits, David would have won lasting fame and goodwill in Israel.

Showing great wisdom, Jonathan brings the whole situation back to God. David did the killing, but "the LORD wrought a great salvation" (v. 5). In this way, Jonathan urges Saul to forget his petty squabble and trust in God's plan for the country. Every God-follower's main goal should be to glorify God and do His work. How important it is to surround ourselves with godly friends, who lead us to accept God's will rather than continue in bitterness that our blood-family might model.

Jonathan reminds Saul that instead of hating David for his military victories, he should be glad that God has been helping Saul's nation survive. Jonathan knows not to mention how all the people of Israel support David, but he does remind Saul of the times when he too loved David and David's actions. Saul himself "didst rejoice" because of David's actions. Jonathan asks, "Wherefore then…" or "So why…" did Saul want to punish David for those same actions now?

In his last question to Saul, Jonathan returns to his first point, that killing David would be a sin. Jonathan does not strictly appeal to the law, though. "Innocent" (Heb. *naqi*, naw-**KEY**) and "without a cause" (Heb. *chinnam*, kheen-**NOM**) are not legal terms. Jonathan does not mean to clear David as though in a court of law. He speaks with Saul informally. He has not built up an air-tight case for David; he has spoken out of his heart. He speaks about a friend, not a defendant. Jonathan knows Saul's change of heart against David is a move of emotion, rather than logic. Therefore, he makes an emotional appeal to Saul to change his mind.

Much could be praised in Jonathan's show of devotion to his friend. Don't we all want a friend who can sing our praises like Jonathan does David's? Even though our friends hold so much sway in our lives as children and teenagers, adults often struggle to gain and maintain friendships with their peers. This leads to unhealthy isolation. Adult responsibilities of caring for a house, a household, and a job outside of these mean we must consciously take time to foster friendships. The good thing, though, is that all it takes is time. You do not have to maintain a certain activity, schedule, or setting; you simply need to mindfully spend time with people to grow deep friendships.

6 And Saul hearkened unto the voice of Jonathan: and Saul sware, As the LORD liveth, he shall not be slain.

Saul has listened to all of Jonathan's arguments: killing David would be a sin, he has treated Saul well, he has risked his life for the nation, he is a war-hero, God has used him, Saul himself has appreciated David's work in the past, shedding innocent blood is—again—a sin, and Saul has nothing to fear from David. Faced with this mountain of reasoning, Saul relents. He "hearkened" (Heb. *shema'*, shaw-**MAH**) to Jonathan's voice. This word implies that one not only hears what is spoken but also obeys it.

Saul swears not to kill David. "As the LORD liveth" was a common oath formula, especially during the monarchial period. It is an oath calling God as a witness to this promise Saul is making with Jonathan. This oath formula does not explicitly name a consequence for failing to fulfill the oath, but since God takes oaths so seriously (Numbers 30:2), it is sure to be severe. Jonathan will use this phrase in a later episode with David and uphold his oath (1 Samuel 20:21). Hearing this oath from Saul does not guarantee David's safety, though. Saul has previously broken an oath he swore: "as the LORD liveth" (1 Samuel 14:39, 45). That time it was in Jonathan's favor. This current vow will eventually be broken also.

For the time being, however, Saul promises not to kill David. In fact, he not only promises that he himself will not kill David, but that David "shall not be slain." The use of passive voice here keeps Saul honest from trying to skirt the law later on. Had he merely promised that he would not kill David, he still could have ordered someone else to kill David for him. This is exactly what he tried to do earlier without success as he sent David to fight Philistines. This oath now commits Saul from trying to harm David, even indirectly.

7 And Jonathan called David, and Jonathan shewed him all those things. And Jonathan brought David to Saul, and he was in his presence, as in times past.

Only open communication can bring about an open reconciliation. Jonathan calls to his friend and reports the outcome of his conversation with Saul. With Saul having promised David's safety, both can return to Saul's court with everything back "as in times past." This phrase means David has returned to his position playing his harp for Saul. Saul continues to keep David at the royal house, to keep an eye on him instead of letting him go to his hometown where he can raise up a village of people who might support David rather than Saul (1 Samuel 18:9).

As the last step in his work as a mediator, Jonathan presents David to Saul himself. Jonathan's presence affects both men. It reminds Saul of the promise the king made to Jonathan before God, and it reassures David that nothing bad will happen since Saul would not challenge both of them. The peace Jonathan has achieved here is only temporary. Just two verses after this episode, Saul will again try to spear David as he plays for the court, and David will have to flee for his life. Even a temporary peace, however, is worthwhile. Jesus promises "Blessed are the peacemakers: for they shall be called the children of God" (Matthew 5:9). Jonathan has proven himself to be a child of God in this matter. He knows his position as the child of Saul is far less important than being marked as a child of God.

Sources:

Brueggemann, Walter. *First and Second Samuel.* Interpretation: A Bible Commentary for Teaching and Preaching. Louisville, KY: Westminster John Knox Press, 1990.

Harris, W. *The Preacher's Complete Homiletic Commentary on the First and Second Books of Samuel.* The Preacher's Complete Homiletic Commentary on the Books of the Bible with Critical and Explanatory Notes, Index, etc., by Various Authors. Grand Rapids, Mich.: Baker Books, 1996.

Klein, Ralph W. *1 Samuel.* Word Biblical Commentary. Vol 10. Waco, TX: Word Books, 2000.

Spence, H.D.M. and Joseph S. Exell, eds. *Ruth, I & II Samuel.* The Pulpit Commentary. Vol 4. Peabody, Mass.: Hendrickson Publishers, 1985.

VanGemeren, Willem A., gen. ed. *New International Dictionary of Old Testament Theology & Exegesis.* Vols 2-4. Grand Rapids, Mich.: Zondervan, 2012.

Say It Correctly

Ashkelon. **ASH**-keh-lon.
Ekron. **EHK**-ron.

Daily Bible Readings

MONDAY
Timothy, My Brother, and Coworker
(1 Thessalonians 3:1-6)

TUESDAY
David Slays Philistine with a Stone
(1 Samuel 17:41-51)

WEDNESDAY
David and Jonathan Bond Together
(1 Samuel 18:1-5)

THURSDAY
Saul Jealous of and Fears David
(1 Samuel 18:12-18)

FRIDAY
Jonathan Asserts David as Next King
(1 Samuel 23:14-18)

SATURDAY
David Provides for
Jonathan's Son Mephibosheth
(2 Samuel 9:1-10)

SUNDAY
Saul Promises to Preserve David's Life
(1 Samuel 19:1-7)

Notes

_____

_____

_____

_____

Teaching Tips

Words You Should Know

A. Bless (v. 28) *eulogeo* (Gk.)—To invoke God's favor

B. Do good (vv. 33, 35) *agathopoieo* (Gk.)—To be benevolent; to do good so that someone derives advantage from it

Teacher Preparation

Unifying Principle—Overcoming Self-Interest. We often wonder how we should treat our enemies. How should we respond to them? Jesus taught his disciples to love their enemies by forgiving them, responding to their needs, and being nonjudgmental.

A. Read the Bible Background and Devotional Reading.

B. Pray for your students and lesson clarity.

C. Read the lesson Scripture in multiple translations.

O—Open the Lesson

A. Begin the class with prayer.

B. Ask participants how much they would be willing to risk in order to love their enemies. Discuss, "Are there enemies you could never love? Why or why not?"

C. Have the students read the Aim for Change and the In Focus story.

D. Ask students how events like those in the story weigh on their hearts and how they can view these events from a faith perspective.

P—Present the Scriptures

A. Read the Focal Verses and discuss the Background and The People, Places, and Times sections.

B. Have the class share what Scriptures stand out for them and why, with particular emphasis on today's themes.

E—Explore the Meaning

A. Use In Depth or More Light on the Text to facilitate a deeper discussion of the lesson text.

B. Pose the questions in Search the Scriptures and Discuss the Meaning.

C. Discuss the Liberating Lesson and Application for Activation sections.

N—Next Steps for Application

A. Look for an opportunity to love an enemy while at the same time confronting evil.

B. End class with a commitment to pray for our enemies during the coming week.

Worship Guide

For the Superintendent or Teacher
Theme: Love Your Enemies
Song: "We Must be Merciful and Kind"
Devotional Reading: Isaiah 1:12-17

Love Your Enemies

Bible Background • LUKE 6:27-36
Printed Text • LUKE 6:27-36 | Devotional Reading • ISAIAH 1:12-17

—————— Aim for Change ——————

By the end of this lesson, we will EXPLORE Jesus' teaching about what it means to love our enemies, REFLECT on times when we felt hate toward others or were hated by others, and IDENTIFY ways to love our enemies.

————————— In Focus —————————

Greg looked out the window at all the trash on the lawn and let out a deep sigh. "I'm tired of them knocking our trash cans over every week and I have to clean it up." Greg had a right to be upset. His neighbors, the Jacksons, had been a nuisance to his family since they moved in next door. It first started with the all-night parties and loud music. Greg had asked them to turn it down a notch, and after that, the Jacksons intentionally began to show hostility toward Greg and his family. Knocking down trash cans and taunting Greg was not enough. The Jacksons' oldest son, Dayshawn, began to insult and threaten Greg's son William at school. Greg sighed again as he put on gloves to pick up the trash. "I guess they need a little more love."

William was fuming with anger. "A little more love? I think they need a little more fists, and Dayshawn is going to be the first to get his."

"No, son," interjected Greg. "That may be how they do things, but we do things differently in this family."

What has been the response when you answered injury with kindness?

—————————— Keep in Mind ——————————

"But I say unto you which hear, Love your enemies, do good to them which hate you, bless them that curse you, and pray for them which despitefully use you" (Luke 6:27-28, KJV).

"But to you who are willing to listen, I say, love your enemies! Do good to those who hate you. Bless those who curse you. Pray for those who hurt you" (Luke 6:27-28, NLT).

Focal Verses

KJV **Luke 6:27** But I say unto you which hear, Love your enemies, do good to them which hate you,

28 Bless them that curse you, and pray for them which despitefully use you.

29 And unto him that smiteth thee on the one cheek offer also the other; and him that taketh away thy cloak forbid not to take thy coat also.

30 Give to every man that asketh of thee; and of him that taketh away thy goods ask them not again.

31 And as ye would that men should do to you, do ye also to them likewise.

32 For if ye love them which love you, what thank have ye? for sinners also love those that love them.

33 And if ye do good to them which do good to you, what thank have ye? for sinners also do even the same.

34 And if ye lend to them of whom ye hope to receive, what thank have ye? for sinners also lend to sinners, to receive as much again.

35 But love ye your enemies, and do good, and lend, hoping for nothing again; and your reward shall be great, and ye shall be the children of the Highest: for he is kind unto the unthankful and to the evil.

36 Be ye therefore merciful, as your Father also is merciful.

NLT **Luke 6:27** "But to you who are willing to listen, I say, love your enemies! Do good to those who hate you.

28 Bless those who curse you. Pray for those who hurt you.

29 If someone slaps you on one cheek, offer the other cheek also. If someone demands your coat, offer your shirt also.

30 Give to anyone who asks; and when things are taken away from you, don't try to get them back.

31 Do to others as you would like them to do to you.

32 If you love only those who love you, why should you get credit for that? Even sinners love those who love them!

33 And if you do good only to those who do good to you, why should you get credit? Even sinners do that much!

34 And if you lend money only to those who can repay you, why should you get credit? Even sinners will lend to other sinners for a full return.

35 Love your enemies! Do good to them. Lend to them without expecting to be repaid. Then your reward from heaven will be very great, and you will truly be acting as children of the Most High, for he is kind to those who are unthankful and wicked.

36 You must be compassionate, just as your Father is compassionate."

The People, Places, and Times

The Disciples. The word disciple means learner or student, and it was common for rabbis to take on students as Jesus did. These students of Jesus were distinct from the multitudes that gathered when He preached and performed miracles. The Gospels refer to the Twelve and another larger group of unnamed disciples. Jesus spent intensive time with the Twelve; the other larger group of disciples did not spend as much time with Jesus but accepted and followed His teaching and practices. These close students, rather than a massive crowd, are the main audience for the Sermon on the Plain.

The Sermon on the Plain. Today's text is a portion of what scholars refer to as the Sermon on the Plain, Luke's equivalent to Matthew's Sermon on the Mount. The content of the sermon in Luke emphasizes the ethical aspects of following Jesus. Since Matthew's audience was primarily Jewish, he emphasized the aspects of Jesus' sermon that built off of Mosiac Law. In contrast, Luke's audience was primarily Gentile. They did not have the Law as the basis of their society. Instead, Luke's presentation of Jesus' sermon continues to press Luke's emphasis on inverting current, unjust social orders.

Background

After spending all night in prayer and choosing the twelve apostles, Jesus descended to a plain where a group of disciples and a great multitude from all over the surrounding country were waiting for Him. They had traveled to hear this great teacher and be healed of their diseases and evil spirits. As Jesus came down the mountain and delivered this sermon, He symbolically created a new Israel. Just like Israel at Sinai had a set of laws that governed their behavior as a people, Jesus gave His disciples a set of "laws" that would govern their behavior. This set of laws is called the Sermon on the Plain.

The Sermon on the Plain is one of the most powerful passages in the entire Bible. In it, Jesus gives an agenda for God's kingdom, a set of rules and instructions for His people to live by. The first part of these instructions consists of four blessings and four woes. These are followed by more explicit instructions that do not cover every situation but can all be summed up under the Golden Rule: "Do to others as you would like them to do to you" (6:31, NLT).

At-A-Glance

1. God's People are Called to Live a Distinctive Lifestyle (Luke 6:27–30)
2. Jesus' Strategy (v. 31)
3. The Total Unselfishness of Love (v. 32-36)

In Depth

1. God's People are Called to Live a Distinctive Lifestyle (Luke 6:27–30)

Just as Moses established a "constitution" for Israel at Sinai (Exodus 20), Christ sets forth the foundation of Christianity as He begins His ministry (Matthew 5-7). An important part of this foundation is the principle, "love your enemies." The Pharisees thought they knew the full implication of Moses' Law when they said, "Love your neighbor and hate your enemy" (Matthew 5:43; cf. Leviticus 19:18). However, Christ showed that true righteousness exceeds what the law demands. When others wrong us, we ought to respond with patience—but more than that, Jesus wants action. He commands us to actively do good to those who hate us.

Those who disagree with this philosophy likely do so because they believe others will not respond. Our problem is that we are not willing to obey if others refuse to do so as well. It takes a great amount of trust to perform this simple commandment.

Does failing to love the unlovable indicate a lack of love for God? Explain.

2. Jesus' strategy (v. 31)

Perhaps the best-known principle in the New Testament is this "Golden Rule." Jesus' guideline sums up the main way that His followers will live a distinctive lifestyle: "Do to others as you would like them to do to you" (v. 31, NLT). It is the guiding principle of seeking another's goodwill. We must follow this rule even when it hurts.

Today's society has several common misconceptions about this verse. One is that to be gracious and loving in the face of hostility is a sign of weakness. On the contrary, it takes a great deal of strength to control the urge to fight back. Someone might also claim that these verses will lead to letting evil take over. However, Jesus is demanding that we fight vigorously against evil. Our battle, however, is to be fought by setting a good example.

What makes our understanding of this commandment difficult?

3. The Total Unselfishness of Love (v. 32-36)

Jesus makes it very clear that Christians have no corner on good deeds (v. 32). The non-Christian does good to those who will return the favor and lends to those who can repay. This kind of behavior does not distinguish us as Christians. Good for good is a fair exchange. Good for evil is the mark of a believer.

Jesus lays it all out in verse 35. His followers are to completely sacrifice themselves in love, energy, and possessions—even for the enemy. The basis of this is God and the very nature of His character. God is kind to the unthankful and the evil. He is merciful, bestowing His love for those who don't deserve it. The proof: Christ loved us and died for us while we were still sinners (Rom. 5:6,7). Following the example of loving our enemies shows that we are "children of the Highest." In that relationship, we show that God is our Father. We show mercy to others because he showed mercy to us. The reward for our obedience is not in the favor of men but the favor of God.

How can we keep the principle of God's mercy in the forefront of our minds?

Search the Scriptures

1. Name eight actions mentioned in today's lesson that are expected of Jesus' followers. (6:27-30)

2. What good things do sinners do? And why do they do them? (6:32-33)

3. Do unloving people sometimes look as though they really love others? In what ways? (6:32-33)

Discuss the Meaning

1. Why do you think so many people regard Jesus' commandment to love our enemies to be unrealistic? How are we as believers empowered by God to love our enemies?

2. Give an example of what it means to "turn the other cheek." Some people feel Black people are not "turning the other cheek" when they fight for their rights. What is your opinion? How do we balance loving our enemies with fighting systemic injustice?

Liberating Lesson

As followers of Jesus, one of the ways that we live a distinctive lifestyle is by practicing radical love. We can love those who are considered unlovable because we are loved by God. In this way, we point the way to Jesus and His radical kingdom.

In our efforts to turn the other cheek, we should not conclude that we have no need for protection against lawbreakers. To love our enemies does not mean we allow ungodly behavior. The command to love our enemies actually places a weapon in the hand of the powerless. When deprived of physical, political, and economic power, we still have the power of a righteous life.

Application for Activation

It is almost normal to think of an enemy as someone who attacks us with unkind actions. Too often, we categorize people as enemies because of their religion, ethnicity, or political persuasion. Because we have the favor of God and His Holy Spirit, we can resist labeling people as our enemies and embrace love without looking for it in return. Very likely someone you know will mistreat you, belittle you, or do something to upset you during the coming week. Brainstorm ways to obey God's command, love them, or do something kind to prove your love. Consider having lunch or coffee with that person.

Follow the Spirit

What God wants me to do:

_____

_____

_____

_____

Remember Your Thoughts

Special insights I have learned:

_____

_____

_____

_____

More Light on the Text
Luke 6:27-36

These commandments come at a time of Jewish oppression. Judea was under Roman rule, establishing enmity between the two people groups. Yet in this state —characterized by hatred, exploitation, bitterness, and malice—Jesus taught his disciples to love their enemies. This teaching must have appeared to be heresy because the Jews felt it was justifiable to reciprocate hatred with hatred.

Some believers today are under the oppression of antagonists who act as masters over them. The treatment they are receiving makes it difficult for them to respond in love. However, we must comply with Jesus' instructions to love our enemies because loving our enemies enables us to live the kind of life acceptable to God—a life of love.

27 But I say unto you which hear, Love your enemies, do good to them which hate you, 28 Bless them that curse you, and pray for them which despitefully use you.

It is important to note the opening word, "but," which serves to separate these verses from the woes listed just prior (vv. 24–26). Jesus is addressing His disciples in this passage. The woes do not apply to the disciples, because Jesus counts them among those who both listen to His teachings and obey them because they have ears to hear (cf. Luke 8:8, 14:35; Romans 11:8). They are members of His fold, subject to His teachings and commandments, and so they are meant to know the higher laws of life. This teaching opens by zeroing in on the last beatitude (v. 22; cf. Matthew 5:38–48).

The Greek word translated "love" (*agapao*, ag-ap-**AH**-o) denotes loving "in a social or moral sense." It is a genuine and selfless concern. Love here means to love dearly and sincerely (cf. Romans 12:14–21). This word is used to express the essential nature of God that ought to be found in every disciple of Christ and must be shown to others. To exhibit this love is to behave like Jesus, who defined humility, long-suffering, and compassion. There is a human tendency to hate one's enemy, but Jesus tells us that our attitudes should transcend this tendency in order to fulfill God's requirements. He mentions that love for our neighbors is the second greatest command (Matt. 22:39). One's neighbor is not just the person living next door, but every human being. In this sense, an enemy—no matter how great our antagonism against them—is a neighbor who deserves to be loved.

God has revealed three factors meant to prompt the Christian to exhibit God's nature of love by obeying the commandment of love: the intrinsic nature of God, the command to love, and the fact that every human being needs love. Love should be an exercise of the divine will, be fulfilled by a deliberate choice, and made in obedience and service to God. Love means three things: to do good, to bless, and to pray for one's enemies—which include three types: those who hate you, those who curse you, and those who abuse you.

Jesus commands His disciples to show goodness in response to hatred. The Greek word translated "do good" (*agathopoieo*, ag-ath-op-oy-**EH**-o), means "to do well, to be of benefit to another." Jesus is conditioning His disciples with a positive attitude to enable them to fulfill the law of love against the negative tide of maltreatment from evil people. This commandment of the Lord Jesus is meant to indicate the desired condition of the heart of a disciple. Each Christ-follower must have in themselves the spirit of love. With this spirit, they can tolerate harsh treatment from others, resist the pangs of offense, and develop the willingness to bless the one who curses them.

The Greek word translated "bless" (*eulogeo*, yoo-log-**EH**-o) means "to speak well of, to

invoke a benediction upon a person, to praise." On the other hand, the Greek word translated "curse" (*kataraomai*, kat-ar-**AH**-om-ahee) means "to pray against, to wish evil against a person." The disciple of Christ is required to counter the person who wishes them evil with a blessing.

In addition, we are given the responsibility of praying for those who misuse us. Jesus commands us to pray to God for the souls of those who mistreat us. The Lord Jesus says to pray *for* them rather than *against* them. God hears prayers about someone, when we have obeyed Him concerning that person. The Greek word translated "despitefully use" (*epereazo*, ep-ay-reh-**AD**-zo) denotes "to insult, slander or accuse falsely." Despiteful use is an opposition against us, and we are required to express love to those who oppose us in this manner.

29 And unto him that smiteth thee on the one cheek offer also the other; and him that taketh away thy cloke forbid not to take thy coat also.

Some believe verses 29 and 30 are intentional hyperbole to make a principled point. Jesus places no limits on the self-denial aspect of love. True love is as infinite as God. Verse 29 starts the illustration of concrete examples of actions in response to maltreatment and presents a command to resist continuing violence. If someone hits you or takes from you, don't hit back—in fact, allow another strike. Secondly, we are told to refuse retaliation against extortion. Jesus says if someone takes away our cloak, we should not stop him from taking our coat also.

Is Jesus telling us to stand still and accept abuse or theft? To get the full meaning, we must examine the surrounding scriptures. Verses 27-28 tell us to take four actions regarding those who wrong us: love, do good, bless, and pray for them. The point of offering the other cheek is not about being hit again.

It is an example of refusing retaliation despite the repeated blows by our enemies. This is the non-violent response we saw in Martin Luther King, Jr. and other civil rights advocates who brought shame upon the enemy who thought themselves victorious because of their hatred and violence. To take one's coat has the implication of a violent action taken through authority. This is a reference to abuse by those with societal power. In both cases, the response to those who seek to abuse and humiliate us is to love, bless, do good, and pray. Jesus lived this example when He was tried unjustly, beaten unmercifully, stripped of His clothing, and crucified cruelly. While we will never go to the cross for the sins of others, our actions toward those in authority who seek to gain notoriety by wronging people they see as beneath them are not to retaliate in kind with acts of hatred. Instead, we must respond through actions that reveal our relationship with Jesus Christ. It is that relationship that strengthens us despite the evil around us.

30 Give to every man that asketh of thee; and of him that taketh away thy goods ask them not again.

Verse 30 takes us from the violence of those in authority to the negative actions of neighbors and even friends. To ask (Gk. *aiteo*, ahee-THE-o) means to beg. While "take" in this verse is the same as "take" in the previous verse, here a personal pronoun is used implying a friend who takes from you.

The spirit of love should make us generous without discrimination. Jesus knows that no matter our state we are in a position where we can give help to other people. He commands us to give. "Every man" denotes any kind of person: the poor or rich, the old or young; relatives, friends, enemies, or strangers. "Every man" does not leave room for discrimination based on religion, background, race, color,

beliefs, or social class. In other words, we are to lay down all we have for a friend (John 15:13).

Based on this command, the thief and the cheat become recipients of the love of God that is meant to emanate from the believer despite being the victim. This is the exact kind of giving that Christ showed to pay for our sin on the Cross.

31 And as ye would that men should do to you, do ye also to them likewise.

This verse is considered the Golden Rule: Do unto others as you would have them do unto you. We have a natural desire to receive good treatment from others. We love to be spoken well of; we love to hear kind words, to be encouraged, and to be given gifts. Jesus says that whatever treatment we love to receive from other people, we should also desire to give to others. The Greek word translated "would" (*thelo*, **THEL**-o) expresses a desire or wish. What you wish for yourself is what you should wish for others.

The words of this verse are forever embodied with this line from a famous poem attributed to St. Francis of Assisi (1181–1226), "Where there is hatred, let me sow love." We could also say, "Where there is injustice, let me sow justice." Remember, you might well be the only Bible the person in front of you ever reads. What lesson of faith will that person receive from you?

32 For if ye love them which love you, what thank have ye? for sinners also love those that love them. 33 And if ye do good to them which do good to you, what thank have ye? for sinners also do even the same. 34 And if ye lend to them of whom ye hope to receive, what thank have ye? for sinners also lend to sinners, to receive as much again.

Jesus teaches unconditional love. Love for others should not be spurred by the fact that the other person is capable of reciprocating that love. Sinners show their acts of love to people who they believe are capable of paying them back because they consider it an investment into the lives of these beneficiaries. The motivation behind a sinner's giving is the recompense he or she will receive from the person to whom they give.

Jesus' point here is to define generosity in a new way and to encourage the growth of real relationships, as friends rather than as "business partners" seeking to exchange favor for a favor. The Greek word translated "thanks" (*charis*, **KHAR**-ece) in these verses is usually rendered "grace." It connotes "favor, benefit, pleasure." This means we derive favor and benefit by loving people who are not capable of reciprocating. The whole point of showing grace is that it cannot be repaid. We have been given such an abundance of grace and favor from Christ's gift of salvation. We certainly have enough to spare!

35 But love ye your enemies, and do good, and lend, hoping for nothing again; and your reward shall be great, and ye shall be the children of the Highest: for he is kind unto the unthankful and to the evil.

Jesus poses a different motive for the actions of his followers. He admonishes them to love, do good and give without hope of anything in return. We are inclined to believe that those who have hurt us are undeserving of our love or our acts of kindness. This mentality fosters enmity and is a barrier to entering the realm of agape, selfless love. Jesus' command to love our enemies enables us to break down this barrier in our hearts. While it may be easy and convenient for us to love those we are pleased with or those with whom we have some affinity, it is generally impossible to love our enemies.

According to God's economy, this impossible task of loving enemies leads to the greatest reward from the Lord. The Greek word translated "reward" (*misthos*, mis-**THOS**) means pay received later for services, wages. In this case, however, the term signifies our reward in heaven. Therefore, Jesus commands us to love, to do good, and to lend without expecting anything. God desires a distinction between His people and all others. The command to love our enemies is key to creating this distinction. According to Jesus, our acts of love firmly establish our standing as children of the Highest. God desires a distinction between His people and the people who serve other gods.

36 Be ye therefore merciful, as your Father also is merciful.

When we desire to take punitive measures against those who have done evil to us, Jesus urges us to be merciful to them. Since we are imperfect, liable to err, and likely to be subjected to adverse conditions of life, we inadvertently offend one another and become beset by ills. We all err and we all need mercy from one another. Mercy can be regarded as one side of a coin, with love on the other side: While love gives, mercy forgives. Mercy is a positive reaction in which we show forgiveness and kindness to one who has offended us. Being merciful is the character of God, and so showing mercy to our offenders means manifesting God's character to them. The child of God is called to be merciful like our Father in heaven. This is the best way to maintain relationships with others and to demonstrate our relationship with God.

Sources:

Bock, Darrell L. Luke. *The NIV Application Commentary.* Grand Rapids, MI: Zondervan, 1996. 190–198.

Liefeld, Walter L. "Luke." *The Expositor's Bible Commentary with the New International Version: Matthew, Mark, Luke.* Vol. 8. Edited by Frank E. Gaebelein. Grand Rapids, MI: Zondervan, 1984. 889–894.

Jeffrey, David Lyle. *Luke.* Brazos Theological Commentary on the Bible. Grand Rapids, MI: Brazos Press, 2012. 86–96.

Phillips, John. *Exploring the Gospel of Luke.* The John Phillips Commentary Series. Grand Rapids, MI: Kregel Publications, 2005. 108–117.

Ryle, J. C. *Luke.* The Crossway Classic Commentaries. Wheaton, IL: Crossway, 1997. 73–76.

Stein, Robert H. *Luke.* The New American Commentary, Vol. 24. Nashville, TN: Holman Reference, 1992. 187–190.

Say It Correctly

Assisi. Ah-**SEE**-see
Judea, joo-**DEE**-uh
Mosaic, moh-**ZAY**-ik

Daily Bible Readings

MONDAY
The Lord Is Merciful and Gracious
(Psalm 103:1-14)

TUESDAY
Responding to Unwanted Demands
(Matthew 5:38-42)

WEDNESDAY
Handling Family Difficulties
(Leviticus 25:35-39)

THURSDAY
Home Life of the Faithful
(Psalm 128)

FRIDAY
Forgiving the Ignorant
(Luke 23:32-36)

SATURDAY
Blessed and Rewarded
(Matthew 5:1-12)

SUNDAY
Love and Forgive Your Enemies
(Luke 6:27-36)

Notes

_____

_____

_____

_____

Teaching Tips

Words You Should Know

A. Neighbor (Luke 10:27, 29, 36) *plesion* (Gk.)—One who is near, a fellow person

B. Priest (v. 31) *hiereus* (Gk.)—One responsible for worship and sacrifices at the temple

Teacher Preparation

Unifying Principle—Meeting the Needs of Others. Selfish desires, self-gratification, and self-interests are highly valued in our time. How can we become better neighbors to one another? Jesus challenges us to address the needs and welfare of everyone, including perceived enemies.

A. Read the Bible Background and Devotional Reading.

B. Pray for your students and lesson clarity.

C. Read the lesson Scripture in multiple translations.

O—Open the Lesson

A. Begin the class with prayer.

B. Ask the class, "Are there traffic laws that you don't always follow? How about rules at work? Why do you neglect those rules? The lawyer correctly says loving our neighbor is one of God's most important rules. How do we fail in doing that?"

C. Have the students read the Aim for Change and the In Focus story.

D. Ask students how events like those in the story weigh on their hearts and how they can view these events from a faith perspective.

P—Present the Scriptures

A. Read the Focal Verses and discuss the Background and The People, Places, and Times sections.

B. Have the class share what Scriptures stand out for them and why, with particular emphasis on today's themes.

E—Explore the Meaning

A. Use In Depth or More Light on the Text to facilitate a deeper discussion of the lesson text.

B. Pose the questions in Search the Scriptures and Discuss the Meaning.

C. Discuss the Liberating Lesson and Application for Activation sections.

N—Next Steps for Application

A. Summarize the value of helping those in need, even if it is not your profession.

B. This week, pray for the Lord to show you people you know but have not included as neighbors.

Worship Guide

For the Superintendent or Teacher
Theme: Loving Your Neighbor
Song: "Make Me a Blessing"
Devotional Reading: John 5:1-15

Loving Your Neighbor

Bible Background • LEVITICUS 19:18, 34; LUKE 10:25-37
Printed Text • LUKE 10:25-37 | Devotional Reading • JOHN 5:1-15

—————— Aim for Change ——————

By the end of this lesson, we will EXPLORE the concept of neighbor in the conversation between Jesus and the lawyer, VALUE all people as God does, and SHARE love and mercy with those who are in need, even those who are different from us.

————————— In Focus —————————

She just could not understand him. Truthfully, she had no desire to. He was just too different. The old man did not think like her, look like her, or believe as she did. He had a reputation for being cold and sometimes rude. The neighborhood children were afraid of him, and her neighbors kept their distance. Why should she be the one to reach out now that he was ill? Where were his children? They probably avoided him for good reason. Where were his friends? Ha! He probably didn't have any.

Yet, she felt drawn to him. So, Mary brought Mr. Martinez a meal. He invited her to share it with him. Three hours later, she realized how dreadfully wrong she had been. Mr. Martinez was a man filled with pain as a result of being wrongly accused of a crime. Having been betrayed by a "friend," he was slow to trust. He lost his family in the process and was overwhelmed by guilt and feelings of abandonment. His pride had prevented him from reconnecting with them upon being released from prison. Now he suffered— alone. By serving him one meal, Mary became a true neighbor and gave him hope.

We are exhorted to love God and our neighbors. This lesson reveals the connection between the two and encourages us to expand our definition of neighbor. Do you have more trouble giving help to or accepting help from a stranger?

—————— Keep in Mind ——————

"Which now of these three, thinkest thou, was neighbour unto him that fell among the thieves? And he said, He that shewed mercy on him. Then said Jesus unto him, Go, and do thou likewise." (Luke 10:36-37, KJV)

"'Now which of these three would you say was a neighbor to the man who was attacked by bandits?' Jesus asked. The man replied, 'The one who showed him mercy.' Then Jesus said, 'Yes, now go and do the same.'" (Luke 10:36-37, NLT)

Focal Verses

KJV **Luke 10:25** And, behold, a certain lawyer stood up, and tempted him, saying, Master, what shall I do to inherit eternal life?

26 He said unto him, What is written in the law? how readest thou?

27 And he answering said, Thou shalt love the LORD thy God with all thy heart, and with all thy soul, and with all thy strength, and with all thy mind; and thy neighbour as thyself.

28 And he said unto him, Thou hast answered right: this do, and thou shalt live.

29 But he, willing to justify himself, said unto Jesus, And who is my neighbour?

30 And Jesus answering said, A certain man went down from Jerusalem to Jericho, and fell among thieves, which stripped him of his raiment, and wounded him, and departed, leaving him half dead.

31 And by chance there came down a certain priest that way: and when he saw him, he passed by on the other side.

32 And likewise a Levite, when he was at the place, came and looked on him, and passed by on the other side.

33 But a certain Samaritan, as he journeyed, came where he was: and when he saw him, he had compassion on him,

34 And went to him, and bound up his wounds, pouring in oil and wine, and set him on his own beast, and brought him to an inn, and took care of him.

35 And on the morrow when he departed, he took out two pence, and gave them to the host, and said unto him, Take care of him; and whatsoever thou spendest more, when I come again, I will repay thee.

36 Which now of these three, thinkest thou, was neighbour unto him that fell among the thieves?

NLT **Luke 10:25** One day an expert in religious law stood up to test Jesus by asking him this question: "Teacher, what should I do to inherit eternal life?"

26 Jesus replied, "What does the law of Moses say? How do you read it?"

27 The man answered, "'You must love the LORD your God with all your heart, all your soul, all your strength, and all your mind.' And, 'Love your neighbor as yourself.'"

28 "Right!" Jesus told him. "Do this and you will live!"

29 The man wanted to justify his actions, so he asked Jesus, "And who is my neighbor?"

30 Jesus replied with a story: "A Jewish man was traveling from Jerusalem down to Jericho, and he was attacked by bandits. They stripped him of his clothes, beat him up, and left him half dead beside the road.

31 "By chance a priest came along. But when he saw the man lying there, he crossed to the other side of the road and passed him by.

32 A Temple assistant walked over and looked at him lying there, but he also passed by on the other side.

33 "Then a despised Samaritan came along, and when he saw the man, he felt compassion for him.

34 Going over to him, the Samaritan soothed his wounds with olive oil and wine and bandaged them. Then he put the man on his own donkey and took him to an inn, where he took care of him.

35 The next day he handed the innkeeper two silver coins, telling him, 'Take care of this man. If his bill runs higher than this, I'll pay you the next time I'm here.'

36 "Now which of these three would you say was a neighbor to the man who was attacked by bandits?" Jesus asked.

37 And he said, He that shewed mercy on him. Then said Jesus unto him, Go, and do thou likewise.

37 The man replied, "The one who showed him mercy." Then Jesus said, "Yes, now go and do the same."

The People, Places, and Times

The Road to Jericho. Travel from Jerusalem to Jericho was by way of a steeply descending road that wound through rocky places that easily hid robbers. Jericho was lower in elevation than Jerusalem, and they were about 17 miles from each other. One had to contend not only with the steepness of the road, but also with ravines, caves, and sharp turns that hindered the traveler. The road was especially dangerous because robbers were common and often attacked a person traveling alone, thus earning the road the name, "path of blood."

Laws of Purity. Priests were not to touch a corpse because it was impure. Pharisees even believed that if the shadow of a corpse fell on a person, the person became impure. Priests and Levites were expected to observe high standards of ritual purity for their sacred ministry. When the priest saw the traveler, he did not know whether the man was dead or alive. Therefore, because of the laws governing purity, he did not want to risk defilement by touching him. Such laws were not as strict for Levites, but the Levite also wanted to avoid defilement since any approach to the wounded man would have seriously compromised his position.

Background

Many times the teachers of the law, along with the scribes and Pharisees, questioned Jesus in order to test and trap Him. This was done to discredit Jesus' ministry. They were considered religious and moral authorities and highly revered among common Jews. As proclaimed "protectors" of the Law, lawyers (i.e. scribes) often questioned Jesus on religious matters. The questions were usually popular questions of the day or ones in which whatever answer was given would place you in a particular theological camp. Jesus was a master at not only giving the right answer but challenging the scribes and Pharisees to live a more God-pleasing life through the answers He gave.

The answer He gives to this lawyer is a parable starring a Samaritan. Samaria was the name given to the Northern Kingdom and its capital city. After the Assyrians conquered the Northern Kingdom, they carried off many of its inhabitants, replacing some of them with people from other conquered lands. The people of the region practiced a form of Judaism that did not include worshiping at the Jerusalem Temple, believing their local Mount Gerizim to be a holier site. They also included some of the religions of the foreigners living there. In New Testament times, the Samaritans were considered heretics and were hostile toward the Jews. They were despised by the Jews because of their mixed Jewish-Gentile blood and their different worship practices. The relationship between the two people groups was a hostile one.

How do you respond when questioned about your faith?

At-A-Glance

1. The Test (Luke 10:25–29)
2. The Parable (vv. 30–35)
3. The Moral (vv. 36-37)

In Depth

1. The Test (Luke 10:25–29)

This conversation is considered a typical one between rabbis and their students. Rabbis would often answer a question with a question and affirm (or denounce) students' responses. Perhaps this is what the lawyer was expecting when he begins this conversation with a question about inheriting eternal life. If his aim was to trap Jesus, then he failed. The Living Word caused him to go to the written Scriptures to explain himself. Note that the lawyer knows the answer. Jesus recognizes that the lawyer knows the law theoretically, but not experientially. Jesus responds, "You have answered correctly." This is not implying that eternal life is based on works. It is by faith in Christ alone. One who loves God with all His heart, soul, strength, and mind is one who desires to please Him through obedience (cf. John 15:9–14; 1 John 4:20–21).

As a learned, religious Jew, the lawyer's response was the correct verbal response, but his follow-up question brings out new territory. His question is designed to put Jesus on the spot. The lawyer asks Jesus, "And who is my neighbor?" (v. 29) If he really wants to inherit eternal life, he needs to live out the commands of Scripture. Jesus' response to the follow-up question not only caused the lawyer to give his own answer, but the lawyer's response shows the relationship between the written law and the lived law of love. In short, Jesus' final word is "just do it!"

Have you seen Christians pose questions about the Bible, not for an answer, but to show off their knowledge or "trip up" a teacher or other person? What causes this behavior?

2. The Parable (vv. 30–35)

As an illustration of neighborly love, Jesus tells this parable. A man taking the dangerous journey from Jerusalem to Jericho is robbed, stripped, beaten senseless, and left on the road almost dead (v. 30). Many people during that time did not have extra clothes; therefore, clothing was a valuable item to steal. A person would expect the priest or Levite to aid an injured fellow Jew, but neither the priest nor the Levite helped the injured man. Perhaps they had any number of very sensible reasons including the purity laws, which forbade the priest and Levite touching dead things. Of course, the bottom line is that they valued their positions more than kindness. Because they longed to be right on the letter of the Law, they failed to interpret the meaning of the words.

The Samaritan, however, goes out of his way to help the man. Unexpectedly, the Samaritan sets aside cultural animosity to show compassion. Even though no Jew would like to admit it, the Samaritans knew just as well as the Jews did that God loves to show mercy. This Samaritan is a picture of love to someone with whom he is neither familiar nor has any previous friendship. He was moved with compassion at seeing another's misery. It is undeniable that the Samaritan is the better person—the true neighbor. He illustrates that a neighbor is one who sees another who is in need and uses whatever resources he has to meet that need.

How many times have you been in a situation in which someone of another race or culture stopped to help you?

3. The Moral (vv. 36-37)

The lawyer does not hesitate in answering Jesus' (and his own) question: Who is the injured man's neighbor? The Samaritan clearly acted beyond the norm to do all he could to show love and concern for the injured man. Therefore, the lawyer answered, "He that shewed mercy on him" (from v. 37). Once the lawyer admitted that the definition of neighbor is larger than he assumed it to be, Jesus told the lawyer that he must do as the Samaritan did if he really wanted to inherit eternal life and fulfill the Law.

Race and location keep neighbors from meeting each other, even in some churches. We often look upon anyone who is not a part of our group as an outsider. God commands us to be neighborly to everyone. It does not matter whether the other person is rich, middle-class, or poor; Black, White, or biracial. Everyone is called to enter a relationship with Jesus. Our circle must be wide enough to encompass all of God's creation.

Are their barriers to serving our neighbors today? In what ways can we show mercy to others (e.g., the Samaritan gave money and helped provide healthcare)?

Search the Scriptures

1. What does the lawyer say is the way to inherit eternal life? How consuming is the pursuit (Luke 10:27)?

2. What did Jesus do to illustrate how to be a good neighbor (v. 30)?

3. When the Samaritan saw the injured man, what made him stop to help (v. 33)?

4. What did Jesus encourage the lawyer to practice (v. 37)?

Discuss the Meaning

1. What message should we learn from the priest and the Levite passing the injured man on the road? Were their concerns legitimate?

2. What message can we take personally from the Samaritan's willingness to stop?

Liberating Lesson

Sometimes we will not stop to help someone because we think they will harm us. We are afraid that stopping may do more injury than good. We suspect others of being involved in illicit behavior such as drug dealing or running a scam to steal money or property. Sometimes

this is true, but how do you discern when to help? We look at race, location, and the appearance of the person before determining whether help should be given. We look at all of these things, but God examines hearts first. God stops and listens to our cries of distress no matter what condition we are in and comes to our rescue. The next time you pass someone who is begging or stopped on the side of the road, put yourself in their place. Wouldn't you want someone to stop and help you?

Application for Activation

Consider the cries for help and mercy within your own little world. Can you help? Will you help? Start by engaging your family in a group project. Is there a sick "neighbor" in need of help with house chores, etc.? Could the family adopt a person who is lonely and alone in life? Could the family work together to save money for a needy cause? The ideas are limitless and so are the needs.

Follow the Spirit

What God wants me to do:

_____

_____

_____

_____

Remember Your Thoughts

Special insights I have learned:

_____

_____

_____

_____

More Light on the Text
Luke 10:25–37

Among the Bantu people of sub-Saharan Africa, the most common philosophy about life is called "ubuntu." Ubuntu is centered on the understanding that personhood is impossible in isolation. Thus, one cannot be a person without interacting with others; a person really exists only in relationship with the community. It is community that allows us to function as true, caring persons. Likewise, only through the gathering of persons can we have community. This sense of community is usually seen best when we encounter strangers, especially those strangers who are in need. In fact, the well-being of the stranger is ubuntu's end goal. In this sense then, ubuntu tells us that the answer to the lawyer's question, "Who is my neighbor?" is the entire world, especially those in need. But Jesus points out that love for the neighbor has to be predicated by love for God.

25 And, behold, a certain lawyer stood up, and tempted him, saying, Master, what shall I do to inherit eternal life?

While only Luke records the Parable of the Good Samaritan, both Matthew and Mark join him in reporting a conversation Jesus has with a lawyer (Gk. *nomikos*, no-mee-**KOHS**, an expert of the Jewish law). This dialogue between Jesus and the lawyer is not only a prelude to the parable; it has its own important place in Jesus' work with His disciples. The lawyer was a recognized religious authority, and he tested Jesus, the unskilled Galilean lay teacher, to see if He could give correct answers to tough theological questions. The purpose was to acquire some reason to convict Jesus of blasphemy and ultimately to execute Him.

First, the lawyer calls Jesus "Master" (Gk. *didaskalos*, dee-**DASS**-kal-os, meaning "teacher"). With this title, the lawyer acknowledges Jesus' authority and familiarity with the Word. The use of this word is not an acknowledgment that Jesus is the only begotten of the Father. He concedes only what many outside the Christian faith believe about Christ today: that He was simply a great teacher.

Luke tells us that the lawyer asks Jesus, "What shall I do to inherit eternal life?" He does not seek to say which of the Torah commandments is the greatest, but rather he inquires about the fundamental principle of all the commandments. Pinpointing the goal of the entire law was a common theme in rabbinical debates of that time. The word "inherit" (Gk. *kleronomeo*, klay-rono-**MEH**-oh, to receive an allotted share) is key to understanding that many Jews of the time thought that their eternal destiny was based on their Jewish descent plus their good deeds, believing these qualified them for God's blessing.

26 He said unto him, What is written in the law? how readest thou? 27 And he answering said, Thou shalt love the LORD thy God with all thy heart, and with all thy soul, and with all thy strength, and with all thy mind; and thy neighbour as thyself.

Jesus answers the lawyer's question with two questions, taking him to the Old Testament whose authority the lawyer would not question, being an expert in the same. Jesus wants the lawyer to state his own interpretation of the Scriptures, thereby shifting the dialogue from Jesus' teaching to the lawyer's understanding of the law. Correctly, the lawyer recites two commandments: love God (Deuteronomy 6:5) and love your neighbor (Leviticus 19:18). Together these two commandments formed the heart of Judaism, but they also formed the core of Jesus' own teaching. Thus, Jesus and the lawyer end up at the same place in their conversation.

28 And he said unto him, Thou hast answered right: this do, and thou shalt live. 29 But he, willing to justify himself, said unto Jesus, And who is my neighbour?

Jesus observes that the lawyer is right in his interpretation, commending his answer and exhorting him to do as he stated. However, having answered the question correctly, the lawyer asks for clarification, possibly to test Jesus further. Since loving your neighbor is a matter of life and death, the correct definition of a neighbor is of extreme importance. So, the lawyer asks, "Who is my neighbor?" In other words, he was saying, "Whom do I love?" Of course, he might have hoped that Jesus would understand— and justify—his bias against certain kinds of neighbors—those who did not belong to the Jewish family. Scholars agree that the general Jewish sense of the neighbor at the time was limited to fellow members of the covenant. Since the lawyer might have been a Pharisee, he could easily interpret the commandments in this exclusive manner. He agreed on loving neighbor, but he sought to define neighbor to include only Jews.

In our contemporary context, this question may be used to justify our individualism while neglecting those neighbors that we do not like. Consequently, this question is of extreme relevance in our world where segregation tears the body of Christ apart just as much as it does any other community. Unity in diversity is a thorny subject even among Christians. Divisions take many forms and are prevalent in our communities. Black, White, Hispanic, Asian, Orthodox, Pentecostal, Roman Catholic, Lutheran, male, female, rich, poor, educated, and uneducated are just a few of the categories we use to classify our neighbors, usually to choose which neighbor to recognize or not recognize. Unfortunately, these efforts at discriminating between neighbors affects our understanding of the church's mission in the world: to invite all people into God's kingdom without regard to our man-made qualifiers.

30 And Jesus answering said, A certain man went down from Jerusalem to Jericho, and fell among thieves, which stripped him of his raiment, and wounded him, and departed, leaving him half dead. 31 And by chance there came down a certain priest that way: and when he saw him, he passed by on the other side. 32 And likewise a Levite, when he was at the place, came and looked on him, and passed by on the other side.

The conversation takes a twist as Jesus brings in a parable to drive the lesson home. In the parable, a man (supposedly a Jew) runs into robbers who vandalize him, strip him, and leave him half-dead. While he lies half-conscious on the wayside, a priest and a Levite pass by, and upon seeing him, they go to the other side of the road. Both the priest and the Levite are well-known religious figures. The priests are descendants of Aaron and are responsible for everything to do with Temple worship. Levites were a tribe of descendants of Levi but not of Aaron (who was also a descendant of Levi), and they assisted the priests in the Temple. The Levite in this story seems overly inconsiderate as he "came and looked" at the wounded man and proceeded without offering help. Jesus' audience, however, might have expected that at the sight of a wounded fellow Jew, both the priest and the Levite would stop by to help him. There could be several reasons for their lack of action, among them: (1) their religious responsibilities may have prevented them from helping the wounded man since he might have appeared dead, as the law prohibited them from touching a corpse, (2) they might have been afraid of being attacked by the same robbers, and (3) they might have simply wanted nothing to do with the wounded person. It is possible that they were not indifferent to the wounded man, but their compassion might have been overcome by their commitment to religious purity. Jewish customs—not God's Word—forbid the Jews from such contact, and the priest and Levite displayed their preference for man's rules over godly love and mercy.

33 But a certain Samaritan, as he journeyed, came where he was: and when he saw him, he had compassion on him, 34 And went to him, and bound up his wounds, pouring in oil and wine, and set him on his own beast, and brought him to an inn, and took care of him. 35 And on the morrow when he departed, he took out two pence, and gave them to the host, and said unto him, Take care of him; and whatsoever thou spendest more, when I come again, I will repay thee.

The parable invites the audience to expect a Jewish layman to be the third traveler who responds to the wounded man, but Jesus brings a very unlikely person from a community hated by the Jews into the story—a certain Samaritan. The significance of the Samaritan in this parable cannot be overstated. If Jesus told the story to us today, He would choose another kind of person who we would be equally surprised to see show compassion, like a leather-clad biker or hard-beaten gangbanger.

The relationship between Jews and Samaritans was one of constant hostility. The Jews considered the Samaritans to be second-class citizens, the half-breed descendants of Jews who had intermarried with foreigners (see 2 Kings 17:24–40). In return, the Samaritans had occasionally troubled Israel. The ancient Jewish historian Josephus claims that in the years between 6 and 9 A.D., Samaritans defiled Passover by scattering bones in the Temple. Because of the Samaritans' ancestry, Jews believed that their faith was diluted, thereby making them unclean and detestable. Not only did "the Jews have no dealings with

[them]" (John 4:9), but they also believed the Samaritans to be demon-possessed (John 8:48).

Still, we have here a Samaritan traveling in Jewish territory. His attending to the wounded Jew jeopardized his life because he could have been easily blamed for the robbery. In addition, the Samaritans were bound by the same religious laws that bound the Jews, and therefore, the Samaritan risked defilement to take care of the possibly dead man—bandaging his wounds, pouring on oil and wine. Being a Samaritan, he could not expect any such kindness from the Jews. However, unlike the priest and the Levite, he fulfilled the law, showed compassion, and helped the wounded man.

He was moved by "compassion," which here comes from the Greek word *splagchnizomai* (splonk-**NEED**-zo-my), which means "to be moved in one's gut." The guts—inward parts, entrails—were thought to be the seat of love and pity. This show of compassion mirrors that of Jesus in three instances: healing a multitude of sick people (Matthew 14:14), feeding the 4,000 (Matthew 15:32), and healing two blind men (Matthew 20:34). In each of these scenes, a feeling of pity prompted a work of mercy. Love, empathy, and mercy are motivated by someone else's needs while withholding mercy is essentially an act of selfishness or self-protection.

Jesus' parable contrasts the lack of compassion shown by the two members of the Jewish priesthood with the Samaritan's compassion and obedience to the Law. Any Jew would be deeply humiliated by this account which not only suggests that love can be found in unlikely places but also paints a picture in the Samaritan that may—or must—be emulated. The mercy of the Samaritan made him give generously of his own supplies for the life of the wounded stranger. His oil and wine cleansed and soothed the wounds. He bandaged and bound the injuries and his own animal carried the man to safety. He used his own money to pay for the man's care at the inn, promising to pay for any further expenses his care would require. In cultures like those of Africa, this Samaritan would be said to be a muntu—one who has ubuntu—and thus, a person. The personhood of the priest and the Levite was diminished for not giving of themselves to help the needy. Love humanizes both the giver and the receiver— and that is what it takes to be a neighbor.

36 Which now of these three, thinkest thou, was neighbour unto him that fell among the thieves? 37 And he said, He that shewed mercy on him. Then said Jesus unto him, Go, and do thou likewise.

Jesus again puts the lawyer on the spot. He asks the lawyer for his opinion on who acted neighborly, based on the lawyer's knowledge of the Law and his response in verse 27. The lawyer, as Luke's narrative indicates, does not use the word "Samaritan." Although he understands the message behind Jesus' parable, the same arrogance that spurred him to justify himself in verse 29 would not allow him to confess verbally that the Samaritan acted more righteously than the priest or the Levite. His obstinacy shows how humans will refuse to give credit where credit is due. In the lawyer's eyes, Samaritans could do nothing noble or admirable, a misconception that led to this being labeled the parable of the "good Samaritan." The play on words shows how God can use what's thought of as the "worst" of society to do what's best for His kingdom.

Jesus then reinforces His answer in verse 28. He advises the lawyer to do as the one who showed mercy on the beaten man had done, trying to get him to realize that keeping the letter of the Law is not enough to inherit eternal life. Love, mercy, and grace must exceed the limits of the Law, and those seeking everlasting life must exhibit these traits through faith in Jesus Christ.

Sources:

Cosby, Michael R. *Portraits of Jesus: An Inductive Approach to the Gospels*. 1st ed. Louisville, KY: Westminster John Knox Press, 1999. 86–87.

Dunn, James D. G., and J. W. Rogerson. *Eerdmans Commentary on the Bible*. Grand Rapids, MI: W.B. Eerdmans, 2003.

Hebrew-Greek Key Word Study Bible, King James Version. Chattanooga, TN: AMG Publishers, Inc., 1991.

Josephus. *The Antiquities of the Jews*. 18.2.2.

Keener, Craig S. *The IVP Bible Background Commentary: New Testament*. Downers Grove, IL: Intervarsity Press, 1993. 217–218.

Marshall, I. Howard. *The Gospel of Luke: A Commentary on the Greek Text*. Grand Rapids, MI: Eerdmans, 1978. 440–450.

Plummer, Alfred. *A Critical and Exegetical Commentary on the Gospel According to St. Luke*. 5th ed. Edinburgh: T. & T. Clark, 1975. 283–288.

Radmacher, Earl D., ed. *Nelson Study Bible, New King James Version*. Nashville, TN: Thomas Nelson Publishers, 1997. 1618–1619, 1714–1715.

Ryrie, Charles C. *Ryrie Study Bible, New International Version*. Chicago, IL: Moody Press, 1986. 1423.

Thompson, Richard P., and Thomas E. Phillips. *Literary Studies in Luke-Acts: Essays in Honor of Joseph B. Tyson*. Macon, GA: Mercer University Press, 1998.

Unger, Merrill F. *The New Unger's Bible Dictionary*. Chicago, IL: Moody Press, 1988. 762–765, 1116–1119.

Walvoord, John F., and Roy B. Zuck, eds. *The Bible Knowledge Commentary: New Testament*. Wheaton, IL: Victor Books, SP Publications, Inc., 1983. 233–234.

Say It Correctly

Samaritan. sah-**MARE**-ih-ten.
Assyria. ah-**SEER**-ee-ah.

Daily Bible Readings

MONDAY
Help Your Neighbor in Need
(Deuteronomy 15:7-11)

TUESDAY
Love God and Brothers and Sisters
(1 John 4:16-21)

WEDNESDAY
Adopt the First Commandments
(Mark 12:28-34)

THURSDAY
Jesus Accepts Thanks
from Healed Samaritan
(Luke 17:11-19)

FRIDAY
Jacob Lives with Joseph in Egypt
(Acts 7:9-15)

SATURDAY
Jesus Offers Samaritan
Woman Living Water
(John 4:1-15)

SUNDAY
Follow the Samaritan's Example
(Luke 10:25-37)

Notes

_____

_____

_____

_____

Teaching Tips

Words You Should Know

A. Charity (1 Corinthians 13:1) *agape* (Gk.)—Love, fellowship, affection, benevolence, or specifically divine kindness

B. Tongues (v. 1) *glossa* (Gk.)—Languages

Teacher Preparation

Unifying Principle—The Most Excellent Way. Special gifts such as knowledge and wisdom can easily make us lose sight of our obligations to others. How can we avoid being pleased with ourselves? Paul suggested that love is the best way to relate to others and forget one's own status.

A. Read the Bible Background and Devotional Reading.

B. Pray for your students and lesson clarity.

C. Read the lesson Scripture in multiple translations.

O—Open the Lesson

A. Begin the class with prayer.

B. Have the class members list and discuss how they expressed love when they were children and how they define and express love as adults.

C. Have the students read the Aim for Change and the In Focus story.

D. Ask students how events like those in the story weigh on their hearts and how they can view these events from a faith perspective.

P—Present the Scriptures

A. Read the Focal Verses and discuss the Background and The People, Places, and Times sections.

B. Have the class share what Scriptures stand out for them and why, with particular emphasis on today's themes.

E—Explore the Meaning

A. Use In Depth or More Light on the Text to facilitate a deeper discussion of the lesson text.

B. Pose the questions in Search the Scriptures and Discuss the Meaning.

C. Discuss the Liberating Lesson and Application for Activation sections.

N—Next Steps for Application

A. Summarize the value of understanding that love sustains, even when our faith and hope are weak.

B. This week practice loving as an act of the will rather than an action-driven by emotion.

Worship Guide

For the Superintendent or Teacher
Theme: Love Divine
Song: "O Perfect Love"
Devotional Reading: Romans 12:9-21

Love Divine

Bible Background • 1 CORINTHIANS 12:27–14:1
Printed Text • 1 CORINTHIANS 13 | Devotional Reading • ROMANS 12:9-21

Aim for Change

By the end of this lesson, we will DEFINE Paul's understanding of love as the apex of the Spirit-led life, APPRECIATE love as motivation to share our God-given gifts, and ACT in love when sharing our God-given gifts.

In Focus

Gayle was president of the church's usher board. She was always on time, impeccably uniformed, and knew all of the hand signals. Whenever Gayle was on duty, the members had their envelopes and fans before they requested them; she would immediately move forward when she heard crying babies—firmly removing them from their parents' arms and delivering them to the nursery so the services could proceed without disruption.

As she moved about the sanctuary this morning, Gayle was clearly irritated. She had met with the pastor on Saturday afternoon, and he had been critical of her work. The pastor had complimented Gayle on her faithfulness and dedication. However, the pastor had gone on to tell her that, while she clearly enjoyed being an usher, he was concerned that she didn't love the members. "Nothing can replace our love for others," he had said. "Working on their behalf is fine, but it is meaningless unless our work is motivated by love. Christian love is essential to make any ministry effective."

Gayle was so distracted thinking about the pastor's rebuke that she dropped the offering plate during service. It clanged loudly and spilled its contents on the floor. As congregants helped her pick everything up, Gayle realized her attitude was keeping the services from proceeding as much as her loud disruption just did. Gayle took a calming breath and prayed God would fill her with patience, kindness, and all the attributes of love.

When have you had to remind yourself to minister in love rather than just fulfill a church obligation?

Keep in Mind

"And now abideth faith, hope, charity, these three; but the greatest of these is charity" (1 Corinthians 13:13, KJV).

"Three things will last forever—faith, hope, and love—and the greatest of these is love" (1 Corinthians 13:13, NLT).

Focal Verses

KJV **1 Corinthians 13:1** Though I speak with the tongues of men and of angels, and have not charity, I am become as sounding brass, or a tinkling cymbal.

2 And though I have the gift of prophecy, and understand all mysteries, and all knowledge; and though I have all faith, so that I could remove mountains, and have not charity, I am nothing.

3 And though I bestow all my goods to feed the poor, and though I give my body to be burned, and have not charity, it profiteth me nothing.

4 Charity suffereth long, and is kind; charity envieth not; charity vaunteth not itself, is not puffed up,

5 Doth not behave itself unseemly, seeketh not her own, is not easily provoked, thinketh no evil;

6 Rejoiceth not in iniquity, but rejoiceth in the truth;

7 Beareth all things, believeth all things, hopeth all things, endureth all things.

8 Charity never faileth: but whether there be prophecies, they shall fail; whether there be tongues, they shall cease; whether there be knowledge, it shall vanish away.

9 For we know in part, and we prophesy in part.

10 But when that which is perfect is come, then that which is in part shall be done away.

11 When I was a child, I spake as a child, I understood as a child, I thought as a child: but when I became a man, I put away childish things.

12 For now we see through a glass, darkly; but then face to face: now I know in part; but then shall I know even as also I am known.

13 And now abideth faith, hope, charity, these three; but the greatest of these is charity.

NLT **1 Corinthians 13:1** If I could speak all the languages of earth and of angels, but didn't love others, I would only be a noisy gong or a clanging cymbal.

2 If I had the gift of prophecy, and if I understood all of God's secret plans and possessed all knowledge, and if I had such faith that I could move mountains, but didn't love others, I would be nothing.

3 If I gave everything I have to the poor and even sacrificed my body, I could boast about it; but if I didn't love others, I would have gained nothing.

4 Love is patient and kind. Love is not jealous or boastful or proud

5 or rude. It does not demand its own way. It is not irritable, and it keeps no record of being wronged.

6 It does not rejoice about injustice but rejoices whenever the truth wins out.

7 Love never gives up, never loses faith, is always hopeful, and endures through every circumstance.

8 Prophecy and speaking in unknown languages and special knowledge will become useless. But love will last forever!

9 Now our knowledge is partial and incomplete, and even the gift of prophecy reveals only part of the whole picture!

10 But when the time of perfection comes, these partial things will become useless.

11 When I was a child, I spoke and thought and reasoned as a child. But when I grew up, I put away childish things.

12 Now we see things imperfectly, like puzzling reflections in a mirror, but then we will see everything with perfect clarity. All that I know now is partial and incomplete, but then I will know everything completely, just as God now knows me completely.

13 Three things will last forever—faith, hope, and love—and the greatest of these is love.

The People, Places, and Times

Corinth. The city of Corinth was the capital of the Roman province of Achaia, which included the southern half of Greece. The ancient Greek city-state of Corinth had been completely destroyed in 146 BC when the Romans conquered the area. In 44 BC, Julius Caesar ordered that the city be rebuilt as a Roman colony. Corinth was a major trade city located on an isthmus that connects cities in northern Greece, like Athens and Delphi, with cities on the Peloponnesian peninsula, like Sparta and Olympia. It also benefitted from maritime trade on the Aegean Sea to the east and on the Gulf of Corinth to the west. This location made Corinth a bustling trade and cultural center.

Corinth was socially, culturally, and religiously diverse. In fact, in AD 49 a good number of Jews who were expelled from Rome resettled in Corinth. The Christians of Corinth reflected the diversity of the city. Congregations included wealthy persons, merchants, slaves, and former slaves. During the time in which Paul wrote, Corinth was known for its wanton sexual immorality. The Greek word *korinthiazesthai*, which means to live like a Corinthian, meant that one lived immorally.

Background

Paul wrote 1 Corinthians while he was living and ministering in the city of Ephesus. The letter was written between AD 53 and 55. During his time in Ephesus, he had also received a letter from the church at Corinth (7:1) expressing confusion about marriage, divorce, corporate worship, bodily resurrection, and living in a pagan society. Paul wrote to encourage the Corinthians and to emphasize the importance of holiness. He also wrote to correct their misunderstanding and abuse of spiritual gifts, which he discussed in chapter 12. Chapter 13 is often misinterpreted, which leads to its improper application as merely an ode to the virtues of love. Paul was using 1 Corinthians 13 to address specific issues in the Corinthian church: selfishness, division, abuse of gifts, and envy.

The Greek term for love (KJV: charity) used in this chapter is *agape* (ah-**GAH**-pay). This word is closely associated with the Hebrew word *chesed* (**KHESS**-ed), which refers to God's covenant love for His people. Because of this association, agape became a keyword for describing God's character and took on the meaning of a divine love that is deeply loyal. Believers should emulate this love.

At-A-Glance

1. Love is Superior (1 Corinthians 13:1-3)
2. Characteristics of Love (vv. 4-7)
3. Love Endures (vv. 8-13)

In Depth

1. Love is Superior (1 Corinthians 13:1–3)

The Corinthians held eloquence in especially high esteem and were somewhat preoccupied with the gift of tongues. However, even the most sophisticated gift of tongues is just noise if not exercised in love. Prophecy, though a desirable gift (14:1), is useless without love. Knowledge of the deepest mysteries of God has no value apart from love. Faith, even when great enough to move mountains, is nothing apart from love. Likewise, boundless generosity is not profitable without love. Willingness to suffer, even to the point of martyrdom, is worthless in the absence of love.

Love is essential. Spiritual gifts are nothing without love; they can even be destructive when not practiced in love. Love is what enriches the gifts and gives them value. Whatever our gifts, love should be the motivating factor and pleasing God our objective.

If works without love are useless, should we stop making an effort to give of ourselves?

2. Characteristics of Love (vv. 4–7)

Paul gives a beautifully elaborate and poetic description of love that can be summed up in verse 7: love bears, believes, hopes, and endures all things. Paul's use of language implies that love must be active at all times. Love "beareth all things." It withstands the assault and protects those under its sphere of influence. Love "believeth all things." It is always willing to give the benefit of the doubt. Love "hopeth all things," and does not despair. Love "endureth all things," including temptation or testing.

Paul highlights the character of love as Christians should express it. His descriptions of love are active, indicating that love is something one does, not merely an emotion. As Christians, we have received the love of God. Therefore, we are to love others. Contrary to what many believe, love is not an abstract notion. Love is practical and must be put into practice on a daily basis. Christians must constantly be aware of their actions and ask themselves, "Did I show love in that situation or toward that person?" Paul explains that love results in characteristics that can be seen and heard.

Describe how you have seen these aspects of love shown in Christians you admire.

3. Love Endures (vv. 8–13)

Love surpasses all the other spiritual gifts because they will pass away, while love endures forever. Prophecy, tongues, and knowledge are limited (v. 9). Further, a time will come when those gifts will not be necessary. They are given by the Spirit for the building and maturation of the church. We will not need such things in heaven but will experience love there.

We exercise our gifts imperfectly. Our knowledge is imperfect, like seeing indirectly, as if through a bronze mirror. (Corinth was well known for its bronze artistry and bronze mirrors.) However, imperfection will give way to perfection, enabling us to see perfectly. In the perfection of heaven, we will experience love eternally. Because love is eternal and is superior to the other spiritual gifts, it is childish to focus on spiritual gifts to the exclusion of love.

Not only is love superior to spiritual gifts, but it is also superior to faith and hope. Just as in heaven we will no longer need prophecy or tongues, we will also no longer need faith when we finally see God. At that point, all hope will be fulfilled (cf. Romans 8:24). Since love outlasts all of these, love is the greatest gift of all.

How are we to "put away childish things" but still retain child-like faith?

Search the Scriptures

1. Why is love superior to the other spiritual gifts (1Corinthians 13:8)?

2. Make a list of what specifically Paul says love does (vv. 4-8)

3. After other spiritual gifts cease to exist, what will remain (v. 13)?

Discuss the Meaning

1. As we continually experience the love of God, how can we show His love to others? How can we demonstrate more love in our relationships? How can we express love in difficult situations?

2. Paul writes to the Corinthians in response to their abuse and misunderstanding of spiritual gifts. What are some of the practical ways we can work to ensure that all members of the body of Christ, regardless of their spiritual gifts, are loved and valued?

Liberating Lesson

Over 500,000 children in the U.S. currently reside in some form of foster care. Two-thirds of these children are African American, and they stay in foster care longer. The challenges of these children are complex and may include blaming themselves and feeling guilty about removal from their birth parents, feeling unwanted if awaiting adoption for a long time, and feeling helpless about multiple changes in foster parents over time. These children are in desperate need of love. How can you help? In many states across the U.S., you are probably eligible to become a foster or adoptive parent. You must be over the age of 21 and financially stable. You must also meet certain safety requirements such as criminal and child abuse screening. There are no preferences made to race or ethnic origin, educational background, marital status, occupation, or homeownership. How might helping or even fostering these children show the love of God? Consider becoming a foster parent.

Application for Activation

True love comes from God. It is the very nature of God. We demonstrate our love for God when we show our love for one another. We are often frustrated in our church work, especially when it feels as though others are not as committed as we are. Over the next week, pray and ask God to reveal to you areas where you may have failed to demonstrate love toward your co-laborers. Then, ask God what you can do to remedy the situation. Also, ask Him how to show love to those who don't show it to you. It may call for you to make apologies, seek forgiveness, or even forgive others; but it will be worth it.

Follow the Spirit

What God wants me to do:

_____

_____

_____

_____

Remember Your Thoughts

Special insights I have learned:

_____

_____

_____

_____

More Light on the Text
1 Corinthians 13

Paul spends time explaining the character of *agape* (Gk. **AH**-gah-pay) to the Corinthian church. In the King James Version, *agape* is translated "charity." When we think of charity, we usually think of giving to others, an active expression of Christian love. This is not the limit of the meaning of "charity." In the King James Version of the Bible, "charity" is understood as it relates to the similar word "cherish." To show charity to someone is to show that you cherish them. This includes, but also goes far beyond, giving alms or offerings, as Paul further explains.

When Paul speaks of "charity," we should read that word as "love." More importantly, we should know that Paul is speaking of a specific form of love. He is not talking about *eros*, or the sensuous or erotic form of love. Nor is Paul describing *philia*, which means "a brotherly affection or friendship." Rather, Paul is describing *agape*, "a commitment of the will to cherish and uphold another person." In the Bible, this is the form of love that is always used when we describe God's love. *Agape* describes our willful and deliberate decision to treat others with the utmost care and concern. Hope allows us to esteem the best interests of our brother or sister above our own.

1 Though I speak with the tongues of men and of angels, and have not charity, I am become as sounding brass, or a tinkling cymbal. 2 And though I have the gift of prophecy, and understand all mysteries, and all knowledge; and though I have all faith, so that I could remove mountains, and have not charity, I am nothing.

Love is a radical reordering of priorities and ultimate values. The person is no longer the center of his or her universe or ultimate concern; "the other" is now in the center. Without love, everything we do is for our own self-glorification and benefit. With love, what we do is for God and others. Love is not a feeling; it is what we do for others without regard for self. It is partaking in the very nature of God because He is love (1 John 4:8).

Spirit-inspired speech spoken in ecstasy, different languages, brilliant human rhetoric, or superhuman entreaties mean nothing if they are not of God. Any intention whose source is not the God of love is in vain. If the Spirit of God animates the body, love holds it together. Tongues without love are only noise. The gift of prophecy or preaching is mere entertainment or scolding and has no effect if the speaker is not motivated by love. The gift of intellectual accomplishment without love leads to contempt and snobbery. The gift of great faith that gives much or sacrifices greatly can lead to false pride. None of these gifts edifies the body of Christ or pleases God unless they are done in love.

3 And though I bestow all my goods to feed the poor, and though I give my body to be burned, and have not charity, it profiteth me nothing.

Benevolence and even self-sacrifice can be great for those on the receiving end or in the eyes of the world. In terms of our own spiritual maturity, it means nothing without love. To give out of obligation, self-promotion, or even contempt can profit those who are poor and needy, but it does not profit the giver unless the spirit of love is present.

The Corinthian Christians were missing the motive and the goal of the gifts, making the means to become their own end. But for Paul, love says it all. It is not an issue of love versus gifts. Paul stresses that the focus and end of the gifts is love. The gifts are not for their own sake. For gifts to be effectual, love must guide their use.

4 Charity suffereth long, and is kind; charity envieth not; charity vaunteth not itself, is not puffed up, 5 Doth not behave itself unseemly, seeketh not her own, is not easily provoked, thinketh no evil; 6 Rejoiceth not in iniquity, but rejoiceth in the truth;

Paul describes a life characterized by love (vv. 4-6). He presents an other-centered life in action.

1) Love "suffereth long" (Gk. *makrothumeo*, mah-kro-thoo-**MEH**-oh)—or endures patiently—the errors, weaknesses, and even meanness of people. Love makes us slow to anger. It will suffer many things for the sake of the relationship. If God's love is in us, we will be longsuffering to those who annoy us and hurt us.

2) Love is kind. Kindness is demonstrated in simple acts, such as giving a cup of water to the thirsty (Matthew 25:42).

3) Love "envieth not" (Gk. *zeloo*, zay-**LOH**-oh). It does not earnestly covet another's good fortune. Love does not get angry at another's success.

4) Love "vaunteth not," or does not brag about itself. It is not boastful or stuck up. Love does not parade itself: Love in action can work anonymously. It does not have to have the limelight or the attention to do a good job or to be satisfied with the result. Love gives because it loves to give without the praise of showing itself off.

5) Love is not "puffed up" (Gk. *phusioo*, foo-see-**OH**-oh), snobbish, or arrogant. Loving people esteem others higher than themselves. To be puffed up is to be self-focused or, as we would say today, have a "big head."

6) Love does not behave rudely, that is, it is not ill-mannered or brash. Where there is love, there will be kindness and good manners. A person who loves does not just speak his or her mind but minds his or her speech. Love does not go around hurting others' feelings. It always uses tact and politeness.

7) Love does not seek its own, an idea that Paul expresses in a slightly different manner in Romans 12:10 and Philippians 2:4. This is being like Jesus in a most basic way: being an other-centered person instead of a self-centered person. Love never demands its rights but seeks its responsibilities toward others. It is not self-centered or self-assertive.

8) Love is not easily provoked. It is neither touchy nor irritable. Love does not fly off the handle. It does not lose its temper. It is not easily exasperated at people.

9) Love thinks no evil. It does not store up the memory or keep an account of any wrong it has received. It forgives the evil that people do to it. It does not carry a grudge. Love does not like to hear about the moral failures of others. It does not get pleasure out of the misfortune of others.

10) Love does not rejoice in iniquity: "I told you so," and "It serves you right," do not reflect the language of love. Love desires the best for others and does not derive personal satisfaction from the failure of others.

11) Instead, love rejoices in the truth. Love is happy to hear what is right, no matter how painful. Love rejoices when what is true, correct, and righteous win the day regardless of how that may impact it directly.

7 Beareth all things, believeth all things, hopeth all things, endureth all things.

Paul ends the discussion of the characteristics of love on a positive note, summarizing the things that love does. It bears all things, believes all things, hopes all things, and endures all things. The Greek word *pantos* (**PAHN**-toce), translated "all" can also be interpreted as "always" (1 Corinthians 13:7). Paul's point is that love never tires of what it does. Most of us do the work of love, but only for a while. The greatness of agape is that it keeps on going!

Love "beareth" (Gk. *stego*, **STEH**-goh) the errors and faults of others. Other translations will say love "protects." This verb is related to the Greek noun meaning "shield," which can be viewed from either side of the battle. If you are the attacker, a shield is protecting your target. If you are the defender, a shield is bearing up under the assault.

Love "believeth" the best, trusts in the object of its love, has confidence in him or her, and gives credit that might otherwise not be self-evident except through the eyes of love. Love can bear all things because it believes all things with the special insight that only a loving relationship can bring.

Love "hopeth" with joy, full of confidence in eager expectation that the salvation of the Lord is to come. It bears all things because it believes with only the insight of God, thus it can wait for the true nature of people to be revealed. Love trusts in the eventual reconciliation with God.

Love "endureth" (Gk. *hupomeno*, hoo-po-**MEN**-oh) and continues to be present; it does not perish or depart in spite of errors, faults, or wrongs done. The verb carries the image of "remaining or abiding under" hardship. Love is not going anywhere; it will endure.

8 Charity never faileth: but whether there be prophecies, they shall fail; whether there

be tongues, they shall cease; whether there be knowledge, it shall vanish away.

The verse begins Paul's conclusion on the topic of love. He has been addressing the over-emphasis of the Corinthian Christians on the gifts of the Holy Spirit. Here, Paul attests to the permanence of love as he continues to put the spiritual gifts and virtues in perspective.

Love is eternal; it never comes to an end. It is absolutely permanent. Whereas all the gifts in which the Corinthians pride themselves are transitory at best, love is transcendent. The gifts were given by the Spirit as instruments to be used in this age. Paul anticipates that these gifts will no longer be needed when the next age occurs, marked by the return of Christ and fulfillment of the reign of God. Prophesies, tongues and knowledge will pass away with the old age. Love, on the other hand, is essential and will never pass away.

9 For we know in part, and we prophesy in part. 10 But when that which is perfect is come, then that which is in part shall be done away.

Love, like God, is complete. On the other hand, we are imperfect creatures who can only comprehend reality—both material and spiritual—in an incomplete manner. Therefore, we can only preach or prophesy in an imperfect and partial way. For Paul, the kingdom of God is near, but not yet. It is not fully revealed in this age, so our knowledge and prophecy of it can only be partial.

The "perfect" (Gk. *teleios*, **TEH**-lay-ose) maturity or completeness will come with the end of this present, imperfect age and the beginning of the new, perfect age. Paul describes the times the Corinthians live in as transitory. Thus they should not make gods or idols out of the gifts they esteem so highly.

11 When I was a child, I spake as a child, I understood as a child, I thought as a child: but when I became a man, I put away childish things. 12 For now we see through a glass, darkly; but then face to face: now I know in part; but then shall I know even as also I am known.

Paul poses a metaphor of the maturing spiritual human being who grows from childhood to adulthood. Paul, who had called the Corinthians "babes in Christ," chides them once again to grow up and put away the trappings of childhood, in this case, using their gifts for the wrong reasons (3:1). It is wrong to suggest that verses 11-12 see tongue-speaking and prophecy as childishness, particularly considering Paul, himself, claims to do both. What Paul is saying is that there is an appropriate age to do so and that now is that age. When the completion of that age finally arrives, then it will be time to set aside what was appropriate and needful for that age.

The word translated as glass (Gk. *esoptron*, eh-**SOHP**-trone) is another word for mirror. Mirrors were a primary industry in the city of Corinth. Mirrors made in Corinth were finely polished silver or bronze. The image was often concave and distorted, much like today's amusement park house of mirrors. Thus, we see only dimly through the distorted reflections of our own limited understanding. However, when Jesus returns and makes His dwelling place among His people, we will see Him face to face (cf. Revelation 21:22–23). We not only come to know, but we will also be known.

13 And now abideth faith, hope, charity, these three; but the greatest of these is charity.

After everything has been said we come to the conclusion of the matter. Spiritual gifts are given for a particular purpose, and for a particular time. It is childish to esteem them too highly. We, like the Corinthian Christians, must remember that giftedness is not the measure of maturity. The display of love is.

It is by faith that we are saved according to the grace of God. In hope, we wait upon the return of Jesus and the coming of the reign of God. All this is due to God's love for us. These are what remain when one matures in Christ.

However, when Jesus returns, the reign of God is fulfilled. We have no need for hope. When we stand face-to-face with God. When we clearly see all that there is to see, then we will have no need for faith. Yet we will continue to love and be loved by God. Love never ends. It is eternal and the greatest gift of God.

Sources:
Adewuya, J. Ayodeji. *A Commentary on 1& 2 Corinthians*. London: SPCK, 2009. 95.
Bruce, F. F. *The Epistle to the Hebrews, Revised: New International Commentary on the New Testament*. Grand Rapids, MI: Eerdmans. Reprint, 1985.
English Standard Version Study Bible. Wheaton, IL: Crossway, 2007.
Guthrie, Donald. *Tyndale New Testament Commentaries: Letter to the Hebrews*. Grand Rapids, MI: Eerdmans, 1983.
Henry, Matthew. *Matthew Henry's Commentary on the Whole Bible: Complete and Unabridged in One Volume*. Peabody, MA: Hendrickson, 1994.
Johnson, Luke Timothy. *Hebrews: A Commentary*. The New Testament Library. Louisville, KY: Westminster John Knox Press, 2006.
Lane, William L. *Hebrews 9-13*. Word Biblical Commentary, Vol. 47B. Dallas, TX: Word Inc., 1991.
Prime, Derek. *Opening Up 1 Corinthians. Opening Up Commentary*. Leominster, UK: Day One Publications, 2005.
Utley, Robert James. *Paul's Letters to a Troubled Church: I and II Corinthians*. Study Guide Commentary Series, vol. 6. Marshall, TX: Bible Lessons International, 2002.
Walvoord, John F., and Roy B. Zuck. *The Bible Knowledge Commentary: An Exposition of the Scriptures*. Dallas Theological Seminary. Wheaton, IL: Victor Books, 1985.
Wiersbe, Warren W. *The Bible Exposition Commentary*. Wheaton, IL: Victor Books, 1996.

Say It Correctly

Achaia. ah-**KIE**-ah.
Peloponnesian.
peh-low-pow-**NEES**-ee-an.
Aegean. ah-**GEE**-an.

Daily Bible Readings

MONDAY
Activists and Supporters Share Victories
(1 Samuel 30:21-25)

TUESDAY
The New Life in Christ
(Romans 12:1-8)

WEDNESDAY
Live by the Mind of Christ
(Philippians 2:1-11)

THURSDAY
Faith, Hope, and Love in Action
(Colossians 1:3-8)

FRIDAY
Gifts for the Good of All
(1 Corinthians 12:4-11)

SATURDAY
Pray with the Mind and Spirit
(1 Corinthians 14:13-19)

SUNDAY
The Life of Love
(1 Corinthians 13)

Teaching Tips

Words You Should Know

A. Wash (John 13:5) *nipto* (Gk.)—To cleanse the hands, feet or face, especially to perform ceremonial cleansing.

B. Clean (v. 10) *katharos* (Gk.)—Free from pollution or dirt; spiritually pure or clear.

Teacher Preparation

Unifying Principle—Upside-Down Love. Multiple definitions of love lead people to be confused about how to love. What is the bottom line ("end") when it comes to love? Jesus taught that our love for one another should be manifested in our service to others.

A. Read the Bible Background and Devotional Reading.

B. Pray for your students and lesson clarity.

C. Read the lesson Scripture in multiple translations.

O—Open the Lesson

A. Begin the class with prayer.

B. Have class members rank a list of ten jobs from the most important to the least important. Point out that people generally believe that service jobs are unimportant jobs.

C. Have the students read the Aim for Change and the In Focus story.

D. Ask students how events like those in the story weigh on their hearts and how they can view these events from a faith perspective.

P—Present the Scriptures

A. Read the Focal Verses and discuss the Background and The People, Places, and Times sections.

B. Have the class share what Scriptures stand out for them and why, with particular emphasis on today's themes.

E—Explore the Meaning

A. Use In Depth or More Light on the Text to facilitate a deeper discussion of the lesson text.

B. Pose the questions in Search the Scriptures and Discuss the Meaning.

C. Discuss the Liberating Lesson and Application for Activation sections.

N—Next Steps for Application

A. Summarize the value of serving others in humility.

B. End class with a commitment to pray this week for the divine power to counter ambition and pride in their lives and the life of the church.

Worship Guide

For the Superintendent or Teacher
Theme: Loving by Serving
Song: "Love Lifted Me"
Devotional Reading: John 15:18—16:4

Loving by Serving

Bible Background • JOHN 13:1-35
Printed Text • JOHN 13:1-15, 34-35 | Devotional Reading • JOHN 15:18–16:4

Aim for Change

By the end of this lesson, we will CONSIDER the significance of Jesus washing the disciples' feet, REPENT of pride that has prevented serving selflessly, and SERVE others as an expression of Christian love.

In Focus

Pastor John Ricks was giving last-minute instructions to the Courtesy Committee. "We are to serve over 100 guests from Blessed Hope Church. They will be coming here from Boston next week to fellowship with us and we want to be sure they are treated kindly," said the pastor.

After the meeting, Joan and her friend Barbara walked to their respective cars. Barbara was the first to speak. "I'm not serving anyone. Every time a church comes here, we are always the ones called on to serve. Isn't there anyone else in this church who can work?"

"Barbara, you shouldn't be that way. After all, we're the Courtesy Committee. It's our job to serve wherever we are needed and help in whatever area we can," said Joan.

"Yeah, but I'm not a servant," said Barbara. "I didn't come to this church to work like a slave. I just came to worship the Lord."

If Jesus didn't mind humbling Himself and being obedient to the Father, shouldn't we have the same attitude? This week we will see how Jesus, the Son of God, decided to show His disciples the mark of a true servant by washing their feet.

Keep in Mind

"For I have given you an example, that ye should do as I have done to you"
(John 13:15, KJV).

"I have given you an example to follow. Do as I have done to you" (John 13:15, NLT).

Focal Verses

KJV **John 13:1** Now before the feast of the passover, when Jesus knew that his hour was come that he should depart out of this world unto the Father, having loved his own which were in the world, he loved them unto the end.

2 And supper being ended, the devil having now put into the heart of Judas Iscariot, Simon's son, to betray him;

3 Jesus knowing that the Father had given all things into his hands, and that he was come from God, and went to God;

4 He riseth from supper, and laid aside his garments; and took a towel, and girded himself.

5 After that he poureth water into a bason, and began to wash the disciples' feet, and to wipe them with the towel wherewith he was girded.

6 Then cometh he to Simon Peter: and Peter saith unto him, Lord, dost thou wash my feet?

7 Jesus answered and said unto him, What I do thou knowest not now; but thou shalt know hereafter.

8 Peter saith unto him, Thou shalt never wash my feet. Jesus answered him, If I wash thee not, thou hast no part with me.

9 Simon Peter saith unto him, Lord, not my feet only, but also my hands and my head.

10 Jesus saith to him, He that is washed needeth not save to wash his feet, but is clean every whit: and ye are clean, but not all.

11 For he knew who should betray him; therefore said he, Ye are not all clean.

12 So after he had washed their feet, and had taken his garments, and was set down again, he said unto them, Know ye what I have done to you?

13 Ye call me Master and Lord: and ye say well; for so I am.

14 If I then, your Lord and Master, have washed your feet; ye also ought to wash one another's feet.

NLT **John 13:1** Before the Passover celebration, Jesus knew that his hour had come to leave this world and return to his Father. He had loved his disciples during his ministry on earth, and now he loved them to the very end.

2 It was time for supper, and the devil had already prompted Judas, son of Simon Iscariot, to betray Jesus.

3 Jesus knew that the Father had given him authority over everything and that he had come from God and would return to God.

4 So he got up from the table, took off his robe, wrapped a towel around his waist,

5 and poured water into a basin. Then he began to wash the disciples' feet, drying them with the towel he had around him.

6 When Jesus came to Simon Peter, Peter said to him, "Lord, are you going to wash my feet?"

7 Jesus replied, "You don't understand now what I am doing, but someday you will."

8 "No," Peter protested, "you will never ever wash my feet!" Jesus replied, "Unless I wash you, you won't belong to me."

9 Simon Peter exclaimed, "Then wash my hands and head as well, Lord, not just my feet!"

10 Jesus replied, "A person who has bathed all over does not need to wash, except for the feet, to be entirely clean. And you disciples are clean, but not all of you."

11 For Jesus knew who would betray him. That is what he meant when he said, "Not all of you are clean."

12 After washing their feet, he put on his robe again and sat down and asked, "Do you understand what I was doing?

13 You call me 'Teacher' and 'Lord,' and you are right, because that's what I am.

14 And since I, your Lord and Teacher, have washed your feet, you ought to wash each other's feet.

15 For I have given you an example, that ye should do as I have done to you.

34 A new commandment I give unto you, That ye love one another; as I have loved you, that ye also love one another.

35 By this shall all men know that ye are my disciples, if ye have love one to another.

15 I have given you an example to follow. Do as I have done to you."

34 "So now I am giving you a new commandment: Love each other. Just as I have loved you, you should love each other.

35 Your love for one another will prove to the world that you are my disciples."

The People, Places, and Times

Foot Washing. Wearing open sandals on dusty roads made it necessary to wash one's feet frequently; therefore a host would customarily provide water for his guests upon their arrival, so that they might wash their feet (see Genesis 18:4; 19:2; 24:32; 43:24; Judges 19:21). Sometimes a servant performed this service for the guests (1 Samuel 25:41). It was considered the most menial task a servant could perform (see Mark 1:7). Not washing one's own feet, on the other hand, was a sign of deep mourning (2 Samuel 19:24).

As recorded in John's Gospel the act of foot washing has a two-fold significance. First, it is a symbolic prophecy of Jesus' atoning death, which would cleanse from sin and make it possible for His disciples to inherit eternal life with Him. Second, it is a lesson in humility. Some have also seen the foot-washing as alluding to the sacraments of baptism and the Lord's Supper.

John's Gospel. John's Gospel differs from the other writers' and puts a unique emphasis on particular events. It is more philosophical than the other accounts and was likely written last of the four. John is the only Gospel that outlines certain events in the Upper Room, such as the foot-washing and the identifying of Judas as the betrayer by the dipping of the bread. Matthew, Luke, and Mark all mention Jesus instituting the Last Supper. John does not. John underscores Jesus' teaching concerning these events and their meaning, rather than just reporting the facts of the occasion.

Background

With the beginning of John 13, Jesus' public ministry has ended and He is alone with the Twelve. Of the Gospel writers, only John provides us with this intimate view of Jesus' private teaching and prayer during His last days before death (John 13–17). John 13 records the events of the night before the Crucifixion—the eating of the Passover and the institution of the Lord's Supper (cf. Matthew 26:17-29; Mark 14:12-25; Luke 22:7-38).

Luke's Gospel account informs us that sometime early during the Passover meal, an argument broke out among the disciples concerning who would obtain the highest rank in the coming kingdom. Jesus rebuked their self-centered arrogance. "In this world the kings and great men lord it over their people, yet they are called 'friends of the people.' But among you, it will be different. Those who are the greatest among you should take the lowest rank, and the leader should be like a servant" (Luke 22:25–26, NLT). Then He washed their feet, which visually demonstrated humble servanthood.

The Gospel of John does not record this heated discussion between the disciples or Jesus' rebuke, but John does record for us the powerful, dramatic response on behalf of the Master Teacher. He demonstrated the meaning of true humility by washing the disciples' feet.

At-A-Glance

1. Jesus Displays Servanthood
(John 13:1-5)
2. Jesus Defines Servanthood (vv. 6-11)
3. Jesus Explains Servanthood
(vv. 12-15, 34-35)

In Depth

1. Jesus Displays Servanthood (John 13:1-5)

Jesus and the disciples were ready to celebrate the Passover. Ordinarily, the lowest servant on the staff washed the feet of the guests before the meal. In those times, the roads were dirty, and the people wore sandals. The tables were low, about the height of today's coffee tables. Dinner guests reclined on pillows at the table. Therefore, clean feet were essential to the enjoyment of the meal. However, this meal with Jesus and His disciples was private with no servant to do the washing. This is the backdrop to why Jesus took off His robe, placed Himself in the position of a lowly servant, and one by one washed the dirty feet of each disciple.

John interjected into his account of this moving Upper Room experience an interesting fact. The devil had already taken over the heart of Judas to betray Jesus. Jesus served not only the faithful disciples, but Jesus also served His enemy. Judas' feet were washed along with all the rest.

What "things" did the Father give to Jesus' hands?

2. Jesus Defines Servanthood (vv. 6-11)

Jesus' actions puzzled the disciples, yet only Peter said anything. Peter didn't understand Jesus' apparent role reversal and told Jesus that he would never allow Him, the Master, to do the menial job of washing feet. Jesus responded to Peter's emphatic statement with one of His own: "If I do not wash you, you have no part with Me" (from v. 8).

Symbolically, the word "wash" alluded to washing away one's sins. Apart from this type of cleansing, one cannot have any part of Jesus Christ. The idea of Jesus as a servant was a new concept to the disciples. Like Peter, we must learn not to try to dictate the terms by which Jesus will move in our lives.

Jesus knew but refused to reveal the identity of the one who was not "clean" (vv. 10-11). He wanted Judas Iscariot to know that He knew Judas' plan to betray him and that he was not going to hinder him, though his actions were evil.

How do you explain Peter's not wanting Jesus to wash his feet?

3. Jesus Explains Servanthood (vv. 12-15, 34-35)

After His act of humility, Jesus asks the disciples if they know what He has done (v. 12). Jesus explains that He is certainly their honored Master, yet He has taken the place of a servant and washed their feet. He is not so above them that He cannot show them an example of humility.

The Old Testament demanded that one not only love God but one's neighbor as oneself. Thus, the command to love is old. However, Christ not only commanded His disciples to love, but also to do "as I have loved you" (v. 34). The latter part is new. The kind of love He had is everlasting (v. 1), humbling (v. 5), and willing to die a sacrificial death for undeserving sinners.

Love acts. Christ demanded this kind of love from the disciples as a sign to all people that they were His disciples. Their love for each other would not only be a sign of identification with Him, but the exercise of that love would enable them to survive in a hostile world.

Is the command to "Love one another" a new commandment?

Search the Scriptures

1. Where was Jesus eventually going? (John 13:1, 3)

2. What meal was taking place in this passage (v.1)

3. Describe the process of Jesus preparing to wash their feet (vv. 4-5)

4. How will "outsiders" react when they see that kind of love? (vv. 34-35)

Discuss the Meaning

1. Why is it so important that we serve others? Is it more important for us to allow others to serve or that we serve? Explain.

2. What was Jesus attempting to convey to His disciples and why?

Liberating Lesson

Our society emphasizes the importance of getting ahead, heaping praise and attention on those with the most power. What would happen if those with power and privilege followed Christ's example of humility? How would the "foot washing" principle of humble, loving service be enacted: a) between employers and employees in a Christian business? b) between the pastor and deacons, trustees or stewards? c) between the tenants and the building superintendent or owner? d) between the president and his Cabinet members? Take steps this week to demonstrate humility in the relationships you have with others.

Application for Activation

Think of ways you can be a servant to those in your church who may not feel comfortable being served. Find at least one person in your church or at your workplace who is not as blessed as you are. Do something for that person that expresses your love by an act of humble service. Whatever it is, give of yourself that someone may be blessed.

Follow the Spirit

What God wants me to do:

_____

_____

_____

_____

Remember Your Thoughts

Special insights I have learned:

_____

_____

_____

_____

More Light on the Text
John 13:1-15, 34-35

The events recorded in chapters 13 through 17 relate to the last day before the Passover. Jesus is with His disciples, and He is about to teach them in practical terms some of the most important doctrines. Here Jesus gives them some final instructions before His departure from this world. The picture is like that of a father, or the head of a family, about to take a long trip from home. Because He is going to be away for a long time, Jesus gathers His disciples to give them instruction on how to live with one another until He returns. Jesus encourages and instructs them regarding how to live as children of God in a world full of evil. He talks to them about serving one another and living in love and harmony.

Love is the trademark of all believers. Through love for one another, the world will know that we are His disciples. Through love, the world will recognize that He is truly from the Father. Through love, we show that we love Him. We keep His commandment when we love one another, for love to Him is the greatest commandment.

1 Now before the feast of the passover, when Jesus knew that his hour was come that he should depart out of this world unto the Father, having loved his own which were in the world, he loved them unto the end. 2 And supper being ended, the devil having now put into the heart of Judas Iscariot, Simon's son, to betray him;

John gives a summary statement of the spiritual importance of the events that are about to follow (vv. 1-3). Note Jesus' deep awareness of the dawning of the "hour" (time) for the fulfillment of His mission—that is, His death—His consistent love for His people, and the work of the devil, which results in His betrayal. This summary includes Jesus' awareness of the divine origin and destiny of His work.

John starts his narrative by telling us the time period of the events—the eve of the Feast of the Passover. Jesus is aware "that his time has come." John uses this phrase six other times in his Gospel (John 2:4; 7:30; 8:20; 12:23, 27; 17:1). The first five instances are in the negative while this verse and 17:1 are in the positive sense. The significance of the statement is notable. It tells of the divine nature of Christ. Although He walked on earth as a human, He maintained His divine nature. He was totally aware of all things, including the purpose of His coming to earth, and precisely the time for His departure. This separates Him from ordinary humans.

John introduces here the subject of love, which will play an important role in the narrative. Love, as noted above, is the hallmark of all things that Jesus did. The phrase "having loved His own which were in the world, He loved them unto the end" shows Christ's readiness to give up Himself on behalf of His people. The phrase "The devil having now put into the heart of Judas Iscariot, Simon's son, to betray him" (v. 2) qualifies the arrival of the time for His departure. It is one of the signs of the time.

3 Jesus knowing that the Father had given all things into his hands, and that he was come from God, and went to God;

Verse 3 also explains the fact of Christ's divinity. "Jesus knowing" (Gk. *eido*, **AY**-doh) refers to His being "aware, having the knowledge, or being conscious" that the Father had given all things into His hands. John says that Jesus is conscious of the authority He has from the Father.

It seems that His knowledge both of the coming moment of His departure and His divine authority and glory were basic to this teaching. The foot-washing was also triggered by the disciples' argument about who would be "the greatest" among them (Luke 22:24).

Before this time, Jesus had rebuked this type of spirit or given other examples. In Matthew 18:1-10, He set a little child in their midst saying that they had to become as little children in humility and not seek to lord over one another. He rebuked this spirit on other occasions as well (Matthew 20:20– 28; Mark 10:35–45). It seems, however, that they have not yet learned their lesson on this subject. With the time for His departure drawing near, He seeks to teach further about this worldly passion. He uses a visual aid to teach the same truth.

4 He riseth from supper, and laid aside his garments; and took a towel, and girded himself. 5 After that he poured water into a basin, and began to wash the disciples' feet, and to wipe them with the towel wherewith he was girded.

The feast is over and, as people often do, the disciples sit talking at the table. They are so absorbed in their conversation that apparently no one notices what Jesus is doing. While everyone is selfishly debating their positions in the kingdom, Jesus gets up, takes off His outer robe, ties a towel around Himself, and pours water into a basin and starts to wash their feet. Interestingly we know that this is Jesus' final meal before he goes to the Cross, yet He is not absorbed in His own thoughts as they are. He sees a need to demonstrate an important lesson and moves to prepare the items He needs.

Apart from the real teaching of this event of humility and servitude (v. 12 ff), Jesus is following the Jewish custom. It is customary for a host to wash the feet of his guests as a symbol of affection and reverence. Supplicants who are making important requests also practiced it. However, to Greeks and Romans, the washing of feet was the duty of the lowest slave. It is in this context of servitude that Jesus presents this teaching. He takes off His own garment and girds Himself with the towel, the same towel he would use to dry their feet. He fetches the water, fills the basin and goes from man to man, washing their feet.

6 Then cometh he to Simon Peter: and Peter saith unto him, Lord, dost thou wash my feet? 7 Jesus answered and said unto him, What I do thou knowest not now; but thou shalt know hereafter. 8 Peter said unto him, Thou shall never wash my feet. Jesus answered him, If I wash thee not, thou hast no part with me.

Peter understands the lowliness of this act so well that when it is his turn, he refuses to have the Lord wash him. The question here, "Lord, dost thou wash my feet?," is rhetorical. Notice the word "Lord" (Gk. *kurios*, **KOO**-ree-oss) that Peter uses in verse 6. This is translated "owner" or "master," and means one with full authority. It is also used as a title of honor or respect. It is the opposite of servanthood. Peter's

use of this word signifies how highly he regards the Lord, and how lowly he sees himself. Peter emphasizes that he is not worthy for the Lord to wash him. Peter, ignorant of the spiritual and moral implications of this act, refuses to be washed by Jesus. Jesus makes it clear to Peter that there is a motive behind what He is doing and promises to explain it shortly to him. Still, Peter stubbornly refuses to yield to the washing and emphatically says to Jesus "Thou shalt never wash my feet."

The word "wash" (Gk. *nipto*, **NIP**-toh), which means to cleanse, is used about seven times to describe the act of washing part of the body (see Matthew 6:17; 15:2; John 9:7–15). Peter's understanding of this act is only physical. But he later learns that something more than mere washing of feet is involved here. There is also a spiritual dimension. Jesus' reply to him, "If I wash thee not, thou hast no part with me," brings out this dimension. The word "part" (Gk. *meros*, **MEHR**-oss) can also mean "share, portion, piece, or allotment." Some suggestions include that Peter's refusal would mean that he would not share or participate in the work of Christ. The washing of feet, therefore, is more than an example. It is characteristic of the way the disciples could participate in His humiliation and suffering.

9 Simon Peter saith unto him, Lord, not my feet only, but also my hands and my head. 10 Jesus saith to him, He that is washed needeth not save to wash his feet, but is clean every whit: and ye are clean, but not all. 11 For he knew who should betray him; therefore said he, Ye are not all clean.

After Jesus' explanation, Peter goes to the other extreme, asking Christ to clean more of him. Once again, Jesus patiently replies, "He that is washed needeth not save to wash his feet." Just as in the natural life, a man who has bathed needs only to wash the dust off his sandaled feet when he returns home, so in the spiritual life a person who has been cleansed from his or her sins through faith in Christ need only confess those sins to be entirely clean again (1 John 1:9).

Jesus takes this opportunity as He talked about cleanliness to point out that not everyone in the room is clean. He is referring to Judas Iscariot. Jesus wants Judas to know that He is fully aware of Judas' intentions and that this act will mark him as unclean. Here, just hours before the betrayal, was an opportunity for Judas to repent. But there was no confession or repentance on the part of Judas.

12 So after he had washed their feet, and had taken his garments, and was set down again, he said unto them, Know ye what I have done to you? 13 Ye call me Master and Lord: and ye say well; for so I am. 14 If I then, your Lord and Master, have washed your feet; ye also ought to wash one another's feet. 15 For I have given you an example, that ye should do as I have done to you.

After washing their feet, Jesus proceeds to teach the application of this service and the implications of His action. He asks them whether they understand what He has done. Of course, the answer is no. He knows how limited their understanding is. His intention is to get their attention and to make them think.

To answer His own question, Jesus appeals to His relationship with them and reminds them of that Lord and servant relationship. They call Him their Master and Lord. The word translated here as "Master" is the Greek word *didaskalos* (did-**AHS**-kahl-oss), meaning "one who teaches." The word translated "Lord" is the Greek word *kurios* (**KOO**-ree-oss), which is sometimes translated "Master." Jesus uses His double title of Teacher and Lord to strike an important note, which He would explain later. The disciples by inference know what it means

to be a teacher or lord. It does not include the washing of feet.

That is the puzzling thing about the whole event. To the ordinary Jew, Greek, or Roman, it does not make any sense for a teacher to stoop down and wash his servants' feet. With this understanding, Jesus now goes on to make His point, which is the climax of the narrative—how to serve one another as disciples and, yes, as Christians. The message is clear. He says, "If I, being your Master and Lord, would condescend to do this, you should be willing to do the lowest service for one another." This act is revolutionary since humility was despised in the ancient world as a sign of weakness. Before the Bible, the idea of humility was completely tied up with the idea of humiliation. In that highly stratified society, you always knew who was above your station and who was below. Being "humble" and voluntarily placing yourself in a station below your rightful place was unheard of. Jesus made humility a virtue when it was not before.

Jesus calls on His followers "to wash one another's feet." This is specific in the context of Jesus' act, but the principle is clear. They are to serve one another. He tells them that He has set an example for them to follow and calls on them to imitate Him.

13:34 A new commandment I give unto you, That ye love one another; as I have loved you, that ye also love one another. 35 By this shall all men know that ye are my disciples, if ye have love one to another.

John 13 through 17 constitutes the last discourse of Jesus with His disciples on the eve before His passion. There He taught them the greatest and most important doctrine, as one who is going away for good (v. 33). For Jesus, love is the central theme that ties all teachings and the foundation on which Christianity is built. Emphasizing the importance of love, Jesus says that He is giving a new commandment and that is to "love one another." "New," *kainos* (Gk. **KIE**-noce), means renewed or fresh. Jesus has the idea of renewing the old commandment and refreshing the disciples' memory of readings from the Old Testament (Leviticus 19:18) or on the other hand, of giving them a fresh commandment. It seems that Jesus is doing both: giving them a new perspective on the old theme of love. The new perspective is to love one another in the way that He loves them. Jesus calls His disciples to follow His example of love, i.e., to be ready even to lay down their lives for one another and for others (Compare John 15:12-14, Romans 5:8-11; Luke 6:27-31). To Jesus, love is the emblem or flag by which Christians are to be identified.

Jesus says that people will be able to recognize that we are His disciples if we have love for one another. Love, Jesus says, is the trademark of all Christians (1 John 3:11-18; 4:7-21) and this love should not be restricted to our fellow Christians and families, but extended to our neighbors, i.e., whoever we meet, as we have discussed.

Sources:
Orr, James. *The International Standard Bible Encyclopedia*. Vol. 2. Grand Rapids, MI: Eerdmans, 1982. 333.

Say It Correctly

Iscariot. iss-**CARE**-ee-ott.

Daily Bible Readings

MONDAY
Laban Arranges to Wash Servant's Feet
(Genesis 24:24-33)

TUESDAY
Brothers Provided Water to Wash Feet
(Genesis 43:20-25)

WEDNESDAY
Servants and Masters, but Same Lord
(Ephesians 4:6-9)

THURSDAY
Peter Denies Jesus Three Times
(John 13:36-38; 18:15-18, 25-27)

FRIDAY
Jesus Betrayed by a Trusted Disciple
(Psalm 41:8-10; John 13:21-30)

SATURDAY
Mary Anoints Jesus' Feet with Perfume
(John 12:1-7)

SUNDAY
Jesus Loved Disciples; Washed Their Feet
(John 13:1-15, 34-35)

Teaching Tips

Words You Should Know

A. Abide (v. 4ff) *meno* (Gk.)—Remain; continue, dwell in one place.

B. Branch (v. 5) *klema* (Gk.)—A young, tender branch that needs a steady supply of nourishment

Teacher Preparation

Unifying Principle—The Love Connection. We try to love, but we feel beaten down by the world's greed and jealousy. How can we love one another in the face of the world's selfishness? Jesus declares that we will be able to love one another if we keep the commandments and abide in His love.

A. Read the Bible Background and Devotional Reading.

B. Pray for your students and lesson clarity.

C. Read the lesson Scripture in multiple translations.

O—Open the Lesson

A. Begin the class with prayer.

B. Have the class members who garden tell how a gardener measures success? How can a gardener ensure success?

C. Have the students read the Aim for Change and the In Focus story.

D. Ask students how events like those in the story weigh on their hearts and how they can view these events from a faith perspective.

P—Present the Scriptures

A. Read the Focal Verses and discuss the Background and The People, Places, and Times sections.

B. Have the class share what Scriptures stand out for them and why, with particular emphasis on today's themes.

E—Explore the Meaning

A. Use In Depth or More Light on the Text to facilitate a deeper discussion of the lesson text.

B. Pose the questions in Search the Scriptures and Discuss the Meaning.

C. Discuss the Liberating Lesson and Application for Activation sections.

N—Next Steps for Application

A. Summarize the value of pruning unproductive attitudes and practices

B. End class with a commitment to pray for and exercise joy and strength on a daily basis.

Worship Guide

For the Superintendent or Teacher
Theme: Abiding Love
Song: "Abide with Me"
Devotional Reading: Psalm 80:7-19

Abiding Love

Bible Background • JOHN 15:4–17
Printed Text • JOHN 15:4–17 | Devotional Reading • PSALM 80:7–19

———————————— **Aim for Change** ————————————

By the end of this lesson, we will COMPREHEND how the metaphor of the vine and the branches applies to Jesus and those who follow Him; YEARN for a more intimate, life-giving relationship with Jesus; and COMMIT to keeping Christ's commandments and abiding in his love.

———————————— **In Focus** ————————————

Jordan met Mr. Mason at Shady Acres Retirement Home. He thought about Pastor Thomas' words to them on Sunday about service and sacrificial love. And yet, he wondered if he had made the right choice when he had agreed to lead worship at Shady Acres.

Mr. Mason vigorously shook Jordan's hand. "I am so happy that you are here. Come this way, we have been waiting for you! My mother has been asking for a church service for so long."

"Well, Mr. Mason, I've never done anything like this before. But when I heard Pastor Thomas talk about the needs here, I decided to try to help."

Mr. Mason led Jordan to the recreation room. Seated inside were ten elderly residents, waiting for them. With a calming breath, Jordan moved to the room's piano and pulled out his music, some sermon notes, and his Bible. "Hi, my name is Jordan. I'm here to worship the Lord with you. I thought that we could begin with a word of prayer."

As he prayed, he felt his uneasiness melt away. Forty-five minutes later, Jordan, Mr. Mason, and the residents were singing and clapping. As he led them in a closing hymn, Jordan knew he made the right choice.

How has Christ blessed you to see the fruit of your labor when you trusted His love and followed Him?

———————————— **Keep in Mind** ————————————

"I am the vine, ye are the branches: He that abideth in me, and I in him, the same bringeth forth much fruit: for without me ye can do nothing" (John 15:5, KJV).

"Yes, I am the vine; you are the branches. Those who remain in me, and I in them, will produce much fruit. For apart from me you can do nothing" (John 15:5, NLT).

Focal Verses

KJV **John 15:4** Abide in me, and I in you. As the branch cannot bear fruit of itself, except it abide in the vine; no more can ye, except ye abide in me.

5 I am the vine, ye are the branches: He that abideth in me, and I in him, the same bringeth forth much fruit: for without me ye can do nothing.

6 If a man abide not in me, he is cast forth as a branch, and is withered; and men gather them, and cast them into the fire, and they are burned.

7 If ye abide in me, and my words abide in you, ye shall ask what ye will, and it shall be done unto you.

8 Herein is my Father glorified, that ye bear much fruit; so shall ye be my disciples.

9 As the Father hath loved me, so have I loved you: continue ye in my love.

10 If ye keep my commandments, ye shall abide in my love; even as I have kept my Father's commandments, and abide in his love.

11 These things have I spoken unto you, that my joy might remain in you, and that your joy might be full.

12 This is my commandment, That ye love one another, as I have loved you.

13 Greater love hath no man than this, that a man lay down his life for his friends.

14 Ye are my friends, if ye do whatsoever I command you.

15 Henceforth I call you not servants; for the servant knoweth not what his lord doeth: but I have called you friends; for all things that I have heard of my Father I have made known unto you.

16 Ye have not chosen me, but I have chosen you, and ordained you, that ye should go and bring forth fruit, and that your fruit should remain: that whatsoever ye shall ask of the Father in my name, he may give it you.

17 These things I command you, that ye love one another.

NLT **John 15:4** Remain in me, and I will remain in you. For a branch cannot produce fruit if it is severed from the vine, and you cannot be fruitful unless you remain in me.

5 Yes, I am the vine; you are the branches. Those who remain in me, and I in them, will produce much fruit. For apart from me you can do nothing.

6 Anyone who does not remain in me is thrown away like a useless branch and withers. Such branches are gathered into a pile to be burned.

7 But if you remain in me and my words remain in you, you may ask for anything you want, and it will be granted!

8 When you produce much fruit, you are my true disciples. This brings great glory to my Father.

9 I have loved you even as the Father has loved me. Remain in my love.

10 When you obey my commandments, you remain in my love, just as I obey my Father's commandments and remain in his love.

11 I have told you these things so that you will be filled with my joy. Yes, your joy will overflow!

12 This is my commandment: Love each other in the same way I have loved you.

13 There is no greater love than to lay down one's life for one's friends.

14 You are my friends if you do what I command.

15 I no longer call you slaves, because a master doesn't confide in his slaves. Now you are my friends, since I have told you everything the Father told me.

16 You didn't choose me. I chose you. I appointed you to go and produce lasting fruit, so that the Father will give you whatever you ask for, using my name.

17 This is my command: Love each other.

The People, Places, and Times

Commandment. This term is used in the English Bible to translate a number of Hebrew and Greek words including law, ordinance, statute, word, judgment, precept, saying, and charge. The idea of authority conveyed by these words comes from the fact that God as the sovereign Lord has a right to be obeyed. The instruction of Jesus is full of ethical teachings that have the force of divine commandments. That is true even when He does not use the word "commandment" or its equivalents as He often does. The Bible is clear that God is not satisfied with mere external compliance with His commandments but expects willing and joyful obedience.

Vine. The grapevine was common to western Asia south of the Caspian Sea. Grape vineyards flourished in Palestine, especially in the central highlands near Hebron, Shiloh, and Shechem. The vine is often used in the Bible literally and figuratively. The vine is a symbol of prosperity and a sedentary life (1 Kings 4:25), which was the ideal for the once-nomadic nation of Israel. The vine is also a picture of God's people (John 15:2; Psalm 80:8; Isaiah 5:2). Since every vine will produce sterile branches, the gardener must trim away unproductive and old branches, lest the vitality of the vine is diverted from its function of bearing fruit.

Background

In John chapters 13 through 17, Jesus privately teaches His disciples. This is their last time together before His crucifixion. Jesus spends His last hours in His final preparation of them, explaining how to know and practice intimate fellowship with God. He taught first by example; He humbled Himself and washed their dirty feet (John 13:4-10). He told them about His departure, their future in heaven, the coming of the Comforter, the Holy Spirit, and how to experience real peace. Jesus gives the secrets of successful Christian living. He tells how we can have peace, joy, and answered prayer by abiding in Him.

As we begin today's study, Jesus teaches His disciples about the relationship they must have with the Father, with Him, and with one another. Unless they abide in the Father and in Him, the disciples would not be able to bear fruit or love one another, which would show the world they belong to Him. As Jesus and the disciples get up from the table to walk to the Garden of Gethsemane, He continues to speak words of encouragement. He instructs His disciples about the needed connection between Him and the Father, and Jesus and His followers. As we abide in Jesus, we can "bear fruit" (John 15:8) and love others as He commands us.

At-A-Glance

1. The Father's Provision (Luke 15:4-8)
2. Abiding in Love (vv. 9–11)
3. Abiding as Jesus' Friends (vv. 12-17)

In Depth

1. The Father's Provision (Luke 15:4-8)

The picture of the vine and the branches was a beautiful and natural illustration of how Jesus' disciples would be able to do His work. It is only by remaining in close, vital contact with the vine that the branch can bring forth any fruit at all. Such a vital connection with Jesus is necessary for disciples to bring forth deeds of obedience for God's glory.

To abide in Christ (v. 4), recognizing Christ as our true source of spiritual life, is how we allow the love of Jesus to flow into our lives. Our fellowship with Christ through the Word of God, daily prayer, and obedient worship and service will result in close, fruitful living with Him. Every fruit-bearing branch gets pruned so that more fruit will be produced (15:2). God expects us to bear fruit in obedience to Him.

The metaphor works not only to show what happens to a good vine, but also what happens to an unfruitful vine. Those who refuse to abide in Christ are branches that have withered and been set aside. Apart from Christ, we are helpless to do God's work or to please Him. If we act in our own power, our actions cannot bear fruit for God. We cannot glory in our own actions or become proud of our own achievements, because all we have and are depends on Him.

When have you experienced the importance of being attached to Christ?

2. Abiding in Love (vv. 9–11)

We learn that the basis for "abiding" with Jesus is the love that God and Jesus share with each other. Jesus, then, likens His love for the disciples to the type of love His Father has for Him. It is this relationship of love that we must remain faithful to.

In verse 10, Jesus comes to the essence of His message to the disciples: The only way the disciples (or any believer) will continue to abide in God's love is if they, like Him, practice obedience and keep His Father's commandments. Obedience is essential to an abiding relationship with Jesus, whose relationship with the Father was also one of obedience (Hebrews 5:8). Our obedience makes us one with God the Father and we, therefore, share in the fellowship that Jesus shares with the Father. By heeding Jesus' words, we also receive His joy.

What would need to happen in our lives so we can abide in the Father's love?

3. Abiding as Jesus' Friends (vv. 12-17)

Jesus called the disciples His friends because He shared the divine plans with them. So it is with us. God wants us to know His divine plan for our lives so that we may walk victoriously in Him. In abiding in Christ, we have the privilege of asking God's favor and grace upon our lives (v. 18) and experiencing the fullness of His love so that we may glorify the Father.

Jesus reminded His disciples that His commandment was: "that you love one another as I have loved you" (v. 12). If we are to be His disciples and abide in His love, we must love one another. True friendship with Jesus is not based on keeping a set of rules, going to church every day, or even serving on boards and committees. Jesus says the test of real friendship is that we "do" whatsoever He has commanded us, which is to love one another as He has loved us.

How deeply do you yearn to be known as a friend of Jesus? How do you portray this level of love and friendship in your life?

Search the Scriptures

1. What does it mean to remain in Christ and why is this important (John 15:5-7)?

2. What proves our love to Jesus (v. 10)?

3. Jesus gives the disciples a direct command in verse 12. Explain how Christ loved people during His time on Earth. What are some ways in which we can love as Christ loved?

Discuss the Meaning

1. How can a Christian tell they are really producing fruit? Should all Christians produce the same amount and in the same way?

2. If all our prayers aren't answered, does that mean we are not abiding in Christ or in the will of God? How does a Christian understand unanswered prayers in the light of verses 7 and 16?

Liberating Lesson

In today's society, many Christians believe that obeying God begins and ends with going to church once a week. While God commands us to meet with the "body," He expects us to continue to walk in His light daily. A part of that walk should include spreading the Gospel so that nonbelievers may be saved and weak Christians may be strengthened. We must be actively sharing, reaching out, and building godly relationships that glorify our Father and bear fruit for God's kingdom.

People today depend on all kinds of resources for their power and strength. Some say that strength comes from human perseverance. Others say it is education and mental stimulation. Still others say it comes from social action groups. These are worthy endeavors and have their place in our lives. However, the love of Christ enacted through our lives will always prove to be the most productive change agent and strengthening power we can have. When these endeavors of seeking education, social action, and perseverance are enacted with love, Christ is glorified in all we do.

Application for Activation

This week think of areas in your life that need pruning. Ask God to show you how to bear more fruit in service and love toward Him. Be prepared to share what you learned about yourself with others next week.

Think about your own fruitfulness. Pray that God would fill you with the Holy Spirit and enable you to do His will. Then act on sharing God's command to love others. Make a plan to share the love of Christ by helping, listening, encouraging, and giving to someone who may not usually hear about Christ. Next week, be prepared to share your efforts with the class.

Follow the Spirit

What God wants me to do:

_____

_____

_____

_____

Remember Your Thoughts

Special insights I have learned:

_____

_____

_____

_____

More Light on the Text

Luke 15:4-17

4 Abide in me, and I in you. As the branch cannot bear fruit of itself, except it abide in the vine; no more can ye, except ye abide in me.

To "abide" (Gk. *meno*, **MEN**-oh, to remain" or "to not depart") is the heart of the entire metaphor and the main point of the entire passage. While it seems obvious, Christians struggle with abiding versus not abiding in Christ when they fail to see how critical it is to their very survival. Even when Christ draws an explicit parallel with a physical branch and repeats Himself numerous times on the importance of abiding, how many have yet to transfer the meaning of the metaphor to their lives? A branch on a fruit vine doesn't exist just to be a branch but to produce fruit, so we exist not for ourselves, but to produce God's fruit. This is possible only with His nourishment, which we receive only when we abide in Him.

5 I am the vine, ye are the branches: He that abideth in me, and I in him, the same bringeth forth much fruit: for without me ye can do nothing.

Jesus points over and over to the reality of nourishment from the True Vine, which alone produces true branches, which in turn produce true fruit. This word for branch comes from the Greek word *klema* (**KLAY**-mah), which specifically refers to a young, tender branch, especially the flexible branch of a vine or a vine sprout. This young branch needs a steady supply of nourishment. As Christians, we have no other source for true fruit and no other chain of supply outside of God.

It is this vital connection to the True Vine to which every believer must attend and that he or she must continually monitor and strengthen. It is also this vital connection that we share with all other believers. No vine produces only one branch. Each produces many branches. Thus, our relationship to other branches is communal or familial, representative of our community of faith.

6 If a man abide not in me, he is cast forth as a branch, and is withered; and men gather them, and cast them into the fire, and they are burned.

The context informs us that a branch becomes fruitless only when it is no longer connected to the vine; branches that abide continue to receive nourishment and effortlessly produce fruit because that is their sole purpose and design. If a branch cannot be pruned, cleansed, and restored so it will become fruitful again, it will be cut off and destroyed. Therefore, any fruitless branch is a disconnected branch. The Master Gardener sees to it that every genuinely born-again Christian receives nourishment and produces fruit for his or her entire life. That is also why the Master Gardener prunes our lives so that we may be fruitful and not viewed as useless. What is unmistakable is that abiding in Christ should not be seen as an "option" by Christians.

7 If ye abide in me, and my words abide in you, ye shall ask what ye will, and it shall be done unto you.

A vine shares a genuinely symbiotic relationship with its branches. The vine can't produce its own fruit without branches, and the branches can't provide their own nourishment in order to produce fruit. When we abide in Christ, when we are attached to the Vine, His nourishment flows into us, just as in reality His Spirit indwells us (John 14:7; Romans 8:11), we receive His Word into our hearts, and we are predictably fruitful (Luke 8:15). Only in this context—as connected, fruitful believers infused with the Spirit and the Word—will we be able to pray in faith and receive that for which we ask. We receive because our will is conformed to Christ's. We are warned in James 4:2–3 not to "ask amiss," but we are also admonished that we have not because we ask not. The qualifications are steep, but the rewards, freedom, and resulting power are immeasurable.

In their connection with Christ, the believer will find the greatest fulfillment, the most exceptional joy, and the answer to prayer (v. 7). Verse 7 should be taken literally. Jesus will honor His promise. But we must see it in the light of the conditions that Jesus made and in connection with the will of God. Praying in Jesus' name is not some magical tag tacked onto the end of prayers. We must assume that "abiding" in Christ includes being in the will of God. Our prayer desires must be in the will of God before they can be fulfilled. When like-mindedness in Christ grows within us, all of our working and willing become transformed into harmony with His.

8 Herein is my Father glorified, that ye bear much fruit; so shall ye be my disciples. 9 As the Father hath loved me, so have I loved you: continue ye in my love.

While the primary meaning of "fruit" is that of the vine or tree, the word also refers to works (Gk. *karpos*, kar-**POS**). Just as a grape does the branch no personal good, our fruit is not for ourselves but for others, for the continuance of the vine, and for the glory of God.

Jesus zeroes in on what has been called the ultimate fruit—love. Repeatedly, we are told of God's love for His Son, such as in 2 Peter 1:17, which recalls the pronouncement at Jesus' baptism: "This is my beloved Son, in whom I am well pleased." Jesus loved His disciples with His Father's love, even though, unlike them (and us), He alone was worthy of such great love. While "continue" (*meno*, **MEN**-o) is a valid translation of the Greek verb used here, it obscures the repetition present in the original language. It is more akin to the phrase "keep abiding." In fact, it is translated as "abide" in the other verses of the passage.

10 If ye keep my commandments, ye shall abide in my love; even as I have kept my Father's commandments, and abide in his love. 11 These things have I spoken unto you, that my joy might remain in you, and that your joy might be full.

We are never asked to do what Christ would not do. In the book of John, it is well established that Christ proved His love for His Father by His obedience to Him (John 8:29, 12:49, 14:31, 17:4). Following suit, the disciples proved their love by their obedience, and we, in turn, prove our love for Christ by our obedience to Him, and receive His promise of abiding in Him.

It was only because of the joy that lay ahead of Him that Jesus was able to endure the Cross (Hebrews 12:2). James writes that we should consider trials as pure joy (James 1:2), and Nehemiah tells the believers that the joy of the Lord is their strength (Nehemiah 8:10). When we do all that Jesus commands (especially love others), our reward both on earth and in heaven is His great joy, a gift truly beyond compare and priceless above all precious things.

12 This is my commandment, That ye love one another, as I have loved you.

At first, Jesus' discourse must have seemed more an exhortation, until the point when it changed to a commandment. Commandments were familiar to Jesus' disciples, and it must have given them pause to hear Him talk about loving one another as a commandment. At the same time, a commandment coming from Jesus couldn't be compared to the commandments they had grown up with under Mosaic Law. While Jesus had taught this previously (Matthew 22:39), considering the many other things the disciples had failed to grasp at first, one wonders if He sensed their lack of understanding and thus felt the need to repeat Himself three times in a single teaching. To obey Jesus' command to love one another is to love as He Himself loved us in obedience to His Father. Indeed, it is the greatest commandment.

13 Greater love hath no man than this, that a man lay down his life for his friends.

Teachers and coaches understand that when a bar is set too low, there is no challenge and consequently no improvement. When the bar is set higher, we have to work to reach the goal, and the challenge makes us grow. The higher the bar, the greater the required effort, so Jesus here sets the bar at the highest point possible: that of actually sacrificing one's life in order to attain the highest imitation of His love. Many through the ages have been put to this very test, and it makes us question whether we would have what it takes if that terrible choice would ever present itself to us. In essence, this verse shows the ultimate sacrifice paid for our salvation.

14 Ye are my friends, if ye do whatsoever I command you. 15 Henceforth I call you not servants; for the servant knoweth not what his lord doeth: but I have called you friends; for all things that I have heard of my Father I have made known unto you.

In Christ, we are much more than servants; we are sons and daughters (2 Corinthians 6:18). Here, we are called friends (for whom He would lay down His life). This speaks volumes to us about all that Christ means as a friend and brother, but it also speaks eloquently of His perfect love—He who offers so much to those who once were enemies. In fact, Christ laid down His life while we were still enemies (Romans 5:8, 10; Colossians 1:21). When Jesus told us to love our enemies, He spoke from personal experience (Matthew 5:44).

Jesus called the disciples "friends" because of the revelation He disclosed to them. It made them close to Jesus. It wasn't the Father's will that everything that could be known should be made known, but everything that God wanted to be known was communicated through Christ (Matthew 11:27, 24:36).

16 Ye have not chosen me, but I have chosen you, and ordained you, that ye should go and bring forth fruit, and that your fruit should remain: that whatsoever ye shall ask of the Father in my name, he may give it you.

Christ reminds His disciples (His friends) that He chose them and has given them a task. As with them, when we abide in Christ, we receive His nourishment, we are fruitful, we fulfill our purpose as branches, we please the Gardener, we feed and nourish others, we produce seeds for planting, and we become eligible for pruning (cleansing) so that we will become even more productive. This is fruit and work that endures (John 6:27), and such a believer has fulfilled the qualifications for prayers being answered, just as God answered His people's prayers in times past: "he was intreated of them; because they put their trust in him" (1 Chronicles 5:20).

17 These things I command you, that ye love one another.

According to 2 Peter 1:5–7, we start with faith and add the various fruit of the Spirit, finally adding love, as if it were the highest attainment of the faith that the Master intended from the beginning. The New Testament places emphasis on exhorting believers to love, to learn to love, to seek love, to become love. Because it is the highest, it is the hardest; because it most closely resembles Christ, it requires greater surrender and sacrifice. We are virtually surrounded with Scriptures that exhort us to make love our highest priority, to pursue love, and to let love transform us into the very image of Christ, who is love (Romans 12:2; 1 Timothy 6:11; 2 Corinthians 3:18).

Sources:
Tenney, Merrill C. *The Zondervan Pictorial Bible Dictionary*. Grand Rapids, MI: Zondervan, 1963. 177.
Unger, Merrill F. *Unger's Guide to the Bible*. Wheaton, IL: Tyndale House Publishers, Inc., 1974. 603.

Say It Correctly

Caspian. **CASS**-pee-in.
Shiloh. **SHY**-low.

Daily Bible Readings

MONDAY
God Is Disappointed with Israel
(Isaiah 5:1-7)

TUESDAY
God Will Redeem Israel
(Isaiah 27:2-6)

WEDNESDAY
Believers Continue God's Work
(John 14:8-14)

THURSDAY
Jesus Freely Lays Down His Life
(John 10:11-18)

FRIDAY
Facing the World as Jesus Did
(John 15:18-25)

SATURDAY
Jesus Tends to His Vineyard
(John 15:1-3)

SUNDAY
Always Love One Another
(John 15:4-17)

Notes

_____

_____

_____

_____

Teaching Tips

Words You Should Know

A. Laid down (1 John 3:16) *tithemi* (Gk.)—To place, to put, to set or appoint

B. Beloved (v. 21) *agapetos* (Gk.)—Dearly loved one

Teacher Preparation

Unifying Principle—Loving Others. Hatred toward others sometimes seems far easier to attain than love. How can we show love for others? The willingness of Jesus to die for us and his command that we live for others brings that confidence.

A. Read the Bible Background and Devotional Reading.

B. Pray for your students and lesson clarity.

C. Read the lesson Scripture in multiple translations.

O—Open the Lesson

A. Begin the class with prayer.

B. Brainstorm ways hatred tears at your community. Then brainstorm ways to counter that hatred with love.

C. Have the students read the Aim for Change and the In Focus story.

D. Ask students how events like those in the story weigh on their hearts and how they can view these events from a faith perspective.

P—Present the Scriptures

A. Read the Focal Verses and discuss the Background and The People, Places, and Times sections.

B. Have the class share what Scriptures stand out for them and why, with particular emphasis on today's themes.

E—Explore the Meaning

A. Use In Depth or More Light on the Text to facilitate a deeper discussion of the lesson text.

B. Pose the questions in Search the Scriptures and Discuss the Meaning.

C. Discuss the Liberating Lesson and Application for Activation sections.

N—Next Steps for Application

A. Summarize the value of countering hatred in the world with God's love.

B. Encourage class members to pray this week for a person they need to show God's love despite the person not showing love to them.

Worship Guide

For the Superintendent or Teacher
Theme: Confident Love
Song: "They'll Know We Are Christians by Our Love"
Devotional Reading: Hebrews 13:1-8

Confident Love

Bible Background • 1 JOHN 3:11-24; 2 JOHN 1:4-11; 3 JOHN 1:5-8
Printed Text • 1 JOHN 3:11-24 | Devotional Reading • HEBREWS 13:1-8

Aim for Change

By the end of this lesson, we will EXPLORE the many dimensions of loving others according to 1 John 3, EMBRACE God's commandments to love with obedience and expectation, and IDENTIFY ways to grow in our faith in Jesus and our love for others.

In Focus

Claudia was excited about the opportunity to engage her church in the largest community holiday event in her city. God had opened the door for the invitation and the pastor's approval. Everyone was excited and advertisements had gone out to the community. A few weeks before the event, a new church coordinator was hired, and Claudia was asked to work with her on final details. Two weeks before the event, the coordinator called and said the event was canceled.

Claudia was devastated and angry. She suspected that the coordinator was jealous that the idea was not hers, but to cancel everything was ridiculous! Claudia was also ashamed that she had done something wrong. This was to glorify God not to put a bad light on the church. She called the pastor in tears to apologize. The next day the pastor called to say that everything was on track. Claudia was relieved and thanked him. She also prayed about how she could forgive the coordinator for such cruelty.

When have you been hurt and found it difficult to forgive the person? Did you seek God's forgiveness for your attitude? What action did you take to forgive the person?

Keep in Mind

"And he that keepeth his commandments dwelleth in him, and he in him. And hereby we know that he abideth in us, by the Spirit which he hath given us" (1 John 3:24, KJV).

"Those who obey God's commandments remain in fellowship with him, and he with them. And we know he lives in us because the Spirit he gave us lives in us" (1 John 3:24, NLT).

Focal Verses

KJV **1 John 3:11** For this is the message that ye heard from the beginning, that we should love one another.

12 Not as Cain, who was of that wicked one, and slew his brother. And wherefore slew he him? Because his own works were evil, and his brother's righteous.

13 Marvel not, my brethren, if the world hate you.

14 We know that we have passed from death unto life, because we love the brethren. He that loveth not his brother abideth in death.

15 Whosoever hateth his brother is a murderer: and ye know that no murderer hath eternal life abiding in him.

16 Hereby perceive we the love of God, because he laid down his life for us: and we ought to lay down our lives for the brethren.

17 But whoso hath this world's good, and seeth his brother have need, and shutteth up his bowels of compassion from him, how dwelleth the love of God in him?

18 My little children, let us not love in word, neither in tongue; but in deed and in truth.

19 And hereby we know that we are of the truth, and shall assure our hearts before him.

20 For if our heart condemn us, God is greater than our heart, and knoweth all things.

21 Beloved, if our heart condemn us not, then have we confidence toward God.

22 And whatsoever we ask, we receive of him, because we keep his commandments, and do those things that are pleasing in his sight.

23 And this is his commandment, That we should believe on the name of his Son Jesus Christ, and love one another, as he gave us commandment.

24 And he that keepeth his commandments dwelleth in him, and he in him. And hereby we know that he abideth in us, by the Spirit which he hath given us.

NLT **1 John 3:11** This is the message you have heard from the beginning: We should love one another.

12 We must not be like Cain, who belonged to the evil one and killed his brother. And why did he kill him? Because Cain had been doing what was evil, and his brother had been doing what was righteous.

13 So don't be surprised, dear brothers and sisters, if the world hates you.

14 If we love our brothers and sisters who are believers, it proves that we have passed from death to life. But a person who has no love is still dead.

15 Anyone who hates another brother or sister is really a murderer at heart. And you know that murderers don't have eternal life within them.

16 We know what real love is because Jesus gave up his life for us. So we also ought to give up our lives for our brothers and sisters.

17 If someone has enough money to live well and sees a brother or sister in need but shows no compassion—how can God's love be in that person?

18 Dear children, let's not merely say that we love each other; let us show the truth by our actions.

19 Our actions will show that we belong to the truth, so we will be confident when we stand before God.

20 Even if we feel guilty, God is greater than our feelings, and he knows everything.

21 Dear friends, if we don't feel guilty, we can come to God with bold confidence.

22 And we will receive from him whatever we ask because we obey him and do the things that please him.

23 And this is his commandment: We must believe in the name of his Son, Jesus Christ, and love one another, just as he commanded us.

24 Those who obey God's commandments remain in fellowship with him, and he with them. And we know he lives in us because the Spirit he gave us lives in us.

The People, Places, and Times

Cain. The eldest son of Adam and Eve, Cain became the tiller of the soil while his brother Abel was a keeper of sheep. Both had brought a sacrifice to the Lord (Genesis 4:3–4). Abel acted in faith by bringing a sacrifice more suitable than that of Cain (Hebrews 11:4). The latter's rage burned out of control against God's rejection. In retaliation, he slaughtered his brother, whose gift had been accepted (Genesis 4:5–8). The Lord confronted Cain with his guilt, judged him, and marked him, sending him out of the land.

Commandments to Love. In the Gospels, our Lord had already charged His disciples to love their enemies (Matthew 5:43–45) and love their neighbors as themselves (Luke 10:25–37). The "new commandment" required that Christians love each other (John 15:12, 17). This did not overrule the other two love commandments. Jesus' command to love those within the church was initiated to create persuasive evidence for those outside the church. It would provide them discernible proof (1) that His followers were Christ-like in their love toward one another, (2) that the foundation for vigorous human community could be found in Christ, and (3) that, by extension, Jesus' declaration about Himself in concert with the miracles He accomplished was really true (John 13:35, 17:20–23, 21:24–25).

Background

In Jesus' day, many assumed that by obeying the commandments, they could show themselves worthy of God's blessings (Galatians 3:2). However, Jesus made it very clear that love was a natural result of God's blessing, not a precondition for it.

This letter was written to members of the churches in Asia Minor. The epistle served as a reminder to the children of God to love one another. The apostle John is prepared to show the church how to put the love of God into action. The commandment to love is an expression of how Christ's disciples should act. This love has been shed abroad by the Holy Spirit in their hearts. Without showing love toward others, it is doubtful that one can really say that he or she loves.

At-A-Glance

1. Love and Life and Death
(1 John 3:11-16)
2. Showing Our Love (vv. 17-20)
3. Confidence in Love and Spirit
(vv. 21-24)

In Depth

1. Love and Life and Death (1 John 3:11-16)

The true test of discipleship is that we love one another (v. 11). No one can claim to be a child of God and not have love for another child of God. An attitude like that would be like Cain, Adam's oldest son who murdered his brother Abel (Genesis 4:8-10). Cain's actions were motivated by jealousy and hatred. We must carefully guard our hearts against envy and jealousy against other people. God knows what each of us needs and desires, and we should thank God that His blessings are available to all His children. We have no business being jealous or envious of other Christians. They are our brothers and sisters too.

The early Christian's were persecuted to the point of death simply for their love for Christ. John's audience was no doubt afraid and uncertain of their paths knowing that the world hated them, families had cast them out, and old communities were no longer welcoming to them. But John admonishes the church to be steadfast in the face of opposition. The apostle affirms that one who has passed from spiritual death to spiritual life is one who loves others. In contrast, one who cannot love fellow Christians remains in spiritual darkness which is, in reality, spiritual death. One cannot claim to be spiritual without having love for his/her brothers and sisters. Since God is love and Jesus Christ is the manifestation of love, how can we abide in Him without loving others? As far as John is concerned those who do not love are spiritually dead.

What does John mean when he says "marvel not" if the world hates you? How does this apply to our lives today?

2. Showing Our Love (v. 17-20)

Our love for others is evidenced by our willingness to give to others. Genuine Christian love gives to others and expects nothing in return. The apostle exhorts us to display our love by doing. We should not just love "in word, neither in the tongue." This means love should be more than just a matter of speech. It is easy to say we love one another, as long as nothing is required of us. That is why John says to love "in deed and truth." In other words, put your love into action.

Since we know that Jesus' death is the means for our salvation, John suggests that Christians ought to be willing to sacrifice their time, talents and treasure, for the good of someone else, just as Jesus did. That's really putting love in action.

Love is more than mere lip service. We cannot really love another without doing something for them. True love is manifested in action.

Verse 20 says, "God is greater than our heart". What does this mean?

3. Confidence in Love and Spirit (vv. 21-24)

If we fail to love, we are left with feelings of guilt that hinder our confidence in the Lord. When our actions are motivated by love, we can approach God with boldness and receive what we ask of Him. His is not a magic formula. When we love as He directs and engages in those actions that please Him, we can have confidence that we are in His will. When we obey God's commands He honors our requests.

Verse 23 states the commandment clearly. It requires that we believe in the name of Jesus and acknowledges that He is the Son of God, our Savior, and Lord. It requires that we love each other, especially those in the body of Christ. We must also remain in fellowship with God, which means staying connected to Him through meditating on the Word and praying. But the commandment to live also means that we must stay connected with other Christians. When we obey God's commandments and live in intimate fellowship with Jesus, others will witness a change and ask what fuels our joy. There is no greater witness to the saved and unsaved than expressing the love of God! Our confidence and our love are anchored in the fact that we know Christ lives in us and we live for Him.

What is the proof that Christ abides in us?

Search the Scriptures

1. What proves that we have passed from death to life (1 John 3:14)?

2. How did God show His love for humanity, and how are we to display love (vv. 16-18)?

3. What is the most basic commandment to which we should adhere? (v. 23)

Discuss the Meaning

1. Based on John's writings, a Christian is one who loves. Does that mean we are to love everyone, including those who desire to hurt us? Explain.

2. Given our diversity in our world today, how can you love someone who looks and thinks differently than you or someone who has hurt you? 3. Why do loving God and loving others go hand-in-hand? Can they be separated?

Liberating Lesson

Tragedy dominates media attention. The more horrific the crime, the more news coverage it receives. With this kind of media frenzy, wickedness appears to have taken an exalted position in our society, leaving many to question the true value of love. It is no wonder so many feel love is trivial and irrelevant. Yet, this lesson reminds us that no matter what happens in the world, we are commanded to love one another. Consider what the church can do to promote love and unity in a world that seems to be torn by strife, hatred and confusion. Are there answers to these problems, and if so, should the church or the government be leading the way to solve them?

Application for Activation

Love is a basic human desire and the evidence that we belong to the body of Christ. Love is more than a word. It is a repeated commandment from the Lord: Love one another. Christian love for others is shown by what we do for others. List things believers can do to show love for other members of the church, for family members, and for people, we don't even know. Choose one item from each category and commit to fulfilling these acts of love this week. Be prepared to share your experiences with the class next week.

Follow the Spirit

What God wants me to do:

_____

_____

_____

_____

Remember Your Thoughts

Special insights I have learned:

_____

_____

_____

_____

More Light on the Text

1 John 3:11-24

11 For this is the message that ye heard from the beginning, that we should love one another.

John's message is clear: Love for one another is an integral part of the Gospel message. It is a command that Jesus gave to the disciples during the Upper Room discourse (John 13-14). It is also the command that He declared was the second greatest commandment outside of loving God Himself. From the outset, love was a vital part of Jesus' teachings. If love for one another is absent in a community, then they are not following the way of Jesus.

In this verse, John states that love should not be an afterthought. Obedience to Jesus' command to love one another as He loves us is expected of anyone who accepts the Gospel message. Love shows us that the Gospel includes both the benefits of salvation and the responsibility of Christians to love one another. Salvation and love go hand in hand. They are not separate or tangential to the Christian faith. The message of the Christian faith is love, obedience to the command, and imitation of the life of Jesus Christ.

12 Not as Cain, who was of that wicked one, and slew his brother. And wherefore slew he him? Because his works were evil, and his brother's righteous.

Cain is cited here as an example of one who did not show love for his brother. Cain is characterized as belonging to "that wicked one." The word "wicked" (Gk. *poneros*, poh-nay-**ROHS**) is also translated as "hurtful" or "evil" and refers to someone who would cause harm. John is explicitly saying that Cain belonged to Satan. Saying Cain belonged to Satan is John's way of pointing out that the way we treat each other is part of the larger cosmic battle between good and evil. If we are characterized by love, it will affect our behavior. Likewise, if we are characterized by hatred, it will certainly show in our behavior.

Cain slew his brother Abel because Cain's "works were evil." Notice that same Greek word, *poneros* (poh-nay-**ROHS**), translated earlier in the verse as "wicked one," is now also used to describe the quality of Cain's works. Cain's murderous act was most assuredly not motivated by love, but by hatred. From the example of Cain, we see that hatred facilitates envy, violence, and murder. While we may not literally murder people, we may assassinate their character and reputation because of hatred (cf. Matthew 5:21–22).

13 Marvel not, my brethren, if the world hate you. 14 We know that we have passed from death unto life, because we love the brethren. He that loveth not his brother abideth in death. 15 Whosoever hated his brother is a murderer: and ye know that no murderer hath eternal life abiding in him.

"The world" here is representative of all those opposed to God. John is saying that we as Christians should not be surprised because the world hates us. It is the expectation for Christians to love one another in obedience to Christ's command. But those who have not experienced the love of Christ are characterized by their lack of love. They are still dead in their sin. Such acts of love, then, translate into acts of righteousness.

Obeying Christ's command to love one another gives Christians an inner knowledge and assurance of their passage from spiritual death to spiritual life. Love for fellow Christians is a dynamic experience that testifies to the reality of our spiritual journey. John compares brotherly love to a rite of passage. It is representative of a significant change or progress in one's spiritual life. It is crucial to note that John does not say our salvation is achieved simply by loving others. That would be salvation by works. Rather, his point is that having a love for others is evidence of one's maturity and the passage from the death of sin to a life based on faith in Christ. Love is the evidence of, and not the means of, salvation.

A nominal Christian who does not demonstrate love has not matured in this spiritual journey. The absence of love for others shows that they have yet to come alive spiritually; they have not allowed the Holy Spirit, who enables us to produce the fruit of love, to act upon their hearts.

This is an echo of Cain's experience from verse 12. John presents the serious consequence of hatred and establishes the parallel between hate and murder. Anyone who, like Cain, hates his brother is also a murderer. Having established this link with Cain, John now concludes that hatred of others is the spiritual equivalent of murder and that no murderer is entitled to eternal life.

The word for "abiding" is from the Greek word *meno* (**MEH**-noh), which means to remain, last, or endure. As John states, those who hate their brothers (and sisters) are murderers and do not have eternal life abiding in them. They are not "heaven-bound." Thus, hatred is the equivalent of spiritual death.

16 Hereby perceive we the love of God, because he laid down his life for us: and we ought to lay down our lives for the brethren.

Quite opposite of those who do not love God and who would kill their brothers with hatred are those who do follow God are willing to die for their brothers. The Greek word *ginosko* (ghee-**NOOS**-koh), translated here as "perceive," refers to obtaining knowledge. John is saying that we will obtain knowledge of the love of God by looking at the life of Jesus. Very practically, God demonstrated His love to us by sending His Son to lay down His life on our behalf. This demonstration of divine love is the heart of the Gospel. Christ gave His own sinless life to pay the penalty incurred by our sins. He now offers the pardon resulting from this sacrificial act of love to all who will accept it by faith in Him.

Divine love is giving love. God gave His Son for love. The Son gave His life for love. The Greek word *agape* (ah-**GAH**-pay), translated here as "love," finds its ultimate definition in Jesus' unconditional act of giving. If Christians follow this model of divine love, then they too ought to give something of themselves to express their love for others. Jesus says, there is no greater love than this self-sacrificing love (John 15:13). Christians are called to a self-sacrificing love rather than a self-preserving love. As beneficiaries of this kind of love, it is incumbent on us to love others in the same way.

17 But whoso hath this world's good, and seeth his brother have need, and shutteth up his bowels of compassion from him, how dwelleth the love of God in him?

John says that when any Christian has the material means to help the needy but refuses to give compassionately, the existence of Christlike love in them is open to question. Using a rhetorical question, John shows that God's love does not exist in anyone who can refuse to help those in need. At issue is not whether God loves the person, but whether such a person possesses God's kind of love toward others.

Our material possessions are not given to us only for self-indulgence. God's command to love others requires that we use our possessions to obey that command. Some regard worldly possessions as an end in themselves. But John says they are a means for expressing God's love, opening the door of compassion in us, and enabling us to reach out to others in need.

The Greek word *splagchnon* (**SPLANGKH**-non) literally means "bowels" or "intestines," but figuratively means "tender mercy or inward affection." It indicates that compassion is a quality of one's inner emotions. We use similar metaphors when we talk about feeling something deep down, in our "gut," or with our heart. As such, love must be present inside before it can show outwardly. Anybody can perceive a need, but not everybody has the compassion to help others.

18 My little children, let us not love in word, neither in tongue; but in deed and in truth.

Addressing his readers as children not only suggests that John is advanced in years but also shows the family atmosphere he is trying to create among God's people. There is no better institution that reflects the kind of sacrificial love John is writing about than the family. Believers should be aware that blood ties are temporary and end with the death of the relative. Spiritual ties, on the other hand, are eternal and have no end.

Including himself in the admonition, he says, "Let us not love in word, neither in tongue." The construction suggests like a father giving advice, John was asking them to stop merely talking about love, but show it through deeds and truth. Christian love is more than a feeling: It involves the essential ingredient of giving. Many times when people say they love another, their only real action is from their mouth (i.e., "in tongue"). An expression of love that is backed up by only the tongue is not true love like Christ's self-sacrificing love. True love engages in actions centered on others. The world is tired of passive love; only active love will attract outsiders and make them want to join God's family.

19 And hereby we know that we are of the truth, and shall assure our hearts before him.
The word "hereby" (Gk. en *touto*, enn **TOO**-toe, here meaning "by this") refers to verse 18 and points to an active expression of love that corresponds to Christ's self-sacrifice. When Christians demonstrate this kind of active love, they know they belong to the "truth" (Gk. *aletheia*, ah-**LAY**-thay-ah). This can be defined as "what is true in things pertaining to God and the duties of man, morality, and religious truth." In the parable of the sheep and the goats, the sheep on Christ's right were commended for their acts of love toward others and were rewarded accordingly by Christ (Matthew 25:31–46). In the future, when Christ returns, we will all stand before Him to be judged and rewarded according to our deeds.

20 For if our heart condemn us, God is greater than our heart, and knoweth all things.
The Greek word *kardia* (kar-**DEE**-ah) refers to the heart organ, but figuratively denotes the center of all physical and spiritual life. Therefore, if the testimony of our heart is negative, then we have not been sacrificially reaching out to

love others like Christ. The Greek word for "condemn" is *kataginosko* (kah-tah-ghee-**NOHS**-koh), which is a compound word from *kata-* "against" and *ginosko* "to know" (as in v. 16). Our heart knows all that can be held against us. Fortunately, God is greater than our hearts and knows our motives for service. Just as we cannot deceive ourselves, we cannot deceive God. He knows (Gk. ginosko) all things, not just that which would condemn us.

21 Beloved, if our heart condemn us not, then have we confidence toward God. 22 And whatsoever we ask, we receive of him, because we keep his commandments, and do those things that are pleasing in his sight.
As Christians, we must learn to listen to our inner voice so we can have confidence before God. The Greek word for "confidence" is *parresia* (par-ray-**SEE**-ah), which means openness, or speaking or acting without concealment. It may be easy to deceive others, but God knows our hearts. Therefore, John says, if our hearts are open and honest, we can go confidently before the throne of grace and petition God. Verse 22 discusses the benefits of a positive testimony of the heart. If we have a confident heart because we keep God's commandments and do the things that please Him, then we also have the assurance that we shall receive whatever we pray for that is in line with His will. John's point is that disobeying Christ's command to love can hinder our prayers, so we should obey Him. When Christians act in obedient, self-sacrificing love, we gain confidence toward God.

23 And this is his commandment, That we should believe on the name of his Son Jesus Christ, and love one another, as he gave us commandment.
In this verse, John provides the crux of his epistle. Faith in Christ and love for one another bring us into a new relationship with God where

we become His children. Believing on the name of Jesus Christ includes accepting the fact that He is the Son of God who gave His life to pay the penalty for our sins, reconciling us to God.

The second part of the commandment is to love one another. The sequence is important. The command is that we both have faith in Christ and also love one another. Faith in Jesus Christ is the basis of our new relationship with God, and love for one another is the expression of that saving faith.

24 And he that keepeth his commandments dwelleth in him, and he in him. And hereby we know that he abideth in us, by the Spirit which he hath given us.

To keep God's commands, which includes loving one another, is to abide in Him and to have Him abide in us. As referenced previously in verse 15, the word "abideth" (Gk. *meno*, **MEH**-noh) means to continually be present. This mutual indwelling characterizes the relationship between God and His Son Jesus and points to their unity (John 17:21). The believers' mutual indwelling with God is also a reference to the familial union between God and His believing children.

God is present in believers through His Holy Spirit, who dwells in them (cf. Romans 8:9, 11). Through the presence of the Holy Spirit, Christians have a sense of belonging in God's family. By the Spirit, we know we are children of God (v. 16). Since God is love, His children should also be characterized by love. Just as we love members of our earthly family and enjoy getting together with them, so believers will enjoy helping others if they have the love of Christ in them.

Sources:

Comfort, Philip W., and Walter A. Elwell, eds. *Tyndale Bible Dictionary*. Wheaton, IL: Tyndale House Publishers, 2001. 719–728.

Key Word Study Bible. New International Version. Grand Rapids, MI: Zondervan Bible Publishers, 1996. 1437.

Life Application Study Bible. New International Version. Wheaton, IL: Tyndale House Publishers, 1991. 1909, 2279–80.

Marshall, I. Howard, A.R. Millard, J.I. Packer, D.J. Wiseman, eds. *New Bible Dictionary*. 2nd ed. Downers Grove, IL: InterVarsity Press, 1982. 157.

The New Oxford Annotated Bible. New Revised Standard Version. New York: Oxford University Press, 2001. 386.

Rainbow Study Bible. New International Version. Grand Rapids, MI: Zondervan Bible Publishers, 1992. 1375.

Unger, Merrill F. *The New Unger's Bible Handbook*. Chicago, IL: Moody Press, 1998. 634.

Say It Correctly

Cain. **KEYN**
Abel. **EY**-bul

Daily Bible Readings

MONDAY
Example of Faith and Obedience
(1 Thessalonians 2:1-10)

TUESDAY
Then Darkness, Now Light
(Ephesians 5:8-16)

WEDNESDAY
Live by the Light
(John 3:16-21)

THURSDAY
Children of God Love One Another
(1 John 2:28-3:10)

FRIDAY
Walking Faithfully in the Truth
(3 John 1:1-4)

SATURDAY
Imitate What Is Good, Not Evil
(3 John 1:9-12)

SUNDAY
Believe Jesus Christ; Love One Another
(1 John 3:11-24)

Teaching Tips

Words You Should Know

A. Gave up the Ghost (v. 5) *exepsychen* (Gk.)—Literally "breathed out"; died

B. Church (v. 11) *ekklesia* (Gk.)—The people of God gathered as a convened assembly

Teacher Preparation

Unifying Principle—Sharing Love in Truth. In every community, there are people who have less than they need to maintain healthy lives. How can we best meet the needs of everyone in our communities? As the first believers in Jesus shared everything in common, the needs of everyone were satisfied.

A. Read the Bible Background and Devotional Reading.

B. Pray for your students and lesson clarity.

C. Read the lesson Scripture in multiple translations.

O—Open the Lesson

A. Begin the class with prayer.

B. Have class members make a list titled "My Time, Talents, and Treasure." Everyone should write out what their time, talents, and treasures are and where they mostly use them.

C. Have the students read the Aim for Change and the In Focus story.

D. Ask students how events like those in the story weigh on their hearts and how they can view these events from a faith perspective.

P—Present the Scriptures

A. Read the Focal Verses and discuss the Background and The People, Places, and Times sections.

B. Have the class share what Scriptures stand out for them and why, with particular emphasis on today's themes.

E—Explore the Meaning

A. Use In Depth or More Light on the Text to facilitate a deeper discussion of the lesson text.

B. Pose the questions in Search the Scriptures and Discuss the Meaning.

C. Discuss the Liberating Lesson and Application for Activation sections.

N—Next Steps for Application

A. Revisit the "My Time, Talents, and Treasure" lists. In light of the lesson, ask if the participants feel they should alter their uses. Do they have another item they forgot to add to the list?

B. End class by asking class members to make a commitment to using at least one resource in a different way this week.

Worship Guide

For the Superintendent or Teacher
Theme: Sharing Love
Song: "All to Jesus I Surrender"
Devotional Reading:
2 Corinthians 6:1-10

Sharing Love

Bible Background • ACTS 4:32–5:11
Printed Text • ACTS 4:32–5:11 | Devotional Reading • 2 CORINTHIANS 6:1-10

—————— Aim for Change ——————

By the end of this lesson, we will EXPLORE the Jerusalem church's practice and witness of communal sharing, REPENT of any idolatrous attachment to material goods, and CREATE a plan to increase our giving for the common good.

—————— In Focus ——————

Ann had grown up in a family with little money, but in college, she met Jim, a man from a well-off family. Ann and Jim got engaged a couple of years after they graduated and planned a modest wedding in Ann's home church. The night before the wedding, Ann and Jim held a dinner for their families following the rehearsal. The food was fine, everyone got along just fine and it looked like the start of a great relationship between two families. When it came time for the parents to give speeches toasting the bride and groom, Jim's father ended his speech saying, "It's so wonderful to see our two very different families joined—one rich, one poor—through the great love of Ann and Jim. To Ann and Jim, may you have a long and happy life together."

As Jim's father sat down, Ann smiled and said to her father-in-law-to-be, "That was a wonderful speech—but I have to say, I've never considered my family poor." Jim's father immediately apologized, "I'm so sorry. I shouldn't have said that." Ann's mother chimed in, "Here at this church, none of us had a lot of money, but we always shared what we had. When twenty different families come in and share what they have, everyone feels rich."

Jim's parents left the rehearsal dinner that night with a new understanding, that wealth could mean something more than money, and to rethink their biased beliefs about people.

How does your church family share its resources?

—————— Keep in Mind ——————

"And the multitude of them that believed were of one heart and of one soul:
neither said any of them that ought of the things which he possessed was his own;
but they had all things common." (Acts 4:32, KJV)

"All the believers were united in heart and mind. And they felt that what they owned was not their own, so they shared everything they had." (Acts 4:32, NLT)

Focal Verses

KJV **Acts 4:32** And the multitude of them that believed were of one heart and of one soul: neither said any of them that ought of the things which he possessed was his own; but they had all things common.

33 And with great power gave the apostles witness of the resurrection of the Lord Jesus: and great grace was upon them all.

34 Neither was there any among them that lacked: for as many as were possessors of lands or houses sold them, and brought the prices of the things that were sold,

35 And laid them down at the apostles' feet: and distribution was made unto every man according as he had need.

36 And Joses, who by the apostles was surnamed Barnabas, (which is, being interpreted, The son of consolation,) a Levite, and of the country of Cyprus,

37 Having land, sold it, and brought the money, and laid it at the apostles' feet.

5:1 But a certain man named Ananias, with Sapphira his wife, sold a possession,

2 And kept back part of the price, his wife also being privy to it, and brought a certain part, and laid it at the apostles' feet.

3 But Peter said, Ananias, why hath Satan filled thine heart to lie to the Holy Ghost, and to keep back part of the price of the land?

4 Whiles it remained, was it not thine own? and after it was sold, was it not in thine own power? why hast thou conceived this thing in thine heart? thou hast not lied unto men, but unto God.

5 And Ananias hearing these words fell down, and gave up the ghost: and great fear came on all them that heard these things.

6 And the young men arose, wound him up, and carried him out, and buried him.

7 And it was about the space of three hours after, when his wife, not knowing what was done, came in.

NLT **Acts 4:32** All the believers were united in heart and mind. And they felt that what they owned was not their own, so they shared everything they had.

33 The apostles testified powerfully to the resurrection of the Lord Jesus, and God's great blessing was upon them all.

34 There were no needy people among them, because those who owned land or houses would sell them

35 and bring the money to the apostles to give to those in need.

36 For instance, there was Joseph, the one the apostles nicknamed Barnabas (which means "Son of Encouragement"). He was from the tribe of Levi and came from the island of Cyprus.

37 He sold a field he owned and brought the money to the apostles.

5:1 But there was a certain man named Ananias who, with his wife, Sapphira, sold some property.

2 He brought part of the money to the apostles, claiming it was the full amount. With his wife's consent, he kept the rest.

3 Then Peter said, "Ananias, why have you let Satan fill your heart? You lied to the Holy Spirit, and you kept some of the money for yourself.

4 The property was yours to sell or not sell, as you wished. And after selling it, the money was also yours to give away. How could you do a thing like this? You weren't lying to us but to God!"

5 As soon as Ananias heard these words, he fell to the floor and died. Everyone who heard about it was terrified.

6 Then some young men got up, wrapped him in a sheet, and took him out and buried him.

7 About three hours later his wife came in, not knowing what had happened.

8 And Peter answered unto her, Tell me whether ye sold the land for so much? And she said, Yea, for so much.

9 Then Peter said unto her, How is it that ye have agreed together to tempt the Spirit of the Lord? behold, the feet of them which have buried thy husband are at the door, and shall carry thee out.

10 Then fell she down straightway at his feet, and yielded up the ghost: and the young men came in, and found her dead, and, carrying her forth, buried her by her husband.

11 And great fear came upon all the church, and upon as many as heard these things.

8 Peter asked her, "Was this the price you and your husband received for your land?" "Yes," she replied, "that was the price."

9 And Peter said, "How could the two of you even think of conspiring to test the Spirit of the Lord like this? The young men who buried your husband are just outside the door, and they will carry you out, too."

10 Instantly, she fell to the floor and died. When the young men came in and saw that she was dead, they carried her out and buried her beside her husband.

11 Great fear gripped the entire church and everyone else who heard what had happened.

The People, Places, and Times

Barnabas. Barnabas means "son of encouragement" in Aramaic. This was the name given by the apostles to Joses, a Levite from Cyprus. Barnabas was an early convert to Christianity. His character and faith soon brought him into a position of leadership in the church. When Paul was first converted, many of the believers were afraid to accept him. Barnabas eased their fears by speaking to the church on behalf of the apostle. Barnabas was one of Paul's companions during the early part of his ministry.

Levite. The Levites were the priestly tribe of Israel. All of Israel's priests are descended from this tribe. However, there is a fundamental difference between priests and Levites. All priests come from the tribe of Levi; however, not all Levites can become priests. They must be descendants of Aaron. Priests are consecrated and were the only ones that could minister at the altar and enter into the holy places. Levites were purified and were set aside to help the priests in performing their duties.

Background

Luke notes at the beginning of Acts that his first book, which we know as the Gospel according to Luke, was an account of all that Jesus "began to do and teach." This statement suggests that the book of Acts is to be understood as a book that is fundamentally about Christ's continuing work in the world through his body, the church. In Acts 4:32-37, the focus of the narrative in Acts shifts from a focus on Peter and John to a focus on the new Christ-following community. At this point in the story, Peter and John have just been released from the custody of the Sanhedrin and they have told the community of faith about God's faithfulness to them in the midst of political persecution. This then sets the context for what is recounted in these verses, specifically the fact that the believers shared all they had with each other. As we witness the generosity of the community of faith, we also witness the heightened stakes of the first years of the Church in the story of Ananias and Sapphira in Acts 5:1-11. In each of these narratives, the reader is encouraged to consider the fact that the communal life to which Christ calls those in union with Him is a radical one.

At-A-Glance

1. Gospel Generosity (Acts 4:32-37)
2. Holiness vs. Hypocrisy (5:1-11)

In Depth

1. Gospel Generosity (Acts 4:32-37)

Acts 4 begins with the imprisonment of Peter and John. This is typical of what the new Christians would face. Following the death of Jesus, the early Christians were persecuted and often treated as outcasts from their Jewish community and family. Despite the persecution, the church community is described as a Spirit-filled, praying, loving and united community. That unity is shown economically through the sharing of goods. In the first few years of the church, followers of Christ voluntarily sought to meet one another's needs because they recognized that they were, in a real sense, united with one another in their faith in Christ. The giving is not merely a one-on-one meeting of needs but a giving to a common pool under the authoritative wisdom of the apostles, who would then distribute according to need. This reveals both the generosity of this community and their trust in their Christ-ordained leadership.

The context of this early church community is important to keep in mind here. Most importantly, they are a model of sacrificial giving. They give because their identities are rooted in the sacrificial giving of their Lord, Jesus Christ. As Jesus graciously gave His life for the forgiveness of sins and as Jesus graciously took on human flesh in order to save humanity, so also the community of faith is encouraged to give sacrificially to one another and to those in need. In those terms, this is not a suggestion, but rather an imperative. If the church is to be the body of Christ, they must exhibit the sacrificial love that Christ showed and commanded.

How should today's church view the actions of the early church? Are we supposed to live communally now?

2. Holiness vs. Hypocrisy (5:1-11)

In the Garden of Eden, sin was met by expulsion. In the wilderness after their emancipation and exodus, when the covenant people of God grumbled against their Redeemer, they were punished with wandering until the resistant generation died. At these pivotal moments in the history of God's covenant community, the stakes are extremely high and it is a constant biblical theme that the Spirit of God holds His community to a high standard. After a beautiful example of gospel generosity, we are given a terrifying account of heinous hypocrisy.

Ananias and Sapphira are not struck dead for mere stinginess. After all, contributing one's goods to the apostles was a purely voluntary act. Ananias and Sapphira are struck dead because they lie to the apostles and the One from whom the apostles received their authority, the Spirit of Christ. Peter explains this (Acts 5:3), reminding Ananias that there was no obligation to give. Ananias lied in order to appear generous. This hurt the faith community and the Holy Spirit would not let that stand.

The text ends with the first reference to "the church" (Gk. *ekklesia*) in the book of Acts. From this point forward, this is the term used to describe the people of God, placing them in continuity with God's Old Testament *ekklesia*, the Israelites. God's standards do not change throughout the Scriptures, but the resources that He has given His people have increased. The greatest of those gifts have been the giving of His own Son and His own Spirit.

What prompted Ananias and Sapphira to lie? Do we see such hypocrisy in the church today?

Search the Scriptures

1. How is the unity of the Christian described (Acts 4:32)?

2. What types of items were sold to support the community (4:34)?

3. How is Barnabas described (4:35-36)?

Discuss the Meaning

1. Contrast Barnabas with Ananais and Sapphira. What makes the difference?

2. What examples have you seen of Barnabas-like generosity in the church?

Liberating Lesson

This text drives home the fact that the Christian life is not an individualistic one. The community's sharing of goods reminds us that when our brothers and sisters suffer, we suffer. The Scripture reminds us of our commitment to the needy because we are a covenant community of God. This does not mean that Christians do not have the joyous opportunity and responsibility to serve those outside the church, but it does mean that meeting the needs of our brothers and sisters in Christ ought to proceed from our hearts without controversy. This means that those among us who are poor, widows, orphans, single mothers, immigrants and all who are marginalized and oppressed must be lifted up. Here one can hear echoes that resonate with the African philosophy of ubuntu, often translated, "I am because we are." In the body of Christ, individual and communal identity cannot be separated. The bond that connects us is not merely our common humanity, but even more deeply, our union with Christ. The call then is to concretely love our neighbors, especially our Christian neighbors. That is how the world will know us: by our love.

Application for Activation

Individual application of this passage is rather simple and yet one of the hardest things for many of us to do. Money is often an indication of one's priorities and for the people of the early church, there was clearly the recognition that their money was not to be used just for their own pleasure, but rather it was a resource that God could use for the uplifting of their brothers and sisters. So the call then also goes out to each Christian to consider their finances in the light of the grace that they have been shown in Christ. What kind of generosity does that call you to?

This call applies to the individual and the community. As you consider your role in your family, in your church community, in your city, and in your country, what kind of steward are you being? In the light of Christ's sacrifice and the high stakes of the Christian life, we must devote ourselves to prayer and communion with each other and with our God to make good use of the resources that He has given us to be beacons of His gospel in His world.

Follow the Spirit

What God wants me to do:

_____

_____

_____

_____

Remember Your Thoughts

Special insights I have learned:

_____

_____

_____

_____

More Light on the Text

Acts 4:32–37; 5:1–11

4:32 And the multitude of them that believed were of one heart and of one soul: neither said any of them that ought of the things which he possessed was his own; but they had all things common. 33 And with great power gave the apostles witness of the resurrection of the Lord Jesus: and great grace was upon them all.

Luke gives a general description of the life of the early Christians in Jerusalem. Verses 32–33 showcase the community life of the early Christians as marked by four things: their unity in mind and soul (v. 32a), their partnership of ownership (v. 32b), the power and witness of the apostles (v. 33a), and the grace of God, which rested upon them (v. 33b). The overarching concept was their unity, their fellowship in the Spirit (cf. *koinonia*, koy-no-**NEE**-ah; Acts 2:42). The unity of the believers and the sharing of their possessions provide more clear and ample evidence of the continuing presence of the Holy Spirit. The latter is described in two ways. First, "neither said any of them that ought of the things which he possessed was his own," that is, "no one claimed that any of their possessions was only theirs." The picture is one of unqualified sharing, of not claiming owner's rights, of saying "what's mine is yours." It was a partnership of ownership. Though the Sadducees had reacted violently to the preaching of the Resurrection, the early believers continued to preach it for it was the Resurrection that validated Christ's sacrifice for sin (cf. Romans 4:25). Recognizing the crucifixion without the Resurrection will leave us with no Gospel to preach. A further significant description of the early believers is that great grace was upon them all. God's grace, present in abundant measure, made the early believers gracious in attitude and action, in word and work.

34 Neither was there any among them that lacked: for as many as were possessors of lands or houses sold them, and brought the prices of the things that were sold, 35 And laid them down at the apostles' feet: and distribution was made unto every man according as he had need.

One proof of God's grace among the early believers was the love and generosity within the new community. Such love, created by the Holy Spirit, prompted and enabled some believers to help those in need by selling their properties and placing the proceeds at the feet of the apostles. The proceeds were then distributed to the needy among them. The practice was wholly voluntary. It was neither compulsory nor universal, but at that time it was a way for the early Christians to share with those who had less or nothing at all.

There was no transfer of ownership, no control of production or income, no requirement to surrender one's property to the community. They sold their property and brought the proceeds to the apostles as needs arose. There was not a requirement for the abolition of private property, as conclusively demonstrated by two facts in the context.

First is the example of Barnabas in vv. 36–37. His sale of the property would hardly be a sterling example if the surrender of property were obligatory. Second is the example of Ananias and Sapphira. Peter clarified for Ananias that his sin was in lying about his charity. The land remained his to do with as he pleased; he was under no obligation to give the proceeds to the church (5:4). The money was his to use as he wished. The early Church practiced extreme, genuine, consecrated stewardship. That is still Christ's demand of those who would be His followers.

36 And Joses, who by the apostles was surnamed Barnabas, (which is, being

interpreted, The son of consolation,) a Levite, and of the country of Cyprus, 37 Having land, sold it, and brought the money, and laid it at the apostles' feet.

Luke concluded his treatment of the early Christian sharing with two specific examples. In verses 36-37, Barnabas sold a field and placed all the receipts at the apostles' feet. Not much detail is provided about Barnabas here other than that he was a Levite from Cyprus. According to the Old Testament (Deuteronomy 10:9; Number 18:20, 24), Levites were not supposed to own land, but that no longer seemed to apply in Barnabas' day. Indeed, Jeremiah, a priest, owned land (Jeremiah 32:6–15). Though his birth name was Joses, he had acquired the nickname Barnabas, presumably for his outstanding abilities to offer "consolation" or encourage to others.

5:1 But a certain man named Ananias, with Sapphira his wife, sold a possession, 2 And kept back part of the price, his wife also being privy to it, and brought a certain part, and laid it at the apostles' feet. 3 But Peter said, Ananias, why hath Satan filled thine heart to lie to the Holy Ghost and to keep back part of the price of the land?

If Barnabas, as portrayed in the preceding verses, was a positive example of the community's sharing, the story of Ananias and Sapphira provides a sharp contrast. Ananias, whose name means "Jehovah is gracious," in collusion with the wife Sapphira, acted contrary to his name. They too sold a piece of property, pledging the proceeds to the community of believers. But they held back part of the proceeds; and a terrible judgment followed, resulting in both their deaths. The use of a rare Greek verb (*nosphizomai*, nos-phi-dzo-mai, v. 2) to describe his action in holding back part of the money is striking. It means to pilfer, to purloin, to embezzle. Peter knew that Ananias'

gesture was a lie and confronted him with his duplicity (v. 3). We are not told how Peter knew it was an incomplete sum. They were the community of the Holy Spirit, and in this community, they placed all their trust, found their identity and their security. But this was not so with Ananias. His heart was divided. He had one foot in the community and the other still groping for a toehold on the worldly security of earthly possessions. To lie with regard to the sharing was to belie the unity of the community and the Spirit that undergirded that unity. That is why Peter accused Ananias of lying to the Spirit. Like Judas, Ananias was motived by money (cf. Luke 22:5). But in filling the heart of one of its members, Satan had now entered for the first time into the young Christian community as well.

4 Whiles it remained, was it not thine own? and after it was sold, was it not in thine own power? why hast thou conceived this thing in thine heart? thou hast not lied unto men, but unto God.

Peter reminded Ananias that he had been under no compulsion (v. 4). They were under no obligation to give. He did not have to sell his land. Even if he sold it, he still could have retained the proceeds. The act of dedicating the land to the community was strictly voluntary. Once pledged, however, it became a wholly different matter. It had been dedicated to the community. In lying about the proceeds, he had broken a sacred trust. Ultimately, he had lied to God. Ananias' sin was not in his failure to give but in his deception. He betrayed the community and in so doing lied to the Spirit.

5 And Ananias hearing these words fell down, and gave up the ghost: and great fear came on all them that heard these things. 6 And the young men arose, wound him up, and carried him out, and buried him.

Here we find the high price of hypocrisy. The phrase "gave up the ghost" is one word in the Greek, *expsucho* (eks-**PSOO**-ko), which is literally "breathed out." Was it from shock from overwhelming guilt and remorse upon the exposure of his sin? Was he struck down by God? The text does not say. The note that great fear came on all them that heard these things would indicate that they at least saw the hand of God in it all. The manner in which his funeral was handled would likewise indicate that divine judgment was seen in the whole affair. The immediate and quick burial also shows the gravity of the judgment. The young men were back in three hours (vv. 7, 10). This was a most unusual procedure. Burials were often fairly hasty in Palestine, but not that hasty, not, that is, except for death under unusual circumstances, such as suicides and criminals—and judgments from God.

7 And it was about the space of three hours after, when his wife, not knowing what was done, came in. 8 And Peter answered unto her, Tell me whether ye sold the land for so much? And she said, Yea, for so much. 9 Then Peter said unto her, How is it that ye have agreed together to tempt the Spirit of the Lord? behold, the feet of them which have buried thy husband are at the door, and shall carry thee out. 10 Then fell she down straightway at his feet, and yielded up the ghost: and the young men came in, and found her dead, and, carrying her forth, buried her by her husband.

About three hours later Sapphira appeared on the scene. Rather than be honest and tell the truth, she joined her husband in the conspiracy with the funds. She would also join him in death. Peter confronted her about the sale price, just as he had confronted Ananias. In giving an affirmative answer to Peter's question, she confirmed her guilt by continuing the lie.

It is significant to note that in both cases Peter did not pronounce a curse. His questioning of Sapphira left her the opportunity of repentance, and one can probably assume the same for Ananias. Peter's role was to confront—not to judge. The judgment came from God. But Peter had to lay before her the consequences of her action. She had joined with her husband in "testing" the Spirit of the Lord. This time the expression was not of lying to the Spirit but of testing him, to see how far he would go in his tolerance. Not very far, was Peter's answer: "The feet of the men who buried your husband are at the door, and they will carry you out also." This was the first Sapphira had heard of her husband's death, and she fell down immediately at Peter's feet, dead. Peter's words scarcely sound redemptive. He was fulfilling the prophetic role of the divine mouthpiece, pronouncing God's judgment on her for her complicity with her husband. She may have died of shock; but if so, it was inevitable, for Peter already knew and informed her that her doom was sealed. One can scarcely miss the irony of the situation. She lay at Peter's feet, in the place of her money. She had joined her husband in the conspiracy. Now she would join him in the grave.

11 And great fear came upon all the church, and upon as many as heard these things.

Sapphira's story and subsequent death end in the same way as that of her husband (cf. v. 5b): "Great fear came upon all the church, and upon as many as heard these things." The repetition is not by chance: it is the whole point of the story. By the power of this spiritual presence in its midst, the young community worked miracles, witnessed fearlessly, and was blessed with incredible growth. The Spirit was the power behind its unity, and its unity was the power behind its witness. But just as with God there is both justice and mercy, so with the Holy Spirit there is also his judgment. This is what Ananias and Sapphira experienced. The Spirit is not to be taken lightly. As the Spirit of God, He must always be viewed with fear in the biblical sense of that word: reverent awe and respect.

It might be noted that this is the first time the word "church" (*ekklesia*, ek-kle-si-a) occurs in Acts, which denotes the people of God gathered as a convened assembly. The church thrives if it lives within the total trust of its members. Where there is unity of trust and oneness of heart and mind, the church flourishes in the power of the Spirit. The witness of the Church fails where duplicity and distrust exist. We must be careful not to relegate the sin of Ananias and Sapphira to the past. Their sin is no more despicable as that of many professed believers today. We often sing, "All to Jesus I surrender, all to Him I freely give," but our actions and lifestyle often contradict our confession.

Sources:
Arrington, French L. *Acts of the Apostles: Introduction, Translation and Commentary*. Peabody, MA.: Hendrickson Publishers, 1988.
Boice, James Montgomery. *Acts*. Grand Rapids, Michigan: Baker Books, 1997.
Carter, W. Carter and Ralph Earle. *The Acts of the Apostles*. Grand Rapids: Zondervan Publishing House, 1973.
Johnson, Luke Timothy. *The Acts of the Apostles*. Sacra Pagina vol. 5.
Mayfield, Joseph M. and Ralph Earle. *John*. Acts. Beacon Bible Commentary Vol. 7. Kansas City: Beacon Hill Press, 1965.

Say It Correctly

Ananias. an-a-**NIGH**-as
Barnabas. **BAR**-na-bas
Sapphira. suh-**FIE**-ra

Daily Bible Readings

MONDAY
Preparing to Become a Deacon
(1 Timothy 3:8-13)

TUESDAY
Healing Ministry Grows the Church
(Acts 5:12-16)

WEDNESDAY
Church Sharing Plan Enlarged
(Acts 6:1-7)

THURSDAY
Stephen's Ministry Opposed
(Acts 6:8-15)

FRIDAY
Sharing All of Life Together
(Acts 2:42-47)

SATURDAY
Prayer for Boldness and Signs
(Acts 4:23-31)

SUNDAY
Sharing All Possessions
Challenges the Church
(Acts 4:32-5:11)

Teaching Tips

Words You Should Know

A. Respect [of person] (v. 1) *prosopolempsia* (Gk.)—Partiality

B. Vile (James 2:2) *rhuparos* (Gk.)—Dirty, cheap, or shabby

Teacher Preparation

Unifying Principle—A Community of Equals. Favoring one person or group over others is a common occurrence in human relationships. Why is it unacceptable to show partiality to certain people or groups? James reminds us that love requires us to treat everyone equally.

A. Read the Bible Background and Devotional Reading.

B. Pray for your students and lesson clarity.

C. Read the lesson Scripture in multiple translations.

O—Open the Lesson

A. Begin the class with prayer.

B. Ask participants to identify ways discriminating harms those who discriminate.

C. Have the students read the Aim for Change and the In Focus story.

D. Ask students how events like those in the story weigh on their hearts and how they can view these events from a faith perspective.

P—Present the Scriptures

A. Read the Focal Verses and discuss the Background and The People, Places, and Times sections.

B. Have the class share what Scriptures stand out for them and why, with particular emphasis on today's themes.

E—Explore the Meaning

A. Use In Depth or More Light on the Text to facilitate a deeper discussion of the lesson text.

B. Pose the questions in Search the Scriptures and Discuss the Meaning.

C. Discuss the Liberating Lesson and Application for Activation sections.

N—Next Steps for Application

A. Summarize the value of the true judgment that can result only from an impartial spirit.

B. Challenge the class to note when they find themselves showing favoritism this week.

Worship Guide

For the Superintendent or Teacher
Theme: Impartial Love
Song: "In Christ There is No East or West"
Devotional Reading: Matthew 12:1-8

Impartial Love

Bible Background • JAMES 2
Printed Text • JAMES 2:1-13 | Devotional Reading • MATTHEW 12:1-8

——————— Aim for Change ———————

By the end of this lesson, we will UNDERSTAND the difference between showing partiality and treating others equally, AFFIRM that all people are equally valued and loved by God, and PRACTICE James's call to fulfill the "royal law" of loving one's neighbor as oneself.

——————— In Focus ———————

Standing before the congregation in his freshly laundered white robe, Pastor Philip "opened the doors" to the church for the call to salvation. It was communion Sunday, his favorite ritual of the church. Two men came down to the altar to give their lives to Jesus Christ. One was well-dressed; the other man was unkempt. He obviously had not had a bath in weeks.

The custom Pastor Philip had begun at the church was to have the congregation come and hug those who had just given their lives to Jesus Christ. With both men standing next to him and the unkempt man standing closest, Pastor Philip knew he would have to hug him. Pastor Philip's first thought was of his freshly laundered white robe. As he began to privately repent to Jesus, he turned to the man, welcomed him into the body of Christ, and fully embraced him, welcoming him to the church.

Partiality contradicts loving one's neighbor as oneself. What are some ways the body of Christ can genuinely embrace those not like us in order to show them God's love?

——————— Keep in Mind ———————

"Hearken, my beloved brethren, Hath not God chosen the poor of this world rich in faith, and heirs of the kingdom which he hath promised to them that love him?"
(James 2:5, KJV)

146

"Listen to me, dear brothers and sisters. Hasn't God chosen the poor in this world to be rich in faith? Aren't they the ones who will inherit the Kingdom he promised to those who love him?" (James 2:5, NLT)

Focal Verses

KJV **James 2:1** My brethren, have not the faith of our Lord Jesus Christ, the Lord of glory, with respect of persons.

2 For if there come unto your assembly a man with a gold ring, in goodly apparel, and there come in also a poor man in vile raiment;

3 And ye have respect to him that weareth the gay clothing, and say unto him, Sit thou here in a good place; and say to the poor, Stand thou there, or sit here under my footstool:

4 Are ye not then partial in yourselves, and are become judges of evil thoughts?

5 Hearken, my beloved brethren, Hath not God chosen the poor of this world rich in faith, and heirs of the kingdom which he hath promised to them that love him?

6 But ye have despised the poor. Do not rich men oppress you, and draw you before the judgment seats?

7 Do not they blaspheme that worthy name by the which ye are called?

8 If ye fulfil the royal law according to the scripture, Thou shalt love thy neighbour as thyself, ye do well:

9 But if ye have respect to persons, ye commit sin, and are convinced of the law as transgressors.

10 For whosoever shall keep the whole law, and yet offend in one point, he is guilty of all.

11 For he that said, Do not commit adultery, said also, Do not kill. Now if thou commit no adultery, yet if thou kill, thou art become a transgressor of the law.

12 So speak ye, and so do, as they that shall be judged by the law of liberty.

13 For he shall have judgment without mercy, that hath shewed no mercy; and mercy rejoiceth against judgment.

NLT **James 2:1** My dear brothers and sisters, how can you claim to have faith in our glorious Lord Jesus Christ if you favor some people over others?

2 For example, suppose someone comes into your meeting dressed in fancy clothes and expensive jewelry, and another comes in who is poor and dressed in dirty clothes.

3 If you give special attention and a good seat to the rich person, but you say to the poor one, "You can stand over there, or else sit on the floor"—well,

4 doesn't this discrimination show that your judgments are guided by evil motives?

5 Listen to me, dear brothers and sisters. Hasn't God chosen the poor in this world to be rich in faith? Aren't they the ones who will inherit the Kingdom he promised to those who love him?

6 But you dishonor the poor! Isn't it the rich who oppress you and drag you into court?

7 Aren't they the ones who slander Jesus Christ, whose noble name you bear?

8 Yes indeed, it is good when you obey the royal law as found in the Scriptures: "Love your neighbor as yourself."

9 But if you favor some people over others, you are committing a sin. You are guilty of breaking the law.

10 For the person who keeps all of the laws except one is as guilty as a person who has broken all of God's laws.

11 For the same God who said, "You must not commit adultery," also said, "You must not murder." So if you murder someone but do not commit adultery, you have still broken the law.

12 So whatever you say or whatever you do, remember that you will be judged by the law that sets you free.

13 There will be no mercy for those who have not shown mercy to others. But if you have been merciful, God will be merciful when he judges you.

The People, Places, and Times

James. The New Testament mentions two people named James: James, the son of Zebedee, who was among the first disciples (Mark 1:19; 5:37; 9:2; 10:35); and James, the half-brother of Jesus, a prominent leader of the Jerusalem church (Mark 6:3; Acts 15:13–29; Galatians 2:1–14). The book was likely written in AD 46, but the son of Zebedee was martyred around AD 44 (Acts 12:2). The other James, who was not martyred until AD 62, therefore, is generally assumed to be the author of this letter. Even though the apostle James was a half-brother of Jesus Christ, he expressed his relationship to Jesus as "a servant of God and of the Lord Jesus Christ" (1:1). He also identifies himself as a teacher (James 3:1).

The book of James is referred to as one of the "catholic epistles" (i.e. universal letters) because it is not addressed to a particular church, but rather appears to be a general letter written to several churches. Many think it was written to Christians scattered throughout Palestine due to persecution, to believers whose behavior contradicted their faith in Jesus Christ (1:1, 2).

Background

James' epistle explains the love Christians are to show others in the world. His tone is direct and reflects the wisdom of a seasoned Christian. Although James does not directly quote Jesus, he uses phrases and ideas that originated with Jesus. In fact, much of what James has written shows a direct relationship to Jesus' Sermon on the Mount.

The letter from James was written to people under pressure. Christians were suffering from economic persecution and oppression, and the church was struggling under the strain. In response to the difficulties they faced, James admonished believers to pull together and help one another. Otherwise, they would compromise with the world and become divided. Helping one another would have been the ideal choice, but these believers were more focused on the struggle to get ahead in the world.

James has just informed his readers what pure religion was all about: serving those who are less fortunate—the orphans and the widows (James 1:27). The early Christians must not forget a primary function of the Church's ministry—to help the poor. Now James looks at some situations where professing Christians might not be living out their faith, beginning here with the rich and the poor.

At-A-Glance

1. Exhortation Against Favoritism
(James 2:1-7)
2. Encouragement to Love (vv. 8-13)

In Depth

1. Exhortation Against Favoritism (James 2:1-7)

As a concerned leader of the Christian church, James begins with a warning about moral behavior to the believers: favoritism is unacceptable (v. 1). James uses the illustration of two men, one rich and one poor, who join in worship (v. 2). Partiality begins when the believer pays more attention to the man of higher status, offering him the best seat. At the same time, the poor man is directed to sit apart from the rest of the congregation (v. 3). James points out that the tendency to show a preference to those with prestige and position over the poor and less fortunate is incompatible with the teachings and actions of our Lord Jesus.

Throughout the Bible, Jesus teaches His followers to love their neighbors as themselves. All should receive honor and concern equally. By preferring the rich, the believers were guilty of sin against Jesus Christ. After all, Jesus did give them the commandment that emphatically states the poor, who are so often dishonored and oppressed by the rich (vv. 6–7), are not only welcome but celebrated in the kingdom of God (Matthew 5:3). Since God honors the poor, they should not be dishonored by those who profess to be His children. Verse 7 explains that giving preference to those with status "blasphemes" the name of the Lord.

The early Christians were rebuked for their behavior. Are we any different in our worship practices? If a homeless person comes into a church, how likely is it that he or she will be seated in the first row? If a famous person visited the church, how much attention would they get? Where would they be seated? Perhaps we would do well to heed James' warning in our worship settings.

How inclusive are today's churches?

2. Encouragement to Love (vv. 8-13)

James continues to teach by saying that it is not enough to merely tolerate poor people and refrain from mistreating them. Rather, believers must go farther and actively show love to the less fortunate, even as we love ourselves (v. 8). James continues to show the believers their harsh treatment of the poor also violated the law of love. James refers to this commandment as "the royal law" (cf. Leviticus 19:18). Often called the Golden Rule, this is a prevailing theme in Jesus' ministry and in early Christian teaching, "Do to others as you would have them do to you" (Luke 6:31). Jesus requires us to put this command into action in our relationships with others.

James refers to those who commit favoritism as "transgressors," which means God's law has been broken (v. 9). As a result of committing one disobedient act against God, that individual becomes guilty of violating God's law in its entirety (v. 10). The law of love, on the other hand, is a "law of liberty" (2:12). God's love frees a person from speaking and acting foolishly.

Love frees us from psychological enslavement to our enemies. And it frees us to help our friends.

James ends this teaching by admonishing his readers to show their obedience and allegiance to God by speaking and acting toward one another with mercy because the day will come when all believers will receive their just reward. This is God's way, and as believers, we have been given the mandate to follow God's way of having mercy for others in order to receive mercy in return (v. 13).

Why can't a Christian just focus on loving God? Why is loving our neighbor/brother needed?

Search the Scriptures

1. What virtues does James attribute to the poor as a class of people (James 2:5)?

2. What is the royal law according to the Scriptures? (v. 8)

3. By what law shall believers be judged? (v. 12)

4. What virtue will rejoice against the judgment? (v. 13)

Discuss the Meaning

1. What should be the attitude of the believer be toward the rich and the poor in our congregations?

2. What are some distinct ways believers in the church today mistreat members or visitors?

Liberating Lesson

In many metropolitan areas, it appears as if highways are built so that commuters don't have to drive through poor communities. This strategy represents an extreme attempt to keep poor people trapped in a marginalized state where society can avoid the issue of improving their quality of life. But God has called His church to be impartial disciples who do not show partiality toward the rich. Instead, we are to fulfill God's royal law and show the love of God to all people, treating everyone as we would like to be treated—with no respect to a person's social status. To the extent that an unfortunate situation involving favoring the rich and ignoring the poor affects African Americans, and therefore African American Christians, we must soberly consider what we can do to help improve the economic conditions of poor neighborhoods. Why are people poor? Is there a way out of poverty?

As a class, plan a project that can be used to meet a critical need of a specific family or person in the church.

Application for Activation

• At least three times this week make a sacrifice to show practical acts of love to someone. Ask God to lead you and then keep your eyes open for the opportunities. They will come.

• Do a self-evaluation to discover a time you judged someone unfairly. Repent and ask the Lord to help you fulfill James 2:13.

Follow the Spirit

What God wants me to do:

_____

_____

_____

_____

Remember Your Thoughts

Special insights I have learned:

_____

_____

_____

_____

More Light on the Text

James 2:1-13

1 My brethren, have not the faith of our Lord Jesus Christ, the Lord of glory, with respect of persons.

The Palestine of James' day showed special consideration to the wealthy by giving them special rank and status. Such favoritism was often shown in legal matters, and even in the Jewish synagogue, where people were often seated according to their rank in society. Here James continues his admonitions from chapter 1 by instructing believers that they are to emulate the Lord Jesus Christ with regards to how they treat and view other people. James is trying to help believers understand that they were no longer to have the world's attitudes. They, as followers of Christ, were not to show personal favoritism.

James makes it very clear that as believers who claim to have faith in the Lord Jesus Christ, they must follow God's Word. He is taking a direct approach to the danger of showing respect of persons. The apostle Peter also brought out the truth that God Himself is no respecter of persons (Acts 10:34). How, then, can one claim to be a believer in Christ if that person displays behavior that is contrary to what our Lord expects? This is James' message to the church.

2 For if there come unto your assembly a man with a gold ring, in goodly apparel, and there come in also a poor man in vile raiment; 3 And ye have respect to him that weareth the gay clothing, and say unto him, Sit thou here in a good place; and say to the poor, Stand thou there, or sit here under my footstool: 4 Are ye not then partial in yourselves, and are become judges of evil thoughts?

James then gave an example of how believers might actually be showing favoritism toward people without even realizing it. By pointing out that they were "having respect" (Gk. *epiblepo*, eh-pee-**BLEH**-poe) for the rich man over the poor man, James was drawing upon a common practice in the temples and courts of his society. In ancient Rome, the wearing of gold rings and fine robes spoke to membership in an elite class that always received favored treatment in Roman courts. Since the synagogue had become the place that served both as the house of prayer and as the community court, some of this same kind of favoritism was creeping in there as well. James counseled believers against adopting such ways. The practice of showing such favoritism was strictly forbidden in Jewish law (cf. Leviticus 19:13), and it was contrary to the ideals established by the Lord Jesus Christ.

James poses a scenario that illustrates what he is attempting to convey. Imagine two men coming into the church at the same time. These two people have extremely different appearances. One man is wearing fine clothing and a gold ring, and the other man is poorly dressed in tattered clothing. James suggests that if anyone offers the man who is well dressed a prominent seat while communicating to the poor man that he is unworthy and relegating him to a lesser seat, that person is exercising judgment based on outward appearances. James stresses this type of behavior is clearly unacceptable to God.

James was forced to ask the question in verse 4, "Are ye not then partial in yourselves, and are become judges of evil thoughts?" "Partiality" (Gk. *prosopolepteo*, pro-soh-poe-layp-**TEH**-oh) means to make distinctions among people based on their rank and influence. The person who is guilty of such action has, in effect, made himself a judge of both the wealthy and the poor. These thoughts are in direct contradiction to God's Word. James rightfully states that such bias comes from an evil motive.

5 Hearken, my beloved brethren, Hath not God chosen the poor of this world rich in faith, and heirs of the kingdom which he hath promised to them that love him? 6 But ye have despised the poor. Do not rich men oppress you, and draw you before the judgment seats? 7 Do not they blaspheme that worthy name by the which ye are called?

James asks a very serious question that believers of any era cannot avoid. His question makes his point very clear in verse 5. He reminds those that have a tendency toward showing favoritism that God, in His infinite wisdom, has favored those considered by the world to be poor. God has given to those who are considered the least in society the ability to be rich in faith. Having faith in God demonstrates a love for God; therefore, these circumstances are pleasing in God's sight and He has decreed that the poor will inherit His kingdom.

There is a sense of bewilderment in James' voice as he asks believers how they could be guilty of despising the poor in the same fashion that the rich did. The rich were the ones oppressing them and dragging them to court. By "despising" or treating poor believers with contempt and dishonor, they were showing by their actions that they had not really heard the Word of God. They were behaving just like the unsaved world around them, and that was unacceptable. James then reminds his hearers that the godless people they were emulating were the same ones who "blaspheme" the name of the very Lord to whom they had given themselves. Jesus Christ, who is worthy of reverence, has allowed believers to be identified with Him. James then directs his readers to consider their own situations and points out that the rich people are treating them the same way they are treating the poor.

8 If ye fulfill the royal law according to the scripture, Thou shalt love thy neighbor as

thyself, ye do well. 9 But if ye have respect to persons, ye commit sin, and are convinced of the law as transgressors.

When Christ was asked to identify the greatest commandment, He said to love God with all their hearts, souls, and minds, and then to love their neighbors in the same way that they loved themselves (Matthew 22:37–40). James called this the "royal" law. It represents the whole law of God as revealed in Moses and stated by Jesus Christ. James affirms that fulfilling the royal law is pleasing to God because that person is showing genuine love to someone else, called here "thy neighbor." The Jewish society of James' day viewed a neighbor only as a fellow Jew. But James is guiding his listeners into understanding that their view of what made someone a neighbor had to be expanded. Anyone bearing the name of Christ belonged to His kingdom and was to be included as a neighbor.

On the other hand, the person who fails to follow the royal law is a "transgressor" (Gk. *parabates*, par-ab-**AT**-ace) or breaker of the law. James points out that showing favoritism stands in direct opposition to obedience to the royal law. When God's people are guilty of having the respect of persons, they are committing a sin against God.

10 For whosoever shall keep the whole law, and yet offend in one point, he is guilty of all. 11 For he that said, Do not commit adultery, said also, Do not kill. Now if thou commit no adultery, yet if thou kill, thou art become a transgressor of the law.

James drives home the point that the smallest transgression of God's law makes one guilty of violating the whole law. A chain with a single broken link is a broken chain. James is trying to help his listeners understand that they were not to pick and choose when it comes to obeying God's commands. By choosing the imagery of

someone who would not commit adultery but would kill, James might have had in mind the zealots who were so pious that they would never commit adultery but who also had no problem with assassinating those they deemed worthy of death. God is not honored when we follow some of His commands and not others because we find some more acceptable than others.

Since it is the same God who has declared what constitutes sin, one cannot differentiate on the basis of individual sin. Even though a person commits one type of sin but refrains from committing another form of sin, in essence, that person is rejecting the whole of God's authority and is, therefore, guilty of committing sin. All people are one in Christ (Galatians 3:28). When partiality and distinctions are shown based on race, gender, position, power, or wealth, sin has entered in and God's law has been violated.

12 So speak ye, and so do, as they that shall be judged by the law of liberty. 13 For he shall have judgment without mercy, that hath shewed no mercy; and mercy rejoiceth against judgment.

Finally, James cautions his listeners to speak and act as those who would be judged by the law of liberty, which was the standard that was set by the Lord Jesus Christ (see 1:25). James is again reminding believers that because they accepted Christ as Lord, the Spirit of Christ was at work transforming their nature into something that was pleasing and acceptable to God. This transformation should show itself in their speech and actions.

Jewish teachers often defined God's character by two attributes: mercy and justice. Mercy (Gk. *eleos*, **EL**-eh-os) meant to show kindness or goodwill toward others, while justice (Gk. *krisis*, **KREE**-sis) meant condemnation. Both belong to the providence of God. James states the truth that God's mercy will be shown to those who themselves show mercy, and God's condemnation will fall on anyone who does not show mercy. Believers who show kindness and goodwill toward others, then, need never fear being on the receiving end of God's judgment because Jesus has declared that the merciful will receive God's mercy (Matthew 5:7).

James counsels his readers to talk and act as though they truly believe what they claim to believe. They must live up to the faith that they profess with their mouths and refrain from betraying God's law of love by showing preferential treatment. It is clear from his teaching that part of living by God's standards involves helping those who are in need. If we show no mercy to others, then we cannot expect mercy from God in return.

James warns that believers will be judged with the same type of judgment they show to others. If we take heed to James's instructions and follow Jesus' words, we will avoid the trap of deceiving ourselves. In other words, we will fulfill the commandment of God by becoming doers of the Word ,by showing love and mercy to our brothers and sisters.

Sources:
Barker, Kenneth, ed. *The NIV Study Bible*. Grand Rapids, MI: Zondervan Publishing House, 1995.
Draper, Charles W., Chad Brand, and Archie England, eds. *Holman Illustrated Bible Dictionary*. Grand Rapids, MI: Holman Reference, 2003.
Dunn, James D. G., and John W. Rogerson. *Commentary on the Bible*. Grand Rapids, MI: Wm. B. Eerdmans Publishing Company: 2003.
Keck, Leander E. gen. ed. *The New Interpreter's Bible*, Vol. XII. Nashville, TN: Abingdon Press, 1998.
Keener, Craig S. *The IVP Bible Background Commentary: New Testament*. Downers Grove, IL: IVP Academic, 1994.
Myers, Allen C., John W. Simpson, Philip A. Frank, Timothy P. Jenney, and Ralph W. Vunderink, eds. *The Eerdmans Bible Dictionary*. Grand Rapids, MI: Wm. B. Eerdmans Publishing Company, 1996.
Radmacher, Earl D., Ronald B. Allen, and H. W. House, eds. *Nelson Study Bible (NKJV)*. Nashville, TN: Thomas Nelson Publishers, 2001.
Tasker, R. V. G. *The General Epistle of James: An Introduction and Commentary*. Grand Rapids, MI: Wm. B. Eerdmans Publishing Company, 1982.
Vincent, Marvin R. *Word Studies in the New Testament*. Peabody, MA: Hendrickson Publishers, 1888.

Say It Correctly

Zebedee. **ZEH**-buh-dee.

Daily Bible Readings

MONDAY
Extending Mercy
More Important than Sacrifice
(Matthew 12:1-8)

TUESDAY
Love One Another from the Heart
(1 Peter 1:17-23)

WEDNESDAY
In Christ Gentiles
Share Abraham's Faith
(Galatians 3:6-9, 13-14)

THURSDAY
Faith of Levite Mother Saves Moses
(Exodus 2:1-10)

FRIDAY
Unexpressed Faith Has No Value
(James 2:14-17)

SATURDAY
Faith and Works
Complement Each Other
(James 2:18-26)

SUNDAY
Disdain the Practice of Partiality
(James 2:1-13)

Call in The New Testament

This quarter examines God's call in stories from the New Testament. The greatest call came to Jesus. Other calls in the New Testament led to the extension of Christian ministry into the world.

UNIT 1 • The Beginning of a Call

This unit has four sessions from the Gospel of Matthew. Lesson 1 highlights the heritage of Jesus. Lesson 2 tells the story of Jesus' birth. Lesson 3 speaks of the witness of the Magi to Jesus' call as the Messiah. Lesson 4 tells of the call of John the Baptist.

Lesson 1: December 6, 2020
Called through Heritage
Hebrews 1:1-5; Matthew 1:1-6, 16–17

Where we come from often speaks volumes about what we are like. How are people rooted in what has come before? Hebrews affirms the ultimate origins of Jesus in the very life of God and Matthew explains how he was the product of his long biblical heritage.

Lesson 2: December 13, 2020
Called Before Birth
Matthew 1:18–25

A newborn baby inspires us to wonder about the potential of every human life. How do we understand the designs of our lives? Joseph's call to form a family with Mary suggests that God calls us to give hope to the world through our families.

Lesson 3: December 20, 2020
A Regal Response to Holy Light
Matthew 2:7–15

As our world gets smaller, we are more and more exposed to people who differ from us in race, culture, and religious values. Where can we find unity in such a world? By summoning wise men from far-off lands to worship Jesus, God demonstrated that this newborn King would transcend the differences that divide us.

Lesson 4: December 27, 2020
Called to Prepare the Way
Matthew 3:1–12

Important projects require thoughtful preparation. What endeavors demand our greatest efforts in preparation? John called for people to repent of their sins and thus be ready to welcome the soon-coming Messiah.

UNIT 2 • Jesus and Calls in His Ministry

This unit presents four lessons about Jesus' ministry. Luke emphasizes Jesus' call to proclamation and ministry and identifies Jesus as one who calls followers. Mark speaks to Jesus' call to a ministry of healing. John gives us a look at Jesus' call as the intercessor for those who follow Him.

Lesson 5: January 3, 2021
Called to Proclaim
Luke 4:14–22

People hear conflicting messages and proclamations all of the time. What message would provide answers to life's deepest problems? The worshipers at Nazareth listened to Jesus' proclamation of justice and compassion and were amazed at His gracious words.

Lesson 6: January 10, 2021
Called to Significance
Luke 5:1–11

People seek significance and purpose. Are we on earth just to eke out a living or can we be part of something greater? Jesus called Simon and his cohorts to follow Him and find fulfillment in doing the work of God's kingdom.

Lesson 7: January 17, 2021
Called to Heal
Mark 2:1–12

The limitations of human existence make genuine wholeness an elusive goal. Where can we find true healing? By declaring a paralyzed man's sins forgiven and restoring his physical health, Jesus demonstrated that God had called Jesus to heal infirmities of the soul as well as the body.

Lesson 8: January 24, 2021
Called as the Intercessor
John 17:14–24

People often look for ways to appeal for assistance on behalf of others. How can people respond to the urge to intercede in a meaningful manner? Jesus' prayer for His disciples serves as a call to use intercessory prayer for the sake of others.

UNIT 3 • The Call of Women

This five-week study highlights women in ministry. The first lesson focuses on prophesying women mentioned in the New Testament. The second lesson focuses on the Samaritan woman's evangelistic ministry. Lesson 3 explores Mary Magdalene's call to unwavering discipleship. Lesson 4 gives an opportunity to study the impact of Priscilla's ministry. The final lesson focuses on Lydia's call to service and hospitality.

Lesson 9: January 31, 2021
Prophesying Daughters
Luke 2:36–38; Acts 2:16–21; 21:8–9

All people have a unique purpose in life. How do we affirm each individual's purpose? The Gospel of Luke and the book of Acts provide examples of women responding to God's call.

Lesson 10: February 7, 2021
Called to Evangelize
John 4:25-42

Some people wonder if they are good enough to give direction to others. What is the best way to share or witness to others? The woman at the well was considered an outcast, but after meeting Jesus she eagerly became a witness and brought others to Jesus.

Lesson 11: February 14, 2021
Mary Magdalene: A Faithful Disciple
Luke 8:1–3; Mark 15:40; John 20:10–18

Being a truly committed follower of someone is often difficult, but some people reveal consistent loyalty no matter what happens. How do you show your loyalty and faithfulness? Mary Magdalene demonstrated her unwavering discipleship and loyalty to Jesus through her actions.

Lesson 12: February 21, 2021
Priscilla: Called to Minister
Acts 18:1–3, 18–21, 24–26; Romans 16:3–4

Encounters that bring together people with similar gifts and talents can lead to greater opportunities for service in other arenas. How can common traits or experiences lead to meaningful engagement in ministry or service? Priscilla and Aquila shared their tent-making business with Paul, and Paul shared his ministry of the Gospel with them.

Lesson 13: February 28, 2021
Lydia: Called to Serve
Acts 16:11–15, 40; 1 Corinthians 1:26–30

Many people have been recipients of generous hospitality or have been in a position to extend hospitality to someone. In what ways can openness and a listening ear provide opportunities to serve? Lydia was an attentive woman who responded to the Gospel message with faithfulness and generous hospitality.

Callings of God

by Luvell Anderson, PhD

We are called to a covenant community. It is made evident in the Pentateuch (the first five books of the Bible, called the books of the Law) that God desires a covenant community that will display His glory to a watching world. Moses, while speaking to the Israelites, informed them of their special status: " For thou art an holy people unto the Lord thy God, and the Lord hath chosen thee to be a peculiar people unto himself, above all the nations that are upon the earth" (Deuteronomy 14:2, KJV). While there is a tremendous benefit in being a member of God's covenant community, membership should also be recognized as a tremendous privilege. God's choice of people is based purely on His grace alone. No one can boast that it was because he or she was so great that God had to let that person into His community. Speaking through Moses, God explicitly made His gracious choice clear: "The LORD did not set his love upon you, nor choose you, because ye were more in number than any people; for ye were the fewest of all people" (Deuteronomy 7:7, KJV). Having awareness of the basis of God's choice ought to humble us and compel us to express gratitude for His grace.

The theme for this quarter's study is designed to teach us how we are to live as members of God's covenant community. Across the majority of the Pentateuch, Moses sets forth God's instructions and decrees for the newly emancipated Israelites, who were being brought in to "a land flowing with milk and honey" (see Exodus 3:8, Leviticus 20:24, Deuteronomy 6:3). The phrase paints a rich image of the abundance and sweetness of the land. Therefore, as a nation, they would be blessed with an abundance of land and possessions. God didn't just call the Israelites to be a people for His possession but He also provided instruction for living life the way He intended it to be lived.

After all, it is in Him that "we live, and move, and have our being" (Acts 17:28, KJV). Consequently, an omniscient (all-knowing) God would know what is best for our lives. The lessons in this quarter are centered on calls in the New Testament, but it will be helpful before that to review calls in the Old Testament. While looking at God's call to His people in the Pentateuch, we see three main themes: (1) how God called Israel out of Egypt; (2) how God called Israel to be His people; and (3) how God called Israel to choose life. These three themes cover the initiation into the covenant community, identity as a member of the community, and finally, the responsibilities that come with being a member of the community.

Initiation

As we have already seen, God's choice to make Israel His covenant community was based on His grace alone. We begin to see the extent of His grace in the way He initiates them into the community. As is often noted in Old Testament passages, Egypt is commonly understood to be a symbol of oppression and suffering. The people of Israel, after initially enjoying several years of peace and prosperity, found themselves slaves in the land. Moses explains that their lives were made "bitter with hard bondage" (Exodus 1:14, KJV). Yet, even in the face of cruel slavery, signs of God's favor upon them were still evident: "But the more they afflicted them, the more they multiplied and grew" (from Exodus 1:12, KJV). As a result of their ever-increasing numbers, Pharaoh ordered the murder of every male Hebrew child (Exodus 1:22). Of course, this action only compounded the amount of sorrow and suffering endured by the Israelites. Yet, it is in the midst of this suffering that God makes His power known. Through the plagues brought upon Egypt and the parting of the Red Sea, God made it clear that He desired to rescue Israel from their bondage.

God's call to Israel, to come out of Egypt, was also a command. They were not just being emancipated from their slavery but they were also being called to leave behind their former way of life. Having spent more than 400 years in an idolatrous land such as Egypt, it is reasonable to expect that the Israelites would have been influenced by the Egyptian culture, especially its idolatrous practices. We also see at one point Israel desiring to return to Egypt (see Numbers 14:1-4). So, God's call was a call to embrace freedom as well as for them to leave behind their former life of bondage.

Called to be God's People

In addition to the call to come out of Egypt, God called Israel to be His people. As a result, He placed a distinctive mark on Israel. They had been brought out of Egypt by miraculous acts. God displayed His choice of them as "His representatives" in a very visible way. Now God was calling them to assume a unique identity as the people of God.

It is through this person that God chose to make Himself known. We see that in the incident where Moses and Aaron went to Pharaoh to tell him of God's command for Pharaoh to free God's people. Of course, Pharaoh did not respond favorably: "And Pharaoh said, Who is the LORD, that I should obey his voice to let Israel go? I know not the LORD, neither will I let Israel go" (Exodus 5:2, KJV). By the end of the plagues, it is clear that Pharaoh came to know who the Living God truly is (Exodus 12:31). He was the God of Israel, His chosen people.

God's call to Israel to be His people also included a call to exclusive worship. The first commandment, tells of God's desire to be the sole object of their affection. God instructed, "Thou shalt have no other gods before me" (Exodus 20:3, KJV). Therefore, to be God's people meant to worship Him alone. Unfortunately, Israel found this a bit difficult to internalize. Not long after God emancipated them from Egyptian slavery— while Moses was still receiving the Law from God Himself on Mount Sinai— the people decided to erect a golden calf to worship (Exodus 32). As a result, there were serious repercussions (vv. 27–29). So we see that the call to be God's people also has ramifications for worship.

A Call to Choose Life

The third and final theme of this quarter has to do with God's call to choose life. After rehearsing God's laws and decrees, telling them what is expected of them, Moses told the Israelites, "I call heaven and earth to record this day against you, that I have set before you life and death, blessing and cursing: therefore choose life, that both thou and thy seed may live" (Deuteronomy 30:19, KJV). It seems obvious that with the choices of life and death before you, choosing life would be a no-brainer. But, if you recall, there were several moments when the Israelites desired to go back to the death in which they once were enslaved (see Exodus 16:3; 17:3; Numbers 14). Even though the life God designed for Israel was clearly better, the familiarity of their past experience still had a stronghold on the Israelites. Consequently, for Israel to enjoy the fullness of salvation, it was not enough to just have the shackles loosened; Israel also had to intentionally embrace freedom by making a deliberate choice. As we will see, choosing life meant obeying God's Law (Deuteronomy 4:1). Israel had been in slavery for more than 400 years, so its perspective on life was distorted. God is the only one who has the perfect vantage point—He has a perspective that is situated above all distortions. Obviously, He can tell us what truly constitutes life. That is why Moses urges the people to obey God's statutes and rules, so they can truly live (Deuteronomy 4:1).

God's call is deep and all-encompassing. Its effects have ramifications for every part of our lives. Let us take comfort in the promise Paul expounded on in his letter to the Romans: "Moreover whom he did predestinate, them he also called: and whom he called, them he also justified: and whom he justified, them he also glorified" (Romans 8:30, KJV).

—————

Luvell Anderson obtained his bachelor's degree in philosophy from the University of Missouri at St. Louis, and his PhD in philosophy from Rutgers.

159

Calling, Character, and Compassion

by Dena Dyer

John met Sam, a youth pastor at a local church, at his health club. At first, John scoffed at Sam's profession and made fun of the minister's commitment. But after a while, their surface relationship took a deeper turn as Sam answered John's questions about faith with sincerity and thoughtfulness. Soon, they were meeting for breakfast once a week to discuss their lives and "shoot the breeze."

"Commitment" is defined as a binding, as by a promise or pledge. When we invite Christ to be the Lord of our lives, we promise or bind ourselves to Him. This pledge changes our lives and, if we follow Christ daily, it can change our relationships and the world.

Many times, Christians are taught that commitment is the fruit of belief in Christ. However, I believe that commitment is the seed (planted by belief) that leads to other fruit like calling, character, compassion, and, ultimately, converts.

First of all, Scripture teaches us that we are chosen or called from the womb. David sings, "In thy book all my members were written, which in continuance were fashioned, when as yet there was none of them" (from Psalm 139:16). The prophet Isaiah affirms, "The LORD hath called me from the womb" (from Isaiah 49:1).

Our calling leads us to a cause: bringing justice, mercy, and hope to a broken planet, one person at a time. When the Holy Spirit reigns in us, God helps us to not falter or be discouraged in our wounds. Then, as part of His perfect plan, God transforms and uses our hurts as healing tools.

Paul writes, "Blessed be God, even the Father of our Lord Jesus Christ, the Father of mercies, and the God of all comfort; Who comforteth us in all our tribulation, that we may be able to comfort them which are in any trouble, by the comfort wherewith we ourselves are comforted of God" (2 Corinthians 1:3-4). In other words, God holds our hand through our trials so that we can hold others' hands when they go through pain.

Several years ago, my friend Jamie lost her daughter in a tragic car accident on Christmas Day. Though she would never have chosen to suffer such a loss, she has seen God use her suffering many times to help other grieving parents and families. In my own life, God has brought good out of a miscarriage and depression by opening doors to ministry that otherwise would have been closed.

Several months into his friendship with Sam, John's wife, Amy (who was pregnant with their second child), had to be hospitalized to try to prevent premature labor. Sam rallied his church members (most of whom didn't even know John) to provide meals for the family. In addition, Sam's youth group took turns mowing the family's lawn, babysitting, and keeping groceries in the refrigerator.

"Why are you doing this?" John asked his buddy during one of Sam's visits to the hospital.

"I've been where you are," Sam said. *"And my church family took care of me and my wife and kids. That's what we do as brothers and sisters in Christ."*

In Isaiah, God says over and over that He is our strength, and that He will equip us to help the weary and downtrodden. When Isaiah draws a portrait of the Suffering Servant, we can find comfort in knowing we are not abandoned during painful seasons in our lives. Jesus was despised, rejected, and spat upon so that He could identify fully with us. Praise God, we are never alone!

As the Apostle Peter wrote, "Beloved, think it not strange concerning the fiery trial which is to try you, as though some strange thing happened unto you: But rejoice, inasmuch as ye are partakers of Christ's sufferings; that, when his glory shall be revealed, ye may be glad also with exceeding joy" (1 Peter 4:12-13). Part of that glory is a new depth of character, the second fruit of commitment, which emerges out of the flames of suffering (cf. James 1:2-4).

Other facets of character that come from the seed of commitment include temperance, self-control, kindness, hospitality, gentleness, contentment, sincerity, and sound doctrine, which are all qualities that Paul urges Timothy to develop and to seek out in potential church leaders. That's what we'll become if we continue to seek after Christ and model ourselves after Him.

What man or woman of faith do you admire? It's likely that they have gone through intense grief. Former missionary and prolific author Elisabeth Elliot tells the story of one of her fans coming up to her and saying, "Oh, I wish I could write as you do!" Elisabeth replied, "Do you want to suffer as I have?"

Like Elliot or biblical heroes such as Shadrach, Meshach, and Abednego, we can become strengthened in faith, prayer, and holiness through the fiery furnaces (death, divorce, despair, etc.) in our lives. In those times, we are more likely to rely on God and cling to His hand. And if we submit to God's chisel and the heat of the flame, other people will come to believe in Jesus, too.

As John and Amy faced the fact that they were not in control of what happened to their unborn child, they began to cling to each other and to question their former resistance to God and the church. Each act of kindness by Sam's youth group pried their spirits open a little bit more. By the time the baby was born—small but healthy—they had agreed to visit the church.

"I'm floored by the people I've met," John told Sam. *"I can't believe they would sacrifice so much for someone they don't know."*

Sam smiled and replied, "Jesus died for us and He never met us." John let the words sink in.

Truly, our commitment to Christ leads to the fruit of compassion for others. Like our Savior, we have been anointed by the Holy Spirit to preach the Good News, bind broken hearts, free prisoners, comfort the mourning, and proclaim God's favor. A tall order? Perhaps. But God's gifts (mercy, grace, faith, and love) make sharing His salvation possible, often through the meeting of practical needs.

What is amazing is that our compassion for others can even spark a revolution. In the book titled *A Revolution of Compassion: Faith-Based Groups As Full Partners in Fighting America's Social Problems* by Dave Donaldson and Stanley W. Carlson-Thies, the authors quote J.C. Watts Jr. as saying, "There is a revolution of compassion in our nation to unite Americans who want to help the poor, addicted, hungry, and homeless no matter what their race, religion, or background happens to be... I am convinced more than ever that the foundation of our country must be laid upon strong family values, unflappable character, and the determination to make life better for every citizen regardless of race or creed."

Indeed, cooperation, dedication, and humility are vital because whether it's done by groups or individuals, the true meeting of needs is the heart of the Gospel. Since we model Christ when we clothe the naked, feed the hungry, or visit prisoners, our faithfulness makes the person of Jesus attractive to nonbelievers.

John and Amy visited Sam's church with their young family. Slowly, they began to get involved in Bible studies and small groups. One Sunday morning, John and Amy accepted Christ as their Savior. Not long after, their oldest son made a profession of faith as well. Sam's commitment (and that of his church body) was the seed that bore fruit in calling, character, and compassion.

Ultimately, it flowered into John and Amy's conversion. Now, the new believers are taking their commitment seriously, and there is no telling what fruits will follow.

What fruit has God developed in you? Have you viewed commitment as an end in itself, rather than a means to other ends? Maybe it's time to discern your calling, discipline your character, deepen your compassion, and develop converts for Christ.

Dena Dyer is a writer, speaker, and actress from Granbury, Texas.

162

WILLIAM STILL

(1821–1902)

UNDERGROUND RAILROAD LEADER AND REFORMER

One of the legendary leaders of the Underground Railroad was a freeborn Black man named William Still. His father, Levin Steel, was a former slave from Maryland. After buying his freedom, Steel went to New Jersey and waited for his wife, Sidney, to join him. After her second attempt to escape, Sidney managed to join her husband with all but two of their children. To avoid recapture, the family changed its name to Still and the mother's name to Charity. Later, William was born, the youngest of eighteen children.

As a boy, William helped his father on the family farm. In his early twenties, he left the farm and a few years later went on to Philadelphia. Having had very few educational opportunities as a boy, William taught himself to read and write.

In 1847, William married Letitia George, with whom he later had four children—two boys and two girls. In 1847 he also became secretary of the Pennsylvania Society for the Abolition of Slavery. At that time the Society consisted of a few white members who had little experience with the practical needs of runaway slaves. William, remembering his family's struggles to become free, became such a helpful member of the Society that in 1851,

he was elected its chairman. He later became director of the General Vigilance Committee of Philadelphia, managing its finances and funding Harriet Tubman's numerous raids. He established a network of safe houses from the upper part of the South to Canada. He kept a careful record of each fugitive so family and friends could later locate them in their newfound freedom. For a while, William hid his records in a cemetery, eventually publishing them in a book, *The Underground Railroad*, in 1872.

As a leading conductor of the Underground Railroad, William used his large house as a station. He kept it stocked with food and clothing for the frightened runaways for fourteen years. About 649 slaves were helped in their escape to freedom. William even helped John Brown's widow and daughter when they passed through Philadelphia. In his classic book, William accounts for about 800 escaped slaves, including 60 children, who were helped during eight years. Black churches offered extensive aid, and while some few white churches offered help, most were hostile to runaways. Unfortunately, spies of both races were often present, looking for an opportunity to sell out escaped slaves for money. Even so, the system worked so well that the slave hunters came up with the term "Underground Railroad." Often, while pursuing slaves, the trackers would lose all trace of the runaways. In their frustration and bewilderment, some suggested there must be an underground railroad the fugitives were escaping to, and although it was spoken in bitter sarcasm, the term came into popular use.

As runaways arrived at Underground Railroad stations in his network, William Still personally interviewed them. His meticulous records, along with the accounts of other observers of the runaway phenomenon, show that thousands of slaves vanished daily from the plantations as the numbers of field workers steadily dwindled. He helped dispel the notion that runaway slaves were aided chiefly by white abolitionists and Quakers by documenting the aid that Black churches, institutions, and

especially ex-runaways gave to themselves and each other.

William Still also found time to help organize an association to collect data on Black people. He set up an orphanage for the children of Black soldiers and sailors in Philadelphia and helped organize the first YMCA for Black men. He went into the stove and later, coal business and obtained a modest fortune. He remained active in helping his people develop their potential and gain more civil rights until his death in 1902.

Sources:

Russell L. Adams, Great Negroes Past and Present (Afro-Am Publishing Co., Inc., Chicago, 1969). 31.

Wm. Still Underground R. R. Foundation, Inc., 1998.

Charles L. Blockson, The Underground Railroad (Prentice Hall Press, New York, 19870. 217, 229, 233, 135.

Dumas Malone, Dictionary of American Biography (Charles Scribner's Sons, New York, 1936), Vol. 9, Part 2. 22-23.

Teaching Tips

Words You Should Know

A. Begat (Matthew 1:2) *gennao* (Gk.)—To be the father of, by direct parentage or ancestral ties

B. Express Image (Hebrews 1:3) *charakter* (Gk.)—A stamp or imprint left by a seal on sealing wax; a replica

Teacher Preparation

Unifying Principle—Fulfilling One's Calling. Where we come from often speaks volumes about what we are like. How are people rooted in what has come before? Hebrews affirms the ultimate origins of Jesus in the very life of God, and Matthew explains how he was the product of his long biblical heritage.

A. Read the Bible Background and Devotional Reading.

B. Pray for your students and lesson clarity.

C. Read the lesson Scripture in multiple translations.

O—Open the Lesson

A. Begin the class with prayer.

B. Say: "It's been said that no one comes to faith in Christ without someone else praying for them. What is your spiritual heritage? What people or experiences have shaped you and your faith?"

C. Have the students read the Aim for Change and the In Focus story.

D. Ask students how events like those in the story weigh on their hearts and how they can view these events from a faith perspective.

P—Present the Scriptures

A. Read the Focal Verses and discuss the Background and The People, Places, and Times sections.

B. Have the class share what Scriptures stand out for them and why, with particular emphasis on today's themes.

E—Explore the Meaning

A. Use In Depth or More Light on the Text to facilitate a deeper discussion of the lesson text.

B. Pose the questions in Search the Scriptures and Discuss the Meaning.

C. Discuss the Liberating Lesson and Application for Activation sections.

N—Next Steps for Application

A. Summarize the value of Jesus being God's final word, the one who completes God's plan for humankind.

B. End class with a commitment to praise God for the scope of God's plan throughout history.

Worship Guide

For the Superintendent or Teacher
Theme: Called Through Heritage
Song: "Faith of Our Fathers"
Devotional Reading: Psalm 102:12–22

Called Through Heritage

Bible Background • MATTHEW 1:1–17; HEBREWS 1 | Printed Text • MATTHEW 1:1–6, 16–17; HEBREWS 1:1–5 | Devotional Reading • PSALM 102:12–22

Aim for Change

By the end of this lesson, we will GRASP the significance of Jesus' earthly heritage and His heavenly origins, WONDER at the depth and scope of God's eternal plan to bring salvation through Jesus, and WORSHIP Jesus as God's definitive word to humanity.

In Focus

Lydia loved to study her family genealogy. She found it so interesting to learn about the different people in her past. Connecting with her history gave her a stronger sense of who she was on many levels. As a result of her genealogy research, Lydia discovered why she couldn't settle down. Like many of her ancestors, she shared an inherent need to be free. Lydia didn't think "commitment" would ever be part of her vocabulary.

One thing Lydia didn't have in common with the people in her past was faith in God. She couldn't even commit to the people in her life. How could she commit to a God she couldn't even see? Joe was probably the closest to a best friend that Lydia had ever had. He was a Christian and had witnessed to Lydia on several occasions, but she was a hard case. Joe was aware of her interest in genealogies, so he challenged Lydia.

Joe told her, "If you research the genealogy of Jesus and still come to the conclusion that He's not really the Messiah, then I'll never bother you about your unbelief again."

Lydia accepted the challenge. Two weeks into her research, she accepted Jesus as her personal Savior and Lord. Ironically, Lydia discovered that real freedom requires commitment. By committing her life to Jesus, she was freed from the chains of sin. Now, Lydia tells people how her love of genealogy led her to Christ.

In today's study, researching the ancestry of Jesus will bless you, too, with a closer walk with Him. What meaning does your family history hold for you today?

Keep in Mind

"[God] hath in these last days spoken unto us by his Son, whom he hath appointed heir of all things, by whom also he made the worlds" (Hebrews 1:2, KJV).

"And now in these final days, he has spoken to us through his Son. God promised everything to the Son as an inheritance, and through the Son he created the universe" (Hebrews 1:2, NLT).

Focal Verses

KJV **Matthew 1:1** The book of the generation of Jesus Christ, the son of David, the son of Abraham.

2 Abraham begat Isaac; and Isaac begat Jacob; and Jacob begat Judas and his brethren;

3 And Judas begat Phares and Zara of Thamar; and Phares begat Esrom; and Esrom begat Aram;

4 And Aram begat Aminadab; and Aminadab begat Naasson; and Naasson begat Salmon;

5 And Salmon begat Booz of Rachab; and Booz begat Obed of Ruth; and Obed begat Jesse;

6 And Jesse begat David the king; and David the king begat Solomon of her that had been the wife of Urias;

16 And Jacob begat Joseph the husband of Mary, of whom was born Jesus, who is called Christ.

17 So all the generations from Abraham to David are fourteen generations; and from David until the carrying away into Babylon are fourteen generations; and from the carrying away into Babylon unto Christ are fourteen generations.

Hebrews 1:1 God, who at sundry times and in divers manners spake in time past unto the fathers by the prophets,

2 Hath in these last days spoken unto us by his Son, whom he hath appointed heir of all things, by whom also he made the worlds;

3 Who being the brightness of his glory, and the express image of his person, and upholding all things by the word of his power, when he had by himself purged our sins, sat down on the right hand of the Majesty on high:

4 Being made so much better than the angels, as he hath by inheritance obtained a more excellent name than they.

5 For unto which of the angels said he at any time, Thou art my Son, this day have I begotten

NLT **Matthew 1:1** This is a record of the ancestors of Jesus the Messiah, a descendant of David and of Abraham:

2 Abraham was the father of Isaac. Isaac was the father of Jacob. Jacob was the father of Judah and his brothers.

3 Judah was the father of Perez and Zerah (whose mother was Tamar). Perez was the father of Hezron. Hezron was the father of Ram.

4 Ram was the father of Amminadab. Amminadab was the father of Nahshon. Nahshon was the father of Salmon.

5 Salmon was the father of Boaz (whose mother was Rahab). Boaz was the father of Obed (whose mother was Ruth). Obed was the father of Jesse.

6 Jesse was the father of King David. David was the father of Solomon (whose mother was Bathsheba, the widow of Uriah).

16 Jacob was the father of Joseph, the husband of Mary. Mary gave birth to Jesus, who is called the Messiah.

17 All those listed above include fourteen generations from Abraham to David, fourteen from David to the Babylonian exile, and fourteen from the Babylonian exile to the Messiah.

Hebrews 1:1 Long ago God spoke many times and in many ways to our ancestors through the prophets.

2 And now in these final days, he has spoken to us through his Son. God promised everything to the Son as an inheritance, and through the Son he created the universe.

3 The Son radiates God's own glory and expresses the very character of God, and he sustains everything by the mighty power of his command. When he had cleansed us from our sins, he sat down in the place of honor at the right hand of the majestic God in heaven.

4 This shows that the Son is far greater than the angels, just as the name God gave him is

thee? And again, I will be to him a Father, and he shall be to me a Son?

greater than their names. The Son Is Greater Than the Angels

5 For God never said to any angel what he said to Jesus: "You are my Son. Today I have become your Father." God also said, "I will be his Father, and he will be my Son."

The People, Places, and Times

Joseph and Mary. Both of Jesus' earthly parents were descendants of King David. Joseph was Jesus' earthly and legal father—though not His biological father—and was engaged to Mary when Jesus was conceived by the Holy Spirit. Joseph was a righteous man (Matthew 1:19), meaning he had spiritual discernment and was sensitive to the guidance of the Lord, regardless of the consequences. Mary was chosen by God Himself to be Jesus' mother—to carry, bear, and raise the Savior of the world. The couple had children together after Jesus' birth.

Genealogical Lists. Bible genealogies, though cumbersome for the modern reader, are essential for the worldview of the Bible's original audiences. The lists let the audience feel the weight of the incredible span of years through which God has been working out His plan of cultivating a people for Himself. Genealogies also link Scriptural stories, which can seem far off, with physical, verifiable history. The term "begat" or "fathered" in Scripture can denote an ancestor, not necessarily a direct, biological parent (1 Kings 15:11; 2 Kings 18:3; 22:2). This is not done in a duplicitous manner to obscure timelines or unsavory relations, but to streamline the story and highlight the ancestors who are relevant to the author's purpose.

Background

The Gospels are about the birth, life, death, and resurrection of our Savior. The Old Testament in its entirety lays the groundwork for the birth of the Messiah. It is a bridge connecting the humanness of Jesus—the son of Mary and step-son of Joseph—to the supernatural Christ the King, the Son of God. Delving into the human genealogy of Christ far surpasses the mystery of uncovering our family ancestry. As we search name by name—from Abraham, to Boaz, to Solomon—we realize that all the pieces fit together and give us a perfect picture of Christ.

The original readers of the Letter to the Hebrews faced a dilemma. As Jews, they practiced Judaism all their lives. When the apostles and other Christian believers presented the Good News of salvation to them, many turned to Christ as Lord and Savior. However, some were beginning to wonder how an unknown son of a carpenter from an obscure village called Nazareth could be greater than their forefathers and prophets like Moses. These harried believers needed to be reminded of the essential truth of their new faith. The writer of Hebrews demonstrated that Jesus Christ is superior to all others because He was born of God.

At-A-Glance

1. Jesus' Diverse Ancestry
(Matthew 1:1–6)
2. Jesus' Place in History (vv. 16–17)
3. Jesus' True Heritage (Hebrews 1:1-5)

In Depth

1. Jesus' Diverse Ancestry (Matthew 1:1–6)

Matthew begins by summarizing that Jesus is descended from Abraham and David. God made a covenant with Abraham that from his lineage all the earth would be blessed (Genesis 12:3). God also promised David that an Eternal King would come from his seed (Psalm 89:3–4). This King and global blessing is Jesus Christ.

While establishing Christ as the heir of the covenant and the throne, Matthew's genealogy also refuses to hide the sinners and Gentiles in Jesus' family tree. Tamar resorted to prostitution to force her father-in-law Judah to fulfill his promise of a child through his family. The twins, Perez and Zerah, were the result of that union and have their place in Christ's family (Genesis 38). The Canaanite Rahab was a pagan and perhaps a prostitute (Joshua 2:11), but heard of the awesome power of God and decided to join God's people. Rahab's son Boaz married another foreigner who became a faithful follower of God, Ruth. Even the great King Solomon was born from a marriage that began with deceit and murder (2 Samuel 11:2–17).

In what ways has God redeemed the negative parts of your family history and made them into something beautiful? How has your family included those who were not born into the family?

2. Jesus' Place in History (vv. 16–17)

While Joseph was the man who reared Jesus, he is not Jesus' true father. Nevertheless, Jesus was heir to all the genealogical history of earthly ancestry. Despite what we might see as family "baggage" He "grew in wisdom and in stature" (Luke 2:52, NLT).

Through the list of his earthly heritage, Matthew grounds Jesus in Jewish history. Abraham was the Father of the Faith. David was the king of the Promise. The period of the Babylonian exile saw the vast loss of life and the loss of God's presence in the Temple. Just as fourteen generations passed between each of these major events in Jewish history, now fourteen more generations have passed since the exile. In this presentation of lineage, Matthew shows the progression of God's plan in salvation history.

Matthew's genealogy emphasizes the Jewishness of Jesus. How would you present your genealogy to emphasize your ethnicity? Are you able to trace the genealogy of your faith through those who led you to salvation?

3. Jesus' True Heritage (Hebrews 1:1-5)

As already mentioned, Joseph is not Jesus' true father. While Matthew communicates Jesus' humanness through His earthly father's genealogy, the writer of Hebrews affirms Jesus' divinity through His Heavenly Father. To support this argument, the author turns to Scripture. He first quotes from a messianic psalm (Psalm 2:7). While this psalm's promise was already metaphorically fulfilled in the reigns of David and Solomon, the Promise finds its full, literal completion in Jesus. The second quote likewise is initially, partially fulfilled in Solomon (2 Samuel 7:14). God's covenant with David promised that David's "son" would be an eternal king over God's people. Solomon inherited these blessings but ultimately failed to live up to God's standard. As later prophesied, David's "son," Jesus, demonstrated faithfulness through His life and death. As prophesied, Jesus inherited the blessings of the Davidic covenant. The idea of inheritance (v. 4) is a key concept in Hebrews. Since Jesus is the Son of God, He is able to pass an eternal inheritance to those who follow Him. Jesus' followers become one with Christ and therefore inherit all that Christ inherits.

What would our faith mean if Jesus were not divine?

Search the Scriptures

1. What is significant about each of the women mentioned in Jesus' genealogy? (Matthew 1:3, 5–6, 16)

2. After completing His sacrifice on Calvary for the forgiveness of our sin, where did Jesus go? (Hebrews 1:4)

3. What are two reasons Jesus is superior to angels? (v. 5)

Discuss the Meaning

Many in the world will challenge your belief in Jesus Christ. They will say He was a great teacher, a good moral example, but just a man. He is often given the same status as Buddha, Confucius, Muhammad, or other great religious leaders. What would you say to them about who Jesus really is?

Liberating Lesson

Believers today can marvel at the scope of God's plan—creating a people through Abraham, establishing a nation through David, and making all humanity a part of both through Jesus. Even if you do not know your heritage, you can claim this spiritual heritage. Every Christian, no matter their biological parentage, stands on the spiritual heritage of all our spiritual forefathers from Abraham and Paul, to St. Augustine and Martin Luther King, Jr.

Application for Activation

Jesus is the culmination of God's work of bringing salvation to the world through one sinful family line. Jesus is God's final and definitive word for humanity. He is our perfect example of living into the great faith heritage you inherit from your family. He is also our perfect example of rising above the family drama that can hold you back from fulfilling God's plan for your life. This week think of one family member who imitated Christ's example

for you and thank that person (in person or spirit) for helping you in your spiritual walk.

Follow the Spirit

What God wants me to do:

_____

_____

_____

_____

Remember Your Thoughts

Special insights I have learned:

_____

_____

_____

_____

More Light on the Text

Matthew 1:1-6, 16-17; Hebrews 1:1-5

Matthew 1:1 The book of the generation of Jesus Christ, the son of David, the son of Abraham.

From the fourth word of his Gospel, Matthew clearly asserts that Jesus is the Christ. "Christ" (Gk. *Christos*, **KHREES**-toce) in Hebrew is "Messiah" (*mashiyach*, maw-**SHEE**-akh). Both titles mean "anointed." In the Old Testament, the term anointed is frequently applied to kings and priests, and sometimes to prophets. Jesus Christ fulfilled all three functions of king, priest, and prophet.

Jesus was "the son of David, the son of Abraham" (Matthew 1:1). David and Abraham are the two most important names in Jesus' genealogy. David's name shows that Jesus is of royal descent and the Messiah (see 9:27; Acts 2:30). Jews consider "son of David" as a messianic title (Isaiah 9:7). Abraham's name points to Jesus' Jewish origin (Genesis 22:18). With these first words, Matthew presents Jesus as the Messiah directly descended from the royal house of David and the seed of the patriarch Abraham, to whom the divine promises were first given.

2 Abraham begat Isaac; and Isaac begat Jacob; and Jacob begat Judas and his brethren;

Matthew's genealogy begins with Abraham, to whom the promise of blessing all nations was made. While Luke traces Jesus' genealogy to Adam (Luke 3:38), to show Christ's authority over all humanity, Matthew is more interested in highlighting Jesus' Jewishness. In Abraham, the Jewish faith began—a faith that withstands much testing (Hebrews 11:17–19). Abraham is called "the Friend of God" (James 2:23), "faithful" (Galatians 3:9), and "the father of us all" (Romans 4:16). Abraham was declared by God to be the father of a multitude and called by God for the specific purpose of blessing the world (Genesis 12:2-3, 7).

Abraham's son Isaac is a type of Christ because he was a child of promise. Also like Christ, he was to be sacrificed by his father, in his case, he was miraculously saved. One of Isaac's sons, Jacob (later renamed Israel) was chosen as the heir of the promise from inside the womb (Genesis 25:23). God's grace chooses him over his older twin brother Esau. Matthew lists Jacob as Jesus' earthly ancestor. "Judas" is the Greek spelling of "Judah" (NLT), one of Jacob's sons. As we see, the ancestors' list is not an exhaustive inventory of Jesus' family tree.

3 And Judas begat Phares and Zara of Thamar; and Phares begat Esrom; and Esrom begat Aram;

Judah was the fourth son of Jacob and Leah. Judah participated in the plot to kill his brother Joseph but then intervened to save his life by selling him into slavery instead (Genesis 37:26-27). He took a lead in the affairs of the family and was given a blessing of leadership by his father Jacob (Genesis 46:28; 49:8-12). Judah resided among the Canaanites at Adullam for a time and married a Canaanite woman.

Judah's son Er also married a Canaanite woman, named Tamar (Greek spelling: Thamar). Er died prematurely (Genesis 38:1–7) and although Judah tried to help provide for Tamar at first (having his second son marry her to provide her with an heir), his generosity gave out when his second son also died. Judah withheld his third son from Tamar, caring more for his own heir than for his twice-widowed daughter-in-law. Tamar, in turn, stooped to posing as a prostitute and slept with Judah to gain progeny. The twin sons born to Tamar were named Perez and Zerah (Greek spelling: Phares and Zara), one of whom became an ancestor of the Messiah.

4 And Aram begat Aminadab; and Aminadab begat Naasson; and Naasson begat Salmon; 5 And Salmon begat Booz of Rachab; and Booz begat Obed of Ruth; and Obed begat Jesse;

Aram is not mentioned outside of genealogical lists, but "Nahshon son of Amminadab" is one of the leaders of Israel in the wilderness (Numbers 1:7). We also find these names in David's genealogy (Ruth 4:19) and Moses' (Exodus 6:23).

Like Judah, Nahshon's son Salmon enters what we would today call an interracial marriage. We must not confuse racism with God's prohibition against marrying outsiders. The issue is not the color of the skin, but religious affiliation. Rahab's (Greek spelling: Rachab) willingness to take risks, because she had faith in the God who delivered the Hebrews from Pharaoh, led her to assist Joshua in his conquest of Jericho (Joshua 2-6). In return for her help, Joshua spared her and her household when the Israelites destroyed Jericho (Joshua 6:17-25). Because of her faith in Yahweh, she was naturalized into the people of God and married Salmon. Rahab is regarded as one of the heroes of faith (Hebrews 11:31).

The son born to Salmon and Rahab was Boaz, whom we know from the book of Ruth. He was a wealthy relative of Naomi's deceased husband. When Naomi returned to her homeland after the death of her husband, her daughter-in-law, Ruth, went with her. Ruth had to glean grain in the fields to sustain her mother-in-law and herself. In the process, she met Boaz who showed her favor. Knowing the customs of her people, Naomi instructed Ruth to lie down at Boaz's feet. This was the traditional way of showing that Boaz was responsible for her care. Boaz became her kinsman-redeemer. From this union with yet another outsider came a son named Obed, who had a son named Jesse.

6 And Jesse begat David the king; and David the king begat Solomon of her that had been the wife of Urias;

Jesse had seven sons and two daughters (2 Chronicles 2:13-16), but of all these children, only David is mentioned in this list. David was chosen by God through the prophet and received the promise of a royal Messiah in his lineage. The addition of "the king" (Gk. *basileus*, bah-see-**LAY**-ooce) emphasizes the royal importance of Jesus' ancestry.

Yet again, Matthew mentions the mother of Jesus' ancestor and reminds the audience of the scandalous nature of this union's inclusion in the Messiah's genealogy. Uriah (Greek spelling: Urias) was a Hittite and one of David's top fighting men (2 Samuel 11:3). His wife was Bathsheba, whom David lusted

after, seduced, and impregnated. When David could not scheme to quickly get Uriah to sleep with her and suppose the child to be his, David resorted to having Uriah killed in battle (11:15). Although God took the child conceived in that particular sinful union, God chose David and Bathsheba's next son, Solomon, to be the special recipient of His blessing (12:24).

A curious characteristic of the list of Jesus' ancestors is the mention of four women: Tamar (v. 3), Rahab (v. 5), Ruth (v. 5), and "the wife of Uriah" (v. 6). Women's names seldom appear in Jewish genealogies yet these four are prominent although Tamar, Rahab, and Ruth were Gentiles. Besides this, Tamar posed as a prostitute, Rahab is called a prostitute, Ruth was a Moabite, and Bathsheba was the widow of a Hittite marriage. Yet all of these women are listed as part of God's plan for the salvation of the whole world. Their lives are lessons about the universality of the Gospel and the grace of God toward humanity.

16 And Jacob begat Joseph the husband of Mary, of whom was born Jesus, who is called Christ. 17 So all the generations from Abraham to David are fourteen generations; and from David until the carrying away into Babylon are fourteen generations; and from the carrying away into Babylon unto Christ are fourteen generations.

From David and Solomon, Matthew lists the kings of Israel and Judah until the fall to Babylon and exile, then from the exile to Jesus. Matthew affirms the Jewishness of this genealogy by referencing the numbers of generations. Fourteen is significant because it is seven twice, and seven is the number of completion. His point is that the timing of Jesus' birth fits perfectly with the whole God's plan since He first called Abraham's descendants to be His people. Matthew lists three sets of fourteen generations before the Messiah, and three is a number showing divinity and completion.

Matthew actually excluded four kings of Israel (Ahaziah, Joash, Amaziah, and Jehoiakim) to reach the number fourteen between David and the exile. The word "begat" (Gk. *gennao*, genn-**NAH**-oh) denotes ancestral linkage, without necessarily implying direct parentage. Matthew would expect his audience to know the line of kings of Judah, otherwise, he would not place them so prominently in his Gospel.

Hebrews 1:1 God, who at sundry times and in divers manners spake in time past unto the fathers by the prophets, 2 Hath in these last days spoken unto us by his Son, whom he hath appointed heir of all things, by whom also he made the worlds;

The letter of Hebrews begins with God as the subject. The writer's perspective is noticeably God-centered. He is the omnipresent God who intervened in human history with His sovereign Word addressed to humankind. However, His ultimate Word was One who has a unique relationship with God.

As opposed to a full revelation of His Word, the word "sundry" refers to the gradual uncovering of the mind and will of God revealed his intent through his prophets. "In divers manners" refers to the various methods of communication. In the time of the forefathers, God spoke to Moses in the burning bush (Exodus 3:2 ff.); to Elijah in a still, small voice (1 Kings 19:12 ff.); to Isaiah in a vision in the Temple (Isaiah 6:1 ff.); to Hosea in his family circumstances (Hosea 1:2); and to Amos in a basket of summer fruit (Amos 8:1).

Jesus' divine nature makes Him the right and only capable bearer of God's complete revelation. Jesus is more than a prophet. Jesus Christ alone brings to humanity the full revelation of God. First, he has been "appointed heir of all things." The word "heir" (Gk. *kleronomos*, klay-row-**NO**-moce) denotes one who obtains a lot or portion, especially of an inheritance. If the father had only one son, there was only one heir. Christ, being God's only Son, is the heir of all things. His exaltation to the highest place in heaven after His work on earth was completed, marked His restoration to His rightful place (cf. Philippians 2:6–11).

Second, it is by or through the Son that God made the worlds (cf. John 1:3). This reveals that Jesus is co-Creator with the Father. He is with God in the beginning, just as John also states (John 1:2-3). The word translated as "worlds" is *aionas* (eye-**OH**-nass) in Greek. It literally means, ages or times. This reveals that Jesus is also co-eternal with the Father.

3 Who being the brightness of his glory, and the express image of his person, and upholding all things by the word of his power, when he had by himself purged our sins, sat down on the right hand of the Majesty on high:

Verse 3 continues the description of the Son. He is the "brightness" (Gk. *apaugasma*, ah-**POW**-gas-mah) of God's glory. The meaning of the word *apagausma* is not entirely clear. It could mean something like "radiance or splendor." If the word is understood this way, Jesus is the revelation of the brightness of God's glory. The word could also mean "reflection," in this case Jesus is the reflection of God's glory. In either case, God's glory is manifested in Jesus, and we see His glory as it really is. God in heaven is inapproachable, but Jesus makes it possible to know Him truly and intimately. What a blessing!

Next, the Son is described as "the express image" (Gk. *charakter*, kha-rack-**TARE**) of God's person or being. The word *charakter* refers to the stamp or imprint left by a seal on sealing wax. The imprint has the exact form of the intricately cut seal stone. Thus, Jesus is the exact image or representation of God. When you look at Jesus the Son, you see God perfectly.

Furthermore, the Son is the One "upholding all things by the word of his power." Creation is not left on its own. Jesus is the Sustainer of creation—He carries it along. The Son not only was active in the event of Creation (v. 2) but also maintains an interest in it by continuing to move it toward the accomplishment of God's plan. He does all this by the "word of his power." The "word" (Gk. *rhema*, **HRAY**-mah; not logos) refers here to a command.

The word translated as "purged" is the Greek word *katharismos* (kah-thah-reese-**MOCE**), which means "cleansing" or "purification." It is most often used in the New Testament of ritual cleansing (Mark 1:44). However, it also has ethical implications (1 Corinthians 5:6–7). Here, it refers to the removal of sin. The Good News is that Christ has effected a complete cleansing at Calvary. Jesus is the Redeemer.

Verse 3 ends with the exaltation of Christ. "Sat down on the right hand of the Majesty on high" shows that Christ's saving work is done and that He is now in the place of highest honor. The writer of Hebrews will return to the implicit power behind this image of Christ sitting down, showing how Christ's sacrifice is better than the high priests' sacrifices (Hebrews 10:11-12).

4 Being made so much better than the angels, as he hath by inheritance obtained a more excellent name than they.

To counter the worship of angels, the writer shows the real position of the angels in relation to Christ. In the first century, angels were of great interest in both Jewish and Greek religious thinking. One of the most commonly held beliefs about angels was that they served as intermediaries between God and humans. Fortunately, because of who Jesus is and His sacrifice on the Cross, we have direct access to God. There is no need for anyone else to intercede between humans and God.

The author gives various reasons Jesus is better than the angels. For example, He has "obtained a more excellent name than they." In ancient times, a name meant much more than a differentiating mark or label. Instead, a person's name was an indication of his or her character. Paul tells the Philippian church that Jesus' sacrifice on the Cross earned Him the "a name which is above every name," a name that must be honored by angels, humans, and demons (Philippians 2:9-11).

5 For unto which of the angels said he at any time, Thou art my Son, this day have I begotten thee? And again, I will be to him a Father, and he shall be to me a Son?

Verse 5 is a combination of two Old Testament quotations: Psalm 2:7 and 2 Samuel 7:14. The writer clearly views Psalm 2 as messianic and as bestowing great dignity on Jesus as the Son with God as the Father. In the Old Testament, angels are sometimes designated as "sons of God" (cf. Job 1:6; 2:1). But the truth that Jesus uniquely fit the bill was announced from heaven at Jesus' baptism (Mark 1:10-11) and preached by Paul (Acts 13:33-34).

The second quotation comes from 2 Samuel. Although the words were originally used by Solomon, the writer of Hebrews sees how the Messiah fulfills them more completely than Solomon did. The quotation points to the Father-Son relationship as the fundamental relationship between God and Christ. No angel can claim such a relationship. By joining Psalm 2:7 and 2 Samuel 7:14, the writer provides strong biblical support for the claim that the position of the angels is subordinate to the status of the Son. Christ alone enjoys a unique relationship with the Father with the designation of "my Son."

Sources:

Henry, Matthew. *Matthew Henry's Commentary on the Whole Bible: Complete and Unabridged.* Peabody, MA: Hendrickson, 1991.

McGee, J. Vernon. *Thru the Bible.* Nashville, TN: Thomas Nelson, 1983.

Mills, Watson E., et al., eds. *Mercer Dictionary of the Bible.* Macon, GA: Mercer University Press, 1990.

Zodhiates, Spiros. *Complete Word Study of the New Testament with Greek Parallel.* Iowa Falls, IA: World Bible Publishers, 1992.

Say It Correctly

Perez. **PEA**-rez.
Zerah. **ZEE**-rah.
Hezron. **HEZ**-ron.
Amminadab. ah-**MIN**-uh-dab.
Nahshon. **NAH**-shon.
Salmon. **SAL**-mon.
Bathsheba. bath-**SHEE**-buh.
Uriah. you-**RIE**-uh.

Daily Bible Readings

MONDAY
God's Anointed Ruler of All Nations
(Psalm 2)

TUESDAY
Blessed and Chosen in Christ
(Ephesians 1:1–14)

WEDNESDAY
Christ, Head Over All People/Things
(Ephesians 1:15–23)

THURSDAY
In the Family Line of David
(Matthew 1:6–15)

FRIDAY
God Anoints Jesus King
(Hebrews 1:6–9)

SATURDAY
Jesus, Creator and Eternal Ruler
(Hebrews 1:10–14)

SUNDAY
Expectations of Jesus Before His Birth
(Matthew 1:1–6, 16–17; Hebrews 1:1–5)

Notes

Teaching Tips

Words You Should Know

A. Save (Matthew 1:21) *sozo* (Gk.)—To provide deliverance, protection, well-being, wholeness, healing, and preservation

B. Fulfill (vv. 22) *pleroo* (Gk.)—To make replete, or completely full

Teacher Preparation

Unifying Principle—Called to Participate in a Promise. A newborn baby inspires us to wonder about the potential of every human life. How do we understand the designs of our lives? Joseph's call to form a family with Mary suggests that God calls us to give hope to the world through our families.

A. Read the Bible Background and Devotional Reading.

B. Pray for your students and lesson clarity.

C. Read the lesson Scripture in multiple translations.

O—Open the Lesson

A. Begin the class with prayer.

B. Have volunteers explain the reason they or other children were given a particular name. Were they named for a relative, a celebrity of the time, or a significant event or holiday?

C. Have the students read the Aim for Change and the In Focus story.

D. Ask students how events like those in the story weigh on their hearts and how they can view these events from a faith perspective.

P—Present the Scriptures

A. Read the Focal Verses and discuss the Background and The People, Places, and Times sections.

B. Have the class share what Scriptures stand out for them and why, with particular emphasis on today's themes.

E—Explore the Meaning

A. Use In Depth or More Light on the Text to facilitate a deeper discussion of the lesson text.

B. Pose the questions in Search the Scriptures and Discuss the Meaning.

C. Discuss the Liberating Lesson and Application for Activation sections.

N—Next Steps for Application

A. Summarize the value of combining justice and mercy.

B. End class with a commitment to pray to obey God, even when doing so involves taking risks.

Worship Guide

For the Superintendent or Teacher
Theme: Called Before Birth
Song: "I Know of a Name"
Devotional Reading: Isaiah 42:1–9

Called Before Birth

Bible Background • MATTHEW 1:18–25
Printed Text • MATTHEW 1:18–25 | Devotional Reading • ISAIAH 42:1–9

—————— Aim for Change ——————

By the end of this lesson, we will REMEMBER the story of the angel's announcement to Joseph of Jesus' birth, REJOICE that the birth of Jesus fulfilled God's promise to be with His people, and LIVE with greater awareness of God's abiding presence.

—————— In Focus ——————

Mackinsie and Michael looked at their new baby boy in awe. They were thankful for Mackinsie's mother being able to stay at their house with their other children, giving the parents time alone with their new youngest child. They were also thankful that Michael's Grandmother Opal was on her way to the hospital to meet her newest great-grandbaby. Just two months ago, the family lost Grandpa Steve, Opal's husband, the patriarch of the family. Opal was still grieving deeply, but she felt seeing this new life born so soon after the death of her Steve would be good for her soul.

Grandma Opal held the baby in her arms with practiced grace.

"We wanted to tell you in person, Grandma Opal," Michael said. "Mackinsie and I want to name him Steve, after Grandpa."

The new baby made Grandma Opal smile. But the news of the baby's name sprinkled tears in her eyes. "It's good to have a new Steve in the family," Opal said. "Look how strong that grip is! He'll have Steve's dedication to working hard, for sure," Opal said.

"I hope he'll have Grandpa Steve's sense of humor," Michael said.

"I hope he'll have Grandpa Steve's dedication to the Lord," Mackensie said. "I love that best about this family, how much you boldly show Christ to the world. Be praying for us, Grandma Opal, that we can give little Stevie as good a Christian home as Grandpa Steve gave his kids."

What spiritual heritage did you inherit from your family?

—————— Keep in Mind ——————

"Joseph, thou son of David, fear not to take unto thee Mary thy wife: for that which is conceived in her is of the Holy Ghost. And she shall bring forth a son, and thou shalt call his name JESUS: for he shall save his people from their sins" (from Matthew 1:20-21, KJV).

"'Joseph, son of David,' the angel said, 'do not be afraid to take Mary as your wife. For the child within her was conceived by the Holy Spirit. And she will have a son, and you are to name him Jesus, for he will save his people from their sins'" (from Matthew 1:20-21, NLT).

Focal Verses

KJV **Matthew 1:18** Now the birth of Jesus Christ was on this wise: When as his mother Mary was espoused to Joseph, before they came together, she was found with child of the Holy Ghost.

19 Then Joseph her husband, being a just man, and not willing to make her a public example, was minded to put her away privily.

20 But while he thought on these things, behold, the angel of the LORD appeared unto him in a dream, saying, Joseph, thou son of David, fear not to take unto thee Mary thy wife: for that which is conceived in her is of the Holy Ghost.

21 And she shall bring forth a son, and thou shalt call his name JESUS: for he shall save his people from their sins.

22 Now all this was done, that it might be fulfilled which was spoken of the Lord by the prophet, saying,

23 Behold, a virgin shall be with child, and shall bring forth a son, and they shall call his name Emmanuel, which being interpreted is, God with us.

24 Then Joseph being raised from sleep did as the angel of the Lord had bidden him, and took unto him his wife:

25 And knew her not till she had brought forth her firstborn son: and he called his name JESUS.

NLT **Matthew 1:18** This is how Jesus the Messiah was born. His mother, Mary, was engaged to be married to Joseph. But before the marriage took place, while she was still a virgin, she became pregnant through the power of the Holy Spirit.

19 Joseph, to whom she was engaged, was a righteous man and did not want to disgrace her publicly, so he decided to break the engagement quietly.

20 As he considered this, an angel of the Lord appeared to him in a dream. "Joseph, son of David," the angel said, "do not be afraid to take Mary as your wife. For the child within her was conceived by the Holy Spirit.

21 And she will have a son, and you are to name him Jesus, for he will save his people from their sins."

22 All of this occurred to fulfill the Lord's message through his prophet:

23 "Look! The virgin will conceive a child! She will give birth to a son, and they will call him Immanuel, which means 'God is with us.'"

24 When Joseph woke up, he did as the angel of the Lord commanded and took Mary as his wife.

25 But he did not have sexual relations with her until her son was born. And Joseph named him Jesus.

The People, Places, and Times

Prophet. The biblical prophet is a speaker for God. God communicates directly with him or her sometimes with future predictions and sometimes with commands from God. When He led the Israelites out of slavery and when He gave Moses the Ten Commandments, God spoke to Moses face to face (Exodus 33:11). God spoke frequently to His Old Testament people through the major and minor prophets (Isaiah through Malachi). God still speaks through individuals today, but not in a way that brings novel revelation because we now have the complete Word of God, the Bible, which speaks to all people everywhere.

Angels. The Greek word *aggelos* (**ON**-gell-oce) means "messenger," and can refer to an earthly or heavenly being. Although angels have an exalted position, we are warned never to worship them (Colossians 2:18). Angels serve many functions, but their primary functions are as messengers and ministers of God to humanity (Hebrews 1:14). They bring God's specific commands (Judges 6:11-23; 13:3-5). They assist people in times of distress (1 Kings 19:5-7) and even carry out military missions (2 Kings 19:5-7; Daniel 10:13, 21; 12:1). Jesus indicated the existence of personal guardian angels (Matthew 18:10; cf. Psalm 91:11).

Why does God communicate differently at different times, whether through prophets, angels, or His Son?

Background

The book of Matthew is called the Jewish Gospel because its intended audience is Jewish. It is rooted in Old Testament prophecy related to the coming King through the lineage of King David. The first chapter of Matthew, presents Jesus' royal lineage, describing His kingly line and rightful place as heir to David's throne. His legal inheritance comes through the line of Solomon through Joseph, Jesus' earthly father (Luke 3:23; 4:22). Jesus' lineage proves that He has the right to be called the King of the Jews.

Jesus was conceived by the Holy Spirit, which gives Him the right to be called the Son of God (Matthew 1:18-25). He is fully God and fully human; He is the Living Word who came down from heaven, clothed in human flesh, and dwelled among people (John 1:1-4; Luke 1:26-35; 2:1-7). His virgin birth fulfilled the prophetic utterances of Isaiah (Isaiah 7:14). The sinless and divine nature of Jesus makes Him the only man capable of shedding divine blood on the Cross and becoming the final atonement for our sin.

What does it tell us about God to know that Jesus fulfilled so many prophecies?

At-A-Glance

1. Divine Conception (Matthew 1:18-19)
2. Divine Correction (vv. 20-23)
3. From Divine Clarity to Human Obedience (vv. 24-25)

In Depth

1. Divine Conception (Matthew 1:18-19)

Having laid out the historical background of the Messiah's birth, Matthew introduces an unexpected divine element. When Matthew says that "before they came together, she was found with child of the Holy Ghost," he introduces a problem to the Jewish mind—for them, the Messiah was nothing more than a human being. By stating it this way, Matthew sets the stage to argue that this human being is also God.

Joseph is described as a righteous man. Unlike the Pharisees, who insisted on a rigid reading of the law's justice, Joseph understood the compassion of the Lord. Pregnancy before the actual wedding would render Mary unfaithful. Fully applying the letter of the law, though, would lead to Mary's being stoned to death. Joseph was unwilling to expose her to the disgrace of public divorce. He, therefore, chose a quiet divorce. Thus Joseph would satisfy the requirement of the law and fulfill his sense of covenant righteousness and his compassion.

What do Joseph's actions say about him?

2. Divine Correction (vv. 20–23)

God sent an angel to Joseph in a dream to stop the divorce. The dream imparted three key things. First, Joseph was reassured that Mary had not been unfaithful (v. 20). Joseph must see this child as God's Child, and this event as a God-event. When God speaks into our situation, we see more clearly and our relationships are put in the right perspective. Second, Joseph was told the baby's sex and what He was to be named. The name "Jesus" is a Greek form of the Hebrew name Joshua, which means "the Lord saves." Third, he was told the baby's divine purpose: "he shall save his people from their sins" (v. 21).

God also clarifies the situation by pointing back to Scripture. All this can be understood by what God had already said through the prophet Isaiah. Our belief in God is not wishful thinking. Rather our faith, like Joseph's acceptance of Mary, is grounded in prophetic insight coming directly from God.

3. From Divine Clarity to Human Obedience (vv. 24-25)

Too many of us spend time fighting with God when we should take a lesson from Joseph and stop worrying about how God guides us. God would only command us to do something consistent with His Word. After God told Joseph what to do, human opinion no longer mattered. Instead, he chose to please the One who was in charge of his life. Once God clarifies the events to Joseph and reveals that this was God's work, Joseph married Mary and named the child Jesus as instructed.

God never makes mistakes. He didn't pick just any virgin or any carpenter—and there were likely scores of both in Nazareth. Instead, God chose the couple who would, individually and together, place His will above all else. Their individual and collective actions made the family that paved the way for the new community that would be known as one that fosters belonging and acceptance.

Search the Scriptures

1. Where and why did the angel of the Lord appear to Joseph (Matthew 1:20)?

2. Why was Joseph instructed to name his son Jesus (v. 21)? Why is the prophesied name Emmanuel important (v. 23)?

Discuss the Meaning

1. What does it mean to be "a just man" and "son of David"?

2. Why did God reveal the truth about Mary's miraculous conception only privately to Joseph in a dream? Why not also tell her family or the whole town?

Liberating Lesson

We never hear Joseph speak. When Joseph was disgraced and humiliated by the news of his betrothed's pregnancy, we never hear him speak. When Joseph is told to marry the woman with whom by law he should have severed ties, we never hear him speak. When Joseph learns of Herod's plot to kill Mary's baby, we never hear Joseph speak. When Joseph learns about Herod's death, we never hear him speak. When Joseph realizes that he must take his young bride and the baby Jesus to live in the despised and unimportant town of Nazareth, we never hear Joseph grumble or complain. Why? Is he not human like the rest of us? Surely he must have had strong feelings about the stress and mess of life.

Whatever his feelings may have been, Matthew portrays Joseph as one who guards his tongue. Given all the pressures that crowded in upon Joseph, why do we never hear him vent his feelings? Joseph's aim in life was obedience. The only speaking that Joseph does is through his active response to the Lord's commands.

Application for Activation

As Joseph found, divine clarification must lead to the practical application of God's Word. God reveals things to us so that we might act in concert with the movement of His Spirit in the world. Insights are not given to us so that we can harbor and hoard them for self-promotion, but to create within ourselves a motion to action. God can use us to unfold this divine will, just as He did with Joseph. All we need to do is listen to the Word of God.

This week, reflect on the question: How committed am I to obeying God's Word? Pray and ask God to help you make decisions and govern your family life and relationships in ways that reflect obedience to His will. Make your speech and actions reflect your dedication to doing the will of God.

Follow the Spirit

What God wants me to do:

_____

_____

_____

_____

_____

Remember Your Thoughts

Special insights I have learned:

_____

_____

_____

_____

_____

More Light on the Text

Matthew 1:18-25

18 Now the birth of Jesus Christ was on this wise: When as his mother Mary was espoused to Joseph, before they came together, she was found with child of the Holy Ghost.

The beginning of this verse resumes the story announced in Matthew 1:1. Matthew's goal here is to show the uniqueness of Jesus' birth. We are introduced to Mary who is betrothed to Joseph. Before they are actually married and have sexual relations, Mary is pregnant by the Holy Spirit.

Matthew said Mary was "espoused" (Gk. *mnesteuo*, muh-nace-**TEW**-oo, "to be promised in marriage, to be betrothed") to Joseph. This was not the same as being engaged, though it was similar. In Jesus' day, Jewish marriage consisted of three stages. First came engagement, which was usually arranged (sometimes when the boy and girl were still children) by the parents or a marriage broker. When they were old enough to marry, a formal commitment, to which the man and woman agreed, was made. It required the confirmation of two witnesses. The betrothal agreement, the requirement of witnesses, and a betrothal period indicated intention and deliberation for marrying, not a necessity. Once the couple was betrothed or espoused, they were referred to as husband and wife—note Joseph is "her husband" and Mary is "thy wife" (vv. 19–20). After that agreement, the couple was considered married, though they did not begin living together until after a wedding ceremony: the third stage. That often came about a year later. Dissolving a betrothal required divorce, not annulment, and sexual unfaithfulness during the betrothal period was considered adultery, not promiscuity, for which the penalty was death by stoning (see Deuteronomy 22:23–24).

Mary being found pregnant before coming together with her husband could have been disastrous. No doubt such a scandal was nothing new to Matthew's original audience, as it is not for modern readers. However, this twist is startling when presenting the story of the Messiah's birth, seeming to imply the birth of the world's Savior began in sin. Matthew has a further twist, however, and states that Mary's being with child is not a result of Joseph or any other man, but the Holy Spirit. The Greek word *hagios* (**HAH**-gee-oce), translated as "holy," implies that Mary's condition of being pregnant resulted from something sacred, physically pure, morally blameless, religiously righteous, and ceremonially clean. In the Jewish context, this being could only be God.

19 Then Joseph her husband, being a just man, and not willing to make her a public example, was minded to put her away privily

Note here that Joseph is referred to as the husband of Mary. Even though they are not technically married yet, they are legally bound to be faithful to each other. In truth, since Mary was to be Joseph's wife, Jewish tradition demanded that she should be killed for conceiving a child by another person. But we read that Joseph is righteous (Gk. *dikaios*, dee-**KYE**-oce, "just"). It means that Joseph was equitable in character and practice. It implies that he was innocent and holy. Being "a just man" means that he lived by the laws of God. Jesus often criticized the Pharisees because though they kept the Mosaic Law technically, they often failed to obey its intention. Joseph, however, was not a legalistic Jew. He obeyed God's laws literally, but also, and just as importantly, spiritually.

Mary was pregnant. By law, he had the right to divorce her or to have her stoned to death. Yet, he decided to privately dissolve the engagement. His just nature shows not in terms of giving someone what they deserve, but connotes a sense of mercy and compassion. What made Joseph "just" was the fact that he was determined to take a different position from that of the crowd. Rather than let the sanction of the law take its course, he chose the mercy of the law. To "will" something is to be inclined or glad to do a thing. Just people do not delight or desire to see others hurt even when they are wronged.

The single Greek word translated into the phrase "make her a publick example" is *paradeigmatizo* (pah-rah-dage-mah-**TEED**-zo) means to put to open shame. When a single woman has a baby in a small town, everyone is going to know eventually. Nazareth was no different. Joseph, however, wants to avoid airing his business and seeking legal action. Therefore, he decides to divorce her "privily," that is, privately and quietly. Even though he and Mary are only engaged, breaking off that engagement is still as serious as a divorce. Jesus uses the same word that is used here, "to put her away" (Gk. *apoluo*, ah-po-**LOO**-oh) when He discusses divorce (Matthew 5:31-32, 19:7-9)

We see Joseph not only as an innocent man but as a deeply religious man whose profound reflection on divine things led him to act in ways that set him apart from his generation.

20 But while he thought on these things, behold, the angel of the LORD appeared unto him in a dream, saying, Joseph, thou son of David, fear not to take unto thee Mary thy wife: for that which is conceived in her is of the Holy Ghost.

We find a divine messenger bringing tidings to many of God's people in times of confusion. In Joseph's confusion, he went into contemplation, and in the middle of his contemplation, a heavenly messenger was sent (cf. Acts 10:19). This messenger is meant to lead him into the proper actions. God sent this messenger to bring clarity and drive the confusion away.

The angel addresses Joseph by name and calls him "son of David." This was to remind Joseph of who he really is. Joseph's connection with David immediately reminds him of the covenant promise given to his ancestor David regarding the coming Messiah. Since the Gospel of Matthew was addressed primarily to Christians from a Jewish background, Joseph's Davidic ancestry needed to be clearly shown.

With this familiar and covenant frame of mind, the angel then addresses the issue at hand. The angel speaks to the psychological situation of fear that was keeping Joseph from doing what he knows to be right. In addressing the present situation, the angel did not avoid the fact that Mary was pregnant but assured Joseph that the child was one of divinity.

21 And she shall bring forth a son, and thou shalt call his name JESUS: for he shall save his people from their sins.

In this verse, the angel announces to Joseph that the child is to be named Jesus. After having an angel put his life in historical perspective and explain what was going on in the present, Joseph was probably left with the question: What is the purpose of all this? First, the angel dealt with the immediate future—the child will be a son. Second, the child shall be named Jesus. Jesus (Gk. *Iesous*, **YEAH**-soos) is the Greek form of Joshua (Heb. *Yehoshua*, ye-ho-**SHOO**-ah), which means "Yahweh is salvation." This probably reminded Joseph of the great warrior conqueror who delivered the Children of Israel from their enemies by the power of God. Finally, the angel connects the name of the child with the future act of the child, "he shall save his people from their sins." Jesus was an often-used name for boys then, so Jesus' name not only communicated God's spiritual purpose for Him but at the same time identified Him with the sinful humanity that needed God's forgiveness. God sent Jesus to earth and, in obedience, Jesus came to fulfill His name.

Even though the modern Christian quickly thinks of eternal salvation as the word "save" (Gk. *sozo*, **SOAD**-zo), the use of the word here addresses the salvific view of the people of the Jews. Living amid oppression, Joseph would have understood this term in relation to deliverance and protection. The term "save" also implies healing and preservation. In this period of Israel's oppression, this term also spoke to their need for well-being and wholeness. Many Jews wanted, and most expected, a Messiah who would set them free politically from Roman domination to become a powerful nation again. What made Jesus unique and brought about His rejection was that God's purpose for Him was to set people free spiritually from domination by sin.

22 Now all this was done, that it might be fulfilled which was spoken of the Lord by the prophet, saying,

Here again, we see Matthew's deep entrenchment in Israel's prophetic tradition as he points us back to the Old Testament. Matthew insists throughout his Gospel that Jesus is the Messiah because He fulfills all the prophecies in astonishing ways. He tells us that everything that is happening here has been spoken by the prophets. This sets the coming of Jesus in a larger context. It was not a circumstance of luck or human will. Jesus' birth was the fulfillment of the divine purpose, a long process of development, the continuity within history. "That it might be fulfilled" is a common refrain throughout Matthew's Gospel (see 4:14; 8:17; 12:17).

Isaiah prophesied in a message to King Ahaz about a coming birth and the salvation of God's people (Isaiah 7:10-16). A key term here is "fulfill" (Gk. *pleroo*, play-**ROW**-oh), which means to make replete, to make completely full. Thus, this experience furnishes Joseph with an explanation of the text in the Old Testament. In a sense, God inspired the word of the prophet with meaning for the reader. It also means that what has been promised is now being executed.

23 Behold, a virgin shall be with child, and shall bring forth a son, and they shall call his name Emmanuel, which being interpreted is, God with us.

185

God's revelation of His divine plan for us is amazing here. Isaiah and Matthew understand the fulfillment of this prophecy differently. When Isaiah first spoke those words to King Ahaz, he did not realize it was a messianic prophecy. At that time, Isaiah saw the Israelite and Aramite armies joining to fight the nation of Judah and spoke God's words to the king: before a young woman could conceive and give birth, it would be obvious that God was with His people. Before the child would learn right from wrong, the land would be even more prosperous than before (Isaiah 7:14-17).

The Hebrew word Isaiah used here is 'almah (**AL**-maw) which refers to a young female. At this stage of life, a woman would be ready for marriage or just married. In biblical times, females married at a very early age and the bride was expected to be a virgin. The word's meaning emphasizes the woman's youth, though she is also understood to be virginal. When the Old Testament was translated into Greek, the word used here was *parthenos* (**PAR**-theh-noce). This is the word used for the equivalent stage of life, but the idea of virginity comes more to the fore.

The name Emmanuel explains the nature of the child who is to be born. Emmanuel is the combination of *im* (Heb. **EEM**), which means with; a suffix meaning us (-*nu*, **NEW**); and the word *el* (Heb. **ELL**), which means God. Isaiah spoke of how God's blessings would reveal Him to be the "With-us God," but Matthew shows his audience that Jesus is the incarnate "With-us God."

By referencing this prophecy, Matthew shines a spotlight on an amazing revelation from God. Isaiah saw his prophecy come true. In less than a year (time for a maiden to marry, to conceive, bear, and name her child), Judah was indeed delivered from the army's threat. But then the Greek translation of Isaiah's words brought out a further understanding. This is what Matthew highlights as he reports Christ's birth. More than just a young girl having a baby, a young girl who had never even had sexual relations would have a baby. More than just feeling God's presence in His blessings on His people, God's people would truly, physically experience His presence. God had already kept His word to Isaiah. With the birth of the Messiah, He keeps His word again. This time its fulfillment abundantly overflows to an extent that few had hoped for.

24 Then Joseph being raised from sleep did as the angel of the Lord had bidden him, and took unto him his wife: 25 And knew her not till she had brought forth her firstborn son: and he called his name JESUS.

When Joseph awakens from this dream, he immediately goes about obeying its message. Joseph agreed to the solution that the angel had proposed. It also implies that Joseph committed himself to continue to exercise himself fully in the Word of God revealed to him. What God had ordained was now going to be his purpose. His reason for rising up was not to transgress the law but to live out the revelation.

When Matthew said Joseph "took" Mary as his wife, that simple word says so much. First, it means he accepted her as his wife. Second, he abandoned any suspicion about infidelity by Mary. Third, although the Scripture gives no specifics, Joseph likely went ahead with the wedding and the Jewish traditions that went with beginning a marriage. Fourth—and most important—he became indispensable in preparing for the Savior's life during Mary's pregnancy.

The phrase "knew her not" means that Joseph had absolutely no sexual relationship with her. The next word "till" suggests that Joseph continued in a state of abstinence until or for as long as Mary was pregnant. After Jesus was born, Joseph and Mary would live together as husband and wife for many years and have several of their own children. However, Joseph wants there to be no mistake, no reason to suspect that Jesus was his biological son. He knows the Child is destined for a holy task and he is dedicated to doing all he can to help Him along the way.

Sources:
Baab, O.J. "Virgin," *Interpreters Dictionary of the Bible*. Vol. 4. R–Z. Nashville, TN: Abingdon Press, 1962.

Filson, Floyd V. *The Gospel According to St. Matthew*. Peabody, MA: Hendrickson Publishers, 1987.

Green, Michael. *Matthew for Today: Expository Study of Matthew*. Dallas, TX: Word Publishing, 1988.

Hobbs, Herschel H. *The Gospel of Matthew*. An Exposition of the Four Gospels, Vol. 1. Grand Rapids, MI: Baker Book House, 1965.

Lightfoot, John. *A Commentary on the New Testament from the Talmud and Hebraica*. Matthew–1 Corinthians. Vol. 2. Matthew–Mark. Grand Rapids, MI: Baker Book House, 1979. (Reprinted from 1859 edition.)

Schweizer, Eduard. *The Good News According to Matthew*. Atlanta, GA: John Knox Press, 1975.

Say It Correctly

Davidic. dah-**VID**-ik.
Aramite. **AIR**-am-ite.

Daily Bible Readings

MONDAY
Sign of God's Presence
(Isaiah 7:10–15)

TUESDAY
Called a Light of the Nations
(Isaiah 42:1–9)

WEDNESDAY
Called to Mission Before Birth
(Isaiah 49:1–7)

THURSDAY
Birth of Jesus Foretold to Mary
(Luke 1:26–38)

FRIDAY
Simeon Foretells Jesus' Ministry
(Luke 2:34–38)

SATURDAY
Mary, in the Lineage of Ruth
(Ruth 4:9–17)

SUNDAY
Miracle of the Holy Spirit Conception
(Matthew 1:18–25)

Notes

Teaching Tips

Words You Should Know

A. Enquired Diligently (Matthew 2:7) *akriboo* (Gk.)—To perfectly follow a law; to thoroughly understand a subject

B. Young Child (v. 11) *paidion* (Gk.)—The life stage after infancy

Teacher Preparation

Unifying Principle—International Honor for the King of the World. As our world gets smaller, we are more and more exposed to people who differ from us in race, culture, and religious values. Where can we find unity in such a world? By summoning wise men from far-off lands to worship Jesus, God demonstrated that this newborn King would transcend the differences that divide us.

A. Read the Bible Background and Devotional Reading.

B. Pray for your students and lesson clarity.

C. Read the lesson Scripture in multiple translations.

O—Open the Lesson

A. Begin the class with prayer.

B. Facilitate a discussion in class asking about how to present the Gospel to a member of another religion. Should a Christian start with tenants of the other religion that are similar to Christianity and find common ground or is it better to emphasize the differences between the religions?

C. Have the students read the Aim for Change and the In Focus story.

D. Ask students how events like those in the story weigh on their hearts and how they can view these events from a faith perspective.

P—Present the Scriptures

A. Read the Focal Verses and discuss the Background and The People, Places, and Times sections.

B. Have the class share what Scriptures stand out for them and why, with particular emphasis on today's themes.

E—Explore the Meaning

A. Use In Depth or More Light on the Text to facilitate a deeper discussion of the lesson text.

B. Pose the questions in Search the Scriptures and Discuss the Meaning.

C. Discuss the Liberating Lesson and Application for Activation sections.

N—Next Steps for Application

A. Summarize the value of working to bring healing and reconciliation in the areas of racial, cultural, and religious division.

B. End class with a commitment to pray for people who suffer innocently for the brokenness and sin in the world.

Worship Guide

For the Superintendent or Teacher
Theme: A Regal Response to Holy Light
Song: "The Coventry Carol"
Devotional Reading: Exodus 1:8–22

A Regal Response to Holy Light

Bible Background • MATTHEW 2:7–15
Printed Text • MATTHEW 2:7–15 | Devotional Reading • EXODUS 1:8–22

—————————— Aim for Change ——————————

By the end of this lesson, we will EXPLAIN how the wise men point to the universality of Jesus' mission, GRIEVE for those who suffer innocently due to the world's brokenness and sin, and JOIN with peoples of every ethnicity and culture to worship Jesus, the King of all nations.

—————————————— In Focus ——————————————

Rather than exchanging gifts, Kathy's family went on a Christmas tour of the Holy Lands, beginning in Egypt. They did all the touristy things—seeing the great pyramids, sailing up the Nile River, and even getting on camels for pictures. Their tour guide focused on the time the Israelites were enslaved in Egypt, but Kathy was thinking of Mary, Joseph, and young Jesus seeking sanctuary here while King Herod was carrying out his plan to murder any potential rival king. Kathy followed the tour guide through a market teeming with brown and black people, some matching her own skin tone. She thought that the white people often portrayed in Bible art would surely stand out in a crowd like this. A more historically accurate portrayal of the holy family would blend right in, here in Mother Africa.

Kathy's son, Stephen, had begun saying that Jesus was only for white people. "Not only was Jesus first imposed on us by slave owners," Stephen would say, "He also doesn't seem to care about black issues like police brutality, colorism, or badly funded schools." Here in Egypt, though, Kathy could see that idea was wrong. Jesus was no "white Savior"; He was everyone's Savior. That night she shared her photos and thoughts with Stephen. Kathy's trip to Egypt and Israel made her feel even closer to Jesus.

What happens when we view historic happenings through only one cultural lens? How do we make sure we are not blind to the unique perspectives of other cultures' lenses?

—————————————— Keep in Mind ——————————————

"And when they were come into the house, they saw the young child with Mary his mother, and fell down, and worshipped him: and when they had opened their treasures, they presented unto him gifts; gold, and frankincense and myrrh" (Matthew 2:11, KJV).

"They entered the house and saw the child with his mother, Mary, and they bowed down and worshiped him. Then they opened their treasure chests and gave him gifts of gold, frankincense, and myrrh" (Matthew 2:11, NLT).

Focal Verses

KJV **Matthew 2:7** Then Herod, when he had privily called the wise men, enquired of them diligently what time the star appeared.

8 And he sent them to Bethlehem, and said, Go and search diligently for the young child; and when ye have found him, bring me word again, that I may come and worship him also.

9 When they had heard the king, they departed; and, lo, the star, which they saw in the east, went before them, till it came and stood over where the young child was.

10 When they saw the star, they rejoiced with exceeding great joy.

11 And when they were come into the house, they saw the young child with Mary his mother, and fell down, and worshipped him: and when they had opened their treasures, they presented unto him gifts; gold, and frankincense and myrrh.

12 And being warned of God in a dream that they should not return to Herod, they departed into their own country another way.

13 And when they were departed, behold, the angel of the Lord appeareth to Joseph in a dream, saying, Arise, and take the young child and his mother, and flee into Egypt, and be thou there until I bring thee word: for Herod will seek the young child to destroy him.

14 When he arose, he took the young child and his mother by night, and departed into Egypt:

15 And was there until the death of Herod: that it might be fulfilled which was spoken of the Lord by the prophet, saying, Out of Egypt have I called my son.

NLT **Matthew 2:7** Then Herod called for a private meeting with the wise men, and he learned from them the time when the star first appeared.

8 Then he told them, "Go to Bethlehem and search carefully for the child. And when you find him, come back and tell me so that I can go and worship him, too!"

9 After this interview the wise men went their way. And the star they had seen in the east guided them to Bethlehem. It went ahead of them and stopped over the place where the child was.

10 When they saw the star, they were filled with joy!

11 They entered the house and saw the child with his mother, Mary, and they bowed down and worshiped him. Then they opened their treasure chests and gave him gifts of gold, frankincense, and myrrh.

12 When it was time to leave, they returned to their own country by another route, for God had warned them in a dream not to return to Herod.

13 After the wise men were gone, an angel of the Lord appeared to Joseph in a dream. "Get up! Flee to Egypt with the child and his mother," the angel said. "Stay there until I tell you to return, because Herod is going to search for the child to kill him."

14 That night Joseph left for Egypt with the child and Mary, his mother,

15 and they stayed there until Herod's death. This fulfilled what the Lord had spoken through the prophet: "I called my Son out of Egypt."

The People, Places, and Times

Herod. The Herod featured in today's Scripture passage is known as "Herod the Great." He was a descendant of Antipater, an Edomite who converted to Judaism in the 2nd century BC. An exceptionally cruel king, Herod ordered the murder of one of his wives, mother-in-law, brother-in-law, uncle, and at least three sons. Although the Jews did not like him because of his friendliness with the Romans, he brought enough stability to Galilee and Judea that he gained some independence from Rome for the Jewish people. He is also remembered as a great builder. His biggest achievement was renovating the second temple in Jerusalem, which was not completed until 68 years after his death.

Magi. The words "wise men," translated Magi (singular: magus), refer to a group of men who may have studied the stars. Because the Bible says they came from the East, many scholars believe they were Babylonian astrologers. The wise men first come to Jerusalem because of a star, a special manifestation from God to indicate a Jewish king's birth. They then come to Bethlehem following the star again and find Jesus. Tradition says there were three of them, but Scripture never gives a number. The idea that there were three of them comes from the number of gifts they offered to the Christ Child (v. 11).

Background

Matthew 2 opens with wise men coming from the East in search of the newborn King of the Jews. Although we are familiar with the non-biblical story of three wise men, Scripture says that they were all from the East. To people of New Testament days, that would probably have been from Persia, modern-day Iran. This was a center of much belief in astrology. The Bible makes very clear that the study of horoscopes is wrong (Deuteronomy 4:19). It ascribes divine plans to the created stars and moon. Yet God uses His creation to unexpectedly bring people to Himself. In calling these Gentiles from far away, God showed that Christ came for us all.

The wise men were astrologers and saw some sort of unusual star (possibly a conjunction of planets) that indicated to them that a new king of the Jews was born. So they traveled to Jerusalem, the capital, where they expected to see this baby. They almost certainly arrived in a great caravan with many servants. Hearing that a new Jewish king has been born, Herod instantly knows this must be the Messiah. The jealous and power-hungry king asks his scholars where the Messiah was predicted to be born.

At-A-Glance

1. Foreigners Before a King
(Matthew 2:7–8)
2. Foreigners Before the King (vv. 9-11)
3. The Messiah in a Foreign Land
(vv. 13-15)

In Depth

1. Foreigners Before a King (Matthew 2:7–8)

The paranoid King Herod took no chances on a potential rival, even if it was just a baby. After Herod's scholars told him where the Messiah was to be born, he has a private meeting with the wise men. He tells them to bring him back the news of the Messiah's whereabouts after they find Him. Herod says this is so he can worship Him, too. Of course, Herod has no such intentions.

We see in this story different responses to Jesus. In Herod, we see outright opposition. Even though Herod is king of the Jews, he does not rejoice at his promised Messiah's birth. He sees Jesus, instead, as a rival, one who could take control away from him. Then we see the wise men—foreigners without much biblical understanding—and yet these were the ones who set aside everything else in their lives to truly know Him.

Herod knew a great deal about the Messiah. Why would anyone who knows about Jesus Christ, sit on the information rather than respond positively to it?

2. Foreigners Before the King (vv. 9-11)

After leaving Herod, the wise men continued their search. As they traveled, the star reappeared and guided them from Jerusalem to Bethlehem. By the supernatural light of that star, the wise men found the Perfect Light, Jesus.

Mary and Joseph were married and living in a house in Nazareth (Luke 2:39). When the wise men arrived, they immediately knelt and worshiped the holy Child. The wise men worshiped Christ before He performed any miracles, preached any sermons, or healed any sick. Their worship was based solely on who He was, not what He did. They honored Him with special gifts worthy of His divine station (v. 11). We should all do as the wise men: find Jesus, accept Him as Lord and Savior, and worship Him!

The Magi did not listen to what King Herod told them to do. A higher authority spoke to them through a dream and told them not to return to Herod. God warned them and they obeyed His warning, returning home a different way.

Share about a time you had to disregard an authority figure to follow God's guidance instead.

3. The Messiah in a Foreign Land (vv. 13-15)

After the wise men departed, God also warned Joseph about Herod's plan. In a dream, Joseph learned that Herod was searching for the child with the intent of killing Him. Joseph was instructed to pack up and move his family to Egypt. When Herod found out that the wise men were aware of his scheme and had left the country by another route, he was furious (v. 16). He ordered his soldiers to go to Bethlehem and kill every male two years old and under. This tragedy fulfilled another prophecy. The destruction caused by sinful, evil humans sets a sorrowful stage that God will soon turn to joy (Jeremiah 31).

Joseph follows the angel's directions and moves to Egypt, returning home only when Herod was dead. Because Jesus' childhood followed this journey, Matthew notes that He fulfills yet another prophecy of coming "Out of Egypt."

How have you noticed God's protection in your life as you followed His direction?

Search the Scriptures

1. What information did Herod want from the wise men? Why did King Herod say he wanted it? (Matthew 2:8)

2. How did Jesus' flight to Egypt help prove He is the Messiah? (v. 15)

Discuss the Meaning

1. Both the Magi and Herod have a high social standing in their lands. Why is their reaction to Jesus' birth so different?

2. Even though God tells His people not to trust astrology, He uses His creation to communicate with the Magi. What does this reveal about God's nature?

Liberating Lesson

The Enemy is happy to remind us of any excuse to cut ourselves off from one another, creating distance and mistrust between groups that could enjoy unity. Believers must work to bring healing and reconciliation in the areas of racial, cultural, and religious division. How does the Gospel especially resonate with minority, refugee, immigrant, or foreign voices?

Application for Activation

The Magi came to Jesus and worshiped their way, by bowing to the ground and giving gifts. Are you welcoming to other cultures' worship traditions in your church? Jesus' family left their ancestral land and lived in another country. How would you continue to worship God and be a witness of the Gospel in a foreign country? Work with a local charity or immigrant population to invite immigrants to lead a worship service at your church.

Follow the Spirit

What God wants me to do:

_____

_____

_____

_____

_____

_____

Remember Your Thoughts

Special insights I have learned:

_____

_____

_____

_____

_____

_____

More Light on the Text

Matthew 2:7-15

7 Then Herod, when he had privily called the wise men, enquired of them diligently what time the star appeared. 8 And he sent them to Bethlehem, and said, Go and search diligently for the young child; and when ye have found him, bring me word again, that I may come and worship him also.

Having discovered where this King would be born, Herod called the wise men unto him "privily," or secretly. From other usages of the word (Matthew 1:19; Acts 16:37), we can infer that the word implies trying to avoid a public outcry. Jerusalem is already in an uproar over the Magi's arrival (Matthew 2:3).

We read further that he inquired of them the exact or specific time of the star's appearance. Why does he want to know the time the star appears? The Magi understood that the star had risen at the time of the child's birth. By Herod's later acts, we can surmise that the Magi saw the star up to two years prior (v. 17).

The verb "enquired diligently" (Gk. *akriboo*, ah-kree-**BOW**-oo) is related to the adverb "diligently" (Gk. *akribos*, ah-kree-**BOCE**) in v. 8. It is related to ideas of perfectly following a law or thoroughly understanding a subject. Instead of spending his efforts to thoroughly understand the Messianic prophecy, which he knew, Herod diligently listens to what the Magi tell him so that he can destroy the baby he perceives as a rival to his throne. At least to some extent, Herod believes the Magi are tipping him off to the coming of the Messiah. This is an event the Jews have been eagerly anticipating for centuries. Now Herod learns that the Messiah has come and instead of joy, this fills him with murderous dread. Note also that Herod wants to get the child before He could be of any physical or political threat to him. He is now going to use these men of wisdom to do his dirty work.

9 When they had heard the king, they departed; and, lo, the star, which they saw in the east, went before them, till it came and stood over where the young child was. 10 When they saw the star, they rejoiced with exceeding great joy.

The wise men leave Herod for the six-mile journey south from Jerusalem to Bethlehem. Herod's instruction to "search diligently" is disrupted by the star, which at this point truly becomes a guiding star for the first time. The reappearance of the star confirms the correctness of looking for the child in Bethlehem, and it guides the wise men to the specific location. An important word here is the Greek word *proago* (pro-**AH**-go), which is translated "went before." The star is now seen as a princely messenger leading an audience into the presence of a powerful king. They were led by the light, not by their own wisdom.

We are told that the sight of the star made the Magi "[rejoice] with exceeding great joy." The word "rejoice" comes from the Greek word *chairo* (**KHYE**-ro) which means "to be cheerful or well-off" (cf. Philippians 4:8). Not only does Matthew use the word *chairo*, but he adds *sphodra*. The Greek word *sphodra* (**SFOD**-rah) is translated in the King James Version as "exceeding." As used here, it really means violently or vehemently. As if these were not enough, Matthew also adds another Greek word, *megas* (**MEH**-gass) which literally means big. Translated, they were high in the spirit or they became loud in a mighty way.

11 And when they were come into the house, they saw the young child with Mary his mother, and fell down, and worshipped him: and when they had opened their treasures, they presented unto him gifts; gold, and frankincense and myrrh.

Just as persistent a tradition as there only being three wise men is the tradition that they were at the stable the very night Jesus was born. Some traditions celebrate Epiphany or Kings Day to remember the coming of the wise men, separating it from the shepherds coming the night He was born. Still, this is observed on January 5, which allows only twelve days for the Magi's travels. This verse gives evidence that this was not so. The Magi enter a house (Gk. *oikia*, oy-**KEE**-ah), which refers to the abode or residence of the family—there is no animal manger in sight. Further, it has been almost two years since Jesus' birth. He is a "young child" (Gk. *paidion*, pie-**DEE**-on), rather than the "babe" (Gk. *brephos*, **BREH**-foce) the shepherds met (Luke 2:16). Although *paidion* can be used to refer to infants (Luke 1:59; 2:21), it is more widely used to refer to young children who can walk and talk (Matthew 11:16; Luke 9:47).

It was customary in the ancient East for those who came into the presence of royalty or who sought the favor of the monarch, to present gifts. For example, the Queen of Sheba brought a small fortune to Solomon when she came to hear his wisdom (1 Kings 10:1-2, 10). The "treasures" opened by the Magi were treasure chests containing their valuables. From these, they presented the child, King Jesus, with gifts that were prophetic symbols of the roles He would fulfill in His lifetime. The gold was a gift presented to royalty, thus symbolizing Jesus' role as the long-awaited King of the Jews, the Messiah. The word for "frankincense" (Gk. *libanos*, **LEE**-bah-noce) refers to a tree and the incense made from its sap. The gift of frankincense suggested the divinity or the priesthood of the Child, as it was an incense burned on altars. Myrrh (Gk. *smurna*, **SMOOR**-nah) is similarly extracted from tree resin and was an ointment used for burial in many African traditions. Myrrh is a much-valued spice or scented oil that is still used in many parts of Africa and Asia. Myrrh suggested the role Jesus would play as the One who would die for the sins of the world (John 1:29; 11:49-52). Note that while the Magi now physically opened their treasures, they would not have been opening up these treasures if they had not first opened their hearts to God's revelation. They gave Him gifts that were valuable to them and honored Him, as we should in our worship.

12 And being warned of God in a dream that they should not return to Herod, they departed into their own country another way.

This verse deals with the intervention of the Lord into the wise men's lives to save them from serving as instruments of Herod's work. We are told that the Lord spoke to them. There was a divine intimation that gave them firmness to deal with the business. For the first time in all of these signs and their long journeying, God speaks directly to the Magi. God tells them not to return to Herod. Going back to Herod would have been appropriate according to human thought. It would have been in accord with their perception of themselves as men of honor. Further, since Herod was king, he might have rewarded them immensely for their work. But God gave them a strict injunction. When God gives instructions, they must be followed.

13 And when they were departed, behold, the angel of the Lord appeareth to Joseph in a dream, saying, Arise, and take the young child and his mother, and flee into Egypt, and be thou there until I bring thee word: for Herod will seek the young child to destroy him. 14 When he arose, he took the young child and his mother by night, and departed into Egypt:

For a second time, the angel of the Lord appears to Joseph in a dream. Joseph is just as faithful to obey God's message this time as he was the last. Abraham went by faith even though he didn't know where God was leading,

so Joseph is going by faith even though he doesn't know how long the journey will last. While in Egypt, Joseph must always be ready for God's word to come, telling him to return to the homeland. Again the word "until" indicates a continued need to look and listen closely for God's guidance (cf. v. 9). For secrecy, they leave "by night," though not necessarily that very night.

The Holy Family must leave for Egypt because Herod wants to "destroy" (Gk. *apollumi*, ah-**POLL**-loo-me) Jesus. This word can have a variety of meanings. Throughout Luke 15, the word is used to mean "lost," but in other contexts, the word clearly has more dire connotations. The Pharisees will also want to "destroy" Jesus (Matthew 12:14), a plot that culminates in His crucifixion. Herod here wishes to kill Jesus. He sets himself up directly at odds with Christ and His mission. Christ has come to free us from such tyranny, promising that "the Son of man is come to save that which was lost [*apollumi*]" (Matthew 18:11).

Egyptian territory at that time was a journey of at least 200 miles from Bethlehem. God specifically tells Joseph to go there instead of any closer destination. While going north to Syria was possible, it might have been a dangerous path because it went through Jerusalem, where Herod lived. The holy family could have also gone west to the Mediterranean Sea and set sail as far away from Herod as they wished, but that is not what God instructed. Egypt at this time, while out of Herod's jurisdiction was still under Roman rule, much like Judea except that the province reported more directly to the emperor than Herod did. By fleeing to Egypt, however, Jesus would fulfill prophecy Matthew tells us (v. 15).

Again Joseph displays his obedience to God. He gives prompt, diligent care and protection to Mary and Jesus. He sets a living example of how to respond to God's commands. His example remains as a model of the importance of exhibiting righteous behavior, for church members before each other and especially for Christian parents before their children.

15 And was there until the death of Herod: that it might be fulfilled which was spoken of the Lord by the prophet, saying, Out of Egypt have I called my son.

Matthew's use of Hosea 11:1 as a messianic prophecy causes questions to arise just as they did for Isaiah's prophecy about Emmanuel. The context must drive our interpretation of the text. The prophet Hosea was speaking to the nations of Israel and Judah soon before the Northern Kingdom's fall to the Assyrians. He warned of the Assyrian invasion and the Babylonian exile. After speaking of the sorrow the Israelites will endure in exile, Hosea 11 begins with God's words to His people. He reminds them of their history together, of His great love for them that brought them out of slavery in Egypt. "Out of Egypt have I called my son," was not a prophetic prediction of the future. It had already happened. In the next line of Hosea, God laments that even after He brought them out of Egyptian slavery, the Israelites insisted on worshiping Baal in Canaan (Hosea 11:2). In taking this verse as messianic prophecy, surely Matthew does not mean to imply that this whole section of Hosea describes the Messiah's coming.

Rather, the connection that God is revealing through Matthew's Gospel is that Jesus is the perfect embodiment of Israel. Just as Israel came out of Egypt, so Jesus comes out of Egypt. Further, just as the patriarchs and Israel had to flee from the threat of death, so did Jesus. Moving from place to place repeatedly, especially at a young age, makes one feel they do not have a home. Because of this, Jesus knows the nation's sorrows. This is another way that Christ fulfills Isaiah's prophecy of being "acquainted with grief" (Isaiah 53:3) and how He accomplishes the Messiah's role of living our temptations so that He can be a compassionate High Priest (Hebrews 2:18). Jesus' personal history mirrors Israel's cultural history. Matthew sets up a contrast in highlighting the Hosea prophecy, too. Unlike Israel as Hosea goes on to describe them, Jesus does not worship idols and suffer the punishment of exile. Jesus follows God in the way Israel was supposed to. While Jesus' experiences mirror those of Israel, His reaction to the experiences is perfect. Because He perfectly endured all these trials, He is worthy to be our Savior.

Sources:
Adeyemo, Tokunboh, gen. ed. *Africa Bible Commentary*. Grand Rapids, MI: Zondervan, 2006. 1110–1111.
Hoehner, Harold W. "Herodian Dynasty." *The Oxford Companion to the Bible*. Bruce M. Metzger and Michael D. Coogan, eds. New York: Oxford University Press, 1993. 280–284.
Stagg, Robert. "Herod." *Holman Illustrated Bible Dictionary*. Trent C. Butler, Chad Brand, Charles Draper, and Archie England, eds. Nashville, TN: Holman, 2003. 753–755.
Carson, Matthew. *Expositors Bible Commentary Series*. Vol. 8. Zondervan. 89.
Shaw, Ian, ed. *The Oxford History of Ancient Egypt*. New York: Oxford University Press.
University of Illinois Extension. "Frankincense and myrrh." Illinois ACES. https://aces.illinois.edu/news/frankincense-and-myrrh. Posted November 14, 2012.

Say It Correctly

Antipater. an-**TEE**-pah-tare.
Magus. **MAY**-gus.

Daily Bible Readings

MONDAY
Midwives Frustrate Pharaoh's Decree
(Exodus 1:15–22)

TUESDAY
God Answers Solomon's Dream
(1 Kings 3:5–14)

WEDNESDAY
Insight into the Meaning of Dreams
(Daniel 1:8–17)

THURSDAY
In Christ No Divisions Allowed
(Galatians 3:25–29)

FRIDAY
Gracious Ruler to Come from Bethlehem
(Micah 5:1–5)

SATURDAY
Successful Return from Egypt
(Matthew 2:19-23)

SUNDAY
Safe in the Midst of Danger
(Matthew 2:7-15)

Notes

_____

_____

_____

_____

Teaching Tips

Words You Should Know

A. Wilderness (Matthew 3:1) *eremos* (Gk.)—An uninhabited, deserted place

B. Repent (v. 2) *metanoeo* (Gk.)—To have a changed mind; to think again

Teacher Preparation

Unifying Principle—Get Ready. Important projects require thoughtful preparation. What endeavors demand our greatest efforts in preparation? John called for people to repent of their sins and thus be ready to welcome the soon-coming Messiah.

A. Read the Bible Background and Devotional Reading.

B. Pray for your students and lesson clarity.

C. Read the lesson Scripture in multiple translations.

O—Open the Lesson

A. Begin the class with prayer.

B. Divide the class into groups. Have each group look at Isaiah 40:3-5 and Malachi 4:5-6 and write a job description for the forerunner to the Messiah. Evaluate John's message in today's text using that job description.

C. Have the students read the Aim for Change and the In Focus story.

D. Ask students how events like those in the story weigh on their hearts and how they can view these events from a faith perspective.

P—Present the Scriptures

A. Read the Focal Verses and discuss the Background and The People, Places, and Times sections.

B. Have the class share what Scriptures stand out for them and why, with particular emphasis on today's themes.

E—Explore the Meaning

A. Use In Depth or More Light on the Text to facilitate a deeper discussion of the lesson text.

B. Pose the questions in Search the Scriptures and Discuss the Meaning.

C. Discuss the Liberating Lesson and Application for Activation sections.

N—Next Steps for Application

A. Summarize the value of a life demonstrating repentance.

B. End class with a commitment to pray for preachers in the public eye as they try to prepare people's hearts for Jesus.

Worship Guide

For the Superintendent or Teacher
Theme: Called to Prepare the Way
Song: "Deep River"
Devotional Reading: John 1:19-34

Called to Prepare the Way

Bible Background • MATTHEW 3
Printed Text • MATTHEW 3:1–12 | Devotional Reading • JOHN 1:19–34

—————————— Aim for Change ——————————

By the end of this lesson, we will RECOGNIZE the reality of sin and the necessity of repentance, IDENTIFY with John the Baptist in his call to prepare the way for Christ, and REPENT of their sins and bear witness to this repentance through their deeds.

———————————— In Focus ————————————

From center stage, Quentin practiced with his gospel band. They were good—really good. However, Quentin was concerned about their drummer's attitude. Adrian liked being the center of attention. When they had started the band, it wasn't a big deal, but now that they were trying for a serious career, Adrian's antics diminished the band's ability to minister.

"Adrian, you're drowning us out," Quentin yelled yet again from his position at the mike. Oblivious to Quentin's rising frustration, Adrian continued to drum fast and loud. The rest of the band stopped and glared at him until Adrian finally noticed.

"I'm sorry, Adrian," Quentin said, "But you can't play at our next engagement. You seem unaware of the difference between ministry and performance. We minister through music to prepare the way for people to receive Christ. I want you in the band, but your attitude has to change. What do you say?"

"I say this is bogus. I quit!" Throwing down his drumsticks, Adrian stormed out. A half-hour later, he returned looking apologetic. "I was wrong. Please forgive me. All this is not about me, but about being a 'voice in the wilderness,' like John the Baptist was. Can we all worship together?"

Working in any community requires a willingness to repent and a commitment to community purposes, guidelines, and leaders. What difficulties do leaders face when going into a new phase of the community, like when John the Baptist led the people of God into the church age?

—————————— Keep in Mind ——————————

"For this is he that was spoken of by the prophet Esaias, saying, The voice of one crying in the wilderness, Prepare ye the way of the Lord, make his paths straight." (Matthew 3:3, KJV)

"The prophet Isaiah was speaking about John when he said, 'He is a voice shouting in the wilderness, Prepare the way for the LORD's coming! Clear the road for him!'" (Matthew 3:3, NLT)

Focal Verses

KJV **Matthew 3:1** In those days came John the Baptist, preaching in the wilderness of Judaea,

2 And saying, Repent ye: for the kingdom of heaven is at hand.

3 For this is he that was spoken of by the prophet Esaias, saying, The voice of one crying in the wilderness, Prepare ye the way of the Lord, make his paths straight.

4 And the same John had his raiment of camel's hair, and a leathern girdle about his loins; and his meat was locusts and wild honey.

5 Then went out to him Jerusalem, and all Judaea, and all the region round about Jordan,

6 And were baptized of him in Jordan, confessing their sins.

7 But when he saw many of the Pharisees and Sadducees come to his baptism, he said unto them, O generation of vipers, who hath warned you to flee from the wrath to come?

8 Bring forth therefore fruits meet for repentance:

9 And think not to say within yourselves, We have Abraham to our father: for I say unto you, that God is able of these stones to raise up children unto Abraham.

10 And now also the axe is laid unto the root of the trees: therefore every tree which bringeth not forth good fruit is hewn down, and cast into the fire.

11 I indeed baptize you with water unto repentance. but he that cometh after me is mightier than I, whose shoes I am not worthy to bear: he shall baptize you with the Holy Ghost, and with fire

12 Whose fan is in his hand, and he will throughly purge his floor, and gather his wheat into the garner; but he will burn up the chaff with unquenchable fire.

NLT **Matthew 3:1** In those days John the Baptist came to the Judean wilderness and began preaching. His message was,

2 "Repent of your sins and turn to God, for the Kingdom of Heaven is near."

3 The prophet Isaiah was speaking about John when he said, "He is a voice shouting in the wilderness, Prepare the way for the LORD's coming! Clear the road for him!'"

4 John's clothes were woven from coarse camel hair, and he wore a leather belt around his waist. For food he ate locusts and wild honey.

5 People from Jerusalem and from all of Judea and all over the Jordan Valley went out to see and hear John.

6 And when they confessed their sins, he baptized them in the Jordan River.

7 But when he saw many Pharisees and Sadducees coming to watch him baptize, he denounced them. "You brood of snakes!" he exclaimed. "Who warned you to flee the coming wrath?

8 Prove by the way you live that you have repented of your sins and turned to God.

9 Don't just say to each other, 'We're safe, for we are descendants of Abraham.' That means nothing, for I tell you, God can create children of Abraham from these very stones.

10 Even now the ax of God's judgment is poised, ready to sever the roots of the trees. Yes, every tree that does not produce good fruit will be chopped down and thrown into the fire.

11 "I baptize with water those who repent of their sins and turn to God. But someone is coming soon who is greater than I am—so much greater that I'm not worthy even to be his slave and carry his sandals. He will baptize you with the Holy Spirit and with fire.

12 He is ready to separate the chaff from the wheat with his winnowing fork. Then he will clean up the threshing area, gathering the wheat into his barn but burning the chaff with never-ending fire."

The People, Places, and Times

John the Baptist. John was a miracle child, born to childless, elderly parents—the priest Zacharias and his wife Elisabeth (Luke 1:5–25). While still pregnant, Elisabeth received a visit from her cousin Mary, who also had been divinely chosen to bear a child—Jesus. The baby in Elisabeth's womb jumped at Mary's voice (Luke 1:44).

John was the prophesied forerunner of Jesus even before his birth. The public reception of John's ministry was tremendous (Mark 1:5). John took no credit for the response to his preaching but properly relegated himself to the role of messenger, rather than savior.

Wilderness. In the Old and New Testaments, the wilderness served as a place God chose to meet with, chastise, and revive His children. The wilderness was also the place where Jesus endured a forty-day fast, encountered Satan, and overcame temptation (Matthew 4:1–11). We often think of wildernesses as deserts, because the wilderness the Israelites wandered before entering the Promised Land is in an arid region. The word, however, merely refers to a region with a low population, a place of solitude. Because John did not venture into the cities to preach, people had to come out of those cities into the wilderness to hear him.

How have places of solitude been important in your spiritual journey?

Background

After a long prophetic silence, John bursts onto the scene. This sudden appearance further emphasizes the silence the Israelites have been enduring from God. The last time God had spoken to His people was through the prophet Malachi, around 400 BC. Fittingly though, Malachi was the very prophet to foretell the ministry of John (Malachi 3:1; 4:5). There is also a long lapse of time between the end of Matthew 2 and the beginning of Matthew 3. Near the end of Matthew 2, we leave Jesus as a young child growing up in Nazareth (see Matthew 2:21-23). By the time we reach Matthew 3, John, who was born only several months before Jesus, is a grown man "preaching in the wilderness of Judaea."

John's ministry was preaching and baptizing ministry that anticipated the ministry of Jesus. John's ministry called people to a confession of sins, to repentance, and to the acknowledgment of the coming one who cleanses us from sins and provides the Spirit who enables living right (Matthew 3:6-12). John's baptism was a public affirmation that the repentant and now-baptized participants were positioned to receive God's saving grace and presence. They had repented, been cleansed, and were ready to follow the imminent Messiah.

If you have been baptized, what did it symbolize to you? How is baptism viewed in your church?

At-A-Glance

1. Preaching the Kingdom
(Matthew 3:1–4)
2. Baptizing the Repentant (vv. 5-6)
3. Rebuking the Dishonest (vv. 7-10)
4. Prophesying the Messiah (vv. 11–12)

In Depth

1. Preaching the Kingdom (Matthew 3:1–4)

The people recognized John as a prophet. God had promised to send Elijah before the coming of the Day of the Lord (Malachi 4:5). When John came dressed in camel's hair with a leather belt, he even appeared like Elijah (2 Kings 1:8). John's ministry being in "the wilderness of Judaea" fulfills a prophecy of Isaiah, and again links John to Elijah, who often spent time in the wilderness (1 Kings 17:5–7; 19:4, 15).

John's ministry had two emphases. First, his ministry called people to repentance. John was intent on calling people to turn from their old ways and pursue God's righteousness. Second, his ministry announced the nearness of the kingdom of heaven. God's kingdom coming soon further urges people to repent, but also gives hope of forthcoming improvement. The coming of God's kingdom on the Day of the Lord is a time of judgment. The Jews would desire to make themselves pure so they could pass God's judgment.

2. Baptizing the Repentant (vv. 5-6)

People responded to John's message and came from all over the Jordan Valley. When they confessed their sin, he baptized them in the Jordan River. While we cannot be certain of the source of John's practice of baptism, it is likely based on various common purification rituals of the time. It is obvious from the context that his baptism was offered as a public sign that those being baptized had received and accepted his message.

Despite John's rough clothing and limited diet, people were attracted to John because of the quality and content of his preaching. There is a lesson in this for today's church. We like to have beautiful worship facilities, hopefully as a sign of our honor to God, rather than a show for ourselves. Ultimately, though, our beautiful buildings or fashionable dress is not what attracts people to Jesus Christ. Real Christian disciples are made as a result of clear and perceptive handling of the Gospel.

3. Rebuking the Dishonest (vv. 7-10)

While John's ministry was successful, it did not go unchallenged. Even though the Pharisees and Sadducees had their differences, they were united in their opposition to John's ministry. In return, he calls them "vipers" and questions their sincerity. The religious leaders are in danger of God's judgment, as John reveals in his metaphor about the ax and tree. Their aim is solely to escape God's punishment for sin, rather than demonstrating a commitment to abandon their evil behavior and lead righteous lives.

John the Baptist also questions their pride in their religious heritage. He reminds them that God could easily turn something as commonplace as a stone into a faithful follower. Rather than automatically conferring a holier status on the Jews, being a child of Abraham means they have a clearer revelation of how God expects them to act.

How can we be sure to produce "good fruit" and avoid God's punishment?

4. Prophesying the Messiah (vv. 11–12)

John is emphatic about the relationship of his ministry to that of Jesus. John's purpose is to call people to repentance. Jesus' purpose is to save us all. In other words, John awakens people's desire for righteousness. Jesus provides the righteousness of God to those who believe and empowers us to live righteously through the Holy Spirit (Romans 3:22; Acts 1:8). Both ministries are needed even today. If the unchurched are to accept Christ and live righteously, they need someone to awaken within them the desire for righteousness.

John uses the pictures of fire and the threshing floor to explain Jesus' ministry. Fire suggests the purification of metal, which must suffer extreme heat to burn away its impurities. Sometimes as we go through hard times, God is using them to purify our characters. On a threshing floor, harvested wheat is tossed into the air and the breeze blows away the lightweight, useless chaff, leaving the heavy grain to fall to the ground. The farmer then stores the wheat and burns away any chaff that remains. Likewise, God will diligently and easily separate His true followers from the hypocrites.

Search the Scriptures

1. What was John the Baptist's primary message (Matthew 3:1–2)?

2. What did the people do before John baptized them (v. 6)?

3. According to John, how would Jesus baptize (vv. 11–12)?

Discuss the Meaning

John's baptism was a baptism of repentance only. His baptism was to prepare people's hearts for the coming of the Messiah. Several Scripture passages talk about the baptism of John being insufficient after the death and resurrection of Jesus Christ (for instance, see the story of Apollos in Acts 18:24–26). Read Romans 6:4 and discuss the symbolism of Christian baptism and how it goes beyond simple repentance. Discuss your understanding of the meaning of baptism when you were baptized. Can you think of ways to make baptism more meaningful at your church?

Liberating Lesson

Given the ever-present temptation of sin and evil, the church still needs John's kind of preaching ministry. Moral standards must be set and people need to be reminded of their potential for growth in the things of God. The message of repentance, forgiveness, and the call to live right can revitalize and bring spiritual renewal to people. The ministry of sharing our testimony and giving witness of Jesus Christ is the call and responsibility of every believer. Like John the Baptist, we too are to seek to awaken in people a desire for righteousness. We are to do this in the confidence that when desire is awakened, God will grant salvation through faith in Jesus Christ and convey righteousness by the power of the Holy Spirit to all who will believe.

Application for Activation

While the desire to avoid divine retribution may be a motive for right living, it is not the best motive. We should desire to live right because it is the right thing to do in response to God's love for us. It is far better to pour one's energies into bringing forth fruit suitable for repentance to glorify God, rather than to pour one's energies into merely avoiding the wrath to come. God is concerned about right motive, as well as right behavior. Repentance that is acceptable to God results in right behavior that is sustained not by a fear of hell, but by unconditional love for God.

This week, examine your reasons for following Christ and doing the work of the church. Are you motivated by your love for God or by fear? If you feel any fear—whether of rejection, failure, or inadequacy—meditate instead on God's great love for you and see how that can change your motivation.

Follow the Spirit

What God wants me to do:

_____

_____

_____

_____

Remember Your Thoughts
Special insights I have learned:

_____

_____

_____

_____

More Light on the Text
Matthew 3:1-12
While Jesus is growing up in Nazareth, preparing for His role as the Son of God, a major new development occurs with the appearance of John the Baptist. John was a prominent prophet. He had his own ministry and a significant group of followers. Moreover, John's ministry continued for some time after his baptizing Jesus in the River Jordan (see Matthew 9:14; 11:2-3). In important ways involving preview and prototype, John's ministry anticipates the ministry of Jesus. Matthew often shows the cousins' similarities: (1) The two men say similar things (compare Matthew 3:2 with 4:17; 3:7 with 12:34; 3:10 with 7:19); (2) Matthew introduces them in similar fashion (compare 3:1 with 3:13); (3) the Pharisees and Sadducees oppose them both (compare 3:7–10 with 23:33); (4) Both men act on God's authority (21:23-32); (5) The people understand that both men are prophets (11:9; 14:5); (6) John and Jesus are rejected by officials and executed as criminals (14:1–12; 26–27); and (7) Both John and Jesus are buried by their disciples (14:12; 27:57–61). Despite these similarities, as we shall read later, John understood he was not Jesus' equal (3:11–13).

1 In those days came John the Baptist, preaching in the wilderness of Judaea,
Matthew leaves the narratives regarding Jesus' childhood and begins to talk about John as a grown man involved in a vital preaching ministry. Our best understanding of the phrase "in those days" is that it refers to the time Jesus resided in Nazareth (2:23). With this phrase, Matthew leaps many years. Since Jesus comes to John as an adult, a whole generation has passed since Joseph took Mary and Jesus to Nazareth.

The location of John's ministry draws on the biblical tradition of end-time renewal in the wilderness (Ezekiel 20:33–38; Hosea 2:14–23). The word "wilderness" (Gk. *eremos*, ER-ray-mos) means "an uninhabited place," a place which is deserted, though not necessarily a desert. John the Baptist positions himself away from the distractions of everyday life. While traveling in the Sinai wilderness, God had first begun to reveal His will to the Israelites. While hiding in the wilderness, Elijah saw the presence of God revealed in a still, small whisper (1 Kings 19:11–13). Now in the Judean wilderness, John the Baptist called the Jews to turn to God in repentance and baptism and experience His forgiveness anew.

2 And saying, Repent ye: for the kingdom of heaven is at hand.
John's message of repentance places him within the tradition of the Old Testament prophets. Again and again, God commissioned prophets—from Moses to Malachi—to call God's chosen people to turn back to Him. Given God's anticipated judgment and redemption, responding to the call to turn one's life around and live righteously is the only sane and responsible thing to do.

Like Malachi said he would, he warns that repentant people would avoid the coming judgment. "Repent" is *metanoeo* (Gk. meh-tah-NOE-oh), meaning "to have a changed mind," similar to the English word which literally means "to think again." This change in internal thought should naturally lead to a change in external action. The apostle Peter summarized beginning the Christian life as laying aside the sin in a person's life (1 Peter 2:1).

"Is at hand" translates a Greek single word (*eggizo*, eng-**EED**-zo) which means "to be close by." Even though the English translation uses a present tense "is at hand," the Greek uses the perfect tense, more literally translated "has come near." The perfect tense indicates a past event that has a continuing effect in the present. John implies that he is not just announcing the Kingdom is here, but that its presence will affect our lives.

3 For this is he that was spoken of by the prophet Esaias saying, The voice of one crying in the wilderness, Prepare ye the way of the Lord, make his paths straight.

This verse describes John's prophesied function as a mouthpiece for God. John's role is referenced in Isaiah 40:3, which Matthew quotes in his continued goal of showing that Christ's coming was predicted and confirmed by the Word of God. Matthew, Mark, and Luke all relate Isaiah 40:3 to John, the one whose ministry is to prepare the way for the long-awaited Messiah.

Old Testament prophecies can be fulfilled multiple times, especially when revealed to be Messianic prophecy. God will let His people see the fulfillment of His words, and then the Messiah will unexpectedly fulfill the prophecy again to a greater degree. This verse is no different. Isaiah spoke of a rejuvenation of Jerusalem after the exile in Babylonia. The prophet spoke of the Almighty God's imminent arrival and exhorted the people to prepare a road for Him through the wilderness. God's coming would bless Jerusalem and put all other nations to shame. This happened as the Israelite state was renewed through the work of Nehemiah and Ezra. The Gospel writers saw this prophecy coming true again with the Messiah. God through Jesus was literally coming to Jerusalem. John the Baptist declared the place to prepare for Jesus' coming was in their individual lives, through repentance, which was then confirmed by baptism.

4 And the same John had his raiment of camel's hair, and a leathern girdle about his loins; and his meat was locusts and wild honey.

John's description indicates that he lived roughly and simply. His "leathern girdle" was a strip of hide worn at the waist and used to hold a garment in place. There is an implied comparison here with the prophet Elijah's clothing (2 Kings 1:8), again pointing to John being a type of Elijah, the prophesied forerunner of the Messiah. John's diet of honey and locusts parallels his simple apparel. Levitical law names locusts as the only winged insects not to be treated as unclean (11:20-23). "Wild honey," produced without beekeepers' assistance, is mentioned in the Old Testament as nourishment (Judges 14:8; 1 Samuel 14:25–27; Deuteronomy 32:13). This verse does not mean to imply that these were the only things that John ate, simply that they were the staples of his diet.

5 Then went out to him Jerusalem, and all Judaea, and all the region round about Jordan.

Matthew wants his readers to know the extent of John's influence. The imperfect tense of the Greek verb *ekporeuomai* (ek-por-**YOO**-oh-my) indicates that they were repeatedly coming out over a period of time to hear John. Although Matthew does not attach a specific number to indicate how many people were attracted to John's ministry, the implication is that, in spite of some opposition, there was a great and unusual response.

The Jewish historian Josephus also emphasizes John's great reputation and influence over the people. Besides what is given in the New Testament, the primary source for biblical scholars of information on John the Baptist comes from Josephus. John's influence leads Herod Antipas to fear John would incite a rebellion, which Josephus gives as the reason behind Herod's execution of John the Baptist. Josephus describes John's practice of baptism as purification of the body by water following the purification of the spirit by righteousness.

6 And were baptized of him in Jordan, confessing their sins.

It should be noted that these baptisms took place in connection with the people's confessions of their sins. Essentially, people could come to John confess their sins in his presence and, because John was acting as God's representative, they could be assured that through the act of baptism God accepted their confessions.

Christian baptism, anticipated in Matthew 28:18, develops out of John's practice of baptism. John baptized people in the Jordan River, though we do not know where along the river's 156–mile length he did this. It is believed that John's practice of baptism grew out of Old Testament practices involving the use of water. Those rituals were concerned with purification and sanctification for service rather than cleansing of sin and guilt. However, that idea does emerge in the Old Testament with suggestions of calls for self-washing or washing by God (Psalm 51:7–9; Isaiah 1:16–17; 4:2–6; Jeremiah 4:14; 33:8).

Ancient bathing practices frequently involved pouring water on someone (known as "effusion") or partial immersion. While some scholars believe that John baptized by sprinkling, other scholars believe he used immersion, since *baptizo* (Gk. bap-**TEED**-zo) means "to dip" or "immerse." The apostle Paul uses several metaphors to explain the theological importance of baptism, including dying and rising, walking under a cloud, and walking through the sea (Romans 6:3–6; 1 Corinthians 10:1–2). But these are metaphors, and as such, they lack the specific informational elements that would prove helpful to us in discussions of how water was used in ancient baptisms.

7 But when he saw many of the Pharisees and Sadducees come to his baptism, he said unto them, O generation of vipers, who hath warned you to flee from the wrath to come? 8 Bring forth therefore fruits meet for repentance:

It is doubtful that the Pharisees and Sadducees were coming to be baptized. The message of repentance was offensive to the two major Jewish parties, the Pharisees and the Sadducees. The Pharisees were a sect that preached strict adherence to the law of Moses, plus stricter laws just to make sure they kept Moses' laws. The Sadducees were generally wealthier and more politically connected. Therefore, both groups were confident that they were good enough in God's eyes and had little need to repent (Luke 18:9-14). Possibly Jewish leaders sent emissaries to hear John, apparently not because of interest as much as to investigate and evaluate the threat his popularity posed to them (John 1:19-22). Matthew's careful language supports this when it says they came "to his baptism" rather than came "to be baptized."

John has a keen perception of God's prophet and harshly questions their motives. In essence, John asked: "Since you show no signs of repentance, why are you coming to this place of baptism?" His statements in verses 8 and 9 provide a logical challenge.

9 And think not to say within yourselves, We have Abraham to our father: for I say unto you, that God is able of these stones

to raise up children unto Abraham. 10 And now also the axe is laid unto the root of the trees: therefore every tree which bringeth not forth good fruit is hewn down, and cast into the fire.

The intent of John's harsh comment is clear. The Pharisees and Sadducees cannot escape the judgment of God by hiding behind their father Abraham's religious legacy. If He chooses to do so, God can "raise up children unto Abraham" from cobblestones. As Moses reminded the Israelites in the wilderness (Deuteronomy 7:7), there is nothing innate about being an Israelite that attracts God to them. He could remake the entire nation of Israel in a moment just from common rocks on the ground. It is a humble and contrite heart that draws God's approval (Psalm 34:18; 51:17), not one's family heritage. After all, the grace of God extends beyond Jewish and family borders.

Like everybody else, the Pharisees and Sadducees have a decision to make and they must make it quickly. For while the kingdom is drawing near, so is God's judgment. Both the kingdom and God's judgment are imminent. John uses the metaphor of an unfruitful tree to talk about the consequences of an unrepentant life. Fruit-bearing trees that bear no fruit are cut down, a message which Jesus Himself will exactly echo in His own ministry (Matthew 7:19). In like manner, people who were created to live for God, but who refuse to do so will ultimately encounter God's retributive justice.

11 I indeed baptize you with water unto repentance: but he that cometh after me is mightier than I, whose shoes I am not worthy to bear: he shall baptize you with the Holy Ghost, and with fire:

John does more than preach, point out people's sins, and baptize; he foretells the coming of Christ and His baptism of the Holy Spirit. John realized that his ministry was much less significant than the ministry of Jesus, just as John was so much less important than Christ Jesus. The difference in status between John and the One to come is highlighted by the phrase "whose shoes I am not worthy to bear." Any true minister of the Gospel must point to our Lord and not to self.

John says a greater baptism is to follow his. It is the baptism of God's conveyance of His righteousness by the Holy Spirit, which enables us to do justice, and to love mercy, and to walk humbly before God (Micah 6:8). God's act is concurrent with one's repentance and continues to empower and purify those who live in obedience to God's will.

John's prophecy concerning Jesus' baptism is both a promise and a threat. Although at the time of John the Baptist there was not a complete understanding of the Holy Spirit, Jews were familiar with Old Testament prophecies, such as when God told Ezekiel that He was going to put His Spirit in His people (Ezekiel 36:26–27). But as a prophet speaking God's words, John said that the Messiah was coming and that He would baptize people with the Holy Spirit and with fire. Baptism by the Holy Ghost functions as purification experienced by those who respond to John's call to repent. Fire carries a destructive purpose experienced by those who reject it. John said that Jesus would baptize with fire, indicating a purifying process to those who receive His Word. John was telling people to repent because Jesus was coming and would not tolerate sin. He is holy, and He is God.

12 Whose fan is in his hand, and he will thoroughly purge his floor, and gather his wheat into the garner; but he will burn up the chaff with unquenchable fire.

John uses the agricultural metaphor of threshing wheat to describe the process of the final judgment. The "fan" was a shovel-like tool used in the winnowing process to separate the wheat from the chaff. The verbs here are intense: the winnowing process will not just purge, but "thoroughly purge"; the chaff will not just burn, but "burn up." John leaves his audience with this frightful image to call them to repentance. Just as the witness of John the Baptist helped to awaken a desire for righteousness in his day, so also can our faithful witness awaken a desire for righteousness in our day.

Sources:
Aland, Kurt, ed. *Synopsis of the Four Gospels.* 10th ed. Stuttgart, Ger.: German Bible Society, 1993.
Barclay, William. *The Gospel of Matthew:* Volume 1. Philadelphia, PN: Westminster Press, 1958. 34–54.
Blount, Brian K., et al., eds. *True to Our Native Land: An African American New Testament Commentary.* Minneapolis, MN: Fortress Press, 2007.
Josephus. *Antiquities of the Jews.* 18.5.116–119.
Nolland, John. *The Gospel of Matthew: A Commentary on the Greek Text.* Grand Rapids, MI: Eerdmans, 2005.
Walvoord, John F. and Roy B. Zuck, eds. *The Bible Knowledge Commentary: An Exposition of the Scriptures.* New Testament Edition. Wheaton, IL: Victor Books, 1983. 24–25.

Say It Correctly

Malachi. **MAL**-uh-kie.
Judaea. joo-**DAY**-uh.

Daily Bible Readings

MONDAY
A Voice Cries, "Comfort My People"
(Isaiah 40:1–5)

TUESDAY
John the Baptist Is the Greatest
(Matthew 11:2–15)

WEDNESDAY
The Baptist's Testimony of Faith
(John 1:19–34)

THURSDAY
Jesus, the Father's Beloved Son
(Matthew 17:1–8)

FRIDAY
In John, Elijah Has Come
(Matthew 17:9–13; Malachi 4:4–5)

SATURDAY
John Baptizes Jesus in the Jordan
(Matthew 3: 13–17)

SUNDAY
John Prepares the Way for Jesus
(Matthew 3:1–12)

Teaching Tips

Words You Should Know

A. Bruised (Luke 4:18) *thrauo* (Gk.)— Shattered or completely crushed

B. Wondered (v. 22) *thaumazo* (Gk.)—To admire, marvel, or have admiration as at a miracle

Teacher Preparation

Unifying Principle—An Amazing Messenger. People hear conflicting messages and proclamations all the time. What message would provide answers to life's deepest problems? The worshipers at Nazareth listened to Jesus' proclamation of justice and compassion and were amazed at his gracious words.

A. Read the Bible Background and Devotional Reading.

B. Pray for your students and lesson clarity.

C. Read the lesson Scripture in multiple translations.

O—Open the Lesson

A. Begin the class with prayer.

B. Ask the students to recall the campaign promises of the last election. How would the students rate the likelihood of those promises being kept in the coming term?

C. Have the students read the Aim for Change and the In Focus story.

D. Ask students how events like those in the story weigh on their hearts and how they can view these events from a faith perspective.

P—Present the Scriptures

A. Read the Focal Verses and discuss the Background and The People, Places, and Times sections.

B. Have the class share what Scriptures stand out for them and why, with particular emphasis on today's themes.

E—Explore the Meaning

A. Use In Depth or More Light on the Text to facilitate a deeper discussion of the lesson text.

B. Pose the questions in Search the Scriptures and Discuss the Meaning.

C. Discuss the Liberating Lesson and Application for Activation sections.

N—Next Steps for Application

A. Summarize the value of standing with Jesus, even when others reject his claims.

B. End class with a commitment to pray for the message of freedom to be spread to the poor, ill, and oppressed.

Worship Guide

For the Superintendent or Teacher
Theme: Called to Proclaim
Song: "Live Into Hope"
Devotional Reading:
Deuteronomy 8:1-11

Called to Proclaim

Bible Background • LUKE 4
Printed Text • LUKE 4:14-22 | Devotional Reading • DEUTERONOMY 8:1-11

———————————— **Aim for Change** ————————————

By the end of this lesson, we will COMPREHEND the meaning and significance of Jesus' inaugural sermon in Nazareth, SENSE the impact of Jesus' pronouncement at Nazareth, and ALIGN our faith response with Jesus' call and mission.

———————————— **In Focus** ————————————

Pastor Greenborough took to the podium on Sunday morning. "I want to talk this morning about my vision for our community. I won't be so bold as to say I have a dream. But…well, I have a dream." He smiled and shuffled with his notes.

"I want us to do something about these poor folk who stand around on our street corners. I know you say, 'But Pastor if we give them money, they'll buy booze and drugs.' Let me tell you, I would buy booze too if I hadn't showered in a month, hadn't had fresh socks and underwear for two weeks, hadn't had a proper sleep in five days, and hadn't had a proper meal in two days. We must do something.

"I want us to do something about our brothers and sisters suffering from depression, PTSD, and suicidal thoughts. I know you say, 'But Pastor, faith will make those people whole. They just need to pray harder.' Let me tell you, they do pray. They pray every day that they could spare the time and money and self-respect to talk to someone trained to help them out of their dark thoughts. They pray every day that God would send them a friend. We must do something, Church."

As Pastor Greenborough went on, sister Patsy sat placidly in her pew. It was great rhetoric, she had to admit and of course she wanted to help all God's children, but still… it was all too great a task for her. What was this "something" their church was supposed to do? Would it really even help?

How do you react to the message of Jesus and the Church's mission in the world?

———————————— **Keep in Mind** ————————————

"The Spirit of the Lord is upon me, because he hath anointed me to preach the gospel to the poor; he hath sent me to heal the brokenhearted, to preach deliverance to the captives, and recovering of sight to the blind, to set at liberty them that are bruised, To preach the acceptable year of the Lord" (Luke 4:18-19, KJV).

"The Spirit of the LORD is upon me, for he has anointed me to bring Good News to the poor. He has sent me to proclaim that captives will be released, that the blind will see, that the oppressed will be set free, and that the time of the LORD's favor has come" (Luke 4:18-19, NLT).

Focal Verses

KJV **Luke 4:14** And Jesus returned in the power of the Spirit into Galilee: and there went out a fame of him through all the region round about.

15 And he taught in their synagogues, being glorified of all.

16 And he came to Nazareth, where he had been brought up: and, as his custom was, he went into the synagogue on the sabbath day, and stood up for to read.

17 And there was delivered unto him the book of the prophet Esaias. And when he had opened the book, he found the place where it was written,

18 The Spirit of the Lord is upon me, because he hath anointed me to preach the gospel to the poor; he hath sent me to heal the brokenhearted, to preach deliverance to the captives, and recovering of sight to the blind, to set at liberty them that are bruised,

19 To preach the acceptable year of the Lord.

20 And he closed the book, and he gave it again to the minister, and sat down. And the eyes of all them that were in the synagogue were fastened on him.

21 And he began to say unto them, This day is this scripture fulfilled in your ears.

22 And all bare him witness, and wondered at the gracious words which proceeded out of his mouth. And they said, Is not this Joseph's son?

NLT **Luke 4:14** Then Jesus returned to Galilee, filled with the Holy Spirit's power. Reports about him spread quickly through the whole region.

15 He taught regularly in their synagogues and was praised by everyone.

16 When he came to the village of Nazareth, his boyhood home, he went as usual to the synagogue on the Sabbath and stood up to read the Scriptures.

17 The scroll of Isaiah the prophet was handed to him. He unrolled the scroll and found the place where this was written:

18 "The Spirit of the LORD is upon me, for he has anointed me to bring Good News to the poor. He has sent me to proclaim that captives will be released, that the blind will see, that the oppressed will be set free,

19 and that the time of the LORD's favor has come."

20 He rolled up the scroll, handed it back to the attendant, and sat down. All eyes in the synagogue looked at him intently.

21 Then he began to speak to them. "The Scripture you've just heard has been fulfilled this very day!"

22 Everyone spoke well of him and was amazed by the gracious words that came from his lips. "How can this be?" they asked. "Isn't this Joseph's son?"

The People, Places, and Times

Synagogue. After Solomon's Temple was destroyed and many of the Hebrews were sent into exile, it became necessary to develop local centers of worship and instruction in the Jewish faith. Even after their return from exile and the Jerusalem Temple was rebuilt, these local centers of worship continued. Most communities of size had at least one synagogue and some had several. Jewish sources hold that a synagogue was to be built wherever there were ten or more Jewish men. The primary meeting was held on the Sabbath (Saturday). The usual worship service consisted of the recitation of the Shema (Deuteronomy 6:4-9), prayers, Scripture readings from the Law and the Prophets, a sermon, and a benediction. Often the community appointed a ruler who cared for the building and selected those who participated in the worship service. Jairus of Capernaum (Mark 5:22), and Crispus and Sosthenes of Corinth (Acts 18) were rulers at their local synagogues. On many occasions, Jesus encountered opposition and conflict in the synagogues both for His teaching (Mark 6:1-6) and His miracles (Luke 4:31-37). As opposition grew, Jesus warned His disciples of a time in the future when they, too, would be persecuted in the synagogues (Matthew 10:17; 23:34; Mark 13:9; Luke 12:11; 21:12).

What similarities do Jewish synagogues have with modern Christian churches?

Background

At the age of thirty, Jesus submitted Himself to baptism as a sign of obedience and to initiate His public ministry, even though He was without sin. Following His baptism, the Holy Ghost led Him into the wilderness, where He endured forty days and nights of fasting and isolation. This was a period of physical weakness but spiritual strength. Three times Satan tried to tempt Jesus, making Him offers that might appeal to His humanness. But in His divine nature, Jesus endured this period and refused the devil's temptations.

Luke 4:1 says that it was the Spirit that gave Jesus the victory over Satan in the wilderness and led Him to Galilee. There, He was able to teach in the synagogues and He was well received, gaining popularity among the people there. Jesus was glorified by all those around Him. The accolades Jesus received in Galilee did not represent the true glory of Jesus, which was to come. Still, Jesus' ministry began and ended with Him being glorified.

Jesus' ministry was initiated after sacrifice and obedience. What lessons might this pattern teach us?

At-A-Glance

1. Returning by the Spirit (Luke 4:14–17)
2. The Spirit is Upon Me (vv. 18–19)
3. Scripture Fulfilled (vv. 20–22)

In Depth

1. Returning by the Spirit (Luke 4:14–17)

Here we find the opening scene of Jesus' ministry—in Galilee. From a glorious reception in Galilee, Jesus' next stop was His hometown, Nazareth. The phrase "where he had been brought up" gives the impression that Jesus had not been in Nazareth for a while before this visit (Luke 4:16). Jesus had been raised by devout Jewish parents who reared Him to participate in the tenets of His faith. Therefore, as His custom was, He went to the synagogue on the Sabbath day. It was normal and usual for Him to participate in worship.

Anyone could be invited to read the Scripture lesson for the synagogue services. Scholars are uncertain as to how the reading from the Prophets was chosen. Perhaps the particular reading was left to the discretion of the man reading. Possibly Jesus chose this passage, as indicated by the phrase, "he found the place where it was written" (v. 17).

2. The Spirit is Upon Me (vv. 18–19)

The reading from Isaiah points back to the very nature of Jesus' ministry. His purpose was to bring the Good News to the poor, brokenhearted, captives, blind, and oppressed (bruised). The Gospel is the Good News to those whose hope lies in Almighty God to act on their behalf. Jesus identifies Himself with the social, religious, and economic outcasts of His day.

Throughout the Old Testament, God is clearly on the side of the poor and oppressed (Isaiah 58:6; Psalms 103:6; 146:7; 72:12-14).

"The acceptable year of the Lord" (Luke 4:19) to which Jesus referred to was likely the jubilee year described in Leviticus 25. The Year of Jubilee was a time when the economic and social inequities accumulated through the years were to be crossed off and all God's people would begin again at the same point. Jubilee meant that slaves were to be set free, and people who were in servitude because of debts they couldn't pay were given back their ancestral lands and set free to return to their families.

3. Scripture Fulfilled (vv. 20–22)

After His reading, the congregation was still. All eyes were fastened on Him, expecting this budding rabbi to offer a sermon on this prophetic text. Jesus broke through the silence with a simple, yet powerful declaration, "This day is this scripture fulfilled in your ears" (v. 21). There He was, in their midst. Jesus of Nazareth was the Messiah of God's promise. The acceptable year of the Lord had been launched in the person and ministry of Jesus. Jesus was ushering in a new age of salvation. The Good News of the kingdom was indeed the fulfillment of the Old Testament Messianic hope.

Initially, those who heard His words responded favorably. They wondered at the gracious words He had just spoken. Still, they were confused about His identity. They could not move beyond the fact that He was Joseph's son. How could a carpenter's son declare Himself to be the Son of God?

Think of a time a speaker has unexpectedly blown you away with their message. What was surprising about the message?

Search the Scriptures

1. What did Jesus do once He arrived at Nazareth (Luke 4:16)?

2. What responsibilities had Jesus been given because the Spirit of the Lord was upon Him (vv. 18-19)?

Discuss the Meaning

1. Jesus often fulfilled prophecy in one way during His earthly ministry, but will also fulfill the same prophesy even more fully when His Kingdom comes. How is it the day of the Lord's favor today? How much more of the prophecy do we still await?

2. What did Isaiah's prophecy mean to its original audience?

Liberating Lesson

We are not redeemed simply to console ourselves in the Spirit, but to be a hand extended to the unchurched and the hurting. People today are looking for peace in their lives. As believers in Christ, we know that Jesus is the answer. But it is of no consequence if we do not get the message to people who really need to hear it. The African American and the global African population is disproportionately influenced by poverty and imprisonment. Make plans to implement one practical way that the class can be a Christ-like influence in your community by doing each of these in the following weeks:

1. Preaching the Gospel to the poor
2. Preaching deliverance to prisoners
3. Helping the blind see
4. Setting the oppressed free

Application for Activation

Isaiah refers to Jubilee in the context of a restoration of Israel after the nation's enemies had humbled her (Isaiah 61:2). Jesus referred regarding the new day He would bring. This week use your Bible and Bible reference tools to do some research on the year of Jubilee (Leviticus 25:8–55). Spend time meditating on how the deliverance Jesus brings compares and contrasts with the freedom of the Jubilee year. Share your thoughts with the group next week.

Follow the Spirit

What God wants me to do:

_____

_____

_____

_____

Remember Your Thoughts

Special insights I have learned:

_____

_____

_____

_____

More Light on the Text

Luke 4:14-22

Jesus has been baptized (Luke 3:21) and led into the wilderness by the Spirit where the devil tempted Him for forty days (4:1-13). Having overcome all the temptations of the devil and being filled with the power of the Holy Spirit, Jesus returns to the region of Galilee, where He officially begins His ministry (cf. Matthew 4:12; Mark 1:14). He is now about thirty years old (Luke 3:23). According to Jewish law, this is the age priests begin their duties (Numbers 4:23; 1 Chronicles 23:3). From the context, Jesus has been teaching in other cities in this region (e.g., Capernaum; see Luke 4:23), especially in their synagogues, before He goes to His hometown of Nazareth. His fame has spread all over the place because of the miracles and the authority with which he taught them (Luke 4:14-15; Mark 1:21-28; 3:32ff).

14 And Jesus returned in the power of the Spirit into Galilee: and there went out a fame of him through all the region round about.

Jesus' ministry was filled with the power of the Holy Spirit and His leading. We first hear of the Holy Spirit descending upon Jesus at His baptism. Next, the Spirit led Him into the wilderness to be tempted. Now, we read that He returned "in the power of the Spirit." Later in His ministry, Gospel-writers link Jesus' power of the Spirit with His authoritative teaching and His miracles. Either or both of these would certainly make the "fame of him" spread throughout the region.

The region of Galilee was surrounded by Gentile (non-Jewish) nations. Because of this, the people were exposed to a variety of ideas, which made them very open in their attitudes. According to the Jewish historian Josephus, they were a very courageous people, many of whom became leaders of rebellions. It was also a very fertile region, so it was able to support many people, probably as many as three million. This was the region where Jesus grew up. God planted His Son in an area in which people would at least be open to hearing Him.

15 And he taught in their synagogues, being glorified of all.

During the exile, when the Temple had been destroyed and people lived far from their home in Israel, the Jews began meeting for worship in synagogues—a town could have a synagogue if there were at least ten adult Jewish men. There were no sacrifices in the synagogues, but the worship services on the Sabbath days had a fairly consistent routine.

Worship began with prayer, which was followed by the reading of Scripture. Seven people from the congregation read from different parts of the Old Testament. Since few were able to understand the original Hebrew, the reading was followed by a translation into either

217

Greek or Aramaic. After the Scripture reading, there was a sermon or teaching. There was no professional minister, but each synagogue had an administrator. This administrator might invite a distinguished person to speak on the Scripture. This would be followed by discussion and questions.

In this context, Jesus may have begun by asking the synagogue administrator for the opportunity to read the Scripture and comment on it. This was not the first time Jesus had spoken in a synagogue, but it was at the beginning of His ministry and His clear, authoritative messages were like a breath of fresh air to the people. "Glorified" is the normal translation of the Greek word used here (*doxazo*, doke-**SOD**-zo) and usually refers to honoring God. In this context though, it more likely has the meaning of celebrating someone or holding them with honor. The people praised Jesus and His sermons; no opposition had yet begun.

16 And he came to Nazareth, where he had been brought up: and, as his custom was, he went into the synagogue on the sabbath day, and stood up for to read.

Continuing His itinerary in the Galilee region, Jesus comes to Nazareth, His hometown. Nazareth was a town in the southern part of Galilee where Jesus spent His boyhood (Matthew 2:23). Nazareth was a small, but beautifully secluded town nestled in the southernmost hills of the Lebanon mountain range. Although it was near major roads, Nazareth itself, though, was isolated from nearby traffic because of the area's hills. This apparent isolation contributed to the fact that Nazareth was regarded as a less important part of the national and religious life of Israel. Coupled with its seclusion, Nazareth had a bad reputation both morally and religiously. It is also believed that Nazareth had a certain crude dialect in the Galilean region. All this seems to make Nazareth notorious and probably prompted Nathanael, when he first learned of Jesus of Nazareth, to ask, "Can anything good come from Nazareth?" (John 1:46, NLT).

At Nazareth, Jesus went into the synagogue on the Sabbath day, a habit He had formed from childhood (Luke 2:41–50). He grew up in the city and the synagogue. Therefore He was a familiar face. He also was familiar with the worship rituals. It was customary during a synagogue service on the Sabbath for seven people to read from the Scriptures: a priest, a Levite, and five ordinary Jews. Therefore, it was not strange that Jesus is handed the Scripture to read.

17 And there was delivered unto him the book of the prophet Esaias. And when he had opened the book, he found the place where it was written,

As we have already noted, the reading of Scripture formed an integral part of synagogue worship. Indeed, Scripture reading remains the most important part of worship in the Jewish religion even today. Before and during Jesus' time, the Jewish people read the Scripture systematically. Readings from the Law and the Prophets followed a schedule of 155 specific lessons, which were designed to allow completion of the entire Pentateuch in three years. In both Palestine and Babylon, the verses were read from the Hebrew text. This was followed by an Aramaic translation, the familiar language of the Middle East.

Jesus is then handed the book of the prophet Isaiah (KJV: Esaias). Even though the word "book" (Gk. *biblion*, bee-**BLEE**-on) is used, we should not imagine a codex with stacked pages bound in a spine, like modern books. The Hebrew Scriptures were written on scrolls, as were most writings until the 4th century AD. In the Hebrew Bible scrolls, the prophetic books were in single volumes (except the twelve minor prophets, which were written collectively on one scroll). Isaiah is the longest of the prophetic books, and the scroll could have been almost two feet thick when rolled up. Jesus unrolls the scroll to the prophetic passage which summarizes His earthly mission. Whether Jesus looked for a passage He wished to read, He just opened the book and His eye fell upon that particular passage, or it was the passage assigned for that Sabbath day, we do not know.

18 The Spirit of the Lord is upon me, because he hath anointed me to preach the gospel to the poor; he hath sent me to heal the brokenhearted, to preach deliverance to the captives, and recovering of sight to the blind, to set at liberty them that are bruised. 19 To preach the acceptable year of the Lord.

Jesus reads from Isaiah 61:1-2 and includes a single phrase from 58:6. He probably read in Hebrew and translated into Aramaic, the commonly spoken language at the time. He reads, "The Spirit of the Lord is upon me," which means that He is filled with the power of the Holy Spirit. As we see in verse 21, Jesus identifies Himself as the subject of Isaiah's prophecy. Here, He says that He has the Holy Spirit for a specific ministry. Christ promised the Holy Spirit to His disciples before He ascended, and its power is demonstrated repeatedly in the Gospels. We should note that He has the Holy Spirit because He has been "anointed." This seems to indicate that the filling or the possession of the Holy Spirit is consequent to the anointing. The word "anointed" here is translated as the Greek word *chrio* (**KHREE**-oh), which means to consecrate, ordain, or set apart a person for a particular service. It is the same word from which we get "Christ," the Anointed One. In the Old Testament, people or things were anointed, as symbolized by the pouring of oil to signify holiness and separation unto God— like the tabernacle and its furniture (Exodus 30:22ff), priests (Exodus 28:41), kings (Judges

9:8; 2 Samuel 2:4; 1 Kings 1:34), and prophets (1 Kings 19:16). The anointing also symbolized authority, appointment, and equipping for a special function or service to God. It was usually associated with the outpouring of the Spirit of God (1 Samuel 10:1, 9; 16:13). The anointing was always regarded as an act of God, and it was sometimes used to mean the bestowal of divine favor (Psalm 23:5; 92:10). The same idea is also carried over into the New Testament (Acts 10:38; 1 John 2:20, 27) and generally refers to the anointing of the Holy Spirit.

The "Gospel" did not originate in the New Testament but had its beginning in Old Testament prophetic literature. The Old Testament prophets talked about God ushering in a new era of justice, righteousness, and peace. During a time of great wickedness, injustice, and oppression, the prophet wrote, "Let judgment run down as waters, and righteousness as a mighty stream" (Amos 5:24). It is clear from the Gospels that Jesus understood His mission as being the fulfillment of this Old Testament hope. When He gave His inaugural address in the synagogue, He used as His Scripture text Isaiah 61:1-2, which spoke of preaching the Good News to the poor and afflicted, binding up the brokenhearted, proclaiming liberty to the captives, and opening the prison to those who are bound.

Here the writer declares that Jesus has been consecrated, as evidenced by the power of the Holy Spirit for a twofold ministry—to preach and to heal. He is called "to preach the gospel" (Gk. *euaggelizo*, yew-ang-gell-**EED**-zo), that is, to announce good news, or glad tidings, to the "poor." This probably includes the physically and spiritually poor. He is called to preach "deliverance to the captives"—those who were bound and imprisoned in sin, sickness, and death (Acts 10:38; Ephesians 4:8-10; Hebrews 2:14-15). He is also sent "to preach [proclaim to all] the acceptable year of the Lord." The "acceptable year of the Lord" is a day salvation, and that day is now (2 Corinthians 6:2, quoting Isaiah 49:8), a time of receiving inheritance and comforting those who mourn (Isaiah 61:2). However, it is also a time of vengeance for the Lord. It is speaking of the end times, but they begin now. This understanding of Christ's role is called "inaugurated eschatology." Christ inaugurated the reign of God's kingdom in His life and ministry. The blessings—and the work—begin now, but will be consummated at the Second Coming. The atonement of Christ is fully embraced when the poor, sick, sinful, and helpless are restored to prosperity, health, holiness, power, and dominion over Satan and receive membership and communion in the family of God.

The second function of the anointing is for healing, both spiritually and physically. Jesus is sent "to heal the brokenhearted." This includes those who are broken in mind and soul (Luke 7:44-50). He will bring comfort and hope to the destitute in heart. The anointing is also for the "recovering of sight to the blind"—body, spirit, and soul—for those in darkness (Matthew 4:16; Acts 26:18). Jesus healed many people who were physically blind, but also often spoke of spiritual blindness (John 9). Jesus is also sent to liberate those "that are bruised" (Gk. *thrauo*, **THROU**-oh, shattered or completely crushed, broken into many pieces). This speaks of the oppressed and broken (Isaiah 58:6-14). Although this passage refers to the immediate situation of Israel's captivity, the reality is to be fulfilled in the future by Christ's ministry.

It is important to remember that while there are spiritual interpretations of poverty, blindness, and oppression, there is also the physical reality. Many people in the world today worry about where their next meal will come from—if it comes today at all—or worry about where they will sleep tonight, or if they can make rent this month. They are too occupied with these worries to think about spiritual matters. As Christ's hands and feet, Christians must work to help meet people's immediate physical needs and fight systems of oppression with justice, while also helping meet people's spiritual need for hope and salvation. Jesus inaugurated this work and showed us how to do it by His ministry. He then anointed us with the Holy Spirit so that we can continue today and work till Jesus comes.

20 And he closed the book, and he gave it again to the minister, and sat down. And the eyes of all them that were in the synagogue were fastened on him. 21 And he began to say unto them, This day is this scripture fulfilled in your ears.

Luke now resumes his narrative. After reading the lesson for the day, Jesus handed the scroll back to the minister, sat down, and was about to start a sermon. Sitting was the usual position for those giving a sermon in the synagogue. As He sat down to preach, all the people in the synagogue focused their attention on Him. Jesus explained to them the Scripture. We do not have the full content of Jesus' teaching, but only a summary of the main theme of Christ's words: "This day is this scripture fulfilled in your ears." Luke indicates that this is just a summary by saying Jesus "began" to say.

Jesus declares to them that the words which He has read to them have finally been fulfilled in their presence; in essence He says that He, Jesus, is the One anointed by God, endued with the Holy Spirit, spoken of in the Old Testament to proclaim the Good News of salvation and deliverance and to heal all manner of diseases. He was sent to proclaim the "acceptable year of the Lord" (v. 19)—the Messianic age and the year of Jubilee. This is an age ushered in by His presence, a period in which God has planned to grant salvation to all types of people. With this, Jesus takes on Himself to fulfill all the prophecies of the Suffering Servant (Isaiah 42:1-4; 49:1-6; 50:4-7; 52:13-53:12), claiming publicly to be the Messiah.

22 And all bare him witness, and wondered at the gracious words which proceeded out of his mouth. And they said, Is not this Joseph's son?

At first, the people's reaction was that of wonder and excitement. All have a positive connotation. "Wondered" (Gk. *thaumazo*, thou-**MOD**-zoh) means to admire, marvel, or to have admiration. Jesus spoke with such grace and authority that the people marveled as they would at a miracle. His words and His claim were so startling and amazing to them that they began to question within themselves, "Is not this Joseph's son?"

Although they had known Him, they had never heard such words from Him in the 30 years He had lived among them. Moreover, they reflected on Jesus' background and family—He was only the son of Joseph, an ordinary person. How could He make such a claim? This was the turning point. They changed from an attitude of awe and wonder to doubt, skepticism, and prejudice. They must have thought, "How can Jesus, whose father Joseph is poor, be the One anointed to preach to the poor?" Jesus endured such prejudice repeatedly as recorded in the Scriptures (cf. Mark 6:3; John 1:46; 7:52).

Although they are simply amazed and incredulous now, soon some would be filled with indignation and anger at Jesus' words. As Jesus finishes this very sermon, the people of Nazareth drag Him out to throw Him off a cliff (vv. 28-30).

Say It Correctly

Shema. shuh-**MAH**.
Jairus. **JIE**-russ.

Daily Bible Readings

MONDAY
Live By God's Word
(Deuteronomy 8:1–11)

TUESDAY
Jubilee, Year of God's Favor
(Leviticus 25:8–17)

WEDNESDAY
Miracle of the Meal and Oil
(1 Kings 17:8–16)

THURSDAY
Naaman's Leprosy
Healed in Jordan River
(2 Kings 5:1–14)

FRIDAY
Jesus Overcomes
the Devil's Temptations
(Luke 4:1–13)

SATURDAY
Jesus Driven out of Nazareth
(Luke 4:23–30)

SUNDAY
Jesus' Mandate for Ministry Announced
(Luke 4:14–22)

Sources:
Holman Bible Dictionary. Trent Butler, general editor. Nashville, TN: Broadman & Holman Publishers, 1991. 1311- 1312.
Josephus. *The Life of Flavius Josephus*.
Mishel, Lawrence, Josh Bivens, Elise Gould, and Heidi Shierholz. "Poverty." *State of Working America Key Numbers. Economic Policy Institute*. Ithaca, NY: Cornell University Press, 2012.

Teaching Tips

Words You Should Know

A. Master (Luke 5:5) *epistates* (Gk.)—Teacher, emphasizing the teacher's position of respect

B. Beckoned (v. 7) *kataneuo* (Gk.)—To signal by nodding one's head

Teacher Preparation

Unifying Principle—The Ultimate Fish Story. People seek significance and purpose. Are we on earth just to eke out a living, or can we be part of something greater? Jesus called Simon and his cohorts to follow him and find fulfillment in doing the work of God's kingdom.

A. Read the Bible Background and Devotional Reading.

B. Pray for your students and lesson clarity.

C. Read the lesson Scripture in multiple translations.

O—Open the Lesson

A. Begin the class with prayer.

B. Think of some influential leaders from the twentieth century. How were they able to inspire others to join their causes? What were they able to accomplish?

C. Have the students read the Aim for Change and the In Focus story.

D. Ask students how events like those in the story weigh on their hearts and how they can view these events from a faith perspective.

P—Present the Scriptures

A. Read the Focal Verses and discuss the Background and The People, Places, and Times sections.

B. Have the class share what Scriptures stand out for them and why, with particular emphasis on today's themes.

E—Explore the Meaning

A. Use In Depth or More Light on the Text to facilitate a deeper discussion of the lesson text.

B. Pose the questions in Search the Scriptures and Discuss the Meaning.

C. Discuss the Liberating Lesson and Application for Activation sections.

N—Next Steps for Application

A. Summarize the value of making sacrifices to spread the Gospel.

B. End class with a commitment to pray for sensitivity to the call of Jesus in serving Him.

Worship Guide

For the Superintendent or Teacher
Theme: Called to Significance
Song: "I Have Decided to Follow Jesus"
Devotional Reading: Luke 9:57-62

Called to Significance

Bible Background • LUKE 5:1-11
Printed Text • LUKE 5:1-11 | Devotional Reading • LUKE 9:57-62

—————— Aim for Change ——————

By the end of this lesson, we will CONTEMPLATE a miraculous catch of fish, REFLECT on Simon's changing attitude toward Jesus, and HEAR Jesus' instructions and eagerly obey them.

—————— In Focus ——————

Marilyn always heard that if you find a career you love, it will never feel like work. She had the career, but work never felt fulfilling. Marilyn knew this was where God wanted her, but also felt she could do more to minister.

She found that ministry when her mother's friend, Miss Sandra, yet again invited her to serve at the Neighbor-to-Neighbor Breakfast at her church. Miss Sandra's invitations were nothing if not persistent. Even though Marilyn always said she didn't have the time, Miss Sandra invited her every week. Finally, Marilyn cleared her schedule to go.

That morning, Marilyn entered the Fellowship Hall, not knowing what to expect. She found rows and rows of tables with homeless people—whom Miss Sandra always called "our unhoused neighbors"—chattering among themselves while waiting to be fed. She looked for Miss Sandra and found her at the front of the room, near the kitchen. As Marilyn threaded her way through the crowd, Miss Sandra called for quiet. Everyone gave Miss Sandra their full focus as she prayed before the volunteers started serving.

After the prayer, Marilyn spent the next hour moving from the kitchen to the tables, with trays full of plates of scrambled eggs, turkey bacon, and fruit salad. In the corner of her eye, she could see Miss Sandra doing the same while joking and laughing with the neighbors, offering a friendly word or a warm touch—or, best of all, a bit of hope. That hope touched Marilyn's heart. She said a prayer of thanks that Miss Sandra had invited her to serve, and she knew she would come back to serve again.

Are we humble enough to accept the blessing of being in service to others?

—————— Keep in Mind ——————

"Jesus said unto Simon, Fear not; from henceforth thou shalt catch men"
(from Luke 5:10, KJV).

"Jesus replied to Simon, 'Don't be afraid! From now on you'll be fishing for people!'"
(from Luke 5:10, NLT).

Focal Verses

KJV **Luke 5:1** And it came to pass, that, as the people pressed upon him to hear the word of God, he stood by the lake of Gennesaret,

2 And saw two ships standing by the lake: but the fishermen were gone out of them, and were washing their nets.

3 And he entered into one of the ships, which was Simon's, and prayed him that he would thrust out a little from the land. And he sat down, and taught the people out of the ship.

4 Now when he had left speaking, he said unto Simon, Launch out into the deep, and let down your nets for a draught.

5 And Simon answering said unto him, Master, we have toiled all the night, and have taken nothing: nevertheless at thy word I will let down the net.

6 And when they had this done, they inclosed a great multitude of fishes: and their net brake.

7 And they beckoned unto their partners, which were in the other ship, that they should come and help them. And they came, and filled both the ships, so that they began to sink.

8 When Simon saw it, he fell down at Jesus' knees, saying, Depart from me; for I am a sinful man, O Lord.

9 For he was astonished, and all that were with him, at the draught of the fishes which they had taken:

10 And so was also James, and John, the sons of Zebedee, which were partners with Simon. And Jesus said unto Simon, Fear not; from henceforth thou shalt catch men.

11 And when they had brought their ships to land, they forsook all, and followed him.

NLT **Luke 5:1** One day as Jesus was preaching on the shore of the Sea of Galilee, great crowds pressed in on him to listen to the word of God.

2 He noticed two empty boats at the water's edge, for the fishermen had left them and were washing their nets.

3 Stepping into one of the boats, Jesus asked Simon, its owner, to push it out into the water. So he sat in the boat and taught the crowds from there.

4 When he had finished speaking, he said to Simon, "Now go out where it is deeper, and let down your nets to catch some fish."

5 "Master," Simon replied, "we worked hard all last night and didn't catch a thing. But if you say so, I'll let the nets down again."

6 And this time their nets were so full of fish they began to tear!

7 A shout for help brought their partners in the other boat, and soon both boats were filled with fish and on the verge of sinking.

8 When Simon realized what had happened, he fell to his knees before Jesus and said, "Oh, Lord, please leave me—I'm such a sinful man."

9 For he was awestruck by the number of fish they had caught, as were the others with him.

10 His partners, James and John, the sons of Zebedee, were also amazed. Jesus replied to Simon, "Don't be afraid! From now on you'll be fishing for people!"

11 And as soon as they landed, they left everything and followed Jesus.

The People, Places, and Times

The Lake of Gennesaret is also known as the Sea of Galilee. It is called Gennesaret because the fertile Plain of Gennesaret lies on the northwest side of the lake (Matthew 14:34). The Old Testament calls it the Sea of Chinnereth because of the shape of it (Hebrew "harp-shaped," Numbers 34:11) and "Chinneroth" (Joshua 12:3) from the town so named on its shore. Gennesaret is probably the corruption of the name Chinneroth. The Sea of Tiberias is another designation (John 6:1; 21:1), associated with the capital of Herod Antipas. All of the names of this single body of water were derived from places on the western shore. The lake is located some 60 miles north of Jerusalem.

The Sea of Galilee was the focus of Galilee's wealth. Nine cities with a population of 15,000 or more stood on its shores. To the northwest was Capernaum, the home of Simon and Andrew (Mark 1:29) and where Matthew sat at custom (Matthew 9:9). It was also the scene of much of Jesus' Galilean ministry.

Background

Previously in Luke, the Lord Jesus was in Capernaum (Luke 4:31) healing many people who came to Him after the Sabbath (vv. 40-41). After these many mighty works, Jesus slipped away to pray in a deserted place near the city. His disciples found Him and reported how many people wanted Jesus to stay there among them. But Jesus told them that He had to go to the other cities and preach the kingdom of God, for that is what He was sent to do (v. 43). His mission was not to call others from a single place but to go to people throughout Judea—where they worked, where they lived, where they studied—and call them as they were, where they were. Jesus left Capernaum to preach in other cities of the Decapolis (see Matthew 4:25). His first stop was Lake Gennesaret (i.e., the Sea of Galilee) where He makes contact with a crowd of people and with some of the men whom He would call to be His disciples.

At-A-Glance

1. The Teaching (Luke 5:1-3)
2. The Miracle (vv. 4-7)
3. The Commitment (vv. 8-11)

In Depth

1. The Teaching (Luke 5:1-3)

On a certain morning Jesus was on the shore of Lake Gennesaret, near Capernaum. As a result of His fame at that time, a great multitude had already collected around Him there early in the morning to listen to His teaching. In order to be able to address the multitude more effectively, the Lord entered into Simon's ship—one of two that were standing by the shore of the lake. He then asked Simon to push the boat out a little further from land and from there He taught the multitude out of the ship. Jesus used an unusual setting from which to teach. It was not in a synagogue, but in a boat (v. 3). In other words, Jesus taught where the people were. The Bible tells us to "Go ye into all the world" (from Mark 16:15); it does not tell the world to come to us. Wherever the opportunity, be ready and committed to do what you can to share the Good News of God!

When have you shown a willingness to share about God in unexpected places?

2. The Miracle (vv. 4-7)

After He finished teaching, Jesus commanded Simon to launch out from the shore into the deep part of the lake and fish there. They were going to have to launch out further in the deeper part of the lake (v. 4). Simon then objects that they had toiled all night to catch fish but had caught nothing. They had already washed their nets, apparently to put them away until another day (v. 5:2). After all, the best time for fishing with nets was during the night. Everything appears to be so unfavorable for fishing and Simon and his friends were probably exhausted and frustrated from their night's work, nevertheless, at Jesus' words, they obeyed His command.

Jesus rewards their faith. They catch so many fish in their nets that they have to call their partners in another boat to come and help them out. And even then both boats become so full of fish that they could not hold the catch.

We need "nevertheless" kind of faith in our lives today. "Nevertheless" faith means that, no matter what the obstacles are, we are going to move forward at Jesus' Words. Do you have "nevertheless" faith?

3. The Commitment (vv. 8-11)

The Lord's revelation of power in the field of Simon's particular calling makes a powerful impression on him. He falls before the Savior, overwhelmed by His divine glory and with a deep realization of his utter sinfulness. When we come into the presence of the Lord, we too must confess that we are sinful and need to be made whole. Jesus understands Simon's state of mind and speaks reassuringly to him. Unexpectedly, Simon receives a divine calling to evangelism. Simon, James, and John committed to the Lord Jesus Christ that they were going to follow Him to the end. They have no idea what they were going to be involved in, only that they would "catch men" (v. 10). Still, they dropped what they were doing and followed Him. We should have that kind of commitment today. We should be willing to forsake all and follow Jesus.

What have you forsaken for the sake of Christ? What do you still cling to?

Search the Scriptures

1. What was Jesus' command to Simon? How did Simon respond to Jesus' command (Luke 5:3–5)?

2. Why did Simon tell Jesus to depart from Him (v. 8)?

3. What did Jesus mean when He said: "thou shalt catch men" (v. 10)?

Discuss the Meaning

1. What does it mean to "forsake all" and follow Jesus today? What kind of commitment does it take to follow Jesus? Is following Jesus difficult? Give reasons for your answers.

2. Should all ministers work for the kingdom full-time or is there space for bi-vocational ministers?

Liberating Lesson

Today, as in Jesus' day, thinking of walking away from your job to pursue full-time ministry is frightening. However, Jesus did not call His disciples to leave everything they knew. They would pivot from fishing for fish to fishing for people. Some of the same skills and natural talents would be applied differently. What natural talents do you use in your occupation that can be used to spread the Gospel?

While the fishermen left their nets to follow Jesus, the men also had a network of support that freed them to focus on full-time ministry. How can your Bible study group or church lend background support so others are financially able to devote themselves to the ministry?

Application for Activation

Think about the commitment you've made to Jesus. Are you still excited about it? If not, ask Him to give you a new excitement this week so you can become "fishers of men" (Matthew 4:19). Encourage each student to write out a prayer to the Lord giving over their life, particularly in those areas where He is not fully

Lord. Encourage honesty. Suggest that students pray to be willing to do this, if necessary.

Follow the Spirit

What God wants me to do:

_____

_____

_____

_____

Remember Your Thoughts

Special insights I have learned:

_____

_____

_____

_____

More Light on the Text

Luke 5:1-11

1 And it came to pass, that, as the people pressed upon him to hear the word of God, he stood by the lake of Gennesaret.

This event took place on the shore of the Sea of Galilee, a body of water that goes by many names. This is the only verse in which the lake is called by the Greek name of the town located on the northwest shore of the lake, Gennesaret. Usually, the Gospel writers call it after the larger Jewish district to the west of the lake, Galilee. The same water body is also called by the name of the sea of Chinneroth in the Old Testament and Tiberias (the name of a town on its southwest shore) two times in John. Whereas Luke uses the word "lake," the other evangelists follow the pattern of the Old Testament and call it a sea. The Sea of Galilee measures 13 miles north to south and 7 miles east to west.

After Jesus' baptism and temptation in the wilderness, He started His ministry in Galilee. He became known all over Galilee (4:14). His preaching ministry, backed with the signs and wonders, gathered crowds around Him (4:42). The people wanted to listen to the word coming from God; not just a message about Him, but a revelation from Him. The people of the area were "amazed" by the grace and authority of His words (4:22, 32). This explains the pressure of the crowds on Him by the shore of the Sea of Galilee.

2 And saw two ships standing by the lake: but the fishermen were gone out of them, and were washing their nets.

After each day of fishing, the equipment was readied for the next expedition by cleaning and repairing if needed. The boats were pulled out of the water to prevent them from drifting away or into the shallow water close to land. Fishing boats normally worked in pairs dragging a net between them. An average fishing boat would be about twenty to thirty feet long.

These two boats were empty because their work had been fruitless. It implies a lot for people who live by fishing to spend an entire night on their venture and achieve nothing. Many Americans today could not handle the financial shock of missing just one payday. It was likely a little different for these fishermen to miss one day's worth of fish. They were probably planning other fishing expeditions with equally uncertain results. This sounds much like what many people go through in life, running their affairs with a kind of monotony regulated by failure and success.

3 And he entered into one of the ships, which was Simon's, and prayed him that he

228

would thrust out a little from the land. And he sat down, and taught the people out of the ship.

Jesus chose one of the boats and requested that its owner should move away from the shore. Jesus had an earlier encounter with Simon when he healed Simon's mother-in-law from fever (Luke 4:38). There was likely an acquaintance between them that is why Jesus could step in his boat before making the request. The fact that Simon heeds Jesus' request means that he was available, selfless, but also respectful of Jesus' character due to the past event he witnessed. He did not just base his response on his physical condition of exhaustion, even though he must have been after a long night's work.

It is a real convenience for Jesus to teach from the boat because it lessens the pressure of the crowd on Him. The position also helps make His voice clear for all to hear and not be drowned out by the crowd. The crowd itself cannot get closer without getting wet. This is perhaps not the only time Jesus instructed his disciples to make available a boat for Him in case He was crowded (Mark 3:9). The people think they just need to touch Jesus to be healed, but Jesus wants their focus to be on His teaching at the moment, so He avoids their touch.

4 Now when he had left speaking, he said unto Simon, Launch out into the deep, and let down your nets for a draught.

After Jesus completes His preaching, He focuses on Simon and says to go where it is deeper. The word "Launch out" is singular and then the order to "let down" the nets is plural. This suggests that Jesus addresses Simon as the captain of the boat to take his fishing team out with him and work as a team to put down the nets, which required two to four men to deploy. The Greek word used for net is *diktuon* (**DEEK**-too-on). In context with the nets, Jesus' use of the word "draught" (Amer. spelling:

draft) refers to things that are drawn or pulled, implying these are a type of dragnet. These nets were made of linen, which would be visible to fish during the day. Further, cooler water can hold more oxygen for the fish to breath, so they will be more active when the water of the Lake is cooler, as at nighttime. That is why Simon's crew fished at night. Therefore for the nets to be able to catch fish in broad daylight was a real miracle.

5 And Simon answering said unto him, Master, we have toiled all the night, and have taken nothing: nevertheless at thy word I will let down the net.

Simon demonstrates respect. Although Simon is a professional fisher, he does not despise the instruction of Jesus. Simon was probably brought up in this trade, as children inherited the trade of their parents and began learning it at an early age. Simon could convincingly state that there was no need trying again. However, Simon has already seen Jesus' supernatural intervention when He healed Simon's mother-in-law. It is worth following Jesus' suggestion. As his own experience could not yield any result for him, he acts upon the utterance of Lord. As Christians we would be better off if only we respond faithfully to the Lord's guidance, even in spite of our skills, experience, or frustrations.

Simon also demonstrates selflessness. Though tired and probably worried about last night's failure, he avails not only himself but also his ship and crew to be used by Lord. He exemplifies the one who cares about others more than himself. Above all, we should care about God's kingdom and His work more than ours. And the result will be a tremendous blessing.

The Greek word used for "master" is *epistates* (eh-peese-**TAH**-tace). In the New Testament, the word only appears in Luke and is used when addressing Jesus, replacing the title of rabbi and teacher that are used in the other Gospels. It essentially still means "teacher" and is used to address a person of high status, particularly regarding his role in leadership. It implies an authority of any kind, not just that of a teacher. The word emphasizes the "master" and the speaker's respectful and intimate relationship, as we can hypothesize since the word is used primarily by disciples.

6 And when they had this done, they inclosed a great multitude of fishes: and their net brake. 7 And they beckoned unto their partners, which were in the other ship, that they should come and help them. And they came, and filled both the ships, so that they began to sink.

What a contrast from the beginning of the passage! The two empty boats were now full of fish and about to sink. Acting upon Jesus' command brought the unexpected. Both types of instruments they used were overflowed by their catch. First, their nets were about to tear when they transferred their catch from the nets to the boats, then the boats were on the verge of sinking.

The Greek word used for "beckoned" is *kataneuo* (ka-ta-**NEW**-oh). It literally means "to signal by nodding one's head," suggesting that Simon's company could not wave to their partners in other boats. Indeed, they made such a tremendous catch, their hands were busy pulling the nets out of the water. The partners from the other boats responded to Simon's nod.

8 When Simon saw it, he fell down at Jesus' knees, saying, Depart from me; for I am a sinful man, O Lord.

Simon has never witnessed such a thing before. He becomes suddenly aware that this man has divine potential in Him. Unlike earlier when he used the title "master" for Jesus (v. 5), here he uses Lord (Gk. *kurios*, **KOU**-ree-oce). The word can be used for expressing politeness, however, it is also used to address God. Simon's awareness of the person he is dealing with is heightened.

Simon's requesting Jesus to leave him suggests his sense of unworthiness in comparison to Christ's greatness and holiness. When Simon sees Jesus as the Anointed One of God who has not only healed his mother-in-law (Luke 4:38) but also has power over this situation, he is immediately brought under the conviction that indeed he is a sinful man. Many people in the Bible, when the face the divine presence, reacted like Simon. Isaiah saw the Lord and realized that his lips are unclean and needed to be purified (Isaiah 6:5). Manoah, Samson's father, also encountered the angel of Lord and feared for his life (Judges 13:22). None of us can come before God in our own selves. We need the cleansing power that only Jesus can provide for us. He is ready to cleanse us and make us whole today.

Even though Simon correctly assesses the condition of his heart and the glory of Christ, his reaction is not salvific. Simon still has spiritual growth to achieve, because his understanding of God and his place in His heart is incomplete. Jesus has just miraculously and freely gifted Simon with a greater income than he has ever dreamed of earning. He gives this freely to the fisherman. But Simon's immediate response is to ask Jesus to go away. Instead of wanting to be cleaned and united with God's glory so that he may enjoy God's presence, Simon cowers in fear. Simon can only admit that he is a sinner. He understands God is powerful and pure, but he does not yet realize that God is also a loving Father, longing to bless His children and live in relationship with them.

9 For he was astonished, and all that were with him, at the draught of the fishes which they had taken: 10 And so was also James, and John, the sons of Zebedee, which were partners with Simon. And Jesus said unto Simon, Fear not; from henceforth thou shalt catch men.

The magnitude of the catch is portrayed by not only Simon's amazement but also that of his other colleagues. But Jesus calms Simon's fear. He now changes the destiny of Simon and his fishing colleagues to henceforth become fishers of men. Jesus' commission of Simon, who readily admits he is a sinner, lays the groundwork for Jesus' ministry of forgiveness and the growing reputation of Jesus as a friend of sinners.

Jesus is not looking for perfect people to serve Him. Rather He is after those who are aware of their own shortcomings and unworthiness, but who are still willing to boldly respond to the challenge by faith. This experience sets a break with the past for Simon and his colleagues. Henceforth, they will have a changed mindset and a new vocation. Simon exhibits a willingness to learn. He knows he is lacking and sinful but obeys the Master's voice to see what God can do. May we be so curious!

Jesus called working men in amid their labor to a life of labor of a different sort. The objective of their first career of fishing was to feed their families and make money. However, when Jesus called them to become "fishers of men" He called them to labor that was not about making money but about remaking the world. Jesus invited them to invest their lives not in man-centered careers but a God-centered one.

11 And when they had brought their ships to land, they forsook all, and followed him.

When they reach the dry land, they decide to leave their past behind to follow Jesus. These men are so convinced that Jesus will meet all their needs from here on out that they were willing to entrust themselves to His providential care. Jesus states that whoever wants to follow Him must forsake himself. In Jesus, James, John, and Simon have found a more fulfilling life than fishing.

Even before this encounter, they knew of Jesus as a teacher and healer. After establishing this groundwork, Jesus calls them to His service. The immediacy of their reaction is expected in their society, given the Jewish religious education system. All Jewish boys went to school to learn the Torah. If a student showed promise, he was invited to keep studying the Prophets, but if not, he went to learn the family trade. If a student showed promise in studying the Prophets, he was invited to the honor of further study of the poetic Writings of the Hebrew Bible. If the boy did not seem bright enough to keep studying, he would be sent back home to learn the family trade. If a student showed promise after learning the Torah, Prophets, and Writings, a rabbi would tell him simply, "Follow me." The student would never turn down the great honor of studying under a rabbi. Simon and his companions were going about their family trade the day Jesus performed this miracle. This means at some point in their education, they were told they were not gifted enough to continue. No rabbi would want them. What a blessing that this rabbi, Jesus, came to them and invited them to be His students! Jesus does not care what the world says about a person, or how the world has evaluated them. He knows our hearts and calls those who will to just follow Him.

Sources:

Baird, W. *The Interpreter's one-volume commentary on the Bible.* Nashville, TN: Abingdon Press, 1971.

Blight, R. C. *An Exegetical Summary of Luke 1:1-11.* Dallas, TX: SIL International, 2007.

Bock, D. L. *The IVP New Testament Commentary Series: Luke.* Downers Grove, IL: InterVarsity Press, 1994.

Green, J. B. *The New International Commentary on the New Testament: The Gospel of Luke.* Grand Rapids, MI: Wm. Eerdmans, 1997.

Kapusta, Philip P. *A King James Dictionary: A Resource for Understanding the Language of the King James Bible.* Murrells Inlet, SC: New Covenant Press, 2012.

Marshall, H. *New International Greek Testament Commentary: Commentary on Luke.* Exeter, UK: Paternoster Press, 1978.

Morris, L. *Tyndale New Testament Commentaries: Luke.* Grand Rapids, MI: William Eerdmans, 1984.

Nolland, J. *Word Biblical Commentary: Luke 1-9:20.* Dallas, TX: Words Books, 1989.

The Zondervan Pictorial Bible Dictionary. Grand Rapids, MI: Zondervan Publishing Co., 1963. 296-297.

Say It Correctly

Gennesaret. geh-**NESS**-are-ett.
Draught. **DRAFT**.
Chinneroth. **CHI**-ner-oth

Daily Bible Readings

MONDAY
Called to Lead Israelites from Egypt
(Exodus 3:1–12)

TUESDAY
Called to Deliver Israelites
from Midianites
(Judges 6:11–16)

WEDNESDAY
Called and Cleansed for Ministry
(Isaiah 6:1–8)

THURSDAY
Single-Mindedness
Required to Follow Jesus
(Luke 9:57–62)

FRIDAY
Repentance, Goal of God's Kindness
(Romans 2:1–11)

SATURDAY
Jesus Calls Peter to Ministry
(John 21:15–19)

SUNDAY
Don't Be Afraid to Catch People
(Luke 5:1–11)

Notes

Teaching Tips

Words You Should Know

A. Perceived (Mark 2:8) *epiginosko* (Gk.)—To know, recognize, or acknowledge; to be fully acquainted with

B. Amazed (v. 12) *existemi* (Gk.)—To be put out of one's wits, be beside oneself; to be astounded, astonished, or insane

Teacher Preparation

Unifying Principle—Healing for the Whole Person. The limitations of human existence make genuine wholeness an elusive goal. Where can we find true healing? By declaring a paralyzed man's sins forgiven and restoring his physical health, Jesus demonstrated that God had called Jesus to heal infirmities of the soul as well as the body.

A. Read the Bible Background and Devotional Reading.

B. Pray for your students and lesson clarity.

C. Read the lesson Scripture in multiple translations.

O—Open the Lesson

A. Begin the class with prayer.

B. Discuss with the students if they agree or disagree with following statement: "Being healthy means more than having a sound body."

C. Have the students read the Aim for Change and the In Focus story.

D. Ask students how events like those in the story weigh on their hearts and how they can view these events from a faith perspective.

P—Present the Scriptures

A. Read the Focal Verses and discuss the Background and The People, Places, and Times sections.

B. Have the class share what Scriptures stand out for them and why, with particular emphasis on today's themes.

E—Explore the Meaning

A. Use In Depth or More Light on the Text to facilitate a deeper discussion of the lesson text.

B. Pose the questions in Search the Scriptures and Discuss the Meaning.

C. Discuss the Liberating Lesson and Application for Activation sections.

N—Next Steps for Application

A. Summarize the value of relying on our Great Physician.

B. End class with a commitment to pray for forgiveness from sins in addition to healing in our bodies.

Worship Guide

For the Superintendent or Teacher
Theme: Called to Heal
Song: "There's Room at the Cross for You"
Devotional Reading: Psalm 103:1-14

Called to Heal

Bible Background • MARK 2:1-12
Printed Text • MARK 2:1-12 | Devotional Reading • PSALM 103:1-14

—————— Aim for Change ——————

By the end of this lesson, we will STUDY Mark's account of Jesus healing the man who was paralyzed, APPRECIATE how one's physical, emotional, social, and spiritual needs are intertwined, and PRAY for God's healing grace to touch us at our particular point of need.

————————— In Focus —————————

Brenda listened to the small group's prayer requests. They were going to pray for Lee's cousin who had cancer, Jordan's knee replacement surgery, and Georgie's nephew who had an opioid addiction. Brenda thought hard, but her family was blessed with good health at the moment. She had just video-chatted with her parents a couple of days ago and everyone was happy and healthy.

Especially in the face of the other serious prayer requests, she felt embarrassed to ask about what was really weighing on her heart. She often suffered from mild Seasonal Affective Disorder. She had felt it settling in over her once Christmas vacation back home in Mississippi was over and she had come back to Virginia where she worked. When it was her turn, Brenda took a deep breath and shared, "I feel silly asking this, but could you guys pray for my mental health?" Brenda met the small group's sympathetic gazes. "I usually have seasonal depression and I'm worried this year will be worse than usual since this is my first winter here away from my family."

"No need to feel silly at all, Brenda. Thanks for letting us know how to help you," the small group leader Jordan said. "I've had some bouts with depression myself and I am happy to talk with you about it, if you want."

God cares about our wholeness in all aspects of our beings—bodily, mentally, and spiritually. How can we work as the church to make sure we minister to the whole person?

—————— Keep in Mind ——————

"Whether is it easier to say to the sick of the palsy, Thy sins be forgiven thee; or to say, Arise, and take up thy bed, and walk?" (Mark 2:9, KJV)

"Is it easier to say to the paralyzed man 'Your sins are forgiven,' or 'Stand up, pick up your mat, and walk'?" (Mark 2:9, NLT)

Focal Verses

KJV **Mark 2:1** And again he entered into Capernaum after some days; and it was noised that he was in the house.

2 And straightway many were gathered together, insomuch that there was no room to receive them, no, not so much as about the door: and he preached the word unto them.

3 And they come unto him, bringing one sick of the palsy, which was borne of four.

4 And when they could not come nigh unto him for the press, they uncovered the roof where he was: and when they had broken it up, they let down the bed wherein the sick of the palsy lay.

5 When Jesus saw their faith, he said unto the sick of the palsy, Son, thy sins be forgiven thee.

6 But there was certain of the scribes sitting there, and reasoning in their hearts,

7 Why doth this man thus speak blasphemies? who can forgive sins but God only?

8 And immediately when Jesus perceived in his spirit that they so reasoned within themselves, he said unto them, Why reason ye these things in your hearts?

9 Whether is it easier to say to the sick of the palsy, Thy sins be forgiven thee; or to say, Arise, and take up thy bed, and walk?

10 But that ye may know that the Son of man hath power on earth to forgive sins, (he saith to the sick of the palsy,)

11 I say unto thee, Arise, and take up thy bed, and go thy way into thine house.

12 And immediately he arose, took up the bed, and went forth before them all; insomuch that they were all amazed, and glorified God, saying, We never saw it on this fashion.

NLT **Mark 2:1** When Jesus returned to Capernaum several days later, the news spread quickly that he was back home.

2 Soon the house where he was staying was so packed with visitors that there was no more room, even outside the door. While he was preaching God's word to them,

3 four men arrived carrying a paralyzed man on a mat.

4 They couldn't bring him to Jesus because of the crowd, so they dug a hole through the roof above his head. Then they lowered the man on his mat, right down in front of Jesus.

5 Seeing their faith, Jesus said to the paralyzed man, "My child, your sins are forgiven."

6 But some of the teachers of religious law who were sitting there thought to themselves,

7 "What is he saying? This is blasphemy! Only God can forgive sins!"

8 Jesus knew immediately what they were thinking, so he asked them, "Why do you question this in your hearts?

9 Is it easier to say to the paralyzed man 'Your sins are forgiven,' or 'Stand up, pick up your mat, and walk'?

10 So I will prove to you that the Son of Man has the authority on earth to forgive sins." Then Jesus turned to the paralyzed man and said,

11 "Stand up, pick up your mat, and go home!"

12 And the man jumped up, grabbed his mat, and walked out through the stunned onlookers. They were all amazed and praised God, exclaiming, "We've never seen anything like this before!"

The People, Places, and Times

Palsy. This disability is due to the loss of motor function of muscles or certain nerves. It refers to all forms of paralysis. The word "palsy" translates the Greek word *paralutikos* (pah-rah-loo-tih-**KAHSS**) from which we derive the English words paralytic and paralysis. The man in this week's Scripture is paralyzed, hence he is unable to walk by himself to meet Jesus. Matthew records the Capernaum centurion asking Jesus to heal his servant of paralysis, which causes him terrible suffering. (Matthew 8:5-6). The apostles also healed those who suffer from this condition (Acts 8:7; 9:33-34).

Scribes. Often called lawyers, doctors, or teachers of the law (Matthew 22:35), they were not considered a Jewish sect or a party, nor were they priests. The title scribe referred to their capacity as transcribers of the Hebrew Bible. They would copy the entire Old Testament by hand onto new scrolls when a new copy was needed. This careful, precise copying of the entire Law, Prophets, and Writings gave them great knowledge of the Scriptures. Mark presents the scribes as often in the company of Pharisees and of the chief priests and coming from Jerusalem.

Have you had special training or a profession that gave you expertise in a subject? How do you and others value that skill?

Background

The news of Jesus, the worker of miracles, spread throughout Capernaum. This was an exciting time. The community had never experienced a healer and teacher like Jesus. No wonder Mark 1:32-33 speaks of the townspeople bringing all the sick and demon-possessed to Jesus. And in Jesus' great compassion He healed every one of them, but He too needed a time of restful healing. So the next morning He departed to be alone with the Father.

The Scriptures do not tell the length of Jesus' solitude, but His time was shortened by the disciples' appearance. Jesus did not appear to be irritated by the disciples' presence, but informed them that He must preach in other places: "Let us go into the next towns, that I may preach there also: for therefore came I forth" (from Mark 1:38). Of a certainty there were more people in need of healing in Capernaum, but Jesus knew His mission was to spread the Gospel to everyone, so He traveled to other towns.

Do you make time to recharge with periods of solitude?

At-A-Glance

1. Jesus Preaches (Mark 2:1-4)
2. Jesus Pardons (vv. 5-9)
3. Jesus Heals (vv. 10-12)

In Depth

1. Jesus Preaches (Mark 2:1-4)

When Jesus entered Capernaum (v. 1), He preached "the word," meaning the Gospel of God's kingdom. Mark's description of the enthusiastic crowd that gathered suggests that it filled the house, jammed the doorway, and spilled out into the street. What a tribute to the ministry of Jesus!

Four men carrying "one sick of the palsy" joined the crowd but were unable to access Jesus through the doorway. Therefore, to get within touching distance of Jesus, they carried the paralytic up the outside stairway to the roof of the house. The oriental house structures in those days were one or two stories, built in a rectangle or square. They had one door that opened into an open space called the porch. Often the porch contained a stairway that led to the roof. So these friends saw the roof as a means to reach

Jesus. They tore the roof open and lowered the paralytic on his bed down through the opening to where Jesus stood preaching. What a scene!

Share about a time you have worked hard to help a friend hear the word of God.

2. Jesus Pardons (vv. 5-9)

Jesus knows this extraordinary action was based on extraordinary faith. He pardons the crippled man's sin. The teachers of the law said nothing but were outraged as they pondered Jesus forgiving the sins of another. Based on Old Testament laws (Exodus 34:6–7), the scribes knew only God had the authority to forgive sins. In their view, Jesus had committed blasphemy (Leviticus 24:15-16), a serious charge that was punishable by death. Even though the scribes do not voice their concerns aloud, Jesus knows their thoughts, which serves as further proof that He is the all-knowing, all-powerful God. Jesus declares His authority as One who is able not only to heal but also to forgive sins. Jesus' words convey to the scribes that forgiving sins are no harder than healing. Since Jesus can heal, as the scribes had seen Him do, then He can also forgive sins.

3. Jesus Heals (vv. 10-12)

Jesus turns His attention to the paralytic and commands him, "Arise, and take up thy bed, and go thy way into thine house" (v. 11). The healing verified Jesus' claim to grant forgiveness. Since the healing was real and impossible for any but God, the claim to forgive sins is also real. The paralytic immediately arose, took up his bed, and walked out in full view of the crowd. This amazed everyone and they praised God—they had never seen anything like this!

Every healing that takes place is cause for rejoicing and praising God. God still heals, but we all know instances where healing didn't occur. Sometimes in the face of our illness, our faith demonstrates God's higher purpose

(John 9) and our relationship with Him. Our faith, despite the absence of physical healing, can recognize the grace of God's peace and strength amid our weakened state. God's healing may be physical, emotional, or spiritual. Even in the absence of healing (2 Corinthians 12:7), we must remember that His grace is sufficient and our faith is the trademark of our relationship with Him—a relationship based on the forgiveness of our sins and reconciliation with our God.

Search the Scriptures

1. What was the main thing that Jesus noticed about the four men who brought their friend to Him? (v. 5)

2. What did Jesus do before He told the man to "take up thy bed, and walk"? (v. 9)

3. What was the reaction of the people when Jesus healed the paralytic? (v. 12) What about when He forgave his sins?

Discuss the Meaning

1. Why did Jesus perform the miracle of forgiveness before performing the miracle of healing (Mark 2:10)?

2. Given their commitment to upholding Jewish law, were the scribes justified in their accusations against Jesus? What motivated their thinking?

Liberating Lesson

Illness and infirmity in body, mind, and soul afflict everyone today. May those who have not yet found physical healing continue seeking it in the faith, believing that God does heal physical illnesses. Yet He does not heal in every situation.

Whether God offers you healing to overcome your illness or strength to continue despite it, you have witnessed the power of God in your life. Paul tells us that God comforts us so that we can comfort others (2 Corinthians 1:4). The testimony of God's presence in your life at a time when healing or deliverance was needed, provides an opportunity for you to share how God sustained you through that time. Whether He has brought you out or continues to help you through, simply sharing with other hurting people helps them know they are not alone.

Application for Activation

Think of someone you know who is suffering from a physical illness. Pray that God might grant wisdom and a deeper understanding of the role of faith in their healing process. Dare to believe that when physical illness prevails, there is more to pray for than a cure. We can pray for God to give us grace and increased faith amid our pain.

Make a list of the times God has healed you physically, emotionally, or spiritually. Reflect on how that healing changed your life and deepened your faith. If you are still awaiting healing, reflect on the blessings He has given you during your situation.

Follow the Spirit

What God wants me to do:

_____

_____

_____

_____

Remember Your Thoughts

Special insights I have learned:

_____

_____

_____

_____

More Light on the Text
Mark 2:1–12

The first chapter of Mark records the beginning of Jesus' ministry, a ministry characterized by teaching, healing, and miracles. People noticed his teaching at the synagogue was better than that of the scribes. He cast out a demon while there at the synagogue, then went to Peter's house and healed his mother-in-law. With these remarkable happenings, Jesus' fame spread all over the region. As a result, people from all walks of life came to Jesus bringing the sick, both to hear Him and to be healed. Among them when Jesus returned to Capernaum were four people who brought to him a man sick of palsy.

1 And again he entered into Capernaum after some days; and it was noised that he was in the house. 2 And straightway many were gathered together, insomuch that there was no room to receive them, no, not so much as about the door: and he preached the word unto them.

Verse 1 states that Jesus "was in the house." Many scholars assume this is Peter's house, which became His headquarters in Capernaum (Matthew 4:13; 9:1; Mark 1:21, 29). It does seem the natural base of operations, as He had been there previously, and Peter was a natural leader among the disciples.

People were drawn to Jesus—His presence, His words, His wisdom, His actions, His attitude, and the grace of God that rested upon Him. As the Son of God, His nature drew people as well. They desired to be close to Him, to be in His presence, to listen to His words, to hear His voice. They wanted to see Him as He touched the lives of the people.

The Lord Jesus preached the Word of God to them. Mark had previously told us that Jesus' message was of the coming kingdom and repentance. He preached God's wisdom, God's counsel, and God's compassion. Jesus was both the Messenger and the Message. He was a living example of what He preached and taught. He never spoke or preached a word that He did not live out. He was the living testimony of the Word He preached and taught. He is the Word of God indeed!

3 And they come unto him, bringing one sick of the palsy, which was borne of four. 4 And when they could not come nigh unto him for the press, they uncovered the roof where he was: and when they had broken it up, they let down the bed wherein the sick of the palsy lay.

To understand the full impact of this passage, one needs knowledge of the Palestinian houses' layout of this time. It is believed that houses were flat-roofed with railings so that people would not fall off (Deuteronomy 22:8; Judges 16:27; 2 Samuel 11:2). On top of some houses, there was access via outside stairs. These types of houses are still common in the northern part of the African continent, especially in northern Nigeria. Houses there are built flat-roofed with mud and wooden beams and thatch covered them.

As Jesus teaches in the small one-room house, four people bring a man "sick of the palsy" to be healed. As they arrive, they discover that there is no room or access through the doorway by which they can get to the Lord. The crowd is too intent on listening to Jesus to allow space for the passage of another person who also desperately needs Jesus. The four helpers are determined, however, and carry the sick man up the outside stairs to the roof of the house. They lower the man down to Jesus. They dig through the thatch or roof tiles (Luke 5:19) and lower the man in front of Jesus. There the sick man lay at Jesus' feet. Their actions in opening up the roof were not an example of reckless destruction of property. Apparently, they realized that a roof can be repaired. These four men wanted to see

to it that this paralyzed man would get to Jesus and receive his healing. They understood that this man's healing was much more important than a roof. Their actions remind us that people are always much more important than things.

How refreshing, encouraging, and uplifting it is to us when we have Christian friends who touch our lives with their faith. Friends who love the Lord, love us, and support us in prayer and encouragement are special gifts to us from God. Friends who will sacrifice themselves on our behalf are precious. When we have genuine Christian friends who support us in these ways, they are more valuable than gold.

We do not know much about these four men who carried the paralyzed man to Christ, but we can recognize faith at work in them. They are men of great faith. Obviously, they believed that the Lord Jesus could and would heal this man or they would not have made the effort to bring him to the Lord. They were also selfless; they put this man and his needs before concern for themselves and material things.

While it is important to keep our attention on Christ, we must also not forget others who are seeking Christ. There is always room for everyone to come to Jesus. We must make sure that our presence does not hinder anyone's progress to God. Instead, we should open ourselves to inviting them in.

5 When Jesus saw their faith, he said unto the sick of palsy, Son, thy sins be forgiven thee.

Jesus is not angry about the hole in the roof. Rather, the Lord Jesus acknowledges "their" faith, the plural indicating not just the man with paralysis, but also the four with him. Their faith is demonstrated in their action—carrying the man to the house and the creativity and perseverance in getting him to Jesus in spite of the obstacles. He responds to their faith first by speaking words of forgiveness to the paralyzed man, whom He calls "son" (Gk. *teknon*, **TEK-**non). This address shows the affection which Jesus holds for the man. Even though this is the first time they meet, Jesus addresses the man with the loving care of a father. This term would also be used by a teacher's followers. Since the man and his helpers have already shown their great faith in Jesus' ability to heal and their awareness of their great need for Jesus specifically, Jesus does not hesitate to include the man among His followers.

Of course, forgiveness is not what the man or his friends are looking for. It does not mean that the man is particularly sinful. The pronouncement of forgiveness here illustrates the common belief in the Old Testament that every suffering is embedded in man's alienation from God. To Jesus the man's deepest need is the healing of the soul (conversion and the forgiveness of sins), then the physical. Jesus, therefore, calls the people's attention to this need by proclaiming forgiveness to the man. This single act provokes controversy and conflict against Jesus among the scribes and Jewish authorities. It is also, according to Mark's record, the beginning of the conflict in Christ's ministry on earth.

6 But there were certain of the scribes sitting there, and reasoning in their hearts, 7 Why doth this man thus speak blasphemies? who can forgive sins but God only?

Among the crowd gathered in the house to hear Jesus are some scribes—"teachers of religious law" (Mark 1:22, NLT). Their purpose in coming is not made known. However, they might have come out of curiosity upon hearing the news of the nature of His teaching as compared with their own (1:22) and the numerous miracles He had already performed. At other points in Gospel accounts, they come to ensnare Him on theological issues.

This opportunity comes as Jesus proclaims forgiveness to the sick man.

The scribes who were present were immediately critical of Christ's action. They thought that Jesus did not have the authority to forgive sins. To claim to be able to forgive sins was blasphemy since the forgiveness of sin is a task for God alone. Blasphemy is ultimately the charge they bring against Jesus to demand His execution on the Cross (Mark 14:64). Indeed, since all sin is ultimately an affront to God Himself, only God has the right and authority to forgive sin. For a mere human to claim such power would be heresy.

However, Jesus is not a mere human. The scribes failed to realize Jesus actually did have the inherent authority to forgive iniquities. Jesus was and is God the Son and God Himself, the Second Person of the Triune Divinity. He can forgive transgressions. Praise Him that He does!

8 And immediately when Jesus perceived in his spirit that they so reasoned within themselves, he said unto them, Why reason ye these things in your hearts? 9 Whether is it easier to say to the sick of the palsy, Thy sins be forgiven thee; or to say, Arise, and take up thy bed, and walk?

Through the Spirit, Jesus discerns their thoughts right away. Both actions (vv. 7-8) are simultaneous, as quick as the thoughts themselves. Mark uses the adverb "immediately," *eutheus* (Gk. yew-**THAY**-oce), a word he uses frequently in his Gospel also which can be translated "forthwith" or "straightway." Mark portrays Christ's ministry as very active.

As the scribes contemplate this in their hearts, Jesus through the Holy Spirit perceives it. The word "perceived" is from the Greek verb *epiginosko* (eh-pee-gee-**NOCE**-koh) meaning to recognize or acknowledge. It has the idea of not just being acquainted with but being fully acquainted with or having full knowledge of.

Even though the scribes do not say a word, Jesus understands them completely. This is further proof Christ is the omniscient God. Although they have not expressed their thoughts openly, through His question Jesus implicitly makes them know who He is because only God can know and discern the inner thoughts of people.

Humanly speaking, to the scribes, both forgiving sins and healing the man are impossible. Simply saying someone has forgiveness could be easier, since its fulfillment is not verifiable. However, asking a paralyzed man to get up and walk is subject to verification. Jesus criticizes the people for their unbelief. They have already seen Him perform healings that are impossible for any human and yet they still think He cannot do the equally impossible task of forgiving sins.

10 But that you may know that the Son of man hath power on earth to forgive sins, (he saith to the sick of the palsy,) 11 I say unto thee, Arise, and take up thy bed, and go thy way into thine house.

The Lord Jesus points out that He has both the power to forgive sin and the power to heal this man. In receiving Christ's forgiveness, the man has the guilt of sin taken away. In receiving his healing, the man receives from the Lord the gift of wholeness in his body.

Jesus reveals His true identity as the "Son of man" to the scribes. The "Son of man" is the title Christ most often applies to Himself. It is an Aramaic way to refer to the "everyman," but it is also a declaration of His divinity because it is an allusion to ancient prophesy (Daniel 7:13). To show them that He has authority on earth to forgive sins—contrary to their belief—He heals the paralytic. The paralytic man shows surprisingly little agency in this healing account. Usually, Jesus talks with the sick person about if and how to heal them. Jesus, however, has already seen that the man

with palsy has faith in Him. Christ's actions now intend to grow the faith of the scribes. The man's physical and outward healing corroborates His claim of authority to forgive sins. It makes the crowd realize that since He can do the miracle of healing, which they can see, He can also do the other miracle, which they cannot see.

12 And immediately he arose, took up the bed, and went forth before them all; insomuch that they were all amazed, and glorified God, saying, We never saw it on this fashion.

The Lord Jesus, with authority and power, commanded the paralyzed man to arise, take up his bed, and go home. The man obeyed. His obedience was an act of faith. Through his faith and obedience, he received his healing. The response of the people who witnessed this miracle was powerful. The people were amazed, astonished, and they glorified God. This and other miracles of the Lord Jesus were signs that pointed people to the Lord and the salvation that He has provided.

The sick man is restored not just to health, but to strength. Even after a short time without the use of one's legs, muscles begin to shrink and weaken. Jesus heals the damaged nerves causing palsy in the man's legs and goes further to strengthen the legs so that he can "immediately" stand, lift his bedding, and walk through the crowded room. Just moments ago, this feat involved four people and the destruction of a roof. Now the man can do it all by his own power.

The sick man's healing and his response is instant. He picks up his bed, according to Jesus' command, and walks away to the amazement of all in the crowd, including the teachers of the law who have challenged His authority to forgive sins. The word "amazed" comes from the Greek verb *existemi* (ex-**ISS**-tay-mee) which literally means to be put out of one's wits, be beside oneself, to be astounded, or astonished, or to become astounded, or insane. The reaction of the crowd moves from being "amazed." They praise God because never before have they seen anything like that. The main thrust of this story is not rooted in terms of Jesus' pity on and healing of the helpless paralytic, but on His ability to forgive sins. Sin is the sick man's (indeed, all humanity's) major problem, to which Jesus first declares forgiven and thereby proclaims the presence of the kingdom of God to mankind—the thrust of His earthly mission.

Sources:

Thayer, Joseph Henry. *A Greek-English Lexicon of the New Testament.* New York: American Book Company, 1996.

Strong, James. *The New Strong's Exhaustive Concordance of the Bible.* Nashville, TN: Thomas Nelson, 2003.

Vine, W.E. *Vine's Complete Expository Dictionary of Old and New Testament Words.* Nashville, TN: Thomas Nelson, 1996.

Say It Correctly

Capernaum. kah-**PEER**-nah-um.
Palsy. **PALL**-zee.

Daily Bible Readings

MONDAY
Peace and Healing Will Come
(Isaiah 57:14–21)

TUESDAY
Healed by Christ's Wounds
(1 Peter 2:18–25)

WEDNESDAY
Canaanite Daughter Healed by
Mother's Faith
(Matthew 15:21–28)

THURSDAY
Anoint Sick with Oil and Prayer
(James 5:13–16)

FRIDAY
Woman Healed by Her Faith
(Mark 5:21–34)

SATURDAY
The Sick Need a Physician
(Mark 2:13–17)

SUNDAY
Jesus Heals and Forgives the Paralytic
(Mark 2:1–12)

Teaching Tips

Words You Should Know

A. Sanctify (John 17:17) *hagiazo* (Gk.)—To set apart for holiness, to be separated from the profane for sacred use; to consecrate

B. Perfect (v. 23) *teleioo* (Gk.)—To make complete and one, to thoroughly finish, to come to the end

Teacher Preparation

Unifying Principle—Standing in the Gap. People often look for ways to appeal for assistance on behalf of others. How can people respond to the urge to intercede in a meaningful manner? Jesus' prayer for His disciples serves as a call to use intercessory prayer for the sake of others.

A. Read the Bible Background and Devotional Reading.

B. Pray for your students and lesson clarity.

C. Read the lesson Scripture in multiple translations.

O—Open the Lesson

A. Begin the class with prayer.

B. Write several titles on small cards: attorney, member of Congress, union negotiator, real estate agent. Ask volunteers to pick a card and hold it to their foreheads without looking at it. Have other class members give your volunteers clues concerning their identities, helping them guess what it is. Afterward, point out that all of these professionals serve as intercessors, tasked with representing the best interest of others.

C. Have the students read the Aim for Change and the In Focus story.

D. Ask students how events like those in the story weigh on their hearts and how they can view these events from a faith perspective.

P—Present the Scriptures

A. Read the Focal Verses and discuss the Background and The People, Places, and Times sections.

B. Have the class share what Scriptures stand out for them and why, with particular emphasis on today's themes.

E—Explore the Meaning

A. Use In Depth or More Light on the Text to facilitate a deeper discussion of the lesson text.

B. Pose the questions in Search the Scriptures and Discuss the Meaning.

C. Discuss the Liberating Lesson and Application for Activation sections.

N—Next Steps for Application

A. Summarize the value of enduring trials, rather than merely escaping from difficulty.

B. End class with a commitment to pray for each other and ask other believers to pray for them.

Worship Guide

For the Superintendent or Teacher
Theme: Called as the Intercessor
Song: "Standing in the Need of Prayer"
Devotional Reading: 1 Timothy 2:1-7

Called as the Intercessor

Bible Background • JOHN 17:14-24
Printed Text • JOHN 17:14-24 | Devotional Reading • 1 TIMOTHY 2:1-7

—————— Aim for Change ——————

By the end of this lesson, we will EXPLORE Jesus' intercessory prayer for His disciples, LONG for Jesus' prayer to be answered more fully in their lives and the church, and PRAY for others and work for unity in the body of Christ.

————————— In Focus —————————

The idea came from a pamphlet Anthony picked up somewhere called "The Power of 30 Days." The pamphlet presented a simple way to deal with problems and trials we all face: Choose a prayer partner and every day for 30 days you and your partner come together in prayer and present the need to God.

Anthony discussed the idea with his wife and they agreed to come together each day and pray that God would do something about the drug house on the corner of their block. As they prayed, they continued to raise awareness of the problem among their neighbors and village officials. They knew God would provide the perfect solution to the dangerous activities that house promoted. Three weeks into their prayer vigil, the drug house burned down. No one was hurt, but the building was burned down so the city had to demolish the remaining structure.

Anthony and his wife were so overjoyed with the results of their prayer experiment that they shared the news with their church. Soon others were joining in the "Power of 30 Days" prayers and many people were reporting miraculous results. In the cases where God had not yet moved, the participants reported a renewed vitality in their prayer lives. Some people who previously did not pray often had started praying regularly.

Prayer does, in fact, change things. When we communicate our love, gratitude, and needs to our heavenly Father, He is moved to act on our behalf. In today's lesson, we will examine Jesus' "High Priestly Prayer" for His followers.

—————— Keep in Mind ——————

"Neither pray I for these alone, but for them also which shall believe on me through their word" (John 17:20, KJV).

"I am praying not only for these disciples but also for all who will ever believe in me through their message" (John 17:20, NLT).

Focal Verses

KJV **John 17:14** I have given them thy word; and the world hath hated them, because they are not of the world, even as I am not of the world.

15 I pray not that thou shouldest take them out of the world, but that thou shouldest keep them from the evil.

16 They are not of the world, even as I am not of the world.

17 Sanctify them through thy truth: thy word is truth.

18 As thou hast sent me into the world, even so have I also sent them into the world.

19 And for their sakes I sanctify myself, that they also might be sanctified through the truth.

20 Neither pray I for these alone, but for them also which shall believe on me through their word;

21 That they all may be one; as thou, Father, art in me, and I in thee, that they also may be one in us: that the world may believe that thou hast sent me.

22 And the glory which thou gavest me I have given them; that they may be one, even as we are one:

23 I in them, and thou in me, that they may be made perfect in one; and that the world may know that thou hast sent me, and hast loved them, as thou hast loved me.

24 Father, I will that they also, whom thou hast given me, be with me where I am; that they may behold my glory, which thou hast given me: for thou lovedst me before the foundation of the world.

NLT **John 17:14** I have given them your word. And the world hates them because they do not belong to the world, just as I do not belong to the world.

15 I'm not asking you to take them out of the world, but to keep them safe from the evil one.

16 They do not belong to this world any more than I do.

17 Make them holy by your truth; teach them your word, which is truth.

18 Just as you sent me into the world, I am sending them into the world.

19 And I give myself as a holy sacrifice for them so they can be made holy by your truth.

20 I am praying not only for these disciples but also for all who will ever believe in me through their message.

21 I pray that they will all be one, just as you and I are one—as you are in me, Father, and I am in you. And may they be in us so that the world will believe you sent me.

22 I have given them the glory you gave me, so they may be one as we are one.

23 I am in them and you are in me. May they experience such perfect unity that the world will know that you sent me and that you love them as much as you love me.

24 Father, I want these whom you have given me to be with me where I am. Then they can see all the glory you gave me because you loved me even before the world began!

The People, Places, and Times

God as Jesus' Father. Jesus' relationship with the Father is unique because He is the eternal Son of God. Jesus expressed His unique intimate relationship to God by referring to Him as "Abba" (Mark 14:36). *Abba* is an Aramaic word that denotes a warm sense of intimacy. On several occasions, Jesus spoke of God as "My Father" (Matthew 7:21; 10:32; 16:17). The personal pronoun is expressive of their relationship. The claim that Jesus had a unique Father-Son relationship with God was shocking to the religious leaders of Jesus' time. His claim not only violated their traditions, but the Jewish leaders understood that Jesus was making Himself God's equal.

The World. In the New Testament specifically, the Greek word *kosmos* (**KOS**-mos) carries a variety of meanings. In some verses, it carries a positive denotation of all humanity (John 3:16: "the world"). John most often uses it to refer to the realm of sin and human affairs in alienation and opposition to God (1 John 4:5; 5:19). John declares the nature of the world is ruled by lust and pride and dominated by Satan, God's enemy. The world's system has an inherent hatred toward God. In the end, the world and its wares are passing away. However, those who believe in Christ and obey God's Word will abide forever (cf. 2:8).

Background

The prayer in Matthew 6:9-13 is commonly called "The Lord's Prayer." However, that prayer is actually a model for the prayers of believers. The true Lord's Prayer is the prayer of John 17. This is Jesus' farewell prayer for His disciples. In the prayer of Matthew 6, Jesus explains what His disciples should desire for themselves. In the prayer of John 17, Jesus petitions God on behalf of His disciples. Jesus and His disciples had just finished eating the Passover meal. And "Jesus knew that his hour was come that he

should depart out of this world unto the Father" (from John 13:1). Jesus gave the disciples their final instructions. He told them of the coming betrayal, going to the Father to prepare a place for them, and the coming of the Holy Spirit (John 13-16).

After completing His final teaching, called the "Upper Room Discourse," Jesus offered up His longest recorded prayer, called the "High Priestly Prayer." The prayer was likely prayed in the presence of the disciples either in the Upper Room or on the way to the Garden of Gethsemane.

If you could only give one last prayer for your children or another group you lead, what would you pray for them?

At-A-Glance

1. The Believers' Protection
(John 17:14-16)
2. The Believers' Sanctification
(vv. 17-19)
3. The Believers' Unity (vv. 20-24)

In Depth

1. The Believers' Protection (John 17:14-16)

In this final prayer before His Passion, Jesus petitions God for His followers. The Lord realizes that His earthly ministry is drawing to an end. Soon He will return to His rightful place in heaven. So He commits His followers to the Father's care. Jesus affirms that He has completed part of His mission already: He has given the disciples the Father's Word. Jesus Himself is the Word of God. By His teaching, preaching, and His holy presence, He has imparted the Father's Word to His followers. Although believers are separated from the world, Christ does not expect us to withdraw from the world. Instead, He asks that we be protected from the world's evil influences. The "evil one" is Satan, the devil, who always seeks to drag people away from God. Though the disciples will be in the world, they belong elsewhere (namely heaven), just like Jesus Himself. Their allegiance and citizenship have changed to the kingdom of heaven.

2. The Believers' Sanctification (vv. 17-19)

Jesus' second petition is for sanctification: "Sanctify them through thy truth" (v. 17). To sanctify means to set apart for God and His holy purposes. Every believer has been set apart to carry on the work of Christ (v. 18). Each Christian has been appointed some divine task and equipped to carry it out. God sent Jesus with a specific mission to enlighten all humanity that involved a great deal of courage, prayer, and self-sacrifice. This is exactly what He expects from us, exactly what he has prepared and personally "sanctified" us for.

Jesus set Himself aside from all defilement and resisted all temptation so that He could successfully carry out His spiritual responsibility. He did this so that others "might be sanctified through the truth." The truth is God's active Word that must be obeyed. Jesus in His incarnation was God's truth personified (14:6) and all of His followers know the truth (8:32) and abide in it (8:44). For their sakes, He has consecrated Himself as a living sacrifice and stood in the gap on our behalf.

How have you sanctified yourself to God's purpose? How do you manifest that promise in everyday life?

3. The Believers' Unity (vv. 20-24)

This prayer can be summed up as a desire for a unity that would mimic the unity that Jesus has with the Father. Up to this point, Jesus has focused His prayer primarily on His disciples. Now He looks to the future and prays for the universal church throughout the ages. The Father and Son provide the best example of Christian unity (John 17:21). Christians will find themselves united with each other as they unite with Christ. The glory of Christ unites Christians with Him. Our common salvation unites us as one and serves as a sign to the world that Christ came from God and lives within us. Jesus asks that the unity of believers would show the world that Jesus was sent by the Father and would cause the world to believe in Him as Savior. All believers should join with Christ in praying that God be glorified and that believers everywhere be protected, sanctified, and unified.

How has the lack of unity in the Church, the body of Christ, contributed to why the world has not been convinced of the Gospel?

Search the Scriptures

1. What did Christ ask God to do to protect believers from the world's evil system? (v. 17)

2. Aside from His disciples, whom else did Jesus include in His prayer? (v. 20)

3. What does Jesus want His followers to see when He brings them to heaven? (v. 24)

Discuss the Meaning

1. Jesus prays for believers to be one with each other. How is this made possible? And how do we maintain unity as the church?

2. Is the church currently a unified witness of Christ? Why or why not?

Liberating Lesson

Many of the problems in our communities could be better addressed by a united effort on the part of God's people. What effect might such unity have on crime, immorality, and social ills?

Application for Activation

This week select a community or church problem that you want God to answer. Then choose a prayer partner. You and your partner will spend at least ten minutes each day praying for this problem. Be prepared to report back to class next week with your experiences.

Follow the Spirit

What God wants me to do:

_____

_____

_____

_____

Remember Your Thoughts

Special insights I have learned:

_____

_____

_____

_____

More Light on the Text

John 17:14–24

14 I have given them thy word; and the world hath hated them, because they are not of the world, even as I am not of the world

This section of Jesus' prayer begins with His assurance that He has imparted "thy word" to the disciples. Repeatedly throughout His ministry, Jesus says that His teachings are straight from God the Father (John 5:19; 8:28; 12:49). Jesus' teaching has not been His own, but God the Father's. Now at the end of His time on earth, Jesus' mission to preach the Gospel is complete. He has completely revealed Himself—and therefore the Father—to the disciples in His teaching.

From much earlier in Jesus' ministry, He has acknowledged that the world hates Him (John 7:7). The reason He gave then was the world's resentment that Jesus was a witness against the world's evils. No one likes to have their flaws pointed out, especially when they believe they are doing well. Because the world sets itself against Jesus, it reflects the need for Jesus' correction. Instead of listening to Jesus' Word and improving, the world stubbornly ignores Jesus and hates that He even mentions its flaws.

Jesus will assert several commonalities between Him and His disciples in these verses; this verse contains the first one. The disciples do not belong to this world any more than Christ Himself. It is easy to see why the Messiah would not feel He belongs to this sinful world. He is patient, kind, powerful, loving, and self-sacrificing. His soul is the stuff of heaven. Here Jesus says all those reasons He does not belong to this world also apply to His followers.

15 I pray not that thou shouldest take them out of the world, but that thou shouldest keep them from the evil. 16 They are not of the world, even as I am not of the world.

Take note of the tone of the prayer. Jesus is not asking that God should take them away from the world, but rather that He should protect them. Jesus does not pray that God should destroy Satan, nor that the disciples should die and leave this world to escape the onslaught of the evil one, nor that they should be separated and given a different world of their own so that they would be free from evil. Rather He prays that God should protect them from the temptations and persecutions that await them. He prays that, although they are in a world that is full of evil, they may live as lights and examples of God.

This small community of believers would be persecuted in the world, but Jesus does not wish them to be completely spared from the hostility. The only way to accomplish this would be to bring the disciples home to heaven immediately. This would fulfill the disciples' unity with Christ and the Father, but it would leave the world to its own devices and deprive the rest of humanity of learning to follow God. Paul faced a similar quandary in his ministry, telling the Philippian church that he had "a desire to depart, and to be with Christ; which is far better" (Philippians 1:23), but that he was needed here on earth to continue his ministry to churches, like the one in Philippi.

He instead asks the Father to protect them from the "evil one." Sometimes, in the face of persecution and death, it seems that they were not protected at all. However, their protection is guaranteed, they are the apple of the Lord's eye, and whatever persecution they encounter, God is always in control. Jesus has told them they are blessed when persecuted for His sake (Matthew 5:11–12). Since they do not belong to this world, God will not leave them alone.

Given His fast-approaching departure, Jesus specifically prays for the disciples' protection from the "evil one," which here refers undoubtedly to Satan, the prince of the world (John 12:31; 14:30; 16:11). Jesus, realizing the power and presence of Satan in the world and his work against the people of God, prays for divine protection and strength. Evil comes in many forms, so Jesus prays His disciples would be protected from all of it. But we must also remember that evil is not just an amorphous, chaotic, mindless force of fallen nature. A malevolent spiritual enemy is trying to keep Christ from winning souls. That enemy sets himself against Christ's disciples in many ways.

Here He compares Himself with the disciples, attesting to their unity and the disciples' holiness as He has done previously (15:3, 19). He says, "They are not of the world" as He is also not of the world. John records Jesus' words about the world (*kosmos*), which dominate this prayer. There are many ways to use the word

kosmos, whether to refer to all the people of the world, the globe itself, or sinful humanity at odds with heaven. Throughout His ministry, as recorded by John, Jesus uses the word *kosmos* to refer to all people. When we look at the context, we see those people need saving. Here in the final days of Jesus' ministry, the meaning shifts to a picture of the sinful systems of humanity that have set themselves against God and His workers. Three times Jesus refers to the "prince of this world (*kosmos*)," implying that the sinful systems of humanity are evil because they are merely following their leader, Satan.

However, Christ contends, neither He nor His disciples are from that sinful world. Christ again confirms that He and we disciples share a unity, which implies disunion with the world. Because we are not one with the world, it recognizes us as its enemy.

17 Sanctify them through thy truth: thy word is truth. 18 As thou hast sent me into the world, even so have I also sent them into the world. 19 And for their sakes I sanctify myself, that they also might be sanctified through the truth.

Then Jesus makes another specific request, asking God to sanctify the disciples. The word "sanctify" is the Greek word *hagiazo* (haw-gee-**ODD**-zo). It means to set apart, to be separated from profane things for sacred use. It has the idea of consecrating, or being consecrated, or making holy. The idea is akin to being separated from the world, a thought Jesus started in the previous verse (v. 16).

He prays that God would continue to keep them separated from the world through the Word of God, which is equated with truth. The Word refers to the teachings of Christ. They are to be separated to continue His ministry on earth (v. 18). As the Father commissioned Him to the ministry, so He commissions them to minister the word of truth in the world (cf

Matthew 28:20; Mark 15:15-20; John 14:12; 20:21). For this purpose and the benefit of the disciples, Jesus says that He separates Himself. He consecrates Himself in order to carry out the work of redemption. He, therefore, sets an example for believers to follow (See 1 John 1:7; Ephesians 5:26).

He does not leave us in the dark as to how we will be sanctified. It is by the truth. And we need not even question as Pilate does, "What is truth?" (John 18:38). Jesus tells us: "thy word is truth" (v. 17). We do not need to be confused at this further step of logic because Christ has already said He has given the disciples God's Word (v. 14)! He has completely prepared His followers with God's Word, which is truth, which is how to be sanctified.

This sanctification involves their consecration for the task entrusted to them and their endowment with all the spiritual resources for carrying out the task. This work is done by the Holy Spirit through the Word of truth—in John, Jesus is both the Word and Truth.

Jesus was sent by the Father into the world and now He sends His disciples into the same world. The Greek word here for "sent" is *apostello* (ah-poe-**STEL**-low), which means "to order to go to an appointed place" or "to send away." We get the English word apostle from this same root. The disciples need to be consecrated to serve as apostles—the "sent ones." The entire Christian community is, thus, to be sanctified as an apostolic community sent by Christ to be His witnesses in the world. This is why, when many Christians recite the Apostles' Creed on Sundays, they pledge their belief in the holy, universal, and "apostolic" church. The entire church has been "sent out" by Christ into the world.

With the impending Cross on His mind, Jesus sets a basis for the disciples' obedience later by resolving afresh to do the Father's will—which in His case means death on the Cross. Jesus sets Himself apart (i.e. sanctifies Himself) to perform the redemptive work on the Cross so that the beneficiaries of that work might set themselves apart from the world that hates them. He shows the disciples that the Father's will reigns supreme and the disciples' best response to God's will is surrender.

20 Neither pray I for these alone, but for them also which shall believe on me through their word; 21 That they all may be one; as thou, Father, art in me, and I in thee, that they also may be one in us: that the world may believe that thou hast sent me.

In verses 21-24, Jesus concentrates on unity within the Body of Christ—the Church—that is the mark of authenticity of their relationship with the Father and the Son. The unity to which the Church aspires is exemplified in the unity between the Father and the Son and is to be maintained by a persistent relationship with both the Father and the Son. This ardent request is made four times in this section and once in verse 11.

The Church's manifest oneness would give public confirmation both of their relationship with Jesus and that of Jesus with the Father. This expanding unity would generate multiplying witnesses throughout the world and that is how the church grows. Such love is only possible through God's power and not only human effort. What Jesus says here is that the Church cannot be complete as a body if there is a lack of unity. Should that happen, the Church will be fragmented, and Christ is not glorified. Jesus here offers a very important antidote for the world's rejection of Christ's authority and purpose on earth—and that is unity in the Church. If Christians want the world to know God, then they should determine to be one as God and Christ are one.

22 And the glory which thou gavest me I have given them; that they may be one, even as we are one: 23 I in them, and thou in me, that they may be made perfect in one; and that the world may know that thou hast sent me, and hast loved them, as thou hast loved me.

Not only do we share Christ's otherworldly origins and belonging, but here He says we also share in His glory. John often speaks of the glory of God and Christ. As early as his opening summary, John says the disciples saw Jesus' glory, "the glory as of the only begotten of the Father" (John 1:14), as Christ performed His miracles (John 2:11, 11:4). Jesus says this is the glory which He shared with the Father "before the world was" (John 17:5), and John sees the glory of God give light to the New Jerusalem (Revelation 21:23). We understand from these last two verses that the glory of God is tied closely with His presence. It only makes sense then that is given the glory of Christ would result in unity with each other and with Christ. The glory of the believers is to be evidenced in their interrelationship with one another and with Christ and the Father.

It is in oneness that the church will "be made perfect (Gr. *teleioo*, teh-lay-**OH**-oh) in one." This does not mean that the church will be completely without fault and good in all we do. The word perfect here means completed or thoroughly done, so Jesus here prays that our unity would be thoroughly accomplished as we receive His glory and allow Him to dwell in us as the Father dwells in Him. A thorough unity in the church not only helps the world believe God sent Jesus (cf. v. 21), but it also shows that God loves us as He loves Jesus. Here we see yet another commonality between us and the Savior: God loves us just as much as He loves Jesus, His only begotten, beloved Son.

24 Father, I will that they also, whom thou hast given me, be with me where I am; that they may behold my glory, which thou hast given me: for thou lovedst me before the foundation of the world.

Jesus appeals to His pre-existence here. It is important to remember that Christ did not suddenly appear for the first time in Bethlehem. Rather, He is co-eternal with the other two Persons of the Trinity. Jesus is the same deity as the God seen in the Old Testament.

Jesus concludes this prayer by requesting that all persons that the Father has given Him may be with Him where He is (John 14:1-3), i.e. heaven. When Christ's followers join Him in heaven, they will see the glory which Christ had before the world was made and prior to His incarnation into the world. The believers' destiny to behold the glory of Christ is predicated on the merits of Jesus our High Priest who makes this request. One must note how Jesus closes this earnest prayer with its deep theology, with a request for companionship. In the end, the reason Christ came and died on the Cross—the reason for all of salvation history—was to restore the relationship between God and His creation. Christ's most dear request is restored unity with us, just so we can all be together in perfect unity.

Sources:

Abraham, Kenneth A. *The Matthew Henry Study Bible, King James Version*. Dallas, TX: World Bible Publishers, 1994. 2155–2158.

Brown, Raymond Edward. *The Gospel According to John Xiii–Xxi: A New Introduction and Commentary*. Garden City, NY: Doubleday, 1966.

Bruce, F. F. *The Gospel of John: Introduction, Exposition and Notes*. Grand Rapids, MI: Wm. B. Eerdmans, 1983.

Carson, D. A. *The Farewell Discourse and Final Prayer of Jesus: An Exposition of John 14–17*. Grand Rapids, MI: Baker Book House, 1980. 173–207.

Meyer, F. B. *Gospel of John: The Life and Light of Man, Love to the Uttermost*. Fort Washington, PA: Christian Literature Crusade, 1988.

Morris, Leon. *The Gospel According to John: The English Text with Introduction, Exposition and Notes*. Grand Rapids, MI: Eerdmans, 1971. 716-738.

Unger, Merrill. *Unger's Bible Dictionary*. Chicago, IL: Moody Press, 1981. 596.

Zodhiates, Spiros, Baker, Warren. eds. *Hebrew Greek Key Word Study Bible, King James Version*. 2nd ed. Chattanooga, TN: AMG Publishers, 1991. 1709, 1717.

Say It Correctly

Aramaic. air-ah-**MAY**-ik.
Gethsemane. geth-**SEH**-muh-nee.

Daily Bible Readings

MONDAY
Prayer for Peter in Prison
(Acts 12:5–11)

TUESDAY
Pray for a Successful Ministry
(Romans 15:22–33)

WEDNESDAY
Pray for Inner Strength and Power
(Ephesians 3:14–21)

THURSDAY
Pray the Prayer of Our Lord
(Matthew 6:7–13)

FRIDAY
Pray for Your Abusers
(Luke 6:22–33)

SATURDAY
Pray to Avoid Trials
(Luke 22:39–46)

SUNDAY
Jesus Prays for His Disciples
(John 17:13–24)

Notes

Teaching Tips

Words You Should Know

A. Redemption (Luke 2:38) *lutrosis* (Gk.)—Ransoming, deliverance

B. Pour out (Acts 2:17) *ekcheo* (Gk.)—To pour forth, bestow, gush, run greedily out, shed abroad, spill

Teacher Preparation

Unifying Principle—Women Speak Out. All people have a unique purpose in life. How do we affirm each individual's purpose? The Gospel of Luke and the Book of Acts provide examples of women responding to God's call.

A. Read the Bible Background and Devotional Reading.

B. Pray for your students and lesson clarity.

C. Read the lesson Scripture in multiple translations.

O—Open the Lesson

A. Begin the class with prayer.

B. Have class members write a thank-you note to a Christian woman (living or dead) who greatly influenced their spiritual development.

C. Have the students read the Aim for Change and the In Focus story.

D. Ask students how events like those in the story weigh on their hearts and how they can view these events from a faith perspective.

P—Present the Scriptures

A. Read the Focal Verses and discuss the Background and The People, Places, and Times sections.

B. Have the class share what Scriptures stand out for them and why, with particular emphasis on today's themes.

E—Explore the Meaning

A. Use In Depth or More Light on the Text to facilitate a deeper discussion of the lesson text.

B. Pose the questions in Search the Scriptures and Discuss the Meaning.

C. Discuss the Liberating Lesson and Application for Activation sections.

N—Next Steps for Application

A. Summarize the value of the contributions of great Christian women, both past and present.

B. End class with a commitment to seek God's will in prayer as to the role they are to play in building the kingdom of God.

Worship Guide

For the Superintendent or Teacher
Theme: Prophesying Daughters
Song: "He Has Done Great Things for Me"
Devotional Reading: Joel 2:28-32

Prophesying Daughters

Bible Background • LUKE 2:36-38; ACTS 1:12-14, 2:16-21, 21:8-9
Printed Text • LUKE 2:36-38; ACTS 2:16-21, 21:8-9 | **Devotional Reading** • JOEL 2:28-32

—————— Aim for Change ——————

By the end of this lesson, we will EXAMINE how God called and empowered women to proclaim His message, AFFIRM contributions of godly women to the church's mission, and ADVOCATE for greater recognition of God-called women in the church.

In Focus

Gina had enjoyed the company of elderly folks since she was a child. Now, as an adult, Gina worked taking care of them. She had seen so much heartache. The physical suffering was bad enough, but it was the emotional suffering like abandonment and loneliness that hurt them the most.

In the past year, there had been several elderly folks in Gina's church who had succumbed to poor health and were no longer able to attend services. Gina genuinely missed seeing their faces in church on Sunday morning. She began to pray for the folks she missed, and the more she prayed, the greater her burden became. Her burden began to expand beyond the boundaries of her church and extended to the elderly folks who needed to hear the Gospel of Jesus Christ.

The Holy Spirit was at work in Gina's heart. Surely she wasn't the only one in her church who saw the need for outreach in this area. Gina spoke with her pastor, and with his prayer and support, she launched a visitation and outreach program for the elderly in her community. The outreach team found that some of the elderly folks wanted to hear nothing about a Savior or the gift of salvation. They began to pray that the Holy Spirit would soften those hardened hearts and that He would empower them in their ministry. One by one, lost souls were led to Christ—not only the elderly but their family members and caregivers as well.

Today's story illustrates how the empowerment of the Holy Spirit, at work in one faithful heart, can reach out to lost, hurting souls and unite a community.

—————— Keep in Mind ——————

"And it shall come to pass in the last days, saith God, I will pour out of my Spirit upon all flesh: and your sons and your daughters shall prophesy, and your young men shall see visions, and your old men shall dream dreams" (Acts 2:17, KJV).

"'In the last days,' God says, 'I will pour out my Spirit upon all people. Your sons and daughters will prophesy. Your young men will see visions, and your old men will dream dreams'" (Acts 2:17, NLT).

Focal Verses

KJV **Luke 2:36** And there was one Anna, a prophetess, the daughter of Phanuel, of the tribe of Aser: she was of a great age, and had lived with an husband seven years from her virginity;

37 And she was a widow of about fourscore and four years, which departed not from the temple, but served God with fastings and prayers night and day.

38 And she coming in that instant gave thanks likewise unto the Lord, and spake of him to all them that looked for redemption in Jerusalem.

Acts 2:16 But this is that which was spoken by the prophet Joel;

17 And it shall come to pass in the last days, saith God, I will pour out of my Spirit upon all flesh: and your sons and your daughters shall prophesy, and your young men shall see visions, and your old men shall dream dreams:

18 And on my servants and on my handmaidens I will pour out in those days of my Spirit; and they shall prophesy:

19 And I will shew wonders in heaven above, and signs in the earth beneath; blood, and fire, and vapour of smoke:

20 The sun shall be turned into darkness, and the moon into blood, before the great and notable day of the Lord come:

21 And it shall come to pass, that whosoever shall call on the name of the Lord shall be saved.

Acts 21:8 And the next day we that were of Paul's company departed, and came unto Caesarea: and we entered into the house of Philip the evangelist, which was one of the seven; and abode with him.

9 And the same man had four daughters, virgins, which did prophesy.

NLT **Luke 2:36** Anna, a prophet, was also there in the Temple. She was the daughter of Phanuel from the tribe of Asher, and she was very old. Her husband died when they had been married only seven years.

37 Then she lived as a widow to the age of eighty-four. She never left the Temple but stayed there day and night, worshiping God with fasting and prayer.

38 She came along just as Simeon was talking with Mary and Joseph, and she began praising God. She talked about the child to everyone who had been waiting expectantly for God to rescue Jerusalem.

Acts 2:16 No, what you see was predicted long ago by the prophet Joel:

17 'In the last days,' God says, 'I will pour out my Spirit upon all people. Your sons and daughters will prophesy. Your young men will see visions, and your old men will dream dreams.

18 In those days I will pour out my Spirit even on my servants—men and women alike—and they will prophesy.

19 And I will cause wonders in the heavens above and signs on the earth below—blood and fire and clouds of smoke.

20 The sun will become dark, and the moon will turn blood red before that great and glorious day of the LORD arrives.

21 But everyone who calls on the name of the LORD will be saved.'

Acts 21:8 The next day we went on to Caesarea and stayed at the home of Philip the Evangelist, one of the seven men who had been chosen to distribute food.

9 He had four unmarried daughters who had the gift of prophecy.

The People, Places, and Times

Upper Room Women. Jesus instructed His followers to go to Jerusalem and wait for the coming of the Holy Spirit. They obeyed and 120 men and women assembled in the Upper Room. The Scripture clearly states that certain women were included in this number. Mary, the mother of Jesus, was mentioned by name (Acts 1:14) and the wives of the apostles (cf. 1 Corinthians 9:5). Also, in this assembly were the female followers of Jesus devoted to Him throughout His ministry (Luke 8:2–3). So, when the Holy Spirit came, He fell on men and women, just as Joel prophesied.

Pentecost. Celebrated fifty days after Passover, Pentecost was also called the "Feast of Harvest" and the "Feast of First Fruits" (Leviticus 23:5–21). Pentecost is also celebrated as Shavuot or the Feast of Weeks, which celebrates Moses receiving the Ten Commandments on Mount Sinai. Christians celebrate Pentecost as a commemoration of the outpouring of the gifts of the Spirit. While Shavuot also represents the Jews being freed from slavery to Egypt, Pentecost represents humankind being freed from slavery to sin.

What has God freed you from and how do you share that redemption with others?

Background

Joseph and Mary carried the baby Jesus into the Temple in Jerusalem to fulfill two Jewish ceremonial obligations: the redemption of the firstborn and the purification of the mother after childbirth (Exodus 13:2; Numbers 8:17; 18:14-16; Leviticus 12:1-8). There they met the prophets Simeon and Anna.

Thirty-three years after these prophets proclaimed their message about Christ, another prophet's words were fulfilled when both men and women played a significant part in the Day of Pentecost. The Holy Spirit had been active since the beginning of time, throughout the Old Testament, and during Jesus' ministry. However, after the Day of Pentecost, the role of the Holy Spirit expanded. The power of God's Spirit equips the believer to live the Christian life and carry out Christ's mission (Ephesians 1:13–14).

Acts 21 states that Paul and his company stayed with Philip the evangelist and his four daughters for some time. The daughters, each called prophetess, and their father may have given Luke (the author of Luke and Acts), information about their ministry and the spreading of the Good News in Caesarea and the surrounding areas.

While Anna and Philip's daughters have only a small mention, we will always remember them because they are in Scripture. What act of Christ-like goodness will you always remember?

At-A-Glance

1. A Woman Called to Declare the Messiah (Luke 2:36-38)
2. All Believers Called to be Filled with the Holy Spirit (Acts 2:16-21)
3. Women called to Prophecy (Acts 21:8-9)

In Depth

1. A Woman Called to Declare the Messiah (Luke 2:36-38)

The Gospel of Luke highlights a prophetess named Anna, from the Israelite tribe of Asher. Anna's husband died after seven years of marriage. Afterward, she devoted the rest of her long life in absolute surrender to God. Faithfully, she prayed, fasted, and served in the Temple in Jerusalem. Anna was so devoted that she "departed not from the temple" (v. 37), where she was certain to gain great knowledge and experience in God's ways.

Anna longed to see the Messiah's face. God granted her heart's desire when Mary and Joseph walked into the Temple with the baby Jesus. Anna immediately recognized the long-awaited Messiah. She praised and thanked God for allowing her to see Jesus and witness the unfolding of the messianic prophecies. Anna, inspired by the Holy Spirit, spoke boldly about the coming Messiah, declaring the baby Jesus is, in fact, the promised one bringing salvation and redemption.

2. All Believers Called to be Filled with the Holy Spirit (Acts 2:16-21)

On the Day of Pentecost, Peter addressed the crowd in Jerusalem. He clarified that it was the partial fulfillment of Joel's prophecy as it pertained to the church (Joel 2:28-29). Christians are now God's temple, the dwelling place of the Holy Spirit (1 Corinthians 3:16). At one time the operation of the Spirit was most prominently recorded as the revelation to a few people and one particular nation—Israel. Today God connects and communicates His desires through people in every walk of life, not merely through the Jewish leadership. Following the Day of Pentecost, people from all nations, cultures, and people groups regardless of gender, race, and social status can be filled with the Holy Spirit, empowered to speak out God's words. Both young and old; men and women; those who might be considered as insignificant and those who are high ranking in society; the educated, the unlearned; the rich and the poor can be recipients of God's divine salvation and filled with His Spirit.

While Joel also predicted changes in the physical atmosphere, those signs will be fulfilled in the end times (Revelation 6:12, 8:12).

In what way was Joel's prophecy seen on the day of Pentecost? What aspects of his prophecy will be deferred?

3. Women Called to Prophesy (Acts 21:8-9)

Philip was one of the first seven deacons (Acts 6:1-6). He witnessed to an Ethiopian eunuch and then the Holy Spirit led him to Azotus where he preached in Caesarea and the surrounding area (Acts 8:26–40). Twenty years later, Philip continued to reside in Caesarea (Acts 21:8–9).

Paul, Luke, and eight others visited Philip whose four unmarried, virgin daughters lived with him. Some scholars believe their unmarried status was an indication of their solidarity and devotion to the Lord (cf. 1 Corinthians 7:34). The Scripture offers no extensive details about these four prophetesses. They are unnamed and nothing was recorded about their mother or specific involvement in ministry except that they prophesied. Philip committed himself to follow the lead of the Holy Spirit, boldly talking about Christ. As is often seen even today, when parents are involved in ministry their children are likely to be involved as well.

Search the Scriptures

1. How does the mention of Anna, the women in Acts 2, and Philip's daughters contribute to Jesus' ministry? (Luke 2:38, Acts 1:14, Acts 21:8).

2. Who were the recipients of the Holy Spirit (Acts 2:16-17)?

3. What was Anna's message and to whom did she prophesy (Luke 2:38)?

Discuss the Meaning

1. How is Anna a role model for men and women?

2. How do you account for the unity of men and women in the Upper Room (Acts 1:14; 2:21)?

3. Why did Luke see the mention of Phillip's daughters as significant?

Liberating Lesson

Some churches and denominations debate women's roles in the furtherance of the Gospel.

How do the passages in today's lesson address this issue?

Application for Activation

The statements regarding women in today's passages, declare the role of women in speaking out as the Spirit of the Lord divinely inspires. Have you ever felt the urgency of speaking in faith under God's Word? How did you respond? What was the result? Seek God for the boldness to speak in favor of the Gospel.

Follow the Spirit

What God wants me to do:

_____

_____

_____

_____

_____

Remember Your Thoughts

Special insights I have learned:

_____

_____

_____

_____

_____

More Light on the Text

Luke 2:36-38; Acts 2:16-21, 21:8-9

36 And there was one Anna, a prophetess, the daughter of Phanuel, of the tribe of Aser: she was of a great age, and had lived with an husband seven years from her virginity; 37 And she was a widow of about fourscore and four years, which departed not from the temple, but served God with fastings and prayers night and day. 38 And she coming in that instant gave thanks likewise unto the Lord, and spake of him to all them that looked for redemption in Jerusalem.

Anna was a holy woman, whose name means grace or gracious. During this time, prophecy was silent. Some have stated it was 300 years and others say it was 400 years that true prophecy from God did not exist, but the prophecy was now happening again coinciding with the arrival of the Messiah. At the time of Christ's birth, we are introduced to Anna, a prophetess.

Anna was the daughter of Phanuel, from the tribe of Asher, which refers to those descended from Israel's tenth son (Genesis 30:13). She was married for seven years and then her husband died. She never remarried. It is not exactly clear how old Anna is, though it is obvious she is a seasoned saint. "Fourscore and four years" is eighty-four, but it is not clear if this is her age or how long she has been a widow.

She devoted her life to serving the Lord. It is thought that she lived near the Temple. She spent a great deal of time there. She was committed to fasting, praying, and giving thanks unto the Lord. She had devoted herself completely to the Lord's work in the Temple. She was available to work as much as she did because her husband was deceased and she no longer had the responsibilities of being a wife. She focuses her time and energy to be mindful of Godly things (cf 1 Corinthians 7:34).

Because of this devotion, Anna happens to be at the Temple "coming in that instant" (v. 38) when Simeon recognizes Baby Jesus as the Savior. Anna, in turn, announces to all who were looking forward to redemption in Jerusalem: the Messiah has come. She would not keep quiet—she was all about the work of the Lord. Her first work, therefore, is to thank the Lord. When praise and thanksgiving are our first responses to whatever God does, we are in a better mindset to continue serving Him. After thanking God, Anna shares the word that He will bring redemption (Gk. *lutrosis*, **LOO-troh-sees**). Interestingly, Mary and Joseph bring Jesus to the Temple that day to fulfill the law of redeeming the firstborn. The Greek translation of the Old Testament even uses this same root (*lutroo*) when giving the instructions for this rite (Exodus 13:13). This baby who is being redeemed from God with a sacrifice of two doves will be the one to redeem from sin all who are looking for Him.

Even though the greatness of this promise makes it sound far-fetched, Anna is unafraid to speak the prophecy God gave her. By devoting ourselves to God like Anna, we too can joyfully embrace the messages God asks us to share. How good it is to have someone speak a prophecy over you, filling you in on God's great plan for your life!

Acts 2:16 But this is that which was spoken by the prophet Joel; 17 And it shall come to pass in the last days, saith God, I will pour out of my Spirit upon all flesh: and your sons and your daughters shall prophesy, and your young men shall see visions, and your old men shall dream dreams:

"In the last days" is often used in the Old Testament to mean "in a future time." It is used in several Scriptures (Genesis 49:1; Isaiah 2:2; Micah 3:1). The most important time for the Jews was the Messiah's reign. This was not the end of the world by any means, but it was celebrated and anticipated as a long and glorious time under the dominion of the Messiah.

"To prophesy" (Gk. *propheteuo*, **pro-feh-TEW-oh**) has several different meanings. In Matthew, it means foretelling the future. Then in Luke, it is to celebrate the praises of God, being under divine influence. In any case, to prophesy is to be under divine influence, whether telling the future, celebrating the praises of God, giving instruction in the duties of religious purposes or even in speaking foreign languages.

One of the ways the will of God in former times was communicated to the prophets was by visions and dreams. One of the familiar names of the prophets was seers (1 Samuel 9:9). God informed Abimelech in a dream that Sarah was the wife of Abraham (Genesis 20:3). This is one of the ways God would make known His will.

God promises to pour out from the Holy Spirit, not sparingly but freely His influences to refresh or renew and purify or sanctify the soul. To "pour out of" means to be given out in very large amounts, as in pouring from a fountain that has no barriers, hindrances, or restrictions. So God chooses to give freely His influences to refresh and purify the soul. Here when speaking of the "Spirit," in this passage, it is the Holy Spirit, the Third Person of the Trinity. The gifts of the Spirit can be traced back to the Holy Spirit (1 Corinthians 4-10). He is the source of which the gifts will flow. Henceforth, the Holy Spirit will refresh, renew, purify, and sanctify the receiving soul.

The Holy Spirit was liberal in whom He would influence, all kinds of people, old men, young men, sons, and daughters. Whereas before this time, men were normally the only ones recognized to hold the title of prophet, in these days, He was making it clear that women may hold this role. Age will no longer have significance and neither will gender because all of God's children are equally welcome and equally blessed (Galatians 3:28).

18 And on my servants and on my handmaidens I will pour out in those days of my Spirit; and they shall prophesy:

God is not a respecter of persons (Romans 2:11), meaning He does not show favoritism. As a matter of fact, God teaches against showing partiality (James 2:9). It does not matter if you have money or not. It does not matter where you live or grew up or who your parents are. It does not matter if you are old or young. This means people, male or female, of the lowest conditions, are excluded from being able to share in the gifts and graces of receiving the Divine Spirit. The key factor is that you have to be His. You must be a child of God.

The influences of God would not be confined to a particular class of people. In Scripture, the worshipers of God were often referred to as servants of God. Therefore, He is saying He chooses whom He shall pour His Spirit into. The people will not fit in a certain category based on looks or social-economic status. The people will not be ranked according to the standards of men. The standard is God and God alone. He is the one to say who is allowed to have what He gives. He is the Giver and we are the ones to receive according to what He decides. God is the One to offer gifts to His servants and handmaidens with the one special gift: prophecy. The gift of prophecy is often coveted for the wrong reasons (cf Acts 8:18–19). The most important aspect of receiving the gift of prophecy is proclaiming that God's Son came into the world to save the lost and redeem creation.

19 And I will shew wonders in heaven above, and signs in the earth beneath; blood, and fire, and vapour of smoke: 20 The sun shall be turned into darkness, and the moon into blood, before that great and notable day of the Lord come:

To do wrong against another person is one thing, but to do wrong against God is very different. The wrong-doer has to pay for what they did. We can choose to sin, but we cannot choose the consequences of our sin. All the prophets could be clear about one message: the prophecy of judgment was sure to come to pass. This is a very dangerous place to be (Joel 3:14–16).

Here, the "day of the Lord" represents any day God manifests Himself, but in particular when He will come to pass judgment or punish His people. God is good and just. For those who reject the Lord, judgment day is frightful. The fire and smoke also remind us of Sinai, when the presence of God was with the people. The "vapour of smoke" here means a column or shaft of smoke, that is here for a moment and then completely gone (cf James 4:14).

21 And it shall come to pass, that whosoever shall call on the name of the Lord shall be saved.

There is only one way to avoid the prophesied judgment and that is to sincerely call on the name of the Lord. Wouldn't that be wonderful to escape the judgment all together? Who will be able to escape the judgment?

The last days include the days of great salvation. Throughout the last days, people can be saved by calling on the name of the Lord. Once anyone recognizes their need to be saved, they have to know and believe that Jesus is Lord, and be willing to receive Him as Lord and Savior. Those who seek God must admit to being a sinner in need of a Savior. Through God's grace, that person can call on the name of the Lord and be saved (cf Romans 10:9–10, 13).

21:8 And the next day we that were of Paul's company departed, and came unto

Caesarea: and we entered into the house of Philip the evangelist, which was one of the seven; and abode with him. 9 And the same man had four daughters, virgins, which did prophesy.

Philip was a believer chosen to be one of the very first deacons. The business of a deacon was to take care of the poor members of the church (Acts 6:1-6). He was a deacon who truly was on fire for the Lord. His passion for the Lord caused him to receive the title "evangelist." He is the evangelist who had reached Samaria with the Gospel for about twenty years or so before. He matured, developed in the faith, and is now a family man. He now has four daughters. Some think the recognition of the daughters being "virgins" (Gk. *parthenos*, **par-THEH-noce**) alludes to their still being unmarried teens. There is no mention of the girls' names, only their gift. Philip was apparently raising his family in the fear of the Lord so that his children were serving and trusting God. His four unmarried daughters are specifically gifted by the Holy Spirit to prophesy.

Sources:
Acts. The Preacher's Outline and Sermon Bible. Leadership Ministries Worldwide. Chattanooga, TN: Alpha-Omega Ministries, 2003.

Barnes, Albert. *Barnes' Notes on the New Testament*. Grand Rapids, MI: Kregel Publications, 1962.

Black, Mark C. *Luke*. The College Press NIV Commentary. Joplin, MO: College Press Publishing Company, 1996.

Carson, D.A., Walter W. Wessel, and Walter L. Liefeld. *Matthew, Mark, Luke*. The Expositor's Bible Commentary. Vol. 8. Frank E. Gaebelein, general editor. Grand Rapids, MI: Zondervan, 1984.

Henry, Matthew. *Matthew Henry's Commentary on the Whole Bible: New Modern Edition*. Vols. 1-6. Peabody, MA: Hendrickson Publishers, Inc., 2009.

Keener, Craig S. *The IVP Bible Background Commentary: New Testament*. Downers Grove, IL: InterVarsity Press, 1994.

Pfeiffer, Charles F., Howard F. Vos, John Rea, eds. *Wycliffe Bible Dictionary*. Peabody, MA: Hendrickson Publishers, Inc., 1998.

Strong, James. *The New Strong's Exhaustive Concordance of the Bible*. Nashville, TN: Thomas Nelson, 2003.

Thayer, Joseph Henry. *A Greek-English Lexicon of the New Testament*. New York: American Book Company, 1889.

Vine, W.E. *Vine's Complete Expository Dictionary of Old and New Testament Words*. Nashville, TN: Thomas Nelson, 1996.

Walvoord, John F. and Roy B. Zuck. *The Bible Knowledge Commentary: An Exposition of the Scriptures*. New Testament. Wheaton, IL: Victor Books, 1983.

Say It Correctly

Phanuel. **FAH**-noo-ell.
Azotus. **AH**-zoe-tuss.
Caesarea. **KYE**-sare-**EE**-uh.

Daily Bible Readings

MONDAY
Jesus Supports Mary's Choice
(Luke 10:38–42)

TUESDAY
Jesus Responds to Sister's Call
(John 11:1–11)

WEDNESDAY
Jesus Raises Lazarus; Mary Believes
(John 11:38–45)

THURSDAY
Women Carry Resurrection
Message to Apostles
(Luke 24:5–10)

FRIDAY
Jesus' Final Words and Ascension
(Luke 24:44–53)

SATURDAY
Simeon Sees Impact of Jesus' Ministry
(Luke 2:28-35)

SUNDAY
The Spirit Empowers
Daughters to Prophesy
(Luke 2:36-38; Acts 2:16-21; 21:8-9)

Teaching Tips

Words You Should Know

A. Marvelled (John 4:27) *thaumazo* (Gk.)—To wonder or admire

B. Testified (v. 39) *martureo* (Gk.)—To be an earnest witness, telling the truth about what is known

Teacher Preparation

Unifying Principle—No Insignificant Witness. Some people wonder if they are good enough to give direction to others. What is the best way to share our witness to others? The woman at the well was considered an outcast, but after meeting Jesus she eagerly became a witness and brought others to Jesus.

A. Read the Bible Background and Devotional Reading.

B. Pray for your students and lesson clarity.

C. Read the lesson Scripture in multiple translations.

O—Open the Lesson

A. Begin the class with prayer.

B. Introduce today's topic of the Woman at the Well. Ask class members to try to summarize the transformation they have experienced because of Jesus in a single sentence that they could share with others.

C. Have the students read the Aim for Change and the In Focus story.

D. Ask students how events like those in today's Scripture lesson weigh on their hearts and how they can view these events from a faith perspective.

P—Present the Scriptures

A. Read the Focal Verses and discuss the Background and The People, Places, and Times sections.

B. Have the class share what Scriptures stand out for them and why, with particular emphasis on today's themes.

E—Explore the Meaning

A. Use In Depth or More Light on the Text to facilitate a deeper discussion of the lesson text.

B. Pose the questions in Search the Scriptures and Discuss the Meaning.

C. Discuss the Liberating Lesson and Application for Activation sections.

N—Next Steps for Application

A. Summarize the value of students' telling their personal testimony as a way to engage others with the Gospel.

B. End class with a commitment to pray for the direction and strength from the Holy Spirit when sharing the Gospel.

Worship Guide

For the Superintendent or Teacher
Theme: Called to Evangelize
Song: "We've a Story to Tell
to the Nations"
Devotional Reading: John 1:37-51

Called to Evangelize

Bible Background • JOHN 1:37-51, 4:25-42
Printed Text • JOHN 4:25-42 | Devotional Reading • JOHN 1:37-51

—— Aim for Change ——

By the end of this lesson, we will IDENTIFY the barriers Jesus crossed in speaking with the Samaritan woman, SENSE the wonder the Samaritan woman felt in her meeting with Jesus, and SHARE with others the transforming power of God at work in their lives.

In Focus

Thirty-year-old Retha, pregnant and unmarried, sat in her kitchen, staring blankly into her cup of coffee. Ever since her abdomen had started rounding obviously, her neighbors and friends avoided her. So, she was quite surprised when she heard a knock on her door. Retha found herself face-to-face with two elderly women she had never seen before.

"Hi, I'm Artice, and this is Peggy. We're from the senior adult Sunday School class of True Rock Church. We've come to bring you some things for your baby," said Artice.

"Our pastor asked us to scout out the neighborhood to see who we can help. When we saw you walking and looking sad the other day, we decided that you might be one we would help. So, here we are," said Peggy.

Retha could hardly believe her eyes and ears. After sharing a cup of coffee and conversation with the ladies, Peggy spoke up first. "We have some good news for you. We came to tell you that Jesus loves you and we would like for you to go to church with us."

But how could Jesus love me? Retha wondered. Wasn't He going to look down on her just like her family did? Still, they had been nice to her and even offered to come by to take her to church on Sunday. Retha's decision to go to church that week would change her life. Eventually, she would know for herself that Jesus is alive and she too would want to share the Good News of Him with others.

No one is too much of an outcast of society that Jesus cannot reach them and make their lives new. How has your witness helped someone to feel that they were welcomed?

—— Keep in Mind ——

"And many of the Samaritans of that city believed on him for the saying of the woman, which testified, He told me all that ever I did" (John 4:39, KJV)

"Many Samaritans from the village believed in Jesus because the woman had said, 'He told me everything I ever did!'" (John 4:39, NLT)

Focal Verses

KJV **John 4:25** The woman saith unto him, I know that Messias cometh, which is called Christ: when he is come, he will tell us all things.

26 Jesus saith unto her, I that speak unto thee am he.

27 And upon this came his disciples, and marvelled that he talked with the woman: yet no man said, What seekest thou? or, Why talkest thou with her?

28 The woman then left her waterpot, and went her way into the city, and saith to the men,

29 Come, see a man, which told me all things that ever I did: is not this the Christ?

30 Then they went out of the city, and came unto him.

31 In the mean while his disciples prayed him, saying, Master, eat.

32 But he said unto them, I have meat to eat that ye know not of.

33 Therefore said the disciples one to another, Hath any man brought him ought to eat?

34 Jesus saith unto them, My meat is to do the will of him that sent me, and to finish his work.

35 Say not ye, There are yet four months, and then cometh harvest? behold, I say unto you, Lift up your eyes, and look on the fields; for they are white already to harvest.

36 And he that reapeth receiveth wages, and gathereth fruit unto life eternal: that both he that soweth and he that reapeth may rejoice together.

37 And herein is that saying true, One soweth, and another reapeth.

38 I sent you to reap that whereon ye bestowed no labour: other men laboured, and ye are entered into their labours.

39 And many of the Samaritans of that city believed on him for the saying of the woman, which testified, He told me all that ever I did.

NLT **John 4:25** The woman said, "I know the Messiah is coming—the one who is called Christ. When he comes, he will explain everything to us."

26 Then Jesus told her, "I AM the Messiah!"

27 Just then his disciples came back. They were shocked to find him talking to a woman, but none of them had the nerve to ask, "What do you want with her?" or "Why are you talking to her?"

28 The woman left her water jar beside the well and ran back to the village, telling everyone,

29 "Come and see a man who told me everything I ever did! Could he possibly be the Messiah?"

30 So the people came streaming from the village to see him.

31 Meanwhile, the disciples were urging Jesus, "Rabbi, eat something."

32 But Jesus replied, "I have a kind of food you know nothing about."

33 "Did someone bring him food while we were gone?" the disciples asked each other.

34 Then Jesus explained: "My nourishment comes from doing the will of God, who sent me, and from finishing his work.

35 You know the saying, 'Four months between planting and harvest.' But I say, wake up and look around. The fields are already ripe for harvest.

36 The harvesters are paid good wages, and the fruit they harvest is people brought to eternal life. What joy awaits both the planter and the harvester alike!

37 You know the saying, 'One plants and another harvests.' And it's true.

38 I sent you to harvest where you didn't plant; others had already done the work, and now you will get to gather the harvest."

39 Many Samaritans from the village believed in Jesus because the woman had said, "He told me everything I ever did!"

40 So when the Samaritans were come unto him, they besought him that he would tarry with them: and he abode there two days.

41 And many more believed because of his own word;

42 And said unto the woman, Now we believe, not because of thy saying: for we have heard him ourselves, and know that this is indeed the Christ, the Saviour of the world.

40 When they came out to see him, they begged him to stay in their village. So he stayed for two days,

41 long enough for many more to hear his message and believe.

42 Then they said to the woman, "Now we believe, not just because of what you told us, but because we have heard him ourselves. Now we know that he is indeed the Savior of the world."

The People, Places, and Times

Jacob's Well. There is a present-day well near Sychar, which Samaritans believed was built by Jacob. A narrow opening four feet long led from the floor of the vault into the well which was dug through limestone. The ground mentioned by John had been purchased by Jacob (Genesis 33:19). The area was later wrested by force from the Amorites (Genesis 38:22). The well is near the base of Mount Gerizim, which was as holy to the Samaritans as Mt. Zion was to the Jews. Many religious differences like this led to disdain between Jews and Samaritans.

The Woman at the Well. The little we know about the Samaritan woman at the well is gleaned from Scripture. She comes to draw water from the well at noon, even though most women came in the morning and socialized. Jesus gives us a personal detail that perhaps explains this behavior. She has had five husbands and is currently living with a sixth man. Although the woman was possibly widowed more than once, she has likely been divorced at some point. The stigma for divorce, especially for the woman, was high in Jesus' time, and likely the woman draws water at an odd time to avoid the judgment and gossip of the other women of the town.

Background

In John 4, Jesus and His disciples left Judea to return to Galilee. The route led them directly through Samaria. Although Jews and Samaritans both descended from ancient Israel, their religious practices and beliefs were slightly different, and there was long-standing hostility between them. While His disciples went into the city to buy food, Jesus rested by the well in the heat of the day. While Jesus rested, a Samaritan woman came to the well to draw water. Due to the social customs, the woman did not expect Jesus to speak to her. He asked her to draw physical water for Him and promised that He could provide her with living or spiritual water. There at the well, they shared a theological conversation. As the conversation progressed, she realized that Jesus was no ordinary Jewish man. Just before the disciples returned, Jesus revealed Himself to be Israel's long-awaited Messiah.

Have you ever had a life-altering spiritual experience at an unexpected time or in an unexpected place?

At-A-Glance

1. "I Am" (John 4:25-30)
2. Gathering Fruit for Eternal Life (vv. 31-38)
3. Because of the Woman's Testimony (vv. 39-42)

In Depth

1. "I Am" (John 4:25-30)

A common phrase Jesus uses in the Gospel of John is "I am He." The phrase reveals Jesus to be the great "I Am." Although Jesus' disciples struggle throughout the Gospel of John to understand who Jesus is, the Samaritan woman does not struggle to believe that He is the Messiah. When the disciples return from the city, the woman leaves her water jug at the well and runs to tell the good news of the man who had "told her everything [she] had ever done." Although the disciples were surprised to find Jesus speaking publicly with a Samaritan woman, none of them said anything to discourage the conversation. When the woman reported her experience with Jesus in the city, the Samaritans went out to meet Him.

Why do you think the Samaritan woman was so receptive to the idea that Jesus was the Messiah?

2. Gathering Fruit for Eternal Life (vv. 31-38)

While the woman was in the city sharing her testimony, the disciples encouraged Jesus to eat, but they received an unexpected response. Like the woman to whom Jesus had offered living water, Jesus told the disciples that they did not know about the food He had. Mirroring the woman's confusion about living water, the disciples wondered who might have brought Jesus something to eat. However, Jesus explained that His "food" was the work God sent Him to do. He told the disciples that the fields were ripe for harvesting. Hearkening back to the long legacy of Hebrew Bible prophets and teachers, Jesus told the disciples that they entered into the labor which others had already begun. Likewise, when we share the story of Jesus and His love, we stand on the shoulders of those who have labored to spread the good news.

When was the last time you let someone know about God's indescribable love for them?

3. Because of the Woman's Testimony (vv. 39-42)

What impact could your simple testimony have on the people around you? The testimony of the Samaritan woman Jesus met at the well was simple. She believed that Jesus was the Messiah because He had told her everything she had ever done. The woman believed in Jesus because she felt seen by Jesus. For the Samaritans, her honest and straightforward testimony was sufficient. They believed in Jesus because of what she had told them about Him. The group Jesus met that day invited Him to stay with them and He agreed to do so for two days. Upon interacting with Him, even more people believed. They told the woman that they no longer believed because of her words alone. They now believed in Jesus because they had encounters with Him.

Will you walk with a friend, neighbor, or family member as they have personal experiences with Jesus?

Search the Scriptures

1. What evidence did Jesus present that convinced the Samaritan woman that He was the Messiah?

2. What experiences did Jesus have in Samaria that made Him convinced that the fields were ripe for a spiritual harvest?

Discuss the Meaning

1. In what way does Jesus treat the Samaritan woman as a worthy evangelist?

2. How does Jesus' interaction with the Samaritan woman transform the way we understand the roles that women might play in Christian ministry?

Liberating Lesson

Globally, ethnic and cultural groups struggle to relate to each other. Cultural misunderstandings can lead to violence including the abuse of women and children. This passage points us to an alternative model for living. It encourages us to build relationships even when cultural norms discourage us from doing so. It reveals that even when we feel alone, we stand on the shoulders of ancestors who have done the labor that we are now continuing. It reminds us that as followers of Jesus Christ, we can model Christ's sacrificial love, grace, and mercy to everyone we meet. It also reveals that we cannot and should not underestimate the ability of women and girls or anyone regardless of the labels society has placed on them.

Application for Activation

Go tell the Good News of Jesus Christ! You never know who might be transformed by your testimony. Do not be afraid to share what God has done for you. However, we are not only called to share the Good News of Jesus Christ individually. Working as members of church families, we also can share the love of Jesus with our community. As a church, explore the possibility of interfaith or interracial dialogue. The church is the hands and feet of Jesus in the world and we should pursue every opportunity to love others as freely as Jesus has loved us.

Follow the Spirit

What God wants me to do:

_____

_____

_____

_____

Remember Your Thoughts

Special insights I have learned:

_____

_____

_____

_____

More Light on the Text

John 4:25-42

25 The woman saith unto him, I know that Messias cometh, which is called Christ: when he is come, he will tell us all things. 26 Jesus saith unto her, I that speak unto thee am he.

While the Jews and the Samaritans both worshiped the same God, their understanding of the Word of God was very different. The Samaritan Scriptures only included the Pentateuch, the first five chapters of the Old Testament. Their religious tradition rejected the writings of the prophets. Furthermore, they believed that Mt. Gerizim was the true place of worship, not Mt. Zion and Jerusalem. The Samaritans recognized that the Messiah would come, but they expected Him to come as a teacher who would reveal all truth (Deuteronomy 18:15-20).

The conversation between Jesus and the Samaritan woman challenged and clarified her understanding of the Messiah. When the woman explained her view (which was the Samaritan view) of the Messiah, Jesus confessed to be the Christ, the very One she had anticipated. Indeed, His revelation was the summation of the systematic and theological conversation He and the woman had been having at the well. Jesus' revelation of Himself as the Messiah, marked the first time He openly admitted who He was. Prior to His trial, He did not profess it to the Jews. Yet He openly declared to this woman

271

that He was the Christ because He intended to reveal the truth of God to her.

27 And upon this came his disciples, and marvelled that he talked with the woman: yet no man said, What seekest thou? or, Why talkest thou with her?

The disciples had left Jesus at the well and were surprised to find him talking to the woman when they returned. This was an apparent violation of several customs. It was rare for a Jewish teacher to engage a woman in public discourse. Furthermore, the chasm between the Jews and the Samaritans meant that Jews saw the Samaritans as unclean. It was a violation of Jewish laws of purification to eat or drink anything belonging to or coming from the Samaritans. Therefore, when the disciples returned they "marvelled" (Gk. *thaumazo*, **thow-MOD-zo**) or wondered why He was having a conversation with the Samaritan woman. The word itself implies that this was indeed a miracle. This was likely due to the respect they had for Jesus as their leader and teacher. It was also possibly awe since Jesus had so often done what was not expected by challenging traditions and confronting people others would overlook or reject. They respected Him too much to question His behavior.

28 The woman then left her waterpot, and went her way into the city, and saith to the men, 29 Come, see a man, which told me all things that ever I did: is not this the Christ? 30 Then they went out of the city, and came unto him.

While some speculate that the disciples' return broke off the woman's conversation with Jesus, it is more likely that Jesus' work was done when He revealed Himself to be the Messiah. The woman made her way back to Sychar to tell what happened to her at the well. She was so excited, she left her waterpot behind. She had

come to the well to get water but hurried back to the city without it because she had a more important task now. This is a clear indication of the deep impression that Jesus had made on her. It was clear that this stranger who knew all about her past was not just an ordinary man. He was an extraordinary man, the declared Messiah, who had such a profound impact on her that she did not hesitate to tell the men of the town all about Him. She likely told the men because they were the teachers and leaders who would most appreciate a theological discussion with Jesus.

Jesus had forced her to face who she was. She had already come to terms with her need (4:15), her sin (4:19), and her true condition (4:26). In the end, she realized that He was the Messiah and was determined to tell others.

The fact that she was a woman, particularly a woman with a stained reputation, should have meant that any theological or religious information coming from her would not be accepted by the elders of Sychar. The woman's plea was so sincere, however, that the Samaritans left the city and began heading toward Jesus. The urgency of her invitation caused them to seek this man for themselves.

31 In the mean while his disciples prayed him, saying, Master, eat. 32 But he said unto them, I have meat to eat that ye know not of. 33 Therefore said the disciples one to another, Hath any man brought him ought to eat?

While the Samaritans were on their way, Jesus spoke privately with His disciples who had come back to meet Him at the well. John recorded the conversation in verses 31-38. The disciples had come back from getting food from town and were concerned about whether Jesus had eaten. They knew He should have been hungry by then. When Jesus rejected the food, they did not understand. Jesus' words were confusing. Ancient teachers would sometimes use physical food as a figure of speech for spiritual food. The disciples thought that when Jesus used the word "meat" (Gk. *brosis*, **BRO-sees**), He was talking about already having physically eaten. The word "meat" is usually used to refer to physical food of any kind, and where it is used metaphorically, the metaphorical use is made clear (cf 1 Corinthians 10:3). The disciples, therefore, wondered where He could have gotten this physical food. They were baffled. Why wasn't Jesus ready to eat?

34 Jesus saith unto them, My meat is to do the will of him that sent me, and to finish his work.

Jesus realized the disciples were unaware of what He was talking about. He broke it down to them. Jesus' focus was to do His Father's work. He explained that when He does His Father's will, He is satisfied much like their bodies are satisfied when they eat. In this case, His meat had been leading the woman to an understanding of who He was through His revelation of her life. Furthermore, His intention was for His Word to reach the Samaritans. He was satisfied because He was doing the work of His Father. He went on to explain about the food He had to eat. Jesus made a bold statement to say He was being fed by doing what His Father told Him to do.

It was imperative with Jesus to accomplish His Father's work, as it should be with us. For the child of God, doing the will of the Father is a source of our strength and satisfaction. This is where the child of God's purpose lies. Jesus did not look at the work of the Father as a chore or a burden. It was what He had come to do. As believers, we should examine ourselves and the things we do to determine whether we are truly doing the will of God. For Jesus, our Lord, did not look on the Father's will as a heavy burden or a gruesome task. He saw His work as food for His soul. His soul survived on doing the will of the Father.

35 Say not ye, There are yet four months, and then cometh harvest? behold, I say unto you, Lift up your eyes, and look on the fields; for they are white already to harvest.

Jesus likely refers to the four months between planting and harvesting. In March, the barley fields would turn white, showing they were ready for harvest. We tend to focus our attention on the physical harvest, the planting of seed and reaping of grain. Jesus was thinking about the souls of the people, the lost souls He had come to save (Luke 19:10). He was changing the focus of their attention from a worldly perspective to a spiritual one. In essence He told them, "Don't look with your natural eye; look with your spiritual eye. See the souls that need salvation."

Jesus was hungry to see people come to Him. Do we have that same hunger to see people come to Jesus? Are we willing to push past our hunger to minister to others? Are we willing to go to the least likely places when we would rather go home and crawl in bed with a snack? Here we see an example of Christ's humility, His helpfulness, His honesty, and even His hunger.

36 And he that reapeth receiveth wages, and gathereth fruit unto life eternal: that both he that soweth and he that reapeth may rejoice together. 37 And herein is that saying true, One soweth, and another reapeth. 38 I sent you to reap that whereon ye bestowed no labour: other men laboured, and ye are entered into their labours.

In a natural harvest, the person who reaps may be one person, while the person who sows may be another person. Many people must labor and toil working the field long before the actual harvest. This is a team effort although the team members may not work at the same time. It was important for the disciples to understand the principle of uniting sowers and reapers. In verse 37, Jesus explains an ancient truism regarding sowers and reapers. Jesus wanted them to see with their spiritual eyes. The Old Testament prophets had put in the work, doing their part to prepare the soil. The last in their tradition was John the Baptist. Christ also wanted the disciples to understand that this work would continue. It is now the task of our generations to see the unsaved as lost souls, as Jesus does. Our work is to do what the Father has sent us to accomplish: to seek and save the lost.

Paul uses this same metaphor when speaking to the Corinthian church: "I have planted, Apollos watered; but God gave the increase" (1 Corinthians 3:6). God is the key component. He is the One that causes the growth. Each person plays an active role, but there is only one purpose.

39 And many of the Samaritans of that city believed on him for the saying of the woman, which testified, He told me all that ever I did. 40 So when the Samaritans were come unto him, they besought him that he would tarry with them: and he abode there two days. 41 And many more believed because of his own word; 42 And said unto the woman, Now we believe, not because of thy saying: for we have heard him ourselves, and know that this is indeed the Christ, the Saviour of the world.

The Samaritans of the city of Sychar heeded the woman's experience. Jesus had talked to her. He knew all about her sin, her lies, and her secrets, yet He continued to talk to her. The men of the town recognized that Jesus ministered to her, knowing her past, causing her to realize Him to be the Messiah, the One whom they had hoped to see. They saw and believed for themselves.

They were interested because the woman "testified" (Gk. *martureo*, **mar-too-REH-oh**); she was an earnest witness. Witnesses are simply to tell the truth about what they know. As a result these men had to go to the source. At the well, they found Jesus to be a witness. Jesus was a witness who asked probing questions. He was a witness who showed concern for human needs. He was a witness who fully and faithfully explained the Scriptures. He was also a witness by emphasizing the Good News for thirsty people. Now they desired more. They wanted Jesus to stay longer. They wanted more of what He had to offer. They wanted Him to stay with them and He did for two days.

The Samaritans believed because of the woman's testimony. Today, we believe because of the eyewitnesses in the New Testament and throughout the entire Bible. They heard what the woman said. We read what the Scriptures say. They saw her transformation. We see their transformation in the pages of the Gospel. They knew who she was and saw who she became because of this Man, Jesus. We too, come to seek Jesus because of the testimony of others. The testimony of others can lead you to have faith for yourself. Initially, you may come to believe in Jesus based on what someone else testified about Him but coming into a real relationship with Him requires a personal experience that leads to a testimony of your own. The testimony of others will get you so far. However, if you witness specific situations and see Jesus in the midst of them, it will change your perspective and cause you to have a deeper sense of who He is. You begin to recognize His saving power in ways you have never seen before. You come to know Him as the woman at the well did, realizing He already knows more about you than you ever thought anyone would. He knows your secrets. He knows your lies. He came to the well for you for the same reason He came to the well for her, to save your soul.

Her testimony was a good start for them but they needed to know for themselves and they did. It was no longer hearsay. They, too, had become eyewitnesses to who Jesus is, the Savior of the world.

Sources:

Archaeological Study Bible. Grand Rapids, Michigan: Zondervan, 2005.

Bassler, Jouette M, Harold W Attridge, Wayne A Meeks, and Society of Biblical Literature. *The HarperCollins Study Bible: Fully Revised Standard Version, with the Apocryphal/Deuterocanonical Books Student Edition.* New York: HarperCollins, 2006.

Bryant, Beauford H. and Mark S. Krause. *John.* The College Press NIV Commentary. Joplin, Missouri: College Press Publishing Company, Inc., 1998.

Gangel, Kenneth. *John.* Holman New Testament Commentary. Nashville, TN: Holman Reference, 2000.

Keener, Craig S. *The IVP Bible Background Commentary: New Testament.* Downers Grove, Illinois: InterVarsity Press, 2014.

Michaels, J. Ramsey. *The Gospel According to John.* The New International Commentary on the New Testament. Grand Rapids, Michigan: Eerdmans, 2010.

Tenney, Merrill C. *John and Acts.* The Expositor's Bible Commentary, Volume 9. Grand Rapids, Michigan: Zondervan, 1984.

Wiersbe, Warren W. *Be Alive (John 1–12).* Bible Exposition Commentary. Elgin, Illinois: David C. Cook, 2009.

The Zondervan Bible Dictionary. Grand Rapids, Michigan: Zondervan, 1963. 399.

Say It Correctly

Sychar. sih-**CAR**.
Gerizim. **GAIR**-ih-zeem.

Daily Bible Readings

MONDAY
Receive the Water of Life
(Revelation 21:1–7)

TUESDAY
Jesus Declares, "I Am From Above"
(John 8:21–30)

WEDNESDAY
God's Children Led by the Spirit
(Romans 8:12–17)

THURSDAY
Simon and Andrew First Disciples
(John 1:37–42)

FRIDAY
Galileans Philip and Nathanael
Become Disciples
(John 1:43–51)

SATURDAY
Jesus Heals the Son of a Galilean Official
(John 4:43–54)

SUNDAY
Samaritans Come to Jesus
(John 4:25–42)

Notes

Teaching Tips

Words You Should Know

A. Sepulcre (John 20:11) *mnemion* (Gk.)—A tomb; a place of remembrance for a deceased person

B. Steward (Luke 8:3) *epitrophos* (Gk.)—An overseer or regent; person placed in charge of household affairs

Teacher Preparation

Unifying Principle—Showing Loyalty. Being a truly committed follower of someone is often difficult, but some people reveal consistent loyalty no matter what happens. How do you show your loyalty and faithfulness? Mary Magdalene demonstrated her unwavering discipleship and loyalty to Jesus through her actions.

A. Read the Bible Background and Devotional Reading.

B. Pray for your students and lesson clarity.

C. Read the lesson Scripture in multiple translations.

O—Open the Lesson

A. Begin the class with prayer.

B. List a few of the most popular U.S. charities. Have class members imagine that they had $1,000 to donate to charity. Ask them to explain how they would divide their contribution among two or more of those charities. Discuss why people support certain charities.

C. Have the students read the Aim for Change and the In Focus story.

D. Ask students how events like those in the story weigh on their hearts and how they can view these events from a faith perspective.

P—Present the Scriptures

A. Read the Focal Verses and discuss the Background and The People, Places, and Times sections.

B. Have the class share what Scriptures stand out for them and why, with particular emphasis on today's themes.

E—Explore the Meaning

A. Use In Depth or More Light on the Text to facilitate a deeper discussion of the lesson text.

B. Pose the questions in Search the Scriptures and Discuss the Meaning.

C. Discuss the Liberating Lesson and Application for Activation sections.

N—Next Steps for Application

A. Summarize the value of spiritual transformation through Jesus.

B. End class with a commitment to pray for their local church and parachurch ministries that are dear to them.

Worship Guide

For the Superintendent or Teacher
Theme: Mary Magdalene:
A Faithful Disciple
Song: "I Stand Amazed in the Presence"
Devotional Reading: Romans 4:13-25

Mary Magdalene: A Faithful Disciple

Bible Background • MARK 15:40; 16:1-9; LUKE 8:1-3; JOHN 20:10-18 | Printed Text • LUKE 8:1-3; MARK 15:40; JOHN 20:10-18 | Devotional Reading • ROMANS 4:13-25

—— Aim for Change ——

By the end of this lesson, we will DISCERN Mary Magdalene's motivations for committing her life to Jesus, APPRECIATE the sacrifices Mary Magdalene made in order to follow Jesus, and EMBRACE a lifestyle of wholehearted discipleship.

—— In Focus ——

It was a wearying plane ride from San Diego to the military hospital overseas, but Jackie got no rest; she was too anxious. This was not the reunion she wanted for her and her husband Bruce, a lifelong Army officer whose career had taken him to deployments across the United States and around the world.

Every time Bruce was reassigned, they dutifully made the moves, understanding that they were together in marriage no matter where it took them. They packed everything they had and she took on the challenges of settling into new housing, making new friends, and supporting him, even as their family grew from two to three, then four.

But the family wasn't allowed to follow when Bruce was stationed at Camp Arifjan in Kuwait, which meant Jackie leaned harder on her faith that her husband would be safe. Before Bruce left, he gave her a bracelet engraved with the Mizpah: "The LORD watch between me and thee, when we are absent one from another." For months, that carried her through. Then came word that Bruce was injured in a vehicle crash.

Now Jackie stood in a hospital corridor being told Bruce had been moved just before her arrival, but it wasn't clear where. As an Army chaplain and an administrator tried to sort out the confusion, a kind charge nurse saw Jackie's distress.

"Don't let worry overtake you now," she said with a smile. "Believe me, with a loving partner like you in his corner, he'll be fine."

Can we trust God to care for those we love, wherever they are?

—— Keep in Mind ——

"The twelve were with him, And certain women, which had been healed of evil spirits and infirmities, Mary called Magdalene, out of whom went seven devils" (from Luke 8:1–2, KJV)

"He took his twelve disciples with him, along with some women who had been cured of evil spirits and diseases. Among them were Mary Magdalene, from whom he had cast out seven demons." (from Luke 8:1–2, NLT)

Focal Verses

KJV **Luke 8:1** And it came to pass afterward, that he went throughout every city and village, preaching and shewing the glad tidings of the kingdom of God: and the twelve were with him,

2 And certain women, which had been healed of evil spirits and infirmities, Mary called Magdalene, out of whom went seven devils,

3 And Joanna the wife of Chuza Herod's steward, and Susanna, and many others, which ministered unto him of their substance.

Mark 15:40 There were also women looking on afar off: among whom was Mary Magdalene, and Mary the mother of James the less and of Joses, and Salome;

John 20:10 Then the disciples went away again unto their own home.

11 But Mary stood without at the sepulchre weeping: and as she wept, she stooped down, and looked into the sepulchre,

12 And seeth two angels in white sitting, the one at the head, and the other at the feet, where the body of Jesus had lain.

13 And they say unto her, Woman, why weepest thou? She saith unto them, Because they have taken away my LORD, and I know not where they have laid him.

14 And when she had thus said, she turned herself back, and saw Jesus standing, and knew not that it was Jesus.

15 Jesus saith unto her, Woman, why weepest thou? whom seekest thou? She, supposing him to be the gardener, saith unto him, Sir, if thou have borne him hence, tell me where thou hast laid him, and I will take him away.

16 Jesus saith unto her, Mary. She turned herself, and saith unto him, Rabboni; which is to say, Master.

17 Jesus saith unto her, Touch me not; for I am not yet ascended to my Father: but go to my

NLT **Luke 8:1** Soon afterward Jesus began a tour of the nearby towns and villages, preaching and announcing the Good News about the Kingdom of God. He took his twelve disciples with him,

2 along with some women who had been cured of evil spirits and diseases. Among them were Mary Magdalene, from whom he had cast out seven demons;

3 Joanna, the wife of Chuza, Herod's business manager; Susanna; and many others who were contributing from their own resources to support Jesus and his disciples.

Mark 15:40 Some women were there, watching from a distance, including Mary Magdalene, Mary (the mother of James the younger and of Joseph), and Salome.

John 20:10 Then they went home.

11 Mary was standing outside the tomb crying, and as she wept, she stooped and looked in.

12 She saw two white-robed angels, one sitting at the head and the other at the foot of the place where the body of Jesus had been lying.

13 "Dear woman, why are you crying?" the angels asked her. "Because they have taken away my Lord," she replied, "and I don't know where they have put him."

14 She turned to leave and saw someone standing there. It was Jesus, but she didn't recognize him.

15 "Dear woman, why are you crying?" Jesus asked her. "Who are you looking for?" She thought he was the gardener. "Sir," she said, "if you have taken him away, tell me where you have put him, and I will go and get him."

16 "Mary!" Jesus said. She turned to him and cried out, "Rabboni!" (which is Hebrew for "Teacher").

17 "Don't cling to me," Jesus said, "for I haven't yet ascended to the Father. But go find brethren, and say unto them, I ascend unto my Father, and your Father; and to my God, and your God.

18 Mary Magdalene came and told the disciples that she had seen the LORD, and that he had spoken these things unto her.

my brothers and tell them, 'I am ascending to my Father and your Father, to my God and your God.'"

18 Mary Magdalene found the disciples and told them, "I have seen the Lord!" Then she gave them his message.

The People, Places, and Times

Demonic Possession. Demons are evil spiritual beings (Matthew 8:16; 12:43-45) who are enemies of God and have certain power over people (James 2:19; Revelation 16:14). They belong to the number of fallen angels that "kept not their first estate" (Jude 6). Demonic possession is mentioned quite often in the New Testament, with a variety of effects such as muteness (Luke 11:14) and epilepsy (Mark 9:17f). The child's posture in Mark 9 is evidence of the physical exhaustion caused by the intense nervous strain of demonic possession. The Gospel records clearly show that Christ distinguished between ordinary sickness and demon possession. Jesus generally healed sick people by the laying on of hands or anointing. The demon-possessed were delivered when the spirits were commanded to depart (for example, see Matthew 10:8; Mark 6:13; Acts 8:7). Sometimes multiple spirits possess a single person, such as the legion of demons who possessed the man in Gennesaret or Mary of Magdala.

Background

Although some traditions have historically advanced the idea that Mary Magdalene was a prostitute, more recent Biblical scholars have debunked that claim because Scripture does not support it. Possibly the link began with scholars assuming Mary Magdalene (who is first named in Luke 8:2) is the same "sinful woman" who anointed Jesus in Simon's house (Luke 7). In Luke 8:2, what we really learn about Mary

Magdalene is that she was a woman from whom seven demons had gone out and she was a close follower and friend of Jesus. In Mark 15:40, we learn that when Jesus was crucified, Mary was among the group of women who looked on from a distance. When the Sabbath was over, she was also one of the three women who brought spices to anoint Jesus' body. Mary's consistent presence with Jesus and His appearance to her after His Resurrection points to the value Jesus placed on the contributions of women to the spread of the Gospel.

What transforming life experiences have shaped your relationship with Jesus?

At-A-Glance

1. The Twelve and Some Women
(Luke 8:1-3)
2. Refusing to Leave the Scene
(Mark 15:40)
3. Looking for Signs of Resurrection
(John 20:10-18)

In Depth

1. The Twelve and Some Women (Luke 8:1-3)

Jesus' earthly ministry would not have been possible without the support of disciples and friends who traveled with Him as He proclaimed the Gospel. As seen in the Gospel of Luke, Jesus' ministry takes Him all over Galilee. He traveled with twelve disciples to represent the twelve tribes of Israel. However, Jesus did not travel with only His disciples. A group of women also accompanied Jesus. Each of the women who traveled with Jesus had been cured of evil spirits or diseases. Mary was called Magdalene because she was from the town of Magdala on the western shore of the Sea of Galilee. Joanna also traveled with them. She was the wife of Herod's steward, Chuza. Her faithfulness to Jesus possibly indicates her opposition to Herod's rule. Luke also records Joanna as being one of the women (along with Mary Magdalene) who first discovered Jesus' tomb was empty (Luke 24:10). Another woman named Susanna also traveled with them. The women who traveled with Jesus and the disciples provided resources such as food and other support for the group.

What unique resources do you provide to contribute to ongoing Christian ministry?

2. Refusing to Leave the Scene (Mark 15:40)

The women who traveled with Jesus supported Him in life and death. Each of the Gospels presents slightly different details of Jesus' death and resurrection, but the account is briefest in the Gospel of Mark which was the earliest of the four Gospels written. Mark does not indicate that the disciples remained at the foot of Jesus' Cross, but he does note that there were women who looked on from a distance (Mark 15:40). These women included Mary Magdalene. Crucifixion was meant to be a humiliating and shameful execution. People would not normally associate themselves with such a person. Crucifixion also demonstrated the total power of the Roman Empire. People who were crucified served as an example to Roman citizens of what happens when one crosses Rome. These women associated themselves with someone who was a threat to the Empire—Jesus. Though they are not right

at the feet of the Cross (where John records himself and Jesus' mother), they do not fully desert their master as the other disciples did. These three women stay with their Master through His death and are the first to come planning to anoint His body on the morning of His resurrection.

When was the last time you supported someone or something until the end even knowing that you would not receive the result for which you had hoped and prayed?

3. Looking for Signs of Resurrection (John 20:10-18)

Mary is the first to find the empty tomb. She then alerts the Apostles (John 20:1–2). When Peter and John went to Jesus' empty tomb, they thought that someone had taken His body. The two returned home. Like Peter and John, Mary feared that someone had taken the body also, but she was unwilling to leave the tomb without trying to determine where the thieves placed Him. Mary remained at the tomb only because of her devotion to Jesus. Mary's grief prevented her from immediately recognizing Jesus when He appeared to her in His resurrected body. When Mary finally recognized Him, she knew Jesus because of the distinct way He spoke to her. The miraculous had happened and Mary was the first of Jesus' friends to bear witness to the fact that Jesus had risen with all power in His hands. Mary could not wait to share the Good News!

When you receive unexpectedly good news, whom do you tell first?

Search the Scriptures

1. Why did Jesus travel with such a large group of followers? Why did those followers include women? (Luke 8:1-3)

2. Why did Mary Magdalene and others go to the tomb after Jesus' death? (Mark 6:1-2; Luke 23:56; John 20:3-9)

Discuss the Meaning

1. What might these women, especially Mary Magdalene, reveal about what it means to be a faithful disciple of Jesus Christ?

2. What risks did Mary take to support Jesus' ministry?

Liberating Lesson

Crises of conscience plague contemporary society. Mary Magdalene's example to us as individuals is two-fold. First, she reminds us to allow God to transform our lives. Second, she shows us what it means to be a faithful follower and friend. In a world where so much seems temporary and fleeting, Mary teaches the contemporary reader to stay plugged into our relationship with Jesus. Mary's example to our churches is not to be hasty and walk away from the empty tomb. Today's churches often find that they are bombarded with statistics of how people in younger generations are less likely to attend church. These statistics sometimes lead us to change or dilute our message to suit changing times. Mary reminds the church to remain steadfast. There is yet hope.

Application for Activation

Think of someone you know who has experienced a liberating transformation because of Jesus. (Maybe you have yourself.) Ask the person to share their testimony with you. Consider asking the person if you may record their story to share with others in your small group.

Follow the Spirit

What God wants me to do:

_____

_____

_____

_____

Remember Your Thoughts

Special insights I have learned:

_____

_____

_____

_____

More Light on the Text

Luke 8:1-3; Mark 15:40; John 20:10-18

Luke 8:1 And it came to pass afterward, that he went throughout every city and village, preaching and shewing the glad tidings of the kingdom of God: and the twelve were with him,

With the word "afterward," Luke begins this part of his account by connecting it to what came before. A review of the previous verses (Luke 7:36-50) reveals that Jesus accepted an invitation to have dinner at the home of a Pharisee named Simon. It was there Jesus taught a great lesson about forgiveness and demonstrated his power to forgive sins. The parallels of this account are found in Matthew 26:6-13; Mark 14:3-9; and John 12:1-8. Jesus blessed an unnamed sinful woman who sought His forgiveness. He also admonished Simon to have a heart of love, worship, giving, and humble submission, which were traits He saw in the woman needing forgiveness. In essence, Jesus was engaged in His Father's business of ministry to all people by proclaiming the Gospel. Chapter 8 continues to shed light on the dynamic ministry of Jesus and those who traveled with Him.

Verse 1 is clear about Jesus' mission on earth: to travel extensively, preaching and showing Himself as our Redeemer, Savior, and expected Messiah. In Greek, the phrase "shewing the glad tidings" is a single word, *euaggelo* (**ew-ang-GHEL-lo**), from which we get the English word evangelize, and is the verb form of the word usually translated "Gospel." The glad tidings were that He had come and anyone who believed in Him would receive eternal life as a child of God (John 3:16). Jesus had many disciples (Luke 6:13), but this passage tells us that His twelve, inner circle men traveled with Him. Luke elsewhere lists these as "Simon, (whom he also named Peter,) and Andrew his brother, James and John, Philip and Bartholomew, Matthew and Thomas, James the son of Alphaeus, and Simon called Zelotes, and Judas the brother of James, and Judas Iscariot, which also was the traitor" (Luke 6:14-16).

2 And certain women, which had been healed of evil spirits and infirmities, Mary called Magdalene, out of whom went seven devils, 3 And Joanna the wife of Chuza Herod's steward, and Susanna, and many others, which ministered unto him of their substance.

These verses make it clear that men were not the only disciples. Women were disciples and devoted followers of Christ as well (Matthew 27:55). Verses 2 and 3 name specific women who are worthy of inclusion in this Scripture: Mary Magdalene, Joanna, and Susanna. All three women were delivered from demons and illnesses by Jesus and became devoted disciples of Christ. They demonstrated their love and devotion by supporting Jesus' ministry with their personal resources. It is the epitome of humility and love that our Lord, who owns everything (including all riches), allowed His followers to contribute to His sustenance and ministry.

Verse 3 is the first reference to Joanna. We can see she worked with Susanna and Mary Magdalene to support Jesus' ministry. She was very likely present when Jesus was taken

from the Cross and buried. She is named as one of the women at the tomb on the morning of the Resurrection (Luke 23:55; 24:10). The name Joanna is a Greek form of a Hebrew name meaning "God is gracious." Joanna's discipleship was unusual because she was the wife of Chuza, Herod's "steward" (Gk. *epitrophos*, **eh-PEE-trow-foce**). This steward would be in charge of household affairs, as an overseer or regent. Joanna was a woman who had resources because of her husband's position and is comparable to someone today whose spouse has a high-ranking job in government, such as a secretary for a governor or district judge. Can you imagine Herod's reaction if he knew his employee's wife was a disciple of Jesus? This Herod is not Herod the Great who tried to kill Jesus as a small child (Matthew 2), but that Herod's son, Herod Antipas, who had John the Baptist executed (Luke 3:19-20). Joanna's contact with Jesus led to her deliverance and salvation. She was grateful and showed her love and devotion by supporting Jesus' ministry, despite Herod's actions against the ministry of the Gospel and the risks involved in her support.

This is the only Scripture that references Susanna by name, but certainly, she was present in other experiences that involved Jesus. He delivered her from evil spirits and sickness. She became one of His disciples and traveled with Him. She too, worked with women such as Joanna and Mary Magdalene to support the ministry of Jesus. Susanna's name is the Greek form of a Hebrew name meaning lily, rose, or flower. It can be assumed that she was a woman of means, perhaps wealthy in her own right, because her husband is not mentioned, yet she supported Jesus' ministry. She holds a significant place in Scripture because of her dedication to Jesus.

However, of the three women named, it is Mary Magdalene who is referred to the most in

Scripture. She is portrayed as an exceptional, faithful disciple—present at the Cross, the burial, and the Resurrection as all four Gospels record (Mathew 27:56-61; Mark 15:40, 47; 16:1-19; Luke 24:10; John 19:25, 20:1). Mary was and continues to be a very common name even today. During biblical times, Mary was so common that people used other descriptors for those named Mary, such as whom they were related to or where they lived. Mary was probably called "Magdalene" because she was from Magdala, a city in Galilee, located in the northernmost region of ancient Palestine, which is now a part of northern Israel. Magdala was a coastal area where Jesus traveled by boat, after His miracle of feeding 4,000 people (Matthew 15:39).

Of the women in Luke 8:1-3, Mary Magdalene is identified first. The fact that her name is given and that she is first on the list of women, says she is special. The life of Mary Magdalene was greatly impacted by Jesus. He healed these three women from evil spirits and diseases. But for Mary Magdalene, He had to cast out seven demons (Mark 16:9). We know from the account of Jesus' encounter with the demoniac of the Gadarenes that many demons can possess a person at one time (Luke 8:30). Even though seven was thought to be a spiritually powerful number, Jesus' authority over all creation—even demons—is more powerful. Such deliverance at Jesus' hand helps us understand why Mary's transformation led to faith, love, and devotion to Christ.

Traditionally, Mary Magdalene has been conflated with the sinful woman Jesus met in Simon's house (Luke 7). It has also traditionally been assumed that the sinful woman was a prostitute. This is why Mary Magdalene has historically been portrayed as a repentant prostitute. A close reading of the texts, however, shows that this is not necessarily the case. The Gospels do not indicate as to Mary Magdalene's

profession or family history. Like Susanna, she simply is likely a wealthy woman with no husband, whose life was so changed by Jesus that she felt compelled to support His ministry in any way she could.

Mark 15:40 There were also women looking on afar off: among whom was Mary Magdalene, and Mary the mother of James the less and of Joses, and Salome;

Mark identifies the women who witnessed Jesus' execution on the Cross. Mary Magdalene is mentioned again, along with Salome (John 19:25), and another Mary who was the mother of James "the less" and Joses. He was called "James the less" to distinguish him since James was such a common name. James the Less was younger or shorter than another James, perhaps another James in the family or among the disciples. Joses is a Greek spelling of Joseph, a common Hebrew name.

Luke and Mark show us the prominent and significant roles women played in the life of Jesus and the support of His ministry. In African American churches and across the overall population, women are crucially active and comprise the majority of protestant congregations. Certainly, it is very encouraging for all to read these verses and see the value Jesus had for women.

John 20:10 Then the disciples went away again unto their own home. 11 But Mary stood without at the sepulchre weeping: and as she wept, she stooped down, and looked into the sepulchre, 12 And seeth two angels in white sitting, the one at the head, and the other at the feet, where the body of Jesus had lain. 13 And they say unto her, Woman, why weepest thou? She saith unto them, Because they have taken away my LORD, and I know not where they have laid him.

After seeing the empty tomb, Mary Magdalene ran back to tell the disciples. Peter and John ran back with Mary to see for themselves, but soon "went away again" to their homes, perhaps to ponder all they had experienced and to think about what might happen next. Mary Magdalene, however, stayed at the gravesite, overwhelmed and distressed because she thought someone had stolen Jesus' body from the tomb. She didn't recognize the two angels as messengers from God, and she responded to them as she would respond to human beings, perhaps because she was in a state of shock and sobbing. She let it be known that in her mind, Jesus' body should have still been there.

14 And when she had thus said, she turned herself back, and saw Jesus standing, and knew not that it was Jesus. 15 Jesus saith unto her, Woman, why weepest thou? whom seekest thou? She, supposing him to be the gardener, saith unto him, Sir, if thou have borne him hence, tell me where thou hast laid him, and I will take him away.

Mary Magdalene was so distraught, she did not recognize Jesus and thought He was a man that cared for the grounds. Even when Jesus questioned her, she tearfully spoke out of her grief and despair, not knowing where to find Jesus' body. We do not know why she did not immediately recognize Jesus. Perhaps it was a dark early morning, coupled with tear-filled eyes, and compounded grief. The fact remains that she simply did not recognize Jesus. Often in a state of deep despair, a mourner will fixate on one thing, and not be shaken even by good news. Mary Magdalene seems to have been fixated on finding Jesus' body.

It should be noted, however, that Mary was not the only one who could not recognize the resurrected Jesus. Later, Jesus shows Himself to the disciples who do not recognize Him either

(John 21:4). Jesus' two disciples on the road to Emmaus also did not recognize Jesus, until He chose to reveal His identity (Luke 24:16, 31). Mary Magdalene recognized Jesus when He was ready for her to realize His presence.

16 Jesus saith unto her, Mary. She turned herself, and saith unto him, Rabboni; which is to say, Master.

Finally, when Mary Magdalene recognizes Jesus, she sees Him as the Risen Savior. He calls her name. God knows the name of each part of His creation (Isaiah 40:26). He knows the secret name of every follower who overcomes (Revelation 2:17). He knows Mary's name. He sees her. And now, she can see Him. She gives a fitting answer to His call with the appropriate response, "Master" (Gk. *didaskalos*, **dee-DASS-kah-loce**; teacher) The term "rabboni" is perhaps the Galilean pronunciation of "rabbi." This is a Jewish title for respected religious leaders, coming from the Hebrew for "my great one." She acknowledges His true identity as Lord. What a significant event for us to witness through Scripture. She goes from mourning and suffering to joy and jubilation in an instant. Surprisingly, it was not John, the beloved disciple, or one of the other men, but a female disciple in the person of Mary Magdalene who first recognized the Savior.

Jesus opens Mary Magdalene's eyes and she believes it is Him. Praise the Lord that Jesus shows Himself to those who deeply and sincerely seek Him. He will reveal Himself in a way that often goes far beyond expectations. Mary Magdalene had a heart that honestly yearned to find Jesus and He spoke to her. She was a devoted disciple of Jesus and demonstrated faith by her belief in Him as our Resurrected Lord.

17 Jesus saith unto her, Touch me not; for I am not yet ascended to my Father: but go

to my brethren, and say unto them, I ascend unto my Father, and your Father; and to my God, and your God.

In verse 17, the word "touch" in Greek is *haptomai* (**HAP**-toe-my) which means to attach oneself to another. Therefore, a better translation of Jesus' words to Mary would be "don't cling to me" (NLT), rather than "Touch me not" (KJV). We can note that Jesus instructed Thomas to touch Him multiple times before He ascended to the Father (John 20:27). He does not want Mary, however, to cling too tightly to Him because He will soon be gone. Today we know that Jesus ascended to the Father. How wonderful it is that He continually allows us to cling to and hold on to Him without limits or restrictions as we pray to and commune with our Savior.

It is a blessing and a source of hope that Jesus let us and Mary Magdalene know that His Father is also our Father, and His God is also our God. This is the essence of our salvation story, to become children of God the Father because of Jesus' sacrifice on the Cross for us.

18 Mary Magdalene came and told the disciples that she had seen the LORD, and that he had spoken these things unto her.

Everyone who encounters Jesus after the Resurrection is transformed by His appearance. We can see a pattern in the appearances recorded by John. Mary is overcome with grief (20:11); the disciples are filled with fear (v. 19); while Thomas doubted (v. 25, 27). Jesus appears to them right in the middle of all their feelings. He does not expect us to clean ourselves up and get everything straight before encountering Him. Regardless of our status or condition, when we see Jesus our hearts and feelings are transformed. Mary's sorrow turns to mission; the disciples' fear turns to joy; and Thomas' doubt turns to faith.

What a privilege for Mary Magdalene to be the one to deliver Jesus' message to the disciples, a message she received in person! Now that we are transformed as believers, how eager are we to deliver the Gospel message to those who need Christ?

Mary Magdalene was healed by Jesus, traveled with Him in support of His ministry, witnessed His Crucifixion, and was one of the first people to witness His resurrection. The Lord gave her unique, transformative experiences and all believers should see her as a special person and a faithful disciple, indeed.

Sources:

Bassler, Jouette M, Harold W Attridge, Wayne A Meeks, and Society of Biblical Literature. *The HarperCollins Study Bible: Fully Revised Standard Version, with the Apocryphal/Deuterocanonical Books Student Edition.* New York: HarperCollins, 2006.

Benson, Joseph. *Benson's Commentary of Old and New Testaments.*

Guideposts Parallel Bible, King James Version, New International Version, Living Bible and Revised Standard Version. New York: Guideposts, 1981.

Higginbotham, Evelyn Brooks. *Righteous Discontent: The Women's Movement in the Black Baptist Church, 1880-1920.* Cambridge, MA: Harvard University Press, 1993.

Kysar, John, R. *Augsburg Commentary on the New Testament*, John. Minneapolis, MN: Augsburg Fortress Publishers, 1986.

Pew Research Center: Religion & Public Life (January 30, 2009). *A Religious Portrait of African-Americans.* https://www.pewforum.org/2009/01/30/a-religious-portrait-of-african-americans/. Retrieved October 13, 2019.

Smith, William. *Smith's Bible Dictionary.* Philadelphia, PA: A.J. Holman Company, 1973.

Say It Correctly

Magdala. **MAG**-dah-lah.
Salome. **SAH**-low-may.
Chuza. **KOO**-zah.

Daily Bible Readings

MONDAY
Jesus Appears to Paul
(1 Corinthians 15:1–11)

TUESDAY
Present with Jesus at the Cross
(John 19:25–30)

WEDNESDAY
Spices Prepared to Anoint Jesus' Body
(Mark 16:1–8)

THURSDAY
Mary Magdalene Finds an Empty Tomb
(John 20:1–9)

FRIDAY
Angel Confirms Jesus'
Resurrection to Women
(Matthew 28:1–10)

SATURDAY
Jesus Appears, Disciples
Sent into Ministry
(John 20:19–23)

SUNDAY
Mary Magdalene, Faithful Disciple
(Luke 8:1-3; Mark 15:40; John 20:10-18)

Notes

_____

_____

_____

_____

Teaching Tips

February 21
Bible Study Guide 12

Words You Should Know

A. Eloquent (Acts 18:24) *logio* (Gk.)—Skilled in speech, as well as wise and learned

B. Perfectly (v. 26) *akribes* (Gk.)—Accurately, exactly, carefully

Teacher Preparation

Unifying Principle—Risk Taker. Encounters that bring together people with similar gifts and talents can lead to greater opportunities for service in other arenas. How can common traits or experiences lead to a meaningful engagement in ministry or service? Priscilla and Aquila shared their tent-making business with Paul, and Paul shared his ministry of the Gospel with them.

A. Read the Bible Background and Devotional Reading.

B. Pray for your students and lesson clarity.

C. Read the lesson Scripture in multiple translations.

O—Open the Lesson

A. Begin the class with prayer.

B. Invite class members who have experienced moving from another area and joining a new congregation to share with the group the importance and value of finding a new church family after a move.

C. Have the students read the Aim for Change and the In Focus story.

D. Ask students how events like those in the story weigh on their hearts and how they can view these events from a faith perspective.

P—Present the Scriptures

A. Read the Focal Verses and discuss the Background and The People, Places, and Times sections.

B. Have the class share what Scriptures stand out for them and why, with particular emphasis on today's themes.

E—Explore the Meaning

A. Use In Depth or More Light on the Text to facilitate a deeper discussion of the lesson text.

B. Pose the questions in Search the Scriptures and Discuss the Meaning.

C. Discuss the Liberating Lesson and Application for Activation sections.

N—Next Steps for Application

A. Summarize the value of mutual support from being part of a Christian community.

B. End class with a commitment to pray for men and women who work as partners in the workplace and their churches.

Worship Guide

For the Superintendent or Teacher
Theme: Priscilla: Called to Minister
Song: "I'm Gonna Live So God
Can Use Me"
Devotional Reading: Colossians 4:7-15

Priscilla: Called to Minister

Bible Background • ACTS 18:1-26; ROMANS 16:3-4; 1 CORINTHIANS 16:19; 2 TIMOTHY 4:19 | Printed Text • ACTS 18:1-3, 18-21, 24-26; ROMANS 16:3-4 | Devotional Reading • COLOSSIANS 4:7-15

Aim for Change

By the end of this lesson, we will RESEARCH the life and ministry of Priscilla and her husband Aquila, APPRECIATE the ministry of those who explain the Way of God with accuracy, and SEEK opportunities to use our gifts or abilities to further the Gospel.

In Focus

Gloria and Raoul had come to the United States five years ago as refugees from the Democratic Republic of Congo. They had to leave their home because regional infighting was making it dangerous for them. The U.S. would provide a safe place where they could start a family. Even though Gloria and Raoul only knew a few people who had immigrated, they trusted that God would provide for them as they journeyed to this new land.

The couple was grateful to be welcomed into a local church. The church included them in their ministries, and Gloria and Raoul offering their skills at the church's after-school program. Raoul had actually taught algebra before they fled, and Gloria loved looking after little ones.

One day, a new face showed up in the congregation. He was an immigrant from Costa Rica named Julio. Even though he spoke only a little English, he loved the Lord and loved to share that love on the field. He told stories about his time coaching *fútbol* back in his hometown. Gloria insisted Julio come to their house for lunch, and they recruited him to join them at the after-school program, teaching soccer. Julio quickly became invaluable to the ministry. Many students were excited to learn new soccer tricks, but they also learned about Jesus' love for them.

What skills do you have that can be used to directly further the Gospel? How can you use your skills in ways that help others share the Gospel too?

Keep in Mind

"Greet Priscilla and Aquila my helpers in Christ Jesus: Who have for my life laid down their own necks: unto whom not only I give thanks, but also all the churches of the Gentiles" (Romans 16:3-4, KJV).

"Give my greetings to Priscilla and Aquila, my co-workers in the ministry of Christ Jesus. In fact, they once risked their lives for me. I am thankful to them, and so are all the Gentile churches" (Romans 16:3-4, NLT).

was born among the large Jewish population of Pontus, he and his wife had most recently lived in Italy. When Emperor Claudius commanded all Jews to be expelled from Rome, however, the couple left and eventually arrived in Corinth. The Scriptures affirm that Aquila, Priscilla, and Paul were all tentmakers, so the three of them worked at their tentmaking trade, and Paul engaged in ministry on the Sabbath, preaching to both Jews and Gentiles in the synagogue.

Most would agree that Paul was a great apostle and evangelist, but dedicated friends helped Paul achieve many of his accomplishments. Christian friends, like Priscilla and Aquila, are vitally important to ministry and evangelism. God's church is not made of brick and mortar; it is made of people who are codependent on one another and Christ.

2. Expanding the Ministry to Ephesus (vv. 18-21)

Paul and his companions minister for a year and a half among the Corinthians before the stirring of the Holy Spirit prompts them to travel to Syria to further the ministry. Paul leaves accompanied by Priscilla and Aquila and sailed back across the Aegean Sea.

The ship upon which the trio has traveling stops in Ephesus for a short time and Paul takes advantage of the stopover to teach in the local Jewish synagogue. His preaching stirs interest among the Jewish inhabitants of Ephesus, who entreat Paul to stay with them longer. However, Paul desires to return to Jerusalem in time for one of the Jewish festivals and is unable to stay. He promises, however, to return if God will permit it. He also leaves Priscilla and Aquila in Ephesus to carry on what he has begun. Priscilla and Aquila remain in Ephesus for several years and permit their home to be used as the meeting place for the Christian church they help to plant.

3. Apollos Meets Priscilla and Aquila (vv. 24-26)

Sometime later, Apollos, a Jew who was born in Alexandria, comes to Ephesus. Apollos was excited about the Word of God and the Lord Jesus Christ and described as "an eloquent man, and mighty in the Scriptures" (v. 24).

Apollos possesses great biblical skills, having the ability to teach the Word diligently, even though he only knows about the baptism of John. However, Apollos' ministry catches the attention of Priscilla and Aquila. They are impressed with his teaching and his boldness as he speaks in the synagogue, but they realize that Apollos lacks a fuller understanding of Jesus.

Priscilla and Aquila become his mentors in the things of the Spirit. We all need spiritual mentors who can help us expound the Word of God in a more complete way. We should not be afraid to ask others who may be more spiritually mature to help us get a better understanding of the Scriptures.

4. Paul Salutes Priscilla and Aquila (Romans 16:3-4)

At the close of his letter to the Romans, the Apostle Paul greets 26 people by name. At the top of this list is the ministry team, Priscilla and Aquila. He refers to the couple as "my helpers in Christ Jesus." The word "helper" means "fellow worker" and looks back to their love and aid when Paul arrived in Corinth. The apostle says that the couple "laid down their own necks," or risked their lives on his behalf. Scripture does not record the incident when this took place, but at some point the couple was willing to sacrifice their own lives for the Gospel. Paul affirms his gratitude for this couple's work, adding that "also all the churches of the Gentiles" thank them. This shows that Paul considers Priscilla and Aquila's work so influential that every church started by non-Jews owes gratitude to them.

Search the Scriptures

1. Why had Priscilla and Aquila left their home in Rome and relocated to Corinth? (Acts 18:2)

2. What activity helped cement the partnership between Paul and the couple? (v. 3)

3. What phrase did Paul use to describe the couple's ministry with him? (Romans 16:3)

Discuss the Meaning

1. Many people believe that working with one's spouse professionally or in ministry can cause problems in the home because work problems or ministry disagreements follow the couple home and cause friction. Do you believe this? If so, why? If not, why not?

2. What are some of the reasons people do not mentor younger people? How should these issues be resolved?

Liberating Lesson

Christian homes and solid Christian marriages remain two of the best tools for spreading the Gospel. Husband-and-wife teams can be tremendous blessings for the body of Christ. The faithfulness of people like Priscilla and Aquila makes ministry a joy for others. The effectiveness of their ministry says a lot about their personal relationship with each other and with God. Their hospitality became the doorway of salvation for many.

This is why the enemy fights so hard against marriage. More than half the marriages in the United States end in divorce. List some of the positive features and negative hindrances that can affect husband-and-wife businesses/partnerships (and marriages). Report on your list next week.

Application for Activation

In today's lesson, Priscilla and Aquila took young Apollos under their wing and mentored him in the Gospel. Examine your life to see who you are influencing in the body of Christ. If you can't think of anyone, ask God to help you make a specific contribution to someone's life this week. Perhaps making a phone call or writing a letter to lift someone's spirit is a good place to start. Before the class is over today, commit to find someone this week.

Follow the Spirit

What God wants me to do:

_____

_____

_____

_____

_____

_____

_____

_____

Remember Your Thoughts

Special insights I have learned:

_____

_____

_____

_____

_____

_____

_____

More Light on the Text

Acts 18:1-3, 18-21, 24-26; Romans 16:3-4

Acts 18:1 After these things Paul departed from Athens, and came to Corinth:

After the apostle's debate with the philosophers and his sermon in the Areopagus (Acts 17:16), Paul leaves Athens, and arrives in Corinth, at the isthmus connecting southern Greece (the Peloponnese) with northern mainland Greece. This places it advantageously along a north-south land trading route and an east-west maritime trading route. It was the capital of the Roman province of Achaea. The city abounded in riches and luxury and was well-known for its debauchery. The centerpiece of the city was the temple of Aphrodite, the goddess of love and beauty, where no fewer than a thousand prostitutes provided services. Wanton sexual behavior was so prevalent in Corinth that the city's name became a verb. "To Corinth" meant "to fornicate." (A far cry from Paul's last stop: "to Athens" meant "to discuss philosophy.")

2 And found a certain Jew named Aquila, born in Pontus, lately come from Italy, with his wife Priscilla; (because that Claudius had commanded all Jews to depart from Rome:) and came unto them.

Jewish guilds always kept together, whether in the street or the synagogue, so Paul would have little trouble finding a place to apply his trade in the city and to meet others who were similarly employed. He was in such a guild when he first met the husband-and-wife, team Priscilla and Aquila. The couple would prove to be valuable assets to the apostle's ministry.

"Aquila" is a Latin name meaning "eagle." Aquila likely took this name or was given it while he was in Rome. Aquila was born in Pontus, along the southern shore of the Black Sea. Even though this Roman province was nearly 900 miles away from Jerusalem, many Jews—including Aquila's parents—lived there. The name "Priscilla" is also Latin, and means ancient, and thus worthy of veneration and honor. We are not told when these Jews converted to Christianity.

The couple had recently arrived in Corinth from Italy because Claudius, the Roman emperor, "had commanded all Jews to depart from Rome." This Claudius was the fourth emperor of Rome, and this decree was passed about the year AD 51 or 54. It is believed that Claudius issued his edict because the Jews in Rome were continually at odds with the Christians about Jesus being the Messiah. Claudius was afraid that the conflict would lead to unrest, so he banished all the Jews from Rome. At that time, Romans saw no difference between Christians and Jews, so they were all ordered to go. As a result, Priscilla and Aquila were obliged to leave Rome. When Paul found out about the couple, he "came unto them," visiting and staying in their home in Corinth.

3 And because he was of the same craft, he abode with them, and wrought: for by their occupation they were tentmakers.

What attracted Paul to the couple was a shared skill. In Greek, the phrase "same craft" is one word, *homotechnos* (hoe-MOE-tek-noce). The word is composed of the prefix *homo*, meaning the same, and the suffix *technos*, meaning trade. Like Paul, Priscilla and Aquila were tentmakers who "wrought," or worked with their own hands to support themselves. Paul was a stranger in Corinth. He supported himself by tentmaking and would take nothing from the converts because he knew that false teachers might rise among them and accuse him of greed.

Tentmaking was a prosperous trade. Soldier's tents were made of a cheap yet durable cloth made from goat hair or of the leathered skins of various animals sewed together. Other tents were canopies made of linen or other materials and were erected in the summer to shade and screen people from the heat of the sun. Although Paul was a scholar, he was taught a trade to earn a living like every Jewish male child.

18 And Paul after this tarried there yet a good while, and then took his leave of the brethren, and sailed thence into Syria, and with him Priscilla and Aquila; having shorn his head in Cenchrea: for he had a vow.

While teaching a good number of those gathering in the synagogue weekly, Paul "tarried" (Gk. *prosmeno*, pros-**MEH**-no) meaning "to continue" or "to remain with" them for an unspecified length of time, but for what is understood to be a considerable number of days. Paul stayed put, preaching and teaching among them, even after a plot to kill him had failed (18:12-17). Because the people were receptive, the preached Word was effectual in convicting and convincing that Jesus is the Christ. Note that in the previous verse, those gathered were called Jews and Greeks. After Paul's effective and persuasive ministry to them, he now calls them "brethren" (Gk. *adelphotes*, ah-del-**FOE**-tace), which explicitly means a brother by birth, national origin, or friendship. However, within the Christian community, the term became all-inclusive to refer to all who believed, whether Jew or Greek, bond or free, and male or female.

Priscilla and Aquila were present in the synagogue and had found Paul's invitation to join his evangelistic journey irresistible. Companionship and partnership in ministry are empowering, encouraging, and refining. As believers, we should seek accountability and good company in one another—both male and female. In this account, like previous lessons this quarter, women are mentioned as central players in the spread of the Gospel.

The "vow" (Gk. *euche*, yew-**KHAY**) that Paul made earlier was likely a 30-day fast and prayer of thanksgiving to God when he did not shave or drink wine. Shaving his head was simply an outward Jewish expression of his inward sincerity when this period of consecration had ended. Cenchrae was the port city nearest to Corinth, where they actually embarked to sail across the Aegean Sea.

19 And he came to Ephesus, and left them there: but he himself entered into the synagogue, and reasoned with the Jews.

The Roman city Ephesus was located on the sea between Smyrna and Miletus (the place from which Paul would call the elders of the church). While in port at Ephesus, Paul left his companions, Priscilla and Aquila, and went directly to the synagogue to again debate with the Jewish religious and philosophical leaders assembled there. Paul was ever ready and ever seeking to persuade, convince, debate, and prove that Jesus Christ is the Messiah to all who would listen.

The Greek word *sunagoge* (soo-nah-go-**GAY**) is used in various grammatical forms. As a verb, "to synagogue" means "to bring together" as in a harvest or a group of men. As a noun, "synagogue" is a formal assembly of Jewish men gathered to pray, read, and discuss Scripture, which met weekly every Sabbath and feast day. Christians also adapted the word "synagogue" to describe their formal gathering in the early church. "Synagogue" also refers to the very buildings where these religious Jewish assemblies, as well as trials, were held. There was at least one synagogue in every town that had at least ten Jewish men.

20 When they desired him to tarry longer time with them, he consented not; 21 But bade them farewell, saying, I must by all means keep this feast that cometh in Jerusalem: but I will return again unto you, if God will. And he sailed from Ephesus.

Paul's teaching was so efficacious that Jewish religious leaders, some new converts to Christianity, asked him to stay or "tarry" (a related, but slightly different Greek verb than "tarry" in v. 18) with them a while longer. Whereas Paul hastened from the port of Ephesus to meet with those in the synagogue, he was compelled by the Holy Spirit to decline their persistence that he extend his stay. Here, Paul demonstrates that his calling and ministry is unto God's will and not for man's desire. The best good to be found among these new believers paled in comparison to the ministry before Paul as he journeyed to Jerusalem.

Paul gave them an explanation for resisting their hospitality: he had to go to the place of worship. The Jews had three "pilgrimage feasts" (Passover, Tabernacles, and Pentecost) which, if at all possible, were supposed to be celebrated at the Temple in Jerusalem. As a dedicated ethnic Jew, Paul wished to attend. He had set out with this goal and had the means to complete it. Paul held fast to his conviction to move on; however, he did leave them with a caveat. He promised to come back and continue in ministry and fellowship only if God needed him more there! "God willing," was a shared understanding among the pious Jews and Greeks. We must take care to use it (James 4:15), not as doubting God's will for our lives or buffeting a weak promise, but as a faithful declaration to do God's will, in God's time, at God's appointed place!

24 And a certain Jew named Apollos, born at Alexandria, an eloquent man, and mighty in the scriptures, came to Ephesus.

After Paul's departure from Ephesus, while Priscilla and Aquila were there, one of John the Baptist's disciples named Apollos arrived in the city and began preaching the Word. Apollos was a cultured, educated Jew from Alexandria, a thriving Egyptian metropolis that was home to a great number of Jews who were lead scholars of their day. "Apollos" is a Greek name that honors the youthful god of music and light.

Luke describes the young man as being "eloquent." The Greek word for eloquence is *logios* (**LOW**-gee-oce), which means skilled in speech as well as wise and learned. Apollos was also "mighty" in Scriptures. In this case, the Greek adjective *dunatos* (doo-nah-**TOCE**) means capable or excellent, rather than strong or powerful. The word "Scriptures" refers to the Old Testament, the only written revelation from God about Himself at that time. Apollos had thoroughly read them, carefully examined them, could readily cite them, had great knowledge of them, and was capable of explaining them.

25 This man was instructed in the way of the Lord; and being fervent in the spirit, he spake and taught diligently the things of the Lord, knowing only the baptism of John.

The word "instructed" suggests that Apollo's parents, who may have been disciples of John, trained him in the Scriptures. Apollo had only been taught the rudiments of the Christian faith, here called the "way of the Lord." Apollos knew of Christ, but he did not know Christ as Lord and Savior. In spite of his incomplete training, Apollo was "fervent" (Gk. *zeo*, **ZEH**-oh), boiling with enthusiasm to preach the Good News. The word "spirit" in this case refers to Apollos' own spirit; in other words, his soul burned with zeal for the glory of God, and he "diligently" (Gk. *akribos*, ah-kree-**BOCE**) proclaimed the Word according to the measure of grace and knowledge he had received. Apollos taught the people all he knew of the person, work, and office of the Lord Jesus.

The phrase "knowing only the baptism of John" must be understood as the entire ministry of John, including John's doctrine of repentance and remission of sins, which looked forward to the Christ who was to come as well as to His baptism. Scholars are not in agreement, but whatever Apollos was lacking he received from Priscilla and Aquila.

26 And he began to speak boldly in the synagogue: whom when Aquila and Priscilla had heard, they took him unto them, and expounded unto him the way of God more perfectly.

Apollo spoke out boldly in the synagogue without fear of the Jews. While attending a synagogue meeting, Priscilla and Aquila hear Apollo preach and observed that there was some deficiency in his message. Being concerned for the young minister's message, they take him aside and privately converse with him. Over time they explain the Word to him more completely. The word "more perfectly" is from the Greek word *akribes* (ah-kree-**BASE**) and means more accurately. It is related to "diligently" in the previous verse. When Apollos preached an incomplete way of the Lord diligently, Priscilla and Aquila taught him more diligently. In other words, Priscilla and Aquila supplied the knowledge that Apollos was lacking.

Priscilla and Aquila had received a considerable measure of evangelical revelation and knowledge from the Apostle Paul during their time together, and they imparted their knowledge to Apollos. Later, Apollos would become one of Paul's trusted friends and companions (1 Corinthians 16:12; Titus 3:13). He was such an effective preacher that some of the Corinthians put him before Paul and Peter (1 Corinthians 1:12; 3:4-6).

Romans 16:3 Greet Priscilla and Aquila my helpers in Christ Jesus:

This couple is extensively traveled extensively, especially considering the difficulty of travel in those days. Aquila was born in Pontus, moved to Rome at some point, was exiled from Rome around AD 52, lived in Corinth, journeyed from Corinth to Ephesus with Paul, stayed there long enough to help establish a church, and then apparently moved back to Rome and hosted a house church there too.

The date that the couple left Ephesus and returned to Rome is unknown, but at that time either Claudius had died or his edict that ordered the Jews to depart from Rome had been revoked. The couple returned to Rome, and they were there when the apostle wrote this epistle to the church in Rome. Paul salutes them and refers to them as "my helpers in Christ Jesus." The term "helpers" translates the Greek *sunergos* (soon-air-**GOCE**), which could also be translated "co-workers" or "fellow laborers." They are not just lesser helpers in Paul's great ministry; they toil equally alongside the apostle. The couple assisted Paul in spreading the Gospel and promoting the kingdom and Lordship of Christ. They helped encourage young converts and comfort them with their own experiences and therefore they were greatly appreciated by the apostle in the work of the Lord Jesus.

4 Who have for my life laid down their own necks: unto whom not only I give thanks, but also all the churches of the Gentiles.

When Paul says that Priscilla and Aquila have "for my life laid down their necks," he is intimating that the couple exposed themselves to great danger to save his life. The allusion is to the ancient practice of beheading and someone laying down his head and offering his neck to the executioner in place of another. Today, we might say someone "stuck their neck out for me." We should not suppose that Priscilla and Aquila literally did this, but the expression intends that in some way they risked their own lives for Paul's. We are given no further details of this courageous act, but there are a couple of plausible possibilities. The incident may have occurred at the insurrection in Corinth when the Jews dragged Paul to the judgment seat of Galileo and beat Sosthenes, the ruler of the synagogue before him (Acts 18:17). Otherwise, it might have been in Ephesus, where Demetrius and the craftsmen incited a riot against Paul and his companions (Acts 19:24). Aquila and Priscilla were present at both events and were no doubt actively protecting the apostle. Whatever the case, Paul was very grateful for their heroic assistance.

With all his missionary work all over the Mediterranean, Paul knows that the church is growing and flourishing not just because of his own teaching, but also through the work of other faithful Christ-followers. Paul knows thanks are in order. He shares his gratitude for this couple who have sheltered him and continue to shelter the church (both in Ephesus and in Rome). He sends not only his thanks but also the thanks of all "Gentile" churches. The word "Gentile" here is *ethnos* (Gk. **ETH**-noce), which is often correctly translated as Gentile as opposed to Jewish. However, the word can also denote people groups everywhere. Paul here might be referring to churches that began with a non-Jewish population, but he also might refer to the church from all people. What a tribute for all of Priscilla and Aquila's devoted work for the Lord, to be thanked from all over the Christian world!

Sources:

Achtemeier, Paul. *Harper's Bible Dictionary.* New York: HarperCollins, 1985. 173, 182-3.

Strong, James. *The New Strong's Exhaustive Concordance of the Bible.* Nashville, TN: Thomas Nelson, 2003.

Thayer, Joseph Henry. *A Greek-English Lexicon of the New Testament.* New York: American Book Company, 1994.

Vine, W.E. *Vine's Complete Expository Dictionary of Old and New Testament Words.* Nashville, TN: Thomas Nelson, 1996.

Say It Correctly

Cenchrae. kenn-**KRAY**-ah.
Sosthenes. **SOSS**-theh-neez.
Aquila. ah-**QUILL**-ah.

Daily Bible Readings

MONDAY
Paul Reflects on His Ministry
(2 Timothy 4:9–18)

TUESDAY
Greetings to Saints in Jesus Christ
(Colossians 4:7–15)

WEDNESDAY
The Holy Kiss Strengthens
Ministry Bond
(2 Corinthians 13:11–13;
1 Thessalonians 5:23–28)

THURSDAY
Ministry Shifts from Jews to Gentiles
(Acts 18:4–11)

FRIDAY
Roman Official Refuses to Settle Dispute
(Acts 18:12–17)

SATURDAY
Greetings to All Sisters in Ministry
(Romans 16:1–2, 6–7, 12–13, 16)

SUNDAY
Priscilla, Key Outreach Minister
(Acts 18:1–3, 18–21, 24–26;
Romans 16:3–4)

Teaching Tips

Words You Should Know

A. Prayer (Acts 16:13) *proseuche* (Gk.)—A call to God, or a place to call on God

B. Faithful (v. 15) *pistos* (Gk.)—Trustworthy and reliable

Teacher Preparation

Unifying Principle—Showing Generous Hospitality. Many people have been recipients of generous hospitality or have been in a position to extend hospitality to someone. In what ways can openness and a listening ear provide opportunities to serve? Lydia was an attentive woman who responded to the Gospel message with faithfulness and generous hospitality.

A. Read the Bible Background and Devotional Reading.

B. Pray for your students and lesson clarity.

C. Read the lesson Scripture in multiple translations.

O—Open the Lesson

A. Begin the class with prayer.

B. Do a hospitality inventory of your congregation. Imagine being a first-time visitor to your congregation. Make a list of how to make a visitor feel welcome, as well as a list of things that might not feel welcoming. Discuss what your group can do to be more hospitable.

C. Have the students read the Aim for Change and the In Focus story.

D. Ask students how events like those in the story weigh on their hearts and how they can view these events from a faith perspective.

P—Present the Scriptures

A. Read the Focal Verses and discuss the Background and The People, Places, and Times sections.

B. Have the class share what Scriptures stand out for them and why, with particular emphasis on today's themes.

E—Explore the Meaning

A. Use In Depth or More Light on the Text to facilitate a deeper discussion of the lesson text.

B. Pose the questions in Search the Scriptures and Discuss the Meaning.

C. Discuss the Liberating Lesson and Application for Activation sections.

N—Next Steps for Application

A. Summarize the value of embracing unity with other Christians on no other basis than their shared faith in Jesus.

B. End class with a commitment to pray for courage to stand for our faith, even when our beliefs violate cultural norms.

Worship Guide

For the Superintendent or Teacher
Theme: Lydia: Called to Serve
Song: "If It Had Not Been for the Lord on My Side"
Devotional Reading: Psalm 33:1-12

Lydia: Called to Serve

Bible Background • ACTS 16:11-15, 40; 1 CORINTHIANS 1:26-30 | Printed Text • ACTS 16:11-15, 40; 1 CORINTHIANS 1:26-30 | Devotional Reading • PSALM 33:1-12

Aim for Change

By the end of this lesson, we will CONSIDER how Lydia used her gifts and her place in society to support Paul's ministry, REPENT of the times we have looked down on others who have not had the same opportunities or advantages, and SERVE others joyfully through whatever means are at our disposal.

In Focus

William lounged on the couch by the window in the Saturday afternoon sun. His wife Betty was off at her book club across town, and he had the house to himself. So quiet, he thought happily. But as he listened more to the ticking of the clock in the kitchen, he grew restless.

They had lived in this house for over thirty years, long enough to have three kids and see them off to homes of their own. William and Betty were certainly enjoying the time to themselves, but now their empty nest just didn't feel right to him. He almost missed the little feet traipsing loudly upstairs or the chatting teens in the TV room. Dinners at the kitchen table were definitely less lively without the kids and their fiancés.

It seemed to William like a waste of space. He wasn't ready to move to a smaller apartment; he wanted the guest rooms. He wanted to be hospitable. Over dinner, William talked with Betty about the feeling.

"You're right, dear," Betty said. "Things are so different now without the kids. In fact, I was just thinking on my drive over there, how far away my book club is. It used to make sense when Billy's baseball practice was out that way, but that was years ago."

"I was thinking," William said. "How about we tell the church office that we're offering to host something here. Could be a new book club, maybe a small group …"

How can you show God's love to others through hospitality?

Keep in Mind

"And when she was baptized, and her household, she besought us, saying, If ye have judged me to be faithful to the Lord, come into my house, and abide there. And she constrained us" (Acts 16:15, KJV).

"She and her household were baptized, and she asked us to be her guests. 'If you agree that I am a true believer in the Lord,' she said, 'come and stay at my home.' And she urged us until we agreed" (Acts 16:15, NLT).

Focal Verses

KJV **Acts 16:11** Therefore loosing from Troas, we came with a straight course to Samothracia, and the next day to Neapolis;

12 And from thence to Philippi, which is the chief city of that part of Macedonia, and a colony: and we were in that city abiding certain days.

13 And on the sabbath we went out of the city by a river side, where prayer was wont to be made; and we sat down, and spake unto the women which resorted thither.

14 And a certain woman named Lydia, a seller of purple, of the city of Thyatira, which worshipped God, heard us: whose heart the Lord opened, that she attended unto the things which were spoken of Paul.

15 And when she was baptized, and her household, she besought us, saying, If ye have judged me to be faithful to the Lord, come into my house, and abide there. And she constrained us.

40 And they went out of the prison, and entered into the house of Lydia: and when they had seen the brethren, they comforted them, and departed.

1 Corinthians 1:26 For ye see your calling, brethren, how that not many wise men after the flesh, not many mighty, not many noble, are called:

27 But God hath chosen the foolish things of the world to confound the wise; and God hath chosen the weak things of the world to confound the things which are mighty;

28 And base things of the world, and things which are despised, hath God chosen, yea, and things which are not, to bring to nought things that are:

29 That no flesh should glory in his presence.

NLT **Acts 16:11** We boarded a boat at Troas and sailed straight across to the island of Samothrace, and the next day we landed at Neapolis.

12 From there we reached Philippi, a major city of that district of Macedonia and a Roman colony. And we stayed there several days.

13 On the Sabbath we went a little way outside the city to a riverbank, where we thought people would be meeting for prayer, and we sat down to speak with some women who had gathered there.

14 One of them was Lydia from Thyatira, a merchant of expensive purple cloth, who worshiped God. As she listened to us, the Lord opened her heart, and she accepted what Paul was saying.

15 She and her household were baptized, and she asked us to be her guests. "If you agree that I am a true believer in the Lord," she said, "come and stay at my home." And she urged us until we agreed.

40 When Paul and Silas left the prison, they returned to the home of Lydia. There they met with the believers and encouraged them once more. Then they left town.

1 Corinthians 1:26 Remember, dear brothers and sisters, that few of you were wise in the world's eyes or powerful or wealthy when God called you.

27 Instead, God chose things the world considers foolish in order to shame those who think they are wise. And he chose things that are powerless to shame those who are powerful.

28 God chose things despised by the world, things counted as nothing at all, and used them to bring to nothing what the world considers important.

29 As a result, no one can ever boast in the presence of God.

30 But of him are ye in Christ Jesus, who of God is made unto us wisdom, and righteousness, and sanctification, and redemption:

30 God has united you with Christ Jesus. For our benefit God made him to be wisdom itself. Christ made us right with God; he made us pure and holy, and he freed us from sin.

The People, Places, and Times

Purple Cloth. The ancient Mediterranean peoples used a dye from a certain kind of sea snail found in the eastern Mediterranean Sea. This dye was very expensive because of its rarity and the labor intensity of extracting it. Clothing made from this dye was equally expensive and reserved for notable members of society. The color is now called Tyrean purple, after Tyre, the Phoenician city that perhaps discovered the dye.

Philippi. A predominantly Roman city at this time, Philippi was eight miles inland from Neapolis, which was a seaport in northern Macedonia. The city is named for Alexander the Great's father, Philip II of Macedon. The city Philippi was located near two rivers and connected with coastal cities by several good roads; therefore, trade was enjoyed and was financially lucrative. Philippi lay along the Egnatian Way, the major east-west Roman road connecting lands in Greece and Turkey.

Background

After Paul and Barnabas' successful journey planting many churches in Syria and surrounding provinces, a new journey to plant churches was planned—this time throughout the Roman province of Asia. Paul and Silas set out from Antioch and were joined by Timothy while visiting a previously established church in Lystra. Soon after, the Holy Spirit deflected the group's plans to go into Asia and guided the men instead of to Macedonia. At this point, Luke (the writer of Acts) joined the team too, and they set sail from the eastern shore of the Aegean Sea.

After meeting Lydia, the team stays in Philippi preaching. They cast a demon out of a slave girl and her masters provoked an uproar that ended with Paul and Silas in jail. When an earthquake opened the chains of every cell in the prison and the jailer was about to kill himself, Paul and Silas led the man to Christ instead.

Paul and Silas benefited from the hospitality of wealthy converts, but Paul also knew that most Christians did not have much worldly wealth or status to boast of. He wrote to the Corinthian church to show how God uses that fact to His advantage so Christians should feel no shame in their lowly status.

Compare and contrast the conversion of Lydia and the jailer. Describe other biblical and present-day examples of how God works.

At-A-Glance

1. The Ministry at Philippi
   (Acts 16:11-13)
2. The Conversion of Lydia
   (vv. 14-15, 40)
3. The Wisdom of the Cross
   (1 Corinthians 1:26-28)
4. The Benefits of the Cross (vv. 29-30)

In Depth

1. The Ministry at Philippi (Acts 16:11-13)

It took two to five days for Paul and his team to travel from Troas to Macedonia. The first colony they visited in Macedonia was Philippi. On the Sabbath, Paul and the others traveling with him made their way through the city gate and to the water's edge. They had discovered that there was no synagogue in Philippi, indicating that there were not ten Jewish men in the community, as this is the number of men required to hold a Sabbath service. Those who sought to worship God, then, were mostly women and did so down by the riverside, where women often gathered to draw water, do laundry, and enjoy female companionship.

Paul and his friends began to preach Christ to these women. Paul had learned that God did not show favoritism and the women who had converted to Christ had become a major source for the spread of Christianity in other places where he had preached.

Where have you seen women take the initiative to start a gathering when men could not or did not do so?

2. The Conversion of Lydia (vv. 14-15, 40)

Lydia's heart is already open to receive God's Word, so when Paul begins to speak, she listens and accepts the truth of the things he has to say. Lydia became the first convert in Europe. Then after accepting Christ for herself and being baptized, she was blessed to see her entire household baptized into the Christian community of believers. The joy she experienced in Christ must have been tremendous, for after her conversion she invited Paul and his companions to stay in her home as her guests and refused to let them say no.

Paul and the other missionaries traveling with him stayed with Lydia until their ministry in the city had concluded. Her home became the first church at Philippi. Paul later referred to the Philippian church as his "joy and crown" (Philippians 4:1).

Lydia became one of Paul's financial supporters and was a loyal helper in his ministry. Lydia even fearlessly opened her house to Paul and Silas after they were released from prison. She did not let the fear of associating with people accused of rabble-rousing keep her from supporting God's workers.

What effort have you made to lead your family and close friends to Christ?

3. The Wisdom of the Cross (1 Corinthians 1:26-28)

As we have seen in this past month of lessons, God does not hesitate to call people to spread the Word even though society has overlooked them. Lydia was rich, but most converts were poor or working class. Paul tells these converts that formal education, political power, and economic status are not what put you ahead in the kingdom of God.

Instead, God specifically chooses those the world counts as low to show His glory. The Lord ordained twelve social outcasts to be His disciples, to learn from Him, and be empowered with the Holy Spirit. They, in turn, were responsible for sharing the message of the Cross worldwide. Perceived as a powerless baby born in a manger, Jesus escaped the murderous rampage of a king. A despised Cross and physical death, instead of ending Jesus' existence, demonstrated His wisdom and power over sin and the grave itself.

How has God used the weaknesses in your life to show His glory?

4. The Benefits of the Cross (vv. 29-30)

When we look back and remember how the Lord has brought us, sheer necessity compels us to sing, "If it had not been for the Lord on my side, where would I be?" Those who know we would be nothing without God have reason to rejoice and brag. True wisdom is knowing that our rejoicing and bragging is in what God has done for us through Christ Jesus.

God chooses the lowly, and completed the entire work of salvation by Himself, so that no one has anything to boast about to God

(v. 29). The marvel is that God makes Jesus everything—and then includes us! He makes Christ all the deep, lasting, spiritual things we could boast about: wisdom, righteousness, sanctification, and redemption (v. 30). But he doesn't keep them to Himself. He shares them with us. God specifically gives these gifts to the lowly so that the world can see how far a person is lifted solely by the power of Christ.

How have you expressed your gratitude for all God has done for you?

Search the Scriptures

1. Who was baptized along with Lydia (Acts 16:15)?

2. What aspects of the world does God confound, shame, and bring to nothing? (1 Corinthians 1:27)

Discuss the Meaning

1. Why did God lead Paul to Macedonia to the women at the river, but forbid him to go to other places?

2. Why is it significant that Lydia already worshiped God?

3. Christians are not saved because we are wise, strong, or wealthy. In fact, Scripture reminds us of how little merit we have on our own. However, Scripture also reminds us of our unity with Christ, who is everything glorious. In light of these two opposite self-images, how should Christians understand themselves and present themselves to the world?

Liberating Lesson

Missionaries who travel to Africa report that the nature of hospitality is such that within the community whenever anyone needs food or shelter, the members of the church rise up and take them into their own homes until they can correct whatever problem might have caused their circumstance. Such hospitality is not uncommon across the world. What do you think would happen in America if Christians practiced that type of hospitality?

Application for Activation

Through Lydia's successful trade of purple, God equipped her to perform the task of hospitality. When Paul's team came, Lydia faithfully jumped at the chance to make use of the skills and means that God had given her. Take time this week to examine how God has equipped you and presented you with the opportunity to make use of your gifts. Find a way to take that opportunity this week and just like Lydia, don't take no for an answer!

Follow the Spirit

What God wants me to do:

_____

_____

_____

_____

_____

Remember Your Thoughts

Special insights I have learned:

_____

_____

_____

_____

_____

More Light on the Text

Acts 16:11-15, 40; 1 Corinthians 1:26-30

Before arriving at the welcome mat of Lydia's hospitality the principal point of this passage, we are compelled to pause and empathize with these spiritually frustrated disciples. As Paul and his companions zealously set out to fulfill the Great Commission (Matthew 28:18-20), they were held back by the Spirit from following a logical path to the next place to preach and to baptize.

They were restrained by the Holy Spirit from going to places that were conveniently along the way. Before celebrating Lydia's conversion and commitment, it is important that we feel the frustration of releasing our desire to simply do good works in the church. Instead, we should want to mature in the Spirit—to grow up from being generally obedient to becoming strictly obedient to God's will. When we listen to and are led by the Holy Spirit, we can be assured that our fervent efforts will bring God glory.

11 Therefore loosing from Troas, we came with a straight course to Samothracia, and the next day to Neapolis; 12 And from thence to Philippi, which is the chief city of that part of Macedonia, and a colony: and we were in that city abiding certain days.

Paul had the vision, but he told it to his companions who obligingly followed him. As the disciples set sail from Troas, even the wind was in their favor, providing a straight course or smooth sailing in two days. They traveled promptly to the island of Samothracia and stayed overnight. The next day, they sailed to Neapolis. There, they journeyed on foot to their stated destination—the great city of Philippi.

This region of Macedonia is a Roman colony and populated mostly by Roman citizens. Although located away from the center of Rome, this region nonetheless was a military conquest and was regarded as a part of the Roman Empire. The inhabitants of such colonies were protected and governed, therefore, by Roman laws. Paul and Silas will use their status as Roman citizens to embarrass the leaders of the city who unjustly imprison them.

Paul and his companions lodged in the city for several days. No one contacted them. In the past, when the apostles entered new territory, someone was there to meet and greet them (Acts 11:26; 13:14-15). The Jewish community had not spread out from Jerusalem so far as Macedonia, though. The missionary team knew no one in this new land.

13 And on the sabbath we went out of the city by a river side, where prayer was wont to be made; and we sat down, and spake unto the women which resorted thither.

The Sabbath is the seventh day of each week, which was a sacred day when the Israelites were required to abstain from all work. On the Sabbath, it was customary for Paul and all Jews to gather for worship, prayer, and read the Scriptures in the synagogue. There was no synagogue of the Jews in Philippi, though. For a synagogue to be established in a city, ten Jewish men had to convene and lead it. With no synagogue in Philippi at this time, in the absence of ten male heads of household to found a synagogue, the women were still determined to be found faithful, worshiping God in spirit and truth (John 4:23-24) as they could where they could.

The meeting took place located outside the city at a river, likely the Gangites River a mile or two west of Philippi. Although the apostles could have taken a day off from the work of preaching the Gospel, they found out where the local God-fearers worshiped and joined them. At the riverside, they found a small group of proselytized women praying to God. The Greek noun *proseuche* (pros-yew-**KHAY**) or "prayer," describes both a prayer addressed to God and a place of prayer. Traditionally, Jews were supposed to wash their hands before prayer (to be clean when addressing their King), and the river would certainly provide water for such cleansing.

The disciples were drawn to join this woman's prayer meeting and encouraged them to continue to worship the true God, but to worship God through the knowledge of Jesus Christ. The apostles did not bypass or dismiss this gathering of women worshiping God outside the city on the Sabbath. Ever modeling Jesus' radical paradigm of teaching to the outcasts, the disciples were not constrained by gender (Galatians 3:28) nor limited by their surroundings when teaching and preaching God's Word. All they required was that hearts were open to hear what the Spirit was saying to the church!

It is while attending to the divine act of worship that a certain woman and a gathering of women became the first European converts to our Christian faith. May women's work and women's worship ever be heralded in the annals of biblical and local church history as integral, not incidental, to the Good News—to the Gospel preached, taught, and believed!

14 And a certain woman named Lydia, a seller of purple, of the city of Thyatira, which worshipped God, heard us: whose heart the Lord opened, that she attended unto the things which were spoken of Paul.

Lydia was a woman of Thyatira, the city of commerce in western Asia Minor. It was well-known throughout the region for its dyer's guild and textiles. Thyatira is a far distance from Philippi—nearly 400 miles. We are never told why she is living in Philippi.

Roman law did not prevent women, whether freeborn or former slaves, from engaging in business enterprises on their own. No husband was mentioned along with Lydia, so she was likely a widow since a woman who had not yet married would not live on her own. To support herself without a husband, Lydia was a "seller of purple," either the dye or cloth dyed this color. Such cloth was an expensive luxury good, used for official Roman garments. This was a noble profession. Today we also see that successful, professional people are also called to serve Christ. One should not let their professional responsibilities deter them from worship.

The name Lydia is Greek, and Thyatira is in a region of Asia Minor that had been thoroughly Hellenized. It is therefore likely that Lydia was a Gentile. She does, however, worship (Gk. *sebo*, **SEH**-bo) the One True God, a word often used to connote a Jewish proselyte (Acts 13:43, 17:4, 18:7). She worshiped God according to the knowledge she had. When she heard the truth of the Gospel, the Lord opened her heart, and she wanted to know more about it. While attending this prayer gathering, Lydia welcomed the opportunity to hear the apostles preach, to hear the disciples teach, and to learn more about the God she worshiped and Christ, God's Son.

Lydia's enthusiastic and attentive listening was fertile ground for God to open her heart to understand and accept the Gospel. The "heart" (Gk. *kardia*, kar-**DEE**-ah) represents the soul or mind as the resident place of one's thoughts, passions, desires, appetites, affections, purposes, understanding, intelligence, will, character, and intentions. Lydia's "open heart surgery" was appreciably more than an emotional response to a well-crafted sermon and loquacious rhetoric. As she listened, Lydia engaged her thoughts, affections, and understanding about God to believe in Christ Jesus! While Lydia had been seeking God, God was in the background working His way into her heart and this nation.

It is not enough to worship God the Father. We must believe in Jesus Christ the Son. There is no coming to God, but through Jesus Christ as

Mediator. God offers us salvation by His grace through faith in Jesus Christ. Jesus stands at the door to our hearts. It is up to each individual to open their heart to Jesus Christ. The opening is on the inside; the choice is ours. God touched Lydia's heart, and she believed the Gospel of Jesus Christ.

15 And when she was baptized, and her household, she besought us, saying, If ye have judged me to be faithful to the Lord, come into my house, and abide there. And she constrained us.

Lydia's response to accepting the Gospel of Christ Jesus was to be baptized. Lydia's baptism and that of her household marked the beginning of the Philippian church. "Baptized" (Gk. *baptizo*, bap-**TEED**-zo) means to submerge in water. Since they were already gathered praying at the riverside, it was convenient to baptize Lydia and her household immediately following conversion. Such a set up recalls Philip's conversion of the Ethiopian eunuch (Acts 8:36-38). Lydia was not the only person present at the prayer meeting listening to the disciples preach and teach. Her whole household (made up of family members and servants alike) heard the Good News, believed, and were baptized. Baptism into the Christian family is a cause for celebration!

After becoming a baptized member of the family of God, Lydia extended hospitality to her newfound family—the apostles. She was very grateful to Paul, Silas, and Luke, and wanted to show her gratitude by inviting them to stay in her home with her and her family. Although her quantifiable wealth is not recorded, evidently Lydia had the means to comfortably accommodate her household as well as Paul and his companions.

They were at first reluctant because they did not want to impose. However, she insisted that they stay. She was so emphatic to extend hospitality to these brothers in Christ that she "constrained" (Gk. *parabiazomai*, pah-rah-bee-**ODD**-zo-my), or made a persuasive appeal, for them to stay at her home while in Philippi. Central to this plea for them to accept her hospitality was Lydia's assertion that the apostles found her "faithful" (Gk. *pistos*, peese-**TOCE**), meaning trustworthy and reliable.

Lydia extended a hospitality paradigm that is simple to follow: Show kindness to one another, especially to those in the household of faith (Galatians 6:10). When the disciples accepted Lydia's hospitality, she and her household, as well as her Philippian neighbors, had the opportunity to receive more teaching and preaching of the Good News; share in discipleship, fellowship, and good company; and help birth and bless this new Christian community.

40 And they went out of the prison, and entered into the house of Lydia: and when they had seen the brethren, they comforted them, and departed.

After establishing an enthusiastic following in Philippi and leading many to Christ, Paul and Silas are arrested. They had healed a girl of a demon, but this interfered with her master's income, so the master complained to the leaders of the city that Paul's group was preaching things illegal under Roman law. They were not, but since the Romans disapproved of any religion that did not make allowances for the divinity of the emperor, Paul and Silas were beaten and imprisoned. This imprisonment leads to singing praises in chains, a midnight earthquake, and the conversion of the jailer and his whole family. When released, Paul raises objections to their treatment, which should not have been allowed since Paul was a Roman citizen. Although he had not been causing a political or legal stir before imprisonment, he actually did afterward.

Our passage picks up just after Paul and Silas are released from prison. They head to Lydia's house and experience the same hospitality they did at her conversion. Lydia knows their character and knows they did nothing to deserve jail time or a beating. The missionary team recognizes the rest of the town is too hostile to them and decides to leave, but they know Lydia will provide them with one last stay of hospitality. She is not afraid of her own reputation being affected by associating with these men. She takes her stand with God's men, even when it is frowned upon in her city.

1 Corinthians 1:26 For ye see your calling, brethren, how that not many wise men after the flesh, not many mighty, not many noble, are called:

To close the lesson, we have several verses from 1 Corinthians, one of several letters Paul wrote to the church at Corinth about how to live in unity and holiness before God.

God calls us to offer what we have to one another. Lydia had a place where the missionary team could stay, so she offers it. But let us not think that our having something to offer makes us better than the people we are helping. The Corinthian believers thought they had wisdom, strength, and social standing to offer God. Paul reminds them that while such things are impressive and perhaps even helpful to the world's viewpoint, to God such things are all filthy rags. Paul outright tells the Corinthian church that they do not truly have the socially admired attributes they think they have. They are not wise, or strong, or powerful. And yet God calls them.

27 But God hath chosen the foolish things of the world to confound the wise; and God hath chosen the weak things of the world to confound the things which are mighty; 28 And base things of the world, and things which are despised, hath God chosen, yea, and things which are not, to bring to nought things that are:

Even though Paul has just asserted that the Corinthian church has nothing much to offer God to use, he also asserts that God specifically chooses those without much to offer to do His work. The foolish confound the wise. God makes Jesus our wisdom (v. 30) and we are in Christ, so we do not need to worry about how much wisdom we already have before Christ. We will have all the knowledge we need when we are unified with Christ.

The weak confound the mighty, by the work of God. Identifying people who are unlikely heroes is not odd in the life of Israel. This is the way God has been working with His people since the beginning. The nation of Israel was born to an infertile couple. The second king of Israel (David) was the youngest of seven brothers, yet he was anointed to depose a king who had the appearance of a warrior (Saul).

The "base" things are the elementary things, things so obvious and common that no one regards them. These "base" things are exactly what God chooses. "Things which are not" means "things that do not exist" and is paired with the phrase "things that are," meaning "things that do exist." God uses those things that are considered by some as lowly and despised to show up the things that humans consider important. In this case, in the context of the Godhead working out salvation, the "things which are not" likely refers to things that have died or passed away, i.e. Jesus. God chose Jesus, who "was not" considered by the religious aristocracy to be of God, especially after the Cross when they supposed He was dead. But God brought "to nought" the things that they considered important. To bring to "nought" is to bring to nothing "things that are." This is a reference to systems of behavior and interaction that are rendered powerless in

310

light of God's power. God gives us the power we need to bring down strongholds and make a difference in our world.

29 That no flesh should glory in his presence.

Paul says God specifically chooses those who do not have a lot as the recipients of His glory to do His work. God makes this choice, rather than a more qualified candidate, to keep humans from boasting in His presence. We have all known people who, because they have good looks, wealth, or talent, consider themselves better than others. God would have us remember that these things are worthless to Him; they are actually marks of pride.

Had God chosen workers who already had blessings of wisdom, wealth, and the rest, non-believers or new believers might think they deserve some glory for the tasks they completed. In reality, every blessing we have comes from God in the first place, so whoever does well is simply doing so because God allows it and could miraculously end their prosperity at a moment's notice. The only one who deserves glory is God, and His selecting the lowly to be His servants helps us remember that.

30 But of him are ye in Christ Jesus, who of God is made unto us wisdom, and righteousness, and sanctification, and redemption:

Throughout each of these Corinthian verses, we see God is the only one who acts. God does all the choosing, and He makes the arrangements of verse 30. God has placed Christians in Christ. Therefore, Jesus is our only source of wisdom, righteousness, sanctification, and redemption. Jesus Christ did the work of our salvation, but God the Father orchestrated that it should all work the way it did.

After understanding all this—our lowliness, our lack of reason to boast, God's actions placing us in Christ and Christ at His right hand—some would be tempted to cower at the unapproachable majesty of the Father. Note, however, why God does all this. God makes Jesus all that He is "unto us," meaning "for us." All of redemption history was orchestrated for us. God is in full possession of every good thing and is immeasurably glorious, and the one thing He wants is us. God shows us that He can do everything, but then also quietly reminds us that He does everything to restore a rich relationship and a more abundant life with us in Him.

Sources:

Strong, James. *The New Strong's Exhaustive Concordance of the Bible.* Nashville, TN: Thomas Nelson, 2003.

Thayer, Joseph Henry. *A Greek-English Lexicon of the New Testament.* New York: American Book Company, 1994.

Vine, W.E. *Vine's Complete Expository Dictionary of Old and New Testament Words.* Nashville, TN: Thomas Nelson, 1996.

Say It Correctly

Troas. **TROE**-as.
Samothrace. **SAH**-moe-thray-ss.
Neapolis. nee-**AH**-poe-liss.
Thyatira. thigh-ah-**TIE**-rah.

Daily Bible Readings

MONDAY
Don't Complain but Serve One Another
(1 Peter 4:7–11)

TUESDAY
Everyday Expressions of Hospitality
(Romans 12:9–19)

WEDNESDAY
Hospitality Practiced in Jail and Home
(Acts 16:35–40)

THURSDAY
Hospitality Practiced by
Widow and Bishop
(1 Timothy 5:9–10, 3:2)

FRIDAY
Christ, God's Power and Wisdom
(1 Corinthians 1:8–25)

SATURDAY
Know Jesus Christ Crucified
(1 Corinthians 2:1–5)

SUNDAY
Lydia, Model of Hospitality Practice
(Acts 16:11–15, 40;
1 Corinthians 1:26–30)

Notes

Prophets Faithful to God's Covenant

This quarter introduces the ministry of the Old Testament prophets. God employs people who live among Israel and Judah to be spokespeople for God. A formal representative of God, the prophet has a message meant to effect social change that conforms to God's desired standards as prescribed under the Law.

UNIT 1 • Faithful Prophets

"Faithful Prophets" has four lessons drawn from Deuteronomy, Joshua, 1 and 2 Kings, that explore the reasons prophets were necessary for Israel's history. Moses leads the people out of Egypt, thus fulfilling God's promise to bring the people back to Canaan. In Deuteronomy, Moses gives the people God's promise to give them prophets who will speak God's word to them. Stories about Joshua, Huldah, and Elijah illustrate the fulfillment of God's promise given through Moses.

Lesson 1: March 7, 2021
Moses: Prophet of Deliverance
Deuteronomy 18:15-22

Life often confronts us with situations that appear to offer only poor outcomes. How are we to respond when the seemingly impossible is asked of us? Following the command of God, the people of Israel left Egypt under the leadership of a faithful prophet, Moses, who became a model for prophets to come.

Lesson 2: March 14, 2021
Joshua: Prophet of Conquest
Joshua 5:13–6:5, 15-16, 20

Individually and corporately, people face choices. How do we discern what choices are best and organize our actions? Joshua and the people of Israel chose to honor a covenant with God, obeying God's instructions perfectly.

Lesson 3: March 21, 2021
Huldah: Prophet of Wisdom
2 Kings 22:14-20

No one knows all the implications of what they learn. Who can help us understand what the future holds? King Josiah's advisers consulted the prophetess Huldah who shared her God-given insights about the coming days of the nation and the king.

Lesson 4: March 28, 2021 (Palm Sunday)
Elijah: Prophet of Courage
1 Kings 18:5-18

People like to go their own way until faced with crises beyond their control. How shall we respond to the advice of those who have great wisdom and insight? In 1 Kings, God sent Elijah to warn of impending disaster.

UNIT 2 • Prophets of Restoration

This unit has four lessons that reveal the compassion of God during the times in Israel's history when the people continually forsook the ways of God. On Easter, Isaiah's prophetic writings and the Book of Luke are used to portray Jesus as the Suffering Servant and the one through whom believers receive salvation. Passages from the prophecies in Ezra, Nehemiah, and Lamentations show the faith of the prophets as they presented new hope to the Israelites.

Lesson 5: April 4, 2021 (Easter)
Salvation is Sealed
Luke 24:13–16, 22–35
When life reaches its darkest depth, people wonder if there is still hope for the future. Where can we find the promise of joy that will overcome our deepest sorrow? Luke 24 records the encounter of the Emmaus travelers with the resurrected Jesus.

Lesson 6: April 11, 2021
Ezra: Faith and Action Preacher
Ezra 10:1-12
Sometimes people can lose their sense of direction in life and turn away from the values they once held. How can we recapture the values we once cherished? Ezra led the returned exiles in prayer and repentance, and afterward, he read the book of the Law to which the people listened and then joyously worshiped the Lord.

Lesson 7: April 18, 2021
Nehemiah: The Captive Cupbearer Rebuilds a Nation
Nehemiah 2:11-20
People are often contemplative before they make major decisions. How does one or should one react after careful consideration of a major decision? Nehemiah set out to rebuild the wall after praying and surveying the ruins.

Lesson 8: April 25, 2021
A Plea for Restoration
Lamentations 5
People seek restoration when their possessions are taken and relationships are broken. How does one cope with the loss of that which is very important? The writer of Lamentations trusted that God would re-establish a relationship with Israel.

UNIT 3 • Courageous Prophets of Change
This unit has five lessons. These lessons show the boldness of God's prophets in 1 Kings, Isaiah, Jeremiah, Ezekiel, and Jonah. Israel and Judah were released from captivity and charged to rebuild Jerusalem. God sent prophets to call the people to restore their covenant relationship with God. When the people strayed away from their covenant with God, the prophets called them back.

Lesson 9: May 2, 2021
Micaiah: Speaking Truth to Power
1 Kings 22:15–23, 26–28
Telling the truth to those who are in power can be difficult. How does one give a difficult message to powerful people? Micaiah resolved that he would tell King Ahab only what the Lord said to him.

Lesson 10: May 9, 2021
Isaiah: Offering Hope for the Future
Isaiah 29:13–24
Relationships suffer when humans lapse into immorality. What is the result when we or others have been immoral? Isaiah prophesied that God would punish the people of Judah but still be merciful and restore the nation.

Lesson 11: May 16, 2021
Jeremiah: The Suffering Preacher of Doom
Jeremiah 38:14–23
No one wants to be the bearer of bad news or challenging advice. How can we find the courage to speak when what we have to say is likely to cause controversy or hard feelings? Jeremiah frankly discussed his concerns with King Zedekiah and then spoke with confidence that he was delivering a message from God.

Lesson 12: May 23, 2021
Ezekiel: Street Preacher to the Exiles
Ezekiel 18:1–9, 30–32
It is easy to blame our background or upbringing for the misfortunes we face. What is the role of personal responsibility? Ezekiel warns Israel that each person will answer for his or her behavior and that all must repent of their sinful ways and obey God's commands to find favor with God.

Lesson 13: May 30, 2021
Jonah: Do the Right Thing
Jonah 3
Change is often required in life if we are to live in peace with others. What can we do about life situations that threaten us? After hearing God's warning from Jonah, the people of Nineveh repented and God forgave their sin.

The Call of God

by Craig Soaries

Part I

The following article is an excerpt that reminds us of our responses as covenant Christians in relationship with God. Soaries provides insight into our covenant relationship with God as we examine our responsibility, urgency, and continuous response to the Lord. Soaries begins with the topic of our responsibility when we respond, "Yes," to living in a covenant community through Christ.

When considering the call of God—through Jesus Christ—to be a part of His covenant community, one must fully understand what the call of God means. When God calls an individual, it is unlike the call of any human being. The original plan of God includes the active participation of the whole human person (body, soul, spirit) in His purposes. In the beginning, God created the heavens and the earth and formed Adam and Eve. The Lord called, purposed, and designed that Adam and Eve be a part of the design of earth's processes. The design and implementation are through the Father, Son, and the Holy Spirit. Colossians 1:16 clearly identifies that "by (Christ) were all things created, that are in heaven, and that are in earth, visible and invisible, whether they are thrones, or dominions, or principalities, or powers: all things were created by him, and for him."

Before the beginning, God purposed that Jesus would be the center of attraction and creation would be called to glorify God through Christ. Adam was called, assigned, and destined to have the privilege of naming and training the animals. Adam and Eve were also called to enjoy the benefits of a perfect dwelling place, called the Garden of Eden, with the implication that they would live in harmony with God. However, Adam failed to recognize and obey the call of God to be a leader and divine example. Eve failed to obey the call of God to be the mother of commitment to God and the express law given to her husband. Though she came from Adam, she was deceived by Satan to reject her call to be God's help to Adam. As a result, instead of life flowing through Adam and Eve, death was ushered in.

The call to the first family of creation was to exemplify Christ in a model relationship and home. In this quarter, we find that Israel (God's chosen people) was called to demonstrate what a godlike community and culture should be. We look at covenant communities in [such books as] Joshua, Ezra, Nehemiah, [Isaiah, and Luke]. We study how almighty God, in His sovereign power and will orchestrated and facilitated the birth and keeping of His covenant community. He kept His covenant commitment with them, but time and time again, they broke their covenant with Him.

Craig Soaries, DMin

This article is an excerpt and adapted from Craig Soaries' essay "The Call of God through Jesus Christ to be Part of His Covenant Community" from Precepts for Living, 2009-2010.

The Call of God

by Craig Soaries

Part II

The following article is an excerpt from Craig Soaries that reminds us of our responses as covenant Christians in relationship with God. Soaries provides insight into our covenant relationship with God as we examine our responsibility, urgency, and continuous response to the Lord. Soaries begins with the topic of our responsibility when we respond "Yes" to living in a covenant community through Christ.

The Responsibility of the Call

Once humanity fell through Adam and Eve, God the Father immediately purposed that humankind would be redeemed through the life and person of His Son, Jesus Christ. Jesus came in the flesh to make the call directly to humankind. As early as Genesis 3:15, the Word of God reveals God's call and purpose that would be manifested through Jesus Christ. He is to be the propitiation (sacrifice) for our sins. Actually, the responsibility of the call first rests upon God Himself. He initiates the movement toward humankind and puts within the hearts of those chosen the desire to respond to His call.

Once the voice of the Lord calls to the individual, the responsibility to respond and obey the Gospel then rests upon the hearer. "Wherefore, To day if ye will hear his voice, Harden not your hearts" is not a hard text to understand (Hebrews 3:7–8). People are given the free will to choose to accept the call to live for Him in obedience (covenant) or reject the call (the covenant). For two thousand years since the advent of Christ, there has been a direct call to all humankind through the Gospel. He is still calling people to enter into a covenant relationship with Him—to be His people, and He will be their God.

The Urgency of the Call

The call is personal and it is urgent. The urgency is revealed in Scriptures such as the Hebrews 3:7–8 passage. Those who do not understand the urgency of the call open themselves to grave danger from divine wrath. The prophet Isaiah affirms this urgency: "Behold, the day of the LORD cometh, cruel both with wrath and fierce anger, to lay the land desolate: and he shall destroy the sinners thereof out of it" (Isaiah 13:9). Thus, this call of a covenant relationship with the Almighty God is between the individual and God. Rejection of the will of the Lord has grave consequences. Obedience brings eternal blessings and rewards (Revelation 21). Many do not understand the significance of an intimate, personal relationship with a holy God. Others simply ignore the Lord and seemingly have no conviction that Jesus died for their sins and desires them to live for Him. The way has been made to forever clear the negative record of failure that sin creates. The blood of Jesus Christ is available to all that will come and receive its atoning power and grace.

The Call Is Continuous

The call is sent daily throughout the nations. Yet, some do not respond to the mighty call of

God through His Son, Jesus. God needs men and women to fulfill His purpose. The Word must become flesh again through us so that the world may see the manifestation of the invisible God. Once the will of God, through salvation in Christ, is accepted, the Lord then challenges believers to seek a deeper, more specific call to service and lifelong dedication. Again, this is a personal choice and the decision to serve the Lord completely as Jesus did when walking the earth in the flesh. He was to do the will of the Father who sent Him. By doing the will of the Father with a continual surrender of "yes, Lord" the Word continues to become flesh through those who yield their lives, manifesting the presence of the Lord and the glory of the Father. God called Israel to become His covenant community. He is calling you to be a part of it, too!

Craig Soaries, DMin

JOHN HOPE FRANKLIN

(1915—2009)
Historian

John Hope Franklin was an esteemed writer and historian. His works reshaped the way African American history is taught and understood. His most famous work, *From Slavery to Freedom*, was published in 1947. It has since been translated into five languages and has sold more than 3 million copies. The book inspired many to take a closer look at Black history and how Blacks were portrayed. The book looks at the period from ancestral Africa to the present day. Each edition updated information on the current struggle for racial equality.

By the time Franklin was 10 years old, he witnessed the effects of the 1921 race riots in Tulsa, Oklahoma, which reportedly began when mobs of Whites began destroying economically successful businesses built by Blacks. More than 100 Blacks were killed; Franklin's father's law office was destroyed.

In addition to writing *From Slavery To Freedom*, Franklin wrote several essays, books, and a autobiography on his life. He also worked with Thurgood Marshall in 1953 to write briefs in the historic *Brown v. Board of Education of Topeka*, which challenged the equality of segregated schools. Franklin marched with Dr. Martin Luther King, Jr. in Montgomery, Alabama, in 1965 to protest injustice and segregation.

Franklin received his bachelor's degree from Fisk University. He earned his master's and a doctorate in history from Harvard University. He taught at several universities, including North Carolina Central, Duke, and Howard University. Franklin received the Presidential Medal of Freedom, the highest award given to a civilian in the nation, in 1995. He was also appointed by President Bill Clinton to lead a group of advisers on promoting racial understanding and reconciliation.

Sources:
Franklin, John Hope. *From Slavery To Freedom*. New York: McGraw-Hill Education, 1947.
Franklin, John Hope. *Mirror to America: The Autobiography of John Hope Franklin*. New York: Farrar, Straus and Giroux, 2005.

Teaching Tips

Words You Should Know

A. Require (Deuteronomy 18:19) *darash* (Heb.)—To seek; to inquire, consult; to demand

B. Presumptuously (v. 22) *zadon* (Gk.)—Proudly, haughtily, with misplaced confidence

Teacher Preparation

Unifying Principle—Facing the Impossible. Life often confronts us with situations that appear to offer only poor outcomes. How are we to respond when the seemingly impossible is asked of us? Following the command of God, the people of Israel left Egypt under the leadership of a faithful prophet, Moses, who became a model for prophets to come.

A. Read the Bible Background and Devotional Reading.

B. Pray for your students and lesson clarity.

C. Read the lesson Scripture in multiple translations.

O—Open the Lesson

A. Begin the class with prayer.

B. Play a recording of a spiritual such as "Wade in the Water," "Ride on Moses," or "Sweet Canaan's Happy Land." Discuss why biblical allusions were so appropriate in the battle to end American slavery and during the Civil Rights Movement. What can we learn about hope and redemption in these songs and the responsibilities of leaders who are charged to lead God's people through difficult situations?

C. Have the students read the Aim for Change and the In Focus story.

D. Ask students how events like those in the story weigh on their hearts and how they can view these events from a faith perspective.

P—Present the Scriptures

A. Read the Focal Verses and discuss the Background and The People, Places, and Times sections.

B. Have the class share what Scriptures stand out for them and why, with particular emphasis on today's themes.

E—Explore the Meaning

A. Use In Depth or More Light on the Text to facilitate a deeper discussion of the lesson text.

B. Pose the questions in Search the Scriptures and Discuss the Meaning.

C. Discuss the Liberating Lesson and Application for Activation sections.

N—Next Steps for Application

A. Summarize the value of remaining faithful when things seem hopeless.

B. End class with a commitment to pray and study the Scriptures to develop the power of discernment.

Worship Guide

For the Superintendent or Teacher
Theme: Moses: Prophet of Deliverance
Song: "Ride On Moses"
Devotional Reading: Psalm 77:11-20

Moses: Prophet of Deliverance

Bible Background • EXODUS 12:28-50; DEUTERONOMY 18:15-22
Printed Text • DEUTERONOMY 18:15-22 | Devotional Reading • PSALM 77:11-20

———————— Aim for Change ————————

By the end of this lesson, we will STUDY Moses' role as a prophet of God in leading the Israelites out of Egypt, REFLECT on leaders who guide us through seemingly impossible situations, and completely RELY on God in resolving challenging situations.

———————————— In Focus ————————————

Ever since she flipped through that pamphlet on youth homelessness from the display stand at her college, Alex felt the urgency of God's call. That summer, she interned with an organization in Chicago that provided services and counseling to LGBTQ kids who had been forced to leave their homes. Once she completed her degree, Alex left her hometown in South Carolina and moved to Chicago, where she took a permanent job with the organization.

For the first few months, everything was perfect. Alex loved her work and could see the difference it was making. On weekends she visited her parents' college friend Winnie, who lived nearby. But over time, gas, food, and bills started to pile up. Alex took on more shifts and had less time to take care of herself. After three weeks with no days off, she ended up on Winnie's couch, sobbing, her hands so weak she could barely hold the tea she was offered.

"I really want to stay here," she cried, "But I can't do this anymore. I'm so tired."

"Admitting you need help doesn't mean you have to give up. My sister lives in the city," said Winnie. "She's looking for a roommate. We've been talking, and she'd love to live with you. For you, it would be perfect—half rent, less gas, and an amazing roommate!"

"Thank you, Ms. Winnie," breathed Alex, ducking her head to hide her grateful tears. That evening she called Winnie's sister, and the next week they were roommates. She took a weekend to recover, and when she began working again she was careful to leave enough time in her schedule for the people she cared about.

Sometimes God speaks to us through people we wouldn't expect. Who could you reach out to and be vulnerable with?

———————————— Keep in Mind ————————————

"The LORD thy God will raise up unto thee a Prophet from the midst of thee, of thy brethren, like unto me; unto him ye shall hearken" (Deuteronomy 18:15, KJV).

"Moses continued, 'The LORD your God will raise up for you a prophet like me from among your fellow Israelites. You must listen to him'" (Deuteronomy 18:15, NLT).

Focal Verses

KJV **Deuteronomy 18:15** The LORD thy God will raise up unto thee a Prophet from the midst of thee, of thy brethren, like unto me; unto him ye shall hearken;

16 According to all that thou desiredst of the LORD thy God in Horeb in the day of the assembly, saying, Let me not hear again the voice of the LORD my God, neither let me see this great fire any more, that I die not.

17 And the LORD said unto me, They have well spoken that which they have spoken.

18 I will raise them up a Prophet from among their brethren, like unto thee, and will put my words in his mouth; and he shall speak unto them all that I shall command him.

19 And it shall come to pass, that whosoever will not hearken unto my words which he shall speak in my name, I will require it of him.

20 But the prophet, which shall presume to speak a word in my name, which I have not commanded him to speak, or that shall speak in the name of other gods, even that prophet shall die.

21 And if thou say in thine heart, How shall we know the word which the LORD hath not spoken?

22 When a prophet speaketh in the name of the LORD, if the thing follow not, nor come to pass, that is the thing which the LORD hath not spoken, but the prophet hath spoken it presumptuously: thou shalt not be afraid of him.

NLT **Deuteronomy 18:15** Moses continued, "The LORD your God will raise up for you a prophet like me from among your fellow Israelites. You must listen to him.

16 For this is what you yourselves requested of the LORD your God when you were assembled at Mount Sinai. You said, 'Don't let us hear the voice of the LORD our God anymore or see this blazing fire, for we will die.'

17 Then the LORD said to me, 'What they have said is right.

18 I will raise up a prophet like you from among their fellow Israelites. I will put my words in his mouth, and he will tell the people everything I command him.

19 I will personally deal with anyone who will not listen to the messages the prophet proclaims on my behalf.

20 But any prophet who falsely claims to speak in my name or who speaks in the name of another god must die.'

21 But you may wonder, 'How will we know whether or not a prophecy is from the LORD?'

22 If the prophet speaks in the LORD's name but his prediction does not happen or come true, you will know that the LORD did not give that message. That prophet has spoken without my authority and need not be feared."

The People, Places, and Times

Mount Sinai. Also called Mount Horeb and has been referred to as the "mountain of God" (Exodus 3:1) and "mount of the LORD" (Numbers 10:33). This mountain and the surrounding wilderness was one of the first stops the Israelites made after escaping from Egypt. They stayed there for about a year (Numbers 10:11). It would prove to be a place of national trial and triumph. On Mount Sinai, the Israelites experienced defeat (including making the golden calf while Moses was receiving the Ten Commandments; Exodus 32) and victory (including ratifying the Ten Commandments; Exodus 19–24) while encamped there.

Deuteronomy. Deuteronomy is Moses' last sermon to the people of Israel right before they finally enter the Promised Land. In these three discourses (Deuteronomy 1-4; 5-26; 27-34), he reiterates the Law handed down on Mt. Sinai. Many sections of this sermon repeat what has already been stated (Exodus 20, Deuteronomy 5; Exodus 32, Deuteronomy 9; Exodus 21:24, Deuteronomy 19:21). Other sections update the Law from a religion to be practiced in the wilderness to one that is practiced in a stable homeland. Moses looks to the future for the nation. For example, Moses promises that another prophet will follow him, and guides the people in how to accept or reject future prophets.

Background

In this passage, Moses predicts the coming of Christ. The phrases "prophet like me" (Deuteronomy 18:15, NLT) and "prophet like you" (v. 18, NLT) have immediate reference to the line of Israelite prophets. However, they find their ultimate fulfillment in the prophetic ministry of Christ (see Acts 3:19-23). This is one of the earliest references to the coming of the Messiah. Moses himself was considered a prophet of high stature. This early prediction of another "like me" gave the Israelites a glimpse of God's plan. It put Moses, God's servant, in proper perspective in the eyes of the people. As great as the works of Moses were, there was still One greater who would come. Moses' prediction of a prophet "like me" not only points to the greatness of the future Messiah, but gives insight into what a prophet and leader of God's people should be.

At-A-Glance

1. He Comes from the People
(Deuteronomy 18:15-16)
2. He Speaks God's Word (v. 17-18)
3. His Words Come True (vv. 19-22)

In Depth

1. He Comes from the People (Deuteronomy 18:15-16)

Jesus' life proves the accuracy of Moses' prediction that a prophet would arise from "among the people." This phrase can be understood two ways. The primary reference here is to national origin. Jesus was a Hebrew who came through the line of Abraham. The secondary reference highlights the identification of the Messiah as one of the people. Jesus came from common human stock. His earthly parents were ordinary people; His place of birth was lowly; He was reared with the working class; and His occupation (carpentry) was that of a laboring man. Jesus lived among people, understood them (John 2:25), wept with them (John 11:35; 2:1-11). Jesus portrayed the characteristics essential for servant-leadership. A person who has not lived among the people is less likely to understand how common people think and what they need.

How have you seen a leader's humble origins affect their leadership style?

2. He Speaks God's Word (v. 17-18)

Moses spoke of a prophet who would have a direct relationship with God (v. 18). Those who are chosen to publicly lead God's people (pastor, missionary, teacher, writer, or Sunday School worker) are called to speak God's words. Just as Jesus represented God the Father and spoke His words, people in God's service represent Christ and should speak His words. This can only be done when one maintains a close relationship with God through prayer, worship, and studying the Bible.

As a prophet, Moses spoke on God's behalf. Moses was not explaining what God had said in the past like a good preacher does. He came with a new message straight from God. God puts His words in the mouth of His prophets (v.18; Jeremiah 1:7-9). When Jesus spoke, He spoke the words of God. He said in His prayer, "I have given unto them the words which thou gavest me" (John 17:8). He assured His disciples "the word which ye hear is not mine, but the Father's which sent me." (John 14:24). This word has been faithfully passed down, protected by the Holy Spirit, through many generations so that we can read it today.

How do you feel about your current relationship with Jesus? What helps keep it strong? What could make it stronger?

3. His Words Come True (vv. 19-22)

Moses warns against false prophets (v. 20). The test of a true prophet is whether his words come true, though further tests may also be required (Deuteronomy 13:1-5). The death penalty which Moses warns about is played out in the confrontation between Elijah and the prophets of Baal (see 1 Kings 18:20–40). The false prophets of Baal call on the name of a different god and are put to death after Elijah shows the awesome power of Israel's true God.

Predicting what will come to pass is only one aspect of the prophetic gift. A prophet is one who proclaims the truth, warns, exhorts, and encourages.

Think of a person who is called a modern prophet and consider whether that person measures up to the test in these verses.

Search the Scriptures

1. Where did Moses say a prophet like himself would arise? (Deuteronomy 18:15, 18)

2. What did Moses tell the people of Israel to do about this prophet? (v. 15)

3. What did Moses reveal about the message of this prophet? (v. 18)

4. What test should be applied to a prophet's words? (v. 22)

Discuss the Meaning

1. Why does God use intermediaries like prophets to bring His message to His followers?

2. How does God "deal with" (v. 19, NLT) those who do not listen to His prophets? How have you seen this play out in your own life?

Liberating Lesson

Maybe you're heard of the phenomenon in today's society called "call-out culture." When someone perceives an injustice, they will speak out against it, usually on social media. They will set demands for the person or company to correct their problematic behavior, and call on their friends and followers to boycott them until they do. How is this similar to or different from the work of a prophet of God?

Application for Activation

List the characteristics of an effective leader. Which of these characteristics do you possess? Which would you like to acquire? Select a quality. This week, read Philippians 4:13, and seek opportunities to demonstrate the quality you desire.

Follow the Spirit

What God wants me to do:

_____

_____

_____

_____

Remember Your Thoughts

Special insights I have learned:

_____

_____

_____

_____

More Light on the Text

Deuteronomy 18:15-22

It is evident from the Old Testament and particularly Deuteronomy 18:9–22 that one of the most dangerous expressions of the waywardness and ignorance of many people is to seek God's help by the wrong means and from the wrong sources. The Canaanites—whose lands were to be occupied by Israel—were preoccupied with evil practices such as divination, sorcery, and witchcraft. They were given to all kinds of magical and superstitious practices to discover the will of the gods and, sometimes, even to compel the gods to act in certain ways. Their unacknowledged guilt led to God's judgment and expulsion from the land. All such practices were forbidden in Israel and were to be an abomination in the land. Israel is called to be blameless of such practices and conduct; otherwise, they too would incur God's wrath. The privilege of God's chosen people

did not entitle them to a different standard of morality and ethics. If they turn to divination and witchcraft, they too will be expelled from the land. Against this backdrop, God promised to raise a Prophet from among the people. Today spiritualism, astrology, palm-reading and other forms of divination are widely practiced. These injunctions to Israel are as important and relevant now as they were then.

15 The LORD thy God will raise up unto thee a Prophet from the midst of thee, of thy brethren, like unto me; unto him ye shall hearken;

Because Israel will soon enter a land filled with abominable practices, Moses clarifies for Israel the means of discerning a true messenger of God, that is, a true prophet. The Lord will provide a succession of prophets from among the Israelites for their benefit. The true prophet will function as Yahweh's mouthpiece, just as Moses has done. Moses, the model prophet, exhorts his fellow Israelites to pay close attention to the message of any true prophet. In contrast to the surrounding nations, God will raise a Prophet from the midst of His people.

God's will is to be discovered or discerned through a prophet and not through a diviner, a magic worker, or a spiritist. It is important to note that although the New Testament portrays Jesus the Messiah as the ultimate fulfillment of this verse, the Hebrew word *nabi'* (naw-**BEE**) in this and the following verses is a collective noun which suggests that it represents a type of individual. How are God's people to know who the true prophet is when there are competing claims regarding access to the Word of God? The case is easy when we are dealing with a prophet who represents another god. The true prophet is the Mosaic prophet, the one who speaks the Word of God in the tradition of Moses himself. In other words, the ultimate test is the course of actual events in time to come; for the word of the true prophet comes to pass.

Moses gives the first characteristic of an authentic prophet—he or she is not self-appointed. The Lord Himself is to raise up such gifted people and equip them for their strategic work. Their place in the ministry of the Word would be due entirely to God's initiative. The lesson is instructive. No one must pursue Christian ministry unless he or she is sure of God's calling for the task. The authority of the minister and the right to be listened to derive from an assured presence of divine call.

16 According to all that thou desiredst of the LORD thy God in Horeb in the day of the assembly, saying, Let me not hear again the voice of the LORD my God, neither let me see this great fire any more, that I die not. 17 And the LORD said unto me, They have well spoken that which they have spoken.

The place of the prophet in Israel is to be understood in light of the incident at Horeb. When God in His manifested glory terrified the people (v. 16). They could not bear to look upon his radiant presence, nor could they listen to His words because of their transcendent quality. They recognized their own limitations, physically and spiritually. Therefore, what was needed was a mediator who could approach God for them and who then could transmit the divine revelation to them. Moses stepped into this role at Horeb. As he stands now on the edge of the Promised Land it is clear that generations after the departure of Moses would also need such spokesmen to bear the message of heaven. This would be particularly the case when the peculiar role of Moses (and of Joshua after him) as a covenant mediator came to an end. The new situation would require someone to carry on the ministry of revelation and covenant enforcement. This would eventually fall to the order of prophets. Note that Joshua is not a prophet, even though he is Moses' successor. Joshua was Moses' successor as A political and military leader of the Israelites. No longer would Israel combine their political leader with their spiritual leader. For better or worse, this distinction came about after Moses' death.

18 I will raise them up a Prophet from among their brethren, like unto thee, and will put my words in his mouth; and he shall speak unto them all that I shall command him.

Here Moses reveals a second mark of an authentic prophet. The authentic prophet is one who receives and welcomes God's Word. Even though now it is considered rude to "put words in someone's mouth," this is just the image God uses for how He equips prophets to speak. Jeremiah provides a clear example. The Lord spoke to the initially reluctant prophet saying, "I have put my words in thy mouth" (Jeremiah 1:9; 5:14, etc.). It is God who commissions and sends forth the prophet. It is only by divine initiative that God's Words could be proclaimed or expressed through a human mouth, even when it is done reluctantly. This is why the prophet could declare, "Thus says the Lord." The prophet does not only receive the Word but also, more importantly, is tasked with declaring it. God's message is not for the prophet's exclusive possession. The truth is given to the prophet to be shared with God's people. There was no room for a special, elitist, highly favored individuals who receive "hidden" messages for themselves that were not to be communicated to other people. God's Word was for everybody, regardless of status. The prophet must not hold back but speak all that God shall command. The Moses-like prophets, called by God from among the people of Israel, would receive and speak only those things committed to them by the Lord (v. 18).

19 And it shall come to pass, that whosoever will not hearken unto my words which he shall speak in my name, I will require it of him. 20 But the prophet, which shall presume to speak a word in my name, which I have not commanded him to speak, or that shall speak in the name of other gods, even that prophet shall die.

The very character of God stands behind the prophetic message (and messenger). To reject the message of a true prophet represents a rejection of God Himself. In other words, the prophets would be vested with such authority by God that whoever is disobedient to their words would not be counted guiltless before God. Rather, the disobedient would incur God's wrath and displeasure. The disobedient listener who merely hears the Word but does not act on it will be accountable to the Lord for his or her stubborn resistance to the truth. So great would be their prophet's authority that anyone who disobeyed their word would have disobeyed the Word of the Lord and accordingly would be made accountable (v. 19). The word translated "require" (Heb. *darash*, daw-**ROSH**) is used in phrases like this frequently enough for Moses to know his audience would understand: the "it" the Lord is requiring is the unbeliever's life (Genesis 9:5; Ezekiel 33:6).

Having enumerated the marks of the true prophet, Moses goes on to warn the people against false prophets. Moses defines two kinds of falsehood. First, and with an insidious threat, is the person who claims or presumes to speak in the name of the Lord but whose words were his or her own. Second, any people who profess to speak for the Lord but in fact do not, but speak in the name of other gods, would be recognizable as a serious violator of the covenant. Such is a false prophet and must be severely punished by execution (v. 20).

21 And if thou say in thine heart, How shall we know the word which the LORD hath not spoken? 22 When a prophet speaketh in the name of the LORD, if the thing follow not, nor come to pass, that is the thing which the LORD hath not spoken, but the prophet hath spoken it presumptuously: thou shalt not be afraid of him.

One of the major problems associated with the whole prophetic movement then and now was the false prophet, although it is clear that the true prophet had a deep sense of divine commission, not all who claimed to be true prophets were genuine prophets of the Lord. It is much easier to claim being a true prophet than to authenticate it. Furthermore, there would have been occasions when it would have been difficult to judge the falsity or authenticity of a given prophet. As far as those who prophesied in the names of other gods were concerned, there would be no question (v. 20b; cf. 13:1–18).

However, what would be the criteria when a man or woman issued a word in the name of the Lord? The answer in the text is very much to the point: the fulfillment of the prophesied message. Anything short of that would brand the prophet as false and unreliable. He had not spoken from God, but have spoken *zadon* (Heb. zaw-**DONE**; "presumptuously"; proudly). Therefore the Israelites "should not be afraid" of that person as an envoy of the Lord (v. 22). But this evidence could sometimes be matched by the false prophet. Chapter 13 shows that false prophets could indeed produce remarkable predictions and still lead the people astray. It remains therefore that such a litmus test should be somewhat nuanced. Although non-fulfillment would of itself suggest a falsehood, fulfillment could not by itself prove authenticity. This is an important caution to bear in mind when evaluating remarkable apparent successes of soothsaying and prediction in any age, including our own. The passage as a whole provides a clue to making a distinction between true and false prophets. The prophet whom God would raise up would be like Moses. Without doubt, this is an important and qualitative criterion.

There was a standard by which the moral and spiritual credentials could be measured. Those who prophesied smooth paths and pandered to the wickedness of the nation and prophesied for their own material and personal gains were definitely not "like Moses". Those who posed no challenge to the oppressive and immoral governments were not "like Moses." Those who were immoral in their own lives and consumed by self-seeking ambitions were not "like Moses." Today, when we have a multiplicity of "prophetic ministries." Believers should once again take a closer look at Deuteronomy 18:15–22 and take caution before jumping on the bandwagon of any prophetic ministry. However, we must also be careful to not throw out the baby with the bathwater. Both Old Testament prophecy (Joel 2) and several passages in the New Testament (Acts 2:16-18; 11:27-28; 21:8-9) show that there could still be authentic prophets and prophecy in our own time.

Sources:

Brown, Raymond. *The Message of Deuteronomy* The Bible Speaks Today. Leicester, England: InterVarsity Press, 1993.

Christensen, Duane L. *Deuteronomy 1–21:9*, Revised, vol. 6A, Word Biblical Commentary. Dallas, TX: Thomas Nelson, 2001.

Grisanti, Michael A. "Deuteronomy," in *The Expositor's Bible Commentary: Numbers–Ruth* (Revised Edition), ed. Tremper Longman III and David E. Garland, vol. 2. Grand Rapids, MI: Zondervan, 2012.

Merrill, Eugene H. *Deuteronomy*. The New American Commentary, Vol. 4. Nashville, TN: Broadman & Holman Publishers, 1994. 273.

Thompson. J. A. *Deuteronomy*. Tyndale Old Testament Commentaries. Reprint. Leicester, England: InterVarsity Press, 1976.

Wright, Christopher. *Deuteronomy*. New International Biblical Commentary. Peabody, MA: Hendrickson Publishers, 1996.

Say It Correctly

Horeb. **HOR**-ebb.

Daily Bible Readings

MONDAY
Remember God's Acts of Deliverance
(Psalm 77:11-20)

TUESDAY
Listen to Moses, Witness with Authority
(Luke 16:24-31)

WEDNESDAY
Instructions for Observing the Passover
(Exodus 12:43-50)

THURSDAY
Aliens and Unclean Share Passover Meal
(Numbers 9:9-14)

FRIDAY
Consecrate All Firstborn to God
(Exodus 13:1-2; Deuteronomy 15:19-20)

SATURDAY
Observe Festival of Unleavened Bread
(Exodus 13:3-10)

SUNDAY
God Leads through Prophets
(Deuteronomy 18:15-22)

Teaching Tips

March 14
Bible Study Guide 2

Words You Should Know

A. Worship (Joshua 5:14) *shachah* (Heb.)—To bow down as a show of honor or respect

B. Shout (vv. 6:5, 16) *rua'* (Heb.)—To sound an alarm, make a joyful noise

Teacher Preparation

Unifying Principle—Making Wise Choices. Individually and corporately, people face choices. How do we discern what choices are best and organize our actions? Joshua and the people of Israel chose to honor a covenant with God, obeying God's instructions perfectly.

A. Read the Bible Background and Devotional Reading.

B. Pray for your students and lesson clarity.

C. Read the lesson Scripture in multiple translations.

O—Open the Lesson

A. Begin the class with prayer.

B. Discuss this Abraham Lincoln quote: "Sir, my concern is not whether God is on our side; my greatest concern is to be on God's side." Lead into the lesson by discussing the difference between wanting God to be on our side and wanting to be on God's side

C. Have the students read the Aim for Change and the In Focus story.

D. Ask students how events like those in the story weigh on their hearts and how they can view these events from a faith perspective.

P—Present the Scriptures

A. Read the Focal Verses and discuss the Background and The People, Places, and Times sections.

B. Have the class share what Scriptures stand out for them and why, with particular emphasis on today's themes.

E—Explore the Meaning

A. Use In Depth or More Light on the Text to facilitate a deeper discussion of the lesson text.

B. Pose the questions in Search the Scriptures and Discuss the Meaning.

C. Discuss the Liberating Lesson and Application for Activation sections.

N—Next Steps for Application

A. Summarize the value of obeying God's commands on faith rather than having to understand them completely.

B. End class with a commitment to pray for strength to achieve their call in God's agenda.

Worship Guide

For the Superintendent or Teacher
Theme: Joshua: Prophet of Conquest
Song: "Joshua Fit De Battle of Jericho"
Devotional Reading: Hebrews 11:23-31

Joshua: Prophet of Conquest

Bible Background • JOSHUA 5:13-6:27
Printed Text • JOSHUA 5:13-6:5, 15-16, 20 | Devotional Reading • HEBREWS 11:23-31

Aim for Change

By the end of this lesson, we will EXPLAIN how Joshua acted obediently to the vision from God, REFLECT on our inefficiencies when challenges overwhelm us, and COMMIT to obeying God especially in challenging times.

In Focus

In the seven years Thomas had worked at his company, his sales team had performed consistently in the top three percent. Thomas had given his best on the job, and he had earned the right to a promotion. Besides, God had placed this desire in his heart long ago.

However, Thomas had been told by a lot of people, mostly Black, that he would never become a district manager at his company. "They don't promote Black folk to those positions," he was repeatedly told.

Whenever he heard this, however, Thomas simply replied, "Well, the final decision is really in God's hands." Thomas knew what they said was true, but it was a good company to work for and he had put in the time and talent. Thomas was sad that the people who should have been encouraging were most discouraging.

Nevertheless, Thomas followed the desire God gave him and put in his application for the district manager position when it came up in January. He didn't hear anything for a long time, but he just kept praying instead of letting himself worry.

In the spring, Thomas was called to his supervisor's office and told the great news: he got the promotion! One of the vice presidents shared with him that the company wanted to reach the African American community. To do this, they would have to hire Blacks in high-level positions. Thomas said to himself, "Yeah, that might have been the company's reason for promoting me, but I know that God already had His plan in mind."

Why is it necessary to be faithful if God works His will anyway?

Keep in Mind

"And the LORD said unto Joshua, See, I have given into thine hand Jericho, and the king thereof, and the mighty men of valour" (Joshua 6:2, KJV).

"But the LORD said to Joshua, 'I have given you Jericho, its king, and all its strong warriors'" (Joshua 6:2, NLT).

Focal Verses

KJV **Joshua 5:13** And it came to pass, when Joshua was by Jericho, that he lifted up his eyes and looked, and, behold, there stood a man over against him with his sword drawn in his hand: and Joshua went unto him, and said unto him, Art thou for us, or for our adversaries?

14 And he said, Nay; but as captain of the host of the LORD am I now come. And Joshua fell on his face to the earth, and did worship, and said unto him, What saith my Lord unto his servant?

15 And the captain of the LORD's host said unto Joshua, Loose thy shoe from off thy foot; for the place whereon thou standest is holy. And Joshua did so.

6:1 Now Jericho was straitly shut up because of the children of Israel: none went out, and none came in.

2 And the LORD said unto Joshua, See, I have given into thine hand Jericho, and the king thereof, and the mighty men of valour.

3 And ye shall compass the city, all ye men of war, and go round about the city once. Thus shalt thou do six days.

4 And seven priests shall bear before the ark seven trumpets of rams' horns: and the seventh day ye shall compass the city seven times, and the priests shall blow with the trumpets.

5 And it shall come to pass, that when they make a long blast with the ram's horn, and when ye hear the sound of the trumpet, all the people shall shout with a great shout; and the wall of the city shall fall down flat, and the people shall ascend up every man straight before him.

15 And it came to pass on the seventh day, that they rose early about the dawning of the day, and compassed the city after the same manner seven times: only on that day they compassed the city seven times.

16 And it came to pass at the seventh time, when the priests blew with the trumpets, Joshua

NLT **Joshua 5:13** When Joshua was near the town of Jericho, he looked up and saw a man standing in front of him with sword in hand. Joshua went up to him and demanded, "Are you friend or foe?"

14 "Neither one," he replied. "I am the commander of the LORD's army." At this, Joshua fell with his face to the ground in reverence. "I am at your command," Joshua said. "What do you want your servant to do?"

15 The commander of the LORD's army replied, "Take off your sandals, for the place where you are standing is holy." And Joshua did as he was told.

6:1 Now the gates of Jericho were tightly shut because the people were afraid of the Israelites. No one was allowed to go out or in.

2 But the LORD said to Joshua, "I have given you Jericho, its king, and all its strong warriors.

3 You and your fighting men should march around the town once a day for six days.

4 Seven priests will walk ahead of the Ark, each carrying a ram's horn. On the seventh day you are to march around the town seven times, with the priests blowing the horns.

5 When you hear the priests give one long blast on the rams' horns, have all the people shout as loud as they can. Then the walls of the town will collapse, and the people can charge straight into the town."

15 On the seventh day the Israelites got up at dawn and marched around the town as they had done before. But this time they went around the town seven times.

16 The seventh time around, as the priests sounded the long blast on their horns, Joshua commanded the people, "Shout! For the LORD has given you the town!"

20 When the people heard the sound of the rams' horns, they shouted as loud as they could. Suddenly, the walls of Jericho collapsed, and the said unto the people, Shout; for the LORD hath given you the city.

20 So the people shouted when the priests blew with the trumpets: and it came to pass, when the people heard the sound of the trumpet, and the people shouted with a great shout, that the wall fell down flat, so that the people went up into the city, every man straight before him, and they took the city.

Israelites charged straight into the town and captured it.

The People, Places, and Times

Jericho. Situated in the southern portion of the Jordan Valley, Jericho was near the east-west roadway that connected Transjordan with the hill country of Palestine. Jericho was a popular place because it was an oasis situated in a hot plain, isolated from other major settlements. Over the life of the city, Jericho has served as both a busy urban center and a small campsite. As early as the Stone Age, Jericho was a walled town of about 10 acres. Jericho came to have solid defense ramparts and walls. By Joshua's time, the walls of Jericho, which had been built thousands of years earlier, were still being used for defense of the settlement.

The story of Joshua's conquest of Jericho reports many items of significance for Israel's history and subsequent Jewish and Christian theology. From the narrative of the spies at Rahab's house, one learns that Jericho was a walled city with houses, gates, and windows. Some houses were built into the walls of the city (Joshua 2:1). The account of the stoppage of the Jordan's water at Adamah reports the crossing "right against Jericho" (Joshua 3:16).

Why would Joshua's inevitable defeat of Jericho become such a beloved story?

Background

Joshua, the mighty Israelite military commander, knew His God and believed He would give His nation the Promised Land. Militarily, God instructed Joshua to plunge into Palestine and divide it into north and south. Jericho was the first target to conquer since it lay directly in the path of their destination. Jericho lay in the valley of the Jordan River. In this lush tropical climate, palm, balsam, sycamore, and henna trees grew. Great and wealthy, Jericho would be an ideal first fruit sacrifice to God.

Once the Israelites had safely crossed the Jordan, they commemorated the event by taking twelve stones from the riverbed and placing them at the next night's campsite. One man from each tribe was to select a stone. The stones were to serve as a memorial for instructing future generations about the Lord's intervention at the Jordan River. Other memorials were established as well. Teaching children about the faith through the use of memorials was an established Israelite practice.

After they crossed the Jordan, the manna which had fallen from heaven each day ceased. Since Israel had reached the land of promise, the daily provision of manna was no longer necessary.

Do you have special memorials or customs to pass on cultural knowledge to the next generation?

At-A-Glance

1. Messenger of the Plan (Joshua 5:13-15)
2. The Plan to Conquer Jericho (6:1-5)
3. Joshua Obeys the Plan (vv. 15-16, 20)

In Depth

1. Messenger of the Plan (Joshua 5:13-15)

Prior to the siege of Jericho, Joshua had an encounter that was similar to Moses at the burning bush. Joshua saw a man standing in front of him with his sword drawn. Joshua asked the man whether he was an enemy or an ally. "Neither," the man replied (5:14). The man identified himself as the commander of the army of the Lord. Upon hearing this, Joshua fell to the ground face down in reverence. Joshua asked what message the Lord had for him. He was then told to take off his shoes as the place where he was standing was holy.

When has God commanded you to worship in what seemed to be an impossible situation?

2. The Plan to Conquer Jericho (6:1-5)

The residents of Jericho had anticipated an attack and barred their gates. The city was closed to all incoming and outgoing traffic. They were afraid of Israel's might (Joshua 2:8-11).

In giving Joshua instructions, the Lord assured him that the victory had already been won. But, it was not going to be an ordinary capture. They would not take it by direct force, espionage, or siege tactics. Joshua was not going to need battering rams and heavy armor to enter the city. Instead, the men were to walk around the city walls, in silence, once a day, for six days. Seven priests led the procession, escorting the Ark which symbolized God's presence. The Ark went before Israel when they

went into battle. In essence, therefore, the Lord went before Israel in every battle.

On the seventh day, the priests and men of war were to walk around the city seven times. After completing their seventh lap, the priests were to blow the trumpets. This would be the signal for the people to shout. The dual purpose of the battle cry was to inspire the troops as it intimidated the enemy. The walls of Jericho would fall flat (v. 5). The men would then be able to capture the city with ease because it would be taken by the power of the Lord.

Sometimes God gives us instructions that may seem so far-fetched, we just can't believe He is really instructing us. We should remember that God's ways are not our ways and His thoughts are not our thoughts (Isaiah 55:8). He knows what is needed at any given time and He tells us to trust Him. He has never let His people down, as Scripture shows us again and again.

What testimony do you have that confirms God's steadfast deliverance?

3. Joshua Obeys the Plan (vv. 15-16, 20)

Joshua's instructions may have seemed strange to the people, but they performed the first six days faithfully. On the seventh day they got up early. This day they were to increase their daily march and walk around the city seven times. When they had finished marching the seventh time, the priests blew their trumpets and Joshua commanded the people to shout the victory. The Lord had given them the city.

God is able to give us the victory over our enemies when we obey His words and follow His instructions. As long as God's people are obedient to Him, they are witnesses to His mighty power exhibited on their behalf. We may not agree with the Lord's directions for our lives, and we may not even want to accept His principles. But, God is never short on His promises. He will come through for us whenever we submit to Him and follow His word every day!

What encouragement can you give to a new Christians about trusting God?

Search the Scriptures

1. What were the people supposed to do when they heard the horn blow? (v. 5)

2. Why were the people to shout? (6:16)

3. What did the people do on the seventh day? (v. 15)

Discuss the Meaning

1. What significance do you see in the repetition of the number seven in the conquest of Jericho?

2. What lessons can you take from this text about victory in your personal battles?

Liberating Lesson

Miraculous events such as the fall of the wall at Jericho are sometimes difficult for modern-day readers to believe.

To our fore-bearers, however, the fall of the wall at Jericho indicated a stronghold of faith. The Old Negro spiritual "Joshua Fit De Battle of Jericho," tells the story of God's assurance of victory in a battle against the enemies of His people. As a group of oppressed people, Israel found strength in a God of deliverance, a God who could destroy the enemy.

It is critical to always remember that God is a God of deliverance and power.

Application for Activation

Look at your own life. Are you taking time to know God now, far in advance of your troubles? Do you take time to praise Him during the day despite what's happening in your life? How is your prayer life? Do you call on God only when you are in need or do you pray just because it is a tradition? These and other questions should be answered this week as you reflect on this lesson and share it with someone else. At the same time decide today that you are going to follow God no matter where He leads and how impossible it may seem to you. As you open your heart to Him, praise Him for answered prayers.

Follow the Spirit

What God wants me to do:

_____

_____

_____

_____

Remember Your Thoughts

Special insights I have learned:

_____

_____

_____

_____

More Light on the Text
Joshua 5:13-6:5, 15-16, 20

The Israelites have successfully and miraculously crossed the Jordan and are now set to possess the land. The news of this and other acts of God spread all around the regions of Canaan, and their inhabitants are afraid of the Israelites (5:1). The Lord appears to Joshua in the form a man set for battle and instructs him on how to go about possessing the land.

The first battle would be against Jericho, which is the first city to the west of the Jordan.

5:13 And it came to pass, when Joshua was by Jericho, that he lifted up his eyes and looked, and, behold, there stood a man over against him with his sword drawn in his hand: and Joshua went unto him, and said unto him, Art thou for us, or for our adversaries? 14 And he said, Nay; but as captain of the host of the LORD am I now come. And Joshua fell on his face to the earth, and did worship, and said unto him, What saith my Lord unto his servant?

Joshua seems to be alone, near Jericho, when confronted with a messenger from God. Because the man has a drawn sword in his hand, Joshua asks if he is friend or foe. Joshua is remembered primarily as the military leader of Israel after Moses' death, and as the military leader, he is vigilant to protect his people from this strange messenger if need be.

Even though Joshua asks an either-or question, the man answers, "Nay." God is not embarrassed to let us know that our entire paradigm, or way of thinking about the world, is wrong. Joshua should not be worried if intruders are for them or against them, but if they are for or against God. Thankfully, this man is for God, as the captain of the Lord's army.

Joshua is overwhelmed by the honor of this visitation from such a heavenly being. He falls to the ground and "worships" the man. When angels are mistakenly worshiped, they usually insist that they are not worthy of such worship (Revelation 19:10). Only God is. This is not necessarily what Joshua is doing here, however. The verb translated "worship" (Heb. *shachah*, shaw-KHAH) means "to bow down"; this can be done in a worshipful manner (Genesis 22:5) or it can merely show respect for authority (2 Samuel 9:6).

15 And the captain of the LORD's host said unto Joshua, Loose thy shoe from off thy foot; for the place whereon thou standest is holy. And Joshua did so.

The captain of the Lord's armies asks Joshua to respect the holiness of this place by removing his dirty shoes. Joshua is sure to have remembered the story of a similar request made to Moses when the Lord called him to rescue His people while speaking out of a bush. When we approach God, He accepts us as we are. It is important, however, to respect the great honor that God gives to us by allowing us such access to the heavenly throne room. To remind us that we should leave behind the worn, dirty, everyday, earthly worries when talking with God, the captain commands Joshua to remove his shoe so as not to disrupt the holiness of the place where he stands. Joshua obediently does so and listens for the Lord's instructions.

6:1 Now Jericho was straitly shut up because of the children of Israel: none went out, and none came in.

The first verse of this chapter describes the seemingly hopeless and almost impossible situation that confronts the Israelites as they approach Jericho. This difficulty is much like other obstacles they have overcome along the way, such as crossing the Red Sea and the Jordan River. The difference, in this case, is that the city has prepared for war by fortifying their city walls. The verse starts by telling the state of mind of the inhabitants of Jericho when the people of Israel arrive at their borders. "Now Jericho was straitly shut up." The double usage of the word *sagar* (Heb. saw-GAR) is employed here to describe shutting in of the people of the land. Literally the phrase reads, "Jericho was shutting up shut," which means that the city was sealed so that no one was able to go in or go out of the city. They were shut within the walls because they were fearful of the Israelites' coming attack (2:10-11; 5:1).

336

2 And the LORD said unto Joshua, See, I have given into thine hand Jericho, and the king thereof, and the mighty men of valour.

It is important to note that verse 1 is inserted parenthetically here, then the narrator continues the thought which he began in 5:13. The chapter division in 5:15 is somewhat misleading and creates the impression that the Lord's theophany and speech with Joshua ended there. However, the Lord's conversation with him continues (6:2-5) with detailed war plans against Jericho. Joshua and the Children of Israel are at the wall of Jericho, probably gazing at the wall and contemplating how to overcome such a formidable barrier. According to some archaeological sources, the wall of Jericho is a pear-shaped mound 366 meters (400 yards) in length from the north to the south, 183 meters (200 yards) in width, and about 67 meters (70 yards) high.

As Joshua is gazing at this impenetrable wall, the Lord appears in military regalia (5:13-15) and speaks to him. The Lord assures Joshua that He has given him the city of Jericho. "See," the Lord said, "I have given into your hand Jericho" with their king and their army. The language here indicates a completed action. In other words, the Lord seems to say to Joshua, "There is no cause for alarm or worry. I have already won the battle for you. I have already handed the land over to you as I have promised." The Lord's specific mention of the king and his army, not only implies total victory but also indicates and confirms that the inhabitants of Jericho have planned to attack Israel. They are ready to defend their city. The Lord then assures Joshua of victory.

3 And ye shall compass the city, all ye men of war, and go round about the city once. Thus shalt thou do six days. 4 And seven priests shall bear before the ark seven trumpets of rams' horns: and the seventh day ye shall compass the city seven times, and the priests shall blow with the trumpets. 5 And it shall come to pass, that when they make a long blast with the ram's horn, and when ye hear the sound of the trumpet, all the people shall shout with a great shout; and the wall of the city shall fall down flat, and the people shall ascend up every man straight before him.

In verses 3-5, the Lord gives direction for how this battle, which has already been won in the spiritual realm, is to be won physically. The Lord gives Joshua the battle strategy to convey to all the Children of Israel. The instructions are clear:

1. The people, led by the men of war (soldiers), are to march round the city of Jericho once each day for six days. The word "compass" (Heb. *sabab*, saw-**BAB**), means "to surround or circle round." The idea is not to march as in a military parade but go around the walls of the city once a day (v. 3).

2. Seven priests with seven rams' horn trumpets shall go in front of the Ark of the Covenant and lead the way around the city each day (v. 4).

3. The people are to circle the city seven times on the seventh day (v. 4).

4. At the end of the 7th time, the priests shall blow a long blast of the rams' horn and the people "shout with a great shout" (v. 5) before marching straight in to take possession of the land (v. 5).

The phrase, "shout with a great shout" are two Hebrew words from the same root. *Rua'* (roo-**AH**) means "to sound an alarm, make a joyful noise," and *teru'ah* (teh-roo-**AH**) is "an acclamation of joy or battle cry." The cry is for both the intimidation of the enemy and the encouragement of the friendly forces (Numbers 10:9; 23:21). Shouting is frequently associated in many instances with the Ark of the Covenant (1 Samuel 4:5; 2 Samuel 6:15; cf. Numbers 29:1; Psalm 33:3).

It is also noticeable that the priests are to lead the people in wars and take an active part in the affairs of Israel. Ministers of the Lord are to be at the forefront in accomplishing the commands of the Lord (cf. v. 4-6; 3:3, 8, 13-17; 4:3). The result of obeying all these instructions is that the walls of Jericho will "fall down flat" i.e., completely. That means total destruction. It will give way and the people of Israel (everyone) will march straight in to take possession of the land.

15 And it came to pass on the seventh day, that they rose early about the dawning of the day, and compassed the city after the same manner seven times: only on that day they compassed the city seven times. 16 And it came to pass at the seventh time, when the priests blew with the trumpets, Joshua said unto the people, Shout; for the LORD hath given you the city.

Verses 6-14 contain Joshua's instruction to the people and the description of the actual procession (the encircling) of the city from the first day to the sixth day. The narrator now takes us to the events of the seventh day. The Children of Israel have obeyed the Lord and have done everything according to the instruction of Joshua to them. Then early in the morning of the seventh day, which we can refer to here as their "D-Day," the people start early to circle the city. Their starting "early about the dawning of the day," as mentioned here, is important in view of the special instruction regarding the seventh day (from v. 4). Since it would take them longer to march around the city seven times in one day, they need to start early. On this eventful day, the people circle the city just as they have been doing for the past six days, silently with seven priests carrying rams' horns leading the way, followed by those carrying the Ark of the Covenant and the soldiers, and then the people (vv. 8-14). Each march must be completely

around the city. To do that seven times on the last day, and then march in to capture the city afterward would take hard work and faith.

To the Israelites as well, this method looks very strange and foolish, but they act in strict obedience to the Lord, who uses the things that seem foolish to the world to put to shame the wise, and the weak things to defeat the mighty (1 Corinthians 1:27–28). Moreover, they have seen enough of God's mighty deeds along the way especially in the most recent time (Joshua 3–4), that they have to trust and obey Him.

Verse 16 relates the fulfillment of God's promises and the result of total faith in and obedience to the word of God even when it sounds irrational. The people have completed the procession according to the instructions of the Lord. After the priests have sounded the trumpets, Joshua announces to the people to shout (rua') for joy because the "Lord has given you the city," which reminds them of God's promise to give them the city (v. 2; cf 8:1, 18; Judges 3:28; 4:7, etc).

20 So the people shouted when the priests blew with the trumpets: and it came to pass, when the people heard the sound of the trumpet, and the people shouted with a great shout, that the wall fell down flat, so that the people went up into the city, every man straight before him, and they took the city.

Here, the narrator gives us the climax of God's victory over the city of Jericho. "So," i.e., recalling the reader's attention to the event in verse 16, Israel obeys Joshua's instruction. When they heard the sound of the trumpet, "the people shouted with a great shout" (vv. 5-6). At the long blast of the rams' horns, coupled with Joshua's signal, the people raise the battle cry of triumph. As they are shouting, probably in excitement and in obedience to the word of God, the walls of Jericho start to crumble. As the wall falls flat, the people of Israel move in, "every man straight before him, and they took the city."

Scholars have long sought physical reasons for the fall of Jericho. Some believe the walls lowered into the ground like an elevator, allowing Israel to enter the city by walking across the tops of the wall. Others believe the Lord might have used an earthquake to bring about His purpose. Still, others think the trampling and vibrations might have weakened the walls causing them to tumble. No matter how the incident is interpreted, the fall of Jericho's walls served to demonstrate God's power over nature.

Sources:

Bromiley, Geoffrey W. *International Standard Bible Encyclopedia*, Vol. 2. Grand Rapids, MI: William B. Eerdmans Co, 1982. 992-993.

Butler, Trent, gen. ed. *Holman Bible Dictionary*. Nashville, TN: Broadman & Holman Publishers, 1991.

Henry, Matthew. *Matthew Henry's Commentary on the Whole Bible: New Modern Edition*. Vols. 1-6. Peabody, MA: Hendrickson Publishers, Inc., 2009.

Say It Correctly

Paradigm. **PARE**-ah-dime.
Adamah. ah-**DAH**-mah.

Daily Bible Readings

MONDAY
Rahab Rewarded for Her Faithfulness
(Hebrews 11:23-31)

TUESDAY
Jesus Heals Blind Man from Jericho
(Luke 18:35-42)

WEDNESDAY
Enjoying the Manna and Local Produce
(Joshua 5:8-12)

THURSDAY
Marching Around the City of Jericho
(Joshua 6:6-14)

FRIDAY
Rahab and Spies Confirm Rescue Plan
(Joshua 2:15-24)

SATURDAY
Rahab Saved While Jericho Is Destroyed
(Joshua 6:22-25)

SUNDAY
Joshua's Successful Conquest of Jericho
(Joshua 5:13–6:5, 15-16, 20)

Notes

_____

_____

_____

_____

Teaching Tips

Words You Should Know

A. Provoke to anger (2 Kings 22:17) *ka'as* (Heb.)—To cause someone growing vexation; used almost always to describe God's anger against injustice and unrighteousness

B. Tender (v. 19) *rakak* (Heb.)—Soft, fearful

Teacher Preparation

Unifying Principle—Seeking Wisdom for the Future. No one knows all the implications of what they learn. Who can help us understand what the future holds? King Josiah's advisers consulted the prophetess Huldah who shared her God-given insights about the coming days of the nation and the king.

A. Read the Bible Background and Devotional Reading.

B. Pray for your students and lesson clarity.

C. Read the lesson Scripture in multiple translations.

O—Open the Lesson

A. Begin the class with prayer.

B. Discuss specific sources people visit when trying to understand the news of the day. What makes one source preferable to another? What can happen when people listen to the misguided voices or fake news?

C. Have the students read the Aim for Change and the In Focus story.

D. Ask students how events like those in the story weigh on their hearts and how they can view these events from a faith perspective.

P—Present the Scriptures

A. Read the Focal Verses and discuss the Background and The People, Places, and Times sections.

B. Have the class share what Scriptures stand out for them and why, with particular emphasis on today's themes.

E—Explore the Meaning

A. Use In Depth or More Light on the Text to facilitate a deeper discussion of the lesson text.

B. Pose the questions in Search the Scriptures and Discuss the Meaning.

C. Discuss the Liberating Lesson and Application for Activation sections.

N—Next Steps for Application

A. Summarize the value of responding to scriptural warnings by correction of our behavior.

B. End class with a commitment to pray for strength to live up to the high standards God desires in both church and state.

Worship Guide

For the Superintendent or Teacher
Theme: Huldah: Prophet of Wisdom
Song: "Praise the Name of Jesus"
Devotional Reading: Psalm 25:1-10

Huldah: Prophet of Wisdom

Bible Background • 2 KINGS 22
Printed Text • 2 KINGS 22:14-20 | Devotional Reading • PSALM 25:1-10

Aim for Change

By the end of this lesson, we will ANALYZE the prophetess Huldah's message from God for King Josiah, REFLECT on Josiah's behavior after hearing the words of the book of the law, and SEEK godly advice about their future.

In Focus

When Marta's father-in-law moved in with her family, she knew it was going to be a change, but she certainly wasn't expecting it to take the mental and physical toll on her that it did. She ended up moving her transcribing desk into the living room to keep an eye on him; he got anxious if he were left alone for more than fifteen minutes at a time. Marta took care of him and, when she wasn't shuttling the kids around, spent all her time with him. He never voiced his thanks, but sometimes Marta could see sparks of gratefulness in his clouded eyes. As his illness worsened, he needed more and more care; and Marta would often rest against the door frame and pray for strength to serve him with love.

He lived with them for nearly half a year before quietly passing away in his sleep. Marta finally had time to rest and catch up with her old friends.

"It's funny," she told Angelica, a college friend, "I was never comfortable with seniors before. But now I understand them better. There was an older grandfather at the kid's soccer game last night, just standing there, and I was able to help him find a seat and some water. I wouldn't have even felt comfortable offering him anything, before."

"That's wonderful," said Angelica, genuinely impressed. "I never know how to help without sounding awkward."

"Exactly!" exclaimed Marta. "But it's because God let me help my father-in-law for so long that I'm able to help others."

What lessons has God has taught you that you would share with others?

Keep in Mind

"Because thine heart was tender, and thou hast humbled thyself before the LORD, when thou heardest what I spake against this place, and against the inhabitants thereof, that they should become a desolation and a curse, and hast rent thy clothes, and wept before me; I also have heard thee, saith the LORD" (2 Kings 22:19, KJV).

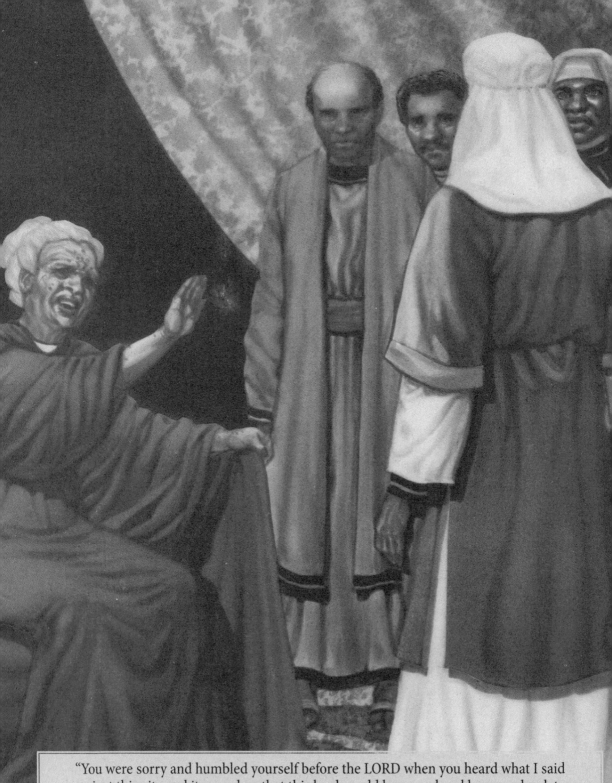

"You were sorry and humbled yourself before the LORD when you heard what I said against this city and its people—that this land would be cursed and become desolate. You tore your clothing in despair and wept before me in repentance. And I have indeed heard you, says the LORD" (2 Kings 22:19, NLT).

Focal Verses

KJV **2 Kings 22:14** So Hilkiah the priest, and Ahikam, and Achbor, and Shaphan, and Asahiah, went unto Huldah the prophetess, the wife of Shallum the son of Tikvah, the son of Harhas, keeper of the wardrobe; (now she dwelt in Jerusalem in the college;) and they communed with her.

15 And she said unto them, Thus saith the LORD God of Israel, Tell the man that sent you to me,

16 Thus saith the LORD, Behold, I will bring evil upon this place, and upon the inhabitants thereof, even all the words of the book which the king of Judah hath read:

17 Because they have forsaken me, and have burned incense unto other gods, that they might provoke me to anger with all the works of their hands; therefore my wrath shall be kindled against this place, and shall not be quenched.

18 But to the king of Judah which sent you to enquire of the LORD, thus shall ye say to him, Thus saith the LORD God of Israel, As touching the words which thou hast heard;

19 Because thine heart was tender, and thou hast humbled thyself before the LORD, when thou heardest what I spake against this place, and against the inhabitants thereof, that they should become a desolation and a curse, and hast rent thy clothes, and wept before me; I also have heard thee, saith the LORD.

20 Behold therefore, I will gather thee unto thy fathers, and thou shalt be gathered into thy grave in peace; and thine eyes shall not see all the evil which I will bring upon this place. And they brought the king word again.

NLT **2 Kings 22:14** So Hilkiah the priest, Ahikam, Acbor, Shaphan, and Asaiah went to the New Quarter of Jerusalem to consult with the prophet Huldah. She was the wife of Shallum son of Tikvah, son of Harhas, the keeper of the Temple wardrobe.

15 She said to them, "The LORD, the God of Israel, has spoken! Go back and tell the man who sent you,

16 'This is what the LORD says: I am going to bring disaster on this city and its people. All the words written in the scroll that the king of Judah has read will come true.

17 For my people have abandoned me and offered sacrifices to pagan gods, and I am very angry with them for everything they have done. My anger will burn against this place, and it will not be quenched.'

18 But go to the king of Judah who sent you to seek the LORD and tell him: 'This is what the LORD, the God of Israel, says concerning the message you have just heard:

19 You were sorry and humbled yourself before the LORD when you heard what I said against this city and its people—that this land would be cursed and become desolate. You tore your clothing in despair and wept before me in repentance. And I have indeed heard you, says the LORD.

20 So I will not send the promised disaster until after you have died and been buried in peace. You will not see the disaster I am going to bring on this city.'" So they took her message back to the king.

The People, Places, and Times

Josiah's Revival. The three decades of Josiah's reign were among the happiest years experienced by Judah. They were characterized by peace, prosperity, and reform. King Josiah dedicated himself to pleasing God and led Israel in their renewed observance of the Mosaic Law. It is a testimony to the grace of God that a wicked king like Amon could have such a godly son and successor. At the age of 16, in the eighth year of his reign, Josiah personally "began to seek after the God of David his father" (2 Chronicles 34:3). It was at this point that he began to purify Judah and Jerusalem from idolatry by destroying whatever he recognized as not belonging to the worship of the true God (2 Kings 22:1–2). The spiritual reform brought about by Josiah climaxes with renovating the Temple, and, in the process, he rediscovered the Book of the Law in the eighteenth year of his reign and the celebration of the Passover (2 Kings 22:8–23; 23). Josiah's aim to turn his people back to true worship was so intense that he and the entire kingdom renewed their covenant with God.

Background

Following Hezekiah's death (2 Kings 20:21) several kings succeeded him. Among them were: Manasseh (2 Kings 21:1); Amon (2 Kings 21:19); and Josiah (2 Kings 22:1). Josiah was eight years old when he became king of Judah. He reigned 31 years. The Bible affirms that he was one of Judah's best kings (see 2 Kings 22:19). Peace, prosperity, and political reform highlighted his reign. In Judah, the Temple had fallen into disrepair (see 2 Kings 21:4-5, 7, 21). So, Josiah gave consent to repair the Temple by sending Shaphan, a scribe to oversee the renovations (see 2 Kings 22:3-4). While the renovation was going on Hilkiah, the high priest, found a copy of the book of the Law in the Temple (v. 8). Shaphan read the book of the Law to Josiah, who tore his clothes after hearing the scribe's reading (v. 11). The king was distressed because he realized that the nation of Judah was far from God in their morality, obedience, and spirituality. Therefore, Josiah called Hilkiah the priest, Shaphan, Ahikam, Shaphan's son, and Asaiah, a servant of the king to inquire of God what the people should do to get right with Him.

At-A-Glance

1. God's Prophetess (2 Kings 22:14)
2. God's Condemnation (vv. 15-17)
3. God's Affirmation (vv. 18-20)

In Depth

1. God's Prophetess (2 Kings 22:14)

Huldah was the wife of Shallum, the wardrobe keeper (either of priestly vestments or royal robes). She lived in Jerusalem, in what was called the second district (not college as in KJV). Apparently, this was in a lower or southern section of Jerusalem. She was consulted on behalf of King Josiah, by Hilkiah the chief priest, Shaphan the scribe and others, following the discovery of "the book of the law in the house of the LORD" (2 Kings 22:8; 2 Chronicles 34:15). Although it is only recorded a few times, God spoke to His people through prophetesses prominently. Miriam (Exodus 15:20), Deborah (Judges 4:4), and Isaiah's wife (Isaiah 8:3) are all described as prophetesses.

Huldah accepted the book as the Word of Yahweh, and with His authority prophesied judgment against Jerusalem and Judah after Josiah's death. It is noteworthy that, although both Jeremiah and Zephaniah were prophesying at this time, it is she who was approached on this matter.

Why do you go to different advisors at different times?

2. God's Condemnation (vv. 15-17)

When Hilkiah, Ahikam, Achbor, Shaphan, and Asaiah arrived at Huldah's, she gives them a message from the Lord God of Israel to take back to Josiah. However, the message was not an encouraging one. As Josiah had anticipated, Huldah's prophecy was that of judgment. Jerusalem and its inhabitants would taste evil days, even as the Book of the Law prescribed. The reason for this impending disaster was clear. The Lord God would not tolerate open violations of His law. Ignorance of the law is no excuse. In 586 BC, destruction did come to Judah when Babylonia brought Judah to its knees.

Huldah told the kings' men that God would bring disaster on the land and the people because they had forsaken Him. God wants us to keep our eyes on Him so we won't fall prey to the "gods" of this world. So often we shift our focus away from God onto ourselves, other people, and other things. Let's make sure we are tuned to what the Lord wants to do so we won't be condemned like Judah.

What daily practices help you remember to worship God alone rather than modern idols of work, or comfort, or success?

3. God's Affirmation (vv. 18-20)

As is so often the case, God's prophecy of doom concludes with a glimmer of hope. The prophetess Huldah speaks another word to the messengers for the king (v. 18). Josiah would experience God's mercy and grace because he humbled himself before the Lord and had a tender heart. Josiah humbled himself when he tore his clothes and wept (v. 11) over what he read in the book of the Law. In God's tender mercies, He indicated through Huldah, King Josiah himself would die before these days of horror appeared. Indeed, Josiah's death occurred in 609 BC, four years before Nebuchadnezzar attacked Jerusalem. Just one good leader can

put off destruction, and give the organization they lead (whether a family, a department, a church, or a country) a little bit more time to turn back to God.

Where are you a leader? How should leaders use their position of power to influence those who follow them?

Search the Scriptures

1. Whom did the Israelites consult to learn God's will? (2 Kings 22:14)

2. What warning did the people of Israel have for the coming disaster? (v. 16)

3. How does God show Josiah mercy? (vv. 19-20)

Discuss the Meaning

1. How do we know when we are out of God's will? Discuss.

2. What should we do when God confronts us with our sin? Is it right for us to confront others about their sins? Why or why not?

3. What are the "idols" that destroy our spiritual lives?

4. How can we convince unbelievers that the Bible is God's authoritative word?

Liberating Lesson

You may feel overwhelmed and inundated by the amount of information from the 24/7/365 news cycle. From those sources, it seems culture is on the wrong track. We look for reliable commentators and analysts to help us understand the events of the day. We know there must be some absolute moral standards but are not always sure where to look for them.

The biblical teaching in this area is fairly straightforward. Yet surprisingly, Christians allow the world to steal their affections and compromise their values. Too many church leaders have forsaken the awesome task of making the Word of God known in the world today. Thank God for those Christian leaders who faithfully teach, preach, and live the Word in our urban society today.

Application for Activation

When was the last time you "consulted" with the Lord by way of His Word? It is so important that we study and meditate on God's Word daily. The Bible tells us to "Study to shew thyself approved unto God, a workman that needeth not to be ashamed, rightly dividing the word of truth" (2 Timothy 2:15). One of the most important ways we commune with God is through His Word. If we don't have a consistent Bible study time we can get "rusty" in our study habits.

This week make a consistent effort to spend at least 15 minutes a day studying the Bible. Write down any questions that might arise in your study. Share your questions with your teacher and others during the week.

Follow the Spirit

What God wants me to do:

_____

_____

_____

_____

Remember Your Thoughts

Special insights I have learned:

_____

_____

_____

_____

More Light on the Text
2 Kings 22:14-20

Two questions about Huldah arise: Why a woman? And, why Huldah in particular? The prophetess Huldah had an important share in the great spiritual revival of the Jewish people under the reign of King Josiah, through her prophecy and influence. Huldah is a unique female prophet in the Old Testament because she is the only woman prophet whose oracle has been preserved in the Bible. Miriam and Deborah are remembered as prophetesses because of the songs that bear their names. Huldah is remembered because of the words she spoke to Josiah. In the light of the contemporary discussion about the role of women in ministry, the story of Huldah the prophetess is significant and is worth examining. One may begin with the question of why the priest and others went to Huldah in the first instance. Just as Hezekiah's representatives once sought Isaiah's advice, so now Josiah's men approach Huldah, God's representative.

14 So Hilkiah the priest, and Ahikam, and Achbor, and Shaphan, and Asahiah, went unto Huldah the prophetess, the wife of Shallum the son of Tikvah, the son of Harhas, keeper of the wardrobe; (now she dwelt in Jerusalem in the college;) and they communed with her.

Nothing is known about Huldah apart from the information offered here concerning her husband and their residence. Her husband Shallum is the "keeper of the wardrobe," likely referring to the special garments of the priests or the king and the royal family. They live in Jerusalem "in the college" (Heb. *mishneh*, meesh-NEH) which is rendered as "the second quarter" by other translations. The word *mishneh* can mean "second," but it also can refer to the oral traditions of the Jewish rabbis, the Mishnah. It was learned "second" after the Torah and actual Scriptures. Although the full tradition of Mishnah writings were not organized at this point in Jewish history, the word could already be in use in Huldah's day to refer to such traditional teachings. To live "in the *mishneh*" would be to live in the area of town where leading scholars gathered to study these teachings, like a college.

Furthermore, little is known about the tradition of female prophets in the society of ancient Israel. Huldah joins the ranks of Miriam (Exodus 15:20), Deborah (Judges 4:4), Isaiah's wife (Isaiah 8:2), and Anna (Luke 2:36) who are also called "prophetesses." Huldah is the only woman prophet mentioned in the history of the Northern (Israel) and Southern (Judah) kingdoms. Other prophets at or very near the time were Jeremiah, whose mission had commenced in Josiah's thirteenth year (Jeremiah 1:2) and Zephaniah, the son of Cushi. Zephaniah's prophecy appears to have belonged to the earliest part of Josiah's reign. One might expect that either of these two prophets would be consulted. Instead, the king sent the high priest, the scribe, and others to Huldah to inquire of God.

Even though this is a unique example in Scripture, the writer uses no literary tools to emphasize Huldah's gender. The Scripture text does not provide any indication that consulting a female prophet was unusual for a king and high priest. There is no discernible difference between male and female prophets concerning their prophetic function. God spoke to Huldah and she delivered His words as instructed.

15 And she said unto them, Thus saith the LORD God of Israel, Tell the man that sent you to me, 16 Thus saith the LORD, Behold, I will bring evil upon this place, and upon the inhabitants thereof, even all the words of the book which the king of Judah hath read:

Huldah's oracle mentions events that would happen in the future. Although many false prophets claimed to speak for God, Huldah spoke concerning what God was about to do to Judah. She knew the character of God, the nature of sin, and the rebellion of the people of Judah. As a prophet, she proclaimed the judgment of God because of the wickedness of the people and their worship of false gods.

Huldah has full prophetic insight and inspiration and delivers God's words, just as Isaiah and Jeremiah do. She spoke a direct message to the king's messengers, confirming the worst fears of Josiah. Her response to Josiah was given in somber tones: God will bring evil upon Judah and its inhabitants thereof, "even all the words," or curses, that are written in the book which they have read before the King of Judah.

17 Because they have forsaken me, and have burned incense unto other gods, that they might provoke me to anger with all the works of their hands; therefore my wrath shall be kindled against this place, and shall not be quenched.

God here speaks in personal terms: the people "provoke [him] to anger" (Heb. *ka'as*, kaw-**OSS**; almost always God's anger against injustice and unrighteousness) with their behavior, so He will execute His wrath on them. He accuses them of the same deeds attributed to Manasseh (2 Kings 21:6), and He confirmed in the same words that His wrath against "this place"—that is, Jerusalem—and shall not be quenched. Here is the gist of their offense, the thing that provoked God's anger. They neglected all the warnings in the Law (Deuteronomy 12:19; 29:25–28; 31:16, 17; 32:15, etc.). It was not a casual breaking of God's commandments but they turned from God altogether and forsaking him.

God's answer provides some important lessons. First, sin has consequences. It is not possible to forsake God and escape the judgment that attends it. Second, God, in the midst of His wrath offers some hope. God's threats against nations are for the most part conditional and may be escaped, or at least their fulfillment may be deferred indefinitely, by repentance, as the example of Nineveh shows (Jonah 3:1–10). But if a nation and individuals persist in sin and wickedness, there comes a time when the sentence can no longer be averted. Real repentance has become impossible, and a pretentious one would only provoke God all the more. For such a state of things, there is "no remedy" (2 Chronicles 36:16), and this was the state of things reached by the nation of Judah.

God's anger against them could not be quenched. The prophet's words make effective use of fire imagery. In response to the Israelites burning offerings to other gods, God kindles His wrath, letting it burn in response. This word for wrath (Heb. *chemah*, kheh-**MAW**) is itself related to a word for "heat." The Israelites' unholy fire for idols has sparked a conflagration of God's righteous wrath that will burn down their nation.

18 But to the king of Judah which sent you to enquire of the LORD, thus shall ye say to him, Thus saith the LORD God of Israel, As touching the words which thou hast heard; 19 Because thine heart was tender, and thou hast humbled thyself before the LORD, when thou heardest what I spake against this place, and against the inhabitants thereof, that they should become a desolation and a curse, and hast rent thy clothes, and wept before me; I also have heard thee, saith the LORD.

The second portion of God's oracle through Huldah concerns Josiah himself. The events of judgment would occur after he died in peace because he was responsive and humble (v. 19) regarding the words of the Lord. This moves

the burning anger of the Lord against Judah farther into the future, at least until after Josiah died. God notes Josiah's motivation (v. 19). Josiah's heart was tender in two ways. First, it was tender to the word of God and was able to receive the convicting voice of the Holy Spirit. Second, it was tender to the message of judgment from Huldah in the previous verses. The word used here for "tender" (Heb. *rakak*, raw-**KOK**) is also used for skin softening when medicine is applied to a wound (Isaiah 1:6), giving the image of Josiah's heart responding to the balm of God's word. The word is also used in contexts of a soft and fearful heart. Indeed Josiah does fear the Lord's judgment for his sinful nation. Rending the garments (v. 11) was an outward act of humiliation. Josiah accompanied this with inward repentance and self-abasement. He had even been moved to tears. A genuine conviction leads to action, and such was the case of Josiah.

The reading of God's word, as it always does, spoke to the heart of the young king and stirred his spirit to conviction and repentance. Josiah feared God in every sense. He was truly afraid of God and what could happen to people who did not fear God enough to keep His commandments. He respected God and His priests. He valued God's house to the extent that he refurbished it, which led to finding the Book of the Law. He did not expect God to pass over the failures and sins of Judah, but he sought God's word from a prophet concerning his situation. Josiah was a model of a true God-fearer who put that awe and respect to work, to bring Judah back into a covenant relationship.

Today, leaders assume they have little power to change the ways of their contemporaries who walk outside of God's ways, so they do not try. But God calls all of us to model righteousness, to warn others against sin, to encourage salvation and opportunities to know Jesus and His Father in heaven (John 17:3).

20 Behold therefore, I will gather thee unto thy fathers, and thou shalt be gathered into thy grave in peace; and thine eyes shall not see all the evil which I will bring upon this place. And they brought the king word again.

There is a seeming contradiction between these words and the fact of Josiah's violent death in battle against Pharaoh Nechoh (2 Kings 23:29). But the contradiction is not a real one. Huldah assured Josiah that, though the destruction of his kingdom and the desolation of Judah and Jerusalem threatened in the Law were at hand, yet they would not come in his day. He would not see the evil time. Before it came he would be "gathered to his fathers," meaning he would die. The promise given him was fulfilled. He died in battle; but he was buried in peace (2 Chronicles 35:24, 25). The enemy who was to destroy Jerusalem and carry the nation into captivity did not make any attack upon the land until three years later when the throne was occupied by Jehoiakim (see 2 Kings 24:1). "The evil which I will bring upon this place" includes the three sieges of Nebuchadnezzar, the destruction of the Temple and city by Nebuzaradan (2 Kings 25:8–10), the deportation of the bulk of the inhabitants (2 Kings 25:11), and the calamities which happened to the remnant left (2 Kings 25:22–26). Josiah did not witness any of this. He was taken away from the evil to come. Hilkiah, Shaphan, and their companions (v. 14) reported to Josiah Huldah's message.

Sources:
"'College' or 'Second quarter' in 2 Kings 22:14 et al.?" KJV Today. http://www.kjvtoday.com/home/college-or-second-quarter-in-2-kings-2214-et-al

Hobbs, T. R. *2 Kings*. Word Biblical Commentary. Vol. 13. Dallas, TX: Word, Inc., 1985. 327.

House, Paul R. 1, *2 Kings*. The New American Commentary. Vol. 8. Nashville, TN: Broadman & Holman Publishers, 1995. 385.

Marshall, I. Howard; J.I. Packer; D.J. Wiseman; A.R. Millard. *New Bible Dictionary*. Downers Grove, IL: Intervarsity Press, 1984. 500.

Phipps, William E. *Assertive Biblical Women*. Westport, CT: Greenwood Press, 1992. 90.

Spence-Jones, H. D. M. ed. *2 Kings*. The Pulpit Commentary. New York: Funk & Wagnalls Company, 1909. 438.

Stökl, Jonathan. "Female Prophets in the Ancient Near East." In *Prophecy and Prophets in Ancient Israel*. Ed. John Day. London: T & T Clark, 2010. 47-61.

Walvoord, John F. and Roy B. Zuck. *The Bible Knowledge Commentary: An Exposition of the Scriptures*. Old Testament. Wheaton, IL: Victor Books, 1985. 581.

Winslow, Karen Strand. *1 & 2 Kings: A Commentary in the Wesleyan Tradition*. New Beacon Bible Commentary. Ed. Alex Varughese and Roger Hahn. Kansas City, MO: Beacon Hill Press, 2017. 259–260.

Say It Correctly

Achbor. **AK**-bohr
Ahikam. ah-**HI**-kuhm
Asaiah. ah-zuh-**HI**-uh
Hilkiah. hil-**KI**-uh
Huldah. **HUL**-duh
Shallum. **SHAL**-uhm
Shaphan. **SHAY**-fuhn
Tikvah. **TEEK**-vah
Zephaniah. **ZEF**-uh-**NI**-ah

Daily Bible Readings

MONDAY
God Loves Covenant Keepers
(Psalm 25:1-10)

TUESDAY
Entering God's Promised Rest
(Hebrews 4:1-11)

WEDNESDAY
New Covenant Made with the Israelites
(Deuteronomy 29:1-6)

THURSDAY
Josiah Prepares to Repair the Temple
(2 Kings 22:1-7)

FRIDAY
Josiah Seeks Guidance
to Confront Disobedience
(2 Kings 22 8-13)

SATURDAY
Josiah Leads in Covenant Renewal
(2 Kings 23:1-3)

SUNDAY
Huldah Confirms Coming Judgment;
Josiah Spared
(2 Kings 22:14-20)

Notes

Teaching Tips

Words You Should Know

A. Troubleth (1 Kings 18:17) *akar* (Heb.)—To stir up, disturb

B. Forsaken (v. 18) *'azab* (Heb.)—To leave, abandon, fall away

Teacher Preparation

Unifying Principle—The Bearer of Bad News. People like to go their own way until faced with crises beyond their control. How shall we respond to the advice of those who have great wisdom and insight? In 1 Kings, God sent Elijah to warn of impending disaster.

A. Read the Bible Background and Devotional Reading.

B. Pray for your students and lesson clarity.

C. Read the lesson Scripture in multiple translations.

O—Open the Lesson

A. Begin the class with prayer.

B. Allow the class to share stories about working for a supervisor who was unpredictable or even cruel. Did they ever find the courage to boldly confront that person's misuse of power?

C. Have the students read the Aim for Change and the In Focus story.

D. Ask students how events like those in the story weigh on their hearts and how they can view these events from a faith perspective.

P—Present the Scriptures

A. Read the Focal Verses and discuss the Background and The People, Places, and Times sections.

B. Have the class share what Scriptures stand out for them and why, with particular emphasis on today's themes.

E—Explore the Meaning

A. Use In Depth or More Light on the Text to facilitate a deeper discussion of the lesson text.

B. Pose the questions in Search the Scriptures and Discuss the Meaning.

C. Discuss the Liberating Lesson and Application for Activation sections.

N—Next Steps for Application

A. Summarize the value of using whatever influence you have for good.

B. End class with a commitment to pray for Christians who face persecution.

Worship Guide

For the Superintendent or Teacher
Theme: Elijah: Prophet of Courage
Song: "Days of Elijah"
Devotional Reading: Luke 19:28-39

Elijah: Prophet of Courage

Bible Background • 1 KINGS 18-19; MATTHEW 17:1-3
Printed Text • 1 KINGS 18:5-18 | Devotional Reading • LUKE 19:28-39

—————— Aim for Change ——————

By the end of this lesson, we will COMPARE Elijah's response to speak to Ahab to that of Obadiah's response to report back to Ahab, GAIN a sense of Obadiah's concerns when reporting Elijah's message to Ahab, and ACT in boldness when speaking the Word of God.

—————————— In Focus ——————————

When Cris fled her abusive husband, she vowed never to depend on another human. She packed her bags and drove across the country to a new job in a strange new town.

She worked hard and at the end of the day she would sit down with a cup of tea and a book. She went to church, but the closest she ever got to anyone was to Mandy, a single mother living in the same apartment complex. She would nod at Mandy as they passed each other in the halls and quickly turn away with a polite little cough.

As the weeks went by, the polite cough became serious and a throbbing pain settled in her chest. The violence she suffered had taken a toll. A series of contradictory doctors discouraged her and slowly her apartment and solitary life started falling into disarray.

Mandy met her one day as she was catching her breath on the stairs. "Hey Cris! Want a hand with those groceries?"

"No, thanks. Actually… yes. That would be great." She accepted Mandy's help but hesitated a bit to let her into the chaos her apartment had become. Cris rested on the couch and Mandy cooked dinner for them.

"I see where you're coming from," said Mandy, after hearing Cris' story, "but shutting yourself off from other people isn't the best way to go. God made us be part of a community, and that means sharing your struggles with other people and listening to their advice."

Cris nodded. "I can see that now. I thought I'd be safer by myself, but it looks like that wasn't meant to be."

Whom could you reach out to for advice and help?

—————————— Keep in Mind ——————————

"And [Elijah] answered, I have not troubled Israel; but thou, and thy father's house, in that ye have forsaken the commandments of the LORD, and thou hast followed Baalim" (1 Kings 18:18, KJV).

"'I have made no trouble for Israel,' Elijah replied. 'You and your family are the troublemakers, for you have refused to obey the commands of the LORD and have worshiped the images of Baal instead'" (1 Kings 18:18, NLT).

Focal Verses

KJV **1 Kings 18:5** And Ahab said unto Obadiah, Go into the land, unto all fountains of water, and unto all brooks: peradventure we may find grass to save the horses and mules alive, that we lose not all the beasts.

6 So they divided the land between them to pass throughout it: Ahab went one way by himself, and Obadiah went another way by himself.

7 And as Obadiah was in the way, behold, Elijah met him: and he knew him, and fell on his face, and said, Art thou that my lord Elijah?

8 And he answered him, I am: go, tell thy lord, Behold, Elijah is here.

9 And he said, What have I sinned, that thou wouldest deliver thy servant into the hand of Ahab, to slay me?

10 As the LORD thy God liveth, there is no nation or kingdom, whither my lord hath not sent to seek thee: and when they said, He is not there; he took an oath of the kingdom and nation, that they found thee not.

11 And now thou sayest, Go, tell thy lord, Behold, Elijah is here.

12 And it shall come to pass, as soon as I am gone from thee, that the Spirit of the Lord shall carry thee whither I know not; and so when I come and tell Ahab, and he cannot find thee, he shall slay me: but I thy servant fear the LORD from my youth.

13 Was it not told my lord what I did when Jezebel slew the prophets of the LORD, how I hid an hundred men of the LORD's prophets by fifty in a cave, and fed them with bread and water?

14 And now thou sayest, Go, tell thy lord, Behold, Elijah is here: and he shall slay me.

15 And Elijah said, As the LORD of hosts liveth, before whom I stand, I will surely shew myself unto him to day.

NLT **1 Kings 18:5** Ahab said to Obadiah, "We must check every spring and valley in the land to see if we can find enough grass to save at least some of my horses and mules."

6 So they divided the land between them. Ahab went one way by himself, and Obadiah went another way by himself.

7 As Obadiah was walking along, he suddenly saw Elijah coming toward him. Obadiah recognized him at once and bowed low to the ground before him. "Is it really you, my lord Elijah?" he asked.

8 "Yes, it is," Elijah replied. "Now go and tell your master, 'Elijah is here.'"

9 "Oh, sir," Obadiah protested, "what harm have I done to you that you are sending me to my death at the hands of Ahab?

10 For I swear by the LORD your God that the king has searched every nation and kingdom on earth from end to end to find you. And each time he was told, 'Elijah isn't here,' King Ahab forced the king of that nation to swear to the truth of his claim.

11 And now you say, 'Go and tell your master, "Elijah is here."'

12 But as soon as I leave you, the Spirit of the LORD will carry you away to who knows where. When Ahab comes and cannot find you, he will kill me. Yet I have been a true servant of the LORD all my life.

13 Has no one told you, my lord, about the time when Jezebel was trying to kill the LORD's prophets? I hid 100 of them in two caves and supplied them with food and water.

14 And now you say, 'Go and tell your master, "Elijah is here."' Sir, if I do that, Ahab will certainly kill me."

15 But Elijah said, "I swear by the Lord Almighty, in whose presence I stand, that I will present myself to Ahab this very day."

16 So Obadiah went to meet Ahab, and told him: and Ahab went to meet Elijah.

17 And it came to pass, when Ahab saw Elijah, that Ahab said unto him, Art thou he that troubleth Israel?

18 And he answered, I have not troubled Israel; but thou, and thy father's house, in that ye have forsaken the commandments of the LORD, and thou hast followed Baalim.

16 So Obadiah went to tell Ahab that Elijah had come, and Ahab went out to meet Elijah.

17 When Ahab saw him, he exclaimed, "So, is it really you, you troublemaker of Israel?"

18 "I have made no trouble for Israel," Elijah replied. "You and your family are the troublemakers, for you have refused to obey the commands of the LORD and have worshiped the images of Baal instead.

The People, Places, and Times

Obadiah. The Obadiah found in 1 Kings 18 is not the prophet and author of the book of Obadiah. This Obadiah worked in King Ahab's administration as a governor, mayor, and one of the top officials. Obadiah held this high position assisting one of Israel's most disobedient kings. However, Obadiah maintained his belief in Jehovah, the true and living God. The Scriptures identify him as a worshiper, one who feared God greatly (1 Kings 18:3). Scholars disagree concerning Obadiah's character. Some call him a hero, while others criticize his timidity, saying he compromised and was afraid to speak out on God's behalf.

Elijah. Little is known about Elijah's birth or family, other than that he came from Tishbeh in Gilead. God called Elijah to prophesy, speaking out against Baal worship in Israel and to actively take part in ending this abomination among God's people. Initially, God kept him secluded near the brook of Cherith where he is fed by ravens for six months. As the drought progressed, God connected Him with a widow and her son. God miraculously provided food for them for the next three years (1 Kings 17:8–16). Just before the end of the drought, Elijah called out the prophets of Baal for a showdown on Mt. Carmel. He challenged the people of Israel to serve the winner of the contest. God victoriously proved his superiority over

Baal and the prophets of the false gods were destroyed (1 Kings 18:17-40).

Ahab. One of the most rebellious kings in Israel's history (1 Kings 16:30). He married Jezebel, a Baal worshiper who hated God's people (1 Kings 18:4). She encouraged his worship of the false gods Baal and Asherah (1 Kings 16:31–33). God sent the prophets Elijah and Elisha to warn him, but he refused to listen. His ultimate downfall came when he made an agreement with a foreign king he was supposed to kill and did nothing when his wife had an innocent Israelite murdered (1 Kings 20-21). Both Ahab and Jezebel died gruesome, tragic deaths.

How does God protect His followers when leaders are unjust?

Background

God's Law clearly commanded never to worship false gods (Exodus 20:3; Deuteronomy 5:7), not to invoke their names (Exodus 23:13), not to marry their adherents or practice any of their customs (Leviticus 20:23; 2 Kings 17:15). King Ahab violated each one of these laws during his 22-year reign in Israel. He married Jezebel, a Phoenician Baal worshiper who had altars and a temple built for Baal. This false god of rain and dew was the supreme male deity of the ancient Phoenicians and Canaanites. Their rituals included illicit sex, ritual prostitution, and child sacrifice. God's prophet Elijah confronted King Ahab. The first time Scripture mentions him, he appears before King Ahab announcing a drought to come upon the whole land because of the nation's sin (1 Kings 17:1–7). This one verbal threat by a lone prophet of God challenged the worship of Baal, who was supposed to control the rain. Instead of Ahab and Jezebel acknowledging God and repenting, they were furious. They desperately sent out soldiers to hunt for Elijah to force him to reverse this curse.

How have you pushed back against God instead of acknowledging Him and repenting?

At-A-Glance

1. God's Providence (1 Kings 18:5-8)
2. God's Servant, Obadiah (vv. 9-16)
3. God's Prophet, Elijah (vv. 17-18)

In Depth

1. God's Providence (1 Kings 18:5-8)

Feeling the effects of the drought, King Ahab and his chief servant Obadiah discuss trying to find grass for the royal horses. The king fears for his safety if his horses died—no army to protect him. Ahab and Obadiah agree to search the area in different directions.

As Obadiah combs the area, Elijah, the missing prophet, walks toward him. King Ahab had looked diligently for Elijah for three and a half years, determined to force him to reverse the drought. The leaders in the surrounding countries joined in the massive hunt for the prophet. No one located him. They swore to the king that no individual had laid eyes on Elijah. However, by the providence of God, Obadiah and Elijah travel down the same path. Obadiah recognizes him, then bows with his face to the ground, in fear, reverence, and respect for God's messenger.

When has God caused you to have an unexpected encounter?

2. God's Servant, Obadiah (vv. 9-16)

Elijah asks Obadiah to deliver a message. He wants a face to face meeting with King Ahab. Obadiah responds with excuses. He thinks his master might be suspicious, assuming he knew the prophet's hiding place all this time. Obadiah images an upset king, angry enough to kill. He also raises another reason for his reluctance. Elijah had a reputation of being in one place, and then the Holy Spirit whisking him away to another. Obadiah lacks confidence in Elijah being in this location for a meeting with the king.

Obadiah continues giving reasons for refusing Elijah's request. He calls himself one who truly worships Yahweh, since his youth. When Jezebel tried to kill all of God's prophets, Obadiah hid one hundred of them in caves, supplying them with food and water. The king's servant urges Elijah to realize how much he'd done already and withdraw his demand.

When one's leader is a tyrant, is it better to covertly honor God as Obadiah did or overtly as Elijah did?

3. God's Prophet, Elijah (vv. 17-18)

Elijah refrains from addressing Obadiah's fears and hesitations. Instead, he speaks about the Mighty God they serve. Elijah walks in the assurance of God's presence, his shield of protection. He boldly intends to challenge King Ahab, resting in the sovereignty of God. He promises Obadiah that when King Ahab arrives, he will be in that very spot. Obadiah never says another word to Elijah but proceeds to go and arrange the meeting.

Finally, Ahab and Elijah face each other. The King accuses Elijah of being the one that disturbed and destroyed his kingdom with the drought. He speaks correctly. Elijah had made the "no rain" declaration. However, Elijah places the responsibility right back on Ahab's shoulders. He tells the king about his willfully ignoring and violating God's Law. Elijah calls for a showdown on Mt. Carmel that will prove the superiority of Jehovah over Baal.

When have you spoken boldly in the presence of fear?

Search the Scriptures

1. What was Elijah requesting of Obadiah and what was his response? (1 Kings 18:9-16)

2. What did Ahab accuse Elijah of doing? How did Elijah respond? (vv. 17-18)

Discuss the Meaning

1. Use the Focus Scriptures to point out words that describe Obadiah and Elijah. Contrast the two men.

2. In what ways were both men instruments in the hand of God?

Liberating Lesson

Speaking the truth today, especially to those who disagree with Christian beliefs is not always easy. Elijah walked in such confidence. He struggled at times with negative thinking and depression, but he also listened to God and followed His instructions. Think of Christians that you know that are bold like Elijah. If possible, have a conversation with them about their journey and glean from their experience.

Application for Activation

Take some time this week to examine your circles of influence, in your family, church, job, or community. Have you spoken up about Christ or have you kept your faith private? Pray about how God may want you to change. Ask the Holy Spirit to point out Scriptures this week to give you more wisdom and understanding. Surrender to the Lord and allow Him to do the transforming.

Follow the Spirit

What God wants me to do:

_____

_____

_____

_____

Remember Your Thoughts

Special insights I have learned:

_____

_____

_____

_____

More Light on the Text
1 Kings 18:5-18

King Ahab was the epitome of evil. He is often referred to as the king that made Israel sin; he led Israel to worship Baal. The Bible describes him as the king that "did more to provoke the LORD God of Israel to anger than all the kings of Israel that were before him" (from 1 Kings 16:33). Whereas good kings of Judah were portrayed as following the example of King David, evil kings of Israel and Judah were described as following the example of Ahab (1 Kings 22:51-52; 2 Kings 8:18, 25-27; 21:1-3). As a consequence for their rebellion against the Lord, Israel was punished with a severe drought.

After three years, the Lord sends Elijah back to announce to Ahab that there would be rain again in the land. Here we encounter God's nature of love, mercy, and grace at work. He does not wait for Israel to repent before changing their circumstances. Meanwhile, the effect of the drought has become so severe that Ahab summons the governor in charge of his house, Obadiah to his palace. Obadiah is known as one that fears God and is credited with saving the lives of a hundred prophets from extermination at the hand of Ahab's wicked wife, Jezebel (1 Kings 18:1-4).

5 And Ahab said unto Obadiah, Go into the land, unto all fountains of water, and unto all brooks: peradventure we may find grass to save the horses and mules alive, that we lose not all the beasts. 6 So they divided the land between them to pass throughout it: Ahab went one way by himself, and Obadiah went another way by himself.

Unlike King David, who repented and sought the Lord during the famine (2 Samuel 21:1), the famine never stirred Ahab to repentance. Rather, Ahab plans to scout the land for food and water. Ahab asks Obadiah to help him go to all "the land, to all fountains and brooks" to see if there is any grass to feed his horses and mules. Ahab is not as concerned about the lives of his people as he is about the lives of his livestock. His concern that "not all the beasts" would die gives a hint at the severity of the famine. Animals were probably dying in great numbers. His concern for the animals is probably motivated by his desire to preserve a strong army. When his military strength appears to be depleted because of the drought, Ahab himself joins in the search for grass to feed the animals used by the army. So the king and Obadiah divide the land between the two; one goes to one side of the land and the other goes to another in search of grass.

7 And as Obadiah was in the way, behold, Elijah met him: and he knew him, and fell on his face, and said, Art thou that my lord Elijah? 8 And he answered him, I am: go, tell thy lord, Behold, Elijah is here.

Elijah is on his way to deliver a challenge from God to King Ahab. Obadiah is on his way to scout for grazing land for the animals. Through divine providence, they meet each other on the road. On seeing Elijah, Obadiah recognizes him and falls on his face in reverence to him. The phrase "he knew him" is translated from the Hebrew root word *nakar* (naw-**KAR**), which means to "acknowledge, recognize, or to take knowledge of." Recognizing it was Elijah, Obadiah asks him, "Art thou that my lord Elijah?" It is not that Obadiah was in doubt of the person he has just met. Rather the question indicates a state of surprise and apprehension, as he will explain later (vv. 9–10). Elijah affirms his identity and instructs Obadiah to tell his master, "Behold, Elijah is here." There is a ring of confidence and boldness in Elijah's instruction in contrast to Obadiah's sense of anxiety and apprehension. Elijah has been sent by God to confront the wicked King Ahab directly; therefore he commissions Obadiah to go and notify Ahab of his presence. Obadiah's anxiety is apparent from his answer to Elijah's order.

9 And he said, What have I sinned, that thou wouldest deliver thy servant into the hand of Ahab, to slay me? 10 As the LORD thy God liveth, there is no nation or kingdom, whither my lord hath not sent to seek thee: and when they said, He is not there; he took an oath of the kingdom and nation, that they found thee not.

Moved by fear, Obadiah asks Elijah what crime he has committed that would warrant his death. Asking him to go and declare that he has seen Elijah, Obadiah believes, is tantamount to sending him to death at the hand of his master, Ahab. Then Obadiah states the reasons it is so dangerous to go to Ahab and inform him that Elijah is around. In case Elijah is inclined to doubt the seriousness of the situation, Obadiah swears, "As the LORD thy God liveth." This is a way of stating an absolute truth: The person's statement is just as true as the statement that the Lord lives.

In case Elijah has missed the news, Obadiah tells him, Ahab has sent people to search for Elijah and often encountered many false leads. Since Elijah prophesied about the drought in the land, Ahab declared him a wanted man all over the region. He deployed people everywhere to search for Elijah—"there is no nation or kingdom" where Ahab has not searched Elijah but all had met with failure. If any nation or kingdom reported that Elijah had not been found there, Ahab would force them to swear an oath that they were telling the truth.

11 And now thou sayest, Go, tell thy lord, Behold, Elijah is here. 12 And it shall come to pass, as soon as I am gone from thee, that the Spirit of the LORD shall carry thee whither I know not; and so when I come and tell Ahab, and he cannot find thee, he shall slay me: but I thy servant fear the LORD from my youth.

Obadiah knows if he tells Ahab that "Elijah is here," and the king comes and fails to find him because the Spirit of the Lord had taken him to an unknown place, the king would suspect Obadiah of conspiracy or lying. That would mean his death. Elijah's disappearance earlier and his sudden reappearance now suggested to Obadiah that God's Spirit was miraculously transporting the prophet about. It should be noted that after Elijah's prophesy of the drought, the Lord ordered him to go hide at the brook Cherith. There was no evidence that the Spirit of the Lord carried him away, although that is something the Spirit does at other times (Acts 8:39).

Obadiah questions his presumed punishment. Elijah's command seems like a death sentence, so Obadiah gives a testimony

of his faith: "but I thy servant fear the LORD from my youth." The name "Obadiah" means "servant of God." It is essential to note the role a name can play in a person's life. As it is with most African traditions, so it is with the Jewish culture where names given often reflect a person's character. Such given names may tell a story about a person, his or her family history, an event, a person's mission in life, or an event that took place. Names in the Igbo culture of Nigeria often reflect who God is and what He has done or express gratitude or praise to God. There are several examples in the Bible too. Moses is named because he was "drawn out of water" (Exodus 2:10). The angel of the Lord told Joseph "name him Jesus, for he will save his people from their sins" (Matthew 1:21, NLT). Obadiah likely had godly parents who gave him this name and practiced the true faith from birth in their household. Indeed, he had feared the Lord from his youth. He also lived out the meaning of his name throughout his life.

13 Was it not told my lord what I did when Jezebel slew the prophets of the Lord, how I hid an hundred men of the LORD's prophets by fifty in a cave, and fed them with bread and water? 14 And now thou sayest, Go, tell thy lord, Behold, Elijah is here: and he shall slay me.

Continuing the argument of why he should not go to face Ahab, Obadiah refers to the good work he did. He proved his ultimate loyalty to God during Jezebel's purge by risking his life to rescue and support one hundred prophets of the Lord. Obadiah states his case by rhetorically asking, "Didn't you hear about that time when Jezebel killed God's prophet? I saved one hundred of them, hid them in two caves, I also fed them with bread and water." Obadiah's tone and line of question seem to imply that Elijah had heard the rumor. Obadiah has already risked his life for God and asks not to have to do it again by going to Ahab.

15 And Elijah said, As the LORD of hosts liveth, before whom I stand, I will surely shew myself unto him to day. 16 So Obadiah went to meet Ahab, and told him: and Ahab went to meet Elijah.

After Obadiah's excuses, Elijah assures him with an oath that he will certainly show himself to Ahab that very day. Elijah's statement "As the LORD of host liveth, before whom I stand," is seen in the Jewish culture as more than a promise of assurance; it is a binding pledge, a word of honor that cannot be broken. Armed with this vow and trusting Elijah as a man of integrity, Obadiah goes off and meets the king. He gives him the message from Elijah, and the king goes to the prophet.

17 And it came to pass, when Ahab saw Elijah, that Ahab said unto him, Art thou he that troubleth Israel? 18 And he answered, I have not troubled Israel; but thou, and thy father's house, in that ye have forsaken the commandments of the LORD, and thou hast followed Baalim.

When Ahab saw Elijah, probably in an attempt to intimidate him, he said to him "Art thou he that troubleth Israel?" The question here might suggest that Ahab was in doubt it was Elijah. That wasn't the case. There is no doubt Ahab recognized Elijah the moment he saw him. However, he must have been stunned to see him after years of searching without success. Therefore the translation that tends to accurately portray the essence of the moment is "So, is it really you, you troublemaker of Israel?" (NLT).

Ahab blames Elijah for how he "troubleth" (Heb. *'akar*, aw-**KAR**) Israel. The word refers to the turmoil caused by great worry, in this case, worry about famine and death caused by the drought that has been ravaging the whole land of Israel. Ahab tried to hold Elijah responsible for the drought and to charge him of a crime against the state worthy of death. Of course, Elijah was in a good company because Paul and Jesus would be labeled "trouble makers" (Luke 23:5; Acts 16:20; 17:6).

But Elijah is not intimidated or afraid of the king. Instead of apologies or pleas for pardon, the prophet boldly throws back the charge to Ahab. He tells him that the national calamity is traceable to him and his family because they do not obey God's laws and worship other gods. Therefore the source of Israel's problem was not Elijah or the drought, but Ahab's breaking of the covenant. Definitely, Ahab knew the terms of the covenant and understood that the blessings of the Lord depended on the king and his people's obedience. Instead, following the example of Ahab and his wicked wife Jezebel, Israel abandoned the worship of the true God.

The sin that always gets Israel into trouble is apostasy. During Ahab's reign as king, his wife Jezebel established Baal and Asheroth as the official gods in Israel. Baal images were often in the shape of a bull, representing strength and fertility. Worship of these gods included ritualistic prostitution and meeting near phallus-like (male organ) pillars; it often included child sacrifice. This confrontation between Ahab and Elijah is the prelude of the famous confrontation between Elijah and the prophets of Baal on Mount Carmel.

Sources:

Keil, C.F. and F. Delitzsch. *Commentary on the Old Testament: New Updated Edition.* Electronic Database. Peabody, MA: Hendrickson Publishers, Inc, 1996.

Strong, James. *The New Strong's Exhaustive Concordance of the Bible.* Nashville, TN: Thomas Nelson, 2003.

Say It Correctly

Jezebel. **JEH**-zuh-bell
Obadiah. oh-buh-**DIE**-uh
Asheroth. **AH**-sure-oth

Daily Bible Readings

MONDAY
Elijah with Moses and Jesus
(Mark 9:2-8)

TUESDAY
John the Baptist, the New Elijah
(Mark 9:9-13)

WEDNESDAY
Elijah Sent to King Ahab
(1 Kings 18:1-4)

THURSDAY
Elijah Challenges Baal Prophets
(1 Kings 18:20-26, 30-33, 36-39)

FRIDAY
Elijah in the Wilderness with God
(1 Kings 19:1-8)

SATURDAY
God Commissions Elijah for New Work
(1 Kings 19:9-15)

SUNDAY
King Ahab Meets Prophet Elijah
(1 Kings 18:5-18)

Notes

_____

_____

_____

_____

Teaching Tips

Words You Should Know

A. Holden (Luke 24:16) *krateo* (Gk.)—Restrained

B. Fools (v. 25) *anoetoi* (Gk.)—Lacking the human capacity of understanding

Teacher Preparation

Unifying Principle—Finding Hope Amid Oppression. When life reaches its darkest depth, people wonder if there is still hope for the future. Where can we find the promise of joy that will overcome our deepest sorrow? Luke 24 records the encounter of the Emmaus travelers with the resurrected Jesus.

A. Read the Bible Background and Devotional Reading.

B. Pray for your students and lesson clarity.

C. Read the lesson Scripture in multiple translations.

O—Open the Lesson

A. Begin the class with prayer.

B. Write these words on the board: proxy, stand-in, surrogate, substitute, understudy. Begin by asking how the class heard one or more of these words used—a substitute teacher, a surrogate mother, etc. Lead into Bible study by asking the group to reflect on the significance of someone taking the place of another.

C. Have the students read the Aim for Change and the In Focus story.

D. Ask students how events like those in the story weigh on their hearts and how they can view these events from a faith perspective.

P—Present the Scriptures

A. Read the Focal Verses and discuss the Background and The People, Places, and Times sections.

B. Have the class share what Scriptures stand out for them and why, with particular emphasis on today's themes.

E—Explore the Meaning

A. Use In Depth or More Light on the Text to facilitate a deeper discussion of the lesson text.

B. Pose the questions in Search the Scriptures and Discuss the Meaning.

C. Discuss the Liberating Lesson and Application for Activation sections.

N—Next Steps for Application

A. Summarize the value of following the example of Jesus who sought to serve rather than dominate others.

B. End class with a commitment to proclaim Jesus' crucifixion as the payment for our sins.

Worship Guide

For the Superintendent or Teacher
Theme: Salvation is Sealed
Song: "Man of Sorrows, What a Name!"
Devotional Reading: Philippians 2:1-11

Salvation is Sealed

Bible Background • ISAIAH 52:13-53:12; LUKE 24:1-35
Printed Text • LUKE 24:13-16, 22-35 | Devotional Reading • PHILIPPIANS 2:1-11

Aim for Change

By the end of this lesson, we will IDENTIFY the connections between the Suffering Servant in Isaiah 52:13–53:12 and the resurrected Christ in Luke 24, AFFIRM the joy of knowing the Suffering Servant is the resurrected Jesus Christ, and SHARE the story of the Suffering Servant, who is the resurrected Jesus Christ.

In Focus

Lisa and Michael's son, Timothy, had been on the organ donor waiting list for five years. He was born with a heart defect and needed a new heart. His parents continually prayed for a new heart to become available. The week of Easter, the hospital called and said they had a new heart for Timothy. His parents rushed to the hospital and waited while the doctors operated on him.

Lisa was anxious for her son but also became very upset as she thought about the parents of the child whose heart Timothy would receive. She could not imagine how sad they must feel. After nine hours of surgery, the doctor reported that the operation was a success. Timothy was in recovery and they could see him in just a few more minutes after the doctors made sure he was settled in his room. The parents rejoiced, but Lisa still could not get the other parents out of her mind. She asked if they could meet the family of the organ donor.

The two sets of parents met in a small private room near the operation wing of the hospital. The other mother wanted them to know that her daughter had died, but a part of her would live on in Timothy. Immediately Lisa's despair turned to joy.

We can often get entangled in our own sense of grief and despair. Where do we find hope to spark our joy again?

Keep in Mind

"And their eyes were opened, and they knew him; and he vanished out of their sight" (Luke 24:31, KJV).

"Suddenly, their eyes were opened, and they recognized him.
And at that moment he disappeared!" (Luke 24:31, NLT).

Focal Verses

KJV **Luke 24:13** And, behold, two of them went that same day to a village called Emmaus, which was from Jerusalem about threescore furlongs.

14 And they talked together of all these things which had happened.

15 And it came to pass, that, while they communed together and reasoned, Jesus himself drew near, and went with them.

16 But their eyes were holden that they should not know him.

22 Yea, and certain women also of our company made us astonished, which were early at the sepulchre;

23 And when they found not his body, they came, saying, that they had also seen a vision of angels, which said that he was alive.

24 And certain of them which were with us went to the sepulchre, and found it even so as the women had said: but him they saw not.

25 Then he said unto them, O fools, and slow of heart to believe all that the prophets have spoken:

26 Ought not Christ to have suffered these things, and to enter into his glory?

27 And beginning at Moses and all the prophets, he expounded unto them in all the scriptures the things concerning himself.

28 And they drew nigh unto the village, whither they went: and he made as though he would have gone further.

29 But they constrained him, saying, Abide with us: for it is toward evening, and the day is far spent. And he went in to tarry with them.

30 And it came to pass, as he sat at meat with them, he took bread, and blessed it, and brake, and gave to them.

31 And their eyes were opened, and they knew him; and he vanished out of their sight.

32 And they said one to another, Did not our heart burn within us, while he talked with

NLT **Luke 24:13** That same day two of Jesus' followers were walking to the village of Emmaus, seven miles from Jerusalem.

14 As they walked along they were talking about everything that had happened.

15 As they talked and discussed these things, Jesus himself suddenly came and began walking with them.

16 But God kept them from recognizing him.

22 "Then some women from our group of his followers were at his tomb early this morning, and they came back with an amazing report.

23 They said his body was missing, and they had seen angels who told them Jesus is alive!

24 Some of our men ran out to see, and sure enough, his body was gone, just as the women had said."

25 Then Jesus said to them, "You foolish people! You find it so hard to believe all that the prophets wrote in the Scriptures.

26 Wasn't it clearly predicted that the Messiah would have to suffer all these things before entering his glory?"

27 Then Jesus took them through the writings of Moses and all the prophets, explaining from all the Scriptures the things concerning himself.

28 By this time they were nearing Emmaus and the end of their journey. Jesus acted as if he were going on,

29 but they begged him, "Stay the night with us, since it is getting late." So he went home with them.

30 As they sat down to eat, he took the bread and blessed it. Then he broke it and gave it to them.

31 Suddenly, their eyes were opened, and they recognized him. And at that moment he disappeared!

32 They said to each other, "Didn't our hearts burn within us as he talked with us on the road and explained the Scriptures to us?"

us by the way, and while he opened to us the scriptures?

33 And they rose up the same hour, and returned to Jerusalem, and found the eleven gathered together, and them that were with them,

34 Saying, The Lord is risen indeed, and hath appeared to Simon.

35 And they told what things were done in the way, and how he was known of them in breaking of bread.

33 And within the hour they were on their way back to Jerusalem. There they found the eleven disciples and the others who had gathered with them,

34 who said, "The Lord has really risen! He appeared to Peter."

35 Then the two from Emmaus told their story of how Jesus had appeared to them as they were walking along the road, and how they had recognized him as he was breaking the bread.

The People, Places, and Times

The Suffering Servant. This enigmatic figure arises out of the complex prophecies of Isaiah. Four "songs" celebrate the fate of the Servant of God: He would bring justice to the nations, bring light to the nations, bring healing and forgiveness, and, most of all, He would suffer (see Isaiah 42:1–4; 49:1-7; 50:4–11; 52:13-53:12). But the Servant's suffering would be redemptive, for "with his stripes we are healed" (Isaiah 53:5). One song explicitly identifies the Servant as Israel (Isaiah 49:3). In their original context, these songs seem to have been an attempt to explain the harsh suffering the nation of Israel would pass through during their exile. It was not for sins, but for the healing of the nations. But the Servant was also God's perfect Servant. This perfection transfers the Servant's identification from the nation to the sinless Christ.

This paradigm makes sense of Jesus' suffering and transcends the Messianic title in another way. It pointed to the Gentiles, the nations, as the object of healing and forgiveness. It is no accident that the first account in Acts that portrays an outreach to Gentiles uses this paradigm: Philip uses the passage about the Suffering Servant to tell the Ethiopian eunuch "the good news of Jesus" (see Acts 8:26–35; 1 Corinthians 15:3; Philippians 2:7; Matthew 12:18–21).

How do you deal with the suffering that arises as part of your spiritual journey?

Background

It had been three days since the crucifixion of our Lord. He had risen from the dead, showing Himself at the tomb to Mary Magdalene who then told the other disciples. The synagogue hierarchy, as well as the Roman government, was upset at this turn of events. When the soldiers who had been guarding the tomb came into the city and reported to the chief priest and other leaders the things which had occurred, they called a meeting and then paid the soldiers hush money to say that the disciples had stolen the body of Christ (Matthew 28:1–15). The elders also promised to take care of the governor over the guards.

In fear, the disciples were either in hiding or getting out of town. The disciples wondered if they had believed in vain. Yes, there was Mary Magdalene who said she saw Jesus, but perhaps it was only a spirit. The disciples wanted a personal appearance from Jesus. They had such a traumatic experience, what act of God would be required to restore faith? Jesus recognized their need and met two disciples on the Emmaus Road.

How do you react when God blesses you with a miracle?

At-A-Glance

1. The Sullen Conversation
(Luke 24:13-16)
2. The Scriptural Exhortation (vv. 22-27)
3. The Surprising Revelation (vv. 28-32)
4. The Sudden Proclamation (vv. 33-35)

In Depth

1. The Sullen Conversation (Luke 24:13-16)

Three days after Jesus was crucified and not all of the disciples heard the good news: He is risen! Instead, many are troubled about Jesus' death. They are grieved at the loss of the Master and disappointed that what they thought would occur—the reestablishment of Jewish power—fell through. At this time, we find two disciples, Cleopas and another on the road to Emmaus, a small town a few miles from Jerusalem.

Into the midst of these disciples' gloom comes Jesus. The Master joins the two of them and begins to walk with them as they are reviewing the events of the past few days. They did not recognize the Savior at the outset, as was the case with others (Matthew 28:17; John 20:14; 21:4). Yet, they are so heavily laden that they take the opportunity to unload their feelings of sullenness to a total stranger.

This is quite a picture of humanity's weakness and God's graciousness. Jesus enters right into the midst of the problems of His disciples and lets them talk through it. The disciples were disappointed and depressed, but Jesus was right there when they needed Him most.

2. The Scriptural exhortation (vv. 22-27)

Once these two disciples finish their story, it becomes their visitor's time to talk. And He opens with a shocker: He calls them "fools" ones who were reluctant to believe the Word of God!

Is that not the problem even today? We tend to pay more attention to portions of Scripture that minister to our present needs. The Jews needed a deliverer. Unfortunately, while looking for immediate deliverance, they did not take into account God's entire program for deliverance which included the crucifixion, death, and resurrection of their Deliverer. And now they were ready to throw out the baby with the wash water.

Jesus starts at the beginning and explains to these disciples everything about Himself that is found in the Pentateuch—the first five books of the Bible—and the "prophets"—which includes historic books like 1 and 2 Kings, major prophets like Isaiah, and minor prophets like Jonah. Hiding in plain sight was the divine message that the things were inevitable for the Messiah before the time of His deliverance would come when He would share in the power and glory of God (vv. 25-26; cf. Luke 22:69).

3. The Surprising Revelation (vv. 28-32)

As the two disciples got nearer the village, they extend customary hospitality to Jesus and He agrees to stay the night with them (v. 29). Before retiring for the evening, the three sit down to have a meal. Even though He is the guest, Jesus plays the part of the host. Jesus takes the bread, gives thanks for it, and shares a piece with each of the disciples (cf. Luke 22:19).

At once these two disciples recognize Jesus for who He is, and Jesus immediately disappears from their presence (v. 31). The disciples realize they should have recognized Jesus all along, just by the way He had explained Scripture to them. Listening to the Lord had been like fire burning in their hearts. They had been filled with joy, enthusiasm, and energy.

4. The Sudden Proclamation (vv. 33-35)

They got up at once and returned seven miles to the place they were escaping—Jerusalem, where the apostles and disciples were gathered. When they arrived, they found the group just as full of excitement as they were. For the Lord was indeed risen from the dead and had appeared to Peter. It was then that the two Emmaus disciples explained how Jesus had appeared to them and their recognition of Him when He broke the bread.

The lesson here is simple. After the Lord reveals Himself to His sullen disciples through the Word, He proceeds to further encourage their hearts through the revelation of Himself in their experience. To encounter Christ in His Word and in life dispels disappointment and replaces it with hope.

Search the Scriptures

1. How did Jesus help the disciples understand who He was? (v. 27)

2. How did the disciples come to recognize Jesus? (v. 30)

3. What did these two disciples learn from the others gathered in Jerusalem? (v. 34)

Discuss the Meaning

1. Why did Jesus conceal His identity from the disciples?

2. Jews looked for a conquering hero. Why was it necessary that the Messiah would suffer?

3. Why was it necessary for Jesus to start with Moses and "expound" (teach, explain, interpret) the prophecies concerning Himself? What elements from the Old Testament might He have explained?

Liberating Lesson

The despairing disciples are seen leaving town or hiding. The Gospel had temporarily ceased flowing in this climate of hopelessness and fear. Those who brought words of hope were shrugged off and discredited until Jesus made personal appearances to the disheartened disciples. What they read in the Scriptures promised a conquering hero. What they ignored in the Scriptures was the suffering Messiah.

Many promises and guarantees have been made to disenfranchise minorities in the United States: African Americans, Native Americans, and Latinos. The fulfillment of those promises and guarantees has been long in coming. There is often a discrepancy between what was expected and what has been done. Like the disciples, many have simply gone into despair and started on the "road to Emmaus," to get away from it all, to forget. Gather members of these and other communities and discuss these questions:

1. How are these three communities (African American, Native American, Hispanic) similar to the disciples?

2. Who are some of the messengers of hope in our communities? Have we listened to them? What has been the general reaction?

3. What should we do with gains already made?

4. What can we do to make further progress?

Application for Activation

Are there promises God has made to you and perhaps fulfilled, but because it is not the way you expected, you might not have recognized them? You may even be walking around in despair because you have not seen what you expected. This week, sit down, write out what you have asked God for, what He promised, and what has happened so far. Look for what might have been hidden from your eyes because you were not looking for what God has done concerning your petition and His promise. Thank Him, and allow yourself to move on!

As you continue to read the Bible thoroughly, find Jesus in every book. His presence and the foreshadowing of His great works are found in every single book of the Bible. Take your pencil, start at the beginning and see how much of Jesus you can find.

Follow the Spirit

What God wants me to do:

_____

_____

_____

_____

Remember Your Thoughts

Special insights I have learned:

_____

_____

_____

_____

More Light on the Text

Luke 24:13-16, 22-35

After the account of Jesus' ministry up to His death, Luke gives some details on the post-resurrection. Jesus died on Friday before the Sabbath, and the women could not embalm the body because of the Sabbath, so they waited until Sunday morning. Early Sunday morning, the women went to the tomb and found that it was empty. Two angels dressed in white told them that Jesus had risen from death. When they returned from the tomb, they reported to the eleven and the other followers. After the report of the women, Peter went and witnessed the emptiness of the tomb. The disciples were mourning the death of Jesus, and it was hard to convince them He had risen.

13 And, behold, two of them went that same day to a village called Emmaus, which was from Jerusalem about threescore furlongs.

After the women's report and Peter's confirmation of an empty grave, two of the disciples decided to go to the village of Emmaus which was about seven miles ("about threescore furlongs") from Jerusalem. The precise location of Emmaus is uncertain because there are multiple possible sites that we know of today. The disciples' motive for going there is also unknown. They may have been residents of Emmaus, prevented by the Sabbath and the surrounding events from getting back to their village. Their journey took place on the first day of the week. The phrase "that same day" indicates that this event took place on the day the women went to the tomb. Chronologically it came after the women's visit to the tomb and probably after Peter's visit to the tomb.

14 And they talked together of all these things which had happened. 15 And it came to pass, that, while they communed together and reasoned, Jesus himself drew near, and went with them. 16 But their eyes were holden that they should not know him.

The two disciples discussed the report of the women and that of Peter. The subject of their discussions is not only on the empty tomb but also on the broader succession of events since the betrayal of Jesus. Jesus joined them early in their journey probably. They should have rejoiced because the one whom they were discussing has joined them and is alive. However, they are kept from recognizing Him. Their eyes are "holden" (Gk. *krateo*, krat-EH-oh), meaning "restrained" from recognizing Him. This unbelief might have been due to their sorrow—because Mark 16:10 mentions that the disciples were mourning and weeping—or it may be that God intentionally prevented them from recognizing Him. Mark, also referring to this event, said that Jesus "appeared in another form" (Mark 16:12), so it might also be that Jesus looked different than what the disciples

369

were used to, after the torture of crucifixion and gaining a new, heavenly body.

22 Yea, and certain women also of our company made us astonished, which were early at the sepulchre; 23 And when they found not his body, they came, saying, that they had also seen a vision of angels, which said that he was alive. 24 And certain of them which were with us went to the sepulchre, and found it even so as the women had said: but him they saw not.

The three people walk along together, and Jesus asks about their topic of conservation. The disciples share with Jesus all that had happened with His betrayal and death. The disciples admit they were hoping Jesus was the Messiah but did not think He had accomplished His mission to deliver Israel. The disciples conclude with the most shocking news of all: the new rumor that Jesus is alive.

In two separate scenes, Jesus' resurrection is evident, but they did not immediately believe it. Before this, two angels appeared at the tomb and asked the women why they were seeking the living among the dead, reminding them that Jesus Himself had said that the Son of Man would be arrested, crucified, and resurrected. Also "certain of them which were with us" (i.e. Peter and John, Luke 24:24; cf John 20:3-10) went and confirmed the women's story that the tomb was empty. They, however, did not see the angels or Jesus Himself, so the disciples are still too astonished to decide if they believe the women's "vision" or not.

25 Then he said unto them, O fools, and slow of heart to believe all that the prophets have spoken: 26 Ought not Christ to have suffered these things, and to enter into his glory? 27 And beginning at Moses and all the prophets, he expounded unto them in all the scriptures the things concerning himself.

Jesus has heard enough and rebukes them for not understanding that everything that happened to Him was necessary for fulfilling Scripture. Jesus calls them fools (Gk. *anoetoi*, ah-**NOH**-ey-toy), which indicates that they lacked the human capacity of understanding. "Slow of heart" has a similar meaning. In ancient times, the heart was considered to be the seat of both emotions and cognition, so it was central to a person's whole being. To call the disciples slow of heart indicates that both their intellectual and emotional response to the prophets was not what it should be.

Jesus' reference to His glory (v. 26) may refer to His resurrection, His ascension, or both. The two are separate events in the Gospels and Acts, but they are not mutually exclusive. In the Transfiguration scene, Peter and the other disciples saw Jesus' glory, and Moses and Elijah standing with Him (Luke 9:32–33). The Greek word for "glory" in both passages is *doxa* (**DOHK**-sah), which refers to light and radiance. The Transfiguration scene on the mountain echoes the scene of Moses on the mountain with God where the appearance of God's glory was like fire (Exodus 24:17), after which his face shone (34:29). There is a sense of brightness or radiance in divine glory, both in Exodus and Luke 9. Furthermore, the Transfiguration contains literary parallels to both the Resurrection and the Ascension. Luke's claim that the Messiah needed to suffer all these things to enter into His glory is a complex statement, but in Christ's case one thing is for sure—suffering, arrest, crucifixion, and burial preceded glory.

The term "Moses and all the prophets" refers to all of the Old Testament Scripture because, in Jesus' time, this was an inclusive way of talking about Scripture broadly (see Luke 16:16). The Jews divided their Scriptures into three major sections: the Law, the Prophets, and the Writings. The Law (Heb. Torah) is the

Pentateuch, the first five books of the Bible. These are traditionally attributed to Moses, so sometimes these five books are referenced by his name. Luke will interchangeably use the phrases "Moses and the prophets" and "the law and the prophets." The Prophets (Heb. Nevi'im) is further divided into the former prophets (Joshua, Judges, Samuel, and Kings), the latter prophets (Isaiah, Jeremiah, and Ezekiel), and the Book of the Twelve (the minor prophets). Even though modern Christians classify the former prophets as historical books, and they are not largely prophetic, the Jews see the guiding presence of prophets like Samuel and Nathan in those books. The Writings (Heb. Ketuvim) is comprised of all other canonical Hebrew books, including such different genres as Psalms, Ruth, Ezra, and the Chronicles. These books were not regularly read at weekly synagogue gatherings, but they were just as authoritative in Jewish theology. Many psalms point to Jesus being the Messiah, so perhaps He included these in His explanation on the way to Emmaus. He certainly includes them soon after this when He appears to His disciples (Luke 24:44).

28 And they drew nigh unto the village, whither they went: and he made as though he would have gone further. 29 But they constrained him, saying, Abide with us: for it is toward evening, and the day is far spent. And he went in to tarry with them. Because it was getting late, they urged Him to stay the night with them.

When they reach Emmaus, Jesus acts as though He will continue His journey. Hospitality is part of Jewish culture, as we can remember, for instance, Abraham accommodating the stranger (Genesis 18:2-5). The writer of Hebrews urges his readers to welcome strangers (13:2). This emphasis on hospitality is significant for our time; the practice of this virtue is rare.

Individualism, mistrust, sad experiences of many hosts with their guests, fear of strangers, lack of free time, and other reasons discourage many Christians from extending hospitality. We should be encouraged to practice hospitality with caution and by the discernment the Spirit grants to believers.

The hospitality these two disciples offered to Jesus strongly suggests that they are from Emmaus. If that were not the case, it would have been difficult for them to host someone else, had they been themselves guests. Many people from the villages went to Jerusalem for the Passover (John 11:55), and perhaps these disciples were returning home to Emmaus now that the Passover was done. The powerful way Jesus explained the Scripture to them had certainly also played a role in their invitation. They might have been willing to hear more and the sudden parting of their companion would have deprived them.

30 And it came to pass, as he sat at meat with them, he took bread, and blessed it, and brake, and gave to them. 31 And their eyes were opened, and they knew him; and he vanished out of their sight.

While on the Emmaus Road, the disciples fail to recognize Jesus. Even His explanation from the Scripture and verbal rebuke could not help them. For this reason, once they got indoors and were about to eat, Jesus took the responsibility of sharing the bread. This was the responsibility of the host, not the guest. The breaking of bread that Jesus undertook must have been a particular choice with a known pattern as in His previous breaking of bread (Luke 22:19), to give them now a hint of the identity of their guest.

Their eyes, which had prevented them from recognizing Jesus, were enlightened now by the act of the breaking of bread. Now that they saw the resurrected Savior, they no longer needed to doubt the testimony about the empty tomb from the women or Peter. Instead, their own eyes had seen the Savior. However, they did not enjoy His presence for long because He disappeared from their sight. This disappearance does not make Jesus' resurrected body immaterial. Had it been so, He could not have eaten with them. In addition, we know that Philip was taken away similarly after baptizing the Ethiopian eunuch (Acts 8:39). Though some suggest it was not a supernatural occurrence, the testimony of Jesus' different appearances and sudden disappearances testifies that it was supernatural and may be a characteristic of the resurrected body.

Jesus' fleeting presence parallels the disciples' fleeting understanding of Him, His death, and resurrection; even when He appeared again, they still thought He was a ghost (v. 39). Luke reminds us once again of the fragile human capacity to understand Jesus' purpose, especially in His death and resurrection. We require constant reminders of the true significance of His life.

32 And they said one to another, Did not our heart burn within us, while he talked with us by the way, and while he opened to us the scriptures?

Now that the disciples have recognized Him, they then analyze their journey as having the companionship of a stranger who talked to them. Not only did their "heart burn within" them but also Jesus allowed them to increase their understanding of the Scripture. His explanation of the Scriptures was progressive.

33 And they rose up the same hour, and returned to Jerusalem, and found the eleven gathered together, and them that were with them, 34 Saying, The Lord is risen indeed, and hath appeared to Simon.

Whatever their reason for coming back to Emmaus, it became secondary in comparison to the news of their encounter with Jesus. They headed back to Jerusalem as soon as they could. The people had pressured Jesus to stay with them because it was getting late but did not mind the seven-mile journey back to Jerusalem as night was falling to tell their good news. The eleven were Jesus' appointed apostles; the number was no longer twelve because of Judas' betrayal of Him. It is not clear where the disciples gathered; perhaps they were assembled in the Upper Room.

While they were bringing good news the other disciples assembled, they probably felt an additional sense of enthusiasm because of the news they were bearing: "The Lord is risen indeed, and hath appeared to Simon (Peter)." This suggests that Peter may have gone again to the tomb. He first went there, did not find the body, and was wondering what had happened (24:12). Before leaving for Emmaus, the two disciples had Peter's first report about the empty tomb (24:24); it is, therefore, right to think that this appearance to Peter was later. The disciples now recognize Jesus as who He claimed to be: the Christ. The term "Lord" applied to Him in Greek is *Kurios* (**KOO**-ree-os), and is the rendering of the Old Testament *Yahweh*. Thomas will be the first to clearly state, "My LORD and my God" (John 20:28). In overcoming death, Jesus proves to be the Lord of lords, the King of kings.

35 And they told what things were done in the way, and how he was known of them in breaking of bread.

The two disciples then confirmed to the others by reporting their own encounter with Jesus with an emphasis on the breaking of bread. That Jesus has risen indeed is an expression of victory and hope.

Sources:

Barr, David L. *The New Testament Story: An Introduction*. Belmont, CA.: Wadsworth Publishing Company, 1987, 27.

Keck, Leander E. *The New Interpreter's Bible*. Vol. 9. Nashville, TN: Abingdon Press, 478.

Pfeiffer, Charles F. *Baker's Bible Atlas*. Grand Rapids, MI: Baker Book House, 2003.

Tenney, Merrill Chapin. *Zondervan Pictorial Encyclopedia of the Bible*. Grand Rapids, MI: Zondervan, 1975.

Say It Correctly

Cleopas. **KLEE**-o-pas.
Emmaus. eh-**MAY**-uhs.

Daily Bible Readings

MONDAY
Isaiah Foretells the Suffering Servant
(Isaiah 52:13–53:3)

TUESDAY
Jesus, The Suffering Servant
(Acts 8:26-35)

WEDNESDAY
Jesus Foretells His Death
and Resurrection
(Luke 18:31-34)

THURSDAY
Christ Suffered and Interceded for Sinners
(Isaiah 53:4-11)

FRIDAY
Jesus, Raised from Death
(Luke 24:1-12)

SATURDAY
Jesus' Disciples Report
the Resurrection to Jesus
(Luke 24:17-21)

SUNDAY
The Risen Christ Appears to Disciples
(Luke 24:13-16, 22-35)

Notes

Teaching Tips

Words You Should Know

A. Taken [a wife] (Ezra 10:2) *yashab* (Heb.)—To dwell, or inhabit; to cause to inhabit or cohabit

B. Put away (v. 3) *yatsa'* (Heb.)—To go forth; to cause to go forth

Teacher Preparation

Unifying Principle—Confession and Correction. Sometimes people can lose their sense of direction in life and turn away from the values they once held. How can we recapture the values we once cherished? Ezra led the returned exiles in prayer and repentance, and afterward, he read the book of the Law to which the people listened and then joyously worshiped the Lord.

A. Read the Bible Background and Devotional Reading.

B. Pray for your students and lesson clarity.

C. Read the lesson Scripture in multiple translations.

O—Open the Lesson

A. Begin the class with prayer.

B. Help your group list immoral behaviors that are sometimes called "victimless crimes," such as media piracy, drug abuse, illegal gambling, etc. Ask whether these crimes are truly victimless or whether they, in fact, victimize others.

C. Have the students read the Aim for Change and the In Focus story.

D. Ask students how events like those in the story weigh on their hearts and how they can view these events from a faith perspective.

P—Present the Scriptures

A. Read the Focal Verses and discuss the Background and The People, Places, and Times sections.

B. Have the class share what Scriptures stand out for them and why, with particular emphasis on today's themes.

E—Explore the Meaning

A. Use In Depth or More Light on the Text to facilitate a deeper discussion of the lesson text.

B. Pose the questions in Search the Scriptures and Discuss the Meaning.

C. Discuss the Liberating Lesson and Application for Activation sections.

N—Next Steps for Application

A. Summarize the value of looking to Scripture, not prevailing mores, for ethical guidance.

B. End class with a commitment to pray and fast for the problems of the nation.

Worship Guide

For the Superintendent or Teacher
Theme: Ezra: Faith and Action Preacher
Song: "Give Us Clean Hands"
Devotional Reading: Ezekiel 18:25–32

Ezra: Faith and Action Preacher

Bible Background • EZRA 9-10
Printed Text • EZRA 10:1–12 | Devotional Reading • EZEKIEL 18:25–32

Aim for Change

By the end of this lesson, we will CONTRAST the people's need for repentance with their joyful response to God's word, BELIEVE that God's truth is eternal, and GROW in determination to serve God in our community and beyond.

In Focus

The official board of First Church called a congregational meeting to discuss the church's constitution. The constitution was written 150 years ago and did not reflect the changing racial structure of the community that the church served.

Deacon Robinson, the moderator, called the meeting to order. He explained to the congregation that the church's constitution had to be reformed if First Church was to survive. Some of the older members were concerned that changing the constitution would mean changing the purpose and character of First Church. However, what was really at stake was the way the church would do ministry in the 21st century.

At one point, old Mr. Johnson stood to speak, "I am the longest attending member of this church. I have been here through three pastors. Change can be a scary word for some people. We are creatures of habit, so it is difficult for some of us to accept changes, whether in our worship style or our personal lives. Certainly one of the most frightening times in our lives is when we move to a new apartment or take on a new job. But I have stayed here through many changes, and I can tell you, they have for the most part, been good ones. This church has a good heart, and we want to follow God. His rules aren't going to change. So maybe ours should."

After three hours of intense discussion and mixed emotions, the congregation gave the board the okay to proceed with rewriting the constitution.

This week we will study God's call through Ezra for the nation Israel to change their lives through religious and moral reform. What are some ways God is guiding you to better walk in obedience to His will?

Keep in Mind

"And Ezra the priest stood up, and said unto them, Ye have transgressed … to increase the trespass of Israel. Now therefore make confession unto the LORD God of your fathers, and do his pleasure: and separate yourselves from the people of the land" (from Ezra 10:10–11, KJV).

"Then Ezra the priest stood and said to them: 'You have committed a terrible sin...
You have increased Israel's guilt. So now confess your sin to the LORD, the God of your
ancestors, and do what he demands. Separate yourselves from the people of the land'"
(from Ezra 10:10–11, NLT).

Focal Verses

KJV **Ezra 10:1** Now when Ezra had prayed, and when he had confessed, weeping and casting himself down before the house of God, there assembled unto him out of Israel a very great congregation of men and women and children: for the people wept very sore.

2 And Shechaniah the son of Jehiel, one of the sons of Elam, answered and said unto Ezra, We have trespassed against our God, and have taken strange wives of the people of the land: yet now there is hope in Israel concerning this thing.

3 Now therefore let us make a covenant with our God to put away all the wives, and such as are born of them, according to the counsel of my lord, and of those that tremble at the commandment of our God; and let it be done according to the law.

4 Arise; for this matter belongeth unto thee: we also will be with thee: be of good courage, and do it.

5 Then arose Ezra, and made the chief priests, the Levites, and all Israel, to swear that they should do according to this word. And they sware.

6 Then Ezra rose up from before the house of God, and went into the chamber of Johanan the son of Eliashib: and when he came thither, he did eat no bread, nor drink water: for he mourned because of the transgression of them that had been carried away.

7 And they made proclamation throughout Judah and Jerusalem unto all the children of the captivity, that they should gather themselves together unto Jerusalem;

8 And that whosoever would not come within three days, according to the counsel of the princes and the elders, all his substance should be forfeited, and himself separated

NLT **Ezra 10:1** While Ezra prayed and made this confession, weeping and lying face down on the ground in front of the Temple of God, a very large crowd of people from Israel—men, women, and children—gathered and wept bitterly with him.

2 Then Shecaniah son of Jehiel, a descendant of Elam, said to Ezra, "We have been unfaithful to our God, for we have married these pagan women of the land. But in spite of this there is hope for Israel.

3 Let us now make a covenant with our God to divorce our pagan wives and to send them away with their children. We will follow the advice given by you and by the others who respect the commands of our God. Let it be done according to the Law of God.

4 Get up, for it is your duty to tell us how to proceed in setting things straight. We are behind you, so be strong and take action."

5 So Ezra stood up and demanded that the leaders of the priests and the Levites and all the people of Israel swear that they would do as Shecaniah had said. And they all swore a solemn oath.

6 Then Ezra left the front of the Temple of God and went to the room of Jehohanan son of Eliashib. He spent the night there without eating or drinking anything. He was still in mourning because of the unfaithfulness of the returned exiles.

7 Then a proclamation was made throughout Judah and Jerusalem that all the exiles should come to Jerusalem.

8 Those who failed to come within three days would, if the leaders and elders so decided, forfeit all their property and be expelled from the assembly of the exiles.

9 Within three days, all the people of Judah and Benjamin had gathered in Jerusalem. This took place on December 19, and all the people from the congregation of those that had been carried away.

9 Then all the men of Judah and Benjamin gathered themselves together unto Jerusalem within three days. It was the ninth month, on the twentieth day of the month; and all the people sat in the street of the house of God, trembling because of this matter, and for the great rain.

10 And Ezra the priest stood up, and said unto them, Ye have transgressed, and have taken strange wives, to increase the trespass of Israel.

11 Now therefore make confession unto the LORD God of your fathers, and do his pleasure: and separate yourselves from the people of the land, and from the strange wives.

12 Then all the congregation answered and said with a loud voice, As thou hast said, so must we do.

were sitting in the square before the Temple of God. They were trembling both because of the seriousness of the matter and because it was raining.

10 Then Ezra the priest stood and said to them: "You have committed a terrible sin. By marrying pagan women, you have increased Israel's guilt.

11 So now confess your sin to the LORD, the God of your ancestors, and do what he demands. Separate yourselves from the people of the land and from these pagan women."

12 Then the whole assembly raised their voices and answered, "Yes, you are right; we must do as you say!"

The People, Places, and Times

Mourning. The ancient Hebrews placed a greater emphasis on external, symbolic acts of mourning than modern Western people do. Upon receipt of bad news or in the presence of sudden calamity it was customary to rend the clothes (2 Samuel 1:2) and to sprinkle dirt or ashes upon the head (Joshua 7:6). Hair cloth, which is scratchy and cheap, was adopted as clothing (Isaiah 22:12). Covering the head or lips also indicated mourning (Jeremiah 13:3; Ezekiel 24:17, 22).

A death in the household set in motion an elaborate ceremony of mourning which lasted a week or more. Family members and their friends gathered around the corpse and indulged in lamentations bordering on hysteria. Professional mourners were often called in for a funeral (Jeremiah 9:17–22; Amos 5:16; Matthew 9:23). In earlier times these were probably to protect the living from the spirits

of the departed, who were greatly feared. By Bible times, however, the professional mourning women were used merely as another manifestation of grief for the departed.

How do you make space to mourn? Why is mourning necessary?

Background

For decades, God sent many prophets to warn Israel and Judah that their disobedience and lack of repentance would ultimately lead to their destruction. These prophecies were fulfilled when Assyria conquered Israel in 722 BC, followed by Judah's fall in 586 BC at the hands of Nebuchadnezzar, king of Babylon. It was then that the Temple was destroyed.

However, the Lord did not leave them without hope, promising the return of a remnant of the people, and rebuilding of the Temple (Jeremiah 27:22). This fulfillment began in 538 BC when Zerubbabel led the first group to Jerusalem to start rebuilding the Temple (Ezra 1–6). The priest, Ezra, led a second group's return. Both returns were authorized and aided by unlikely sources—the kings of Persia, who had conquered Babylon. In this passage, we see Ezra addressing the people who appear to be heading down a similar sinful path as their forefathers. His focus becomes to lead the people to not only a physical return but a spiritual return of their hearts toward the one true God.

Where do you see God at work in your life calling you back to Him and rebuilding your faith?

At-A-Glance

1. The Proposal (Ezra 10:1-4)
2. The Oath (vv. 5-6)
3. The Proclamation (vv. 7-8)
4. The Affirmation (vv. 9-12)

In Depth

1. The Proposal (Ezra 10:1–4)

In chapter 9, several leaders brought to Ezra's attention that some of the men had married pagan women and reproduced with them. Ezra's response was one of lament. God had faithfully delivered them from the seventy years in exile as promised, and here they were, seemingly determined to return to the evil that led to their destruction.

As was ancient Jewish custom, Ezra tore his clothes, then plucked the hair from his head and beard, fasted, prayed, confessed, and wept loudly as a public expression of his grief and astonishment.

Such a public outcry compelled others to join him. Shechaniah was moved to publicly confess, on behalf of the community, a sin that he did not commit (his name is not on the list in 10:18–43). It is possible, however, that his disdain and grief were still personal, as he may

have been related to one of the offenders. He is identified as the "son of Jehiel, one of the sons of Elam," and there is a Jehiel listed among the sons of Elam who defied God's law.

Shechaniah's response was filled with hope, support, and admonishment as he proposed a covenant with the Lord—the utmost binding form of commitment. His solution to send away those wives who still worshiped pagan gods, along with their children, was a difficult one to execute but revealed his commitment to holiness, and the law of God.

2. The Oath (vv. 5–6)

Shechaniah's admonition, "Be of good courage, and do it," was reminiscent of God's command to Joshua as he prepared to lead Israel into the promised land after forty years of wandering, due to their fathers' lack of faith (Joshua 1:6). Generations later, Ezra was now tasked with spiritually leading a remnant of exiled Jews back to the Lord. His call of repentance meant all of Israel would have to swear to keep their promise, under the threat of severe punishment. Twice it is mentioned he "arose," indicating Ezra continued to bow before the Lord in mourning.

Even after Israel swore an oath, he did not celebrate—he returned to the room of the high priest's grandson to resume fasting and mourning because of "the unfaithfulness of the returned exiles" (NLT). This is the way in our lives too sometimes. Even after we realize our mistake and determine to correct it, the guilt and shame of the mistake still need to be atoned for.

3. The Proclamation (vv. 7–8)

Each decision led to another with a broader scope. Shechaniah's proposal to Ezra led to the oath taken by the leaders and those gathered locally. Now a proclamation was sent requiring all of the returned exiles in Judah to come to Jerusalem. A timeline of three days was given as those furthest away from Jerusalem would be no more than 50 miles away—or three days' journey. Failure to come would lead to expulsion and confiscation of property, essentially a stripping away of legal rights. Ezra was granted this authority by King Artaxerxes (7:25–26). Ezra knows giving up a wife and her children is a major decision, and some would hesitate to do it. He is insistent on faithfully keeping God's law, though. If these men do not agree to keep the entire law, they will not be permitted to remain under that law. They will be excluded from the community (by being separated from the congregation) and from the inheritance (by forfeiting their property, especially their land).

4. The Affirmation (vv. 9–12)

As commanded, the people gathered after three days, despite the cold December weather. Ezra records the day as "the ninth month, on the twentieth day of the month" (v. 9). This is Kislev 20 on the Jewish calendar, which begins in the spring, placing their ninth month in the winter, rather than the fall. Because the Jewish calendar is lunar, dates sometimes vary from year to year compared to the common Western solar calendar. However, since we can pin Ezra's account to a specific year in King Cyrus' reign, scholars can calculate the date of this particular Kislev 20 as December 19 on our Gregorian calendar (see NLT, v. 9).

The combination of the fear of God's wrath, and being drenched and cold caused them to tremble. Under these circumstances, Ezra boldly confronted their unfaithfulness and called for their confession and action. The whole assembly agreed. Since it was rainy season (November-March) and the assembly was rather large, it would take three months for all marriages to be investigated. In the end, 113 men (including several priests and Levites) were found guilty of ungodly marriages (vv. 18–43).

Search the Scriptures

1. When did God first forbid Israelites to intermarry and why (Deuteronomy 7:1–6)?

2. Whose idea is it to divorce pagan wives and send them away (Ezra 10:3)?

Discuss the Meaning

It has been said that we do not sin in isolation, which means our individual sin can have communal negative consequences. These consequences can still exist even amid repentance.

1. Who are the people immediately affected by some Israelite men's sin, and their subsequent repentance (Ezra 10: 3, 11, 44)? Discuss how this potentially impacted them.

2. How do Ezra's and Shechaniah's responses to hearing of the sin demonstrate their understanding of this reality?

Liberating Lesson

It is tempting to judge Israel when reading about their cycle of sin, judgment, and repentance. They never quite seem to get it right. Israel's story is our story. Like Israel, we do not sin in isolation; the actions of a few can have dire consequences for the masses. Like Israel, we may often find ourselves in a constant cycle of sin. However, our individualistic approach to holiness hinders us. Our pride prevents us from publicly confessing our sin to one another, therefore, rarely do we see examples of a body or individual willingly confessing the sins of others. Yet Scripture shows that such actions please God, often bringing Israel to a place of healing, true repentance, and restoration.

Application for Activation

When confronted with the magnitude of their sin, the returned exiles took repentance seriously, even though the corrective action would be costly. They had tasted God's faithfulness. He kept His promise to allow them to return. Their reasonable act of service would be to worship the one true God.

Consider your own life. Where have you seen God's faithfulness, grace, and mercy? What sin has He revealed to you lately that requires your attention and repentance? What will the corrective action cost you? Spend time in prayer—mourning, bowing, worshiping, fasting if necessary. Then, "Get up, be strong and take action."

Follow the Spirit

What God wants me to do:

_____

_____

_____

_____

Remember Your Thoughts

Special insights I have learned:

_____

_____

_____

_____

More Light on the Text

Ezra 10:1-12

1 Now when Ezra had prayed, and when he had confessed, weeping and casting himself down before the house of God, there assembled unto him out of Israel a very great congregation of men and women and children: for the people wept very sore.

After the return from exile, Ezra made two significant reforms: the reading of the law in Nehemiah 7-10 and the resolution of mixed marriages in this passage. Informed by the leaders about the issue of marriage with foreign wives, Ezra is in great distress for the sin of people and he expresses his complete displeasure on the matter by a fast (9:1–3). During evening sacrifice time which is around 3 p.m., he falls prostrate and delivers a prayer of confession in front of the Temple for all to see. And indeed, his posture brings the whole community (men, women, and children) around to witness what was going on.

Ezra's act of contrition is portrayed by four elements: prayer, confession, weeping, and throwing himself to the ground. The weeping shows Ezra's contrition for the nation's sin, and by throwing himself on the ground, he showed his abject humility before God. Stirred by the example of humility and contrition of Ezra, the crowd also joins in weeping. They weep even more deeply than Ezra. Ezra's example leads them to realize the seriousness of the sin they have committed. Confession is the first step toward reconciliation with God after a sin is committed. Ezra could confess the sin of the people but a more precise decision needed to be taken to demonstrate to God that the remorse of the people is sincere.

2 And Shechaniah the son of Jehiel, one of the sons of Elam, answered and said unto Ezra, We have trespassed against our God, and have taken strange wives of the people of the land: yet now there is hope in Israel concerning this thing.

There is not much background information on Shecaniah, because there are six different individuals with this name mentioned in Ezra—Nehemiah. It is possible either he or his father was married to a foreign woman, in which case, his role as spokesman is understandable because he would have an interest to the resolution of the case. His speech was to acknowledge the sin of the people, which was mixed marriage. The unfaithfulness of the people to God is expressed in terms of breaking an oath. The word used for marriage in this context is *yashab* (Heb. yaw-**SHAB**) is not the normal Hebrew word for marriage (*chathan*, khaw-**THAN**). It means that these marriages were not legally and religiously valid. This is a further indication of the unlawfulness in which the people find themselves. The Law of Moses forbade mixed marriages (Deuteronomy 7:1–4) to prevent the moral and spiritual corruption of the covenant nation.

The ban on marriages with foreign women was not on racial basis, as clearly attested by the Bible with the story of the mixed multitudes in Exodus who left Egypt with the Israelites (Exodus 12:38) or in the story of Rahab who forsook her people and their gods for the God of Israel (Joshua 2) and Ruth the Moabite who married with Boaz (Ruth 1:16; 4). The ban was not therefore on interracial marriage but on interreligious marriage with its obvious danger of drifting the heart of God's people away from God to worship pagan gods like in the case of Solomon. The phrase "married the daughter of a strange god" (Malachi 2:11) can imply the adoption of all or part of the pagan religion as a result of such marriages.

The sin was too serious for a remnant that had just come out of the exile caused by continuous disobedience to the Law. The atmosphere was that of despair with Ezra completely afflicted by the sin and the people's awareness of their trespass. What should be expected in this kind of situation is a heaviness in the hearts and a somber prospect of the future. However, Shecaniah, in spite of the seriousness of the issue, has confidence that there is still hope. The Hebrew word translated "hope" is found only five times in the Old Testament. Apart from this verse, it is found once in 1 Chronicles 29:15 and three times in Jeremiah (14:8; 17:13; 50:7). In this case, it suggests that all is not lost for the people. There is still a glimpse of light. When things do not seem to move in the direction we expect, we can trust God, for He is our hope. No situation is really hopeless because we can amend our ways and God will always bring restoration. Jeremiah finds hope in the mercies of God that are renewed every morning (Lamentations 3:22–24). In the depth of their fall, hope, and restoration are found in repentance, which consists not only in a confession of sin but also in reparation of the wrong.

3 Now therefore let us make a covenant with our God to put away all the wives, and such as are born of them, according to the counsel of my lord, and of those that tremble at the commandment of our God; and let it be done according to the law. 4 Arise; for this matter belongeth unto thee: we also will be with thee: be of good courage, and do it.

Shecaniah proceeds to give concrete actions that should be initiated to restore the people. First, the people have to resolve to separate themselves from their pagan wives and their children. The move may seem too rigid, but there were too many Israelite women abandoned for the foreign ones. Malachi also deals with the same evils mentioned in Ezra and Nehemiah (Malachi 2:13–14). The inference is that the interreligious marriages were made at the expense of the divorce from Israelite women. The reproach of divorcing their lawfully wedded wives is preceded by the reproach of marrying foreign women. The religious influence of the pagan wives on their children would be a stumbling block for preserving the purity of the religion of the Lord.

The decision to dismiss the pagan wives requires a covenant. Yahweh is a covenant-keeping God who never breaks His covenant with His people. Every altering of the covenant comes from people because His faithfulness endures forever. The covenant was formalized by an oath or a gesture performed by the parties involved. This instance is rather a renewal of the covenant that the people themselves have broken. The word used for divorce, *yatsa'* (yaw-**TSAW**), is not the normal Hebrew term for divorce, (*kerithuth*, ker-ee-**THOOT**). It means that religiously there was nothing wrong with sending these women away. The men made no religious covenant with these women "till death do us part," as we do today. The God who dislikes divorce in Malachi 2:16 (cf. Matthew 19:16; Mark 10:9) would not have ordered them to divorce from these women were they lawfully married. Shecaniah, as a spokesperson, engages the whole assembly in respecting the instruction of Ezra and those he will appoint to sort the matter out. They will pledge to keep the law of God.

Second, Shecaniah calls on Ezra to also take his responsibility and lead the people to correct the wrong they have done. Ezra's sadness over the case is also due to the involvement of even some members of the priesthood. Ezra needed a strong backing and Shecaniah's words were timely and appropriate. Now that the people recognize their sin, the procedure to repair and move to restoration was now contemplated. Ezra the leader who is divinely endowed with leadership, vision, and a scholar's understanding of the law has to indicate the way forward. He is assured of the full cooperation of the entire assembly.

5 Then arose Ezra, and made the chief priests, the Levites, and all Israel, to swear that they should do according to this word. And they sware. 6 Then Ezra rose up from before the house of God, and went into the chamber of Johanan the son of Eliashib: and when he came thither, he did eat no bread, nor drink water: for he mourned because of the transgression of them that had been carried away.

Without delay, Ezra indicates the first thing to be done. He invites the leaders representing the entire assembly to take an oath to confirm that they will do as they have promised. All the leaders take the oath on behalf of the group they represent. All these things are conducted in a consensual manner bringing everyone on board. Now there is a binding covenant on the whole community to act according to their own decision.

After Ezra gets assurance that the people will proceed as they promise, he leaves the spot and goes to the room of Jehohanan son of Eliashib to continue with his fast. This room is probably in the Temple where there were rooms for priests. Ezra himself being a priest, so it is lawful for him to stay there.

Ezra extends his fast because the matter is so serious. Though he was assured by the leaders' oath taken that they were ready to make their ways straight with the Lord, he still needs to continue to mourn because of the unfaithfulness. What is not clear is the length of his fast, whether it was just for the night or up to the three days appointed to gather the people.

7 And they made proclamation throughout Judah and Jerusalem unto all the children of the captivity, that they should gather themselves together unto Jerusalem; 8 And that whosoever would not come within three days, according to the counsel of the princes and the elders, all his substance should be forfeited, and himself separated from the congregation of those that had been carried away.

To complete the process of repentance, a gathering is called within three days for all the returnees from exile to come to Jerusalem. This gathering unlike the previous one is not spontaneous but a well-planned formal meeting. These three days were probably necessary so that people from cities far from Jerusalem needed to make the journey.

In case some decided not to come, they were exposed to the confiscation of their property and ex-communication from the assembly. The confiscated properties might have been sent to the Temple treasury (Joshua 6:19, 24).

9 Then all the men of Judah and Benjamin gathered themselves together unto Jerusalem within three days. It was the ninth month, on the twentieth day of the month; and all the people sat in the street of the house of God, trembling because of this matter, and for the great rain.

The assembly takes place on the twentieth day of the ninth month also known as the month of Kislev, which is the third week of December during the middle of the rainy season. The gathering takes place in the square before the Temple of God. People are exposed to physical and emotional challenges. They assemble under heavy rain in a cold season. It is an indication of the gravity of the matter they are dealing with. There is no possibility of postponement considering the urgency of the matter. Emotionally, they are faced with the prospect of separation from people with whom they built up an emotional bond.

10 And Ezra the priest stood up, and said unto them, Ye have transgressed, and have taken strange wives, to increase the trespass of Israel. 11 Now therefore make confession unto the LORD God of your fathers, and do his pleasure: and separate yourselves from the people of the land, and from the strange wives. 12 Then all the congregation answered and said with a loud voice, As thou hast said, so must we do.

Ezra with the authority of the priesthood stands during the gathering to solemnly declare to the people their sin. He designates the sin in clear terms and stresses the gravity of it. The people have brought more condemnation on themselves than previously. The sense is not that they have committed a greater sin but that their guilt is now higher than before because they have witnessed how God deals with unfaithfulness. They are just back from exile, and it seems they did not learn the lesson taught by these years far from their land.

Ezra calls on the assembly to confess their sin to the Lord, "the God of your ancestors." This reminds them of two things: The God of their ancestors is a just and holy one who will not tolerate sin as He did not with their ancestors, but He is also a God of mercy and longsuffering ever ready to forgive those who will come to Him in humility pleading for His mercies. It is therefore important to come back to Him for restoration that generates hope for His presence, guidance, and assistance.

The confession will not be complete until action is taken to repair the wrong that has been done to God. As suggested above by Shecaniah, Ezra reiterates the call to get rid of the foreign wives. Though religiously, it was expected to send these women away, socially it had to be done wisely to avoid creating a social crisis. The dismissed women and their children would go back to their families. In unison, the whole assembly agreed to do as recommended by Ezra.

Sources:

Alden, R. L. *The Expositors Bible Commentary*. Vol. 7. F. E. Gaebelein, ed. Grand Rapids, MI: Zondervan, 1985.

Baldwin, J.G. *Tyndale Old Testament Commentaries: Haggai, Zechariah, Malachi*. D.J. Wiseman, ed. Downers Grove, IL: InterVarsity Press, 1972.

Douglass, J.D. and Merrill C. Tenney. *The Zondervan Bible Dictionary*. Grand Rapids, MI: Zondervan, 1967. 561.

Fensham, C.E. *The New International Commentary on the Old Testament: The Book of Ezra and Nehemiah*. Grand Rapids, MI: Wm.B. Eerdmans, 1982.

Keener, Craig S. *The IVP Bible Background Commentary: Old Testament*. Downers Grove, IL: Intervarsity Press, 2000.

Kidner, D. *The Tyndale Old Testament Commentaries: Ezra and Nehemiah*. D. J. Wiseman, ed. Downers Grove, IL: InterVarsity Press, 1979.

Noss, P. A., and K. J. Thomas. *An Handbook on Ezra and Nehemiah*. United Bible Society, 2005.

Ryrie, Charles C. *Ryrie Study Bible*. Chicago, IL: Moody Press. 1986.

Walvoord, John F., and Roy B. Zuck, eds. *The Bible Knowledge Commentary: Old Testament*. Wheaton, IL: Victor Books, 1985.

Yamauchi, E. *The Expositor's Bible Commentary*. Vol. 4. F. E. Gaebelein, ed. Grand Rapids, MI: Zondervan, 1988.

Zondervan Study Bible. Grand Rapids, MI: Zondervan Publishers, 2002.

Say It Correctly

Zerubbabel. zeh-**ROO**-bah-bell.
Shechaniah. sheh-**KAH**-nee-uh.
Jehiel. **JEH**-hee-ell.
Elam. **EE**-lam.
Artaxerxes. ar-tah-**ZERK**-sees.
Jehohanan. jeh-**HOE**-ha-non.
Eliashib. ee-**LIE**-uh-sheev.
Kislev. **KEES**-lev.

Daily Bible Readings

MONDAY
A Light to Jews and Gentiles
(Acts 26:19–23)

TUESDAY
Live the New Life in Christ
(Ephesians 4:17–24)

WEDNESDAY
Keep Land Faithful to Godly Practices
(Leviticus 18:24–30)

THURSDAY
Ignoring God's Laws Leads to Judgment
(Zechariah 7:8–14)

FRIDAY
People Anxious to Hear the Law
(Nehemiah 7:73–8:6)

SATURDAY
People Respond Actively to the Law
(Nehemiah 8:9–12)

SUNDAY
Committed to a Life of Obedience
(Ezra 10:1–12)

Notes

Teaching Tips

Words You Should Know

A. Pool (Nehemiah 2:14) *berekah* (Heb.)—A reservoir at which camels kneel as a resting place

B. Reproach (v. 17) *kherpah* (Heb.)—Disgrace or shame; a cause or occasion of blame, discredit, or disgrace

C. Portion (v. 20) *kheleq* (Heb.)—An inheritance; a tract of land

Teacher Preparation

Unifying Principle—Initiating Renewal. People are often contemplative before they make major decisions. How does one or should one react after careful consideration of a major decision? Nehemiah set out to rebuild Jerusalem's wall after praying and surveying its ruins.

A. Read the Bible Background and Devotional Reading.

B. Pray for your students and lesson clarity.

C. Read the lesson Scripture in multiple translations.

O—Open the Lesson

A. Begin the class with prayer.

B. Review practices of your congregation that provide for the security of the church grounds and of worshipers. Discuss when security preparations cross the line from prudent to indicating a lack of faith (see Ezra 8:22).

C. Have the students read the Aim for Change and the In Focus story.

D. Ask students how events like those in the story weigh on their hearts and how they can view these events from a faith perspective.

P—Present the Scriptures

A. Read the Focal Verses and discuss the Background and The People, Places, and Times sections.

B. Have the class share what Scriptures stand out for them and why, with particular emphasis on today's themes.

E—Explore the Meaning

A. Use In Depth or More Light on the Text to facilitate a deeper discussion of the lesson text.

B. Pose the questions in Search the Scriptures and Discuss the Meaning.

C. Discuss the Liberating Lesson and Application for Activation sections.

N—Next Steps for Application

A. Summarize the value of balancing secular and sacred concerns.

B. End class with a commitment to pray for the safety of your church's operation in a secular society.

Worship Guide

For the Superintendent or Teacher
Theme: Nehemiah: The Captive
Cupbearer Rebuilds a Nation
Song: "To the Work!"
Devotional Reading: Daniel 9:4-6, 15-19

Nehemiah: The Captive Cupbearer Rebuilds a Nation

Bible Background • NEHEMIAH 2:11-20; 13:1–22
Printed Text • NEHEMIAH 2:11-20 | Devotional Reading • DANIEL 9:4-6, 15–19

Aim for Change

By the end of this lesson, we will EXAMINE why Nehemiah decided to restore the wall of Jerusalem and reform/revive the Sabbath law, APPRECIATE Nehemiah's feelings and behavior in restoring the wall and reforming Jewish worship, and IDENTIFY ways to restore worn parts of the faith community and revive traditions that honor God.

In Focus

Gathered before Georgia were the leaders of one of the area churches in her denomination. The church was about 20 years old, and until a week ago, they all thought that it was in good condition. Then, the pastor and treasurer had both abruptly resigned, and the remaining church leaders discovered that the church's funds had been seriously mismanaged. The church's checking account was overdrawn by more than $18,000, and checks were being returned for insufficient funds.

The denomination had called this emergency meeting of the Trustee Board. Georgia, the denomination's chief accountant, had only had two days to prepare for it. She had sifted through the years of statements and reports.

While her days had been spent sifting through piles of paper looking for answers, her evenings had been spent asking God how He wanted her to handle this awful situation. Despite the carelessness that had been shown, Georgia knew that these people were hurting. Yes, she wanted to blame them for not recognizing the church's situation for so long and take some corrective actions, but all of that could wait. What they needed right now was to know that she cared about them and what they were going through.

Georgia wisely sought the Lord's counsel about how to proceed, rather than relying solely on her own abilities. When have you shown this wisdom? When have you wished you had acted on God's counsel?

Keep in Mind

"Then said I unto them, Ye see the distress that we are in, how Jerusalem lieth waste, and the gates thereof are burned with fire: come, and let us build up the wall of Jerusalem, that we be no more a reproach" (Nehemiah 2:17, KJV).

"But now I said to them, 'You know very well what trouble we are in. Jerusalem lies in ruins, and its gates have been destroyed by fire. Let us rebuild the wall of Jerusalem and end this disgrace!'" (Nehemiah 2:17, NLT).

Background

Nehemiah is the cupbearer to King Artaxerxes I of Persia, an honorable and prestigious position of great trust. While serving in this position, Nehemiah receives visitors from Jerusalem and asks them about events going on back home (Nehemiah 1:1–2). They give him a very discouraging report about the disgraceful condition of the people and the deplorable state of the city. The crumbling walls had left the city, the Temple, and the people vulnerable to attack and gave their enemies cause to ridicule. Although Ezra was an excellent spiritual leader, the people lacked political leadership. They needed someone to motivate them, show them where to begin, and to direct their activities. On receiving this news, Nehemiah weeps and grieves for some days, fasting and praying. He knows he has to do something about the city's crumbling infrastructure, but what and how?

After prayer, Nehemiah is still very distressed and the king asks what troubling him (2:1–2). By God's grace, Nehemiah obtains permission from the king to go to his native country and rebuild its walls and gates. Nehemiah left the comfort of a king's palace to return to his ancient homeland to challenge his countrymen to get busy and reconstruct the walls. Armed with letters of safe passage and a full military escort provided by the king, Nehemiah faced the almost 1,000-mile trip to Jerusalem.

How have you used your position of privilege to help others?

At-A-Glance

1. Survey the Situation
(Nehemiah 2:11–15)
2. Calls the People to Work (vv. 16–18)
3. Respond to Opposition (vv. 19–20)

In Depth

1. Survey the Situation (Nehemiah 2:11–15)

Although he has the full support of the king, Nehemiah does not immediately rush into action or expose his plan to the people (2:11–12). Instead, Nehemiah secretly inspects the wall to assess the damage and estimate the work needed to rebuild it. After staying in Jerusalem for three days, Nehemiah embarked at night on a survey of the damage. The walls of Jerusalem were in such a state of ruin that rubble and debris had strewn the valley floor so that he could not even ride his mount through it. During his late-night ride, he finds that the reports he had received were true: The walls of Jerusalem and its gates are in ruins. Nehemiah says nothing to anyone until he first explores the extent of the damage for himself. We can take a page from Nehemiah's playbook when we are facing recovery in our own lives. First, we have to acknowledge the truth for ourselves. Then—and only then—should we tell others.

2. Call the People to Work (vv. 16–18)

Nehemiah calls a meeting of the city leaders and discloses why he has come to Jerusalem. Nehemiah appeals to the leaders' pride in Jerusalem as God's holy city. Next, he appeals to their love for God and their desire not to bring Him shame. He acknowledges God and His divine guidance in the plan to rebuild the wall. Then, he tells of King Artaxerxes' support.

Nehemiah uses the pronoun "we" rather than "you" or "I." Wise leaders understand they must identify themselves with the need to motivate others to assist them. This reminds us that a Christian can't live an independent life, because we are called to function in the community of believers.

The religious, political, and other leaders overwhelmingly accept Nehemiah's plans. Collectively, they say, "Let us rise up and build" (v. 18). Nehemiah challenges and inspires the people, and God strengthens them to complete the work. Spirit-led projects carried out under spiritual guidance succeed when measured by God's definition of success.

3. Respond to Opposition (vv. 19–20)

Anytime people start the process of recovery, they should expect to meet with some resistance. The Scriptures tell us that Sanballat, Tobiah, and Geshem tried to stop Nehemiah's rebuilding effort. All three were political leaders from the Persian provinces surrounding Judah to the north, south, and west. Understandably, they did not want Jerusalem to become a strong and well-defended city, because trade routes and economic advantages would shift in favor of Jerusalem. Hence, their attempt to stop Nehemiah was politically motivated.

Nehemiah could have argued that what he was doing had higher political backing. Instead, Nehemiah simply stood on the promises of God. He did not waste a minute of his precious time or energy trading insults with them; he simply spoke the truth. Nehemiah tells them that the land has been given to the Children of Israel, and Sanballat, Tobiah, and Geshem did not have any right to even be in the land of Jerusalem (v. 20).

Whenever we are attacked by circumstances contrary to God's Word, we need to speak the Word to our tormentors and ourselves. We can do this in boldness and rest in God's promise that we now have a share of that great inheritance when Jesus returns and God's kingdom finally comes.

Nehemiah worked carefully to bring the Israelite leaders on board with his plan to rebuild. Why not try to make these foreigners into allies?

Search the Scriptures

1. When Nehemiah revealed his plan, what was the people's response? (Nehemiah 2:18)

2. What did the people in Jerusalem do to show that they were ready to follow Nehemiah in rebuilding the wall? (v. 18)

Discuss the Meaning

1. Why is it important to begin any task with prayer?

2. Making decisions is a part of life. Sometimes what we decide to do or say forces us to oppose the majority. How do we know whether we have made the right decision? How do we encourage people to stand by their decisions?

3. Nehemiah was able to motivate the other Jews to embrace his vision of rebuilding the walls of Jerusalem. What factors determine how flexible you are in sharing a vision with people? When are you flexible, and when are you more assertive?

Liberating Lesson

Many American communities are crumbling around the people who live there. Slumlords, a lack of funding rooted in historical inequities, and unethical policing practices account for much of the problem, but cleanliness and maintenance are problems the residents can solve. Should a church's vision for its community include upkeep and maintenance? What are some ways the church can motivate members to clean up and maintain their neighborhoods? What are some ways the church can pressure the cities' leaders as Nehemiah did so that they take action?

Application for Activation

In today's lesson, we read that once Nehemiah safely arrived in Jerusalem, he went around inspecting the city walls at night and conducted a thorough survey of exactly what damages needed to be repaired. If we are truly concerned about rebuilding parts of our lives, we need to prayerfully assess what will be required. This week, make this a target of prayer in your own life. Be honest with yourself. Ask God to show you exactly what steps need to be taken. Only when we change lazy or sinful habits can we be freed to be what God wants us to be.

Follow the Spirit

What God wants me to do:

_____

_____

_____

_____

Remember Your Thoughts

Special insights I have learned:

_____

_____

_____

_____

More Light on the Text

Nehemiah 2:11–20

The book of Nehemiah is about one man's love, dedication, and faithfulness to both his God and his country. It is a journal or memoir of one man's determination to make a difference for his people—to rebuild, in spite of enormous opposition from their enemies and detractors. The book demonstrates how one person can motivate a whole nation to accomplish things that they would not be able to do under normal circumstances. It demonstrates Nehemiah's love for his nation, his personal sacrifice of an enviable position (2:5) for the cause of his people. This kind of sacrifice exemplifies the type of unselfish and motivational service always

needed when a great work is to be achieved. The narrative also demonstrates God's faithfulness and authority over humankind's affairs, when we put all our problems, wills, and desires into His hands.

11 So I came to Jerusalem, and was there three days. 12 And I arose in the night, I and some few men with me; neither told I any man what my God had put in my heart to do at Jerusalem: neither was there any beast with me, save the beast that I rode upon.

Armed with the king's permission, letters for free passage through the territories, and authorization for the supply of materials for the reconstruction, Nehemiah heads home. He arrives in Jerusalem and spends three days without anyone's knowledge of his presence, most likely praying and resting after a long journey (cf. Ezra 8:32).

After the three days of rest, Nehemiah takes a few men with him by night and surveys the city. He rides around the city to see for himself the extent of destruction. The reason for going by night and taking just a few men is obvious: He wants to keep his actions secret until he ascertains the magnitude of the damage and extent of work to be done. The statement, "neither was there any beast with me, save the beast that I rode upon" indicates that he went around the city without his entourage, which accompanied him from Persia (Nehemiah 2:9–12). The office of a cupbearer in ancient times was a high and respectable position. Such a tour with a person of such prominence, the king's cupbearer, would require a big entourage and fanfare, but Nehemiah chose to tour the city privately to avoid public exposure or attracting attention.

13 And I went out by night by the gate of the valley, even before the dragon well, and to the dung port, and viewed the walls of

Jerusalem, which were broken down, and the gates thereof were consumed with fire. 14 Then I went on to the gate of the fountain, and to the king's pool: but there was no place for the beast that was under me to pass. 15 Then went I up in the night by the brook, and viewed the wall, and turned back, and entered by the gate of the valley, and so returned.

Verses 13–15 give a detailed record of the tour. The mention of different areas and sections of the wall in these verses indicate that he made a thorough inspection and study of the situation to understand the extent of work to be done. The recurring phrase, "I went out by night …" or "… in the night" (vv. 12–13, 15) could show that it takes him more than one night, perhaps several nights to complete the survey: section by section. There is debate as to how far west the city stretched at this time, but we can use the information provided here to track Nehemiah's route around the southern half of the city. The "gate of the valley" is on the southwestern side of Jerusalem, and the "dung port" is at its southern tip. Nehemiah's trek then turns north by the fountain and pool, where he continues on foot to the brook running on Jerusalem's eastern side. From this vantage point, he can see much of the rest of the city walls, including those that stretch north of his position and around the Temple. He then retraces his path back into the city. He finds the ruins just as the delegates have reported—the walls of Jerusalem are broken and their gates consumed with fire. In some of the places, such as the Fountain Gate and King's Pool, the rubble is so extensive that his mount could not get through (v. 14).

16 And the rulers knew not whither I went, or what I did; neither had I as yet told it to the Jews, nor to the priests, nor to the nobles, nor to the rulers, nor to the rest that did the work.

Nehemiah did not tell anyone— the priests, nobles, rulers, or even the rest of the people— what the Lord has led in his heart and the favor He granted him through the king to rebuild the walls. Why did he keep it a secret? One reason is to hide it from their enemies (v. 10) until everything is ready and all plans are finalized so they cannot jeopardize the work. Nehemiah has already seen that Sanballat and Tobiah want to oppose this work and will soon see them do it. Another reason would probably be that he kept them away from the people until everything was in place to avoid discouragement for them because of the immensity of the job facing them.

17 Then said I unto them, Ye see the distress that we are in, how Jerusalem lieth waste, and the gates thereof are burned with fire: come, and let us build up the wall of Jerusalem, that we be no more a reproach.

After getting a handle on the situation, Nehemiah now calls an assembly and tells the leaders his plans. He first calls their attention to their plight, reminding them of their suffering, and the deplorable condition of their city. Nehemiah, as an individual, could be excluded from the suffering (being one of the highest positions of that time, a cupbearer to the most powerful king); however, he identifies with the suffering of his people. He sees himself as a member of the suffering community. He never allowed his personal comfort in the king's palace blind him to the suffering of his people in Judah or to separate him from the community of his people. Rather he includes himself saying, "Ye see the distress that we are in." Great leaders never allow personal gains and comfort entice them away from their calling or accomplishing what they have been called to do.

He reminds them of the humiliation facing them as a result of the desolation of their proud city and "how Jerusalem lieth waste, and the

Teaching Tips

Words You Should Know

A. Reproach (Lamentations 5:1) *kherpah* (Heb.)—Shame, scorn, and disgrace

B. Deliver (v. 8) *paraq* (Heb.)—Redeem

Teacher Preparation

Unifying Principle—Overcoming Losses and Brokenness. People seek restoration when their possessions are taken and relationships are broken. How does one cope with the loss of that which is very important? The writer of Lamentations trusted that God would re-establish a relationship with Israel.

A. Read the Bible Background and Devotional Reading.

B. Pray for your students and lesson clarity.

C. Read the lesson Scripture in multiple translations.

O—Open the Lesson

A. Begin the class with prayer.

B. Ask participants to talk about a song that they used to listen to when they suffered a broken or strained relationship.

C. Have the students read the Aim for Change and the In Focus story.

D. Ask students how events like those in the story weigh on their hearts and how they can view these events from a faith perspective.

P—Present the Scriptures

A. Read the Focal Verses and discuss the Background and The People, Places, and Times sections.

B. Have the class share what Scriptures stand out for them and why, with particular emphasis on today's themes.

E—Explore the Meaning

A. Use In Depth or More Light on the Text to facilitate a deeper discussion of the lesson text.

B. Pose the questions in Search the Scriptures and Discuss the Meaning.

C. Discuss the Liberating Lesson and Application for Activation sections.

N—Next Steps for Application

A. Summarize the value of sharing grief with other believers.

B. End class with a commitment to pray for a deeper trust in God during difficult times.

Worship Guide

For the Superintendent or Teacher
Theme: A Plea for Restoration
Song: "It Is Well With My Soul"
Devotional Reading:
Lamentations 3:22-33

A Plea for Restoration

Bible Background • LAMENTATIONS 5
Printed Text • LAMENTATIONS 5 | Devotional Reading • LAMENTATIONS 3:22-33

Aim for Change

By the end of this lesson, we will UNDERSTAND why the writer of Lamentations pleaded with God for the restoration of Israel, SENSE the writer's feelings over the oppression of his nation, and PRAY for and engage in the restoration of broken relationships with God.

In Focus

Karen and Tim stood with their neighbors, in shock over the fire that was eating up their apartment complex. As they stared in disbelief, Karen broke down and began to wail, "I can't believe what has happened, we lost everything, and so many people have been displaced from their homes all because of someone's negligence."

The fire had spread quickly, taking one whole building and threatening another. The first responders were still putting out the last flames and seeing to those who had breathed too much smoke. Tim wanted to do something to help comfort his neighbors but didn't want to leave Karen, who was heartbroken over the loss of their home. "It's not just the possessions, Tim. It's our history, our life together, your mother's photo albums, my paintings. And now it's all in ashes," she exclaimed. "How can we rebuild?"

Tim suggested they pray, but Karen was still too angry. Overcome with emotion she asked, "God, where are You in this? What did we do to deserve this?"

Tim held his wife and consoled her. "We need to believe God, Karen. We have to trust His love and His promises to never leave us, and that He will sustain us through this crisis." Tim heard Karen take several slow, calming breaths. "Let's just start with figuring out where to stay for the night."

Karen nodded, "Let's call the pastor and his wife. They'll know someone with a guest room."

How has God's Word given you hope amid a crisis?

Keep in Mind

"Turn thou us unto thee, O LORD, and we shall be turned; renew our days as of old" (Lamentations 5:21, KJV).

"Restore us, O LORD, and bring us back to you again! Give us back the joys we once had!"
(Lamentations 5:21, NLT).

Focal Verses

KJV **Lamentations 5:1** Remember, O LORD, what is come upon us: consider, and behold our reproach.

2 Our inheritance is turned to strangers, our houses to aliens.

3 We are orphans and fatherless, our mothers are as widows.

4 We have drunken our water for money; our wood is sold unto us.

5 Our necks are under persecution: we labour, and have no rest.

6 We have given the hand to the Egyptians, and to the Assyrians, to be satisfied with bread.

7 Our fathers have sinned, and are not; and we have borne their iniquities.

8 Servants have ruled over us: there is none that doth deliver us out of their hand.

9 We gat our bread with the peril of our lives because of the sword of the wilderness.

10 Our skin was black like an oven because of the terrible famine.

11 They ravished the women in Zion, and the maids in the cities of Judah.

12 Princes are hanged up by their hand: the faces of elders were not honoured.

13 They took the young men to grind, and the children fell under the wood.

14 The elders have ceased from the gate, the young men from their musick.

15 The joy of our heart is ceased; our dance is turned into mourning.

16 The crown is fallen from our head: woe unto us, that we have sinned!

17 For this our heart is faint; for these things our eyes are dim.

18 Because of the mountain of Zion, which is desolate, the foxes walk upon it.

19 Thou, O LORD, remainest for ever; thy throne from generation to generation.

20 Wherefore dost thou forget us for ever, and forsake us so long time?

NLT **Lamentations 5:1** LORD, remember what has happened to us. See how we have been disgraced!

2 Our inheritance has been turned over to strangers, our homes to foreigners.

3 We are orphaned and fatherless. Our mothers are widowed.

4 We have to pay for water to drink, and even firewood is expensive.

5 Those who pursue us are at our heels; we are exhausted but are given no rest.

6 We submitted to Egypt and Assyria to get enough food to survive.

7 Our ancestors sinned, but they have died— and we are suffering the punishment they deserved!

8 Slaves have now become our masters; there is no one left to rescue us.

9 We hunt for food at the risk of our lives, for violence rules the countryside.

10 The famine has blackened our skin as though baked in an oven.

11 Our enemies rape the women in Jerusalem and the young girls in all the towns of Judah.

12 Our princes are being hanged by their thumbs, and our elders are treated with contempt.

13 Young men are led away to work at millstones, and boys stagger under heavy loads of wood.

14 The elders no longer sit in the city gates; the young men no longer dance and sing.

15 Joy has left our hearts; our dancing has turned to mourning.

16 The garlands have fallen from our heads. Weep for us because we have sinned.

17 Our hearts are sick and weary, and our eyes grow dim with tears.

18 For Jerusalem is empty and desolate, a place haunted by jackals.

21 Turn thou us unto thee, O LORD, and we shall be turned; renew our days as of old.

22 But thou hast utterly rejected us; thou art very wroth against us.

19 But LORD, you remain the same forever! Your throne continues from generation to generation.

20 Why do you continue to forget us? Why have you abandoned us for so long?

21 Restore us, O LORD, and bring us back to you again! Give us back the joys we once had!

22 Or have you utterly rejected us? Are you angry with us still?

The People, Places, and Times

The Exile. Israel and Judah were told that God would lead them away into exile if they became unfaithful to the covenant He made with them through Moses (Deuteronomy 28:36-37, 64; 29:28). When they did break that covenant, Israel and Judah underwent periods of exile and were removed from the Promised Land. Consequently, the Jews were scattered throughout the known world, where they became known as the Diaspora, which is the Greek word for "scattering." The Northern Kingdom of Israel was conquered by the Assyrians in 722 BC. Judah was also defeated three times by the Babylonians. In 605, King Nebuchadnezzar took the royal court and the ablest men of Judah into Babylon. He returned in 597 BC. During the final fall of Jerusalem to Babylonia in 586 BC, the city was burned, and the remaining people of Judah were deported, from which only a remnant returned 70 years later. The phrase "the Exile" is most often associated with the 70-year Babylonian captivity of Judah. The lasting effects of the Exile were profound. Aside from the stress of being removed from their homes and loved ones, while in captivity they had the status of slaves, were unfamiliar with the language, and were sometimes required to worship idols (Daniel 3:4-7).

Background

While some scholars question the authorship of Lamentations, it is traditionally attributed to the prophet Jeremiah as an appendix to his book of prophesy. Jeremiah was known as the "weeping prophet" who spent over forty years calling out Israel's displeasing ways and pleading with them to repent and avert the promised doom for disobedience. After years of predicted warnings of destruction to their homeland, the worst had come to pass. Jerusalem and Judah had been destroyed, and the Israelites were overtaken by enemies on every side until they were dispossessed from their land and taken into captivity. The major theme of Lamentations 1-4 expresses personal and community cries to God for their affliction. However, right in the middle of those cries, Jeremiah digs deep and pivots to place his hope in the God of his salvation (Jeremiah 3:21-26). Jeremiah provides a voice to their overwhelming grief: repentance and hope in God's love and mercy because of His covenant. The book of Lamentations continues to serve as a significant part of Jewish life. The entire book is read publicly as a part of an annual solemn observance to remember the Temple's destruction in 587 BC (Jeremiah 52:12-13).

How are Negro spirituals, hymns, or music from the Civil Rights Movement connecting points between past and current struggles?

401

At-A-Glance

1. A Plea to Consideration
(Lamentations 5:1-6)
2. A Plea For Sins (vv. 7-16)
3. A Plea For Mercy (vv. 17-22)

In Depth

1. A Plea for Consideration (Lamentations 5:1-6)

Jeremiah, as an eyewitness to the calamity, paints the scenes of the devastation through these laments. The people of Israel were enduring great horror and punishment. Such disgrace included loss of their inheritance. Those God commanded them to protect and provide for (widows and orphans) were unprotected as a result of their sins rooted in idolatry and apostasy. The prophet's petition was for the Lord God to intently look upon the reproach and suffering of His covenant people. In essence, all the curses for disobedience God proclaimed through Moses were realized (Deuteronomy 28:15-68). God's commands are sure and yet He provided Israel with opportunity after opportunity through the voice of His prophets to repent, turn from their wicked ways, and return to Him. Israel suffered consequences for no longer depending on God as the source of their life, provision, safety, and identity.

How can we look at troubling times through the lens of God's Word and realize what went wrong?

2. A Plea For Sins (vv. 7-16)

In his distress, Jeremiah calls out that his generation's suffering was a direct result of the sins from past generations. When God formed Israel as a nation, He warned them that iniquity would follow them through generations (Exodus 20:4-5, 34:6-7). But note that God is not temperamental and would later refute the Israelites' idea that the suffering experienced in the current generation was a result of their ancestors (Jeremiah 31:29-30, Ezekiel 18:1-5).

The prophet's lament in these stanzas shares how the basis of their community life had been uprooted and was in peril. The elders were not esteemed or in their rightful place to execute justice in their land. The women were sexually assaulted. There was no one to protect them because the young men were burdened from survival. On behalf of the community, Jeremiah woefully cries out that there is no joy in living, and the glory of Israel is gone as past and present sins are taking their toll.

How can we accept responsibility before God and others for our sins and turn around to do what pleases Him?

3. A Plea For Mercy (vv. 17-22)

Jeremiah expresses how he and his people are heartsick over what they have experienced and are at the end of themselves because the home in which they placed so much of their identity as a people is destroyed. He ends this last stanza of the lament by transitioning his hope to God. He reminds himself of God's power and authority in that His throne remains forever. God's heavenly throne continues even after God's earthly throne in Jerusalem is gone. As any human would amid the depth and length of this suffering, Jeremiah questions why God continues to allow their suffering. Although he feels forsaken by God, he still unshakably believes that God is eternal and almighty. He pleads in true penitence for God to show mercy by restoring and renewing His people and their land. Jeremiah strikes a balance between owning the nation's sins, remembering God's love and mercy, and—with human limitations—still questioning if God will still reject his pleas.

In what ways has God made His love and mercy known to us?

Search the Scriptures

1. How does Jeremiah open his prayer for God's attention to their suffering (Lamentations 5:1-6)?

2. Where does Jeremiah shift his lament to reflect on God's power (v. 19)?

Discuss the Meaning

1. Does Jeremiah's reflection of his people's suffering capture the pain felt by all of the Jews? Is he effective?

2. How does remembering God's sovereignty shift the pleas in this lament to hope in His mercy?

Liberating Lesson

As a community, we have our part for action and inaction as it relates to the status of socio-economic conditions where we live. We are empowered to make our communities safer and more economically sound by working cooperatively, and as in the past, the Church must lead the way. As a people, we have survived the atrocities of slavery, segregation, and systemic injustice with God as our source and strength. As a resilient people, we have to continue to pass down the heritage of how to strategically fight and pray—working across the generations—to realize the true transformation and restoration God promises when we look to Him.

Application for Activation

Life gets discouraging and lamenting on the ills of our world is a common natural response. But after acknowledging the pain, we must turn that complaint to action. There are so many ways for us to get involved individually and collectively to make a social impact. Get to know legislators at every level of government and keep them accountable to their campaign platforms. Develop faith-based programs that share the Gospel or join existing programs that serve the common good. As we engage in social media platforms, focus on solutions and help shift the conversation from the negative to how to make life better.

Follow the Spirit

What God wants me to do:

_____

_____

_____

_____

Remember Your Thoughts

Special insights I have learned:

_____

_____

_____

_____

More Light on the Text

Lamentations 5

The book of Lamentations is a Hebrew poem expressing the destruction of Jerusalem in 587 BC by the Babylonians. Jeremiah, the prophet is believed to be the author. The book is entirely poetical consisting of five poems where the verses are arranged in Hebrew alphabetical order, each verse starting with the next letter of the alphabet. Only Lamentations 5 is not presented in alphabetical acrostic as in the other chapters; instead, it is a prayer that was offered by the lamenting remnant.

1 Remember, O LORD, what is come upon us: consider, and behold our reproach.

The prayer begins by drawing God's attention to the misfortunes that have come upon Judah. The poet, believed to be Jeremiah, is pleading with the Lord to remember the things they have endured during Jerusalem's fall to the Babylonians. He also makes an appeal to God to observe sorrows resulting from what they have suffered. The word "reproach" (Heb. *kherpah*, kher-**PAW**) refers to shame, scorn, and disgrace. This is the same word Nehemiah uses to describe the state of the Jerusalem walls (Nehemiah 2:17; see last week's lesson). The destruction of the city's infrastructure is just part of what is causing shame for the Lord's people, however.

2 Our inheritance is turned to strangers, our houses to aliens.

Now the poet starts to list everything that has befallen the nation of Israel. Their inheritance of foremost importance is the greatest loss. This inheritance was land given to them by God as an everlasting possession. Now this land has been turned over to and has become the property of other nations. Foreign troops occupied the land, like some Edomites who penetrated Southern Judah and settled in south of Hebron and were later followed by other Edomite and Arab groups. The loss of the land, which was a concrete sign of the nation's relation to their God, generated a crisis of faith that constitutes the central theme of Lamentations. The Israelites' own homes would no longer belong to them. The foreigners, in this case, have the good homes, and God's people have become like settlers in their land.

Hospitality and kindness to strangers is a staple of many ancient Near Eastern value systems. The Israelites were commanded many times to be kind to foreigners (Heb. *gar*, **GARE**), remembering their own time in Egypt (Exodus 23:9; Leviticus 19:34; Deuteronomy 10:19). The *gar* wishes to live among God's people for a long time and might be interested in adopting some of their customs. The strangers that Jeremiah calls out here, though, are not the same as those protected by God's law. The Israelites' inheritance has gone to "strangers" (Heb. *zur*, **ZOOR**), a word that also describes prostitutes or unholy sacrifices. Their houses are turned over to "aliens" (Heb. *nokri*, noke-**REE**), people who are from far off lands and know nothing of the Israelites' ways.

3 We are orphans and fatherless, our mothers are as widows. 4 We have drunken our water for money; our wood is sold unto us.

Many men were killed in the battles and sieges, leaving fatherless orphans and widows. Many were involved in war and were, at any rate, the foremost target during battles. The men were faced with death or captivity. Some of them had been spared by the sword, but are far away in captivity. The loss of the paternal leaders of homes will naturally lead to a lack of protection of the more vulnerable segments of society, children and women. If the Law's protection for widows and orphans were still in place, this would not be such a desperate situation; however, the foreign government does not follow God's law about how to treat the poor and destitute.

The resources of the land were no more owned by the remnant. They have to access them filling some conditions. Water and firewood were to be secured by money. They are not even seeking water for irrigating vineyards or timbers for building fine houses. The Jewish remnant simply wants water to drink and wood for a cooking fire.

Jewish law states that foreigners living in the land have to carry water and firewood for the Israelites (Deuteronomy 29:11). The foreigners among the Israelites had the duty to serve them. Now foreigners dictate to the remnants of Judah what to do with their natural resources.

This is a symbol of a nation under domination by foreign forces. This is a further explanation of the difficult socio-economic conditions of the remnant. Life has simply become harder for them.

5 Our necks are under persecution: we labour, and have no rest. 6 We have given the hand to the Egyptians, and to the Assyrians, to be satisfied with bread.

The image of a neck being under persecution is a possible allusion to the ancient practice of a victor placing his foot on the neck of a prostrate enemy to symbolize complete subjugation (Joshua 10:24; Isaiah 51: 23). Verse 6 describes the critical condition of the remnant under Gedaliah (the governor appointed by the king of Babylon upon Judah after the conquest, cf. Jeremiah 40:5), which had worsened to such an extent that they were eager to cooperate with either Egypt or Assyria for survival. The expression "to give the hand to someone" (v. 6) may have two meanings: to make a pact with each other as equals or to surrender. The context of this verse justifies the use of "submitted" by NLT. To make sure they had enough to eat, they needed to bargain with Egypt and Assyria.

7 Our fathers have sinned, and are not; and we have borne their iniquities.

The poet seems to complain about the retribution of sin. The punishment of the ancestors' sin was visited upon the children. The guilty ones did not even live longer to face the judgment they deserved. This is the way it seems to Jeremiah. This view of retribution of sin is based on Exodus 20:5 where the succeeding generation could bear the consequences of their forefathers' sins up to the third or even fourth generations. In the Mosaic Law, God was dealing with Israel as a corporate body. The covenant was with the people as a body and therefore the retribution of sin was also executed in a corporative way. This explains why the sins of the forefathers can be visited on the succeeding generation.

When we take Scripture as a whole, we see that although the remnants' ancestors sinned and rightly deserved the judgment, their offspring also did not turn away from the sinful ways of their forefathers and therefore fell under judgment. In Ezekiel 18 God states through the prophets that consequences of sin will not be doled out based on succeeding generations' crimes but each generation will bear the consequences of its own sin. God emphasizes the individualistic nature of retribution (Ezekiel 18:4, Jeremiah 31:30), paving the way to the new covenant (Jeremiah 31:31).

8 Servants have ruled over us: there is none that doth deliver us out of their hand. 9 We gat our bread with the peril of our lives because of the sword of the wilderness. 10 Our skin was black like an oven because of the terrible famine.

The word "servants" (Heb. 'ebed, EH-**bed**, slave) refers to minor Babylonian officials who could act with disdain and cruelty (cf. 2 Kings 25:24). They are themselves slaves, or servants, to the Babylonian king, but he has set them up to rule over the Jews. Gedaliah urges the remnants not to fear the servants of the Chaldeans who will not harm them. It recalls Proverbs 30:21-22, which depicts the conditions of the rule of a slave.

There were no noble or brave people left to "deliver" (Heb. paraq, paw-**ROCK**) or redeem them from danger. After the conquest, the Babylonian army chief left only the poorest of the land to look after the vineyards (2 Kings 25:12). The king ordered his army to bring to Babylon some of the noble young men of royal lineage (Daniel 1:3). It was a common ancient policy to exterminate or take away to captivity all those who were noble and brave in the vanquished land to prevent them from reorganizing themselves to fight back. Even daily livelihood was secured at the expense of one's own life. One has to face many dangers to get his daily substance. Bedouin marauders from the desert make harvesting crops a dangerous and perilous venture. In the process of gathering enough food to cook, they are baked in the hot drought that has caused a famine. Ovens of the time were large pots set on the wood cooking fire. This would get the pot covered with soot, turning it black. The Israelites feel cooked until they are as black as their pots.

11 They ravished the women in Zion, and the maids in the cities of Judah. 12 Princes are hanged up by their hand: the faces of elders were not honoured. 13 They took the young men to grind, and the children fell under the wood.

Jeremiah also presents how the various segments of society from the vulnerable to the strong are suffering under the rule of the enemies. The women are without protection and prey to the enemy. Lawlessness has reached its climax and has become prevalent under the rule of the enemies, not just in the enemy's stronghold, but across the country. Sometimes during war people will use rape as a weapon against the enemy. Even in some contemporary conflicts, belligerents use this kind of horrific strategy. The aim is to humiliate further the vanquished.

As the women are humiliated by rape, the men are humiliated in their own ways. The "princes" who are the rulers or leaders of Jerusalem with civil authority are being put to death in a shameful, torturous way. The old men in the city, who deserved respect, are now despised by the enemies. The young men were taken captive and used "to grind," that is to work as slaves at a milestone. These young men are humiliated by grinding grain into flour,

performing work usually done by an animal. Children are forced into hard labor. Formerly, according to Deuteronomy, foreigners had to carry firewood for the Israelites; now children of the Judean remnant have to carry on this task for the enemies of Judah. They stumble and fall under the heavy load.

14 The elders have ceased from the gate, the young men from their musick. 15 The joy of our heart is ceased; our dance is turned into mourning. 16 The crown is fallen from our head: woe unto us, that we have sinned!

The usual activities of the city are no longer carried on. The old men are convening at the city gate to discuss matters of the city and make useful decisions for the city life. They are no longer ruling the city. They are treated with contempt and they are not consulted. The young men were the expression of the vitality of the city. They were once carrying on with exuberance and joyful life, making music and dancing. This life of music and dance has come to an end. They can rejoice no more either because they are being mistreated or they are mourning due to a lot of misfortunes. There is no expression of joy in the land. Only mourning has replaced the once vibrant and joyful life of the city. The symbols of honors they were crowned with have disappeared (cf. Isaiah 28:1–4).

The prophet admits that the people know the cause of all this devastation: They have sinned. They have disobeyed God and are now reaping the covenant curses, just as they gained the covenant blessings when they properly obeyed the Lord.

17 For this our heart is faint; for these things our eyes are dim. 18 Because of the mountain of Zion, which is desolate, the foxes walk upon it.

The whole situation leads them to uneasiness. The sicknesses of a weakened heart and dimming eyes are physical but also figurative. They have no more strength to fight their oppressors. Their vision about the prospect of the future is not clear. It is a feeling of being hopeless, discouraged, defeated.

This feeling is the result of the desolation of Jerusalem, the city God consecrated for His glory among the nation. Mount Zion is the hill on which the Temple stood. Here it refers to the location of the Temple and Jerusalem as a whole. The consequence of the desolation is the occupation of the site by unclean animals that usually only live in the wilderness (cf. Isaiah 13:19–22, for the desolation of Babylon).

19 Thou, O LORD, remainest for ever; thy throne from generation to generation. 20 Wherefore dost thou forget us for ever, and forsake us so long time? 21 Turn thou us unto thee, O LORD, and we shall be turned; renew our days as of old.

In spite of all the circumstances described in the preceding verses, God remains the same forever. Though Judah has lost his former status, God's reign and His sovereignty remain untouched. Foxes wander the place where God was once worshiped, but God is not His Temple. Humankind's fortunes or misfortunes do not influence or affect any change in the character of God. He remains the same forever (cf. Hebrews 13:8). Circumstances may change; God remains the same. Even in our generation where evil seems to be so prevalent, God is unchangeable. We can abide by Him, and be assured that even in misfortune, He remains our hope.

The poet pleads for God to remember His people and hasten deliverance. Even though God is eternal, His creations are not. The poet feels the passage of time acutely. He is afraid that God's forgetfulness will last indefinitely, so in the agony of his lament he pursues two parallel questions: "Why did You forget us?" and "Why did You forsake us?" These questions are a way of invoking God's mercy and grace for all they have endured and the poet has listed above. It is a suggestion to God that they have had enough of the suffering and to ask whether God could intervene promptly.

The poet calls for the restoration of God. He pleads with God to turn their hearts to Him once again. He asks God to turn them Himself, rather than asking that they be given strength to turn themselves. The poet knows that if God does it, it will happen, but if they try to change their hearts, they will fail. We cannot turn to God by our will and strength. God must call us to Himself. We cannot force ourselves to commit to a changed lifestyle. God must guide us to keep us from falling back to our old ways. The unchanging God can bring restoration and bring them their former status. It is a prayer or request that acknowledges the separation between God and His people due to their sin.

22 But thou hast utterly rejected us; thou art very wroth against us.

If God does not respond to the previous questions (v. 21), it may imply that He has completely rejected His people. It may also mean that He is still angry with them. During Jewish liturgical reading of this book, verse 21 is usually repeated after verse 22. This ends the reading with a hopeful plea and keeps it from ending with the pessimistic nature of verse 22.

God promised not to forget nor forsake His people (Deuteronomy 31:6; cf. Hebrews 13:5) Tough and trying times may come our way, but we should remember that God works everything for our good (Romans 8:28) in His own time. God's faithfulness is continually renewed (Lamentations 3:22). Even God's punishment is an expression of His profound love for us (Hebrews 12:5). In the meantime, while we may not understand the reason or the purpose of the trying time, we are free to pour our hearts before Him as Hannah did and as Job did. We cannot grasp His ways and doings (Ecclesiastes 11:5), but He will never forget us and never stop loving us. He will come to us with deliverance and song of joy (Psalms 34:5–7).

Sources:

Abraham, A. Kenneth. *The Matthew Henry Study Bible, King James Version.* Iowa Falls IA: World Bible Publishers, Inc. 1994. 1547, 1555-1556.

Attridge, Harold, W. *The Harper Collins Study Bible, New Revised Standard Version.* New York, NY: Harper One, 2006. 1085,-1086, 1095

Cabal, Ted et. al., *The Apologetics Study Bible, Holman Christian Standard*, Nashville, TN, Holman Bible Publishers, 2007. 1175-1176.

Collins, John J., *A Short Introduction to the Hebrew Bible*, Minneapolis, MN, Fortress Press, 2007. 183-184.

Guthrie, H.H. *The Interpreter's One-Volume Commentary on the Bible.* C. M. Laymon, ed. Nashville, TN: Abingdon Press, 1971.

Harrison, R K. *The Tyndale Old Testament Commentaries: Jeremiah and Lamentations, An introduction and commentary.* D.J. Wiseman, ed. Downers Grove, IL: InterVarsity Press, 1973.

Hillers, D.R. Lamentations: *A New Translation with Introduction and Commentary.* 2nd edition. New York: Doubleday, 1972.

Packer, J.I. and M.C. Tenney, ed. *Illustrated Manners and Customs of the Bible.* Nashville, TN: Thomas Nelson Publishers, 1980. 36-43, 500-501.

Reyburn, W. D. *A Handbook on Lamentations.* New York: United Bible Societies, 1992.

Van der Mass, Ed M. *Halley's Bible Handbook: Deluxe Edition (25th Edition).* Grand Rapids, MI: Zondervan, 2007. 377.

Zodhiates, Spiros. *Key Word Study Bible King James Version.* Chattanooga, TN: AMG Publishers, 1991. 995.

Say It Correctly

Diaspora. dee-**AS**-pore-ah.
Edomite. **EE**-dum-ite.

Daily Bible Readings

MONDAY
Praise for God's Wonderful Works
(Psalm 111)

TUESDAY
God's Blessings Intended for All
(Zechariah 8:18-23)

WEDNESDAY
The Lord, Our Sovereign
(Psalm 102:12-22)

THURSDAY
Plea for Mercy for Jerusalem
(Psalm 102:12-22)

FRIDAY
Mourn the Destruction of Zion
(Jeremiah 9:17-22)

SATURDAY
God's Mercy and Love Never Ends
(Lamentations 3:22-33)

SUNDAY
Remember and Restore Us
(Lamentations 5)

Teaching Tips

Words You Should Know

A. Prophesy (1 Kings 22:18) *naba* (Heb.)—To cause to bubble up, to pour forth words abundantly to be inspired, to speak by divine power

B. Lying Spirit (v. 22) *sheqer* (Heb.)—The spirit sent to entice, trick, or deceive. An untruth, lie. A way contrary to God.

Teacher Preparation

Unifying Principle—Speaking Truth Boldly. Telling the truth to those who are in power can be difficult. How does one give a difficult message to powerful people? Micaiah resolved that he would tell King Ahab only what the Lord said to him.

A. Read the Bible Background and Devotional Reading.

B. Pray for your students and lesson clarity.

C. Read the lesson Scripture in multiple translations.

O—Open the Lesson

A. Begin the class with prayer.

B. Pose various bad news situations to the participants. Ask how they would react to such bad news.

C. Have the students read the Aim for Change and the In Focus story.

D. Ask students how events like those in the story weigh on their hearts and how they can view these events from a faith perspective.

P—Present the Scriptures

A. Read the Focal Verses and discuss the Background and The People, Places, and Times sections.

B. Have the class share what Scriptures stand out for them and why, with particular emphasis on today's themes.

E—Explore the Meaning

A. Use In Depth or More Light on the Text to facilitate a deeper discussion of the lesson text.

B. Pose the questions in Search the Scriptures and Discuss the Meaning.

C. Discuss the Liberating Lesson and Application for Activation sections.

N—Next Steps for Application

A. Summarize the value of holding to faith convictions even in the face of opposition.

B. End class with a commitment to pray for believers in countries were governments impose marginalization and even persecution because of people's faith.

Worship Guide

For the Superintendent or Teacher
Theme: Micaiah: Speaking
Truth to Power
Song: "Stand Up, Stand Up for Jesus"
Devotional Reading: 1 John 3:23-4:3;
Deuteronomy 18:19-22

Micaiah: Speaking Truth to Power

Bible Background • 1 KINGS 22:1-40 | Printed Text • 1 KINGS 22:15-23, 26-28
Devotional Reading • 1 JOHN 3:23-4:3; DEUTERONOMY 18:19-22

Aim for Change

By the end of this lesson, we will IDENTIFY with Micaiah's boldness in declaring the word of the Lord, ASPIRE to be like Micaiah when speaking the word of the Lord, and COMMIT to tell those in power what the Lord has said.

In Focus

Martin Fairchild stared at the spreadsheet. There was no way around it, his family would not be able to go on a vacation this year. There just was no money for it. He thought about all the fun vacations they had had in years past and how much the kids looked forward to the week of adventuring. Even though they were teens now and too cool to admit it. But with the extra costs of college admission tests and application fees, plus a new transmission for the car, there just wasn't the extra money.

He broke the news to his family at dinner. The kids quickly offered new ways of getting the money.

"What if we just borrow some money from Uncle Phil?" Raymond asked.

"What if we skip just a week or two of tithing?" Denise asked.

Mrs. Fairchild shook her head. "Your father has made the wisest decision he can in this situation."

Martin nodded to his wife, thanking her for the support. "We are not going into debt just to go someplace. And we are certainly not going to forget to give back to the Lord. I know it's not what you want to hear, but it's what God has provided for us this time."

How have you followed God's guidance even when others didn't like what God had to say?

Keep in Mind

"And Micaiah said, As the LORD liveth, what the LORD saith unto me, that will I speak." (1 Kings 22:14, KJV)

"But Micaiah replied, 'As surely as the LORD lives, I will say only what the LORD tells me to say.'" (1 Kings 22:14, NLT)

Focal Verses

KJV **1 Kings 22:15** So he came to the king. And the king said unto him, Micaiah, shall we go against Ramothgilead to battle, or shall we forbear? And he answered him, Go, and prosper: for the LORD shall deliver it into the hand of the king.

16 And the king said unto him, How many times shall I adjure thee that thou tell me nothing but that which is true in the name of the LORD?

17 And he said, I saw all Israel scattered upon the hills, as sheep that have not a shepherd: and the LORD said, These have no master: let them return every man to his house in peace.

18 And the king of Israel said unto Jehoshaphat, Did I not tell thee that he would prophesy no good concerning me, but evil?

19 And he said, Hear thou therefore the word of the LORD: I saw the LORD sitting on his throne, and all the host of heaven standing by him on his right hand and on his left.

20 And the LORD said, Who shall persuade Ahab, that he may go up and fall at Ramothgilead? And one said on this manner, and another said on that manner.

21 And there came forth a spirit, and stood before the LORD, and said, I will persuade him.

22 And the LORD said unto him, Wherewith? And he said, I will go forth, and I will be a lying spirit in the mouth of all his prophets. And he said, Thou shalt persuade him, and prevail also: go forth, and do so.

23 Now therefore, behold, the LORD hath put a lying spirit in the mouth of all these thy prophets, and the LORD hath spoken evil concerning thee.

26 And the king of Israel said, Take Micaiah, and carry him back unto Amon the governor of the city, and to Joash the king's son;

27 And say, Thus saith the king, Put this fellow in the prison, and feed him with bread

NLT **1 Kings 22:15** When Micaiah arrived before the king, Ahab asked him, "Micaiah, should we go to war against Ramoth-gilead, or should we hold back?" Micaiah replied sarcastically, "Yes, go up and be victorious, for the LORD will give the king victory!"

16 But the king replied sharply, "How many times must I demand that you speak only the truth to me when you speak for the LORD?"

17 Then Micaiah told him, "In a vision I saw all Israel scattered on the mountains, like sheep without a shepherd. And the LORD said, 'Their master has been killed. Send them home in peace.'"

18 "Didn't I tell you?" the king of Israel exclaimed to Jehoshaphat. "He never prophesies anything but trouble for me."

19 Then Micaiah continued, "Listen to what the LORD says! I saw the LORD sitting on his throne with all the armies of heaven around him, on his right and on his left.

20 And the LORD said, 'Who can entice Ahab to go into battle against Ramoth-gilead so he can be killed?' There were many suggestions,

21 and finally a spirit approached the LORD and said, 'I can do it!'

22 'How will you do this?' the LORD asked. And the spirit replied, 'I will go out and inspire all of Ahab's prophets to speak lies.' 'You will succeed,' said the LORD. 'Go ahead and do it.'

23 So you see, the LORD has put a lying spirit in the mouths of all your prophets. For the LORD has pronounced your doom."

26 "Arrest him!" the king of Israel ordered. "Take him back to Amon, the governor of the city, and to my son Joash.

27 Give them this order from the king: 'Put this man in prison, and feed him nothing but bread and water until I return safely from the battle!'"

of affliction and with water of affliction, until I come in peace.

28 And Micaiah said, If thou return at all in peace, the LORD hath not spoken by me. And he said, Hearken, O people, every one of you.

28 But Micaiah replied, "If you return safely, it will mean that the LORD has not spoken through me!" Then he added to those standing around, "Everyone mark my words!"

The People, Places, and Times

Ramoth-gilead. This border city between Aram (Syria) and Israel, modern Tel ar-Ramith, is located on the eastern side of the Jordan River. It is called Ramoth-gilead or Ramoth in Gilead to distinguish it from another city also named Ramoth, which was in the Negev (1 Samuel 30:27). It was declared a city of refuge by Moses (Deuteronomy 4:43) and provided pastureland for the Levites (Joshua 21:38). The city changed hands several times between Syria and Israel. Ahab notes that Syrians occupy the city, even though it belongs to Israel (1 Kings 22:3). He fails to recover it and the Syrians later cement their control of it (2 Kings 10:32-33).

Benhadad. This king of Syria adds to the tumultuous political intrigue of the time. King Asa of Judah bribes Benhadad to break his treaty with King Baasha of Israel and form a treaty with him instead (1 Kings 15:18-20). Later, he attacks Samaria, the capital of Israel. This attack and his attack the following year fail, as the Lord shows His might to defend His people (1 Kings 20). Finally, Benhadad falls ill and asks the prophet, Elisha, if he will recover. Elisha prophesies that he will not and the king's messenger Hazael brings this prophecy about by smothering Benhadad (2 Kings 8:7-15).

Background

In 1 Kings 22, we find the kings of the Northern and Southern Kingdoms having trouble accepting the Word of God from His prophets. The king of the North, the evil Ahab, now holds the upper hand, while the king of the South, the God-fearing Jehoshaphat, has

become his vassal. By treaty, Jehoshaphat is under obligation to help Ahab in any way he asks. Syria was presently at peace with Israel and Judah but held a section of land called Ramoth-gilead. After three years of not receiving Syria's promised tribute, Ahab wants to go to war against Benhadad, the Syrian king. Ahab asks Jehoshaphat, "Will you join me in battle to recover Ramoth-gilead?" (1 Kings 22:4, NLT).

Jehoshaphat has no alternative other than agreeing to help Ahab. But wisdom prevails and Jehoshaphat wants counsel from the Lord (v. 5). Ahab agrees to listen to a god but not the God of Abraham; instead, he listens to the prophets of his own state religion, prophets of Baal (v. 6). These men are false prophets who tell Ahab what he wants to hear. Jehoshaphat wants to hear from a true prophet of God, not these pseudo-prophets, so he asks Ahab if such a prophet is available (v. 7). Ahab then calls his officials to bring forth Micaiah, the son of Imlah (vv. 8-9). This passage is the only place Micaiah is mentioned in Scripture.

At-A-Glance

1. Micaiah's Prophecy (1 Kings 22:15-18)
2. Micaiah's Vision (vv. 19-23)
3. Micaiah Imprisoned (vv. 26-28)

In Depth

1. Micaiah's Prophecy (1 Kings 22:15-18)

Once a true prophet knows the word of God, no one can prevent him from delivering the message. Micaiah did not avoid God's words even when they were unwelcome, discouraging, or negative. No matter if it cost him his life, Micaiah was committed to being true to God and His Word. When Micaiah sarcastically told Ahab to attack and be victorious, the king knew something was wrong because Micaiah never agreed with Ahab's prophets (vv. 15-16). Ahab knew his false prophets were only saying what he wanted to hear and he knew if the truth was to be heard, it was going to come from someone who really knew God. Ahab demanded the truth of Micaiah though he really didn't want to hear it.

Micaiah reported the opposite of what the false prophets had been saying. He told Ahab that he would be killed and his army scattered. This battle, according to Micaiah who spoke on behalf of the Almighty God, would be a disaster. Although Ahab asked for a true word from God, when it was spoken he pushed it aside and blamed the prophet for always being against him.

When you ask God in prayer for the truth about yourself, are you willing to accept His answers?

2. Micaiah's Vision (vv. 19-23)

The prophet spoke about a vision. Micaiah saw the Lord sitting on His throne surrounded by a host of angelic beings. These angelic beings were not there to advise God; instead, they served as witnesses of God's omniscience and omnipotence. The Lord asks how He can persuade Ahab to fight Ramoth-Gilead. One spirit came forth with the plan to lie to the king through his prophets. Then Yahweh gave him permission to go and do so.

Ahab sought to suppress divine authority and truth. God in His omniscience affected His sovereign will by allowing this "lying spirit" to feed the king's own destructive ego through the untruths of his prophets. God gave Ahab what he wanted—his own wish instead of God's truth—and it led to Ahab's death. Our God is the God of those with pure hearts as well as those with perverse hearts. God can and will use any means necessary to carry out His sovereign will (John 12:40; 2 Thessalonians 2:11; Exodus 14:4, 8).

3. Micaiah Imprisoned (vv. 26-28)

Ahab didn't like what Micaiah said so he did what all tyrants do. He put him in prison to shut him up. When a person or a nation stifles the truth by silencing those who speak out for the truth, it is denying a basic right. But also, it is halting the very flow of truth that might be its own salvation. Ahab did not see that Micaiah was warning him of defeat and death. Ahab was too bent on doing what he wanted. But killing a man who tells the truth does not change the truth. Truth will conquer and often with deadly accuracy.

Micaiah was the kind of person who usually had the last word. His final warning to Ahab in verse 28 was, "If thou return at all in peace, the LORD hath not spoken by me." Micaiah had real confidence in the accuracy of the message he received from God. There are times when we have to stand up for what is right and true, even if everyone else is playing loose with the truth.

Shall we follow the way of the crowd and serve ourselves or shall we wait on the word of the LORD however He chooses to send it?

Search the Scriptures

1. Did Micaiah yield to the pressure of the status quo or did he serve the Lord? (v. 15)

2. Can a prison cell stop the word of God from coming to fruition? (vv. 26-28) Explain.

Discuss the Meaning

1. Micaiah resisted the pressure to agree with the rest of those in his profession. He endured the rebuke of the king. He stood for truth at high

personal costs. Discuss the reasons for standing firm for the truth. What are its dangers? What are its rewards? Can you cite examples of how being truthful has paid off well? Or, how lying has caused disaster? (The lies of Watergate illustrate how many people can be brought down by not facing the truth immediately.)

2. Micaiah's prophecy of the divine council shows us a spirit offering a plan of lying and Yahweh approves of this plan. However, we know from parts of Scripture that God hates lying tongues and outlaws false testimony as one of His chief laws. Can God ever be a liar or endorse lying? Discuss.

Liberating Lesson

We live in a society that encourages excuses and glorifies lies. When someone tells the truth, especially biblical truth, most people do not want to hear it. People who want to live in lies and deception often lash out at the person telling the truth. Sometimes it hurts to hear the truth because then we might have to admit we are wrong or confess a sin. To stand for the truth in a difficult situation can be hard. Many times God is the only one pleased with our honest decision. Christians must always weigh the risks of being truthful against the consequences of getting caught in a tangle of lies and inconsistencies. Commit to stand for the truth and speak it in love, no matter the consequences. What statement would your church make to its community about the truths it stands for?

Application for Activation

Micaiah was called to deliver some hard truth. He spoke boldly but also spoke with love for the king and love for the people. Truth must be spoken, yet the Scripture exhorts us to speak "the truth in love" (Ephesians 4:15). It is also necessary to pray and ask God for the best time to speak the truth. God directed Micaiah at this particular time to speak to these kings. When we decide to speak the truth, let's make sure that God—not our flesh, our desire to get back at someone, or our need to dump on someone—is the motivation prompted by the Holy Spirit.

Is there something you've been holding back that God wants you to say? What's your next step?

Follow the Spirit

What God wants me to do:

_____

_____

_____

_____

_____

Remember Your Thoughts

Special insights I have learned:

_____

_____

_____

_____

More Light on the Text

1 Kings 22:15-23, 26-28

15 So he came to the king. And the king said unto him, Micaiah, shall we go against Ramothgilead to battle, or should we forbear? And he answered him, Go, and prosper: for the LORD shall deliver it unto the hand of the king.

King Ahab of Israel was planning to join forces with King Jehoshaphat of Judah to fight against the Syrians to take back the city of

Ramoth in Gilead. Four hundred prophets had been queried and had all agreed that this battle would turn out favorable for these allied kings. However, King Jehoshaphat wanted to be sure they had consulted with all the prophets, so he asked if there were any prophets of Yahweh to ask. So Ahab sent for the prophet, Micaiah, the son of Imlah, to add his voice to the 400 prophets who had been consulted.

Perhaps this is what signaled a problem to King Jehoshaphat. One of the criteria for distinguishing false prophets from true prophets was that the false prophet told the king what he wanted to hear, while the true prophet told the king what was difficult or unfavorable. When Micaiah arrived, he answered the king in the same manner as the other prophets.

16 And the king said unto him, How many times shall I adjure thee that thou tell me nothing but that which is true in the name of the LORD?

Micaiah's response must have sounded completely insincere to King Ahab, too agreeable, and too sweet. Verse 8 indicates that Micaiah and Ahab's relationship had been full of conflict to the point that the king hated this prophet. His opinion would not have even been sought after if it were not for King Jehoshaphat. Ahab did not care to hear what Micaiah had to say, because he knew it would not be good. Ahab knew he must be lying if Micaiah agreed with the others. This alerted King Ahab that there might be a problem because Micaiah had never been agreeable, as King Ahab had done many things to anger the Lord. Under his leadership, altars were built for foreign gods. Micaiah was one of the few prophets who dared to speak out against the king's behavior. King Ahab, in his most pious sounding voice, said, "How often must I tell you to only speak that which is true in the name of Yahweh?" This from the mouth of a king who built altars to Baal!

17 And he said, I saw all Israel scattered upon the hills, as sheep that have not a shepherd: And the LORD said, These have no master: let them return every man to his house in peace.

So Micaiah revealed what the Lord had truly said. He had seen a vision of the army scattered upon the hills in Gilead, confused and wandering aimlessly. The phrase "sheep that have not a shepherd" uses the same imagery of a common term for a king at that time, "the shepherd of his people." If these people are without a shepherd, their king must be dead. The vision was confirmed by the word of the Lord saying, "These have no master." This meant that King Ahab would be killed in the battle and that his death would bring an end to the war. They would not make peace, but the loss of their king would end their desire to fight.

18 And the king of Israel said unto Jehoshaphat, Did I not tell thee that he would prophesy no good concerning me, but evil?

King Ahab was correct. Micaiah's prophecy regarding him was terrible, as expected. That was why he avoided Micaiah. What a demoralizing prophecy to go into battle with. Ahab did not wish to hear anything like this. He had known a truthful prophecy from Micaiah would end this way and hated to be proven right.

There are many people, like Ahab, who think that because they have heard a certain truth before, it no longer merits attention. The person says, "I knew that's what you were going to say." And even though it's the truth, it carries no weight with them because they anticipated it. Such people don't want to hear the truth, only what they want to hear. How often have we made up our minds to do something we know is not best and then get angry at a counselor for warning us away from it? How often do we ignore our conscience, the guidance of the

Holy Spirit, or our own better judgment, simply because we hate their being a spoilsport? It is not wisdom simply to seek advice; wisdom is shown in actually acting on good advice.

19 And he said, Hear thou therefore the word of the LORD: I saw the LORD sitting on his throne, and all the host of heaven standing by him on his right hand on his left. 20 And the LORD said, Who shall persuade Ahab, that he may go up and fall at Ramoth-gilead? And one said on this manner, and another said on that manner.

King Ahab has not yet heard all that the Lord had to say concerning him. Micaiah continues by telling him what the Lord has really said. Micaiah begins to describe a human-like vision of God. God and His angels are spirit-beings and cannot actually sit or stand or have a right hand or left. These bodily images of the spirits are how God reveals Himself to Micaiah's limited human mind.

God, the King of Heaven, is seated on His heavenly throne, with His heavenly army standing around him. This scene is reminiscent of the vision Isaiah described (Isaiah 6). Here, too, the Lord is seated upon His throne, surrounded by angels, delivering unfavorable news to the nation. John would see a similar sight in his vision of the heavenly throne room. The image is one of awesome power.

According to the vision, the Lord inquired amongst the heavenly host (Heb. *tsaba'*, tsah-**BAH**, a large army) to see if any might have a strategy to convince Ahab to go into battle, so that he might meet his end there. As He has from the beginning, God invites His creation to join Him in the unfolding of history. God already knows how He will go about killing the evil king Ahab, but He still asks for the angels' ideas and suggestions.

God means to "persuade" Ahab to ride into battle and meet his death. The word translated "persuade" (Heb. *patah*, paw-**TAW**) carries the sense of causing one to be deceived, or enticed. Various ones answered with differing approaches. But none came up with an acceptable plan to Yahweh.

21 And there came forth a spirit, and stood before the LORD, and said, I will persuade him. 22 And the LORD said unto him, Wherewith? And he said, I will go forth, and I will be a lying spirit in the mouth of all his prophets. And he said, Thou shalt persuade him, and prevail also: go forth, and do so.

This part of the story also reminds one of the story of Job whom Satan sought to harm, but could not do so without God's permission (Job 1). However, it is not useful to think of the agent here as an independent entity of evil. In the eyes of the people, God was responsible for the origin of good and evil. Thus God could be thought of as being responsible for the deception of Ahab. Ahab was not a righteous king. So here we find God participating in his demise, instead of offering protection.

As in Isaiah 6, the Lord prepares to dispatch an agent to accomplish His will. It is believed that the "spirit" referred to here was the Spirit of Prophecy who inspired prophets to speak truth or lies. The Lord wanted to know the details of how this spirit hoped to achieve the results. He responded that he would inspire all of Ahab's prophets to lie. This lying spirit perhaps even influenced Micaiah in his first answer to Ahab's question (v. 15). Thus, even Yahweh's prophet would agree with one voice with Baal's prophets. This seemed like an effective plan, so the Lord gave this spirit permission to do as he had said.

23 Now, therefore, behold, the LORD hath put a lying spirit in the mouth of all these thy prophets, and the LORD hath spoken evil concerning thee.

So concludes Micaiah's story, explaining how it was that all the other prophets agreed upon the plan for battle. Amazingly, the false prophets were prophesying under the power of the true God this time. Even when using them Him in His plan, however, they are filled with a lying spirit and not a trustworthy source of guidance.

It must have required a lot of courage to be the lone dissenting voice when Micaiah knew what King Ahab wanted to hear. Micaiah was already very unpopular with the king, but he never changed the word that he was supposed to deliver from the Lord.

26 And the king of Israel said, Take Micaiah, and carry him back unto Amon, the governor of the city, and to Joash the king's son; 27 And say, Thus saith the king, Put this fellow in the prison, and feed him with bread of affliction and with water of affliction, until I come in peace.

When Micaiah has finished his prophecy, King Ahab is furious with him. Ahab was expecting a negative word, but this was a bit too much. In his fury, King Ahab orders that Micaiah be arrested and taken back to the capital, Samaria. He is to be jailed in the palace, under the custody of the governor and the king's son. Micaiah is given prison food, the bread and water "of affliction" (Heb. *lakhats*, **LAH-**khats) which refers to oppression, pressure, and distress. The only other reference to the bread and water of affliction is in a prophecy of Isaiah, where God promises to be with His people, teaching and guiding them, even when their fare is affliction (Isaiah 30:20).

Ahab planned to return shortly from the battle and then gloat in Micaiah's face. He said, "Until I come in peace" in defiance of Micaiah's prophecy. If he returned, Micaiah would appear the fool and would be discredited forever. Ahab figured that would put an end to this pesky prophet. If he did not return, then Micaiah would die in prison.

28 And Micaiah said, If thou return at all in peace, the LORD hath not spoken by me. And he said, Hearken, O people, every one of you.

Micaiah's reputation as a prophet of the Lord and his life are at stake. Yet he does not back down from what he knows to be the truth. King Ahab would not return. Micaiah calls for the attention of everyone around. The word "hearken" in Hebrew (*shama'*, shaw-MAH) means not just to hear the words, but to internalize them. These people would be witnesses to the words that were spoken. Thus, even in death, Micaiah would be vindicated.

Once again God gives Ahab a chance to repent and to follow His instructions, but he does not take it. This, however, was his last chance. Just as Micaiah had predicted, Ahab does not come back alive. His army was defeated and King Ahab died in battle.

Sources:
Elwell, Walter A., ed. *The Evangelical Dictionary of Theology.* Grand Rapids, MI: Baker Books, 1987. 886.
Henry, Matthew. *Matthew Henry's Commentary on the Whole Bible: New Modern Edition.* Vols. 1-6. Peabody, MA: Hendrickson Publishers, Inc., 2009.
Strong, James. *The New Strong's Exhaustive Concordance of the Bible.* Nashville, TN: Thomas Nelson, 2003.

Say It Correctly

Micaiah. mi-**KIE**-yuh.
Jehoshaphat. jeh-**HOE**-shaw-fat.
Ramoth-gilead.
RAH-moth-**GILL**-ee-add.
Benhadad. **BEN**-haw-**DOD**.

Daily Bible Readings

MONDAY
Elisha Prophesies Truth
to King Jehoshaphat
(2 Kings 3:9-17)

TUESDAY
Kings Propose Battle Against Aram
(1 Kings 22:1-6)

WEDNESDAY
Micaiah Resists Pressure
to Prophesy Falsely
(1 Kings 22:7-14)

THURSDAY
A Lying Spirit Brings Disaster
(2 Chronicles 18:18-22)

FRIDAY
King Ahab Suffers Fatal Injury
(1 Kings 22:29-40)

SATURDAY
Jehoshaphat Promotes Peace with Israel
(1 Kings 22:41-46)

SUNDAY
Prophet Micaiah Speaks the Truth
(1 Kings 22:15-23, 26-28)

Notes

_____

_____

_____

_____

Teaching Tips

Words You Should Know

A. Poor (Isaiah 29:19) *ebyon* (Heb.)—In need or in want; destitute; a beggar, or needy

B. Redeemed (v. 22) *padah* (Heb.)—To ransom, deliver or to rescue

Teacher Preparation

Unifying Principle—Empty Rituals Are Useless. Relationships suffer when humans lapse into immorality. What is the result when we or others have been immoral? Isaiah prophesied that God would punish the people of Judah but still be merciful and restore the nation.

A. Read the Bible Background and Devotional Reading.

B. Pray for your students and lesson clarity.

C. Read the lesson Scripture in multiple translations.

O—Open the Lesson

A. Begin the class with prayer.

B. Ask the students if they have any silly rituals or superstitions they or a friend participates in. Why do they do this?

C. Have the students read the Aim for Change and the In Focus story.

D. Ask students how events like those in the story weigh on their hearts and how they can view these events from a faith perspective.

P—Present the Scriptures

A. Read the Focal Verses and discuss the Background and The People, Places, and Times sections.

B. Have the class share what Scriptures stand out for them and why, with particular emphasis on today's themes.

E—Explore the Meaning

A. Use In Depth or More Light on the Text to facilitate a deeper discussion of the lesson text.

B. Pose the questions in Search the Scriptures and Discuss the Meaning.

C. Discuss the Liberating Lesson and Application for Activation sections.

N—Next Steps for Application

A. Summarize the value of refusing to make any part of life off-limits to God.

B. End class with a commitment to pray against insincerity that leads to hypocrisy and finally leads to faithlessness.

Worship Guide

For the Superintendent or Teacher
Theme: Isaiah: Offering Hope for the Future
Song: "The Potter's House"
Devotional Reading: Jeremiah 29:10-14

Isaiah: Offering Hope for the Future

Bible Background • ISAIAH 29
Printed Text • ISAIAH 29:13-24 | Devotional Reading • JEREMIAH 29:10-14

———————————— Aim for Change ————————————

By the end of this lesson, we will CONSIDER how God's promise of mercy will triumph over God's judgment, BELIEVE that an essential characteristic of God's nature is forgiveness, and REJOICE in the manifestation of God's love in our own lives.

———————————— In Focus ————————————

Pamela was in a bind and needed help with an unexpected car repair, so she called in a favor from her friend Aisha who was always willing to lend a helping hand. What Pamela didn't know was that Aisha was fed up with being her emergency fund and had already determined the next time she made one of her 9-1-1 calls for financial help she was not going to help. The reason: Pamela was not a good steward over her finances and was known for making poor choices. Aisha loved her friend but for her well-being and the sake of their friendship, she had to set that boundary. Also, Pamela was slow to return what she borrowed, and when she did, there was always an excuse for not repaying the full amount.

She called Aisha and asked for a five hundred dollar loan and said: "I promise I will pay you back next week when I get paid. I will set it up to send electronically."

Aisha thought, "My Father in heaven is rich, but I am not your bank!" But instead, she responded, "Girl, I don't have the full amount, but I will give you half. I am so sorry that's all I can do right now."

"I understand," Pamela said, "I have been to your well too many times. I need to make changes."

If someone was a repeat offender, would you continue to give your resources to help them?

———————————— Keep in Mind ————————————

"They also that erred in spirit shall come to understanding, and they that murmured shall learn doctrine" (Isaiah 29:24, KJV)

"Then the wayward will gain understanding, and complainers will accept instruction"
(Isaiah 29:24, NLT)

Focal Verses

KJV **Isaiah 29:13** Wherefore the Lord said, Forasmuch as this people draw near me with their mouth, and with their lips do honour me, but have removed their heart far from me, and their fear toward me is taught by the precept of men:

14 Therefore, behold, I will proceed to do a marvellous work among this people, even a marvellous work and a wonder: for the wisdom of their wise men shall perish, and the understanding of their prudent men shall be hid.

15 Woe unto them that seek deep to hide their counsel from the LORD, and their works are in the dark, and they say, Who seeth us? and who knoweth us?

16 Surely your turning of things upside down shall be esteemed as the potter's clay: for shall the work say of him that made it, He made me not? or shall the thing framed say of him that framed it, He had no understanding?

17 Is it not yet a very little while, and Lebanon shall be turned into a fruitful field, and the fruitful field shall be esteemed as a forest?

18 And in that day shall the deaf hear the words of the book, and the eyes of the blind shall see out of obscurity, and out of darkness.

19 The meek also shall increase their joy in the LORD, and the poor among men shall rejoice in the Holy One of Israel.

20 For the terrible one is brought to nought, and the scorner is consumed, and all that watch for iniquity are cut off:

21 That make a man an offender for a word, and lay a snare for him that reproveth in the gate, and turn aside the just for a thing of nought.

22 Therefore thus saith the LORD, who redeemed Abraham, concerning the house of Jacob, Jacob shall not now be ashamed, neither shall his face now wax pale.

23 But when he seeth his children, the work of mine hands, in the midst of him, they shall

NLT **Isaiah 29:13** And so the Lord says, "These people say they are mine. They honor me with their lips, but their hearts are far from me. And their worship of me is nothing but man-made rules learned by rote.

14 Because of this, I will once again astound these hypocrites with amazing wonders. The wisdom of the wise will pass away, and the intelligence of the intelligent will disappear."

15 What sorrow awaits those who try to hide their plans from the LORD, who do their evil deeds in the dark! "The LORD can't see us," they say. "He doesn't know what's going on!"

16 How foolish can you be? He is the Potter, and he is certainly greater than you, the clay! Should the created thing say of the one who made it, "He didn't make me"? Does a jar ever say, "The potter who made me is stupid"?

17 Soon—and it will not be very long—the forests of Lebanon will become a fertile field, and the fertile field will yield bountiful crops.

18 In that day the deaf will hear words read from a book, and the blind will see through the gloom and darkness.

19 The humble will be filled with fresh joy from the LORD. The poor will rejoice in the Holy One of Israel.

20 The scoffer will be gone, the arrogant will disappear, and those who plot evil will be killed.

21 Those who convict the innocent by their false testimony will disappear. A similar fate awaits those who use trickery to pervert justice and who tell lies to destroy the innocent.

22 That is why the LORD, who redeemed Abraham, says to the people of Israel, "My people will no longer be ashamed or turn pale with fear.

23 For when they see their many children and all the blessings I have given them, they will recognize the holiness of the Holy One of Jacob. They will stand in awe of the God of Israel.

sanctify my name, and sanctify the Holy One of Jacob, and shall fear the God of Israel.

24 They also that erred in spirit shall come to understanding, and they that murmured shall learn doctrine.

24 Then the wayward will gain understanding, and complainers will accept instruction."

The People, Places, and Times

Isaiah. One of the greatest prophets of his time, Isaiah had a vision of God and was called by God to do God's work bringing his nation to repentance to save it from a whirlpool of destruction. His very name means "Yahweh is (the source) of salvation." Isaiah came to the people with messages of judgment tempered with hope. He ministered for 60 years or more and prophesied during the reign of five kings: Uzziah, Jotham, Ahaz, Hezekiah, and Manasseh. He pleaded with the people to turn from their wicked ways back to a loving God who would forgive and restore them. Isaiah saw the deliverance of Jerusalem from her enemies, the Assyrians. It was through his prayers and by the intervention of God that Jerusalem was spared from being destroyed. But even this great show of God's mercy and protection did not sway the people back to the worship of Yahweh alone.

Lebanon. In biblical times, Lebanon was synonymous with the cedar trees that grew there. Cedars were most often referred to as "the glory of Lebanon" (Isaiah 35:2; 60:13). The trees grew very tall (Isaiah 2:13) and had plenty of branches to make shade (Ezekiel 31:3). Much of the Temple, Solomon's palace, and public buildings in Jerusalem were made from Lebanon's cedar.

Background

For sixty years, Isaiah served as the prophet in Judah; he stood as the voice of God amid the people's disobedience and his message was to call them back to God. At the start of Isaiah's divine appointment, Judah experienced military and financial strength. As a result, the elite disregarded God's commands—especially in their treatment of the poor, widows, and orphans—as well as their arrogance. Then neighboring Assyria grew in political and military power. Rather than turn to the God of their salvation for refuge, Judah's government leaders looked to the surrounding nations for safety, which was an insult to God.

Isaiah 29 opens with the prophet making a sorrowful declaration upon Jerusalem using the alias Ariel, which means "lion of God." Isaiah predicted how God would deal with Jerusalem's disobedience. The holy city would be under siege and in mourning because of the coming distress at the hand of their enemies as punishment for their idolatry and self-centeredness. But the message also shifts focus that after enduring punishment, He would also handle those enemies who would rise against His chosen people (vv. 5–7).

Have you experienced times where you thought God's help wasn't needed?

At-A-Glance

1. Far From Center (Isaiah 29:13–16)
2. Return to Center (vv. 17–21)
3. Return to Covenant (vv.22–24)

In Depth

1. Far From Center (Isaiah 29:13–16)

God caused the false prophets, rulers, and seers to fall into deep delusions for choosing to follow after darkness. As a result, Judah was unable to understand the word of the Lord and brought into a drunken stupor (vv. 9–12). Isaiah called them out for their hypocrisy, lip service, and religious performances. The Lord would go on to pronounce spiritual judgment against them through Isaiah, saying that their worship of Him was misguided. While Judah followed what had become man-made rituals, they failed to reach His heart. Further in their conceit, Judah's leaders thought they could outsmart and hide from God and live without His wisdom. He warned that they would soon be met with sorrow for being so high-minded. The Lord God reminded them that nothing is hidden from Him. He is the potter, the one who fashioned and created everything.

What are some instances when worship becomes routine?

2. A Return to Center (vv. 17–21)

The Lord shifts the message to bring forth hope for what is to come. God delivers the message through Isaiah that He would turn from judgment to restoration of Judah. God did a review of His covenant and promised that if the people repented, they would be restored. They would see fruitfulness in the land; the deaf would hear and understand what the Lord says, the blind will see and have the ability to read, those that would humble themselves for Him would be filled with joy and the poor would rejoice in the Holy One of Israel. In contrast, those who were oppressive, corrupt, evil, and deceivers would be killed and banished from the land. The people would be brought back to their place of dependence and trust in the Lord God because their idols would be destroyed.

How does God's promise of redemption give us hope today?

3. Return to Covenant (vv. 22–24)

God reinforces His message to the Children of Israel by reminding them of their forefather Abraham. Although He chastises the people for their waywardness, He assures them that they would no longer live in shame and spiritual poverty. God would continue to fulfill His promise to Abraham that he would be the father of many nations and that his seed would be great in the land (Genesis 12:1–3; 15:1–5). If God's chosen people would return to a position of worship and awe of God, then the spiritual plug would be removed to comprehend and follow God's commands. God's people need only remember to look for how God has remained faithful to the promises He made to Abraham, all those hundreds of years ago. With those blessings of wealth and progeny fulfilled, even those who scoffed at God and ignored His instruction would change their ways.

What does it mean for us that God would remind Judah of His promise to Abraham and reaffirm the nation's position as Jacob's descendants?

Search the Scriptures

1. What was God's accusation against Judah (Isaiah 29:13)?

2. How did Judah insult the Lord (vv. 15–16)?

Discuss the Meaning

1. How can we examine the sincerity of our private worship and watch out for hypocrisy in our public worship?

2. What are the themes of hope in verses 17–24 that connect with your faith to trust God in every situation?

Liberating Lesson

God's love is boundless and He freely lavishes His grace on those who would receive it. God's kindness is intended to lead to repentance. However, He will allow circumstances and experiences to chastise and bring us to a place of surrender. After chastisement, God lovingly restores. What would happen if our current system of justice followed God's model? The intent of the criminal justice system should not only be to punish for offenses, but to be effective it should also be restorative. Offenders should have access to programs within the system that rehabilitates—bringing mental, emotional, and spiritual healing that gets to the root causes of deviant behavior for true transformation. Essential to restoration and cultivating honorable citizens is access to education that teaches life skills and provides opportunities to be productive members of society rather than breeding criminalization. Look for ways your small group or church can support a charity working toward criminal justice reform.

Application for Activation

When you consider God's redemptive work through Jesus Christ, how can you focus your attention on making disciples? How can you mentor and support individual or group their development? Is there a person or population you feel called to serve? What hope from your testimony is an indicator of what you can offer to bring healing to another soul?

Follow the Spirit

What God wants me to do:

_____

_____

_____

Remember Your Thoughts

Special insights I have learned:

_____

_____

_____

More Light on the Text
Isaiah 29:13–24

Isaiah 29 falls within a group of chapters in Isaiah (28–33) that make up a series of prophetic oracles against Jerusalem. Each chapter begins with the word, "Woe!" a translation of the Hebrew, *hoy* (**HOH**-ee). Oracles are generally declarations of warnings for disobedience followed by blessings for obedience. For example in verses 1–4, the Lord pronounces judgment against Jerusalem and in verses 5–8 promises them deliverance and protection from the hands of their enemies (fulfilled in chapter 37). This apparent change is not consequent from pessimism to optimism; it is not derived from or dependent on Israel's positive response or change of heart, but it is derived from God's counsel and attributes—His sovereignty and His covenantal relationship with Israel. This is reflective of the Christian relationship with the Father through Christ Jesus (see Romans 5:8). This assurance of deliverance should have motivated the people to trust and worship properly, but they continued in their defiance and senseless behavior. Therefore the Lord dragged them deep into spiritual sleep and blindness by hardening them, leaving them to act without understanding (vv. 9–12).

13 Wherefore the Lord said, Forasmuch as this people draw near me with their mouth, and with their lips do honour me, but have removed their heart far from me, and their fear toward me is taught by the precept of men: 14 Therefore, behold, I will proceed to do a marvellous work among this people, even a marvellous work and a wonder: for the wisdom of their wise men shall perish, and the understanding of their prudent men shall be hid.

Verse 13 commences with an introductory formula laying out new charges against Jerusalem that would warrant more punishment. With the word, "Wherefore" (i.e. therefore), which points back to the preceding actions, the Lord charges them of hypocrisy in their worship. They outwardly tend to worship and honor God, but not from their hearts. They profess to know God, perform all acts of worship, but their hearts are far from Him and from keeping His precepts. Rather they are more concerned with man-made legalistic rules than with the rules they already covenanted to follow, which encourage mercy, justice, and equity.

Because of that, God would judge them; their wisdom would vanish. This is one major sin of Israel; it is reminiscent of what Hosea prophesied, "And they have not cried unto me with their heart, when they howled upon their beds: they assemble themselves for corn and wine, and they rebel against me" (Hosea 7:14; 8:2; 10:1–2). Prophet Micah decried against this practice of false piety (Micah 3:11; 6:6ff).

This attitude in worship did not end with the Old Testament times, it continued during the time of Christ Jesus too. Jesus quoted this passage to denounce the hypocrisy of the Pharisees' pretentious and ritualistic type of worship (Mark 7:6–7; cf. Matthew 15:8–9). Jesus used this prophetic oracle to make the same point as Isaiah. Here Isaiah denounces the leaders' religious practice, "their fear toward me is taught by the precept of men," and Jesus quotes him to describe the tradition of the elders as rules "taught by men." Jesus' reaction to the Pharisees' hypocrisy mirrors Isaiah's prophecy against Jerusalem. Jesus pronounced judgment to those who practiced empty rituals (Matthew 23:1-36) and blessings to those who live by faith (Matthew 5:1-11). Speaking through Isaiah, the Lord pronounces judgment against the people for their insincerity in worship.

The word "behold" (hinni, heen-NYE), also translated lo! (i.e., look!), is often used to call one's attention to the importance of what is about to follow. In this case, it calls their attention to what God is about to do because of their religious practices without true worship of their God. The phrase "I will proceed to do a marvellous work among this people" tends to suggest that the people are familiar with the consequence for their behavior. With the word "proceed," (yasaf yaw-SAF) means "to continue to do." The idea is that the Lord is saying, "Since you're aware of the outcome of your action, I'll to go ahead and fulfill my own side of the covenant." This covenant, known as the Mosaic covenant, which is conditional and, which simply stated says that "if you do this I will do that." So after stating His case against the people, the Lord says that He is going to do such "marvelous" or "wonderful" things that would astound the people so much that those who think they are wise and intelligent will be confounded and go into hiding (cf. 44:25; Jeremiah 8:9).

15 Woe unto them that seek deep to hide their counsel from the LORD, and their works are in the dark, and they say, Who seeth us? and who knoweth us? 16 Surely your turning of things upside down shall be esteemed as the potter's clay: for shall the work say of him that made it, He made me not? or shall the thing framed say of him that framed it, He had no understanding?

The Lord continues the discourse regarding the foolishness of the "wise" and pronounces "woe" on those who think that they can hide things from God. The people try to keep their plan secret. They think that God does not see, does not know, or is unaware of their secret plans. This perhaps refers to Hezekiah's foolish alliance with Egypt for protection rather than seeking and trusting the Lord for deliverance and protection from their enemies (30:1–5). Indeed the people are not thinking clearly, but acting foolishly thinking that they can hide anything from the Almighty who sees and knows all things. They are delusional like the wicked who think, "God isn't watching us! He has closed his eyes and won't even see what we do!" (Psalm 10:11, NLT). They refuse to understand that God knows everything about us—that He examines our inward thoughts and that we cannot hide anything from Him (Psalm 139). Trying to hide anything from God is foolishness and "turning of things upside down" Doing that is reversing man's and God's roles.

The prophet uses the potter/clay metaphor to describe the foolishness of the people. He argues that giving God lip service and trusting to provide for one's security is a role reversal. The Lord presents His case with a series of rhetorical questions. The answers are obvious—it is impossible for the thing made to deny the artistry of its creator. In the same way, it is foolhardiness for one to deny the One who made him or think that "He had no understanding." Instead of counting on God to be the potter and shape them, Judah was treating God as the clay that can be manipulated by rituals and ceremonies. Isaiah would further denounce this attitude later and the "woe" (sorrow or anguish) that awaits those who challenge or argue with the Lord their maker using the same potter/clay metaphor (45:9; cf. 64:8; see also Jeremiah 18:1–6). This passage is also quoted in part by Paul (Romans 9:20–21) to those who tend to question the sovereignty of God and His authority to do what He pleases.

Unfortunately, this hypocritical attitude in worship did not end in the biblical eras—it continues today. Like the people then, we often fall into routine patterns when we worship. We neglect to give God our full love and devotion, our worship is constantly becoming routine and ritualistic. If we want to be called God's own people, we must be obedient and worship Him in honesty and sincerity. Today people go to church for miracles or what they can gain rather than to worship the living God with all their heart, soul, and mind. Hence false prophets and dubious pastors are on the rise.

17 Is it not yet a very little while, and Lebanon shall be turned into a fruitful field, and the fruitful field shall be esteemed as a forest? 18 And in that day shall the deaf hear the words of the book, and the eyes of the blind shall see out of obscurity, and out of darkness.

Scholars differ in the interpretation of this part of the prophecy. However, based on the patterns of prophetic oracles, it appears a positive change in the land is being prophesied. After the seemingly gloomy situation, there seems to be a ray of hope in the land. Here we encounter another shift in redemption (cf. Isaiah 28:5–8). In spite of the people's falsification in worship, Isaiah declares a change in their situation—there would be restoration in no distant time for Jerusalem. The question, "Is it not yet a very little" is another way of saying in a very short time, the people will experience change.

Lebanon is known for its forest, which will be turned into a fruitful field. On the other hand the "fruitful field" will become "as a forest." This seems to suggest that while God would cut one down, He would build another up. This probably again refers to Jerusalem's deliverance as recorded in chapter 37, where God delivered Jerusalem and destroyed Assyria and their king, Sennacherib. Verse 18 seems to support this idea where there will be a reversal of the people's condition described in the previous verses (29:10–12), which is referred to as the nation's impaired sight.

Nonetheless, this prophecy seems to have both immediate and futuristic interpretations, referring to the coming Messianic Age when things would be different. This tends to suggest that while the nation is perverse, sinful, and hypocritical now, a time of change would come. At that time, the wicked would be transformed and the number of the devout worshipers shall increase. Pure and true worship of God will replace general hypocrisy. Isaiah does not say when this will take place, but simply affirms that it will be "yet a little while" (32:15; 35:1–6).

The phrase "And in that day shall the deaf hear the words of the book" speaks of those who have the law and do not understand it. They seem to be deaf to the word of God, but the time is soon coming when they shall hear and understand it. Likewise, "the eyes of the blind shall see out of obscurity, and out of darkness," simply means the darkness would be removed and the people shall clearly see the truth of God's word. This speaks of when the spiritual deafness and blindness of God's people would be restored; pride would no longer prevent them from hearing God's word or seeing God's work.

19 The meek also shall increase their joy in the LORD, and the poor among men shall rejoice in the Holy One of Israel. 20 For the terrible one is brought to nought, and the scorner is consumed, and all that watch for iniquity are cut off: 21 That make a man an offender for a word, and lay a snare for him that reproveth in the gate, and turn aside the just for a thing of nought.

Continuing the change that would take place, Isaiah says, "The meek shall increase their joy in the LORD," and the "[the poor] shall rejoice (celebrate) in the Holy One of Israel." The word "meek" (*'anav*, aw-**NAWV**) also means the humble, the lowly and poor (in spirit). The word "poor" is a translation of *ebyon* (eb-**YONE**), with an idea of being in need or want; it is the feeling of destitution, a beggar, or the needy. People in these situations are usually unhappy and joyless, but when this prophecy is filled, both the humble (poor in spirit) and physically

poor (the materially destitute) will have joy in the Lord; they will rejoice "in the Holy One of Israel." On the Sermon Mount, Jesus affirms this saying, "Blessed (or happy/joyful) are the poor in spirit: for theirs is the kingdom of heaven" (Matthew 5:3).

The phrases "in the LORD" and "in the Holy One of Israel" mean that both the humble and the poor will rejoice because of their belief and faithfulness in the Lord. On the other hand the "terrible" (*'arits*, aw-**REETS**), i.e. the powerful and the oppressors, will be rendered powerless and brought to nothing. Both the scorner and those who crave iniquity will be consumed and cut off. These are people who unjustly mistreat the poor and humble. They plot evil and frame the innocent and the poor, falsely accusing them. So at that time, everyone will be affected. While the poor and the needy will rejoice in the Lord because of what He will do for them, the cruel and the wicked that deprived the innocent of justice will be punished (cf. Isaiah 29:5).

22 Therefore thus saith the LORD, who redeemed Abraham, concerning the house of Jacob, Jacob shall not now be ashamed, neither shall his face now wax pale. 23 But when he seeth his children, the work of mine hands, in the midst of him, they shall sanctify my name, and sanctify the Holy One of Jacob, and shall fear the God of Israel. 24 They also that erred in spirit shall come to understanding, and they that murmured shall learn doctrine.

Through Isaiah, the Lord makes a profound promise of redemption to the people and reminds them of His activity in the past as a guarantee of its fulfillment. Isaiah assures them that just as the Lord redeemed Abraham their forefather in the past, He will surely do the same for them. To reinforce this promise, Isaiah employs God's personal name, "LORD" or *Yahweh* (**YAH**-way), "self-Existent or Eternal;

Jehovah." Yahweh is the Jewish national name of God—the only true God. The word "redeemed" (Heb. *padah*, paw-**DAW**) means to ransom, deliver or to rescue. This word is generally used in the deliverance of Israel from Egypt under Moses (Exodus 6:6; 15:13). The whole phrase "who redeemed Abraham" refers when the Lord delivered the patriarch from his pagan and idolatrous world, ordering him to "get thee out of thy country, and from thy kindred, and from thy father's house, unto a land that I will shew thee" (from Genesis 12:1ff; cf. Joshua 24:2–3). Therefore based on this historical fact, Isaiah promises that "the house of Jacob" (Israel and Judah) shall no more be "ashamed" or grow pale because of their enemies. Fear makes the face look pale—that means they will no longer be afraid of their enemies. This promise is repeated over three times later in this book and it is a perpetual covenant to God's people: "But Israel shall be saved in the LORD with an everlasting salvation: ye shall not be ashamed nor confounded world without end" (Isaiah 45:17; cf. 50:7; 54:4). This promise will also be for Israel's posterity.

When this is accomplished, they will experience visible change among themselves and their offspring. The house of Jacob will see God's handiwork in their children–and their attitude toward God will change. Every spiritual reformation and change is always God's work alone (Isaiah 60:21; Ephesians 2:10). Consequently, the people will revere God's name and worship Him. Sinners will be changed; they will understand the true worship and reverence of the Lord. Their eyes will spiritually open and their ears spiritually unstopped to see and hear the truth (Isaiah 29:18); their worship will be genuine from the heart and not with their lips only (v. 13). They will then adulate the Lord in truth and in spirit and their murmuring will cease. This speaks of a great revival among God's people.

Sources:

Abraham, A. Kenneth, *The Matthew Henry Study Bible, King James Version*, Iowa Falls IA: World Bible Publishers, Inc. 1994. 1292, 1339-1342.

Attridge, Harold, W. *The Harper Collins Study Bible, New Revised Standard Version*. New York: Harper One, 2006. 948–949.

Barnes, Albert. *Barnes' Notes on the New Testament*. Grand Rapids, MI: Kregel Publications, 1962.

Cabal, Ted et. al., *The Apologetics Study Bible, Holman Christian Standard*, Nashville, TN, Holman Bible Publishers, 2007. 991-992, 1031.

Collins, John J., *A Short Introduction to the Hebrew Bible*, Minneapolis, MN, Fortress Press, 2007. 169-170.

Life Application Study Bible, New Living Translation. Wheaton, IL: Tyndale House Publishers, Inc., 1996. 1055–1056.

Pfeiffer, Charles F., Howard F. Vos, John Rea, eds. *Wycliffe Bible Dictionary*. Peabody, MA: Hendrickson Publishers, Inc., 1998.

Strong, James. *The New Strong's Exhaustive Concordance of the Bible*. Nashville, TN: Thomas Nelson, 2003.

Van der Mass, Ed M. *Halley's Bible Handbook: Deluxe Edition (25th Edition)*. Grand Rapids, MI: Zondervan, 2007. 335–342, 352–353.

Walvoord, John F. and Roy B. Zuck. *The Bible Knowledge Commentary: An Exposition of the Scriptures*. Old Testament. Wheaton, IL: Victor Books, 1983.

Zodhiates, Spiros. *Key Word Study Bible King James Version*. Chattanooga, TN: AMG Publishers, 1991. 854.

Say It Correctly

Sennacherib. seh-**NACK**-rib.
Mosaic. mow-**SAY**-ik.
Assyria. ah-**SEER**-ee-ah.

Daily Bible Readings

MONDAY
Discipline the Immoral Person
with Respect
(1 Corinthians 5:1–5)

TUESDAY
Uphold Justice for All Peoples
(Exodus 23:1–9)

WEDNESDAY
Seek and You Will Find Me!
(Jeremiah 29:10–14)

THURSDAY
Lip Service Is Not Enough
(Mark 7:1–8)

FRIDAY
Jerusalem Punished and Rescued
(Isaiah 29:1–8)

SATURDAY
Judah, Blind to God's Ways
(Isaiah 29:9–12)

SUNDAY
Israel Will Enjoy a Bright Future
(Isaiah 29:13–24)

Notes

_____

_____

_____

_____

Teaching Tips

Words You Should Know

A. Chaldeans (Jeremiah 38:18) *kasdim* (Heb.)—Inhabitants of Chaldea, in the lower Mesopotamia; Babylonians

B. I Beseech Thee (v. 20) *na'* (Heb.)—Please; a particle of incitement and entreaty

Teacher Preparation

Unifying Principle—The Consequences of Giving Challenging Advice. No one wants to be the bearer of bad news or challenging advice. How can we find courage to speak when what we have to say is likely to cause controversy or hard feelings? Jeremiah frankly discussed his concerns with King Zedekiah and then spoke with confidence that he was delivering a message from God.

A. Read the Bible Background and Devotional Reading.

B. Pray for your students and lesson clarity.

C. Read the lesson Scripture in multiple translations.

O—Open the Lesson

A. Begin the class with prayer.

B. Share a personal time you went to a wise counselor for help in a no–win situation. Ask volunteers to share a similar situation.

C. Have the students read the Aim for Change and the In Focus story.

D. Ask students how events like those in the story weigh on their hearts and how they can view these events from a faith perspective.

P—Present the Scriptures

A. Read the Focal Verses and discuss the Background and The People, Places, and Times sections.

B. Have the class share what Scriptures stand out for them and why, with particular emphasis on today's themes.

E—Explore the Meaning

A. Use In Depth or More Light on the Text to facilitate a deeper discussion of the lesson text.

B. Pose the questions in Search the Scriptures and Discuss the Meaning.

C. Discuss the Liberating Lesson and Application for Activation sections.

N—Next Steps for Application

A. Summarize the value of speaking boldly despite consequences.

B. End class with a commitment to pray for understanding current events according to God's perspective.

Worship Guide

For the Superintendent or Teacher
Theme: Jeremiah: The Suffering Preacher
Song: "Lord, Speak to Me That
I May Speak"
Devotional Reading: Jeremiah 38:7-13;
39:15-18

Jeremiah: The Suffering Preacher

Bible Background • JEREMIAH 37-38
Printed Text • JEREMIAH 38:14-23 | Devotional Reading • JEREMIAH 38:7-13; 39:15–18

Aim for Change

By the end of this lesson, we will IDENTIFY Jeremiah's hesitation to give controversial advice to Zedekiah, SENSE Jeremiah's apprehension when talking to Zedekiah, and COMMIT to giving challenging godly advice.

In Focus

Walter was stuck between the proverbial "rock and a hard place." Walter still liked to hang out with his single friends, reveling in his former life, but sought to change his ways, especially for the sake of his marriage. In the past, Walter used his brother Ronald as a cover without his knowledge and rationalized that it was just more comfortable for him not to know so he could avoid the lecture. He hadn't meant to do it again, but then his single friends planned a once-in-a-lifetime trip to Jamaica. Walter promised this would be the last time he tried to cover up his actions with these friends, and told his wife just he and Ronald were going for brother time.

While out at a family function, Tonya asked, "So Ronald, how are plans for your trip to Jamaica? Walter told me you all would be using our timeshare." Ronald was at a loss for words and gracefully excused himself from Tonya to calm down.

Later, Ronald confronted his brother "Hey man, enough is enough, I am not going to be a part of your lies and deception. If you don't tell Tonya the truth, I will!"

Walter replied, "Ronald, what do I do? I just wanted to get away and have some fun with the fellas, and I figured if Tonya thought you were going, she would not ask too many questions."

Walter had no idea how to get himself out of the mess he made, both with his wife and with his brother, but he could not bring himself to face the truth.

Which is harder to expose the truth or remain silent?

Keep in Mind

"Then Jeremiah said unto Zedekiah, If I declare it unto thee, wilt thou not surely put me to death? and if I give thee counsel, wilt thou not hearken unto me?"
(Jeremiah 38:15, KJV)

"Jeremiah said, 'If I tell you the truth, you will kill me. And if I give you advice, you won't listen to me anyway.'" (Jeremiah 38:15, NLT)

Focal Verses

KJV **Jeremiah 38:14** Then Zedekiah the king sent, and took Jeremiah the prophet unto him into the third entry that is in the house of the LORD: and the king said unto Jeremiah, I will ask thee a thing; hide nothing from me.

15 Then Jeremiah said unto Zedekiah, If I declare it unto thee, wilt thou not surely put me to death? and if I give thee counsel, wilt thou not hearken unto me?

16 So Zedekiah the king sware secretly unto Jeremiah, saying, As the LORD liveth, that made us this soul, I will not put thee to death, neither will I give thee into the hand of these men that seek thy life.

17 Then said Jeremiah unto Zedekiah, Thus saith the LORD, the God of hosts, the God of Israel; If thou wilt assuredly go forth unto the king of Babylon's princes, then thy soul shall live, and this city shall not be burned with fire; and thou shalt live, and thine house:

18 But if thou wilt not go forth to the king of Babylon's princes, then shall this city be given into the hand of the Chaldeans, and they shall burn it with fire, and thou shalt not escape out of their hand.

19 And Zedekiah the king said unto Jeremiah, I am afraid of the Jews that are fallen to the Chaldeans, lest they deliver me into their hand, and they mock me.

20 But Jeremiah said, They shall not deliver thee. Obey, I beseech thee, the voice of the LORD, which I speak unto thee: so it shall be well unto thee, and thy soul shall live.

21 But if thou refuse to go forth, this is the word that the LORD hath shewed me:

22 And, behold, all the women that are left in the king of Judah's house shall be brought forth to the king of Babylon's princes, and those women shall say, Thy friends have set thee on, and have prevailed against thee: thy

NLT **Jeremiah 38:14** One day King Zedekiah sent for Jeremiah and had him brought to the third entrance of the LORD's Temple. "I want to ask you something," the king said. "And don't try to hide the truth."

15 Jeremiah said, "If I tell you the truth, you will kill me. And if I give you advice, you won't listen to me anyway."

16 So King Zedekiah secretly promised him, "As surely as the LORD our Creator lives, I will not kill you or hand you over to the men who want you dead."

17 Then Jeremiah said to Zedekiah, "This is what the LORD God of Heaven's Armies, the God of Israel, says: 'If you surrender to the Babylonian officers, you and your family will live, and the city will not be burned down.

18 But if you refuse to surrender, you will not escape! This city will be handed over to the Babylonians, and they will burn it to the ground.'"

19 "But I am afraid to surrender," the king said, "for the Babylonians may hand me over to the Judeans who have defected to them. And who knows what they will do to me!"

20 Jeremiah replied, "You won't be handed over to them if you choose to obey the LORD. Your life will be spared, and all will go well for you.

21 But if you refuse to surrender, this is what the LORD has revealed to me:

22 All the women left in your palace will be brought out and given to the officers of the Babylonian army. Then the women will taunt you, saying, 'What fine friends you have! They have betrayed and misled you. When your feet sank in the mud, they left you to your fate!'

23 All your wives and children will be led out to the Babylonians, and you will not escape. You will be seized by the king of Babylon, and this city will be burned down."

feet are sunk in the mire, and they are turned away back.

23 So they shall bring out all thy wives and thy children to the Chaldeans: and thou shalt not escape out of their hand, but shalt be taken by the hand of the king of Babylon: and thou shalt cause this city to be burned with fire.

The People, Places, and Times

Jeremiah. The son of a priest, Jeremiah was born in Anathoth, a village three miles northeast of Jerusalem. Jeremiah received his calling as a prophet in 626 BC during the thirteenth year of King Josiah's reign. The Book of Jeremiah reveals the inner turmoil and conflict out of which Jeremiah delivered his prophetic burden. Jeremiah resisted his call to prophetic ministry, citing his youth as an obstacle (Jeremiah 1:6-9). But God's will cannot be resisted. Jeremiah followed his calling faithfully, but the road was hard. He was rejected by his people (Jeremiah 15:10). He was frustrated by their hardheartedness (Jeremiah 5:3). In spite of all of the difficulties that Jeremiah experienced, he found that he could not resist God's call to prophesy. He had to declare the word of the LORD as the LORD had directed him. It was a compulsion. It was a dynamic, powerful inner motivation that made him prophesy. "Then I said, I will not make mention of him, nor speak any more in his name. But his word was in mine heart as a burning fire shut up in my bones, and I was weary with forbearing, and I could not stay" (Jeremiah 20:9).

Background

Jeremiah, whose name means "Yahweh appointed," was set apart by God as a prophet from the womb (Jeremiah 1:5). For over forty years he was God's mouthpiece as he called out judgment against Judah for their wickedness. In the fourth year of King Jehoiakim's eleven-year reign, the Lord commanded Jeremiah to provide a written account of everything spoken about Israel, Judah, and all the nations from the time of King Josiah until that present which included His reminders of the disaster to come. God's objective was to extend mercy if hearers would only repent (Jeremiah 36:1-3). King Jehoiakim and his officials heard the prophetic word but rather than repent, the scrolls were burned (Jeremiah 36:1-25).

In spite of the tough words he had to deliver and personal pain experienced, Jeremiah followed through with everything the Lord commanded. In the last days of Jerusalem King Zedekiah, a weaker king was in power and the Lord sent word through Jeremiah that although Judah looked to Egypt as an ally, the other nation would leave them to fend for themselves. He further warned that Judah's nemesis—the Chaldeans—would prevail against them, burn down the city, and scatter them as exiles. However, this destruction would be averted if the king and his leaders would turn back to the Lord. The officials were angered by his prophecy and sought to paint Jeremiah as a traitor to the Chaldeans; he was beaten and thrown into prison (Jeremiah 37:1-16).

What does it mean to speak truth to power?

At-A-Glance

1. A Final Interview (Jeremiah 38:14–18)
2. A Final Response (vv. 19–23)

In Depth

1. A Final Interview (Jeremiah 38:14–18)

King Zedekiah on more than one occasion privately sought out Jeremiah to hear what the Lord had revealed to him. The king had other prophets who told him what he wanted to hear regarding Judah's national security. But those prophets did not align with what the Lord spoke through Jeremiah, who proved to be His true prophet. The Lord delivered Jeremiah from his officials through King Zedekiah (Jeremiah 37:17–21). Jeremiah would find himself in trouble with the king's officials again for delivering the Lord's proclamation of calamity for disobedience and coming Chaldean siege. He was considered a trouble maker who caused unrest in the land and was thrown into a dry cistern by the king's men. The king would later rescue Jeremiah from death, but he would be once again locked up (Jeremiah 38:1–13).

King Zedekiah sought to show honor for the word of the Lord and had Jeremiah brought to him at the Temple to inquire what the Lord might say through him. Jeremiah was hesitant to answer because he recognized that Zedekiah would probably not listen to his counsel. His officials had great power and influence and wanted Jeremiah dead. The king promised in their one-on-one conversation that neither he nor his men would kill Jeremiah because the king wanted to hear what the Lord said. Jeremiah gave the Lord's word by advising the king and his officials to surrender to the Babylonians so that they may live. However, if they did not heed his counsel from the Lord, the city would burn, and they would not escape.

How do you discern when to speak and when to be quiet?

2. A Final Response (vv. 19–23)

After hearing Jeremiah's prophetic word to surrender, King Zedekiah in confidence shares with Jeremiah that he fears what will happen if he follows the instructions given by the Lord. Jeremiah assures the king if he and his officials obey the Lord, the crisis will be suspended and they will be saved. However, if he refuses, the Lord revealed that the Chaldeans would burn the city and the people would be taken captive by Babylon. Further, Jeremiah tells the king that he and his officials would bring disgrace upon themselves as the people who trust them realize they had misled them. Their wives who are the life-givers and their sons who represent their bloodline would be captured. The king and all of his officials would be destroyed. King Zedekiah led Judah through habitual disobedience and bad advice, and Jeremiah foretold the consequences of those decisions. God still provided an opportunity to change their ways if they would only ask for and receive God's mercy.

What are some reasons people dismiss godly advice?

Search the Scriptures

1. What was Jeremiah's response to King Zedekiah's request to hear from the Lord (Jeremiah 38:15)?

2. What was the Lord's advice to King Zedekiah through Jeremiah? What was His warning (vv. 17, 20–21)?

Discuss the Meaning

1. Given Jeremiah's experience as a prophet, was he right to question King Zedekiah's request? What did the king expect to hear from Jeremiah?

2. Are there times when you have been the recipient of advice you did not want to receive but the Lord confirmed it was from Him? How did you respond?

Liberating Lesson

Dr. Martin Luther King Jr. spoke many times about the dangers of keeping silent. There are times when God will compel His people to speak truth to those who will not receive it favorably, but we must stand for righteousness even if it costs. Some believers live in parts of the world where they are faced with persecution daily for boldly living their faith. Those of us blessed with religious freedom must continue to pray and support those who do not have the same freedom. Think of ways your small group or church can help people living in countries were Christianity is actually illegal. Even on our side of the world, we must be intentional to equip ourselves and others in the spirit of God's love to share and defend our faith in the public square amid opposition.

Application for Activation

In our world, we still hear the chant "no justice, no peace," because there is a need to keep speaking out against systemic injustice. The Church must champion against injustice because we are recipients of God's mercy and made equal at the Cross of Jesus. No matter the race, color, or creed injustice against any people does not reflect the God who created humanity in His image with the capacity to love without limit. There are plenty of causes in need of individual and collective voices for social change. Commit to sharing your time, talent, and resources as an individual, a class, or a church to bring God's kingdom of righteousness in the earth.

Follow the Spirit

What God wants me to do:

_____

_____

_____

_____

Remember Your Thoughts

Special insights I have learned:

_____

_____

_____

_____

_____

More Light on the Text
Jeremiah 38:14–23

Jeremiah 37–39 is a chronological narrative of Prophet Jeremiah's life during the reign of King Zedekiah in Jerusalem until its final siege and destruction by King Nebuchadnezzar of Babylonia. In an earlier conquest of the city, Nebuchadnezzar had taken King Jehoiachin captive and replaced him with his uncle, Mattaniah whom he ironically renamed Zedekiah, which means, "Yahweh is righteous" (2 Kings 24:15–17; Jeremiah 37:1). King Zedekiah's life was anything but righteous for he "did what was evil in the LORD's sight" (from 2 Kings 24:19–20, NLT). Zedekiah also made Judah sin against the Lord God. The Lord determined to discipline Jerusalem as a consequence for their rebellion using Babylonia as His instrument. However, the Lord used the prophets including Jeremiah to warn the people of the imminent destruction that awaited them unless they repented. Despite a series of warnings through Jeremiah, King Zedekiah and the people continued to rebel; they refuse to heed the word of God (37:3–10). Rather, they conspire to kill Jeremiah and put him in prison three times for speaking the mind of God (cf. 37:11–16; 38:1–6).

438

14 Then Zedekiah the king sent, and took Jeremiah the prophet unto him into the third entry that is in the house of the LORD: and the king said unto Jeremiah, I will ask thee a thing; hide nothing from me. 15 Then Jeremiah said unto Zedekiah, If I declare it unto thee, wilt thou not surely put me to death? and if I give thee counsel, wilt thou not hearken unto me?

Verses 7–13 record how the Lord used an Ethiopian eunuch, an officer in the royal palace, Ebed-Melech, to rescue Jeremiah from the officials of the city who had plotted to kill him. They had gone to Zedekiah and accused Jeremiah of discouraging the people with his prophecies. To them it was a treasonous act. On their demand for Jeremiah's death (vv. 2–3), Zedekiah handed him over to the officials. They cast him into a dry but muddy cistern and left him there to die. Jeremiah sank into the mud, but for Ebed-Melech's timely intercession to the king, Jeremiah would have died. Zedekiah then gives orders and Jeremiah is rescued from the cistern (vv. 9–13). Jeremiah would later send a special message to Ebed-Melech assuring him that when the city is taken, God would spare his life and he would be delivered (39:15–18).

Later, King Zedekiah invites Jeremiah for a private and secrete consultation. According to records, this is the fourth and last contact King Zedekiah had with Jeremiah before the fall of the city to Babylonia.

On his arrival, Zedekiah takes him "into the third entry that is in the house of the LORD." It has been suggested that this entrance may refer to a private entrance that connected the king's palace with the Temple. Without going directly to his inquiry, the king solicits for Jeremiah's honesty to tell him the truth. The request seems to put Jeremiah in a dilemma because of his past experiences. This is the third occasion Zedekiah called on Jeremiah. The two previous times did not go well. After giving the word of God the

first time, Jeremiah is imprisoned (37:1–16). After the second summons, he is thrown into the cistern (38:1–6).

Based on these previous experiences, Jeremiah is apprehensive; he expresses two objections. First, "If I declare it unto thee, wilt thou not surely put me to death?" That is, if he would say things unfavorable to the king, there is no guarantee the king would not kill him. Second, "if I give thee counsel, wilt thou not hearken unto me?" In other words "there is no need giving you advice because you will not listen." Previously, Jeremiah has warned Zedekiah and the nation of Judah several times of the impending destruction of Jerusalem because of their rebellion, but they have flouted God's words and ignored Jeremiah's counsels. Indeed Jeremiah has become unpopular with the officials for his negative messages regarding the fall of Jerusalem so they plot his death (cf. 26:10–11; 37:11–15; 38:4). King Zedekiah's decision to meet him privately was for fear of the officials (37:17; 18:5).

16 So Zedekiah the king sware secretly unto Jeremiah, saying, As the Lord liveth, that made us this soul, I will not put thee to death, neither will I give thee into the hand of these men that seek thy life.

After Jeremiah has voiced his objections, King Zedekiah secretly vows to Jeremiah using the Lord's name that he would neither kill him nor hand him over to the people. With these specifics, the king stops himself from a loophole. One can imagine an evil twist as the king promises not to kill the prophet, only for him to be handed over to someone else who will kill him. King Zedekiah does not take advantage of that trick, though, and answers Jeremiah's first objection, but not the second. He promises to spare Jeremiah's life but never promises to comply with Jeremiah's messages and counsel.

17 Then said Jeremiah unto Zedekiah, Thus saith the LORD, the God of hosts, the God of Israel; If thou wilt assuredly go forth unto the king of Babylon's princes, then thy soul shall live, and this city shall not be burned with fire; and thou shalt live, and thine house: 18 But if thou wilt not go forth to the king of Babylon's princes, then shall this city be given into the hand of the Chaldeans, and they shall burn it with fire, and thou shalt not escape out of their hand.

Zedekiah probably thought that Jeremiah must have been enticed with the promise of his safety to compromise God's message. Apparently, he must have thought that Jeremiah was as unstable, wobbly and fearful as himself, and therefore would change his message to suit the king. But Jeremiah is stable, obedient, and faithful to God and His word, unlike Zedekiah. Therefore Jeremiah's message remains the same as before (cf. 21:1–10; 37:17; 38:1–3).

Jeremiah boldly declares to him what Lord has revealed to him, this time with emphasis, "Thus saith the LORD" According to the word of God, if Zedekiah would surrender to the Babylonians, then his life would be spared, Jerusalem would be conquered but it would not be burned down, and his family would be spared and safe. However, if Zedekiah refuses to surrender, Jeremiah assures him, Jerusalem would be handed over to the armies of Babylonia who would burn it down and Zedekiah would not escape from their hands (cf. 21:10; 32:3–4, 29; 34:2, 22; 37:8,10; 38:23).

For its authenticity and its fulfillment, Jeremiah identifies the source of his prophecy: it is from the "LORD, the God of host, the God of Israel" using God's divine attributes and identities that are familiar to Zedekiah. The same God in whose name Zedekiah swore to Jeremiah of his safety if he would be honest with him. One would think that on hearing that the order is from the Lord God of Israel, Zedekiah would listen and follow the prophet's advice. But the contrary is the case. Instead of trusting the Lord and obeying His word and in spite of Jeremiah's guarantee of safety if he would follow his advice, Zedekiah prefers to fear his own people rather than God.

19 And Zedekiah the king said unto Jeremiah, I am afraid of the Jews that are fallen to the Chaldeans, lest they deliver me into their hand, and they mock me. 20 But Jeremiah said, They shall not deliver thee. Obey, I beseech thee, the voice of the Lord, which I speak unto thee: so it shall be well unto thee, and thy soul shall live.

King Zedekiah would not follow Jeremiah's advice because of fear. He tells Jeremiah that he is afraid if he surrenders to the Babylonians, they might hand him over to the Jews who had already had gone to Babylon; and they would him to taunt and ridicule. They might maltreat him and his family because of his acts of cruelty toward them in the past. If Zedekiah had trusted in the Lord, he would not have been afraid of either the officials or the deserters. Not minding the spineless king's flimsy and ridiculous excuses, Jeremiah reassures him that the Babylonians would not deliver him to his detractors. Pleading, Jeremiah tries to persuade him to obey God's word. The phrase "I beseech thee" is from the Hebrew word *na'* (**naw**), a particle of incitement and entreaty, that can simply be translated as "please." Jeremiah begs Zedekiah to obey the Lord and to voluntarily surrender to the Babylonians in order to save his life, his family, and Jerusalem. Jeremiah then reiterates the consequences if he refuses to heed the word of God.

21 But if thou refuse to go forth, this is the word that the LORD hath shewed me: 22 And, behold, all the women that are left in the king of Judah's house shall be brought

forth to the king of Babylon's princes, and those women shall say, Thy friends have set thee on, and have prevailed against thee: thy feet are sunk in the mire, and they are turned away back. 23 So they shall bring out all thy wives and thy children to the Chaldeans: and thou shalt not escape out of their hand, but shalt be taken by the hand of the king of Babylon: and thou shalt cause this city to be burned with fire.

Jeremiah's plea to King Zedekiah is followed by a stern warning. Jeremiah warns him that if he fails to surrender to the Babylonians, worse things than what he fears will come upon him. To stress the seriousness of the consequences of his refusal to obey, Jeremiah warns the king affirming that his revelation is from God—it's not man's words or just a made-up story. Therefore Zedekiah should take it seriously because what is coming to him will be worse than what he is afraid of. When the Babylonian army comes and takes the city, all the women would be given to the officers of the Babylonian army. What he feared will then come to him. "The woman," Jeremiah basically tells Zedekiah, "will ridicule you, and mockingly sing to you, 'What fine friends you have! They have betrayed and misled you. When your feet sank in the mud, they left you to your fate!'" In other words, "What type of good friends you have who have betrayed and misled you with false advice and now you are in trouble, they have deserted you and abandoned you to your fate."

Continuing his warning in verse 23, Jeremiah tells King Zedekiah that if he refuses to surrender to Babylonia, he would watch his wives and children be taken away. He himself would be captured and the city of Jerusalem would be burned down as the Lord had spoken (cf. 38:18). The fulfillment of this prophecy is recorded in the next chapter (39:6). Like the coward he is and being afraid of the officials, Zedekiah warns Jeremiah not to disclose their conversation to the officials, and if he did he would lose his life (vv. 24ff). It is no surprise that King Zedekiah disobeyed all the words the Lord had spoken through Jeremiah. That notwithstanding every word of Jeremiah's prophecy was fulfilled.

The question is why would Zedekiah not believe Jeremiah. It has been suggested that one of the reasons could be Ezekiel's prophecy that he would never see Babylon: "I will bring him to Babylon to the land of the Chaldeans; yet shall he not see it, though he shall die there" (Ezekiel 12:13). Both Jeremiah and Ezekiel had agreed in all the prophecies regarding the destruction of Jerusalem and that Zedekiah would be taken captive to Babylon. Zedekiah indeed was taken captive to Babylon just as the prophets had prophesied, but he never saw Babylon. King Nebuchadnezzar had made him watch his sons slaughtered before him, then he gouged out his eyes, bound him in bronze and led him to Babylon (Jeremiah 39:6–7).

Zedekiah means "Yahweh is righteous" ironically given him by Nebuchadnezzar (2 King 24:15–17). He was one of the most unrighteous, wicked and godless kings reigned in Israel and Judah; he was an epitome of evil and led Judah to sin. Jeremiah ministered under him during one of the most difficult times in Jerusalem. Jeremiah's life was threatened constantly and he was often imprisoned—yet he remained truthful and faithful to God's Word. He never compromised; he fearlessly proclaimed the word of God and was never afraid to say the truth. Playing on the meaning of King Zedekiah's name, Jeremiah prophesied that the Lord would send a king worthy of the name. This future King will come from King David's lineage to save his people, taking up the messianic name "Yahweh Is Our Righteousness."

On the one hand, Zedekiah-types are not lacking in our society and in many nations today. It is not rare to find ungodly leaders who, like Zedekiah are disobedient to the word of God and who are leading their countries. Many are fighting the Lord.

On the other hand, Jeremiah-types are rare and almost impossible to find in our churches today. The Gospel is compromised, we have become weak and afraid to proclaim God's word fearlessly; our priority has changed, instead of propagating the Gospel, prosperity is preached and amassing wealth. Private jets and big mansions have become the symbol of success and church growth. Only very few if any can faithfully stand on the truth of God's Word under threat imprisonment or death. May God restore the spirit of Jeremiah among us.

Sources:

Abraham, A. Kenneth, *The Matthew Henry Study Bible, King James Version*, Iowa Falls IA: World Bible Publishers, Inc. 1994. 1414, 1502-1510.

Adeyemo, Tokunboh, gen. ed. *Africa Bible Commentary*. Grand Rapids, MI: Zondervan, 2006.

Cabal, Ted et. al., *The Apologetics Study Bible, Holman Christian Standard*, Nashville, TN, Holman Bible Publishers, 2007. 1085-1086, 1142-1146.

Kapusta, Philip P. *A King James Dictionary: A Resource for Understanding the Language of the King James Bible*. Murrells Inlet, SC: New Covenant Press, 2012.

Harrison, R. K. editor. *The New Unger's Bible Dictionary*. Chicago: Moody Press, 1988. 1382-1383.

Strong, James. *The New Strong's Exhaustive Concordance of the Bible*. Nashville, TN: Thomas Nelson, 2003.

Tabaka, Marla. *"31 Martin Luther King Jr. Quotes to Inspire Greatness in You."* Inc.com. https://www.inc.com/marla-tabaka/31-martin-luther-king-jr-quotes-to-inspire-greatness-in-you.html. (accessed July 15, 2019)

Thayer, Joseph Henry. *A Greek-English Lexicon of the New Testament*. New York: American Book Company, 1889.

Van der Mass, Ed M. *Halley's Bible Handbook: Deluxe Edition (25th Edition)*. Grand Rapids, MI: Zondervan, 2007. 362-363, 370-371.

Vine, W.E. *Vine's Complete Expository Dictionary of Old and New Testament Words*. Nashville, TN: Thomas Nelson, 1996.

Walvoord, John F. and Roy B. Zuck. *The Bible Knowledge Commentary: An Exposition of the Scriptures. Old Testament*. Wheaton, IL: Victor Books, 1983.

Zodhiates, Spiros. *Key Word Study Bible, King James Version*. Chattanooga, TN: AMG Publishers, 1991. 921.

Say It Correctly

Ebed-melek. eh-**BED**-meh-**LEK**.
Zedekiah. zeh-deh-**KYE**-ah.
Jehoiachin. jeh-**HOY**-ah-kin.
Mattaniah. mah-tah-**NYE**-ah.

Daily Bible Readings

MONDAY
Apostles Speak Truth to Council
(Acts 4:13–22)

TUESDAY
Prophet Jeremiah Is
Arrested and Imprisoned
(Jeremiah 37:11–16)

WEDNESDAY
Ebed-Melech's Trust in
Jeremiah Honored
(Jeremiah 38:7–13; 39:15–18)

THURSDAY
Jeremiah Reaffirms
Prophecy of Zedekiah
(Jeremiah 37:17–21)

FRIDAY
Jeremiah's Last Days in Jerusalem
(Jeremiah 38:24–28)

SATURDAY
Jerusalem Destroyed; People Exiled
(2 Kings 25:1–12)

SUNDAY
Zedekiah Must Submit
to Babylonian Conquest
(Jeremiah 38:14–23)

Teaching Tips

May 23
Bible Study Guide 12

Words You Should Know

A. Soul (Ezekiel 18:4) *nephesh* (Heb.)—Meaning, life, person's desire, emotion; the inner being of a person

B. Repent (v. 30) *shub* (Heb.)—To feel sorry for having done wrong, change of mind; to turn back or to weep in grief over an act

Teacher Preparation

Unifying Principle—Take Responsibility! It is easy to blame our background or upbringing for the misfortunes we face. What is the role of personal responsibility? Ezekiel warns Israel that each person will answer for his or her behavior and that all must repent of their sinful ways and obey God's commands to find favor with God.

A. Read the Bible Background and Devotional Reading.

B. Pray for your students and lesson clarity.

C. Read the lesson Scripture in multiple translations.

O—Open the Lesson

A. Begin the class with prayer.

B. Ask the participants to share an excuse they've made or heard recently. Why do excuses rarely address the real problem?

C. Have the students read the Aim for Change and the In Focus story.

D. Ask students how events like those in the story weigh on their hearts and how they can view these events from a faith perspective.

P—Present the Scriptures

A. Read the Focal Verses and discuss the Background and The People, Places, and Times sections.

B. Have the class share what Scriptures stand out for them and why, with particular emphasis on today's themes.

E—Explore the Meaning

A. Use In Depth or More Light on the Text to facilitate a deeper discussion of the lesson text.

B. Pose the questions in Search the Scriptures and Discuss the Meaning.

C. Discuss the Liberating Lesson and Application for Activation sections.

N—Next Steps for Application

A. Summarize the value of moral regeneration rather than putting forth extra efforts to be moral.

B. End class with a commitment to pray for the right attitude toward problems.

Worship Guide

For the Superintendent or Teacher
Theme: Ezekiel: Street Preacher
to the Exiles
Song: "Trust and Obey"
Devotional Reading: Psalm 147

Ezekiel: Street Preacher to the Exiles

Bible Background • EZEKIEL 18
Printed Text • EZEKIEL 18:1-9, 30-32 | Devotional Reading • PSALM 147

Aim for Change

By the end of this lesson, we will EXAMINE behavior in which we blame others as the cause, COMMIT to be responsible for our own behavior, and ENGAGE in responsible behavior that finds favor with God.

In Focus

Alex and Andrew grew up watching their father, Mason, come home drunk. Sometimes Mason would scream at their mom or them or sometimes just go to bed to sleep it off. They saw him miss work because of hangovers and then have nothing to do in the evening but drink some more.

When Andrew moved out of the house, he prided himself on how he could drink responsibly. He would go out for drinks with the guys after work and enjoy himself at a weekend party. It was hard living on his own, though, and soon his treat of a nightcap turned to more and more drinking. Andrew was worried about what he saw his own life becoming, but what could he do? He had never had a positive role model to show him how to deal with life's hardships. His dad had been an alcoholic and now he was borderline too. What had anyone really expected to happen?

Alex watched as his brother descended into the same path their father did. Even though Alex was the spitting image of his dad, they were very different in temperament. Knowing that he would likely have a problem with alcohol if he tried it, he decided to completely abstain. There were plenty of fun things to do with his friends that didn't involve drinks.

How have you followed in your parents' footsteps? When have you decided specifically to not follow their example?

Keep in Mind

"Behold, all souls are mine; as the soul of the father, so also the soul of the son is mine: the soul that sinneth, it shall die" (Ezekiel 18:4, KJV)

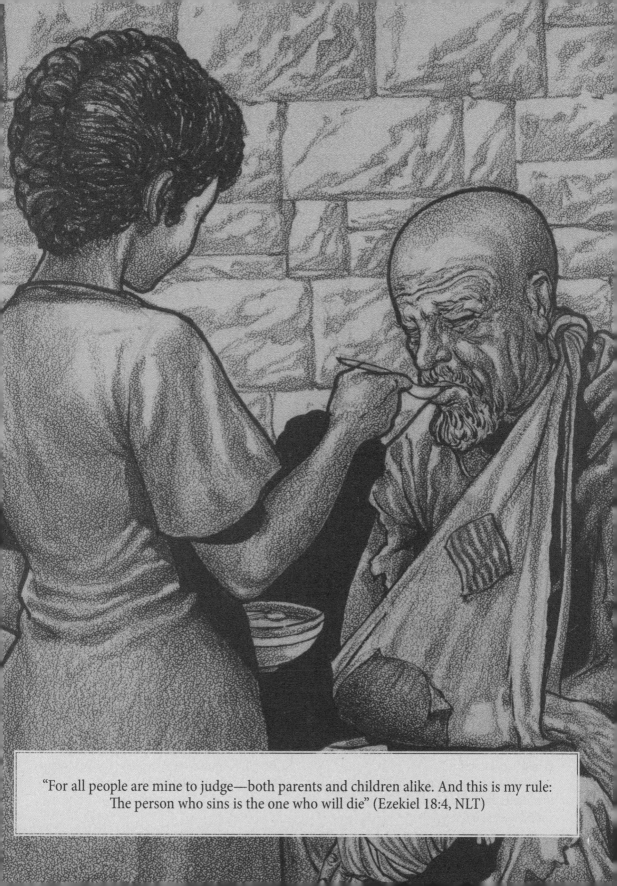

"For all people are mine to judge—both parents and children alike. And this is my rule:
The person who sins is the one who will die" (Ezekiel 18:4, NLT)

Focal Verses

KJV **Ezekiel 18:1** The word of the LORD came unto me again, saying,

2 What mean ye, that ye use this proverb concerning the land of Israel, saying, The fathers have eaten sour grapes, and the children's teeth are set on edge?

3 As I live, saith the Lord GOD, ye shall not have occasion any more to use this proverb in Israel.

4 Behold, all souls are mine; as the soul of the father, so also the soul of the son is mine: the soul that sinneth, it shall die.

5 But if a man be just, and do that which is lawful and right,

6 And hath not eaten upon the mountains, neither hath lifted up his eyes to the idols of the house of Israel, neither hath defiled his neighbour's wife, neither hath come near to a menstruous woman,

7 And hath not oppressed any, but hath restored to the debtor his pledge, hath spoiled none by violence, hath given his bread to the hungry, and hath covered the naked with a garment;

8 He that hath not given forth upon usury, neither hath taken any increase, that hath withdrawn his hand from iniquity, hath executed true judgment between man and man,

9 Hath walked in my statutes, and hath kept my judgments, to deal truly; he is just, he shall surely live, saith the Lord GOD.

30 Therefore I will judge you, O house of Israel, every one according to his ways, saith the Lord GOD. Repent, and turn yourselves from all your transgressions; so iniquity shall not be your ruin.

31 Cast away from you all your transgressions, whereby ye have transgressed; and make you a new heart and a new spirit: for why will ye die, O house of Israel?

32 For I have no pleasure in the death of him that dieth, saith the Lord GOD: wherefore turn yourselves, and live ye.

NLT **Ezekiel 18:1** Then another message came to me from the LORD:

2 "Why do you quote this proverb concerning the land of Israel: 'The parents have eaten sour grapes, but their children's mouths pucker at the taste'?

3 As surely as I live, says the Sovereign LORD, you will not quote this proverb anymore in Israel.

4 For all people are mine to judge—both parents and children alike. And this is my rule: The person who sins is the one who will die.

5 Suppose a certain man is righteous and does what is just and right.

6 He does not feast in the mountains before Israel's idols or worship them. He does not commit adultery or have intercourse with a woman during her menstrual period.

7 He is a merciful creditor, not keeping the items given as security by poor debtors. He does not rob the poor but instead gives food to the hungry and provides clothes for the needy.

8 He grants loans without interest, stays away from injustice, is honest and fair when judging others,

9 and faithfully obeys my decrees and regulations. Anyone who does these things is just and will surely live, says the Sovereign LORD.

30 Therefore, I will judge each of you, O people of Israel, according to your actions, says the Sovereign LORD. Repent, and turn from your sins. Don't let them destroy you!

31 Put all your rebellion behind you, and find yourselves a new heart and a new spirit. For why should you die, O people of Israel?

32 I don't want you to die, says the Sovereign LORD. Turn back and live!"

The People, Places, and Times

House of Israel. This is a phrase used to address the Israelites. It is used throughout the Bible, primarily by the prophets such as Jeremiah, Ezekiel, and Amos. The phrase is often referred to when the Lord through the prophets, begins to speak to Israel. The phrase is normally used as a way of gathering the Israelites' attention before speaking to them. Many examples in the Bible support this theory (Jeremiah 3:20; Ezekiel 33:11; Amos 5:25).

Proverb. A proverb is a short, wise saying used for a long time by many people. The proverbs and the lessons they taught were passed down from generation to generation. It was a condensed parable or fable that was sometimes presented to clearly teach a lesson. The proverbs of the Israelites and other people of the east were primarily "similitudes," which present their wisdom as a pair of truisms that are similar to each other (e.g. Proverbs 26:11). Many proverbs are generally true, as opposed to absolutely consequential. Most are in this category of true (Proverbs 17:22), while others were false (Ezekiel 18:2). The main purpose of a proverb was to help families instruct to their young.

Many proverbs can be found throughout the Bible. The Book of Proverbs lists many wise saying of kings and powerful leaders. Most of these are short, compact statements that express truths about human behavior.

When have you seen a proverb play out in your life?

Background

The Prophet Ezekiel lived during the Babylonian exile and was active as a prophet for approximately 20 years from 593 BC to at least 573 BC. Ezekiel lived as an exile according to the title of the book that bares his name (Ezekiel 1:1-2), he was carried away as a captive with Jehoiachin (1:2; 2 Kings 24:14–16) in about 597 BC. His prophetic call came to him in the fifth

year of Jehoiachin's captivity (593 BC). Ezekiel held a prominent place among the exiles, and was frequently consulted by the elders (Ezekiel 8:1; 11:25; 14:1; 20:1). In the ninth year of his exile, he lost his wife by some sudden and unforeseen tragedy (8:1; 24:1, 18). According to the information in the book's opening, he was the son of the priest Buzi (1:3) and his name in Hebrew meant "God strengthens (this child)" or possibly, "May God strengthen (this person)." Because he was of a priestly family, he probably had a good education, especially in the Law, and his father may even have had some influence in Jerusalem. The time and manner of his death are unknown.

At-A-Glance

1. God Reminds Judah of His Sovereignty (Ezekiel 18:1–4)
2. God Reminds Them What is Righteous (vv. 5–9)
3. God Reminds Them of their Personal Responsibility (vv. 30–32)

In Depth

1. God Reminds Judah of His Sovereignty (Ezekiel 18:1–4)

The prophets had warned of God's judgment for generations. Because of that, the captives blamed their ancestors for their problems. They complained that God was punishing them for something their parents had done, quoting an old Jewish proverb, often used when a person was having trouble and it didn't seem like he'd done anything to deserve it. They failed to realize they were even worse than their ancestors (Jeremiah 16:12). They remembered only the sins of the past, forgetting their sins of the present. Some White Americans tend to have a similar problem. They readily admit the past sin of slavery but protest that they had nothing to do with it. They complain about the demands of Blacks, forgetting their present injustice.

God forbade Judah's complaining. First He reminded them that He is God. He is in charge, and if the people were living in faith they would recognize His work. Even when people rebel, God is in charge of their souls. Second, He assures them that only those individuals who rebel against God will die. He is not unjust. Out of mercy, God waited for generations, looking for repentance. Finally, He had to send His judgment. Each individual soul is responsible for its own sin and will be judged accordingly.

Why do we often feel we are being punished for someone else's missteps?

2. God Reminds Them What is Righteous (vv. 5–9)

However, just because a person has a right to stand as an individual in God's hand doesn't mean all his problems are over. It means he's got to watch how he lives. It means he's got to stick to the standards. It means he's got to uphold the Law.

If you don't want to stand there with your knees wobbling, if you don't want to stand there with fear and trembling, you're going to have to do your bit to live in God's way. The greatest of the commandments is to love the Lord your God and to love your neighbor as yourself. The examples of the commandments we should keep (18:6-8), quite naturally, fit both categories: loving God and loving our neighbor. God never intended anything else.

How do you remind yourself what the right thing to do is?

3. God Reminds Them of Their Personal Responsibility (18:30–32)

God does not enjoy punishing the wicked. He sends punishment so the wicked will repent.

When they do repent, He gives them life and hope. Repentance works in reverse too. The previously righteous man who turns to a wicked life opens himself to God's judgment.

God concluded His comments with a promise. If any wicked man would turn from his wicked ways his life would be saved. The choice was theirs. "Why do you want to die?" God cried. "Seek me and live!" (cf, Deuteronomy 30:19; Amos 5:4). Hinting at the coming Gospel of Jesus Christ, God promised a new heart and a new spirit to any who would live in faithful obedience to Him.

Through the power of the Holy Spirit, the Christian has an even better opportunity to live righteously than the people of Judah during the time of Ezekiel. But modern Christians have the same problem that Ezekiel's hearers had. They have an attitude of self-righteousness, complaining about the sins of others without examining themselves.

Why do we not do the right thing, even after we are given good advice?

Search the Scriptures

1. Why did God say the old proverb should not be used? (Ezekiel 18:1-4)

2. What did God say the people of Judah needed? (v. 31)

3. Does God enjoy punishing people? (18:32) Explain.

Discuss the Meaning

1. What does God do when you try to turn from your old ways, but keep slipping back?

2. God had described Himself as "visiting the iniquity of the fathers upon the children, and upon the children's children, unto the third and to the fourth generation" (Exodus 34:7). Now He says individuals pay for their sins, specifically saying the parents' sin does not lie on the child. Scripture tells us that God is unchanging (Hebrews 13:8). Why does God

seem to be changing His methods? Was He not satisfied with the previous arrangement? Is He admitting that He had made a mistake? Explain.

Liberating Lesson

Many people are familiar with old superstitious sayings passed down through generations. These may include sayings such as: seven years of bad luck for breaking a mirror; you will go to jail if your foot is swept by a broom; you will have bad luck if a black cat crosses your path, or good luck if you eat black-eyed peas at the start of a new year.

If we live our lives according to these kinds of sayings, we not only keep ourselves in bondage, but we also keep generations of our descendants in bondage too. As children of God, we must realize that no superstition or old saying is more powerful than God. On the contrary, we must depend totally on God, because He holds our complete destiny in His hand.

Application for Activation

Think of problems in your life that you feel were caused by someone else. To what extent have you contributed to the problems yourself? What attitude should you have toward people who cause problems for you? What can you do to ease these problems?

Look at the problems you have caused yourself. What attitude does God want you to have toward these problems? What can you do to correct them?

Follow the Spirit

What God wants me to do:

_____

_____

_____

Remember Your Thoughts

Special insights I have learned:

_____

_____

_____

_____

More Light on the Text
Ezekiel 18:1–9, 30–32

The eighteenth chapter of Ezekiel contains a full account of the theme of individual responsibility—God deals with people according to their personal acts of sin or righteousness. The prophet Ezekiel debunks the people's common notion that their suffering or punishment (the Babylonian Exile) is the consequence of their fathers' sin. By holding that idea, they refuse to take responsibility for their actions. Instead they tend to attribute their present plight to consequences of their fathers' wrongs, thus shifting the blame.

1 The word of the LORD came unto me again, saying, 2 What mean ye, that ye use this proverb concerning the land of Israel, saying, The fathers have eaten sour grapes, and the children's teeth are set on edge?

The prophet starts this portion of his prophecy with a word from the Lord. The phrase "the word of the LORD came unto me" means that he heard from the Lord or that God prophetically spoke to him. It is a phrase commonly used among the prophets. Here the Lord calls the prophet's attention to a slogan, which seems to be current among the people during their exile. The Lord, through Ezekiel, questions the people as to what they mean by using the proverb "the fathers have eaten sour grapes, and the children's teeth are set on edge."

449

This proverb turns out to only be as true as the schoolyard retort, "Sticks and stone may break my bones, but words can never hurt me."

The idea of the grapes proverb is that the hardship that the contemporary generation is going through is the fault of the previous generation. It is as if the forefathers ate unripe grapes which taste sour and bitter, but instead of receiving the unpleasant effect, it was transferred to those who never tasted the grapes. This sounds absurd. In Israel's opinion, they are taking the brunt of their ancestors' wrongdoing.

Although the early laws in the Israel's covenant relationship with Lord stipulate individual responsibility for wrong behavior (Exodus 20:22–23:33), the people tend to hold only to the part of the Decalogue where the Lord threatens to punish the children for the sins of their fathers to third and fourth generation (Exodus 20:5; Deuteronomy 5:9). The people choose to ignore the fact that living so closely with one's family and clan as they did in those days, three or even four generations of one family will likely participate or at least be complicit in any sin the family's patriarch commits.

Rather than accepting their faults and repenting from their sins, with this slogan the people accuse God of partiality or bad judgment, and of punishing them for what their forefathers had done in the past. This enables the people to shift blame and deny their sin. By using this slogan, the people also seem to doubt the truth that God is a just and righteous judge. Therefore, the Lord says that the slogan will no more hold.

3 As I live, saith the Lord GOD, ye shall not have occasion any more to use this proverb in Israel. 4 Behold, all souls are mine; as the soul of the father, so also the soul of the son is mine: the soul that sinneth, it shall die.

The Lord continues His instruction to the prophet that the people's notion of transferred guilt will no longer be used as an excuse for evading responsibility. The proverb which they hitherto have been using (cf Jeremiah 31:29) will no more apply because all people are equal in His sight. He introduces this correction with the phrase "As I live," which gives authority and emphasis to what He is about to say. Also the use of "behold" (Heb. *hen*, **HANE**), often used as an interjection, gives an emphatic stress to the point He makes: "all souls are mine." The emphasis here is that God as the sovereign Creator and sustainer of all things has the right to deal with us as He wills without question. He has the right to hand one over to death, just as He can call another to life. Equally, the Lord can hold the child accountable for their parent's deed, just as He can decide to call the parent to question regarding the child's misdeeds. Life and death are in His hands, and judgment is His prerogative. No one, not even Israel, has a right to question His judgment, and He is not accountable to anyone. He does what is right in His sight.

He continues, "the soul the sinneth, it shall die." This means the child will no more carry the brunt of the parent's sin; neither will the parent any more take the responsibility for the child's wrong action. Whoever sins will have to live with it. The clause "the soul that sinneth it shall die" is consistent with God's order of things in other passages of the Bible (cf. Genesis 2:17; Romans 1:29–32; 1 Corinthians 6:9–11; Galatians 5:19–21). At this point, it is necessary to understand the meaning of "death" or "die" in this passage. What does the word "death" or "to die" (used in the passage about 13 times) mean in the context of the passage? Does it mean physical death? Although physical death can be attributed to sin after the fall, physical death is not necessarily always the penalty for sin. Death here evidently means spiritual death and separation from God.

5 But if a man be just, and do that which is lawful and right, 6 And hath not eaten upon the mountains, neither hath lifted up his eyes to the idols of the house of Israel, neither hath defiled his neighbour's wife, neither hath come near to a menstruous woman,

Our God never means to make it too difficult to follow His law. Having warned that the sinner would die, He reminds His people what following Him looks like. This is what it means to be "just" (Heb. *tsadiq*, tsah-**DEEK**), "lawful" (Heb. *mishpat*, meesh-**POT**), and "right" (Heb. *tsedaqah*, tseh-daw-**KAH**). The Hebrew words translated here as "just" and "right" come from a root meaning true or straight, and refers to being in right relationship with God. The Hebrew translated here as "lawful" is in a word family related to judging and judgments. These are God's pronouncements of the law. If a person lives by these true judgments, they will live at peace with God.

The prophecy continues with two further examples of righteous conduct. To have "eaten upon the mountains" is to have partaken of pagan sacrifices. Worshipers would usually not burn up an entire animal as a sacrifice, but would eat much of the meat. Worship usually took place in a high place, like on a mountain. If one has not eaten on the mountains or lifted their eyes to idols, they are free from idolatry.

This righteous man's relationship with Yahweh is pure, and his marriage is also pure. He has not committed adultery with his neighbor's wife (Leviticus 18:20), and he has not had sex with his wife during her period (Leviticus 18:19). It is important to keep his marriage pure because marriage is a revelation of God's relationship with His people (Ezekiel 16:1-8; Ephesians 5:31-33).

7 And hath not oppressed any, but hath restored to the debtor his pledge, hath spoiled none by violence, hath given his bread to the hungry, and hath covered the naked with a garment; 8 He that hath not given forth upon usury, neither hath taken any increase, that hath withdrawn his hand from iniquity, hath executed true judgment between man and man,

The righteous person, as the prophecy future explains, is kind to his neighbor, especially when it comes to money. His actions related to giving loans is all exactly in keeping with the law. God's law explains that if a person taking a loan from you gives you a "pledge" or form of collateral that he'll need (like a cloak), it should be given back at night (Exodus 22:26-27; Deuteronomy 24:12-13). "Giving on usury" and "taking an increase" have to do with the interest charged on a loan. God is clear that the poor should not be charged any interest at all on a loan (Leviticus 25:35-37), so this righteous man does not. He also does not violently steal (KJV: "spoil"), in keeping with the law (Exodus 20:15). Instead, he is generous to those in need, whether they need food or clothes.

He also withdraws himself from evil, and helps his fellow Israelites settle disputes fairly. All of these actions ensure that the righteous person will be in right relationship with everyone: with God, with spouse, with community.

9 Hath walked in my statutes, and hath kept my judgments, to deal truly; he is just, he shall surely live, saith the Lord GOD.

In summary, the righteous person obeys God's law. He "walked" in them, following them in every aspect of his life, and he has "kept" them, stalwartly watching himself so that he stays in line. This is the way to remain "just" (Heb. *tsadiq*) before the Lord. If a person aims to stay true to God, he will live, God promises. It does not matter what people do around you, even your own kin. Every action in these verses has been something anyone can do, no matter what others are doing to them.

30 Therefore I will judge you, O house of Israel, every one according to his ways, saith the Lord GOD. Repent, and turn yourselves from all your transgressions; so iniquity shall not be your ruin.

Although Israel is punished as a community, God still judges individuals based on their response. Although individual sin can affect the whole community, yet the righteous are usually rewarded for their righteousness. God has an excellent track record of sparing singularly righteous followers even amid a community-wide judgment, for example Noah (Genesis 6:8), Lot (Genesis 19:16), and Rahab (Joshua 6:17). God has always judged on an individual basis.

Now comes the climax of the passage: "Repent, and turn yourselves from all of your transgressions; so iniquity shall not be your ruin." The word "repent" is a translation of the Hebrew word *shub* (**SHOOV**), which means turning, or to turn back, to go or come back. It carries the idea of making a right-about turn, to retreat from a certain direction to another. Here it involves turning from their way of sin (transgression) to the way of righteousness. The word "transgression" is the Hebrew noun *pesha'* (**PEH**-shah) derived from the verb *pasha'* (pah-**SHAH**), which means to break away from authority, to trespass, revolt, rebel, or apostatize. Transgression can be against an individual, a nation, or against God. In context, the rebellion is against God and His ordinances.

The Lord invites Israel to turn away from sin and to return to Him so that "iniquity shall not be your ruin." The Lord, through the prophet, calls on the people to turn over a new leaf so that they can live and not die.

31 Cast away from you all your transgressions, whereby ye have transgressed; and make you a new heart and a new spirit: for why will ye die, O house of Israel?

Using a stronger word, the Lord invites them to "cast away" or to get rid of their transgression, and to cultivate "a new heart and a new spirit" so that they will not face the consequences of their transgression. This is a call to transform the inner self. To "cast away" is another way of saying that they should turn away from their rebellion and come back to Him. Emphasizing the need for repentance, the Lord appeals to their reasoning. He does this rhetorically—"for why will ye die, O house of Israel?" In other words, life and death are your choice. You can choose to repent and live or continue in your sin and face death. In a way, here, God is renewing His covenant with Israel, since this language is similar to that of Deuteronomy (30:19). The conditions for salvation are consistent both in the Old Testament and in the New Testament (Acts 2:38; 26:18; Romans 10:9–10; 2 Corinthians 5:17–21).

32 For I have no pleasure in the death of him that dieth, saith the Lord GOD: wherefore turn yourselves, and live ye.

Concluding this oracle, the Lord reiterates His earlier assertion (v. 23) that He does not take delight in the death of the wicked or the righteous who turn away from His righteousness. Rather, He calls again for genuine repentance and change of heart—the only criterion for living.

Sources:
Harrison, R.K. editor. *The New Unger's Bible Dictionary*. Chicago: Moody Press, 1988. 1046.
Strong, James. *The New Strong's Exhaustive Concordance of the Bible*. Nashville, TN: Thomas Nelson, 2003.
Thayer, Joseph Henry. *A Greek-English Lexicon of the New Testament*. New York: American Book Company, 1996.
Vine, W.E. *Vine's Complete Expository Dictionary of Old and New Testament Words*. Nashville, TN: Thomas Nelson, 1996.

Say It Correctly

Jehoiachin. jeh-**HOY**-ah-kin.
Buzi. **BOO**-zee.

Daily Bible Readings

MONDAY
Treat Each Other Fairly
(Deuteronomy 24:14–18)

TUESDAY
Taking Personal Responsibility
(Jeremiah 31:27–30)

WEDNESDAY
The Child Who Sins Suffers Punishment
(Ezekiel 18:10–13)

THURSDAY
The Righteous Child Is Rewarded
(Ezekiel 18:14–18)

FRIDAY
All Are Accountable for Their Sins
(Ezekiel 18:19–24)

SATURDAY
God Is Compassionate and Fair
(Ezekiel 18:25–29)

SUNDAY
Repent and Live Righteous Lives
(Ezekiel 18:1–9, 30–32)

Notes

Teaching Tips

May 30
Bible Study Guide 13

Words You Should Know

A. Overthrown (Jonah 3:4) *hopak* (Heb.)—To turn over, turn back, convert, change, overthrow, or destroy. The word is frequently used regarding acts of God.

B. Repent (v. 3) *nakham* (Heb.)—Having compassion, or easing oneself of anger; to be moved to pity

Teacher Preparation

Unifying Principle—Changing for the Better. Change is often required in life if we are to live in peace with others. What can we do about life situations that threaten us? After hearing God's warning from Jonah, the people of Nineveh repented and God forgave their sin.

A. Read the Bible Background and Devotional Reading.

B. Pray for your students and lesson clarity.

C. Read the lesson Scripture in multiple translations.

O—Open the Lesson

A. Begin the class with prayer.

B. Discuss the phrase "hitting rock bottom." What does the phrase mean, and what does it have to do with making a radical life change?

C. Have the students read the Aim for Change and the In Focus story.

D. Ask students how events like those in the story weigh on their hearts and how they can view these events from a faith perspective.

P—Present the Scriptures

A. Read the Focal Verses and discuss the Background and The People, Places, and Times sections.

B. Have the class share what Scriptures stand out for them and why, with particular emphasis on today's themes.

E—Explore the Meaning

A. Use In Depth or More Light on the Text to facilitate a deeper discussion of the lesson text.

B. Pose the questions in Search the Scriptures and Discuss the Meaning.

C. Discuss the Liberating Lesson and Application for Activation sections.

N—Next Steps for Application

A. Summarize the great love of God that makes repentance possible.

B. End class with a commitment to pray for forgiveness of their sins and the will to live in right relationship with God and others.

Worship Guide

For the Superintendent or Teacher
Theme: Jonah: Do the Right Thing
Song: "Jonah and the Whale"
Devotional Reading: Jonah 2

Jonah: Do the Right Thing

Bible Background • JONAH 3
Printed Text • JONAH 3 | Devotional Reading • JONAH 2

————— Aim for Change —————

By the end of this lesson, we will SURVEY Nineveh's response to Jonah's message, SENSE how the people of Nineveh felt after hearing Jonah's message, and ENGAGE in repentance and right behavior after hearing God's warning.

————— In Focus —————

Darrell had never managed to break loose from his neighborhood gang. They were known for thefts in the area and boosting anything from bikes to phones to cars. Darrell knew stealing was wrong. But, he reasoned, maybe the victim deserved what was coming to them, or he needed the goods more than they did. There was always an excuse.

Then one day, he opened his door to see two police officers. "Mr. Parker," one officer said. "We have a search warrant; we have reason to believe your son, Miles, stole a bike."

Darrell kept his hands still and visible as the cops searched his small apartment. "Do you know where your son is now?"

"Getting groceries, sir."

"Do you think he's mixed up with gangs?"

"No, sir."

"We'll be back in a few days to speak with him."

"Yes, sir." Darrell finally breathed again when the officers left. He knew the cops didn't really have anything on Miles. They had come to scare him. The officers very well could have found the wallet he stole from a guy yesterday. He saw just how close he had come to destruction and how his actions could cost his son his freedom or even his life.

Darrell and Miles had a serious talk that night. Darrell apologized for his reckless behavior. For the first time in years, Darrell prayed to God for freedom from his gang life.

What causes people to make sudden true, lasting repentance?

————— Keep in Mind —————

"And God saw their works, that they turned from their evil way; and God repented of the evil, that he had said that he would do unto them; and he did it not."
(Jonah 3:10, KJV)

"When God saw what they had done and how they had put a stop to their evil ways, he changed his mind and did not carry out the destruction he had threatened." (Jonah 3:10, NLT)

Focal Verses

KJV **Jonah 3:1** And the word of the LORD came unto Jonah the second time, saying,

2 Arise, go unto Nineveh, that great city, and preach unto it the preaching that I bid thee.

3 So Jonah arose, and went unto Nineveh, according to the word of the LORD. Now Nineveh was an exceeding great city of three days' journey.

4 And Jonah began to enter into the city a day's journey, and he cried, and said, Yet forty days, and Nineveh shall be overthrown.

5 So the people of Nineveh believed God, and proclaimed a fast, and put on sackcloth, from the greatest of them even to the least of them.

6 For word came unto the king of Nineveh, and he arose from his throne, and he laid his robe from him, and covered him with sackcloth, and sat in ashes.

7 And he caused it to be proclaimed and published through Nineveh by the decree of the king and his nobles, saying, Let neither man nor beast, herd nor flock, taste any thing: let them not feed, nor drink water:

8 But let man and beast be covered with sackcloth, and cry mightily unto God: yea, let them turn every one from his evil way, and from the violence that is in their hands.

9 Who can tell if God will turn and repent, and turn away from his fierce anger, that we perish not?

10 And God saw their works, that they turned from their evil way; and God repented of the evil, that he had said that he would do unto them; and he did it not.

NLT **Jonah 3:1** Then the LORD spoke to Jonah a second time:

2 "Get up and go to the great city of Nineveh, and deliver the message I have given you."

3 This time Jonah obeyed the LORD's command and went to Nineveh, a city so large that it took three days to see it all.

4 On the day Jonah entered the city, he shouted to the crowds: "Forty days from now Nineveh will be destroyed!"

5 The people of Nineveh believed God's message, and from the greatest to the least, they declared a fast and put on burlap to show their sorrow.

6 When the king of Nineveh heard what Jonah was saying, he stepped down from his throne and took off his royal robes. He dressed himself in burlap and sat on a heap of ashes.

7 Then the king and his nobles sent this decree throughout the city: "No one, not even the animals from your herds and flocks, may eat or drink anything at all.

8 People and animals alike must wear garments of mourning, and everyone must pray earnestly to God. They must turn from their evil ways and stop all their violence.

9 Who can tell? Perhaps even yet God will change his mind and hold back his fierce anger from destroying us."

10 When God saw what they had done and how they had put a stop to their evil ways, he changed his mind and did not carry out the destruction he had threatened.

The People, Places, and Times

Nineveh (NIN-eh-vuh). The site of the ancient city of Nineveh has now been excavated thoroughly. Occupational levels on the site go back to prehistoric times, before 3100 BC. The city was founded by Nimrod (Genesis 10:8-10) and served as the capital of the great Assyrian Empire for many years. Its fortunes rose and fell as Babylonia and Assyria struggled with each other for the dominant position in the ancient world. During some periods Babylonia was stronger, while the Assyrians gained the upper hand at other times.

At the time of Nineveh's greatest prosperity, the city was surrounded by a circuit wall almost eight miles long. This "great city" (Jonah 1:2) had an area sufficient to contain a population of 120,000, as indicated in Jonah 4:11 and 3:2. As a result, it would have required a "three days' journey" to go around the city, and a "day's journey" would have been needed to reach the city's center from the outlying suburbs, just as the Book of Jonah reports (Jonah 3:3).

Although God spares Ninevah when they ask for forgiveness after Jonah's message, in 612 BC Nineveh was destroyed, as prophesied by other Hebrew prophets, especially Nahum. Nahum specifically cites Nineveh's idolatry (1:4) as cause of its destruction, as well as Assyria's habit of enticing other nations into idolatry (3:4).

Background

God called His prophet Jonah to cry out against a neighboring nation, the Assyrian capital of Nineveh. Jonah disobeyed God and attempted to run away from His service. In spite of all this, when Jonah's situation appeared hopeless, God prepared a great fish to rescue him.

Jonah was saved from death by grace. God not only saved his life but also restored Jonah to his position as a prophet. Jonah failed God, but God did not give up on Jonah. God had a job

that He wanted Jonah to do, and Jonah's failure did not disqualify him for the mission.

God's ultimate purpose was to rid Nineveh of evil. He sent Jonah to warn the Ninevites of their impending destruction. God would end the evil of Nineveh through divine judgment or, if they repented, through divine mercy.

Why do we often misunderstand God's plan, especially for people we consider our enemies?

At-A-Glance

1. God's Forgiveness (Jonah 3:1–5)
2. Prayers to God (vv. 6–9)
3. God Relents (v. 10)

In Depth

1. God's Forgiveness (Jonah 3:1–5)

After his experience on the boat and in the belly of the great fish, Jonah was finally ready to submit to God's will. God gave the reluctant prophet a second chance. Once again God commanded Jonah to go to Nineveh and announce His judgment against the city. This time Jonah readily obeyed God and made the 500-mile journey from the sea to Nineveh. When the prophet arrived in the city, he immediately began to proclaim the message of God's judgment to the inhabitants.

Nineveh and its surrounding suburbs had a circumference of about 60 miles. It would take about three days for a person to travel through the entire city and suburbs on foot. Jonah walked through the city shouting out God's message, "In forty days Nineveh will be destroyed." Before he had completed one day's journey, an astonishing event occurred. The people of Nineveh heard Jonah's words, believed his report, and repented of their sin.

When has God given you a second chance? How did you use it?

2. Prayers to God (vv. 6–9)

People today believe that repentance is simply apologizing for sins, but the unbelievers in the lesson text knew that to please God, they had to demonstrate their faith by actions reflective of repentance. As an external sign of their repentance, all the people fasted (cf. 1 Samuel 7:6). They clothed themselves in sackcloth, a coarse material made from goat's hair (cf. Genesis 37:34). Everyone from the king to the lowest beggar participated in the acts of repentance (Jonah 3:6). The people hoped that God would show compassion and turn away from His fierce anger (v. 9). Even the animals were not allowed to eat or drink.

How do you show you are truly sorry when you mess up?

3. God Relents (v. 10)

When the Ninevites humbled themselves and made their outward expressions congruent with their inward sorrow, God saw that they had turned from their evil ways. Then God turned aside from His anger and had compassion on them. The Lord extended His mercy to them by relented from the destruction they so richly deserved. He extended His grace by giving them what they could never deserve, forgiveness. The conversion of Nineveh is the high point in the book of Jonah. The Ninevites not only heard God's word, but they also believed. God forgave Nineveh just as He forgave Jonah.

God is ready to forgive anyone and everyone willing to turn away from their sins and submit to His will. Are you ready?

Search the Scriptures

1. Jonah walked through Nineveh proclaiming that in 40 days the city would be destroyed. How did the people of Nineveh respond to the prophecy of Jonah? (v. 5)

2. When God saw the response of the Ninevites, how did He respond? (v. 6)

Discuss the Meaning

1. The Ninevites were cruel and very wicked people. What did they do to deserve God's mercy and kindness? What can we do to earn His mercy and kindness?

2. What does it mean that a perfect God "changed His mind" and "repented of the evil"?

Liberating Lesson

Jonah's sin was believing that these people were unredeemable and the Jewish people were the only true people of God. Many Black people have difficulty forgiving White people for their atrocities during the days of slavery.

Revelation 7:12 says that people of all races, cultures, and languages will one day stand together before the throne. Shouldn't we be practicing now for that great day?

Application for Activation

Jonah described God as being merciful, compassionate, and patient with the faults of others. Christians are supposed to be physical expressions of our spiritual God to a physical world. This week, look for people to whom you can demonstrate mercy, compassion, and patience.

Follow the Spirit

What God wants me to do:

_____

_____

_____

Remember Your Thoughts

Special insights I have learned:

_____

_____

_____

More Light on the Text

Jonah 3

1 And the word of the LORD came unto Jonah the second time, saying, 2 Arise, go unto Nineveh, that great city, and preach unto it the preaching that I bid thee.

Jonah is returned to dry land by Yahweh's orders to the great fish (1:10). The Lord commissions him again to complete the same mission that he had run away from. With the same words, the Lord orders Jonah again as before (1:2), "Arise, go unto Nineveh, that great city, and preach (*qara'*, kaw-**RAW**, i.e., "to proclaim") unto it the preaching (*qeri'ah*, keh-ree-**AH**, literally, "the proclamation") that I bid thee."

Jonah is to go and preach or declare the Lord's message to the people of Nineveh. The phrase, "the preaching that I bid thee," emphasizes the fact that a preacher (a true preacher) speaks not of himself, but speaks the oracles of God. Jonah knows that he is to preach the message God gives him. However, he was disobedient at first. Now, having experienced the disciplinary hand of God, Jonah obeys the word of God without further argument. However, he does not go enthusiastically, but reluctantly.

3 So Jonah arose, and went unto Nineveh, according to the word of the LORD. Now Nineveh was an exceeding great city of three days' journey.

Jonah obeys the Lord and goes to Nineveh as the Lord commissioned him. The author now mentions that Nineveh is "an exceeding great city of three days' journey," referring to its size. The estimated size of the city of Nineveh proper measured three miles in length and less than a mile and a half in breadth, and that the city wall was about eight miles in length. This does not seem very big; however, when the other surrounding cities that make up the metropolitan area are included, we find that it was indeed an "exceeding great [large] city."

It is believed that to travel through Nineveh and its suburbs was about three days' journey and that the city was about 60 miles around, 18 miles long, and 14 miles wide. It was a well-fortified city with walls about 100 feet high and broad enough to allow 3 chariots abreast on top. The expression "exceedingly great" literally means "great to God" or "great before God" and describes the magnitude of the city in the normal way of expressing a superlative.

"Three days' journey" does not mean how long it would take to reach there, but how long it would take to cover the city because of its magnitude. The repeated mention of the size of the city also seems to indicate the enormity of the task before Jonah.

4 And Jonah began to enter into the city a day's journey, and he cried, and said, Yet forty days, and Nineveh shall be overthrown.

The immensity of the task is soon reduced to a day's journey (or a day's work rather than three), for the inhabitants of the city fall on their knees in repentance as soon as Jonah declares the message from the Lord. The expression, "And Jonah began to enter into the city a day's journey" suggests that he entered Nineveh proper the first day, and started proclaiming the message of the doom awaiting them.

The message is simple: "Yet forty days, and Nineveh shall be overthrown." This is the only prophecy in the book and means, "Within forty days Nineveh will be destroyed." The prophecy here was conditional, but the condition is implicit, as is the agent of Nineveh's destruction. The prophecy is to be fulfilled if the people do not repent before Yahweh. Had the prophecy been unconditional, no mercy would have been shown to them. God would have overthrown or destroyed the city without warning or notice. It would have been unnecessary to send Jonah or any other messenger to the city to preach to them. However, it also would have been impossible for the people to repent without the word of God being preached to them.

5 So the people of Nineveh believed God, and proclaimed a fast, and put on sackcloth, from the greatest of them even to the least of them. 6 For word came unto the king of Nineveh, and he arose from his throne, and he laid his robe from him, and covered him with sackcloth, and sat in ashes.

Although Jonah did not mention any provision or condition to avert the impending doom awaiting them in forty days, the people understood very well the purpose of the preaching—that is, repentance. As they heard Jonah's announcement of doom, they repented and believed God, and declared a national time of fasting and prayer asking for forgiveness.

Note the things Nineveh did to obtain mercy. First, they believed God (v. 5). That means that they accepted God's verdict against them, knew He was their Judge and was also their only hope for salvation. This, of course, was what Jonah feared (4:1–3). Second, they declare a fast and "put on sackcloth," which shows an attitude of sorrow, remorse, and mourning. No one would wear the cheap, coarse cloth used for sacks if they could afford any better. To wear sackcloth was to willingly debase yourself to show humility and dejection.

The king, all the nobles, and all the people, including all domestic animals, join in the national mourning and call on the Lord for forgiveness (vv. 6–9). The king stands up from his throne and instead sits in ashes. He takes off his royal robes and instead wears sackcloth. Even the king repents and shows deference to Yahweh.

7 And he caused it to be proclaimed and published through Nineveh by the decree of the king and his nobles, saying, Let neither man nor beast, herd nor flock, taste any thing: let them not feed, nor drink water: 8 But let man and beast be covered with sackcloth, and cry mightily unto God: yea, let them turn every one from his evil way, and from the violence that is in their hands. 9 Who can tell if God will turn and repent, and turn away from his fierce anger, that we perish not?

The king uses his position of power to get others to repent also. Working together, they show in every way they can that they are sorry and recognize themselves as under God's power. They make an outward show of humility to show they understand where they would be without God's help: they would have no food, no water, and barely any covering. After positioning themselves this way, they must cry "mightily" to God, with strength and force.

This one-time show of humility is not all the king proclaims for the Ninevites, though. They must also change their behavior in the future, turning from their evil ways and violence. The call to "turn" (Heb. *shub*, **SHOOV**) is the word usually used in the context of what we recognize as repenting from sin. Even though these Gentile people have not directly heard all the laws of God, they know they have committed evil. They have broken the laws of their own people. They have heard of the just laws of the Israelites and not tried to improve their community with those guidelines. They recognize the destructive nature of violence (Heb. *khamas*, khaw-**MOSS**), which refers both to physical aggression and to being wrong or false.

At the end of the day, however, these people do not know God. They do not have the cultural history that the Jews do, where God revealed Himself more and more fully over many generations. They only have Jonah's word that Yahweh is ready to destroy them. They can only hope that their efforts will change His mind. These wicked, evil people turned from their sinful ways and turned to a sovereign God who has all power in His hands—power to deliver, power to heal, and power to destroy or not destroy.

10 And God saw their works, that they turned from their evil way; and God repented of the evil, that he had said that he would do unto them; and he did it not.

Here we see what we have assumed throughout the book of Jonah: that God is merciful. God relents from carrying out His judgments against people who turn to Him with their whole heart in repentance. Recognizing the genuineness of their repentance from their evil ways, the Lord changes His mind and forgives them. They "turned (*shub*) from their evil," which means that they turned back from what they were doing before, or turned from their evil ways. It carries the idea of changing course and turning back or changing from one way of life (either positive or negative) to a new way of life. In this case, the Ninevites' change was positive and pleasing to God.

Thus, God "repented" (*nakham*, naw-KHAM), i.e., changed His mind about destroying the city. One should not imply from this verb that God had sinned in planning to destroy the city. God does not sin and does not need to "repent" of sin. Rather, nacham carries the idea of "having compassion," or "to ease oneself of anger," or "to be moved to pity." Moved by compassion and by the evidence of sorrow and repentance from the city, the Lord's anger is abated and He spares them the punishment He had pronounced on them.

Sources:
Strong, James. *The New Strong's Exhaustive Concordance of the Bible.* Nashville, TN: Thomas Nelson, 2003.
Thayer, Joseph Henry. *A Greek-English Lexicon of the New Testament.* New York: American Book Company, 1889.
Vine, W.E. *Vine's Complete Expository Dictionary of Old and New Testament Words.* Nashville, TN: Thomas Nelson, 1996.

Say It Correctly

Nahum. **NAY**-hum.
Assyria. ah-**SEAR**-ee-ah.

Daily Bible Readings

MONDAY
Jonah's Experience Foreshadows Christ's
(Matthew 12:38-42)

TUESDAY
Nineveh's Repentance:
A Lasting Message
(Luke 11:29-32)

WEDNESDAY
Jonah Turns Away from God's Call
(Jonah 1:1-12)

THURSDAY
Sailors Make Vows to the Lord
(Jonah 1:13-16)

FRIDAY
Jonah Resents God's Grace
Toward Others
(Jonah 4:1-5)

SATURDAY
God's Compassion Overrides Jonah's
Personal Comfort
(Jonah 4:6-11)

SUNDAY
God's Mercy Prevails
(Jonah 3)

Confident Hope

The study this quarter looks at God's gift of faith as the source of hope. Sessions from the Gospels illuminate hope and faith in teachings and miracles of Jesus. Sessions from the Epistles show how the early church understood God's gift of salvation through faith in Christ as the source of hope.

UNIT 1 • Jesus Teaches about Faith

This unit has five sessions. They reveal the hope and faith that come through Jesus' teachings and miracles. The sessions from Matthew demonstrate that faith in God is the primary source of hope and confidence. The miracles in Mark and Luke illustrate the power of faith.

Lesson 1: June 6, 2021
Why Do You Worry?
Matthew 6:25–34

Life's uncertainties can lead people to worry about how to obtain their basic needs. Who can we trust to meet all our needs? The Gospel of Matthew points out that our God who is truly sovereign will fulfill our needs.

Lesson 2: June 13, 2021
Why Are You Afraid?
Matthew 8:23-27

People often lose confidence amidst the storms of persecution, rejection, and poverty. Where can we find assurance when beset by the storms of life? Fearing they would not survive the windstorm, the disciples turned to Jesus to save them.

Lesson 3: June 20, 2021
Healed by Faith
Matthew 9:18-26

People often look to others to help them with their health issues. Where does healing come from? Jesus told the woman with the issue of blood that she was healed because of her faith and told Jairus that his daughter was healed and restored to life.

Lesson 4: June 27, 2021
Why Do You Doubt?
Matthew 14:22–33

In the depth of crisis, people are often caught between trust and doubt. Will one trust that one's help will come? Jesus, by walking on water to save His disciples, demonstrated His divine empowerment to be the Savior of all.

Lesson 5: July 4, 2021
An Attitude of Gratitude
Leviticus 13:45–46; Luke 17: 11–19

People often receive mercy but do not acknowledge the one who helped them. Do you show appreciation? Ten lepers, isolated by their skin diseases, were healed; but only one, who was a foreigner, was saved by his faith and offered thanks.

UNIT 2 • Faith and Salvation

This unit has four sessions. They explore in Paul's Letter to the Romans his understanding of the hope of salvation through faith. The letter teaches that God's righteousness is revealed in those who live by faith. Paul illustrates faith through the example of Abraham. He unpacks the teaching about being reconciled to God by justification through faith and teaches that salvation is for all.

Lesson 6: July 11, 2021
The Power of the Gospel
Romans 1:8–17

People often look to be in a relationship that provides them with strength and stability. Where do you find your strength? The Gospel is the power of God that can save all those who believe.

Lesson 7: July 18, 2021
The Faith of Abraham
Romans 4:1–12

People often look to those older than they are for assurance. Who is an example one can trust? Through faith, Abraham, the father of all who believe, proved he was in the right relationship with God.

Lesson 8: July 25, 2021
Justification through Faith
Romans 5:1–11

People often struggle with fractured relationships that they may or may not have caused. How can these relationships be reconciled? Only justification by faith in Jesus Christ reconciles the ultimate ruptured relationship between God and humanity.

Lesson 9: August 1, 2021
Salvation for All Who Believe
Romans 10:5–17

Many people lack confidence in addressing life's circumstances. How can one gain trust? Salvation comes to all who confess Jesus Christ as Lord and believe in their hearts.

UNIT 3 • Faith Gives Us Hope

This unit has four sessions. They focus on faith as essential for the hope of eternal life. Hebrews defines faith in Christ as a basis for hope and tells how faith in Christ gives hope that helps people persevere in all circumstances. 1 John promises that faith conquers the world. 2 Corinthians teaches about hope in God's gift of eternal life.

Lesson 10: August 8, 2021
Meaning of Faith
Hebrews 11:1–8, 13–16

People enduring life's miseries hopelessly plod along the way of life. What can enliven this emptiness of existence? Faith in God assures of hope and conviction of certainty.

Lesson 11: August 15, 2021
A Preserving Faith
Hebrews 10:23–36

People lacking self-assurance feel overwhelmed by life's challenges. What can enable one to face life confidently? Believers in Jesus Christ, who persevere in hope and encourage others in love and good works, develop in faith.

Lesson 12: August 22, 2021
A Conquering Faith
1 John 4:2–3, 13–17; 5:4–5

Faced with the world's allure, people contend with its many appeals. How can one resist this unhealthy allure? Believers through faith in Jesus Christ overcome the world and its seductions with the hope of victory.

Lesson 13: August 29, 2021
Hope Eternal
2 Corinthians 4:16-5:10

People fear the fragility of life and the meaning of death. In weakness and death, where can any assurance be found? God gives believers in Jesus Christ an eternal, unseen place in him that is guaranteed by the Spirit.

Recipe for Hope

One thing we can count on is that at some time in our lives we will go through hard times. As a part of a community or as an individual, you do not need a prophet to predict that you will experience trouble in this journey of life. This is one of humanity's lowest common denominators and many do not know how to sustain hope during the seasons of hardship and suffering that we all experience. When it comes to sustaining hope, the most basic principle is to place your hope in someone or something that is worthy of hope.

Many place their hope in the next political candidate, only to have their hopes dashed when the candidate's promises fail. Others place their hope in relationships, only to see their trust and love abused or taken for granted. Often people place their hope in money, and the economy shows them how unstable riches and wealth can be. The surest way to sustain hope is to place it in God. Even when we do this, our hope can diminish and we can falter along the way. Sustaining hope is about persevering for the long haul. There is a recipe for sustaining hope during the hard times and it consists of four ingredients: promises, people, prayer, and presence.

We Need Promises (Romans 15:4)

Paul explains to the church in Rome that we can persevere and continue in our walk with Christ because of the promises of Scripture. He says that the ultimate goal of the things that were written is that we would have encouragement and hope. These Scriptures written in the past sustain us in the present as we wait for their fulfillment in the future. We can only gain more hope as we learn and think about the fulfillment of what God has promised. What has He promised? He has promised us a kingdom where we live with Him forever (see Matthew 19:29). He has promised that we would have resurrected bodies and overflowing joy (see Psalm 16:9-11). Meditating on promises like these can only serve to steer us toward hope in God.

We Need People (1 Thessalonians 4:13–18)

In 1 Thessalonians 4:13–18, Paul lets the believers know that they do not have to grieve as those who have no hope. He then goes on to explain the hope of the resurrection and the second coming of Jesus. He describes how the Lord will come and that all who believe, whether living or dead, will rise to be with Him forever. Then He says to encourage each other with these words. The way that we can sustain hope is by being surrounded by others who have the same hope. The people we have around us can either discourage us so that we throw that hope away or encourage us so that we keep that hope in our hearts alive. This does not mean that we should avoid at all costs people who have no hope, for Jesus calls us to love and care for those in need. Instead, we must continue to remind each other of the hope in Jesus so that we can make it through the difficulties that we and others face.

We Need Prayer (Psalm 65:5)

The psalmist declares that God faithfully answers the prayers of His people. Then he further adds that the Lord is the hope of everyone on the face of the earth. Prayer, especially answered prayer, increases our hope. When we have seen God do amazing things in our lives, our hope is more steadfast and resilient. We know what God has done and this enables us to trust Him more for future acts. As we lean into prayer, we recall a big God who does big things and our small hope is enlarged to handle the storms of life.

We Need Presence (Romans 5:5 and 15:13)

Paul explains in Romans 5 that we have a hope that doesn't disappoint us. Why? Because the love of God is overflowing in our hearts. We experience God's love. We experience that we are His and He will never leave us or forsake us. How does this happen? Through the presence of his Holy Spirit in our hearts, we know that God loves us. Later, in Romans 15:13, Paul prays that God would give the church in Rome joy and peace and that they would overflow with confident hope through the power of the Holy Spirit. Through the presence of God filling us with joy and peace, we have confident hope as we face the many trials of life. That is the recipe for hope. When disaster strikes and crisis invades our lives, we can sustain hope through God's promises, people, prayer, and presence. Many things may trouble us and douse the fire of our hope.

Every day we read of terrorist attacks, unstable economies, and unspeakable crimes, but we have a hope that will outlast the present age. With this kind of hope we can say like Jeremiah in Lamentations 3:21–23: "This I recall to my mind, therefore have I hope. It is of the LORD's mercies that we are not consumed, because his compassions fail not. They are new every morning: great is thy faithfulness."

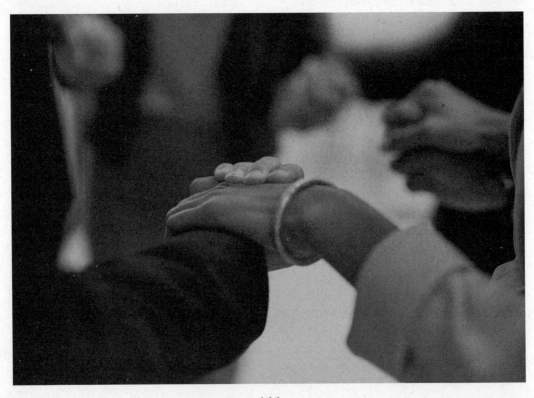

Looking for Hope in All the Right Places

by Rosa Sailes

I once heard a news bulletin announcing the suicide of a businessman who headed the largest financial institution in this country. His quiet, very upscale neighborhood is shocked at his death. His family is devastated. The political insiders (of whom he was one) are no doubt wondering if they, too, would have succumbed to the devastating loss of billions that will now mark his legacy. I cannot berate the man. I will not stomp on his grave with platitudes of rich young rulers and the eye of a needle, but I will ask—where was hope?

His parents had the best intentions for him. They sent him to the finest schools; his career ladder only headed in one direction. I'm sure that from the beginning his family beamed at the offspring who was raised to be successful. His wife married him knowing that, in addition to her personal accomplishments, she had married well. His children no doubt admired him, and his business associates wanted to ride his coattails to the bank. Each person had hope—hope in this man, his ability, his position, his perceived power, his bank account, and his connections. They had hope in their relationship with him and his relationship with others. But where was the man's hope?

Hebrews 11 tells us that hope must be anchored in something. Hope is an active verb that looks eagerly to a particular outcome. For some of us, our hope is anchored in the success and health of our children. For others, hope equates to the sufficiency of our income now and in the future. There are those for whom hope rests in intangibles—love, joy, peace, freedom, justice. College students place hope in a future where they can capitalize on the years they have invested in education. Parents often find themselves hanging their hopes on children who they pray will be caregivers to them, the same children to whom they once gave loving care. Hope truly has a desire.

The desire for hope is best realized by faith. Faith is the substance of the intangible object of our desire. We will study this faith and hope it anchors this quarter in the Gospels and Epistles, but "the Gospel" of hope as preached in the Old Testament by Isaiah as well. Through Isaiah's words, God's people were comforted. In the midst of exile and sorrow, Isaiah spoke of the coming salvation of God—a salvation that was for the captives and the generations after them. Their fears could be cast aside and their strength could be realized because hope spoke of a future without despair. God, who had formed them and made them His own, had not forgotten them. The proof was in the faith to which they clung with the assurance that only hope could give.

Isaiah spoke hope to those who felt a loss of hope. He spoke words of exaltation and gave a vision of hope. His words quickened the faith the nation needed at their lowest point. His preaching painted the picture of a future for God's people even in the midst of their sorrow. Through Isaiah's message, they found the faith to believe the God who had proven Himself to them even before their Red Sea experience.

Isaiah spoke to a nation of captives about God's promise, but we are living on this side of Calvary. We have seen what Isaiah's generation hoped for and yet we appear to have no hope. As African Americans we are, traditionally, a people of hope. We have had to be. But now we are seeing a generation that seems to have lost hope.

With a death rate soaring for teens in urban areas such as Chicago, Los Angeles, and Atlanta, hope has come to have a short life expectancy. With a fluctuating economy that is fueled by injustice and devastated by greed, it is no surprise that so many of our young adults see no future and senior citizens find their dreams of retirement dashed on the rocks of corporate greed and fraudulent behavior.

In the midst of such trials, we must keep faith in the fact that hope took on flesh. Two thousand years ago, Jesus spoke to the disenfranchised, the hurting, and the discounted. His birth, death, and resurrection were the hope that Isaiah had preached. His message was the word of comfort that God had encouraged from Isaiah's lips.

We must keep the faith and keep hope alive because 400 years ago, Jesus' words fit another group of disenfranchised, hurting, and discounted people, a people stolen from a native land, placed in shackles, and made to believe that their entire lives and the lives of their children would forever be without hope. For those people, nobody seemed to care, nobody seemed to hear, and nobody seemed to want to deliver.

Those disenfranchised slaves found a way to express their hope and to wait for their change to come. They started a tradition that remains in African American churches today, a tradition called "Watch Night." It was the way they waited for the New Year and waited for the voice of Jesus

to set them free as He had those people in His time and those who had been devastated by war and captivity in the days of Isaiah.

Watch Night became an expression of hope played out for decades—hoping the change was going to come, hoping that God's light would spring anew and the nightmare of enslavement would end. Those slaves had much to fear, yet they found hope and held on looking for God to open a new way, to light another direction for them, to make clear a path of escape so that they could move forward in the visions and dreams God had placed in their hearts.

On Watch Night those slaves watched and prayed, but each had a different vision of freedom. They each had a different urgency of hope. One wanted to find his mother. Another longed to find her children. Another sought enough to eat or wear. Another's heart cried for the freedom to go unfettered to a new life. Those slaves identified with the disenfranchised listeners who heard the words of Jesus and with the captives who hailed Isaiah's cry. Our fore-parents, though they were slaves in bondage, realized that Jesus knew the fears and doubts that they carried. They heard the words of Jesus and they knew the release that resonated in their souls. They hoped on the eve of a new year and hoped in the dawn of a new day. But Jesus did not only speak to those people on the mountainsides and valleys of Jerusalem. He did not only speak to slaves in small clusters throughout this country who were watching and praying for freedom to come. He also speaks to us. Like children who find themselves in the midst of anticipation waiting for their opportunity to let fly the dreams they have pent up inside, it is time for a new generation to recognize the words of hope and take hold of the faith so many have held before.

Now that the year is half gone, you can reflect. As you ended 2010, where were you looking for hope? After all, you know what you're hoping for. Like those who heard Isaiah's sermons or listened to Jesus' voice, we each define our hope in different ways. Perhaps God has spoken an urgency into your life, reminding you again of the gifts He has given you, a promise that He made to you, or a promise unfulfilled that you made to Him. Like those who cried for freedom from the tyranny of Babylon or who envisioned Watch Night as a means of expressing their hope in God, we must reinvigorate our hopes for 2021, and enter Watch Night 2022 without the burdens of the old year's struggles.

We have the same assurance as those on the mountain and those who were delivered from chains. It doesn't matter what you've been through; it matters that Jesus has declared you to be a light. It doesn't matter that you shed tears; it matters that Jesus has chosen you as His own. You may feel despondent, but Jesus has declared that your effort will make a difference in the world. The words of Isaiah and the sacrifice of Jesus ring forth even now, telling us to turn our sights to the only place we can find hope—in God Almighty, the Great I Am. We must look for hope in Jehovah-Jireh, the God who provides. We must anchor our faith in Jesus Christ, who is the "author and finisher of our faith" (Hebrews 12:2). Jesus Christ is, for each person who has called upon His name, our comfort in our present, our confidence in our future, and the Messiah we long to see.

Rosa M. Sailes, EdD, is the former Director of Editorial Leadership Resources at Urban Ministries, Inc. This article has been edited from its original printing in Precepts for Living®, 2010-2011.

469

PAUL CUFFE

(1759–1817)

Businessman, Sea Captain, Abolitionist

The seed of Pan-Africanism can be seen in the life of Paul Cuffe. Cuffe was born free in Cuttyhunk Island, Massachusetts, in 1759, although his exact date of birth is unclear. He was one of the many enslaved Blacks who could trace their ancestry to the Ashanti empire in West Africa, Cuffe's father Kofi was a skilled tradesman who earned his freedom. He married Paul's mother, Ruth Moses, a Native American. Kofi died when Paul was a teenager. Paul refused the last name of Slocum given by his father's owner and chose to use his father's first name. In choosing the name of his African heritage, Paul Cuffe already was showing small signs of his destiny to make a name for himself and empower African Americans.

During his teenage years, Paul taught himself navigation, mathematics, and other nautical skills. His first journey as a member of a whaling vessel was at age sixteen. From the time of the Revolutionary War until several years after, Paul began to buy shares in different ships and build his shipping enterprise.

Eventually he owned shares in ten ships. Cuffe and his brother David also built their own boat and smuggled supplies through British blockades during the war. Cuffe's success as a whaling ship captain eventually became known along the coast of Massachusetts.

In 1793, he married Alice Pequit and they later had six children: Paul, Mary, Alice, William, Ruth, and Rhoda. During the same year of his marriage, the Fugitive Slave Act gave slave owners the right to retrieve and capture an escaped slave in another state. This new law put Cuffe and his crew in constant danger as they made shipping expeditions up and down the Atlantic coast.

Cuffe became a political activist when he was in his twenties. In 1778, he and his brother John refused to pay taxes, claiming that if they were not allowed to vote, then they suffered from "taxation without representation." He organized a petition to sway the Massachusetts government to allow African and Native Americans the right to vote or free them from taxation. The petition did not influence the Massachusetts General Court to allow them the right to vote, but it did influence the creators of the Massachusetts Constitution to give freedom to all Massachusetts citizens.

Cuffe was a Quaker and his religious beliefs could be seen in his activities as a philanthropist. He donated to many causes and organizations that helped uplift African Americans. One of these causes was the building of a school in his hometown of Westport, Massachusetts. This school was established on his property and was open to children of all races. Cuffe also was an abolitionist who used his connections with free Blacks and other Quakers to rally against slavery and the slave trade. During this time, he advocated for organizations that helped African Americans to participate in the leadership and planning of these organizations.

Cuffe earned a reputation as the wealthiest African American and the largest employer of free African Americans. Although he gained enormous wealth and business success, he became frustrated and discouraged by the status of African Americans in the United States. This led him to believe the best course to take was to establish an independent African nation with returnees from America. In this way, two objectives would be accomplished: gain freedom for African Americans and modernize Africa.

After British abolitionists paved the way in creating the colony of Sierra Leone, Cuffe decided to follow the same path. In January of 1811, he sailed for the West African coast to Freetown. With an entirely African American crew, the expedition safely arrived at their destination. Shortly thereafter Cuffe organized the "Friendly Society of Sierra Leone," which would serve as a trading organization for those Blacks who had returned to Africa.

Cuffe hoped that the long-term goal of this organization would help African Americans spread the Gospel, start new businesses, and abolish slavery and the slave trade.

In 1815, Cuffe led a second expedition to Sierra Leone. The returnees numbered thirty-eight. Once there, they settled into new homes among the former English residents and refugees from Nova Scotia. After this initial success, Cuffe hoped to bring even more returnees and organize larger groups of African Americans who wanted to live a new life of freedom and equality. This plan would soon be overtaken by the American Colonization Society, which was much larger and well-funded. The Society created the colony of Liberia and began a similar emigration program. In the uproar of many White and Black Americans debating the validity of the program, Cuffe's plans were overshadowed and eclipsed. Cuffe died on September 9, 1817.

Sources:
Becker, Chrisanne. *100 African Americans Who Shaped American History*. San Francisco: Bluewood Books, 1995.
"Cuffe, Paul, Sr. (1759-1817)." https://www.blackpast.org/african-american-history/cuffe-paul-sr-1759-1817/. Accessed August 23, 2013.
Julye, Vanessa. "Paul Cuffe (1759-1817)." https://www.fgcquaker.org/sites/default/files/attachments/Paul%20Cuffe.pdf. Accessed August 23, 2013.

Teaching Tips

June 6
Bible Study Guide 1

Words You Should Know

A. Consider (Matthew 6:28) *katamanthano* (Gk.)—To examine or note carefully

B. Ye of little faith (v. 30) *oligopistos* (Gk.)—Lacking trust or trusting too little

Teacher Preparation

Unifying Principle—No Worries. Life's uncertainties can lead people to worry about how to obtain their basic needs. Who can we trust to meet all our needs? The Gospel of Matthew points out that our God who is truly sovereign will fulfill our needs.

A. Read the Bible Background and Devotional Reading.

B. Pray for your students and lesson clarity.

C. Read the lesson Scripture in multiple translations.

O—Open the Lesson

A. Begin the class with prayer.

B. If you have ever had a struggle with anxiety, you may want to share what you've learned with the class this week. Ask for one or two people to briefly share an experience they've had with worry. Ask for one or two people to briefly share their experience with worry and how they coped.

C. Have the students read the Aim for Change and the In Focus story.

D. Ask students how events like those in the story weigh on their hearts and how they can view these events from a faith perspective.

P—Present the Scriptures

A. Read the Focal Verses and discuss the Background and The People, Places, and Times sections.

B. Have the class share what Scriptures stand out for them and why, with particular emphasis on today's themes.

E—Explore the Meaning

A. Use In Depth or More Light on the Text to facilitate a deeper discussion of the lesson text.

B. Pose the questions in Search the Scriptures and Discuss the Meaning.

C. Discuss the Liberating Lesson and Application for Activation sections.

N—Next Steps for Application

A. Summarize the value of committing our worries to God in faith.

B. End class with a commitment to pray their thanks to God for caring for them.

Worship Guide

For the Superintendent or Teacher
Theme: Why Do You Worry?
Song: "Silver and Gold"
Devotional Reading: Ezekiel 34:11-16

Why Do You Worry?

Bible Background • MATTHEW 6:19–34
Printed Text • MATTHEW 6:25–34 | Devotional Reading • EZEKIEL 34:11–16

—————— Aim for Change ——————

By the end of this lesson, we will CONTRAST Jesus' teachings about worry with our own anxieties, APPRECIATE God's care for everything in nature, and EMBRACE the opportunity to trust God in everyday life.

————————— In Focus —————————

Pastor Ricky closed out his sermon about worry. "Job worries, financial problems, health concerns, family issues … each one of these problems is out of our control to some degree. The only thing that is under our control is our response to these difficult issues when they come into our lives."

Then, he passed out blank envelopes and sheets of paper to his congregation. Each person in the church that morning was instructed to list all the things that were troubling them, no matter how big or small. They were then instructed to place the list in the envelopes and to address the envelopes to themselves.

"During the final song, I encourage each one of you to bring those worries you just wrote down to the altar and lay them down. We'll let Jesus take care of them for a while and then we'll see how we feel about those same issues."

One month later, the pastor mailed the envelopes out to his congregation. With few exceptions, most of the congregation saw their month-old concerns in a whole new light. Though some troubles were ongoing in the people's lives, the majority of the worries that seemed so enormous at the time had diminished drastically in urgency and intensity. Bills had gotten paid, arguments had been resolved, problems at work had changed, and health problems had been healed. This simple experiment taught the congregation a lesson about the nature of worry that none of them would soon forget.

What has helped you keep God's eternal perspective on worry in mind?

———————— Keep in Mind ————————

"(For after all these things do the Gentiles seek:) for your heavenly Father knoweth that ye have need of all these things. But seek ye first the kingdom of God, and his righteousness; and all these things shall be added unto you" (Matthew 6:32-33, KJV).

"These things dominate the thoughts of unbelievers, but your heavenly Father already knows all your needs. Seek the Kingdom of God above all else, and live righteously, and he will give you everything you need" (Matthew 6:32-33, NLT).

Focal Verses

KJV **Matthew 6:25** Therefore I say unto you, Take no thought for your life, what ye shall eat, or what ye shall drink; nor yet for your body, what ye shall put on. Is not the life more than meat, and the body than raiment?

26 Behold the fowls of the air: for they sow not, neither do they reap, nor gather into barns; yet your heavenly Father feedeth them. Are ye not much better than they?

27 Which of you by taking thought can add one cubit unto his stature?

28 And why take ye thought for raiment? Consider the lilies of the field, how they grow; they toil not, neither do they spin:

29 And yet I say unto you, That even Solomon in all his glory was not arrayed like one of these.

30 Wherefore, if God so clothe the grass of the field, which to day is, and to morrow is cast into the oven, shall he not much more clothe you, O ye of little faith?

31 Therefore take no thought, saying, What shall we eat? or, What shall we drink? or, Wherewithal shall we be clothed?

32 (For after all these things do the Gentiles seek:) for your heavenly Father knoweth that ye have need of all these things.

33 But seek ye first the kingdom of God, and his righteousness; and all these things shall be added unto you.

34 Take therefore no thought for the morrow: for the morrow shall take thought for the things of itself. Sufficient unto the day is the evil thereof.

NLT **Matthew 6:25** "That is why I tell you not to worry about everyday life—whether you have enough food and drink, or enough clothes to wear. Isn't life more than food, and your body more than clothing?

26 Look at the birds. They don't plant or harvest or store food in barns, for your heavenly Father feeds them. And aren't you far more valuable to him than they are?

27 Can all your worries add a single moment to your life?

28 And why worry about your clothing? Look at the lilies of the field and how they grow. They don't work or make their clothing,

29 yet Solomon in all his glory was not dressed as beautifully as they are.

30 And if God cares so wonderfully for wildflowers that are here today and thrown into the fire tomorrow, he will certainly care for you. Why do you have so little faith?

31 So don't worry about these things, saying, 'What will we eat? What will we drink? What will we wear?'

32 These things dominate the thoughts of unbelievers, but your heavenly Father already knows all your needs.

33 Seek the Kingdom of God above all else, and live righteously, and he will give you everything you need.

34 So don't worry about tomorrow, for tomorrow will bring its own worries. Today's trouble is enough for today."

The People, Places, and Times

Grass. During biblical times, fuel was scarce. Withered plants of all kinds were used for fuel. The term in verse 30 that is translated "grass" actually includes all sorts of vegetation not classified as trees, including the beautiful lilies mentioned in verses 28-29. Even the magnificent plants that displayed God's care in creation ended up as fuel to be used by the people that He valued and loved.

Wealth. Wealth is a blessing from God. Deuteronomy is full of promises of the Promised Land bringing with it fields, vineyards, cattle, and good harvests that meant economic prosperity to the Israelites. Paul speaks of monetary donations from the Corinthian church to the poor in Jerusalem as a "grace" or "mercy" (Gk. *charis*, 2 Corinthians 8-9). However, the Bible also recognizes that material wealth brings with it great dangers. For example, there is the danger of failing to acknowledge that God is the source of the blessing (Deuteronomy 8:17-18; Hosea 2:8). Another spiritual danger associated with riches is materialism; that is, envying and greedily hoarding the things money can buy.

Background

Jesus always used illustrations in His sermon that His listeners could understand. For instance, those who heard this message knew of the wealth of Solomon and could probably visualize how beautifully he was clothed in the richest cloth with elaborate ornamentation. Jesus also used objects that were right in front of Him. As He sat upon the mountain, He spoke of the lilies of the field (Matthew 6:29) and the birds that flew overhead (v. 26) and told the people that they were much more important to God than these creatures. Therefore, to fully understand God's Word, we have to dig a little to discover the setting and ideas of the people of the time in which the Scripture was written. We can also look for contemporary illustrations to help listeners understand what God is saying today.

How does the setting of today's passage on a hillside in Galilee affect our understanding of the text? What would be a similar setting in modern-day?

At-A-Glance

1. Earthly Examples (Matthew 6:25-30)
2. Anxiety's Antidote (vv. 31-34)

In Depth

1. Earthly Examples (Matthew 6:25-30)

Don't worry about the necessities of food and clothes, Jesus counsels because your heavenly Father knows you have these needs. To have excessive concern reflects a lack of trust in an all-wise and loving heavenly Father. What can you change by worrying, Jesus asks. If you cannot add a single hour to your life span, something only God controls, why worry about food and clothes? He will supply these needs just as He supplies life itself.

Jesus provides several reasons and illustrations to support His counsel. First, we must trust God because we cannot do these things ourselves (v. 27). Going into specifics, Jesus secondly reminds us of God's past and present performances. If you doubt God's ability to take care of His creatures, you need only look at what He has done, is doing, and promises to continue doing (v. 26). Third, Jesus reminds us that God can provide better than we can. The flowers do not work or weave their own garments, yet they are more beautifully gowned than the wealthiest king that Israel had ever known (v. 29). Finally, we are reminded that we are worth a lot to God (v. 26, 30). We need only turn to Calvary and see the expression of His love and concern there (Romans 8:32). Christ assures His audience that God cares for all His children. Our faith in Him is well-placed, giving us confidence in our future.

Why do we worry so often about things we cannot alter?

2. Anxiety's Antidote (vv. 31-34)

The phrase "Take no thought" (vv. 31, 34) does not mean that believers are to wait passively on God's provision. It also does not mean that we should not carefully and prayerfully plan for our futures. It means that all of our efforts and planning should be made in confidence. Believers should be assured that God knows exactly what we need and that He will provide for those needs.

In verse 31, Jesus delivers the punch line: If God takes such good care of His simplest creations, then He can be trusted to take care of our needs. Anxiety robs us of our ability to trust God's care for us. Worry leaves us hopeless and fearful. Confidence in God to meet our day-to-day needs, however, frees us to concentrate on those things which are pleasing to Him: God's kingdom and righteousness. The idea is a constant mental preeminence of God's kingdom. We are to always be putting God's kingdom first and other things in proper perspective. When we do this, we have the assurance that the things necessary for survival and comfort will be given to us.

He promises that if we give the Kingdom first place, all our other needs will be met. Our problem is that we do not believe that. Our lack of confident trust in our heavenly Father causes us to hesitate. Only when we begin to take Christ's promise seriously will we begin to experience the joy that comes from confident trust in Him.

What is one area of your life that you worry about? How would seeking God's Kingdom first help alleviate that worry?

Search the Scriptures

1. What do we learn from nature about the goodness of God? (Matthew 6:26-29)

2. In what way should we not be like unbelievers? (v. 32)

3. What is Jesus' instruction about tomorrow? (v. 34)

Discuss the Meaning

1. What makes you more valuable than the flowers or the birds?

2. Should someone trust Christ just so their physical needs will be met?

3. What does it mean and look like, in practical terms, to seek God first? (v. 33)

Liberating Lesson

We live in a very materialistic culture. It is very easy to get locked into the lie that who you are equals the pile of stuff you can accumulate. Those who do not have the ability to contribute financially (the elderly, the ill, the disabled, the unwanted unborn) are assigned a lesser value than those who have big earning power. God, on the other hand, values every person and is not at all impressed by our material possessions.

By learning to seek His kingdom first, you declare to the world around you that you serve a radically different King. Desiring Him above all else will help set everything else in proper, eternal perspective. It has the added bonus of subduing worry, which can also be a powerful statement to the world around you that your King is completely trustworthy.

Application for Activation

In this passage, Christ does not condemn material possessions. He simply warns us of the peril we face when our search for things gets ahead of Him (cf. 1 Timothy 6:17). He reminds us that His Father is available to provide all our needs when we learn to trust Him. May each of us take a hard look at ourselves and our lifestyle. Are we really placing the interests of Christ and His kingdom first? Are we developing that confident trust in our Father that was so characteristic of Christ? There's no better time to start than now!

You might want to try the experiment discussed in the In Focus section, either as individuals or as a group. Make a list of everything that is worrying you today, date it, and place it in an envelope not to be opened for a month. While you are listing your concerns, pray about each one. When you open your envelope a month from now, you will have a fresh perspective (and answered prayer) about today's problems. You can trust God—You are of great value to Him!

Follow the Spirit

What God wants me to do:

_____

_____

_____

_____

_____

Remember Your Thoughts

Special insights I have learned:

_____

_____

_____

_____

_____

More Light on the Text
Matthew 6:25-34

25 Therefore I say unto you, Take no thought for your life, what ye shall eat, or what ye shall drink; nor yet for your body, what ye shall put on. Is not the life more than meat, and the body than raiment?

The preposition, "therefore," that begins this section serves as a transition from the previous verses (vv. 22-24), which emphasizes the need for total focus and undivided loyalty to the Lord God. Therefore, setting our affection and desire on earthly possessions or occupying ourselves with amassing and hoarding earthly wealth will influence our affection, love, service, and loyalty toward God. It will mean making wealth our master rather than God or having two masters, which Jesus says is impossible. If we love money or riches, it follows then that we cannot love God; and if we love God, then our love for riches will be eliminated.

What would cause someone to love money or have money as their master? Needs! These include primarily the necessities of life— food, clothing, and sustenance. Lack of these necessities can lead one into worry and anxiety or doing all sorts of things that might lead to evil. Aware of this, Jesus advises His audience against anxiety and worry. He does this by using two negative imperatives (vv. 25, 31) and develops His arguments by offering positive alternatives. Then He concludes with another negative imperative and positive advice (v. 34).

The phrase "I say unto you" underscores the importance of both what He has already said and what He is about to say, and the truthfulness and certainty of what He is talking about. The prohibition "Take no thought" translates a Greek verb that can be rendered "do not worry, fret, or be anxious." Neither your life nor what to eat or what to wear should concern you. Jesus then follows this statement with two rhetorical questions, "Is not life more than meat and the body than raiment?" Of course, the answer is "yes"—life is more than meat (food) and the body is more than raiment (clothing). The word translated as "life" here is *psyche* (Gk. puh-**SOO**-khay), which also means "soul." These worries might affect our life in our day-to-day activities, but they should never trouble our souls. The importance and implication of these rhetorical questions are not realized until verse 33. In support of His argument against an anxious approach to life, Jesus illustrates His point about food by urging His audience to think about the birds and how they get their food.

26 Behold the fowls of the air: for they sow not, neither do they reap, nor gather into barns; yet your heavenly Father feedeth them. Are ye not much better than they? 27 Which of you by taking thought can add one cubit unto his stature?

Christ points the people's attention to the birds. When one considers how birds eat they would realize that birds do not sow or cultivate their food, reap or harvest what they planted, nor do they worry about storing their food in barns. God provides for them. Therefore, we should learn from how the Lord cares for the birds. He will, in the same way, and even more than that, care for our needs. Stating His providential authority and care over His creation, the Lord made a similar point to Job (Job 38:39-41; cf. Matthew 10:29-31).

Jesus strengthens this truth again with another rhetorical question: "Are ye not much better than they?" Of course, the answer is in the affirmative; human beings are worth more than birds since we are created in the image of God.

It is noteworthy to understand clearly that Jesus is not encouraging laziness or that the disciples do not need to work and expect "manna to fall from heaven" as the saying

goes. Adult birds do not wait for their food to be dropped into their beaks. The point here is that they go about their daily search for food without fretting. God in His providential plan and care provides for them daily. In the same way, we need to trust the Lord for our daily food (see the Lord's Prayer, Matthew 6:11).

In case the audience did not get His point, Jesus poses another rhetorical question (v. 27) to drive home the truth about God's care for them. The point is that worrying is useless and profitless since it cannot "add one cubit" to one's stature. "Cubit" is the Greek word *pechus* (**PAY**-khoos), a measure of length equal to the distance from the joint of the elbow to the tip of the middle finger (approximately 18 inches), so its precise length fluctuates. Many interpreters believe that cubit is used figuratively here to refer to any short length. Hence, the NLT translates verse 27: "Can all your worries add a single moment to your life?" Indeed, it has been medically proven that anxiety causes stress, which is detrimental to health and can cause stroke, heart failure, and in some cases death. Instead of adding to life, worry shortens life.

28 And why take ye thought for raiment? Consider the lilies of the field, how they grow; they toil not, neither do they spin: 29 And yet I say unto you, That even Solomon in all his glory was not arrayed like one of these.

Christ's second argument against the futility of worries focuses on clothing. He questions the rationale of worrying about clothes— what we should wear—and then directs our attention to the lilies or flowers of the field. He uses the verb, *katamanthano* (Gk. ka-ta-man-**THA**-no) translated "consider," and means "to consider well, to examine" or "note carefully," and implying the same level of focus and concentration as "behold" (v. 26). Here Jesus calls on the listeners to thoroughly consider the flowers of the field and "how they grow." They do nothing of themselves to grow, neither "toiling" in the fields to earn money to buy clothes nor "spinning" to make clothing themselves. The lilies or flowers of the field refer to wild plants in general (Psalm 103:15) rather than flowers planted in the garden (see v. 30 where they are described as grass of the field). He then describes the beauty of these grasses by comparing them with the splendor of King Solomon. Their splendor surpasses that of Solomon (the most decorated king of all Israel) with no effort of their own. Who gives them their beauty? The answer is obvious—God.

30 Wherefore, if God so clothe the grass of the field, which to day is, and to morrow is cast into the oven, shall he not much more clothe you, O ye of little faith?

Then the argument follows, just as in verse 26, from the lesser to the greater. If God could clothe the "grass of the field," which has no lasting value, but is destined for the oven to be burned for fuel, "shall he not much more clothe you?" Again, Jesus is not advocating laziness, although the thought here differs slightly from that of the birds. The flowers are as useful as they can be; they grow and they are flammable. Such simple tasks do not require beautiful petals, but God gives it to them anyway. The kind of God who is willing to trouble Himself with making even such a temporary thing beautiful will do so much more for those whom He loves and calls to an everlasting life.

Jesus then rebukes the disciples by calling them *oligopistos* (Gk. oh-lee-**GO**-pees-toce), which means people of "little faith," a term Jesus uses often in the Book of Matthew (8:26; 14:31; 16:8, etc.). *Oligopistos* could mean "lack of trust" or "trusting too little." Nothing affects our faith and trust in the Lord more than anxiety and worry. Most of the people who were listening to Jesus likely had a correct understanding of godly doctrine. Their faith in that sense was

strong. But if they allow themselves to worry, that shows a lack of faith. Likewise today, we can give the right answers to theological questions, but that knowledge must inform our actions and thought patterns or our faith is actually weak.

31 Therefore take no thought, saying, What shall we eat? or, What shall we drink? or, Wherewithal shall we be clothed? 32 (For after all these things do the Gentiles seek:) for your heavenly Father knoweth that ye have need of all these things.

Jesus summarizes His thoughts and reemphasizes the command "do not worry." He gathers the previous statements together with the preposition, "so" or "therefore" (Gk. *oun*, **OON**). That is, in light of God's providential care, there is no need to fret or worry about food, drink, or clothing. Jesus lists the common questions that go through the minds of those who worry. Such questions are useless and unprofitable because they cannot accomplish anything (v. 27). He continues by saying that worrying too much about all the earthly needs is the mark of the Gentiles. Gentiles here are those who have no relationship with the Lord—those who do not trust in the providential power of God to provide for His people.

It is also useless and indeed foolhardy to fret about food, drink, and clothes since the Lord is always aware of our circumstances and knows what our needs are, including the above-mentioned necessities. A hardy faith will remind us that God is in control of His entire creation and that He loves us dearly. As any father would (Matthew 7:9-11), He will take care of His children without their having to fret about the things He will provide. Christ's disciples should, therefore, lead lives different from those of the pagans, who have no trust in God's fatherly care for them and whose fundamental goals are materialistic.

33 But seek ye first the kingdom of God, and his righteousness; and all these things shall be added unto you.

Rather than fretting and worrying about all our needs, and pursuing earthly materials and possessions as the pagans do, we are to seek first the kingdom of God, and God's righteousness. The Lord who knows all our needs (vv. 8, 32) will also give us "all these things." We have the assurance that if we will earnestly pursue His kingdom and hunger and thirst for His righteousness (5:6), God will meet our needs because of who He is and because He cares for us (cf. Philippians 4:6; 1 Peter 5:7). To "seek" (Gk. *zeteo*, dzay-**TEH**-oh) means "to desire, to strive for," or "seek after" or "to clamor for"—the same word is used in reference to the Gentiles seeking earthly things. Therefore, to seek "first" the kingdom of God and His righteousness is to put God and our desire for His kingdom first in our lives. It is to make God our priority in service and worship above everything else. It means to strive to live in a right relationship with God our Father and to allow Him to govern our lives—in all activities of life and in all our relationships with other people. It is to give our absolute allegiance to God, submitting wholeheartedly to His will always.

34 Take therefore no thought for the morrow: for the morrow shall take thought for the things of itself. Sufficient unto the day is the evil thereof.

Jesus concludes this section with another negative imperative: "Do not worry." In view of the assurance that God will meet the needs of those who commit themselves to His kingdom and righteousness, *oun* (Gk. "therefore" or "these things being so"), "take … no thought for the morrow." This is a way of saying, "Leave tomorrow's problems for that day" or "allow nature to take its course," as people would say. Focus on today's issues; they are enough for today. Don't add tomorrow's "evil" (Gk. *kakia*, kah-**KEE**-ah), or trouble, to today's. God's grace for today is just enough for today and should not be wasted on tomorrow's worries. There will be new grace to meet whatever trouble tomorrow may bring (Lamentations 3:23).

Sources:

Ladd, George Eldon. *The Biblical Expositor: The Living Theme of The Great Book*. Carl Henry, ed. Philadelphia, PA: A. J. Holman, 1960. 31.

Peterson, Eugene H. *The Message: The Bible in Contemporary Language*. Colorado Springs, CO: NavPress Publishing Group, 2002. 1755.

Vine, W. E., Merrill F. Unger and William White Jr. *Vine's Expository Dictionary*. Nashville, TN: Thomas Nelson Publishers, 1996. 562–63.

Say It Correctly

Rhetorical. Ruh-**TOR**-ih-cul.

Daily Bible Readings

MONDAY
Worried? Seek God's Counsel
(1 Samuel 9:5-10)

TUESDAY
God Cares for His People
(Ezekiel 34:11-16)

WEDNESDAY
Rich? Set Your Hope on God
(1 Timothy 6:17-19)

THURSDAY
Enlarge Your Faith Practices
(Matthew 17:14-20)

FRIDAY
Overcome Worry through Faith
(Luke 12:22-34)

SATURDAY
Serve God with Your Whole Heart
(Matthew 6:19-24)

SUNDAY
Live Worry-Free Every Day
(Matthew 6:25-34)

Notes

_____

_____

_____

_____

Teaching Tips

Words You Should Know

A. Tempest (Matthew 8:24) *seismos* (Gk.)—To agitate or shake; specifically, an earthquake or violent windstorm

B. Marvelled (v. 27) *thaumazo* (Gk.)—To wonder, be awed, or struck with admiration or astonishment

Teacher Preparation

Unifying Principle—Calming the Storm. People often lose confidence amidst the storms of persecution, rejection, and poverty. Where can we find assurance when beset by the storms of life? Fearing they would not survive the windstorm, the disciples turned to Jesus to save them.

A. Read the Bible Background and Devotional Reading.

B. Pray for your students and lesson clarity.

C. Read the lesson Scripture in multiple translations.

O—Open the Lesson

A. Begin the class with prayer.

B. Ask volunteers to share an incident in their lives that they consider a miracle from God.

C. Have the students read the Aim for Change and the In Focus story.

D. Ask students how events like those in the story weigh on their hearts and how they can view these events from a faith perspective.

P—Present the Scriptures

A. Read the Focal Verses and discuss the Background and The People, Places, and Times sections.

B. Have the class share what Scriptures stand out for them and why, with particular emphasis on today's themes.

E—Explore the Meaning

A. Use In Depth or More Light on the Text to facilitate a deeper discussion of the lesson text.

B. Pose the questions in Search the Scriptures and Discuss the Meaning.

C. Discuss the Liberating Lesson and Application for Activation sections.

N—Next Steps for Application

A. Summarize the value of trusting God's timing.

B. End class with a commitment to pray, thanking God for His power to swiftly restore order and calm to our lives.

Worship Guide

For the Superintendent or Teacher
Theme: Why Are You Afraid?
Song: "Jesus Never Fails"
Devotional Reading: Psalm 107:23–32

Why Are You Afraid?

Bible Background • MATTHEW 8:23–27; MARK 4:35–41; LUKE 8:22-25
Printed Text • MATTHEW 8:23–27 | Devotional Reading • PSALM 107:23–32

——————————— Aim for Change ———————————

By the end of this lesson, we will CONSIDER the feelings of the disciples when a storm overtook their boat while Jesus was asleep, IDENTIFY the crises that cause adults to worry about themselves and their families, and RESPOND to the promised presence of Jesus in bad times as well as good times.

——————————— In Focus ———————————

Shala had gone through a lot in her life: she had lived through a dysfunctional family, mental and physical abuse, and depression. Yet, she found God at an early age and accepted Jesus as her Lord and Savior. She and her husband Bill tried to obey God in every way. Shala had known pain and suffering throughout her life, but it was nothing compared to the pain and suffering she experienced when her daughter Joan rebelled against God.

Joan had grown up in church, been taught about Jesus and His principles, and watched her parents live out those principles daily in their own lives. She said she had given her heart to God as well. However, when Shala was diagnosed with breast cancer soon after her daughter's fourteenth birthday, Joan turned her back on God and her rebellion lasted for over ten years.

Shala could not understand why these things happened. She felt that she and her husband had trained their daughter in the nurture and admonition of God. However, the child still rebelled! Shala and Bill were rocked almost as much as Joan, but through it all, Shala and her husband learned to trust in God. They dug their spiritual roots deep into God through prayer, praise, and reading His Holy Word.

What has been your greatest fear in life? How have you brought the issue to God? How has God helped you in it?

——————————— Keep in Mind ———————————

"And he saith unto them, Why are ye fearful, O ye of little faith? Then he arose, and rebuked the winds and the sea; and there was a great calm"
(Matthew 8:26, KJV).

"Jesus responded, 'Why are you afraid? You have so little faith!' Then he got up and rebuked the wind and waves, and suddenly there was a great calm" (Matthew 8:26, NLT).

Focal Verses

KJV **Matthew 8:23** And when he was entered into a ship, his disciples followed him.

24 And, behold, there arose a great tempest in the sea, insomuch that the ship was covered with the waves: but he was asleep.

25 And his disciples came to him, and awoke him, saying, Lord, save us: we perish.

26 And he saith unto them, Why are ye fearful, O ye of little faith? Then he arose, and rebuked the winds and the sea; and there was a great calm.

27 But the men marvelled, saying, What manner of man is this, that even the winds and the sea obey him!

NLT **Matthew 8:23** Then Jesus got into the boat and started across the lake with his disciples.

24 Suddenly, a fierce storm struck the lake, with waves breaking into the boat. But Jesus was sleeping.

25 The disciples went and woke him up, shouting, "Lord, save us! We're going to drown!"

26 Jesus responded, "Why are you afraid? You have so little faith!" Then he got up and rebuked the wind and waves, and suddenly there was a great calm.

27 The disciples were amazed. "Who is this man?" they asked. "Even the winds and waves obey him!"

The People, Places, and Times

Chaotic Seas. In the Jewish mind, the sea represents chaos and mystery and therefore offers many opportunities to showcase the awesome power of God. He does what He wants with the raging sea, showing that He is sovereign over all creation. This can be seen from the very first lines of Scripture (Genesis 1:2). One of the greatest miracles recorded in the Bible is Israel's crossing of the Red Sea. Jesus displays His divine power over the chaotic seas multiple times, when He calms the storm, and when He walks on the water. The one who divided the waters and the seas from the dry land can also stop them from overwhelming us when they threaten our lives. The water is not sovereign; God is.

Matthew. Matthew, originally named Levi, was a Jewish tax collector who became one of Jesus' Twelve disciples. Matthew responded to Jesus' call and followed Him (Mark 2:14). When Jesus went to Matthew's home, Matthew held a banquet and invited other tax collectors and people who needed to meet and follow Jesus.

Using his skills at record-keeping and attention to detail, Matthew wrote to a Jewish audience about the fulfillment of the Old Testament prophecy which validated Jesus as the Messiah, the everlasting King. The themes in the Gospel of Matthew include: Jesus Christ, the King; the fulfilled prophecy of the Messiah; the kingdom of God; and Jesus' teachings.

Background

To show His power and authority over everything that He has created, the Lord will sometimes personally intervene and override the laws of nature. These miracles most often occur as a result of prayer when God's people call out for help or deliverance. Scripture provides many examples of these kinds of miracles. One such miracle is God personally feeding the Israelites bread from heaven during their extended journey in the wilderness (Exodus 16:4). Another is when God slowed the rotation of the earth, allowing Joshua more time to completely defeat his enemies (Joshua 10:12–14). When calming the storm on the Sea of Galilee, Jesus personally overrode nature at the request of His disciples.

At-A-Glance

1. The Peaceful Savior
(Matthew 8:23–24)
2. The Panicked Sailors (vv. 25–27)

In Depth

1. The Peaceful Savior (Matthew 8:23–24)

The Sea of Galilee is really a small freshwater lake about 600 feet below sea level, about six miles wide and eight miles long. High mountains surround the lake on three sides. The Jordan River flows from the southern end of the Sea of Galilee down to the Dead Sea (about 1300 feet below sea level). The mountains around the lake and the downward flow of the Jordan create a natural funnel. When winds blow down from the mountains through this funnel, they often produce sudden, violent storms. It was in just such a storm that Jesus first demonstrated His power over the elements.

Jesus had been healing many people in the area of Capernaum: the centurion's servant, Peter's mother-in-law, and many others with demons and sicknesses. Jesus wished to leave the crowds behind for a while. After warning some early followers about the cost of being His disciple, the small fishing boat set sail for the opposite shore carrying Jesus and faithful disciples. The eastern shore was much less populated, so Jesus and His disciples would be able to rest and refresh themselves.

As the boat made its way across the lake, Jesus gave in to His weariness. He made His way to the back of the boat, stretched out on a cushion on the steersman's seat, and dropped off into a deep, peaceful slumber. Our Lord's fatigue reminds us that He had the same physical needs and limitations as we have.

How is Jesus able to sleep, even while a storm is raging?

2. The Panicked Sailors (vv. 25–27)

Several men in the boat with Jesus that day were seasoned fishermen. They had probably experienced these storms firsthand and knew what to do when the sea turned ugly. But this storm was something they could not face.

A violent wind swept down toward the lake. Huge waves swamped the boat and the men know their lives were in danger (Luke 8:23). They cannot save themselves. In desperation they turn to Jesus: "Lord, save us! We're going to drown!" (Matthew 8:25, NLT). The second they called on Jesus, He immediately stopped the wind. He taught them a lesson in faith and called them to examine themselves.

Jesus awakes from His slumber and scolds the fearful disciples. "Why are ye fearful, O ye of little faith?" (v. 26). Even early in His ministry, the disciples are beginning to suspect who Jesus truly, fully is. The disciples personally witnessed Jesus perform many miracles, but when the going got tough, they panicked. Jesus rose from the place and spoke to the storm. Immediately, tranquility reigned over the water.

Many are the storms of life that burden our souls; some of them, like the storm, may threaten to overwhelm us. But when problems and trials seem to overwhelm us, we should know that we are not alone. When the storms of life are raging, we can take heart in the fact that Jesus is with us in our situation.

Why do we wait until we run out of options before we call on the Lord?

Search the Scriptures

1. What was Jesus doing while the disciples were fighting to keep the boat afloat in the windstorm? (Matthew 8:24)

2. What did the disciples do when faced with a situation beyond their control? (v. 25)

3. What question did the disciples ask about Jesus after He had rebuked the storm? (v. 27)

Discuss the Meaning

Most believers have experienced God working in their lives during past trials and times of anxiety. Yet, usually when we meet with new difficulty, we tend to give in to fear and often try to handle the situation ourselves. Do you think that Jesus would rebuke us as He did the frightened disciples? When is the last time you were rebuked by the Holy Spirit?

Liberating Lesson

Most people have to experience the fear of thinking they have no way out of a problem. Perhaps you have even become discouraged, feeling overwhelmed by a storm of life. Bad experiences may cause us to believe that no one cares about our problems. We seek assurance when facing these battles. While believers are not exempted from experiencing life's storms, we can trust in God's timing, recognizing His sovereign power over our lives and our world. Even though God might not answer at the immediate sign of trouble in our lives, we can find assurance in knowing that God cares about the issues causing us anxiety and will respond to our earnest pleas for help. When He does move, just watch how God's power is swift to restore order and calm to our lives!

Application for Activation

Make a list of the things in your life that cause you to worry. Then make a second list of things you need the Lord to provide for you. Be careful to list only your needs, not your desires. For the next month, set aside one day each week to pray and fast for these things. At the end of the month check off the prayers the Lord has answered. Be prepared to share your testimony with the class.

Follow the Spirit

What God wants me to do:

_____

_____

_____

_____

_____

Remember Your Thoughts

Special insights I have learned:

_____

_____

_____

_____

_____

More Light on the Text
Matthew 8:23-27

Jesus and the disciples are caught in a terrible windstorm while crossing the Sea of Galilee. The disciples are awed when they see that even the forces of nature must obey the commands of Christ.

23 And when he was entered into a ship, his disciples followed him. 24 And, behold, there arose a great tempest in the sea, insomuch that the ship was covered with the waves: but he was asleep. 25 And his disciples came to him, and awoke him, saying, Lord, save us: we perish.

Most of the disciples had grown up around the Sea of Galilee and several of them were seasoned fishermen. They were familiar with the sudden storms common to the lake. But they had never seen anything like this. The word used (Gk. *seismos*, **SAZE**-moce) is usually translated "earthquake" (Matthew 27:54; Acts 16:26) and is rarely associated with the water.

After doing all they could to keep the boat afloat, the frightened disciples called out to Jesus for help. The fearful men woke the Lord from His peaceful slumber, all shouting at once. One cried, "Master, master, we perish" (Luke 8:24). Another shouted, "Master, carest thou not that we perish?" (Mark 4:38), and a third pleaded, "Lord, save us; we perish" (Matthew 8:25). Their language is that of extreme terror. The three exclamations recorded by the three writers describe three possible responses to the troubles that afflict us. Some of us may think that the Lord is unaware of the depth of our torment. Others realize that God knows all, but because He is not acting the way we think He should, we begin to wonder if He even cares. Finally, some simply cry out in desperation, "Lord, if you don't save me, I'll perish!"

The prayer Matthew records begins by acknowledging the person of Christ as "Lord" and ends with an appeal to His power to "save us." "Lord" (Gk. *kurios*, **KOO**-ree-oce) acknowledges Christ as our Master. Since the disciples belong to Him, it is His responsibility to act on their behalf. Their pleas of "save us" (Gk. *sozo*, **SODE**-zo) means "to deliver from danger or death." It can refer to physical or spiritual peril. Is this not the prayer of all believers? Do we not come to Christ with the initial prayer, "Lord, save me from death"? We continue our walk with the plea, "Lord, deliver me from the evil of the world." Such is the state of the true disciple of Christ. We are completely dependent on Him for deliverance and care. The reason Christ delays or sometimes appears to be sleeping is to bring us to the point of utter surrender, to force us to acknowledge that without Him we will surely perish.

26 And he saith unto them, Why are ye fearful, O ye of little faith? Then he arose, and rebuked the winds and the sea; and there was a great calm.

The Lord's disappointment with His disciples is apparent. Without moving, He looks at the frightened men and scolds them for their lack of faith. Jesus is not upset because the men woke Him from a peaceful sleep. He is displeased because of their fear. The Lord's question, "Why are ye fearful?" is a question all God's children must ask themselves when we are worried or fearful. Fear indicates a lack of trust in Christ. The Lord had told the disciples they were going to the other side of the lake (Mark 4:35). Since Jesus said it, no power in all creation could prevent the safe crossing from taking place. In spite of the apparent hopelessness of their situation, Jesus expected the disciples to have faith in His word.

Echoing His recent teaching in the Sermon on the Mount, the Lord calls them out for their "little faith" (Gk. *oligopistos*, see Lesson 1, More Light on the Text, v. 30). Their faith depended on seeing Him exercise His power. The words of the disciples when they called out to Jesus indicate that they believed the Lord could save them. They feared because they did not understand that their deliverance was already an accomplished fact. The promises of God are always backed by the power of God. Even when we cannot see God's power at work in our lives, we must take comfort in His promises to save, deliver, and work out all situations for our good (Romans 8:1).

After rebuking the disciples for their lack of faith in His Word, the Lord turns His attention to the source of the men's fear and rebukes it too. Rising from His place of rest, the Lord speaks to the storm. Mark provides us with the very words of the Lord's rebuke: "Peace, be still" (Mark 4:39). As soon as the words leave the Lord's lips, the uproarious winds grow silent and the convulsing sea becomes calm.

Since the unpredictable sea is an object of such uncertainty—and therefore fear—in the Jewish mind, a calm sea is seen as a special blessing. The "calm" (Gk. *galene*, gah-**LAY**-nay) here is specifically the calmness of a vast expanse, and also recalls the "still small voice" Elijah encounters as the power and presence of God (1 Kings 19:12).

27 But the men marvelled, saying, What manner of man is this, that even the winds and the sea obey him!

The sudden, quiet stillness of the sea and the wind must have disconcerted the men. Nothing moved, not a sound was heard. The astonished men probably stood for several seconds in open-mouthed wonder and when they spoke, their words expressed their astonishment. They "marvelled" (Gk. *thaumazo*, thow-**MOD**-zo) or were struck with admiration and astonishment at the miracle. Jesus had given them new proof of His control over the forces of nature. Even the winds and waves obeyed Him at a word. The Lord's dominion over the wind and the waves was the dominion God gave to Adam before the fall (Genesis 1:28). The first Adam lost His dominion to the prince of the air (Ephesians 2:2). Christ, the second Adam, used this incident to demonstrate the future restoration of humanity's dominion over creation.

Sources:
Henry, Matthew. *Matthew Henry's Commentary on the Whole Bible: New Modern Edition.* Vols. 1-6. Peabody, MA: Hendrickson Publishers, Inc., 2009.

Strong, James. *The New Strong's Exhaustive Concordance of the Bible.* Nashville, TN: Thomas Nelson, 2003.

Thayer, Joseph Henry. *A Greek-English Lexicon of the New Testament.* New York: American Book Company, 1889.

Say It Correctly

Chaotic. kay-**OH**-tick.
Capernaum. cay-**PUR**-nay-um.

Daily Bible Readings

MONDAY
Do Not Fear the Storm
(Mark 4:35-41)

TUESDAY
Do Not Fear Persecution
(Matthew 24:9-14)

WEDNESDAY
No Separation from God's Love
(Romans 8:31-39)

THURSDAY
I Have Overcome the World
(John 16:25-33)

FRIDAY
Choose to Follow Me Now!
(Matthew 8:18-22)

SATURDAY
Jesus Delivers the Demon-Possessed
(Matthew 8:28-34)

SUNDAY
Jesus Stills the Stormy Seas
(Matthew 8:23-27)

Teaching Tips

June 20
Bible Study Guide 3

Words You Should Know

A. To be whole (Matthew 9:21) *sozo* (Gk.)— To save from sickness, death, or eternal condemnation

B. Put forth (vv. 25) *ekballo* (Gk.)—To forcefully remove, throw or cast out

Teacher Preparation

Unifying Principle—A Healing Touch. People often look to others to help them with their health issues. Where does healing come from? Jesus told the woman with the issue of blood that she was healed because of her faith and told Jairus that his daughter was healed and restored to life.

A. Read the Bible Background and Devotional Reading.

B. Pray for your students and lesson clarity.

C. Read the lesson Scripture in multiple translations.

O—Open the Lesson

A. Begin the class with prayer.

B. Remind participants about things that were happening twelve years ago. Ask participants how their life has progressed since then. Then ask participants to imagine suffering a major medical condition for that entire time. That is how long the woman with the issue of blood was suffering.

C. Have the students read the Aim for Change and the In Focus story.

D. Ask students how events like those in the story weigh on their hearts and how they can view these events from a faith perspective.

P—Present the Scriptures

A. Read the Focal Verses and discuss the Background and The People, Places, and Times sections.

B. Have the class share what Scriptures stand out for them and why, with particular emphasis on today's themes.

E—Explore the Meaning

A. Use In Depth or More Light on the Text to facilitate a deeper discussion of the lesson text.

B. Pose the questions in Search the Scriptures and Discuss the Meaning.

C. Discuss the Liberating Lesson and Application for Activation sections.

N—Next Steps for Application

A. Summarize the value of not being fearful of approaching God with our needs.

B. End class with a commitment to pray for peace in struggles when God does not heal or save our loved ones as we expected.

Worship Guide

For the Superintendent or Teacher
Theme: Healed by Faith
Song: "He Touched Me"
Devotional Reading: Proverbs 3:1–8

491

Healed by Faith

Bible Background • MATTHEW 9:18–26; MARK 5:21–43; LUKE 8:40–56
Printed Text • MATTHEW 9:18–26 | Devotional Reading • PROVERBS 3:1–8

Aim for Change

By the end of this lesson, we will EXAMINE the nature of the faith involved in the healings of the woman and the girl in this passage, SENSE the power of God to bring life and healing to our loved ones, and REJOICE in the healing power of God as manifested in our own lives.

In Focus

Even after Pastor James retired from the pulpit, he felt called to minister to people in need. He volunteered for the prayer line at a local TV station. While answering the phones, he received a call from a young woman by the name of Sandra who was contemplating suicide. Sandra told the pastor about her past abusive relationships and how she consistently failed at everything she attempted. She didn't see any reason to keep going in this world.

Pastor James listened and was overwhelmed with compassion for Sandra and wept for her as he began to pray. He decided to personally follow up on Sandra by phoning her. He received no answer and grew concerned. He prayed much harder.

On his fourth try, Sandra answered. She told the pastor she was very depressed and wanted to commit suicide. She also mentioned she had told God, "If you are real, have someone call and pray for me."

"That's just what God laid on my heart to do," Pastor James said. Because of his compassion, Pastor James was able to bring Sandra to a decision for Christ.

Jesus always responds to those who are desperate, who confess their hopelessness and helplessness. How do you communicate your hopelessness? How do you respond when people share their hopelessness with you?

Keep in Mind

"But Jesus turned him about, and when he saw her, he said, Daughter, be of good comfort; thy faith hath made thee whole. And the woman was made whole from that hour" (Matthew 9:22, KJV).

"Jesus turned around, and when he saw her he said, 'Daughter, be encouraged! Your faith has made you well.' And the woman was healed at that moment" (Matthew 9:22, NLT).

Focal Verses

KJV **Matthew 9:18** While he spake these things unto them, behold, there came a certain ruler, and worshipped him, saying, My daughter is even now dead: but come and lay thy hand upon her, and she shall live.

19 And Jesus arose, and followed him, and so did his disciples.

20 And, behold, a woman, which was diseased with an issue of blood twelve years, came behind him, and touched the hem of his garment:

21 For she said within herself, If I may but touch his garment, I shall be whole.

22 But Jesus turned him about, and when he saw her, he said, Daughter, be of good comfort; thy faith hath made thee whole. And the woman was made whole from that hour.

23 And when Jesus came into the ruler's house, and saw the minstrels and the people making a noise,

24 He said unto them, Give place: for the maid is not dead, but sleepeth. And they laughed him to scorn.

25 But when the people were put forth, he went in, and took her by the hand, and the maid arose.

26 And the fame hereof went abroad into all that land.

NLT **Matthew 9:18** As Jesus was saying this, the leader of a synagogue came and knelt before him. "My daughter has just died," he said, "but you can bring her back to life again if you just come and lay your hand on her."

19 So Jesus and his disciples got up and went with him.

20 Just then a woman who had suffered for twelve years with constant bleeding came up behind him. She touched the fringe of his robe,

21 for she thought, "If I can just touch his robe, I will be healed."

22 Jesus turned around, and when he saw her he said, "Daughter, be encouraged! Your faith has made you well." And the woman was healed at that moment.

23 When Jesus arrived at the official's home, he saw the noisy crowd and heard the funeral music.

24 "Get out!" he told them. "The girl isn't dead; she's only asleep." But the crowd laughed at him.

25 After the crowd was put outside, however, Jesus went in and took the girl by the hand, and she stood up!

26 The report of this miracle swept through the entire countryside.

The People, Places, and Times

Jairus. Coming to Jesus on behalf of his beloved daughter, Jairus oversaw the administration of the synagogue at Capernaum. This was an elected position and a powerful one. Jairus was a devout Jew and leader. He was the father of a 12-year-old daughter whom he loved deeply. Jairus showed strong courage by going to Jesus, who was hated by the religious elders. However, because of his deep love for his daughter and his belief in Jesus, he approached Christ with humility, worship, and faith.

Background

Matthew writes a cluster of miracle narratives, one healing narrative inside the framework of another. First, there is the desperate cry of a synagogue ruler for the life of his daughter. Next, there is the hopelessness of a woman with a 12-year bleeding disorder. Both stories tell of desperation, and each one can stand independent from the others. These narratives demonstrate the authority, power, and compassion of Jesus. His fame had spread throughout the region, and thousands of people were following Him because everywhere He went He cured every disease and sickness (Matthew 9:35).

Today there are many reasons people follow Jesus. Maybe it is what their friends are doing, or maybe they simply want to receive a blessing. The scribes and Pharisees (religious rulers), however, followed Jesus to test the validity of His being the Son of David, the Messiah. Jesus was their king but they would not acknowledge Him. They were trying to discredit Him and find a reason to put Him to death. The Pharisees went so far as to say He casts demons out of people by the power of the ruler of demons (v. 34). But the people were saying, " It was never so seen in Israel" (v. 33). Jesus is moved to deep compassion by what He sees people confused, leaderless, scattered, and dying in their sins!

At-A-Glance

1. Compassion for the Hopeless
(Matthew 9:18–19)
2. Compassion for the Helpless
(vv. 20–22)
3. Compassion for Healing (vv. 23–26)

In Depth

1. Compassion for the Hopeless (Matthew 9:18–19)

Jairus, a leader from the synagogue, interrupts Jesus as He speaks to John the Baptist's disciples. Jairus falls down before Jesus and makes a desperate request for Him to raise his 12-year-old daughter from the dead. The father says, "But if you will come and lay your hands upon her, she shall live" (vv. 18–19). This is also the only reference in the book of Matthew regarding the laying on of hands. We see Jesus and His disciples immediately got up to follow Jairus (v. 19). God immediately

responds to genuine faith because He desires that we should trust and depend on Him. Being interrupted and delayed by the ailing woman could have easily discouraged Jairus. Although the worst had happened, the Son of God has authority over death and the power to restore life. Jesus is touched by the faith Jairus displays.

Jesus knows what is best for us, and we must trust Him to touch our needs. Jairus is an example of how our leaders should approach Christ: in humility, worship, and faith. Most of us have experienced loved ones dying, so we can understand the desperation Jairus felt.

In times of hopelessness, do we ask Jesus for His touch?

2. Compassion for the Helpless (vv. 20–22)

A woman with a chronic bleeding problem touches Jesus' clothing and is healed by her faith in Him (vv. 20–22). Matthew uses the phrase "And, behold," to interrupt the story about the dead girl to introduce the hemorrhaging woman. She was considered to be unclean, contaminated, and unworthy. According to the Mosaic law, she was to be cut off from the Jewish community and ostracized. The woman was desperate and unable to help herself. But she purposed in her heart that if she could just touch the hem, the fringe, the tassel of Jesus' garment, He would never know and she would be healed.

Desperation and faith stir Jesus to compassion, for He who knows all can help all! This poor woman had been cut off from society and family according to Jewish tradition. Jesus turned and saw her, for her faith had touched Him (Mark 5:32). Faith will never go unnoticed or ignored by Christ. Pointedly, Jesus commends this woman's faith and calls her "daughter," even as He makes His way to heal Jairus' daughter. To God, we are each His daughter or His son, each dearly loved, and always welcome in His presence with any of our many needs.

What do we need for Jesus to touch for us? Cancer? Depression?

3. Compassion for Healing (vv. 23–26)

By the time Jesus arrives at Jairus' house, the girl's funeral has begun. The musicians (v. 29) were a Gentile custom. They would play melancholy tunes to stir up the grief and mourning of those in attendance. Jesus sends away all the noisemakers, keeping only those who have faith that Christ can perform this miracle. Despite the hopelessness of the crowds, Jairus' faith called Jesus to his daughter's deathbed, and that simple, yet bold, the request is enough to change the outcome. As Jairus asked, Jesus lays hands on his daughter, and she lives!

Jesus' acts of healing and resurrection were not just personal but restored the woman and the girl to the whole community. Indeed, word of the girl's resurrection goes out to the entire region. When we act on faith and receive God's blessing, it builds the faith of everyone in our community who witnesses our blessing.

How has an act of faith in your community made surprisingly wide ripple effects?

Search the Scriptures

1. What did the Jewish leader ask of Jesus? (Matthew 9:18)

2. The mourners reacted to Jesus with scorn. How did Jesus respond? (v. 25)

Discuss the Meaning

1. Jesus' compassion is seen in His response to the Jewish leader and the hemorrhaging woman. How should we respond to Jesus and His commands knowing He is full of compassion?

2. What should the role of faith be in today's medical practice?

Liberating Lesson

Many people in our society are hopeless, helpless, and desperate. Some are drug addicts, prostitutes, alcoholics, and some are just homeless. Many believers avoid these people and have a difficult time ministering to them, because of fear and lack of willingness to be compassionate. How do you think Jesus feels about this avoidance? Where would we be if God had not shown us His mercy? How could you, your Bible study group, or your church show radical compassion like Jesus did?

Application for Activation

Almost every family is directly or indirectly touched by some form of substance abuse. Many organizations, such as hospitals, halfway houses, and soup kitchens, need volunteers. Right in our neighborhoods and communities, we can make a difference. This week make a special effort to show your faith that God can heal these people. Observe and study people and allow God to demonstrate His mercy through you for their physical and/or spiritual needs.

Follow the Spirit

What God wants me to do:

_____

_____

_____

_____

_____

_____

_____

Remember Your Thoughts

Special insights I have learned:

_____

_____

_____

_____

_____

_____

_____

More Light on the Text

Matthew 9:18–26

18 While he spake these things unto them, behold, there came a certain ruler, and worshipped him, saying, My daughter is even now dead: but come and lay thy hand upon her, and she shall live. 19 And Jesus arose, and followed him, and so did his disciples.

An official of the synagogue comes to Jesus and tells him that his daughter has just died. Matthew does not give much detail about who this man is, but we read from other Gospel writers that his name is Jairus and he is a ruler in the synagogue, a leader in the local assembly (Mark 5:22; Luke 8:41). He comes in respect, and even "worshipped" Jesus. The Greek word here, *proskuneo* (pro-skoo-**NEH**-oh), is common outside of religious worship, referring to people bowing down, whether to God or rulers. Still, Jairus takes time to bow to Jesus, acknowledging who He was before he made his request. He comes in faith, clearly expecting Jesus would raise her from the dead. He goes even so far as to tell Jesus how to do it: "Lay thy hand upon her," he said, "and she shall live."

This man has lost his daughter. Research has shown that the loss of a child is the most devastating death to cope with. No parent ever expects to have to bury their child. But this official does not come asking Jesus why his daughter died. This is the question we are all tempted to ask at times like these. We ask, but we usually get no answer, because the only answer is the one Jesus gives His disciples shortly before His arrest: In the world we will have tribulation (John 16:33).

Jesus responds to the official's faith. He always responds to our faith too. He loves the kind of faith that gives people the boldness to come and ask and to believe He can do something to remedy the situation. Jesus and His disciples begin to follow the official to his house.

20 And behold, a woman, which was diseased with an issue of blood twelve years, came behind him and touched the hem of his garment: 21 For she said within herself, If I may but touch his garment, I shall be whole.

Jesus and the disciples don't get very far before they encounter a woman, another person in need of healing from Jesus. She has been suffering with a hemorrhage for twelve years. It is easy to read that in black and white, but imagine going day after day for twelve years experiencing a serious medical condition.

Jairus had shown boldness to approach Jesus and ask for healing. He might have suffered backlash from the Jewish religious leaders for seeking out Jesus. He simply approaches Jesus in the middle of His teaching and asks Him to perform an unprecedented miracle. The woman with the issue of blood, however, is not bold in the same way that Jairus is bold. She does not approach Jesus directly, but still she approaches. It was taboo for a menstruating woman to touch a man; she was considered unclean. So she has to overcome that barrier as she comes up behind Him and touches the hem of His garment. She had been convincing herself all the way, as she maneuvered through the crowd, "If I can just touch His garment, I shall get well."

The "hem" of Jesus' robe referred to the word used for the tassels Jews are instructed to wear on their clothing at all times as a reminder to keep the Law (Number 15:37-41). Reaching out to touch the tassel expressed the woman's faith in the power of Israel's God to heal as well as faith in Jesus as the one sent from God. Her faith in Jesus' holiness is also on display here. Priests were not supposed to touch unholy things or they would become unholy themselves. This woman is unclean because of her sickness, but when she touches Jesus, instead of Jesus becoming unclean, she becomes clean. Others later took up this approach too, touching Jesus' robe to be healed (Matthew 14:36).

The word for her healing is worth noting here. The Greek word (*sozo*, **SODE**-zoh) translated "to be or be made whole" (vv. 21-22) is elsewhere translated "to save." Matthew's previous uses of this word were when the disciples were afraid they were going to drown in a storm at sea (Mathew 8:25), and the angel's announcement that Jesus would save the people from their sins (Matthew 1:21). It is most often used in the New Testament to refer to eternal salvation, but it is telling to see how salvation is understood as the same word is used to refer to physical healing and to being whole, intact, and perfect.

22 But Jesus turned him about, and when he saw her, he said, Daughter, be of good comfort, thy faith hath made thee whole. And the woman was made whole from that hour.

Jesus recognizes, responds to, and rewards that faith. He first tells her to "be of good comfort" (Gk. *tharseo*, thar-**SEH**-oh). This word is the verb form of the noun "courage." It is the positive command to counter "Fear not" (cf. Matthew 14:27). Often parents are instructed to tell children what they want the them to do, rather than only scolding them for doing something they were not supposed to do. As Jesus calls this woman "daughter" then, it is no surprise that He acts as the parent, telling her that she should have courage, rather than telling her she should not be afraid. Then He gives her the joyous news that her disease has been cured. Her faith makes her well, from that very hour. It is almost as though she is raised from the dead; she certainly has new life after her encounter with Jesus.

Sometimes we have to come to Jesus just like this woman. We have to make our way through the crowd and other obstacles, perhaps crawling, getting to Him any way we can. We need to have the kind of faith that keeps us going, knowing if we can just touch the hem of His garment, Jesus can bring healing and new life into our situations and circumstances.

23 And when Jesus came into the ruler's house, and saw the minstrels and the people making a noise, 24 He said unto them, Give place: for the maid is not dead, but sleepeth. And they laughed him to scorn.

When Jesus arrives at the official's house, He finds they have already begun to mourn. The musicians have been hired and there is a crowd loudly grieving the loss of this girl. In their minds, it is settled—the child is dead. There is nothing left to do but go through the motions of bereavement.

Seeing all these people carrying on, Jesus tells them to "give place" (Gk. *anachoreo*, ah-na-khoe-**REH**-oh). He is not gentle with them as He was with the hemorrhaging woman, to whom He spoke courage. These people, He says, should just go away—far away, as the word is used to speak of people leaving the country. He speaks the truth to them all, saying that the girl is not dead, but asleep. The text says "they laughed him to scorn," jeering and mocking Him. It must have seemed ludicrous, this prophet coming into a house of death and saying these ridiculous things. It seemed just as ridiculous to them then, as it might to some today.

Sometimes the things we believe by faith seem ridiculous to others. When we tell them what we are praying for or believing in, they might laugh us to scorn. But faith in Jesus is no laughing matter. Laughter and disbelief cannot coexist with faith.

25 But when the people were put forth, he went in, and took her by the hand, and the maid arose. 26 And the fame hereof went abroad into all that land.

The people who laughed are "put forth" (Gk. *ekballo*, ek-**BALL**-low). Like Jesus' command for them to go away, this action is forceful. They have to be removed from the house, "thrown out" even. The word is also translated "cast out" like demons (9:33-34). Only then does Jesus perform the miracle; when unbelief is not present. He takes the little girl by the hand and she arises. It is touching to note that Jesus is asked to lay hands on the girl, but when He comes, instead of the authoritative and priestly stance of laying hands on her, He instead chooses simply to hold her hand, bringing her gently back to life.

There is surely a lot of sickness, and many accidents claim the lives of people we love, at all ages. It seems we can come to terms better with the loss of someone older, but no matter how young or old the person is, those left behind experience a lot of pain and grief.

We need to be aware that Jesus weeps with us, just as He wept at the tomb of Lazarus (John 11:35). Jesus knows and feels our pain. He is with us to assure us, just as He assured Martha, that He is the Resurrection and the Life (John 11:25). Jesus has won the victory over death. Because of that, we can know that our loved ones live on in His kingdom, and we can be reunited with them one day. So let us not grieve as those who have no hope (1 Thessalonians 4:13). Let us instead look forward to the kingdom where every tear will be wiped away, and there will be no more death, sorrow, or pain (Revelation 21:4).

The news about Jesus continued to spread. This is truly the Gospel, the Good News Jesus said He was anointed to preach. It is the same Good News we should be spreading today: Faith in Jesus makes you whole.

Sources:

Henry, Matthew. *Matthew Henry's Commentary on the Whole Bible: New Modern Edition*. Vols. 1-6. Peabody, MA: Hendrickson Publishers, Inc., 2009.

Strong, James. *The New Strong's Exhaustive Concordance of the Bible*. Nashville, TN: Thomas Nelson, 2003.

Thayer, Joseph Henry. *A Greek-English Lexicon of the New Testament*. New York: American Book Company, 1889.

Say It Correctly

Jairus. **JEYE**-russ.
Melancholy. **MELL**-an-**KOLL**-ee.
Hemorrhage. **HIM**-ridge.

Daily Bible Readings

MONDAY
Fringe, Aid to Remember
God's Commandments
(Numbers 15:37-41)

TUESDAY
Disciples and Family Witness
Girl's Healing
(Luke 8:40-42, 49-56)

WEDNESDAY
Woman.Testifies to Jesus' Healing Touch
(Luke 8:42-48)

THURSDAY
Jesus Opens Eyes of the Blind Man
(Matthew 9:27-31)

FRIDAY
Jesus Restores Speech to Mute Man
(Matthew 9:32-34)

SATURDAY
Join the Lord's Harvest Today
(Matthew 9:35–10:1)

SUNDAY
Faith in God Heals Many Ills
(Matthew 9:18-26)

Notes

_____

_____

_____

_____

☑ UMI
A Friendly Reminder!

Pre-Order Your 2021-2022 Precepts For Living®

Order Today And Save 10%!
urbanministries.com/pfl
1-800-860-8642

Precepts for Living® is also Available Online!
Get downloadable, easy-to-follow lesson plans, Teaching Tips
Videos and access to the Precepts for Living® Online Community
Forum to discuss the lessons and share insights and more.

preceptsforliving.com

⛊ UMI
A Friendly Reminder!

Pre-Order Your 2021-2022 Precepts For Living®

Order Today And Save 10%!
urbanministries.com/pfl
1-800-860-8642

Precepts for Living® is also Available Online!
Get downloadable, easy-to-follow lesson plans, Teaching Tips Videos and access to the Precepts for Living® Online Community Forum to discuss the lessons and share insights and more.

preceptsforliving.com

Teaching Tips

June 27
Bible Study Guide 4

Words You Should Know

A. Spirit (Matthew 14:26) *phantasma* (Gk.)—A phantom or ghost

B. Fear (v. 26) *phobos* (Gk.)—Dread, terror, especially that which is caused by intimidation or adversaries

Teacher Preparation

Unifying Principle—An Amazing Feat. In the depth of crisis, people are often caught between trust and doubt. Will one trust that one's help will come? Jesus, by walking on water to save His disciples, demonstrated His divine empowerment to be the Savior of all.

A. Read the Bible Background and Devotional Reading.

B. Pray for your students and lesson clarity.

C. Read the lesson Scripture in multiple translations.

O—Open the Lesson

A. Begin the class with prayer.

B. Ask: Do you have a friend whom you can trust in difficult times? Discuss times participants have needed someone to save them from a bad situation.

C. Have the students read the Aim for Change and the In Focus story.

D. Ask students how events like those in the story weigh on their hearts and how they can view these events from a faith perspective.

P—Present the Scriptures

A. Read the Focal Verses and discuss the Background and The People, Places, and Times sections.

B. Have the class share what Scriptures stand out for them and why, with particular emphasis on today's themes.

E—Explore the Meaning

A. Use In Depth or More Light on the Text to facilitate a deeper discussion of the lesson text.

B. Pose the questions in Search the Scriptures and Discuss the Meaning.

C. Discuss the Liberating Lesson and Application for Activation sections.

N—Next Steps for Application

A. Summarize the value of trusting in Christ, even during times of trouble.

B. End class with a commitment to pray for Jesus' help when we feel alone in times of trouble.

Worship Guide

For the Superintendent or Teacher
Theme: Why Do You Doubt?
Song: "Here Comes Jesus (See Him Walking on the Water)"
Devotional Reading: Isaiah 38:16–20

Why Do You Doubt?

Bible Background • MATTHEW 14:22–33
Printed Text • MATTHEW 14:22–33 | Devotional Reading • ISAIAH 38:16–20

—————— Aim for Change ——————

By the end of this lesson, we will RECALL the amazing story of the storm at sea followed by Jesus' appearance walking on the water, REPENT of failing to trust in God when caught up in a crisis, and DEVELOP habits of trust that enable us to overcome our doubt about God's care.

—————— In Focus ——————

Two years had passed and Warren was finally able to find a full-time job that fit his training. He took a job that called for a considerable pay cut. So his family could simply stay afloat, he and his wife Angela had to downsize their lifestyle, which included significant cuts in giving. Warren became more and more frustrated and even angry with God.

A visiting preacher at their church brought a powerful word that encouraged them to trust God for their provision. Warren cried out to the Lord and asked for God's intervention. He knew that this current job was not paying the bills, but he decided to work as hard as he could, expecting God to provide for his family's needs.

In the following weeks, Warren and Angela began to receive several unexpected blessings. One night, they were both too weary to make dinner, but then a neighbor came over to offer them the overflow from a casserole. A friend got back in touch with Angela and returned a loan she had given. But then the biggest blessing came.

While at work, Warren gave excellent service to a frazzled customer. It turned out that the customer was the head of human resources at a company that was expanding. He loved Warren's personality and pursuit of excellence, and he gave Warren his card. Within two weeks, Warren had a job that paid more than his previous job. As he walked into his new workplace, he heard in his spirit, "Why did you doubt My ability to bless you?"

How many times do we doubt the Lord's ability to do the impossible in our lives?

—————— Keep in Mind ——————

"And immediately Jesus stretched forth his hand, and caught him, and said unto him, O thou of little faith, wherefore didst thou doubt?" (Matthew 14:31, KJV).

"Jesus immediately reached out and grabbed him. 'You have so little faith,' Jesus said. 'Why did you doubt me?'" (Matthew 14:31, NLT).

Focal Verses

KJV **Matthew 14:22** And straightway Jesus constrained his disciples to get into a ship, and to go before him unto the other side, while he sent the multitudes away.

23 And when he had sent the multitudes away, he went up into a mountain apart to pray: and when the evening was come, he was there alone.

24 But the ship was now in the midst of the sea, tossed with waves: for the wind was contrary.

25 And in the fourth watch of the night Jesus went unto them, walking on the sea.

26 And when the disciples saw him walking on the sea, they were troubled, saying, It is a spirit; and they cried out for fear.

27 But straightway Jesus spake unto them, saying, Be of good cheer; it is I; be not afraid.

28 And Peter answered him and said, Lord, if it be thou, bid me come unto thee on the water.

29 And he said, Come. And when Peter was come down out of the ship, he walked on the water, to go to Jesus.

30 But when he saw the wind boisterous, he was afraid; and beginning to sink, he cried, saying, Lord, save me.

31 And immediately Jesus stretched forth his hand, and caught him, and said unto him, O thou of little faith, wherefore didst thou doubt?

32 And when they were come into the ship, the wind ceased.

33 Then they that were in the ship came and worshipped him, saying, Of a truth thou art the Son of God.

NLT **Matthew 14:22** Immediately after this, Jesus insisted that his disciples get back into the boat and cross to the other side of the lake, while he sent the people home.

23 After sending them home, he went up into the hills by himself to pray. Night fell while he was there alone.

24 Meanwhile, the disciples were in trouble far away from land, for a strong wind had risen, and they were fighting heavy waves.

25 About three o'clock in the morning Jesus came toward them, walking on the water.

26 When the disciples saw him walking on the water, they were terrified. In their fear, they cried out, "It's a ghost!"

27 But Jesus spoke to them at once. "Don't be afraid," he said. "Take courage. I am here!"

28 Then Peter called to him, "Lord, if it's really you, tell me to come to you, walking on the water."

29 "Yes, come," Jesus said. So Peter went over the side of the boat and walked on the water toward Jesus.

30 But when he saw the strong wind and the waves, he was terrified and began to sink. "Save me, Lord!" he shouted.

31 Jesus immediately reached out and grabbed him. "You have so little faith," Jesus said. "Why did you doubt me?"

32 When they climbed back into the boat, the wind stopped.

33 Then the disciples worshiped him. "You really are the Son of God!" they exclaimed.

The People, Places, and Times

Sea of Galilee. Although not explicit in Matthew's account, it is more clear in Mark's Gospel (6:45–53) that Jesus walked on the Sea of Galilee, located north of Jerusalem. Scholars estimate that Jesus did many of His most notable miracles, at least eighteen, in and around the communities bordering this body of water.

The Apostle Peter. Peter and his brother Andrew were the first disciples Jesus called (Mark 1:16–17). He was known for his impulsive nature and forceful personality, as well as his special relationship with Jesus. Jesus Himself changed his name from Simon to Peter (or Cephas), which means "rock" (Matthew 16:18). Although Peter denied Jesus three times before Jesus' crucifixion, after receiving the gift of the Holy Spirit on the day of Pentecost, Peter was the first to preach to the crowds. He ultimately became one of the Gospel's most passionate and tireless ambassadors, suffering persecution, beatings, and imprisonment until he was martyred around AD 67.

What traits of Peter's faith during his time learning from Jesus are admirable? Which needed further growth?

Background

In the preceding verses, Jesus dealt with the devastating news of the imprisonment and execution of His cousin John the Baptist at the hands of Herod the tetrarch (Matthew 14:1–13). He sought to get away from the crowd and retreated by Himself to a remote place to rest. However, crowds of people from surrounding towns began to seek after Jesus. As the evening set in, the disciples sought to send the people on their way to fend for themselves for dinner, but Jesus objected.

He ordered His disciples to give the people something to eat. The disciples were perplexed at Jesus' command, but it was all a setup for a display of His unquestionable power and convincing proof of His ability to defy natural law. With five loaves and two fishes, Jesus blessed His Father and turned little into overflow, feeding five thousand men, not including women and children (Matthew 14:13–21). After this, Jesus sent the disciples away by boat to the other side of the Sea of Galilee while He recharged in prayer.

At-A-Glance

1. Jesus Replenishes His Power
(Matthew 14:22–23)
2. Jesus Defies the Laws of Nature
(vv. 24–27)
3. Jesus Calls Peter to Step Out
(vv. 28–29)
4. Jesus' Power Declared (vv. 30–33)

In Depth

1. Jesus Replenishes His Power (Matthew 14:22–23)

Jesus, after His exhausting time of ministry and meeting the spiritual and natural needs of the people, again seeks to commune alone with His Father in prayer. Jesus sends the disciples ahead of Him by boat while dismissing the crowds that gathered to see Him.

He sought to be alone with His Father to recharge and regroup. In this scene, we see the humanity of Jesus and the dependency that He had on the Father and the Holy Spirit in His daily life and ministry. Through Jesus, we have a model for how we should carve out time away from the busyness of life to steal away with the Father. In His presence we are refreshed, renewed, and empowered to continue on with His purpose. It sets the perfect stage for the next scene, in which we see the perfect exhibition of the divinity of Jesus Christ.

2. Jesus Defies the Laws of Nature (vv. 24–27)

Matthew shifts the scene. While on the boat, the disciples encounter torrential winds and waves in their travel, which is very unsettling even for the trade fishermen to navigate. In this brewing storm, between 3 and 6 o'clock in the morning, the disciples see a figure walking toward them and become terrified. Out of fear, their imaginations take them to the worst possible scenario, and they conclude that it was a threatening figure. They begin to scream out with terror, "It's a ghost!" not realizing that it was Jesus (v. 26, NLT). Upon their reaction, Jesus immediately calls on His disciples to calm down and "take courage" (v. 27, NLT) because He has arrived on the scene among the waves and wind. Jesus' appearance on the water is not an everyday occurrence, and it is not something that has been repeated. He defies all natural laws by walking on the water.

Scholars are still trying to rationalize how this could have happened, and if it really occurred as recorded. However, as Christians, we accept it as truth because the One who created the seas has the power to walk on them and is sovereign over all the earth.

What should the Christian response be when skeptics try to rationalize away the miraculous works Jesus performed?

3. Jesus Calls Peter to Step Out (vv. 28–29)

Peter, often being the spokesman of the group and bold enough to ask the tough questions, puts Jesus to the test after hearing His voice. Peter responds, "Lord, if it's really you, tell me to come to you, walking on the water" (v. 28, NLT). It was Peter's personality to take Jesus at His word and take risks of faith which would prove to be invaluable for his future role in the church. No one since has successfully walked on water, but in the Spirit, as we receive a word from the Lord to do something, we have the ability to defy the odds through the power of the Holy Spirit.

4. Jesus' Power Declared (vv. 30–33)

As Peter leaves the boat, he notices within his natural senses what is happening around him and becomes afraid. The wind gets stronger, and as it presses his body, he gets nervous, which causes him to take his eyes off Jesus. As Peter becomes frightened, he sinks and cries out to Jesus to save him because he thinks he was going to drown. Matthew notes that Jesus immediately reacts and stretches out His hand to pull Peter from the water and get him to safety. Jesus then asks him, "Why did you doubt me?" (v. 31, NLT). Once Jesus and Peter get into the boat, the winds and waves cease and everything is still and peaceful. All of the disciples worship Jesus, acknowledging He "thou art the Son of God" (v. 33).

How often do we take our eyes off Jesus when things don't look like what we expect, even though we have been given a word from the Lord to go forward in faith?

Search the Scriptures

1. What was Peter's response to the sight of Jesus walking on water (Matthew 14:28)?

2. How did Jesus react to the disciples and Peter's trouble on the water (vv. 27, 31)?)

Discuss the Meaning

1. How can we apply this Scripture to our lives today? Drawing on the example of Scripture, what things can we do corporately and individually to step out on faith?

2. Jesus' response to Peter's cry for help was immediate. What does that mean for when you cry out for help? What keeps us in fear?

Liberating Lesson

God is still performing signs and wonders today as we call on the name of His Son Jesus.

We should seek the Lord's Will for our lives to receive vision and be empowered by the Holy Spirit to get in alignment to make the miraculous happen in our age. The same power that raised Jesus from the dead lives within us. Just as the apostles turned the world upside down at the Word of the Lord to establish the church, we live on as His fruit on the earth.

Application for Activation

We are encouraged to fix our eyes on Jesus, the Author and Finisher of our faith, who for the sake of the joy set before Him endured the Cross and is seated at the right hand of the throne of God (Hebrews 12:2). If we truly believe that Jesus ever lives to make intercession for us, we must trust that we are safe in His arms and follow His lead.

Follow the Spirit

What God wants me to do:

_____

_____

_____

_____

Remember Your Thoughts

Special insights I have learned:

_____

_____

_____

_____

More Light on the Text
Matthew 14:22–33

22 And straightway Jesus constrained his disciples to get into a ship, and to go before him unto the other side, while he sent the multitudes away.

Jesus multiplied bread for five thousand people in a desert place (vv. 13–21) where He had retreated with His disciples. His withdrawal was motivated by a report of Herod's beheading of His cousin John the Baptist and by the king's comments about Him and the miracles He was performing (vv. 1–2, 13).

After feeding the people with the bread, they were overwhelmed and wanted to appoint Him king (John 6:15). Jesus rejected this as a potential threat to His mission on earth. Jesus' purpose on earth was to serve, not to be served (Matthew 20:28; Mark 10:45). This situation led Jesus to constrain His disciples to leave the scene immediately while He dismissed the crowd. The Greek word for constrained is *anagkazo* (ah-nahng-**KAHD**-zo), which means to physically or mentally compel or force somebody to do something. It is derived from *anagke* (Gk. ah-**NAHNG**-kay), which means necessity or need. There was an imperative motive for Jesus to send His disciples ahead.

23 And when he had sent the multitudes away, he went up into a mountain apart to pray: and when the evening was come, he was there alone.

After He sent them away, Jesus climbs the mountain to communicate with the Father. At some critical periods of Jesus' earthly ministry, He isolates Himself from the crowd and even His disciples to pray. Jesus withdraws into the wilderness for prayer in periods of great popularity (Luke 5:16). Jesus entreats us to withdraw in our closet to pray to God (Matthew 6:6). It is therefore important for Christians

507

today to emulate our Lord and retreat from noise and busyness at times to pray. Jesus was alone at evening. We should not be confused about the use of "evening" twice in this chapter in the narrative sequence. The Jews divided the day into three periods: morning, noon, and evening (cf. Psalm 55:17). The evening was in turn subdivided into two parts: the first evening began at sunset (twilight) and the second began when the sun was fully set (dusk) (cf. Exodus 12:6 literally "between the evenings"). The Greek word for evening was *opsios* (**OP**-see-ose) which could refer either to the period before sunset or right after sundown but was sometimes used for the two. In context, however, it is logical to ascribe the first mention of evening (14:15) to the first evening and the current one to after sunset. Jesus was left praying alone when it was night.

24 But the ship was now in the midst of the sea, tossed with waves: for the wind was contrary.

While Jesus was on the mountain praying, the disciples were on the sea tossed with waves. They encountered a contrary wind that would eventually lead them to Gennesaret. Mark tells us that Jesus saw that the disciples were battling with the contrary wind (Mark 6:48). We cannot be certain if Jesus saw them physically or supernaturally. The current event is taking place after they had left the desert place for quite a long time. Still, John states that it was already night when they encountered the wind. It would have been difficult for Jesus to see from such a long distance. In any case, if Jesus at the beginning of His ministry could see Nathanael (John 1:50) from afar, it is not unlikely that He could see the disciples by the divine endowments of the Holy Spirit.

25 And in the fourth watch of the night Jesus went unto them, walking on the sea.

The Jews divided the night into three watches and the Romans divided it into four between 6 p.m. and 6 a.m. Jesus, therefore, came to the disciples between three and six o'clock in the morning.

Around this time, Jesus appeared to them in an unprecedented fashion by walking on the sea. There was probably no boat left for Him to join the disciples, so He joined them the fastest way possible: by walking out to their boat across the water. Great figures of Old Testament history such as Moses, Joshua, Elijah, and Elisha did miracles involving parting of water bodies, but never has it been recorded that anyone else walked on water (Exodus 14:21, 22; Joshua 3:15–17; 2 Kings 2:8, 14). This action of Jesus clearly portrays His divine nature.

26 And when the disciples saw him walking on the sea, they were troubled, saying, It is a spirit; and they cried out for fear.

The disciples saw someone walking on water at night and with a contrary wind. The disciples could not fathom this scene, assuming the being they saw was a spirit. The Greek word for spirit here is *phantasma* (**FAHN**-tahs-mah), meaning phantom or "a ghost" (NLT). Our perception of reality always shapes our responses and reactions. They expressed their inner feelings of fear outwardly by a strident noise. Their fear could have been due to prevailing cultural beliefs of the time. In the ancient Near East, the sea was thought to be the realm of powerful, chaotic beings (cf. Job 41; Revelation 13:1). They undoubtedly thought Jesus was a "ghost" that would do them harm. Their deduction that it was a ghost led them to fear (Gk. *phobos*, **FOE**-bose), which means fear, dread, terror—that which is caused by intimidation or adversaries.

27 But straightway Jesus spake unto them, saying, be of good cheer; it is I; be not afraid.

The Lord is always prompt in coming to rescue us. "Be of good cheer" or "take courage" (NLT) are phrases of encouragement and comfort (cf Matthew 9:22). It resonates when we have a challenging task ahead; it will re-echo if we are in peril or in the face of danger, such as the current case facing the disciples.

The Lord wants us to "be of good cheer" and not be afraid because of His presence. "It is I" is the translation of *ego eimi* (Gk. eg-**O** ay-**MEE**), which echoes the "I am" God's self-revelation to Moses (Exodus 3:14) and other similar passages (Isaiah 43:12). We have this promise of Jesus in Matthew 28:20: "I am with you always, even to the end of the age" (NLT). We should therefore not be afraid even in our darkest circumstances or the most violent storm of our lives.

28 And Peter answered him and said, Lord, if it be thou, bid me come unto thee on the water.

Peter's request was not portraying a doubt about the identity of the one walking on water. Scholars suggest the phrase "since it is you" is an acceptable rendering of "if it be thou." Peter has an extroverted personality. His request might have been guided by the delegation of power Jesus granted them over sicknesses and demons (Matthew 10:8). Knowing Jesus had freely given His disciples power to do all that Christ Himself did, Peter wished to test his ability to perform this new miracle. Since it was the Lord, He can grant Peter with this authority over physical laws also.

29 And he said, Come. And when Peter was come down out of the ship, he walked on the water, to go to Jesus.

Jesus granted Peter's request by the word "come." It should not be perceived here as a mere invitation but rather as a delegation of power or a transfer of authority. Jesus had already deputized His followers to spread the message of the coming Kingdom (Matthew 10), and would later promise them they would do all His miracles and more (John 14:12). Peter therefore took the first step and came out of the ship. Once he was out of the boat and on the sea, he could walk just as Jesus was doing.

30 But when he saw the wind boisterous, he was afraid; and beginning to sink, he cried, saying, Lord, save me.

We can perform greater works by faith as long as we keep on looking at the Lord who instructs us. Anytime we shift our focus from the Lord to the challenge, we will start to experience failure. Here Peter fails to look at the Lord, who instructed him to come but rather focused on the wind. Fear and faith do not coexist. Solid faith will drive out fear, but fear will also drive out faith.

With a wavering faith, Peter's feet on top of the water also wavered. When Peter realized he was sinking, he cried to Jesus, saying, "Lord, save me." Our faith may fail us at times, but ultimately Jesus is our last recourse in peril or danger. Instinctively, Peter cried out of fear and despair for the rescue of the Lord.

31 And immediately Jesus stretched forth his hand, and caught him, and said unto him, O thou of little faith, wherefore didst thou doubt?

Jesus did not tarry in rescuing Peter. Without any delay, He stretched His hand to seize the drowning Peter. Peter walked quite a distance since Jesus could just stretch His hand to get hold of Him.

Jesus rebuked him after He got hold of him. The Greek word for "little faith" is *oligopistos* (oh-lee-**GO**-pees-tose), and it is used only by the Lord to gently rebuke His disciples for their anxiety. Our cry of desperation will always be heard, and God will swiftly deliver us from our trouble, but we must expect a gentle rebuke from our loving Lord. While calling His followers "little faith" must be understood as a rebuke, we can also be encouraged in this name. Jesus will also tell His followers that only a little faith is needed to move mountains (Matthew 17:20).

32 And when they were come into the ship, the wind ceased. 33 Then they that were in the ship came and worshipped him, saying, of a truth thou art the Son of God.

Peter walked back with Jesus to the boat. When the two entered the ship, the wind ceased. With the ending of the storm, the disciples realized the true personality of Jesus. This Man could multiply five loaves of bread for five thousand people, walk on water, and still the wind. Who could that person be except the promised Son of God? The Roman officer and the soldiers made the same confession when they witnessed the events at Jesus' death and were filled with awe (Matthew 27:50–54).

The term used for worship is *proskuneo* (Gk. pros-koo-**NEH**-oh), which signifies to fall prostrate in front of the one being worshiped. The same word is used when Cornelius welcomed Peter into his house. Peter's objection that he was also a man points to the fact that this action is appropriate only to the highest of Lords (Acts 10:25–26).

Sources:

Attridge, Harold et. al. The Harper Collins Study Bible New Revised Standard Version. New York: Harper One, 2006. 1693, 1694, 1736.

Bromiley, G.W. Theological Dictionary of the New Testament. 7th Edition. Grand Rapids, MI: Eerdmans, 1978.

Carson, D.A. The Expositor's Bible Commentary with the New International Version. Grand Rapids, MI: Zondervan Publishing House, 1995.

Fullam, E.L. Living the Lord's Prayer. Lincoln, VA: Chosen Books, 1980.

Green, J. B. The New International Commentary on the New Testament: The Gospel of Luke. Grand Rapids, MI: Eerdmans, 1997.

Hagner, D. A. Word Biblical Commentary: Matthew 14-28 Vol. 33. Dallas, TX: Word Books Publisher, 1995.

Hendriksen, W. New Testament Commentary: Luke. Carlisle, PA: The Banner of Truth Trust, 1978.

Howard, F. D. The Gospel of Matthew: A Study Manual. Grand Rapids, MI: Baker Book House, 1961.

Howard, M. J. The New International Greek Testament Commentary: The Gospel of Luke. Grand Rapids, MI: Eerdmans, 1978.

Keener, C.S. The IVP Bible Background Commentary: New Testament. Downers Grove, IL: Inter Varsity Press, 1993.

Morris, L. Tyndale New Testament Commentary: Luke. Grand Rapids, MI: Eerdmans, 1984.

Nolland, J. Word Biblical Commentary: Luke 9:21–18:34. Vol. 35B. Dallas, Texas: Word Books, 1993.

Richards, Lawrence O. The Expository Dictionary of New Testament Words. Grand Rapids, MI: Zondervan, 1985. 463-464.

Ryrie, C.C. The Ryrie Study Bible: New Testament, King James Version. Chicago, IL: The Moody Bible Institute, 1976.

Tasker, R.V. Tyndale New Testament Commentaries: Matthew. Grand Rapids, MI: Wm. Eerdmans Publishing Company, 1961.

Unger, Merrill. Unger's Bible Dictionary. Chicago, IL: Moody Press, 1981. 387, 388, 847, 848.

Vine, W. E. An Expository Dictionary of the New Testament Words. 7th Edition. Old Tappan, NJ: Fleming H. Revell, 1966.

Wilson, N.S., and L.K. Taylor. Tyndale Handbook of Bible Charts and Maps. Wheaton, IL: Tyndale House Publisher, 2001.

Zodhiates, Spiros, Baker, Warren. eds. Hebrew Greek Key Word Study Bible King James Version. 2nd ed. Chattanooga, TN: AMG Publishers, 1991. 1749, 1766, 51.

Say It Correctly

Gennesaret. juh-**NES**-uh-ret.
Galilee. **GAH**-luh-lee.

Daily Bible Readings

MONDAY
Let's Sing of the Lord's Faithfulness
(Isaiah 38:16-20)

TUESDAY
The Baptist Dies for the Faith
(Matthew 14:1-12)

WEDNESDAY
The Crowd's Hunger Satisfied
(Matthew 14:13-21)

THURSDAY
Believe the One Sent to You
(John 6:22-29)

FRIDAY
The Sick Are Healed
(Matthew 14:34-36)

SATURDAY
Speak Confidently to Civil Authorities
(Mark 13:9-12)

SUNDAY
Savior of the Fearful, Doubter, Needy
(Matthew 14:22-33)

Notes

_____

_____

_____

_____

Teaching Tips

Words You Should Know

A. Mercy (Luke 17:13) *eleeo* (Gk.)—To show compassion or pity; to help the afflicted

B. Give thanks (v. 16) *eucharisteo* (Gk.)—To show gratitude, at times specifically through prayer

Teacher Preparation

Unifying Principle—Wisdom in Action. People often receive mercy but do not acknowledge the one who helped them. Do you show appreciation? Ten lepers, isolated by their skin diseases, were healed; but only one, who was a foreigner, was saved by his faith and offered thanks.

A. Read the Bible Background and Devotional Reading.

B. Pray for your students and lesson clarity.

C. Read the lesson Scripture in multiple translations.

O—Open the Lesson

A. Begin the class with prayer.

B. Ask: How do you feel when God blesses a person you don't think deserves it? Talk about ways such experiences can open our hearts to God's vast depth of love for all humanity, whether they are believers or not.

C. Have the students read the Aim for Change and the In Focus story.

D. Ask students how events like those in the story weigh on their hearts and how they can view these events from a faith perspective.

P—Present the Scriptures

A. Read the Focal Verses and discuss the Background and The People, Places, and Times sections.

B. Have the class share what Scriptures stand out for them and why, with particular emphasis on today's themes.

E—Explore the Meaning

A. Use In Depth or More Light on the Text to facilitate a deeper discussion of the lesson text.

B. Pose the questions in Search the Scriptures and Discuss the Meaning.

C. Discuss the Liberating Lesson and Application for Activation sections.

N—Next Steps for Application

A. Summarize the value of not taking God's blessings for granted, and instead demonstrating thankfulness.

B. End class with a commitment to pray for the needs of people who are regarded as outcasts.

Worship Guide

For the Superintendent or Teacher
Theme: An Attitude of Gratitude
Song: "My Tribute"
Devotional Reading: Isaiah 56:1-8

An Attitude of Gratitude

Bible Background • LEVITICUS 13-14; LUKE 5:12–16; 17:11-19
Printed Text • LEVITICUS 13:45–46; LUKE 17:11–19 | Devotional Reading • ISAIAH 56:1-8

—————— Aim for Change ——————

By the end of this lesson, we will EXPLORE reasons only one of ten healed lepers turned back to Jesus in thanksgiving, SENSE the need in our lives for increased expressions of gratitude to God, and DEVELOP a plan for showing thanksgiving to God and others on a daily basis.

————————— In Focus —————————

Diane listened to the soloist at her church sing "My Tribute" by Andraé Crouch, and began to weep. Her 30th birthday was Monday and she reviewed all the major events of her life. Diane grew up taking care of her mother until cancer finally took her life. Diane, at the tender age of 15, held her mother's body until she breathed her last breath.

Diane married out of high school and got pregnant right away. Soon, she watched her 3-day-old infant die in her arms, from a rare disease attacking the child's heart. Her young husband, George, struggled with the baby's death and ended up on medication for depression. Several times Diana spent long days sitting with him in the mental health facility after he had threatened suicide. Eventually, he got his medication regulated and slowly recovered, but it had been a long, hard road. Diane delivered two more children, but at the end of her last pregnancy, her doctor discovered a tumor in her breast. She had gone through the surgery and chemotherapy, now considering herself a cancer survivor in remission for almost five years. "To God be the glory …" The song spoke to her heart. She had been through so many difficult challenges in life and she was thankful that God carried her through.

God has done so much for us and gratitude is the best response. What are you thankful for right now?

—————— Keep in Mind ——————

"And one of them, when he saw that he was healed, turned back, and with a loud voice glorified God" (Luke 17:15, KJV).

"One of them, when he saw that he was healed, came back to Jesus, shouting, 'Praise God!'"
(Luke 17:15, NLT).

Focal Verses

KJV **Leviticus 13:45** And the leper in whom the plague is, his clothes shall be rent, and his head bare, and he shall put a covering upon his upper lip, and shall cry, Unclean, unclean.

46 All the days wherein the plague shall be in him he shall be defiled; he is unclean: he shall dwell alone; without the camp shall his habitation be.

Luke 17:11 And it came to pass, as he went to Jerusalem, that he passed through the midst of Samaria and Galilee.

12 And as he entered into a certain village, there met him ten men that were lepers, which stood afar off:

13 And they lifted up their voices, and said, Jesus, Master, have mercy on us.

14 And when he saw them, he said unto them, Go shew yourselves unto the priests. And it came to pass, that, as they went, they were cleansed.

15 And one of them, when he saw that he was healed, turned back, and with a loud voice glorified God,

16 And fell down on his face at his feet, giving him thanks: and he was a Samaritan.

17 And Jesus answering said, Were there not ten cleansed? but where are the nine?

18 There are not found that returned to give glory to God, save this stranger.

19 And he said unto him, Arise, go thy way: thy faith hath made thee whole.

NLT **Leviticus 13:45** Those who suffer from a serious skin disease must tear their clothing and leave their hair uncombed. They must cover their mouth and call out, "Unclean! Unclean!"

46 As long as the serious disease lasts, they will be ceremonially unclean. They must live in isolation in their place outside the camp.

Luke 17:11 As Jesus continued on toward Jerusalem, he reached the border between Galilee and Samaria.

12 As he entered a village there, ten men with leprosy stood at a distance,

13 crying out, "Jesus, Master, have mercy on us!"

14 He looked at them and said, "Go show yourselves to the priests." And as they went, they were cleansed of their leprosy.

15 One of them, when he saw that he was healed, came back to Jesus, shouting, "Praise God!"

16 He fell to the ground at Jesus' feet, thanking him for what he had done. This man was a Samaritan.

17 Jesus asked, "Didn't I heal ten men? Where are the other nine?

18 Has no one returned to give glory to God except this foreigner?"

19 And Jesus said to the man, "Stand up and go. Your faith has healed you."

The People, Places, and Times

Priest. Descendants from the tribe of Levi, a priest's duties included representing the people before God, caring for the Temple, teaching God's laws, and administering the Jewish sacrifices and services outlined in the Mosaic Law. Only they could declare a diseased person clean (Leviticus 13–14).

Leper. Someone who contracted the disease of leprosy was called a leper. "Leprosy" in the Bible could refer to any number of contagious skin diseases. The diseased person was quarantined and cut off from the rest of society. The leper was considered unclean according to Jewish law (Leviticus 13:44–46). Whenever they approached a person, the leper was required to yell, "Unclean! Unclean!" As a result, they were isolated socially and spiritually and treated as outcasts.

What is the psychological toll of being a social outcast?

Background

The lepers in this Scripture are not the same as in Jesus' previous encounter with a leper (Luke 5:12–15). In Luke 5, the leper is in the city amidst many other people, indicating that he was not treated in the same way as most lepers, though Luke does not tell us why he's treated differently. Jesus not only talks to the leper but touches and heals him.

This healing was different than Jesus' previous healing of lepers; it did not require His touch. He only commanded them to show themselves to the priests. This type of healing can be classified as a word of command and is very common in the Gospel narratives. When Jesus touched the previous leper, His compassion was more of the focus or theme. Here as He speaks this word of command, absent physical touch, His power is on display, though only one leper recognizes and acknowledges it.

Why is it important for Luke to present not only Jesus' power but also His compassion?

At-A-Glance

1. Living as a Leper (Leviticus 13:45-46)
2. Ten Lepers Ask for Healing
(Luke 17:11–13)
3. Jesus Heals the Ten Lepers (v. 14)
4. One Leper Returns to Thank Jesus
(vv. 15–19)

In Depth

1. Living as a Leper (Leviticus 13:45-46)

Life for a leper in ancient times was extraordinarily unpleasant. First, there was the disease itself to deal with. The leprosy described in the Bible does not always look like the disease that is called leprosy today. In ancient times, "leprosy" covered a broader range of skin diseases. Whether suffering from the modern leprosy of losing the sense of touch or another disease-causing welts, sores, and discoloration on the skin, there was a major physical toll on the body.

Second, there was the isolation. To keep from spreading the physical and ritual uncleanness to others, lepers were to live outside normal settlements until their health improved. Often, however, their health never would improve, exiling them from society for the rest of their lives.

Third, if they ever did need to interact with non-leprous people, they had to take embarrassing precautions. They had to make it obvious to any passerby that they were defiled with leprosy and everyone should keep away from them. Lepers made their clothes, hair, and face evidence of their condition. If that was not enough, they were also to shout out their contaminated state for all to hear.

2. Ten Lepers Ask for Healing (Luke 17:11–13)

Jesus encounters ten lepers who observe Him entering a village. They keep their distance because leprosy was known to be contagious. One of the ten lepers, a Samaritan, lived among the group. Ordinary Jews refused to settle in the same area inhabited by Samaritans. However, the lepers, isolated from the general population, bonded with any they could and ignored ethnicity. They cry out to Jesus, addressing Him as "Master" (v. 13). This title indicates He had authority as a thought leader, rabbi, and teacher. They ask Him to have mercy, desiring for Him to extend compassion and alleviate their misery. They acknowledge Jesus as a worker of miracles, one who had a history of healing incurable diseases (Luke 5:15).

3. Jesus Heals the Ten Lepers (v. 14)

Jesus instructs the lepers to go to the priest, the only authority able to pronounce them clean and permit them to re-enter their communities (Leviticus 13:13). After being observed by the priest and declared cured, the examiner would perform a ceremonial cleansing called the Law of the Leper (Leviticus 14).

All ten men start toward the Temple to find the priest, demonstrating extreme faith. Previously, Jesus healed a leper immediately by touching him (Luke 5:12–13). These lepers did not receive instant healing but acted exclusively on Jesus' word. They were told to report to the priest, spots still covered their bodies. As they make their way down the road, they realize their flesh is healthy.

4. One Leper Returns to Thank Jesus (vv. 15–19)

One leper sees the recovery of his body, stops, and goes back. After finding Jesus, he loudly proclaims God's greatness. Prostrated at Jesus' feet, he expresses gratitude. His posture testifies that Jesus deserved the same honor as God (Psalm 95:6; Revelation 4:10). Jesus asks the one returning leper, "Where are the nine?" (v. 17). The others, after being declared clean by the priest, went on their way, living their lives, seemingly taking their healing for granted. The Samaritan leper obtains more than physical healing: Jesus also says he was made "whole," indicating the leper's salvation (Luke 7:50). For Luke, genuine faith made you not only physically but also spiritually well.

Search the Scriptures

1. How were lepers distanced from society (Leviticus 13:45-46)?

2. What caused the leper to return (Luke 17:15–16)?

3. What caused Jesus to declare the thankful leper whole (v. 19)?

Discuss the Meaning

Are you the one leper who returned or one of the nine who did not? Name some ways we are tempted to take God's blessings for granted. What causes us to not be thankful? It's never a small thing to be thankful to the Lord. What does it mean to be thankful?

Liberating Lesson

Perhaps you have been treated as an outcast because of a characteristic others deem undesirable. Many have been discriminated against because of a condition beyond their control. We know Jesus lovingly ministered to people on the outskirts of society. We too should minister to the needs of the outcasts and the discriminated. As a class, seek ways you can minister to people in need, especially those on the fringes of society.

Application for Activation

We see daily how much easier it is to complain than give thanks. Busy schedules, aggravation, loneliness, anger, and stress all cause us to whine and complain instead of being grateful. The media stirs up an attitude of wanting more and being discontent. The negative attitudes are a result of ignoring God, and not acknowledging Him as the source of all our possessions and well-being.

Read Psalm 100:4–5. Sometime this week make up a prayer, song, poem, praise dance, or something creative based on these verses and the lesson. Share it with a member of your family, friend, or co-worker and ask them to be an accountability person. When you start complaining, tell them to remind you of your creative piece and your desire to be more grateful.

Follow the Spirit

What God wants me to do:

_____

_____

_____

_____

_____

Remember Your Thoughts

Special insights I have learned:

_____

_____

_____

_____

_____

More Light on the Text

Leviticus 13:45-46; Luke 17:11-19

Leviticus 13:45 And the leper in whom the plague is, his clothes shall be rent, and his head bare, and he shall put a covering upon his upper lip, and shall cry, Unclean, unclean. 46 All the days wherein the plague shall be in him he shall be defiled; he is unclean: he shall dwell alone; without the camp shall his habitation be.

Even without knowledge of germ theory and contagious diseases, the Israelites could practice these laws for the treatment of a leper and be fairly safe from the contagion. "The plague" referred to here is not the bubonic plague or Black Death, but a general word for the infection of leprosy. After a detailed and rigorous inspection and waiting period to determine if a patient truly has leprosy, the priests are instructed as to what measures to take. To keep the contagion from spreading, the lepers would tear their clothes (and burn them if they show signs of infection too, v. 52), shave their head (which makes it easier to track the spread of the disease on the scalp), cover their mouths (to prevent spread by coughing or sneezing), and issue an audible warning (so others can stay away). The leper would also be quarantined outside of the camp, away from dense populations.

The ancient Israelites did not see these steps as precautions against germs, however. They saw them as the way to prevent becoming "unclean" or "defiled," both from the Hebrew *tame'* (taw-**MAY**). The word is quite common in the Old Testament and refers to impurity, whether sexual, religious, or ceremonial. Even though sickness is not the sign of moral failing, it does serve as a reminder that cannot be ignored: there is sin, death, and decay in this world. Those contaminated with that decay are not fit to come before God, because our living God is holy. There is no death in Him, nor can death exist in His presence. His community must strive to be holy as He is holy, and so cannot incorporate anything that God abhors.

Luke 17:11 And it came to pass, as he went to Jerusalem, that he passed through the midst of Samaria and Galilee.

This pericope (a self-contained section of the Gospel narrative) is a continuation of the travel narrative found in Luke, which has a limited direct reference to Jesus' travel and begins in 9:51 and ends in 19:27–48. The narrative's focus is not on the travel specifics, but Jesus' interactions with followers, crowds, Pharisees, and others interpreting the Law. His final destination is Jerusalem, the Holy City. There is little telling whom He will interact within this in-between space on the edge of two regions, but the verse suggests He could interact with Samaritans. Previously in Luke's Gospel (9:51–56), Samaria was a site of divisiveness.

12 And as he entered into a certain village, there met him ten men that were lepers, which stood afar off.

This verse presents socio-cultural boundaries that are important to note. The ten men are identified by their physical condition which required physical boundaries. We learn about the geographic limitations of lepers in Numbers 5:2, and lepers are also found gathering near the city entrance in 2 Kings 7:3–5. Leprosy was a disorder with physical, emotional, and spiritual consequences, as those identified as lepers were dislocated from their communities and unable to worship.

13 And they lifted up their voices, and said, Jesus, Master, have mercy on us.

Even if they are on the outskirts of the city because of their condition, the lepers know who has entered the city. They call out to Jesus,

whom they have heard about and believe can respond to their situation. Those who are sick are often thought to be weak, but these men had the strength to cry out. They do not whimper or whine but lift their collective voices to get Jesus' attention.

The title of "Master" used by the lepers is peculiar in the New Testament and is often heard from the disciples. The Greek word used here is *epistates* (eh-pee-**STA**-tase), a word used to identify someone as a "boss" or "chief" with the focus on their power. When Jesus' disciples used the honorary title, it demonstrates their weak faith and limited understanding.

14 And when he saw them, he said unto them, Go shew yourselves unto the priests. And it came to pass, that, as they went, they were cleansed.

To heal them, Jesus tells the lepers to go show themselves to the priests. Lepers were prohibited from entering the Temple and approaching the priests. If the Jews' place of worship was in Jerusalem, then the Samaritans must determine which priests to show themselves to because of the division between the Jews and the Samaritans. Here we begin to see how Jesus becomes the mediator between both groups. The inspection they will undergo by the priests is explained in the Old Testament (Leviticus 14:1–32). Although there was a ritual to identify and ban them from their communities, there was also a ritual if a leper was healed. After being examined by the priest, a leper could be designated "clean."

15 And one of them, when he saw that he was healed, turned back, and with a loud voice glorified God.

On their way to the priests, the lepers realize they were healed; however, one leper does not continue to the Temple to receive clearance from the priests. Instead, he returns to the one who restored him. The Samaritan's healing is not only an account of physical healing but also redirecting his life, which is representative of what occurs with the saving work of Christ. The voice once joining in the collective cry is now a solo voice with a shout. As a leper, he shouted from afar, but as a cleansed and restored man, he can come directly into Jesus' presence.

16 And fell down on his face at his feet, giving him thanks: and he was a Samaritan.

The act of worship exhibited by the Samaritan went beyond just calling Jesus "master"; he has physically shown his submission by falling at Jesus' feet, showing that the one who has healed is worthy to be praised. By indicating that the man is a Samaritan, Luke indicates that God's mercy extends beyond boundaries as will the message of the Gospel.

The Greek term for the Samaritan's thanksgiving is *eucharisteo* (ew-khah-ree-**STEH**-oh), from which we get the word eucharist to refer to Communion. The word means to show gratitude, at times specifically through prayer.

While a reader could become fixated on this man's identification as an outsider, the main point is this man's desire to praise God for the gift of restoration, both physical and spiritual.

17 And Jesus answering said, Were there not ten cleansed? but where are the nine? 18 There are not found that returned to give glory to God, save this stranger.

Though some translations render the Greek *katharizo* (ka-tha-**REED**-zo) here as "healed," the KJV renders the word "cleansed," which better captures the word's possible religious connotations. Although Jesus adheres to the purity standards of the culture and sends the lepers to the priests for clearance, one man could not go on without giving honor to God for the healing no other could grant.

This story is told not to isolate the one leper as the one who did the right thing, but rather focus on the proper response to God's grace. "It is right to give our thanks and praise," suggests the Great Thanksgiving, which is included in the prayers of churches of many traditions (Book of Common Prayer). Thanksgiving is given to Jesus, but glory is given to God because His work is done publicly through Jesus.

The Greek word for foreigner is *allogenes* (al-lo-geh-**NACE**; from another tribe or family) and occurs numerous times in the Greek Old Testament but only here in the New Testament, probably because tribal affiliations were not as central during the Roman Empire and other terms became more widely used, such as the word *ethnos* (**ETH**-nos, a people who associate themselves due to geography, ethnicity, religion and/or political affiliation), which is usually translated as Gentile. Samaritans identified themselves as descendants of Abraham, but historically a rift occurred that caused Samaritans to worship at Mt. Gerizim, while Israelites and later Jews worshiped in Jerusalem. Jesus is emphasizing that, like the Gentiles (7:9), those who are considered outsiders among His Jewish audience sometimes exhibit exemplary faith.

In his Gospel account, Luke shows us that Samaritans and Gentiles often respond with more faith and gratitude than the Jews who are God's chosen people. Luke consistently shows these reversals wherein the one expected to give praise or thanks does not respond accordingly. Thus, Jews and insiders aren't the only ones privileged to receive divine mercy.

19 And he said unto him, Arise, go thy way: thy faith hath made thee whole.

Jesus offers words to the leper echoed in other healing narratives. Previously, healing associated with faith was received by the woman in the crowd who touched Jesus' garment (Luke

8:46–48). As was also the case with the woman with the issue of blood, here again the word translated "whole" is *sozo* (Gk. **SODE**-zo), which also connotes salvation and healing.

Whether it is the restoration of vision or body parts, the one healed or cleansed, in this instance, will rise and walk into their new reality. The healed Samaritan man is now a part of the people of God. He has not only been physically but also spiritually made whole.

Sources:

Henry, Matthew. *Matthew Henry's Commentary on the Whole Bible: New Modern Edition*. Vols. 1-6. Peabody, MA: Hendrickson Publishers, Inc., 2009.

Strong, James. *The New Strong's Exhaustive Concordance of the Bible*. Nashville, TN: Thomas Nelson, 2003.

Thayer, Joseph Henry. *A Greek-English Lexicon of the New Testament*. New York: American Book Company, 1889.

Say It Correctly

Pericope. peh-**RICK**-oh-pee.
Eucharist. **YOU**-kar-ist.

Daily Bible Readings

MONDAY
God Welcomes Foreigners
(Isaiah 56:1-8)

TUESDAY
Naomi's Sorrow Turns to Joy
(Ruth 4:3-6,13-15)

WEDNESDAY
Symptoms and Treatment of Leprosy
(Leviticus 13:1-8)

THURSDAY
Lepers Share Their Good News
(2 Kings 7:3-11)

FRIDAY
Many Samaritans Believe in the Savior
(John 4:39-42)

SATURDAY
Doing What Needs to Be Done
(Luke 17:1-10)

SUNDAY
Cultivate Gratefulness for
Acts of Healing
(Leviticus 13:45-56; Luke 17:11-19)

Notes

_____

_____

_____

_____

Teaching Tips

July 11
Bible Study Guide 6

Words You Should Know

A. Salvation (Romans 1:16) *soteria* (Gk.)—Divine deliverance from sin and to holiness

B. Righteousness (v. 17) *dikaiosune* (Gk.)—State declared by God that places believers in right relationship with Him

Teacher Preparation

Unifying Principle—A Gift to Strengthen You. People often look to be in a relationship that provides them with strength and stability. Where do you find your strength? The Gospel is the power of God that can save all those who believe.

A. Read the Bible Background and Devotional Reading.

B. Pray for your students and lesson clarity.

C. Read the lesson Scripture in multiple translations.

O—Open the Lesson

A. Begin the class with prayer.

B. Discuss why it is helpful for Christians to share with and encourage each other in the faith. How have they, and can they, encourage someone to continue being a strong example of faith.

C. Have the students read the Aim for Change and the In Focus story.

D. Ask students how events like those in the story weigh on their hearts and how they can view these events from a faith perspective.

P—Present the Scriptures

A. Read the Focal Verses and discuss the Background and The People, Places, and Times sections.

B. Have the class share what Scriptures stand out for them and why, with particular emphasis on today's themes.

E—Explore the Meaning

A. Use In Depth or More Light on the Text to facilitate a deeper discussion of the lesson text.

B. Pose the questions in Search the Scriptures and Discuss the Meaning.

C. Discuss the Liberating Lesson and Application for Activation sections.

N—Next Steps for Application

A. Summarize the value of letting people know wherever they go about their faith in Christ.

B. End class with a commitment to pray to be inspired by the example of others to live faithfully.

Worship Guide

For the Superintendent or Teacher
Theme: The Power of the Gospel
Song: "I Am Not Ashamed"
Devotional Reading: Psalm 71:1-6, 17-24

The Power of the Gospel

Bible Background • ROMANS 1
Printed Text • ROMANS 1:8–17 | Devotional Reading • PSALM 71:1–6, 17–24

—————— Aim for Change ——————

By the end of this lesson, we will DISCERN the power of God as illustrated in Paul's faith, AFFIRM the power of God's salvation in family and friends, and PRAY for the salvation of the world, believing it is possible.

—————————— In Focus ——————————

Cheryl was struggling with a sense that God wanted her to make herself available for greater forms of service. Her period of intense prayer and fasting had revealed to her that God had more in store for her. As she looked at the more traditional areas of formal church ministry, she did not see herself in any of those roles. She realized that preparation for her ministry would probably involve enrolling in Bible college or seminary for training.

As Cheryl considered the possibilities for her life, she began to grow concerned about having to give up her current job and standard of living. "I worked so hard to achieve everything," she thought. She also began to fear that her fiancé, Dwayne, might not understand. "Maybe he'll call off the wedding!" she feared.

"Am I willing to give up my career and the man I love to do the Lord's will?" she asked herself over and over. Cheryl grew embarrassed and ashamed. How she wished she could readily respond, "yes!" But she knew she had not yet reached that point in her faith journey.

As she pondered the matter over and over, she could reach no simple solution. Finally, she realized that the dilemma was not hers to solve. She knew that the God she served would show her the right steps to take. "For now," she resolved, "I'll just take the first step. Whatever happens later, I have to trust that the Lord will work it all out."

What aspects of life hinder us from unabashedly following God's will for our lives and personal ministries? How do we push back against those hindrances?

—————— Keep in Mind ——————

"For I am not ashamed of the gospel of Christ: for it is the power of God unto salvation to every one that believeth; to the Jew first, and also to the Greek" (Romans 1:16, KJV).

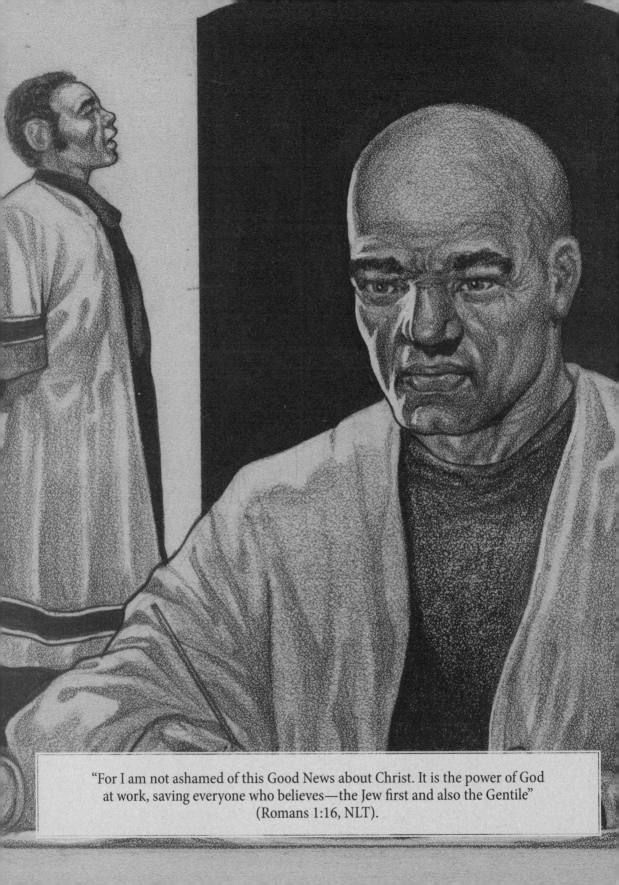

"For I am not ashamed of this Good News about Christ. It is the power of God at work, saving everyone who believes—the Jew first and also the Gentile" (Romans 1:16, NLT).

Focal Verses

KJV **Romans 1:8** First, I thank my God through Jesus Christ for you all, that your faith is spoken of throughout the whole world.

9 For God is my witness, whom I serve with my spirit in the gospel of his Son, that without ceasing I make mention of you always in my prayers;

10 Making request, if by any means now at length I might have a prosperous journey by the will of God to come unto you.

11 For I long to see you, that I may impart unto you some spiritual gift, to the end ye may be established;

12 That is, that I may be comforted together with you by the mutual faith both of you and me.

13 Now I would not have you ignorant, brethren, that oftentimes I purposed to come unto you, (but was let hitherto,) that I might have some fruit among you also, even as among other Gentiles.

14 I am debtor both to the Greeks, and to the Barbarians; both to the wise, and to the unwise.

15 So, as much as in me is, I am ready to preach the gospel to you that are at Rome also.

16 For I am not ashamed of the gospel of Christ: for it is the power of God unto salvation to every one that believeth; to the Jew first, and also to the Greek.

17 For therein is the righteousness of God revealed from faith to faith: as it is written, The just shall live by faith.

NLT **Romans 1:8** Let me say first that I thank my God through Jesus Christ for all of you, because your faith in him is being talked about all over the world.

9 God knows how often I pray for you. Day and night I bring you and your needs in prayer to God, whom I serve with all my heart by spreading the Good News about his Son.

10 One of the things I always pray for is the opportunity, God willing, to come at last to see you.

11 For I long to visit you so I can bring you some spiritual gift that will help you grow strong in the Lord.

12 When we get together, I want to encourage you in your faith, but I also want to be encouraged by yours.

13 I want you to know, dear brothers and sisters, that I planned many times to visit you, but I was prevented until now. I want to work among you and see spiritual fruit, just as I have seen among other Gentiles.

14 For I have a great sense of obligation to people in both the civilized world and the rest of the world, to the educated and uneducated alike.

15 So I am eager to come to you in Rome, too, to preach the Good News.

16 For I am not ashamed of this Good News about Christ. It is the power of God at work, saving everyone who believes—the Jew first and also the Gentile.

17 This Good News tells us how God makes us right in his sight. This is accomplished from start to finish by faith. As the Scriptures say, "It is through faith that a righteous person has life."

The People, Places, and Times

Epistles. Following the letter-writing customs of the day, epistles were written on sheets of papyrus with ink and a reed pen, then rolled or folded, and often sealed for privacy and authentication. The Christian community employed the members of their churches as carriers of the letters. Thus four people were usually involved in any New Testament letter: the writer, the secretary, the carrier, and the readers. In the case of Romans, we have the names of all these people. Writer: Paul (1:1), secretary: Tertius (16:22); carrier: likely Phoebe (16:1-2); and audience: the Roman church (1:7).

Paul. Even before his conversion, Paul was instrumental in causing the church to spread from its Jerusalem roots. His participation in the death of Stephen, the deacon, and frenzied persecution of believers after the Resurrection caused them to flee Jerusalem and take the Gospel to other parts of the world.

After his conversion (Acts 9:1-19), Paul embarked on three missionary journeys spreading the Gospel throughout the Roman Empire. Not only did the apostle personally establish countless churches throughout the world, he also wrote at least 13 epistles that make up a significant part of the New Testament.

How have you changed from who you used to be or stepped out or your comfort zone to share the Gospel or minister to others?

Background

The Apostle Paul had never visited the church in Rome, but he greatly desired to do so. The Roman church was strategically located for world evangelism. In his letter to the Romans, Paul does not address any particular need, problem, or doctrinal error. However, in the Epistle to the Romans, Paul presents a deeply theological discussion of major Christian doctrine. The church was renown for its faith and spiritual maturity (Romans 1:8). The apostle's purpose was to establish the young church in the faith as deeply as possible.

The members of the church were primarily Gentile, with a Jewish minority. This may account for Paul's reminder regarding Christianity's Jewish roots and God's unchanging plan for them (Romans 9-11). The letter to the Roman church plainly sets forth God's plan for both the nation of Israel and the Gentiles.

At-A-Glance

1. Paul's Prayer and Request
   (Romans 1:8–13)
2. Paul's Theme (vv. 14–17)

In Depth

1. Paul's Prayer and Request (Romans 1:8–13)

When Paul prayed for the Christians in Rome he prayed with two things on his mind. One was thanksgiving and the other was a request. And each one had something to do with the Gospel of God. As always the apostle begins by thanking God. He is particularly thankful for the church's faith. In all but one of Paul's letters to the churches, he expresses his gratefulness to God for his fellow Christians.

Because of the city's connections, believers throughout the Roman empire knew of the faith of the believers in Rome. Paul had never visited the church, but he, too, was aware of their great faith. The Roman believers demonstrated their faith by their passion for Christ and their love and devotion to one another. In the heart of an immoral, unjust, and pagan society, the Roman Christians boldly proclaimed the Gospel of Christ and lived virtuous lives.

Devout Israelites might spend several hours each day in prayer and would pray at different periods of the day. Paul mentioned the Roman believers "I always pray for is the opportunity" (v. 10, NLT). There were times when the apostle was incarcerated or incapacitated and could not evangelize. However, there was never a time when He could not pray. Constant faithful prayer is the greatest service anyone can give the kingdom of God.

Paul's request of God was simple: he desired to visit the Church in Rome (v. 10). He had never been to the city. He had made plans to come to Rome, but time and again his plans fell through (v. 13). In his prayers, Paul expressed his longing to visit the city to "impart some spiritual gift to you." Paul desired that the Holy Spirit would use his gifts to bless the believers in Rome, and Paul expresses his belief that the Roman believers would also be a blessing to him (v. 12). Whenever Christians come together there should be mutual blessings. Everyone should give and receive. All believers regardless of ethnicity share a common hope, purpose, and mission.

How does prayer impact your personal Christian walk?

2. Paul's Theme (vv. 14–17)

Paul was aware of his Christian obligation to people regardless of ethnicity or beliefs. The same Jesus who died for him died for all. That is why he was so eager to preach the Gospel in Rome. Those in Rome need not think that Paul did not have much confidence in the Gospel which he had been preaching. Rather, the Gospel was the cause of Paul's glory and he was honored to be able to proclaim it. Paul did proclaim the Gospel, and did so with full confidence in the ability (power) of this God-given message to bring salvation to all who would but believe (v. 16).

Paul simply states, "I am not ashamed of the gospel" (v. 16). Paul is not ashamed of the Gospel for two reasons: "for it is the power of God unto salvation" (v. 16). Whenever believers

share the Gospel message with an unbeliever, they tap into the unlimited power of God. The God of salvation sent the Good News of Christ so that people would believe and receive salvation.

Paul is also not ashamed of the Gospel because through it "is the righteousness of God revealed" (v. 17). The righteousness that comes from God restores believers to a right relationship with God. Perfect righteousness is not the result of good deeds. Rather, it is a righteousness "that is by faith." Faith is both a single act and a continuing attitude. As we continue in our Christian walk, our loyalty and obedience matures to trust and devotion. And faith becomes the driving force in our lives, "as it is written, The just shall live by faith" (v. 17).

What practical steps do you take to live by faith?

Search the Scriptures

1. What aspect of the Roman Christian's relationship with God was Paul especially thankful for? (v. 8)

2. Why was the Apostle Paul so anxious to visit the church in Rome? (v. 11)

3. How did Paul describe the Gospel and who benefited from it? (v. 16)

4. What reasons did Paul give to prove he was "ready" to preach the Gospel? (see Romans 1:14-17)

Discuss the Meaning

Paul declared that the Gospel reveals the power of God for salvation to all regardless of ethnicity. Do African Americans have a responsibility to share the Good News with people of other races? What about in other nations? How can we accomplish this international evangelism?

Liberating Lesson

Today's lesson on how Paul viewed his evangelistic mission raises questions about modern evangelism. Some say we need a new message in modern inner cities because the Christian Gospel is a White folk's Gospel. They claim that the Gospel is ineffective in dealing with the stress and turmoil of today's urban centers. Based on Paul's view of the Gospel, how would you respond to these critics?

Application for Activation

Paul insists that the Gospel is for all people, reminding Christians of the Great Commission's understanding that we will go into all the world (Matthew 28:19-20). This week, write down a prayer seeking God's will for how you are to participate in the salvation of the world. Pray that prayer each day this week and listen for God's answer.

Follow the Spirit

What God wants me to do:

_____

_____

_____

_____

Remember Your Thoughts

Special insights I have learned:

_____

_____

_____

_____

More Light on the Text

Romans 1:8-17

8 First, I thank my God through Jesus Christ for you all, that your faith is spoken of throughout the whole world.

The introduction is complete. "First" in this case does not refer to priority but rather means "in the first place." The phrase "I thank" is from the Greek word *eucharisteo* (eew-kha-rees-**TEH**-oh) which is better translated as "I give thanks." The present tense indicates a continuous rendering of gratitude. Paul's gratitude to God, particularly for fellow Christians, is always uppermost in his thoughts. In all but one of his epistles to the churches, Paul expresses thankfulness for believers. The only exception is the epistle to the Galatians, who had abandoned the Gospel of grace for an opposing teaching (Galatians 1:6).

Giving thanks to God is an expression of joy and therefore a fruit of the spirit (Galatians 5:22). Paul understood this truth and so offered up his thanks "through Jesus Christ." The apostle knew that every good thing that happened, every grace he received and every Christian he met was a blessing from God through his union with Christ. So every act of worship, praise, or thanksgiving was offered up to God through Christ.

The phrase "your faith" can be interpreted in two ways. It could be a reference to the strength of their faith. However, the context seems better served by referring to their Christianity. The way they lived their lives, their Christian walk, was being "spoken of throughout the whole world." The phrase "is spoken of," from the Greek verb *katangello* (ka-ta-ang-**GELL**-oh) is better translated "is being proclaimed." The "world" in this case does not mean the whole world, but rather the Roman Empire.

9 For God is my witness, whom I serve with my spirit in the gospel of his Son, that

528

without ceasing I make mention of you always in my prayers; 10 Making request, if by any means now at length I might have a prosperous journey by the will of God to come unto you.

Paul uses an interesting word to describe his service to God—*latreuo* (lah-**TREW**-oh) which literally means to serve as a priest. It is the Greek word used in the Septuagint (the Greek translation of the Hebrew Scriptures) to refer to the service of priests in the Temple. Paul said that he served God "with my spirit." He considered all Christian service to be an act of worship. Therefore, true Christian service must originate in the spirit because "God is a Spirit: and they that worship him must worship him in spirit and in truth" (John 4:24).

Paul prayed continuously. In Paul's first letter to the Thessalonians, he encouraged them to "pray without ceasing" (1 Thessalonians 5:17). Here Paul demonstrates that he practiced what he preached.

In the introduction of the Roman epistle, the apostle reveals two elements of his prayer life: his thankfulness (v. 8) and his concern for others (v. 9). When Paul says, "I make mention of you" he does not mean the church in general, but he is specifically referring to the Roman church by name. At the end of this letter, Paul mentions by name 26 members of the Roman church—a church that he had never visited before (Romans 16). From this, we can conclude that personal prayer for individuals should always be specific.

Along with praying for others, Paul also requests for himself. He wanted to have "a prosperous journey" to Rome. Paul also reveals submissiveness in his prayer life. Paul made all his requests "by" or "in" the will of God. Thus, the best and surest way of life is always in the will of God. In relying on this divine formula, Paul confirms the teaching of the Apostle John, "If we ask anything according to his will, he heareth us" (1 John 5:14). Paul also follows the example of Christ, the Great Apostle, who prayed, "not as I will, but as thou wilt" (Matthew 26:39).

11 For I long to see you, that I may impart unto you some spiritual gift, to the end ye may be established; 12 That is, that I may be comforted together with you by the mutual faith both of you and me.

The apostle's prayer reflects the desires of his heart. The phrase "I long for you" literally means "I am homesick for you." Paul's desire to visit Rome was so strong that it was comparable to homesickness even though he has never been there before. The motivation for his great longing is three-pronged: "that I may impart unto you some spiritual gift," "[that] ye may be established," and "that I may be comforted together with you."

Paul uses the term "spiritual gift" term in both the natural and spiritual sense. In the natural sense, Paul wanted to share the Gospel message. In the spiritual sense, the apostle refers to the gifts that transcend the ordinary workings of nature known as the "grace gifts" as described in 1 Corinthians 12-14.

The reason Paul gives for the impartation of these "grace gifts" is so that "ye may be established." Note the passivity of the phrase. Paul does not say so that "I" may establish, but rather that "ye" may be established. With all his gifts and eloquent speech, Paul knew that only God could develop, strengthen, and establish Christian character.

Paul is not implying any spiritual weakness on their part nor superior spiritual strength for himself. In fact, it is his hope that they will share in a common strengthening. The word "comfort" from the Greek *sumparakaleo* (soom-pa-ra-ka-**LEH**-oh) is best rendered "strengthen together." Paul hopes that both he and the Roman Christians will be mutually strengthened by his visit.

13 Now I would not have you ignorant, brethren, that oftentimes I purposed to come unto you, (but was let hitherto,) that I might have some fruit among you also, even as among other Gentiles.

The emphatic phrase "I would not have you ignorant" is one of Paul's favorites. Paul uses this phrase five times in his epistles (Romans 11:25; 1 Corinthians 10:1; 12:1; 2 Corinthians 1:8; 1 Thessalonians 4:13). Each time, the apostle employs the phrase to call special attention to what follows.

In this case, Paul calls attention to how often he had "purposed" to visit Rome. "But was let hitherto" is an old English expression that is hardly used anymore. In this usage, it means "hindered" or "prevented." It must have appeared to Paul that there were forces working to hinder his visit to the city. These could have been sinister forces of evil, hoping to slow the progress of the Gospel, or it could have been the protection and guidance of the Spirit (Acts 16:6-7).

The apostle's eventual journey to Rome actually began with a visit to Jerusalem to settle the issue of Gentile circumcision. After his meeting with the church elders, some Jews lied on Paul and incited a riot in the city. Paul was arrested and later kept in protective custody (Acts 21:15–23:10). While Paul was in custody, Christ appeared to him and said, "Be of good cheer, Paul: for as thou hast testified of me in Jerusalem, so must thou bear witness also at Rome" (Acts 23:11). Before finally making it to Rome, the apostle would languish under house arrest for two years (Acts 24:27) and be shipwrecked on the island of Malta (27:1—28:16). In spite of all the hindrances, Paul knew that God wanted him to go to Rome, and the apostle purposed in his spirit to go there.

14 I am debtor both to the Greeks, and to the Barbarians; both to the wise, and to the unwise. 15 So, as much as in me is, I am ready to preach the gospel to you that are at Rome also.

Thus, Paul prayed to visit Rome so that he could preach the Gospel in the capital city of the empire. He had a debt to pay to all humanity, a debt that could never be satisfied. This was a debt to proclaim the Gospel of God. However high or however low, wise Greek or uneducated barbarian, Paul saw them all as fit subjects for the message of Christ. The term "barbarians" referred to those who did not speak Greek. While it did have some connotations to lacking the "civilized" nature of Greek society, Paul cannot be using it to insult here, since he is confessing his debt to them.

The society of Rome was not unlike our society. We too are faced with the so-called cultured "Greeks" and those referred to by the so-called cultured folks as "barbarians." We too have the educated and the illiterate. Yet, to one and all, the Gospel of God is the only hope of salvation, temporal as well as eternal. The power to save comes from God through the message of the Gospel. All we need to do is tell the story, and our society will be saved.

16 For I am not ashamed of the gospel of Christ: for it is the power of God unto salvation to every one that believeth; to the Jew first, and also to the Greek. 17 For therein is the righteousness of God revealed from faith to faith: as it is written, The just shall live by faith.

The preposition "for" marks the transition from the introduction to the heart of the epistle. In these two verses, Paul states the purpose and theme of his letter to the Roman church—the Gospel of Jesus Christ. The Good News of Jesus Christ can be summarized like this: God loves humanity; humanity is essentially sinful; Christ paid the price for our sin; you must be born again.

The language of Paul's declaration, "I am not ashamed," implies that it required some courage to boldly proclaim what was a stumbling block to the Jews and foolishness to the Greeks (1 Corinthians 1:23). The word "ashamed" is a translation of the Greek word *epaischunomai* (eh-pies-**KHOO**-noo-my), which means to have feelings of fear or shame that would prevent a person from taking action. Paul's courage sprang from his knowledge concerning the Gospel. Paul knew that the Gospel is the power of God unto salvation, and it reveals the righteousness of God.

Paul's initial statement about the Gospel relates its power. The keyword here is "is." The apostle does not say that the Gospel has or exerts power. He proclaims that "it is the power." The word "power" comes from the Greek word *dunamis* (**DOO**-nah-mees), from which we derive the word dynamite. It means the inherent strength or power residing in a thing by its nature. Therefore the Gospel is the inherent power of God exerted in the salvation of humanity.

The basic idea of "salvation" (Gk. *soteria*, so-teh-**REE**-ah) is deliverance. It speaks of the divine deliverance from sin to holiness. Salvation is a gift of God's grace that is based on Christ's death (Romans 3:25), resurrection (5:10), and continued intercession on our behalf (Hebrews 7:25). The only requirement for salvation is faith in the Person and work of Jesus Christ (Romans 3:22-25).

This great salvation comes to believers in three stages. In the initial stage, believers are saved from the penalty of sin (Romans 6:23). In its present stage, salvation delivers believers from the power of sin in our daily lives. God accomplishes our deliverance from the power of sin by filling us with the Holy Spirit (1 Corinthians 6:19; Galatians 5:16), which brings us into a new personal relationship with God (John 1:12–13). In the future stage, salvation delivers believers from the actual presence of sin (Revelations 21:1-8).

God's great salvation is available to everyone who believes. As believers, we receive and live our salvation through faith, which is both the acceptance of the truth of the Gospel and complete trust in our Lord and Savior, Jesus Christ. Therefore, faith is both a one-time act and a continuing attitude that grows and is strengthened.

Paul's second statement about the Gospel is this: "for therein is the righteousness of God revealed from faith to faith." The word "righteousness" (Gk. *dikaiosune*, dee-keye-oh-**SOO**-nay) refers to the restoration of right relations between God and believers. No one can approach God based on his or her righteousness because humanity has no righteousness (Romans 3:10). Therefore, God imputes or credits believers with His righteousness through our faith in Christ (Romans 4:5). The phrase "from faith to faith" indicates a progression of faith from a lower to a higher degree (cf. 2 Corinthians 3:18). Faith is the key to initial salvation and to living saved lives.

Paul was able to say "I am not ashamed of the gospel," because he had seen the Gospel's power unleashed in the lives of many believers. This power had freed them from the power of sin and death and empowered them to live godly lives. This same power is available today to all who believe.

Sources:

Bruce, F.F. Romans. *Tyndale New Testament Commentaries*. Book 6. Grand Rapids, Michigan: Eerdmans, 1986.

Henry, Matthew. *Matthew Henry's Commentary on the Whole Bible: New Modern Edition*. Vols. 1-6. Peabody, MA: Hendrickson Publishers, Inc., 2009.

Newman, Barclay M., and Eugene A. Nida. *A Translator's Handbook on Paul's Letter to the Romans*. United Bible Society, 1973.

Packer, J.I., Merrill C. Tenney, William White, Jr. *The Bible Almanac: A Comprehensive Reference Guide to the People of the Bible and How They Lived*. Nashville, TN: Thomas Nelson, 1978.

Ryken, Leland. *The Literature of the Bible*. Grand Rapids, Michigan: Zondervan, 1974.

Strong, James. *The New Strong's Exhaustive Concordance of the Bible*. Nashville, TN: Thomas Nelson, 2003.

Tenney, Merrill Chapin. "Epistles." *Zondervan Pictorial Encyclopedia of the Bible*. Grand Rapids, MI: Zondervan, 1975.

Thayer, Joseph Henry. *A Greek-English Lexicon of the New Testament*. New York: American Book Company, 1889.

Say It Correctly

Tertius. **TER**-she-us.
Phoebe. **FEE**-bee.

Daily Bible Readings

MONDAY
Apollos and Paul, Builders
(1 Corinthians 3:1-11)

TUESDAY
Entrusted to Take Gospel to Gentiles
(Galatians 2:1-10)

WEDNESDAY
Grace and Peace to All
(Romans 1:1-7)

THURSDAY
God's Righteous Wrath
(Romans 1:18-23)

FRIDAY
God's Actions Are Fair and Just
(Romans 1:24-32)

SATURDAY
God's Righteous Actions
for Saints, Sinners
(2 Peter 2:4-9)

SUNDAY
The Gospel Changes Jews and Gentiles
(Romans 1:8-17)

Notes

_____

_____

_____

_____

Teaching Tips

July 18
Bible Study Guide 7

Words You Should Know

A. Faith (Romans 4:5) *pistis* (Gk.)—Assurance, belief, trust, and fidelity

B. Sign (v. 11) *semeion* (Gk.)—An event, activity, or thing that possesses a deeper meaning than a surface level interpretation can provide

Teacher Preparation

Unifying Principle—Seeking Assurance. People often look to those older than they are for assurance. Who is an example one can trust? Through faith, Abraham, the father of all who believe, proved he was in right relationship with God.

A. Read the Bible Background and Devotional Reading.

B. Pray for your students and lesson clarity.

C. Read the lesson Scripture in multiple translations.

O—Open the Lesson

A. Begin the class with prayer.

B. Give each student an index card and ask them to write the name of a Christian they admire (living or dead, person acquaintance or public figure) and then four to six traits about that person that makes him or her a righteous (but not perfect) Christian.

C. Have the students read the Aim for Change and the In Focus story.

D. Ask students how events like those in the story weigh on their hearts and how they can view these events from a faith perspective.

P—Present the Scriptures

A. Read the Focal Verses and discuss the Background and The People, Places, and Times sections.

B. Have the class share what Scriptures stand out for them and why, with particular emphasis on today's themes.

E—Explore the Meaning

A. Use In Depth or More Light on the Text to facilitate a deeper discussion of the lesson text.

B. Pose the questions in Search the Scriptures and Discuss the Meaning.

C. Discuss the Liberating Lesson and Application for Activation sections.

N—Next Steps for Application

A. Summarize the value of setting a good example for new or young Christians.

B. End class with a commitment to pray for relationships with seasoned, stable Christians who can help guide and encourage toward a proper faith walk.

Worship Guide

For the Superintendent or Teacher
Theme: The Faith of Abraham
Song: "The Blessing of Abraham"
Devotional Reading: Genesis 15:1–6

533

The Faith of Abraham

Bible Background • ROMANS 4
Printed Text • ROMANS 4:1-12 | Devotional Reading • GENESIS 15:1-6

—————————— Aim for Change ——————————

By the end of this lesson, we will STUDY the difference between faith and works as manifested in the life of Abraham, REFLECT on the knowledge and wisdom of Paul as seen in his understanding of the Old Testament, and IDENTIFY ways in which we rely on our faith for a relationship with God.

—————————— In Focus ——————————

"Hi, Daddy," said Zona Jackson Moore as her father entered the arid room where families met with inmates. Nelson Jackson could barely recognize his little girl in the face of the woman who stood before him. He had last seen her when she had to move across the country for college years ago. Nelson had only spoken to the man she married in letters. Now Zona had made a special trip back home so everyone could meet her new baby.

"Daddy, this is my husband, Roy, and our baby girl, Faith," introduced Zona.

"Faith, yes, the perfect name," said Nelson. "How I need faith these days. Can I hold her?"

Roy placed the baby in his arms and said, "Mr. Jackson, we have never believed the awful things they said you did. We have faith and we're praying that one day you will be vindicated and released."

It would be another ten years before new DNA tests would prove Nelson's innocence. Waiting at the prison gates the morning of his release were Zona, Roy, and Faith. Though well into his 70s, Nelson ran to hug them and picked up Faith.

"Faith, how precious you are," said Nelson. "And, now that I'm free, I will continue to share my faith with everyone. While I was imprisoned, I never stopped preaching about faith in God, and many men, both inmates and guards, gave their lives to Jesus. God said I'd be cleared, and He kept His promise. Faith in the goodness of God is the hope of the world."

Salvation is a gift to all who will receive it. In today's lesson, we will examine the case that the Apostle Paul makes to show that rules, traditions, and actions that bar people from the gift of God's love and grace have no place in the body of Christ.

—————————— Keep in Mind ——————————

"For what saith the scripture? Abraham believed God, and it was counted unto him for righteousness" (Romans 4:3, KJV).

"For the Scriptures tell us, 'Abraham believed God, and God counted him as righteous because of his faith'" (Romans 4:3, NLT).

Focal Verses

KJV **Romans 4:1** What shall we say then that Abraham our father, as pertaining to the flesh, hath found?

2 For if Abraham were justified by works, he hath whereof to glory; but not before God.

3 For what saith the scripture? Abraham believed God, and it was counted unto him for righteousness.

4 Now to him that worketh is the reward not reckoned of grace, but of debt.

5 But to him that worketh not, but believeth on him that justifieth the ungodly, his faith is counted for righteousness.

6 Even as David also describeth the blessedness of the man, unto whom God imputeth righteousness without works,

7 Saying, Blessed are they whose iniquities are forgiven, and whose sins are covered.

8 Blessed is the man to whom the Lord will not impute sin.

9 Cometh this blessedness then upon the circumcision only, or upon the uncircumcision also? for we say that faith was reckoned to Abraham for righteousness.

10 How was it then reckoned? when he was in circumcision, or in uncircumcision? Not in circumcision, but in uncircumcision.

11 And he received the sign of circumcision, a seal of the righteousness of the faith which he had yet being uncircumcised: that he might be the father of all them that believe, though they be not circumcised; that righteousness might be imputed unto them also:

12 And the father of circumcision to them who are not of the circumcision only, but who also walk in the steps of that faith of our father Abraham, which he had being yet uncircumcised.

NLT **Romans 4:1** Abraham was, humanly speaking, the founder of our Jewish nation. What did he discover about being made right with God?

2 If his good deeds had made him acceptable to God, he would have had something to boast about. But that was not God's way.

3 For the Scriptures tell us, "Abraham believed God, and God counted him as righteous because of his faith."

4 When people work, their wages are not a gift, but something they have earned.

5 But people are counted as righteous, not because of their work, but because of their faith in God who forgives sinners.

6 David also spoke of this when he described the happiness of those who are declared righteous without working for it:

7 "Oh, what joy for those whose disobedience is forgiven, whose sins are put out of sight.

8 Yes, what joy for those whose record the Lord has cleared of sin."

9 Now, is this blessing only for the Jews, or is it also for uncircumcised Gentiles? Well, we have been saying that Abraham was counted as righteous by God because of his faith.

10 But how did this happen? Was he counted as righteous only after he was circumcised, or was it before he was circumcised? Clearly, God accepted Abraham before he was circumcised!

11 Circumcision was a sign that Abraham already had faith and that God had already accepted him and declared him to be righteous—even before he was circumcised. So Abraham is the spiritual father of those who have faith but have not been circumcised. They are counted as righteous because of their faith.

12 And Abraham is also the spiritual father of those who have been circumcised, but only if they have the same kind of faith Abraham had before he was circumcised.

The People, Places, and Times

Abraham. Abraham was originally from Ur, which was Chaldean territory in modern-day Iraq. He was the son of Terah, who was a descendant of Shem, one of Noah's sons. Noah had declared the Lord God's blessing over Shem who, with his brother, covered Noah when he was naked (Genesis 9:18–26). Later, God would declare an even greater blessing over Abraham: he would have fertile land, blessings, and descendants as numerous of the stars and the sand.

Circumcision. In ancient Israel, this act (removing the foreskin of the male sex organ) was performed as a ritual on all male children on the eighth day after birth. In the Jewish faith, it was an external symbol of one's total and complete allegiance and devotion to Yahweh. Controversy arose in the early church over the circumcision of Gentile converts (Acts 15:13-18). During the first century AD, Jews frowned upon non-circumcision among Christians. Apostle Paul played a crucial role in settling the dispute. He determined that physical circumcision was not essential to Christian faith and fellowship. Circumcision of the heart through repentance and faith were the only requirements of the faith.

Background

This letter to Christian believers in Rome was written by the Apostle Paul between AD 56 and AD 58 when he was living in Corinth, a Grecian port city. It is thought that the emerging Christian belief had made its way to Rome from Jewish believers who had heard about Jesus Christ during visits to Jerusalem and on returning to Rome, shared the good news with both Jews and Gentiles. In AD 49, Emperor Claudius expelled the Jews. After he died around AD 54, Jewish Christians returned to Rome and found Gentile believers leading a growing number of Christ-followers.

Well entrenched in the rules and regulations of the Jewish tradition, these Jewish Christians believed that Gentile believers needed to adhere to the practice of circumcision which had been established by the patriarch of their faith, Abraham. The letter to the Romans offers a well-developed explanation of God's interaction with humanity since creation and the fall, the preeminent role of belief in Jesus Christ for humanity's redemption, and the faithful response of believers when they rightly understand that salvation is a gift that had been made available to Jews and Gentiles alike—not through human works—but by belief in the sacrificial life, death, and resurrection of Jesus Christ.

At-A-Glance

1. Faith Builds Relationship
(Romans 4:1-3)
2. Faith Becomes Righteousness (vv. 4-8)
3. Faith Begets Works (vv. 9-12)

In Depth

1. Faith Builds Relationship (Romans 4:1-3)

The Jewish people have always recognized Abraham as a progenitor for their national lineage and monotheistic faith. Abraham was the person who had dared to leave the plurality of gods that his ancestors worshiped to accept an invitation to follow the God who they saw as the One True and Living God. This God blessed Abraham with great riches and gave him an incredible promise—he and his wife Sarah would have a son. As years passed and they were well beyond child-bearing age, their faith in God's promise was tested. Abraham and Sarah would have to continually prevail in faith, trusting in the God who had made the promise, not their ability to get things done through human effort. For Abraham's descendants, Abraham was the model of faithfully walking with God. Humanly speaking, that was a legacy to be proud of. Yet, in the presence of a holy and righteous God, no one, not even Abraham, could brag about accomplishments, natural or spiritual.

Name some of the ways Abraham's and Sarah's faith was tested as they waited for God to fulfill His promise.

2. Faith Becomes Righteousness (vv. 4-8)

Human effort earns human rewards, like large salaries, or trophies, and accolades. Faith in God, however, gives something much more significant—a relationship that puts a person in good standing with God. Abraham was given such right standing, not because he had done any specific work, but because God attached right standing to his faith. Only God could perform the work necessary to bridge the divide that had been created by sin (Genesis 3). To be declared right with God is a gift from God that can only be received, never earned. The appropriate human response to God's merciful initiative is acceptance, obedience, and thankfulness.

Why would the Apostle Paul choose Abraham and David to make his argument that people are saved by faith, not their works?

3. Faith Begets Works (vv. 9-12)

The Apostle Paul points out that Abraham was given right standing with God and received the incredible promise of a son before he was circumcised. This crediting of right standing had been declared roughly two decades before Abraham was circumcised. Circumcision then was a response from Abraham that he had accepted God's pronouncement, and he was thankful for the amazing gift of relationship with God. For uncircumcised Gentiles who

had placed their faith in the redemptive power of Jesus Christ, this message from Paul showed that God's forgiveness and acceptance had been given to someone who was uncircumcised.

Abraham, as presented in Paul's discourse, was to be seen as the father of all who faithfully followed the God of their forefather and the promised Son through whom all the world would be blessed. Abraham was more than the father of those who were circumcised, he also was the father of anyone who put their faith in Jesus Christ.

What role, if any, does works of righteousness have in the life of those who have put their faith in Jesus Christ?

Search the Scriptures

1. In your own words, what is the meaning of "imputed" (Romans 4:6)?

2. Explain why righteousness has to be recognized as a gift and not a reward for right living. (Romans 4:4-8)

Discuss the Meaning

When an African American billionaire announced that he would pay off the college loans of nearly 400 young men at a historically black college, the news went viral. Without such a gift, many of those graduates would have lived under the burden of debt for decades. Two millennia before, another man paid off a significant debt. Jesus Christ wiped out humanity's debt to sin and declared that through faith, anyone can have access to a relationship with Him.

1. Have you ever benefited from the generosity of others? What was your response?

2. What are some ways to make the news of Jesus' gift of salvation go viral?

Liberating Lesson

A woman entered the church wearing a black niqab. *That isn't our look for Sunday worship,* thought a woman whose father was a founder of her denomination. "You can't dress like that here or in heaven," she admonished the visitor. "Find out our traditions and come back next week." The pastor, seeing the visitor heading for the door, left the pulpit and ran to stop her. "Please sit over here," he assured. "The doors of God's church are open to anyone who has the faith and courage to enter."

What do you know about the cultural and religious practices of other religious traditions? What might be the first step toward greater understanding?

Application for Activation

Debates over circumcision rarely arise today, but conflicts over other religious rituals, practices, and norms continue to keep the body of Christ divided about who is in right standing with God. Think about a religious difference you have recently noticed. Take the position of the side you are opposed to and defend it as vigorously as you would defend your position. Identify ways the opposing position extends the redemptive grace of God to more people. What are some ways that you can invite people who hold your point of view to look at the conflict from another's perspective?

Follow the Spirit

What God wants me to do:

_____

_____

_____

_____

Remember Your Thoughts

Special insights I have learned:

_____

_____

_____

_____

More Light on the Text

Romans 4:1–12

1 What shall we say then that Abraham our father, as pertaining to the flesh, hath found?

Nothing. That is the appropriate response to Paul's rhetorical question in this verse. There is nothing that we can say Abraham gained according to the flesh. The term "pertaining to the flesh," is from the Greek words *kata sarka* (**KA**-ta **SAR**-ka). In this letter to the Romans, this phrase depicts the lower and external aspects of human life that are juxtaposed to the higher and internal aspects of human life, especially for the believer. Rather than a life that is *kata sarka*, Paul suggests implicitly here and more explicitly in Romans 8:1-13 (and other places) that believers are to live a life *kata pneuma* (puh-**NEW**-muh) or according to the Spirit. Therefore, Paul seeks to emphasize that Abraham, the ancestor of believers, did not gain anything according to the flesh, but as we will see below, Abraham's faith is a key to how to gain everything according to the Spirit. Similarly, we should make sure that we focus on strengthening our spiritual walk with God rather than focusing on superficial items that will ultimately leave us empty.

2 For if Abraham were justified by works, he hath whereof to glory; but not before God.

Abraham's response to God is critical for this passage and for understanding Paul's thinking.

One of the words that is key for understanding this passage is the word *dikaio* (dee-**KAI**-oh), which has been translated as "justified." This translation both veils and reveals how Paul uses this word. The root of this word is at work behind the two times that "justified" appears in this text, which is clear in verses 2 and 5. However, what is not as clear is that the same word is at the root behind the word translated as "righteousness," which is the Greek word *dikaiosune* (dee-kai-oh-**SOO**-nay) in verses 2 and 5. You can see how the two words are related. If we start with the noun *dikaoisune*, it can provide insight on how to interpret the verbs translated as "justified."

Dikaiosune here is righteousness or better justice, which captures the preferred status in which people should stand in relationship to their covenant with God. This covenantal relationship extends back into the Hebrew Bible. A believer should desire to be in good standing in their covenant with God, which is in a position of justice. The word *dikaoisune* will appear as justice/righteousness throughout this section to remind the reader of this discussion.

The way that one gets into this position is captured in the way that *dikaio* as a verb in verse 2 is in the passive voice. This means that the subject (the believer) does not do the action, but rather the action happens to them. The verb here is communicating how one is placed into a position of justice/righteousness. Therefore, Paul is communicating how Abraham becomes a person of justice/righteousness, first by stating what Abraham did not do to be justified. Abraham was not justified or made into a person of justice/righteousness by "works." Works here refers to the rite of circumcision.

Abraham being a person of justice/righteousness is key for Paul's argument, and that is the reason he lifts him up as an example. As believers, our position as people of justice/righteousness is fundamental to our witness in the world. We cannot fall to the temptation to want to boast about our religiosity or "super" spirituality. Nor can we rest on the fact that we have been placed in right standing in relationship by our covenant with God. Our being in right standing with God implies that our lives should be marked by commitment to being persons of justice/righteousness. To live as that type of person, our spiritual walk has to be nurtured from a deep reserve of faith.

3 For what saith the scripture? Abraham believed God, and it was counted unto him for righteousness.

To further explain how Abraham is justified or made into a person of justice/righteousness, Paul appeals to the Scripture in Genesis 15:6. In that passage, after God tells Abram (later called Abraham) that he would have countless descendants, Abram believed God. And God credited the belief to Abram as justice/righteousness.

Two more words are important for interpreting this passage. The first is the Greek word behind what is translated as "believed." This is the word *pisteuo* (pis-te-**OO**-oh). It can certainly mean to believe, but it also can mean to trust and to be faithful to something. This is the same word in verse 5 behind the term translated "the one who … trusts." This word is also the verb form of the word *pistis*, which is translated as faith. *Pistis* is the noun form of believing, trusting, and being faithful. Therefore, the English words faith, belief, trust, and faithfulness (fidelity) capture the range of meanings that *pistis* has. Because it has such a wide range, the Greek word *pistis* will appear throughout the rest of the lesson to remind the reader of the interpretive possibilities. It is Abraham's faith (*pistis*) to God that God credits as justice/righteousness.

This gets us to the next term *logizetai* (lo-**GEE**-ze-tai). This term is an accounting term, which is why the translation of it as "credit" captures how Paul uses it here. God takes Abraham's faith (*pistis*) and gives Abraham credit as a person of justice/righteousness. God places justice/righteousness in Abraham's account because of his first act of faithfulness (*pistis*) to God. Because Abraham trusts God's promise, God trusts Abraham with righteousness/justice. As believers, our faith (*pistis*) in God uncovers God's faith (*pistis*) in us.

It is important to recognize that not only are we to have faith (*pistis*) in God but to also know that God has faith (*pistis*) in us. God has placed justice/righteousness in our accounts anticipating us to act as agents of justice and righteousness. God is counting on us to be His representatives in the world. Whether at home, work, church, or social groups our faith (*pistis*) should manifest and communicate that we have a covenant relationship with God and that we want to see God's purpose revealed in our lives and the world.

4 Now to him that worketh is the reward not reckoned of grace, but of debt. 5 But to him that worketh not, but believeth on him that justifieth the ungodly, his faith is counted for righteousness.

Paul continues to explain how one becomes credited as a person of righteousness/justice. He uses wordplay and compares the works that did not get Abraham justified (i.e. circumcision) with the work of one who labors for wages. The laborer who works for their wages is not paid out of the benevolence of their employer. Put another way, we do not find our bosses particularly generous when they pay us for the time we worked. The pay is what is owed. However, if one receives money that they did not work for as a bonus, then it is a gift. It is credited or added to a worker without the giver receiving anything in return. The credit adds to the person and impacts how they live

their lives moving forward without necessarily being linked to their past actions or inactions. For Paul, this is how people are placed into position as people of justice/righteousness. It is not because the individual has earned such a position. One does not need to put an item on credit if it has already been earned or paid for.

God would not have to apply righteousness/justice into the account of believers if they had already earned it, but we had not earned it. God had to give it to us on credit anticipating that we would live into it. This is particularly the case for Paul's primarily Gentile audience. The Greek word behind "ungodly" is *asebe* (as-eh-**BAY**), which highlights how Gentiles, from a Jewish perspective, worshiped false gods. In this way, they had a similar background to Abraham, whose father made idols (Joshua 24:2). But after hearing God, Abraham trusted God and God credited him with justice/righteousness. Similarly, Gentiles, who before hearing preaching like Paul's, were not in covenant with the God of Israel and did not pursue justice or righteousness. But now they are granted an opportunity to be a part of the covenant. They can gain access to God's covenant by trusting the One who can even transform immoral idol worshipers into people of justice/righteousness. That type of trust (*pistis*) is what God uses as collateral to credit justice/righteousness into the account of those who exhibit it.

God's miraculous grace manifests toward us and God chooses to credit righteousness/justice to our account even before we live into it. We do not have to earn God's approval or God's plan for our lives. Our trust (*pistis*) starts us on a journey of making God's presence real in our lives and the lives of those around us. Our faith (*pistis*) also allows us to recognize that our opportunity to be in relationship with God is a gift that we did not earn and we can share it with others by expanding the covenant to others and pursuing justice and righteousness in our homes, communities, nations, and world.

6 Even as David also describeth the blessedness of the man, unto whom God imputeth righteousness without works, 7 Saying, Blessed are they whose iniquities are forgiven, and whose sins are covered. 8 Blessed is the man to whom the Lord will not impute sin.

Paul incorporates another passage from the Scripture to further illustrate his point about how God places justice/righteousness into people's accounts. He appeals to Psalm 32 where the word *logizetai* describes the blessed state of one whom the Lord has not credited with sin. This passage serves three purposes for Paul's argument. The first is that it demonstrates that God can credit one with justice/righteousness or with sin. The second purpose assumes that the speaker in the psalm is guilty and that God can choose to discredit one's account, especially of sin, if God chooses to. Both of these elements demonstrate God's sovereignty over how justice/righteousness and sin/iniquity get accounted for in God's ledger. The third purpose is to illustrate that works (particularly circumcision) are not how God credits accounts.

One of the greatest blessings is to know that God is not in heaven primarily keeping a record of our mistakes and shortcomings. God is more concerned with forgiving and transforming us into people of justice/righteousness than condemning us because of our mistakes. This should both prevent us from comparing ourselves with others in boastful ways, and it should remind us of the constant work that we have toward becoming all of who God has called us to be. It is a blessing to not be shackled to the past. The blessing is to not have our past held against us. The blessing is also to avoid recreating our past in the present, and the blessing is to create a future that is not bogged down by that past. That is a state of blessedness indeed.

9 Cometh this blessedness then upon the circumcision only, or upon the uncircumcision also? for we say that faith was reckoned to Abraham for righteousness. 10 How was it then reckoned? when he was in circumcision, or in uncircumcision? Not in circumcision, but in uncircumcision.

These verses highlight Paul's main contention in this passage—the irrelevance of circumcision for Gentile believers. He uses Psalm 32 to interpret Genesis 15. He launches from the blessed state discussed in Psalm 32 into his critique of circumcision as a requirement to be credited as a person of justice/righteousness. He uses Abraham's life as proof positive that circumcision is not a prerequisite for participating in covenant with the God of Israel. This is significant because circumcision could have been a significant deterrent for many male Gentiles who did not practice circumcision. Some of Paul's contemporaries, no doubt, suggested that to participate in covenant with the God of Israel, men had to be circumcised. We find evidence of people having differing views about this issue in Acts 15 and Galatians 2.

Often discussions about works or circumcision lead to interpretations of Romans that suggest that Paul is abandoning the Torah (Law); however, that is not the case. Paul, as a Jewish believer in Christ, would have found it unthinkable to abandon the Law. As a matter of fact, he is using the Law (the book of Genesis, the first book of the Torah) to make his claim about how Gentile men do not need to be circumcised to participate in the covenant and to be credited with righteousness/justice. Paul uses Abraham's life as a legal test case of how God chooses to make people who act in faithfulness to God people of righteousness/justice. Although Paul is primarily addressing a Gentile audience, he makes a Jewish argument to explain that since Abraham was credited with righteousness/justice before he was circumcised, God does not require circumcision before justifying Gentiles.

Paul desires to emphasize that it is faith (*pistis*) that most concerns God. It is faith (*pistis*) that is credited into the believer's account as righteousness/justice. Faith (*pistis*) is more than a creedal assent to certain doctrines or formulas. It is about placing one's life completely in the hands of God and faithfully submitting to God's plan. That is what moves God to credit righteousness/justice into one's account. This type of commitment could not be reduced to following one component of the Law—circumcision. Faith (*pistis*) actually is the foundation for the Law and God's covenantal relationship with God's people. Hence, Abraham had faith (*pistis*) even before he was circumcised.

11 And he received the sign of circumcision, a seal of the righteousness of the faith which he had yet being uncircumcised: that he might be the father of all them that believe, though they be not circumcised; that righteousness might be imputed unto them also: 12 And the father of circumcision to them who are not of the circumcision only, but who also walk in the steps of that faith of our father Abraham, which he had being yet uncircumcised.

Paul describes Abraham's circumcision as a "sign." The Greek word is *semeion* (say-MAY-on) and captures the notion of an event, activity, or thing that possesses a deeper meaning than a surface level interpretation can provide. Circumcision is this type of sign. For Abraham, it is more than a ritual; it is a representation of something much deeper—his faith (*pisitis*) in God.

Paul further explains the sign as a seal. The Greek word *sphragida* (sfra-**GEE**-duh) is the type of seal an official put on a letter to make sure that its contents were not tampered with until it arrived at its destination. Similarly, righteousness/justice through faith (*pistis*) sealed Abraham even though he had not been circumcised. His faith was able to preserve him as a person of justice/righteousness even before his circumcision. Paul uses this to emphasize how our faith (*pistis*) can preserve us even before we know how God wants to use us.

Paul understands God's crediting of justice/righteousness to Abraham before he was circumcised as an indication that God wanted to make Abraham the ancestor of those who have faith (*pistis*) regardless of the status of their circumcision. This means that God's covenant has expanded to include both Jews and Gentiles, both circumcised and uncircumcised. Abraham is the model of faith to the circumcised and the uncircumcised. Even more important than those labels, Abraham is the ancestor and example to all people who have faith (*pistis*).

Abraham becomes a role model without knowing exactly how God was going to do what He has promised because he believed anyway. Abraham became a model for justice and righteousness even when he was still imperfect, because he acted in faithfulness to God anyway. Abraham received a credit to his account that would benefit his descendants because he trusted a covenant that he was the first to participate in. Paul raises Abraham's life as an example to the community in Rome and to believers everywhere to live a life of faith that inspires others to have faith. We are called to make good on the credit of justice/righteousness that God has placed into our account by leaving a faithful legacy that will cause generations after us to be blessed because of our faith.

Sources:
Church, Rev. Leslie F. *Commentary on the Whole Bible by Matthew Henry*, Grand Rapids, MI: Zondervan Publishing House, 1960.
Fitzmyer, Joseph A. *Romans*, New York, NY: Doubleday, 1993.
Jewett, Robert. *Romans: A Commentary*, Hermeneia (Minneapolis: Fortress Press, 2007.
Lopez, Davina. *Apostle to the Conquered: Reimagining Paul's Mission*. Minneapolis: Fortress Press, 2008.
Osborne, Grant R., ed. *Romans*, Downers Grove, IL: InterVarsity Press, 2004.
Pilch, John J. *Galatians and Romans, Collegeville Bible Commentary*. Collegeville, MN: The Liturgical Press, 1983.
Sanders, E.P. *Paul: The Apostle's Life, Letters, and Thought*. Augsburg Fortress Publishers, 2015.
Stendahl, Krister. *Paul Among Jews and Gentiles, and Other Essays*. Philadelphia: Fortress
Stowers, Stanley K. *A Reading of Romans: Justice, Jews, and Gentiles*. New Haven: Yale University Press, 1994.

Say It Correctly

Chaldean. kall-**DEE**-an.
Terah. **TARE**-ah.

Daily Bible Readings

MONDAY
God's Covenant with Abraham
(Genesis 15:1-8)

TUESDAY
All World's Families Blessed
Through Abraham
(Genesis 12:1-9)

WEDNESDAY
Promise Realized by Faith Not Law
(Romans 4:13-15)

THURSDAY
For All Who Share Abraham's Faith
(Romans 4:16-18)

FRIDAY
Abraham Believed
Despite Impossible Odds
(Romans 4:19-21)

SATURDAY
In Christ, Believers Share Abraham's Faith
(Romans 4:22-25)

SUNDAY
Abraham, Father of the Faithful
(Romans 4:1-12)

Notes

Teaching Tips

July 25
Bible Study Guide 8

Words You Should Know

A. Peace (Romans 5:1) *eirene* (Gk.)—The absence of war and hostilities; the tranquility of mind that arises from reconciliation with God

B. Access (v. 2) *prosagoge* (Gk.)—The audience or right of approach granted to someone by high officials or kings

Teacher Preparation

Unifying Principle—Seeking Reconciliation. People often struggle with fractured relationships that they may or may not have caused. How can these relationships be reconciled? Only justification by faith in Jesus Christ reconciles the ultimate ruptured relationship between God and humanity.

A. Read the Bible Background and Devotional Reading.

B. Pray for your students and lesson clarity.

C. Read the lesson Scripture in multiple translations.

O—Open the Lesson

A. Begin the class with prayer.

B. Discuss some recent crimes that have made headlines nationally or in your community. Then ask, "What would repentance on the part of the perpetrators look like? What part does repentance play in reconciliation in these cases?"

C. Have the students read the Aim for Change and the In Focus story.

D. Ask students how events like those in the story weigh on their hearts and how they can view these events from a faith perspective.

P—Present the Scriptures

A. Read the Focal Verses and discuss the Background and The People, Places, and Times sections.

B. Have the class share what Scriptures stand out for them and why, with particular emphasis on today's themes.

E—Explore the Meaning

A. Use In Depth or More Light on the Text to facilitate a deeper discussion of the lesson text.

B. Pose the questions in Search the Scriptures and Discuss the Meaning.

C. Discuss the Liberating Lesson and Application for Activation sections.

N—Next Steps for Application

A. Summarize the value of knowing God as both a Friend and heavenly Parent.

B. End class with a prayer thanking God for the depth of love that moved Him to send Jesus to earth.

Worship Guide

For the Superintendent or Teacher
Theme: Justification through Faith
Song: "Jesus Loves Even Me"
Devotional Reading: Isaiah 53:1-12

Justification through Faith

Bible Background • ROMANS 5:1–11
Printed Text • ROMANS 5:1–11 | Devotional Reading • ISAIAH 53:1–12

——————— Aim for Change ———————

By the end of this lesson, we will IDENTIFY the relationship between faith in Christ and justification in the sight of God, REPENT of personal failures to obtain the peace that God gives, and CELEBRATE our justification through faith in Christ.

——————— In Focus ———————

Jawanda prayed for guidance about the meeting after church with her pastor. A member of her church since she learned to read, her devotion left her refreshed. But this morning Jawanda felt she was on the wrong side of God's love..

When she reached the pastor's office, a thin veil of anger clouded her thoughts. The pastor had asked her to step down as chairperson of the Community Day Committee and serve as co-chair under Sadie, who had been a member for only six months. Her eyes were moist as she relayed her anxiety. "I have tithed and served faithfully in our church my entire adult life. Never have I been asked to step down from a leadership role. Why now?"

The pastor's lips turned down as he began to speak. "Jawanda, this is not about you. This is about Sadie and her Christian walk."

Jawanda spoke in a muffled voice. "Please, Pastor, don't ask me to serve under this young girl. Less than a year ago by her own testimony, she was using heavy drugs and living wildly. How do you expect me to respect her decisions?"

"Listen to me," the pastor said. "This is not a demotion; it is a promotion. If you stand as co-chair, your humility and support will be an instrument of deliverance for God's salvation plan for this young woman. Remember, Jawanda, all Christians have been delivered from sin." It was the pastor's last words that released her anger as she recalled the redeeming grace Christ had given her.

In today's lesson, the apostle Paul explains the blessing that comes from God to all those who have been justified by faith. What happens when we forget about those blessings?

——————— Keep in Mind ———————

"Therefore being justified by faith, we have peace with God through our Lord Jesus Christ" (Romans 5:1, KJV).

"Therefore, since we have been made right in God's sight by faith, we have peace with God because of what Jesus Christ our Lord has done for us" (Romans 5:1, NLT).

Focal Verses

KJV **Romans 5:1** Therefore being justified by faith, we have peace with God through our Lord Jesus Christ:

2 By whom also we have access by faith into this grace wherein we stand, and rejoice in hope of the glory of God.

3 And not only so, but we glory in tribulations also: knowing that tribulation worketh patience;

4 And patience, experience; and experience, hope:

5 And hope maketh not ashamed; because the love of God is shed abroad in our hearts by the Holy Ghost which is given unto us.

6 For when we were yet without strength, in due time Christ died for the ungodly.

7 For scarcely for a righteous man will one die: yet peradventure for a good man some would even dare to die.

8 But God commendeth his love toward us, in that, while we were yet sinners, Christ died for us.

9 Much more then, being now justified by his blood, we shall be saved from wrath through him.

10 For if, when we were enemies, we were reconciled to God by the death of his Son, much more, being reconciled, we shall be saved by his life.

11 And not only so, but we also joy in God through our Lord Jesus Christ, by whom we have now received the atonement.

NLT **Romans 5:1** Therefore, since we have been made right in God's sight by faith, we have peace with God because of what Jesus Christ our Lord has done for us.

2 Because of our faith, Christ has brought us into this place of undeserved privilege where we now stand, and we confidently and joyfully look forward to sharing God's glory.

3 We can rejoice, too, when we run into problems and trials, for we know that they help us develop endurance.

4 And endurance develops strength of character, and character strengthens our confident hope of salvation.

5 And this hope will not lead to disappointment. For we know how dearly God loves us, because he has given us the Holy Spirit to fill our hearts with his love.

6 When we were utterly helpless, Christ came at just the right time and died for us sinners.

7 Now, most people would not be willing to die for an upright person, though someone might perhaps be willing to die for a person who is especially good.

8 But God showed his great love for us by sending Christ to die for us while we were still sinners.

9 And since we have been made right in God's sight by the blood of Christ, he will certainly save us from God's condemnation.

10 For since our friendship with God was restored by the death of his Son while we were still his enemies, we will certainly be saved through the life of his Son.

11 So now we can rejoice in our wonderful new relationship with God because our Lord Jesus Christ has made us friends of God.

The People, Places, and Times

Reconciliation. Reconciliation is at the heart of Pauline theology. The word reconciliation was not used in a religious sense by the other religions of Paul's time. Reconciliation is roughly the same as justification, but is broader and includes the aspect of forgiveness. The same God who judges also reconciles, so through reconciliation the sinner's guilt is removed. Reconciliation comes from God's initiative. Christians are brand-new people (2 Corinthians 5:17-19). The Holy Spirit gives us new life, and we are not the same anymore. We are recreated and live in union with Christ (Colossians 2:6). God brings us back to Himself by blotting out our sins and declaring us righteous. Because we have been reconciled to God, we have the privilege of leading others to do the same. This is our ministry of reconciliation.

Apostle Paul. Apostles were literally "the sent out ones." God called them, equipped them, and then sent them to establish His Word among His people. The Apostle Paul was, as he said, an apostle "born out of due time" (1 Corinthians 15:8) meaning he was late to be called one of the apostles. He was, in fact, an enemy to the early church until God plucked him out from among his Pharisaical brothers. However, Paul showed the same zeal in serving Christ that he had shown in persecuting Him and His people. He was radically changed, completely taken with his Master. His loyalty to Jesus was unimpeachable, and he was driven to get others to follow with the same zeal. He was completely convinced of salvation by grace. In these verses, he shows that this salvation gives a new perspective, one that carries us through even the toughest times.

Background

Before Jesus came, no one could ever be intimate with God. In presenting his case, Paul has proved that all humanity stands guilty before God. He has clearly shown that no one can ever be saved through deeds such as circumcision or obedience to the law. He has used Abraham as an example of how anyone can achieve right standing with God through faith. If Paul's readers stopped reading at this point, they would know that they needed salvation and it was available to them.

In chapter 4, the apostle Paul established that Abraham is the father of the family of faith, not just of the Hebrews. All who believe that God raised Jesus from the dead and receive Him as Lord and Savior are Abraham's spiritual seed. In verse 25, Paul makes a transitional statement concerning Christ being raised for our justification. Paul is now finished with his discussion of Abraham. Justification is the first blessing of the Christian life and carries with it many other blessings. When believers are justified, they receive everything God has to give. In chapter 5, Paul explains the blessing of our salvation: justification brings us peace with God and access to Him by faith, and Christ is the basis of our justification. Paul almost sings with the joy of his confidence in God. Accepting God at His Word has accomplished what human effort could not; it has given believers peace with God.

At-A-Glance

1. The Blessings of Justification
(Romans 5:1-5)
2. The Beauty of Justification (vv. 6-8)
3. The Reconciliation of God Leads to
Our Joy (vv. 9–11)

In Depth

1. The Blessings of Justification (Romans 5:1-5)

We have peace with God because we are justified. Trusting faith has given us what working to keep the law could never give us—peace with God. Christ paid the price for our rebellion and brought about the end of hostilities between the creature and the Creator. Everyone who rejects God's offer of reconciliation through Christ chooses to remain God's enemy.

Because we are justified, we have "access by faith" (Romans 5:2). In the Jewish tabernacle was an inner room called the Holy of Holies, which symbolized the presence of God. The High Priest was the only person ever allowed into the Most Holy Place, and he could only enter once a year on the Day of Atonement. When Christ died on Calvary, the curtain separating the Most Holy Place from the rest of the Temple was split, signifying the acceptance by God of all God's faithful to the throne of grace.

Because we are justified, we have a new standing with God (v. 2). No one could stand the scrutiny of God if and when He begins to pick out the iniquities of the sinful. Thank God that our justification gives us a right standing before Him. The only way this is ever accomplished is through union with Christ. Being in Christ means that we are identified with His death, burial, and Resurrection (Romans 6:1-8). Because of our identification with Christ, we now stand in the place of highest privilege. Not only has God declared us not guilty, but He has also drawn us nearer to Himself.

What enables believers to rejoice in good times or bad? How can one really be happy when facing difficult trials or tragedies? Does our rejoicing mean that we never feel sad or lonely?

2. The Beauty of Justification (vv. 6-8)

After discussing the blessing that results from justification, Paul moves on to discuss the depths of God's love. The apostle highlights the absolute inability of humans to deliver themselves from the grip of sin. We needed a rescuer, and our God sent one from heaven. "Ungodly" refers to those who live impious,

wicked, and sinful lives—people with little regard for God in their minds and hearts. Christ offered Himself up as a sacrifice on the Cross to do for weak, sinful people what they could never do for themselves. What a thought: the godly dying for the ungodly!

Now Paul pens one of the most beloved sentences ever written: "But God commendeth his love toward us, in that, while we were yet sinners, Christ died for us" (Romans 5:8). Christ's death is a clear demonstration of divine love in action. This is what Christ means when He commands us to love our enemies (Matthew 5:44). Humanity was in flat-out rebellion against God. We were servants of the evil one and demonstrated our contempt for God by our lifestyles. Yet God loved us so much that He sent His Son from the glories of heaven to the filth of earth. God clothed holiness in sinful flesh and sent Christ to the Cross on our behalf. No greater expression of love has ever, or will ever, be made.

How can we harmonize God's love and His wrath (vv. 8–9)?

3. The Reconciliation of God Leads to Our Joy (vv. 9–11)

In these final verses of our text, Paul continues to expound on the benefits of our justification. We are justified and therefore saved from wrath. We have atonement with God which gives us joy. We have been reconciled to God and therefore saved by the life of Christ. In verse 9, Paul uses the phrase "much more," and again in verse 10. Then in verse 11 he adds, "And not only so." He piles one benefit upon another. He is overcome with the positive nature of our standing in Christ. Our justification through Jesus' blood has moved us from helplessness to being reconciled, no longer under His wrath but now sharing His life, which leads to our joy.

Here Paul makes an extraordinary statement: God's love reconciled us through Christ. This contrasts with false theologies stating that only Jesus is loving while the Father is vengeful. Instead, Paul explains the truth: God's love brought about our salvation through His Son.

How can we clearly see those who need hope and then share His hope with them?

Search the Scriptures

1. What result does our justification have on our relationship with God (Romans 5:1)?

2. Since we have peace with God, what should our emotional response be in times of difficulty and sorrow (vv. 2-3)?

3. How did God demonstrate His love for us beyond any doubt (v. 8)?

4. Because of sin we were separated from God and considered His enemies. How are we reconciled back to the Father (v. 10)?

Discuss the Meaning

1. Why does Paul emphasize humanity's weakness and our inability to change ourselves? Do you believe that all unsaved people are God's enemies? If so, why? If not, why not?

2. The world can suck up our hope, but it has always been this way. As followers of Christ, we will need to understand how to allow His hope into our lives. How can we connect our redemption to a daily hopeful outlook?

Liberating Lesson

It is interesting that the Scripture never presents living in faith and being hopeful as requests but as commands. We should keep in mind that the Lord is aware of our weaknesses even more than we are. He also knows our enemies and challenges but still requires our victorious outlook. When we are fearful and unsettled, then it shows we are not focused on His assurances.

Our believing brothers and sisters need to see our hope in the Lord. Our hopeless world needs to see our hope as well. When we correct

our relationship with Christ—when our daily walk is firm—we will grow in the ability to share this hope.

Application for Activation

Share the eternal truths of today's lesson with at least two people this week. Explain how Christ's death not only reconciles us to God but also empowers us to live godly lives. Record the reactions of the people you share this Good News with and be prepared to share your experiences with the class next week.

Follow the Spirit

What God wants me to do:

_____

_____

_____

_____

_____

_____

Remember Your Thoughts

Special insights I have learned:

_____

_____

_____

_____

_____

_____

More Light on the Text

Romans 5:1-11

1 Therefore being justified by faith, we have peace with God through our Lord Jesus Christ:

With the close of the fourth chapter, Paul completes his teaching on how God justifies a person. Justification is the initial blessing of salvation, but it carries with it all the other blessings of Christian life. In chapter 5, Paul launches into an explanation of eight attendant blessings of justification by faith. Because we are justified by faith, we have "peace with God" (v. 1); "access" to God's presence and standing in grace, joy, and "hope" (v. 2); "the love of God" and "the Holy Ghost" (v. 5); we are "saved from wrath" (v. 9); and "saved by his life" (v. 10).

A literal translation of verse 1 is: "Since we have been justified by faith, let us have peace with God." "Justified" is in the Greek past tense and points to an accomplished fact. This illustrates that justification is not a process, but rather an instantaneous act that takes place at the moment a sinner receives Christ as Lord.

The phrase "we have peace with God" could also be translated as "let us have peace with God." The "let us" is from the Greek present tense verb *echomen*, which means to keep on having or enjoying our peace with God. It is the privilege of those who are justified to "have peace with God," and Paul is encouraging believers to both realize this privilege and to enjoy it. As believers, we must never allow doubt or fear to rob us of what is rightfully ours. This "peace," translated from the Greek word *eirene*, is first a change in God's relationship to us. Then, as the natural consequence of God's changed relationship to us, we change in our relationship toward Him. Because of our fallen nature, humanity is in a state of hostility with God. In other words, sinners are God's enemies (see v. 10). When we are justified, that hostility is removed and we have "peace with God."

Awareness of our peace with God brings a sense of peace to our souls.

2 By whom also we have access by faith into this grace wherein we stand, and rejoice in hope of the glory of God. 3 And not only so, but we glory in tribulations also: knowing that tribulation worketh patience; 4 And patience, experience; and experience, hope:

Not only does Christ remove the hostility that existed between God and sinners, but He also gives us "access" (Gk. *prosagoge*, pro-sah-go-**GAY**, a bringing to) into His very presence. In the Hebrew Temple, the presence of God was in a room called the Holy of Holies. A thick veil separated this room from the rest of the Temple, and only the high priest was allowed past the veil once a year to purify the altar which has been made unclean by the sins of the people (Leviticus 16:16). This curtain represented the separation of sinful humanity from God.

When Christ died on the Cross, the veil that led to the Holy of Holies ripped down the middle (Matthew 27:51). Ripping the veil represented the elimination of the separation so that all believers now have access to God. Christ's eternal sacrifice on our behalf brings us into the presence of God and allows us to have continuous access to Him.

Being justified by faith also brings us into a new permanent standing with God where we enjoy His divine favor. The basis of our new standing is obtained by grace. No one can stand before God by his own deeds, character, or righteousness. Our new standing is totally the result of God's undeserved favor.

Therefore, we rejoice "in hope of the glory of God." The glory spoken of here is twofold. First, we hope to experience the Divine Presence in heaven. Second and more immediate, we hope to bring glory to God through and in our tribulations.

Paul says we glory or rejoice in tribulation because we realize it is heaven's way of teaching us patience or longsuffering. Patience is the confident endurance of things hoped for or difficulties we wish removed. The spiritual fruit of patience (cf. Galatians 5:22) is seen in the humble endurance of ill because of the realization that nothing comes against us that has not been allowed by God.

This patience then brings about "experience" (Gk. *dokime*, doe-kee-**MAY**), a word also translated as "proof" (2 Corinthians 2:9, 13:3; Philippians 2:22). Proof is the experimental evidence that we have believed through grace.

Believers enter periods of tribulation and patiently endure. Our patient endurance is rewarded with eventual victory over our circumstance, and our victorious experience proves the faithfulness to God to deliver us from future trials. Another meaning for *dokime* is "character." Testings prove or establish our character because it is made evident through patient endurance. Then, experience brings us back to "hope."

We have hope in two distinct ways and at two successive stages of the Christian life. First, immediately upon believing, along with the sense of peace and abiding access to God, we have hope in our new relationship. Next, hope grows after the reality of our faith has been proven by the patient endurance of trials sent to test it. Our hope comes from looking away from ourselves to the Cross of Christ, then looking into ourselves as being transformed into the image of Christ. In the first case, our hope is based on faith and in the second by experience.

5 And hope maketh not ashamed; because the love of God is shed abroad in our hearts by the Holy Ghost which is given unto us.

Our hope of heaven, which presupposes faith, is the confident expectation of future good. Our faith assures us that heaven will be ours, and our hope expectantly anticipates it. This hope in the glory of God will never make us ashamed (like empty hopes do) because it is based on "the love of God"—not our love of God, but His love of us which is "shed abroad" (Gk. *ekkheo*, ek-**KHE**-oh, "poured forth," used literally of blood or wine, and figuratively of love or the Holy Spirit itself). God's love for us is seen in the indwelling presence of the Holy Spirit.

6 For when we were yet without strength, in due time Christ died for the ungodly.

At the appointed time, Christ offered Himself as our eternal sacrifice "when we were yet without strength"—that is, when we were powerless to deliver ourselves and therefore ready to perish. Christ's death reveals three properties of God's love. First, "the ungodly" are those whose character and sinful nature are repulsive in the eyes of God. Second, He did this when they were "without strength"—nothing stood between humanity and damnation but divine compassion. Third, He did this "in due time" when it was most appropriate that it should take place.

The phrase "in due time" shows that God has always been involved in human history. Nothing catches Him by surprise. The good Lord had always planned to send Christ to die for us; He made the initial announcement after humanity's fall from grace (Genesis 3:15). Then, at just the right time, He sent His only begotten Son to teach, minister, and die for the sinful. Whenever we think things in our lives are running out of control, we can remember that God always moves "in due time."

7 For scarcely for a righteous man will one die: yet peradventure for a good man some would even dare to die. 8 But God commendeth his love toward us, in that, while we were yet sinners, Christ died for us.

The apostle now proceeded to illustrate God's compassion. Few, if any people, would be willing to sacrifice their lives for a "righteous man" of exceptional character. A few more might be willing to die for a man who, besides being exceptional, is also distinguished for goodness or a benefactor to society. But God, in glorious contrast to what men might do for each other, displayed His love, "while we were yet sinners"—that is, in a state in of absolute rebellion—"Christ died for us."

9 Much more then, being now justified by his blood, we shall be saved from wrath through him. 10 For if, when we were enemies, we were reconciled to God by the death of his Son, much more, being reconciled, we shall be saved by his life.

Having been "justified by his blood," we shall be saved from wrath through the sacrifice of Christ. Christ's death restored our relationship with God while we were in open rebellion against Him. Since we are now reconciled, "we shall be saved by his life." If Christ's sacrifice was offered for people incapable of the least appreciation for God's love or Christ's labors on their behalf, how much more will He do all that remains to be done? "For since our friendship with God was restored by the death of his Son while we were still his enemies, we will certainly be saved through the life of his Son." (v. 10, NLT). To be "saved from wrath through him" refers to the entire work of salvation—from the moment of justification to the great white throne judgment (Revelation 20:11–15), when the wrath of God shall be revealed to all who ignore the Gospel of Jesus. The Apostle Jude best described Christ's continuing work of salvation when he said that He "is able to keep you from falling, and to present you faultless before the presence of his glory with exceeding joy" (Jude 24).

11 And not only so, but we also joy in God through our Lord Jesus Christ, by whom we have now received the atonement.

"And not only so" refers back to the blessing Paul mentioned previously. We not only find joy in our newfound peace, access, standing, hope, love, indwelling, and salvation, but we rejoice in God Himself. We find joy in our God for what He has done and for who He is. Our joy proceeds from our union with Christ who brought about our atonement.

"Atonement" (Gk. *katallage*, kah-tah-lah-**GAY**) is the noun form of the verb for reconciling in v. 10. It indicates a shift from a negative relationship to a positive one or from a broken relationship to a healthy one. Paul moves beyond the sacrificial language here to focus on the restored relationship that Christ's atoning death provides. This restored relationship with God brings about joy, or more literally boasting (see v. 2).

Atonement is the gracious act by which God restores a relationship of harmony and unity between Himself and believers. The word contains parts that express this great truth in simple but profound terms: "at-one." Through God's atoning grace and forgiveness, we are reinstated to a relationship of being "at one" with God.

Sources:
Henry, Matthew. *Matthew Henry's Commentary on the Whole Bible: New Modern Edition.* Vols. 1-6. Peabody, MA: Hendrickson Publishers, Inc., 2009.
Strong, James. *The New Strong's Exhaustive Concordance of the Bible.* Nashville, TN: Thomas Nelson, 2003.
Thayer, Joseph Henry. *A Greek-English Lexicon of the New Testament.* New York: American Book Company, 1889.

Say It Correctly

Commendeth. kuh-**MEN**-dith.
Peradventure. pur-ad-**VIN**-ture.

Daily Bible Readings

MONDAY
Blessed Are Persecuted Believers
(Matthew 5:9-12)

TUESDAY
Jesus, Not Suffering, Matters
(Philippians 1:12-20)

WEDNESDAY
Suffering for Christ and the Church
(2 Corinthians 11:21-30)

THURSDAY
In Hope Our Salvation Is Secure
(Romans 8:18-25)

FRIDAY
Free Gift of Jesus Brings Justification
(Romans 5:12-17)

SATURDAY
Grace Leads to Eternal Life
(Romans 5:18-21)

SUNDAY
Justified through Faith in Jesus Christ
(Romans 5:1-11)

Notes

_____

_____

_____

_____

Teaching Tips

August 1
Bible Study Guide 9

Words You Should Know

A. Heart (Romans 10:6) *kardia* (Gk.)—The center of one's physical and spiritual life

B. Deep (v. 7) *abussos* (Gk.)—A pit of an immeasurable depth used to hold the dead

Teacher Preparation

Unifying Principle—Seeking Confidence. Many people lack confidence in addressing life's circumstances. How can one gain trust? Salvation comes to all who confess Jesus Christ as Lord and believe in their hearts.

A. Read the Bible Background and Devotional Reading.

B. Pray for your students and lesson clarity.

C. Read the lesson Scripture in multiple translations.

O—Open the Lesson

A. Begin the class with prayer.

B. Ask students to consider whether they extend themselves beyond their personal comfort zones to share the Gospel with others. Discuss the effectiveness of your church's outreach and evangelism ministries.

C. Have the students read the Aim for Change and the In Focus story.

D. Ask students how events like those in the story weigh on their hearts and how they can view these events from a faith perspective.

P—Present the Scriptures

A. Read the Focal Verses and discuss the Background and The People, Places, and Times sections.

B. Have the class share what Scriptures stand out for them and why, with particular emphasis on today's themes.

E—Explore the Meaning

A. Use In Depth or More Light on the Text to facilitate a deeper discussion of the lesson text.

B. Pose the questions in Search the Scriptures and Discuss the Meaning.

C. Discuss the Liberating Lesson and Application for Activation sections.

N—Next Steps for Application

A. Summarize the value of the joy of their relationship established through Christ.

B. End class with a commitment to pray for family members and friends who are not Christians or who refuse to hear the Gospel.

Worship Guide

For the Superintendent or Teacher
Theme: Salvation for All Who Believe
Song: "'Whosoever' Meaneth Me"
Devotional Reading: Psalm 19:1–14

Salvation for All Who Believe

Bible Background • ROMANS 10:5–17
Printed Text • ROMANS 10:5–17 | Devotional Reading • PSALM 19:1–14

——————— Aim for Change ———————

By the end of this lesson, we will EXPLAIN Paul's confidence in the salvation offered in Christ, FEEL justified through our faith in Christ, and EMBRACE with joy the possibility for all.

——————— In Focus ———————

For three months, Cathy had been looking for work. She prayed that the Lord would give her a job where she would have the opportunity to share the Gospel with her fellow workers. Cathy was a trained and certified accountant but no doors were opening for her.

One morning, Cathy received a call from a local rehabilitation center that had gotten her name from a former employee. The center was hiring, but not in the accounting department. The personnel director was so impressed by Cathy's work ethic and resume, he asked Cathy if she would be interested in training men and women who had just been released from prison so that they might successfully return to society and work. She asked for a week to consider.

Cathy continued looking for employment in her field, but nothing materialized. After several sleepless nights, Cathy wondered if this assignment was an answer to her prayer. She decided to step out on faith and take the position.

Within the first month, God gave Cathy favor with her supervisor so that she could start a weekly Bible study. More than 75% of the patients attended and Cathy was able to lead many of them to Christ. Nearly everyone Cathy trained was successful in finding good-paying jobs and becoming witnesses for Christ where they worked.

How has God shown you unexpected ways to make a path to share the Gospel with those around you?

——————— Keep in Mind ———————

"For whosoever shall call upon the name of the Lord shall be saved"
(Romans 10:13, KJV).

"For 'Everyone who calls on the name of the LORD will be saved'"
(Romans 10:13, NLT).

Focal Verses

KJV **Romans 10:5** For Moses describeth the righteousness which is of the law, That the man which doeth those things shall live by them.

6 But the righteousness which is of faith speaketh on this wise, Say not in thine heart, Who shall ascend into heaven? (that is, to bring Christ down from above:)

7 Or, Who shall descend into the deep? (that is, to bring up Christ again from the dead.)

8 But what saith it? The word is nigh thee, even in thy mouth, and in thy heart: that is, the word of faith, which we preach;

9 That if thou shalt confess with thy mouth the Lord Jesus, and shalt believe in thine heart that God hath raised him from the dead, thou shalt be saved.

10 For with the heart man believeth unto righteousness; and with the mouth confession is made unto salvation.

11 For the scripture saith, Whosoever believeth on him shall not be ashamed.

12 For there is no difference between the Jew and the Greek: for the same Lord over all is rich unto all that call upon him.

13 For whosoever shall call upon the name of the Lord shall be saved.

14 How then shall they call on him in whom they have not believed? and how shall they believe in him of whom they have not heard? and how shall they hear without a preacher?

15 And how shall they preach, except they be sent? as it is written, How beautiful are the feet of them that preach the gospel of peace, and bring glad tidings of good things!

16 But they have not all obeyed the gospel. For Esaias saith, Lord, who hath believed our report?

17 So then faith cometh by hearing, and hearing by the word of God.

NLT **Romans 10:5** For Moses writes that the law's way of making a person right with God requires obedience to all of its commands.

6 But faith's way of getting right with God says, "Don't say in your heart, 'Who will go up to heaven?' (to bring Christ down to earth).

7 And don't say, 'Who will go down to the place of the dead?' (to bring Christ back to life again)."

8 In fact, it says, "The message is very close at hand; it is on your lips and in your heart." And that message is the very message about faith that we preach:

9 If you openly declare that Jesus is Lord and believe in your heart that God raised him from the dead, you will be saved.

10 For it is by believing in your heart that you are made right with God, and it is by openly declaring your faith that you are saved.

11 As the Scriptures tell us, "Anyone who trusts in him will never be disgraced."

12 Jew and Gentile are the same in this respect. They have the same Lord, who gives generously to all who call on him.

13 For "Everyone who calls on the name of the LORD will be saved."

14 But how can they call on him to save them unless they believe in him? And how can they believe in him if they have never heard about him? And how can they hear about him unless someone tells them?

15 And how will anyone go and tell them without being sent? That is why the Scriptures say, "How beautiful are the feet of messengers who bring good news!"

16 But not everyone welcomes the Good News, for Isaiah the prophet said, "LORD, who has believed our message?"

17 So faith comes from hearing, that is, hearing the Good News about Christ.

559

The People, Places, and Times

Word of Faith. The apostle's letter reaffirms the basic doctrine of salvation by faith—not works—available to Jews and Gentiles alike. He also affirms that preaching as a form of word-of-mouth promotion continues to be a primary way to spread the Gospel and to build a foundation of faith necessary to desire and receive salvation.

Israel in God's Plan of Salvation. In Romans, the Apostle Paul addresses Israel's past election, present rejection of the Gospel, and their future salvation. How could God's promise to Abraham and the nation of Israel remain valid while the nation of Israel as a whole seems to have no part in the spread of the Gospel? Paul maintains that God's promise to Israel has not failed because the promise was meant only for "true Israel"—meaning, those who were faithful to the promise (see Genesis 12:1-3; 17:19). Paul contends that Israel's failure to respond to Christ is not due to an unconditional decree of God but to their unbelief and disobedience (see Romans 10:3).

The apostle also affirms that Israel's rejection is only partial and temporary. The nation will eventually accept God's salvation in Christ. God has turned Israel's transgression into an opportunity to proclaim salvation to all the world. Belief in Jesus Christ by a portion of national Israel will take place in the future. The Scriptures are full of promises of the eventual restoration of Israel to God through their acceptance of the Messiah. (See Isaiah 11:10-16.)

What role does the modern nation of Israel have in God's salvation plan for Abraham, Isaac, and Jacob's descendants?

Background

Born a Jew, Paul was highly educated in the Jewish faith and understood the doctrine, teaching, and workings of the Law. His education, training, and love for the Law contributed to his zealous opposition of Christians and their teachings. As a former persecutor of Christians, therefore, he understood how zeal for a cause could turn a person into a murderous opponent.

After his dramatic conversion while traveling to Damascus to detain and imprison Christians (Acts 9), Paul became a defender of the faith he had, up to then, despised. More so, he became the apostle to the Gentiles and the one directly called to reach his former enemies.

In addressing the believers at the church of Rome, Paul confesses his fervent prayer that his Jewish brothers would be saved. He relates that he can "bear record" of their zeal without knowledge, referring to his former anti-Christian activities.

Finally, he makes it clear that the church of Rome should not become cocky in their position in Christ, because God plans to restore a remnant of Israel. Rather, Paul admonishes Gentile believers not to get conceited about their faith in light of Israel's present disobedience.

At-A-Glance

1. We Cannot be Saved by the Law (Romans 10:5)
2. We are Saved Through Jesus Christ, the Only Way (vv. 6-7)
3. We Must Become Christians, but How? (vv. 8-13)
4. We Must Take the Good News to Others (vv. 14-17)

In Depth

1. We Cannot be Saved by the Law (Romans 10:5)

Paul enlightens these Gentile and Jewish believers about the futility of trying to be saved by the Law. He shows them and us today that no one can meet such high standards set by the

Law and be saved. After all, we are all sinners. He wants us to appreciate that to be saved by the Law, a person would have to live a perfect life and no one but Jesus Christ Himself could do that. Sinning even one time would mean that we would be lost.

Paul explains further that God gave the Law, not to save us, but to show us how guilty we are before a Holy God; to show us our lostness, our dilemma. The sacrificial system of the Law educated people of their need for a lamb without blemish. That lamb is Jesus Christ (Hebrews 10:1-4).

Why did God give Moses the Law if it could not save?

2. We are Saved Through Jesus Christ, the Only Way (vv. 6-7)

Jesus is the end of the Law. With His death, burial, and Resurrection, He fulfilled the purpose and goal of the Law (Matthew 5:17). Unlike Jesus Christ, however, the Law cannot save anyone. Nothing can bridge the gap between a holy God and sinful man. Receiving Jesus Christ as Lord and Savior is the only way. The salvation that God offers is a gift and we need to respond and receive it, or be lost forever. God's salvation is right in front of us. Paul emphasizes the closeness of salvation, and how simple God has made it to be restored to Him. Faith in Christ is not too high above us, up in heaven where we cannot reach. It is not down in the depths of the earth, in realms of darkness and death.

3. We Must Become Christians, but How? (vv. 8-13)

Sin has cut us off from God, but Paul explains how to get back to God and be saved. It is not a complicated process, but based on a simple faith in the finished work of Jesus on the Cross. God said that if we confess with our mouths that Jesus is Lord, and believe in our heart that

God, Himself, raised Jesus from the dead; then we are saved (v. 9). This profession can be made by both Jews and Gentiles alike (v. 12) because with God there is no favoritism when it comes to salvation (Romans 2:11). Paul wanted both Jews and Gentiles to know in this letter that our sins point out our need for a Savior. We need to be cleansed and made whole—and only Jesus can do that.

4. We Must Take the Good News to Others (vv. 14-17)

God is calling us to bring the Good News of salvation to others. Through our Christian living, loving, teaching, and preaching; they will know that we follow Christ. If God's Spirit is indeed in us, we will obey this command. If this is not true of us, then we need to examine ourselves seriously before the Word.

As Paul explains the process of calling, believing, hearing, telling, and sending, we understand the large network within the Church that evangelism requires to reach souls for the Gospel. Often we think of evangelism as a task for others with that specific spiritual gift, but everyone in the Church should be using their gifts, time, and talents to further the ultimate goal of evangelism everywhere.

Are all Christians responsible for preaching the Gospel to non-Christians? What does that look like?

Search the Scriptures

1. What must a person believe about God and Jesus to receive salvation (Romans 10:9)?

2. How does God use the preacher (v. 14)? Can just anyone be a preacher (v. 15)?

Discuss the Meaning

1. What kind of preaching do we need in order to build faith?

2. Why does God seem to have a special place in His heart for Israel if He shows no favoritism?

Liberating Lesson

God surely has a sense of humor. Religious, racial, and economic barriers separate people and fuel hatred and discord. But, just when we think we know it all and are better than everyone else, God provides a Damascus Road experience to shed light on our own unrighteousness and neediness. Our perceived enemies today may be our mission fields tomorrow. Jesus died and was resurrected because of God's love for all persons. How does knowing this make it easier to share your faith with nonbelievers?

Application for Activation

There are people all around you who need to hear the Good News of salvation. Determine in your heart and carry out the plan of witnessing to someone in your family, on your job, or in your community. Pray first and ask God to show you someone who needs a Savior and then, help you to find the right time, place, and words to obey His command.

Follow the Spirit

What God wants me to do:

_____

_____

_____

_____

Remember Your Thoughts

Special insights I have learned:

_____

_____

_____

_____

More Light on the Text
Romans 10:5-17

Paul's letter to the church in Rome is written to speak to both Jewish and Gentile Christians. It is overflowing with the theme of salvation through faith in Christ, and not of works. Paul is addressing Jewish and Gentile Christians, creating an environment of peace and unity rooted in faith in Christ.

5 For Moses describeth the righteousness which is of the law, That the man which doeth those things shall live by them.

The description the apostle Paul gives of the righteousness of the Law is written in Leviticus 18:5: "Ye shall therefore keep my statutes, and my judgments: which if a man do, he shall live in them." Paul is speaking of God's command to the people to observe and keep the moral law. The word "righteousness" (Gk. *dikaiosune*, dee-kay-oh-**SOO**-nay) means to be in a condition acceptable to God. Righteousness in the Law is directly related to human works, both external and internal. In the Law, the emphasis is placed on human activity, and righteousness is based on one's actions and deeds. The Law required perfect obedience, something impossible for fallen mankind.

6 But the righteousness which is of faith speaketh on this wise, Say not in thine heart, Who shall ascend into heaven? (that is, to bring Christ down from above:) 7 Or, Who shall descend into the deep? (that is, to bring up Christ again from the dead.)

Paul moves his reader from the righteousness of the Law to the righteousness of faith. Paul uses phrases taken from Deuteronomy 30:12-13, inserting commentary in running text with the words of Scripture, as was common in Jewish Midrash teaching. Just as Moses left the Children of Israel without an excuse as they promised to keep God's Law as they prepared to enter Canaan, Paul is leaving both his original audience and his modern-day readers without an excuse. The righteousness of faith is not a mystery. It is not hidden in the heavens, nor is it buried in the deep. The righteousness of faith is not attainable by human actions. It is not necessary or possible for any person to go to heaven or to launch into the deep to bring Christ and have Him revealed. Christ has done all the work necessary for humans to obtain the right standing with God.

Christ descended from heaven, took on human form, and fulfilled all the righteousness of the law by living a life free of sin. He bore the penalty of sin, suffered on the Cross, died, and rose again so that we might be declared righteous, regardless of the sins we have committed.

8 But what saith it? The word is nigh thee, even in thy mouth, and in thy heart: that is, the word of faith, which we preach;

Continuing to echo Moses' words, Paul reminds us that the word is near us, in our mouth and heart; it is not based on what we will or will not do but is based solely on faith. It is not what we must do, but what we must believe. The mystery of salvation, the righteousness of faith, has been revealed in Christ. "Word" here (Gk. *rhema*, **RAY**-mah) means that which is or has been uttered by the living voice, the spoken word. The word is the message here. The way of righteousness has come to you. It is not in the Law, works, deeds, or behaviors; but it is in your mouth and in your heart. The word of faith—righteousness based on faith—is what the apostle Paul is proclaiming.

Paul's message to the church in Rome is equally relevant to the modern Christian regardless of location. We should not focus on outward deeds as a measuring tool for inward righteousness. Our focus on "works" righteousness will prevent us from seeing Christ (Romans 9:32). The message is to believe that God exists, He is the Creator, and that He provides salvation and right standing to His creation through Jesus Christ. This is the message that exceeds time and supersedes context and culture. Our justification and righteousness are rooted in our proclamation with our mouth and our belief in our heart that Jesus is Lord.

9 That if thou shalt confess with thy mouth the Lord Jesus, and shalt believe in thine heart that God hath raised him from the dead, thou shalt be saved.

The Greek word for "saved" is *sozo* (**SODE**-zo) meaning to save a suffering one from perishing. Notice the difference between the conditions of the Law and the righteousness of faith. The requirements of the Law were impossible. Yet salvation by faith is simple and easily attainable by anyone willing to confess and believe. This inward belief and outward confession speaks to both Jesus as man and Jesus as God. We are not saved by our actions, so there is nothing magical about speaking the words "the Lord Jesus." Rather, the change comes because, when we confess Jesus as Lord, we must allow Him to reign over us in total. It should also speak of our ability, through Christ, to live a life that represents Christ internally on the inside of us. Our outward life should be a testimony of our inward faith. While we are not perfect, let us continue to press toward perfection in Christ Jesus (Philippians 3:14).

The belief that God raised Jesus from the dead speaks of His triumph over sin, death, and the grave. It grounds Christian belief in the historical fact of the Resurrection, and it affirms God the Father's complete power and authority over all creation.

10 For with the heart man believeth unto righteousness; and with the mouth confession is made unto salvation.

Righteousness begins in the heart. It is belief with all your heart that Jesus took on human nature, walked among mankind, lived a life free of sin, died on the Cross, and was resurrected from the dead. Belief is the key requirement for God to impart righteousness, right relationship with Him. This belief in our heart is confirmed and reaffirmed by the confession of our mouth.

"Salvation" (Gk. *soteria*, so-tay-**REE**-ah) means deliverance and preservation. Salvation then comes from God through Christ and is not based on one's works of righteousness, but through believing in the heart and confessing with the mouth. We must refrain from any attempt to add to the requirements of salvation. Notice it does say that you must not do this, or stop doing that. Salvation is simple and easy and is accessible to even a small child with limited understanding. The belief in the heart and the confession of the mouth provides the Christian with redemption from the wages of sin and preservation from eternal damnation. The salvation of the Christian is both in the present and the future. The Christian is called to live victoriously and abundantly in this life, and in the life to come.

11 For the scripture saith, Whosoever believeth on him shall not be ashamed. 12 For there is no difference between the Jew and the Greek: for the same Lord over all is rich unto all that call upon him. 13 For whosoever shall call upon the name of the Lord shall be saved.

Paul touts the inclusiveness of the Gospel of Jesus Christ. "Whosoever" does not omit anyone willing to believe in their heart and confess with their mouth the Lordship of Jesus Christ. The "whosoever" is not contingent upon race, gender, economic status, educational achievements, or human accolades. The "whosoever" bridges the gap between those that "have" and those that "have not." Paul speaks to both the Jewish and Gentile Christians. Christ is the common denominator and liberates us from the keeping of the Law. Christ moves beyond the Law of Moses and Jewish custom and opens the door for all to access the covenant blessings of God.

Christ is the ultimate example of God's impartiality toward His creation, and His desire to see all mankind redeemed. God is ready to pour out His abundance upon all those who call upon Him. Verse 13 is taken from Joel 2:32 and is used to show that God is rich in mercy and is ready to receive all who ask and dispense grace and salvation—deliverance from the penalty of judgment.

Salvation through faith in Jesus Christ moved beyond Jewish custom and culture practices. In the same manner, we are unable to earn our salvation through good works, church culture, and tradition. So often the church gets hung up on how one should interact with the world or how one should act in church that they almost seem to add works and requirements to God's salvation. We must also strive to live a life that represents Christ and the power of the Holy Spirit to operate as Lord in and over our life. A life in Christ should differ from a life void of Christ. However, our distance from the world will look different from region to region, from generation to generation, and even from person to person. Christians must be careful to not judge one another based on outward actions.

14 How then shall they call on him in whom they have not believed? and how shall they believe in him of whom they have not heard? and how shall they hear without a preacher? 15 And how shall they preach, except they be sent? as it is written, How beautiful are the

feet of them that preach the gospel of peace, and bring glad tidings of good things!

Salvation comes through faith in Jesus Christ and the Resurrection. In order to believe, you must first hear the Gospel. In order to hear the Gospel, it must be preached. Who will preach the Good News for all to hear? Paul's charge to preach should be embraced by every Christian. Who will be sent to preach, proclaim, and share the Gospel? Anyone willing to go. You don't have to be a pastor, minister, or special person to share the Gospel, though. Be willing to share your testimony of salvation through faith in Jesus Christ to all who will listen. Preaching the Gospel is not limited to the Sunday preacher, for they can only reach those few who will come into the church. Every Christian has a responsibility to share Sunday's message with the friends, family, and co-workers they encounter throughout the week. The only sermon that some will hear will be the one you preach. The only Bible that some will read will be the life you live.

We need not be afraid to share the Gospel. Jesus promises to give us the words when we need them. Even if we do not lead people all the way to salvation, we can help them along the way. Remember, what we share is *good* news. Christian faith is not about limitations and rules; it is about relationship with an amazing God.

16 But they have not all obeyed the gospel. For Esaias saith, Lord, who hath believed our report? 17 So then faith cometh by hearing, and hearing by the word of God.

Not all Jews who heard the message of Jesus Christ embraced and believed unto salvation; neither did all the Gentiles. However, that did not keep Paul and others from preaching the Good News, that Jesus the Messiah had come, died, and rose from the grave. The same is true today. Not everyone who hears the message of Jesus Christ will accept the invitation to salvation. However, that does not relieve us of our responsibility to preach to all we can. We have a commission to spread the Gospel throughout the world (Mark 16:15). Our commission to preach the Good News is independent of the hearers' response to the message preached.

Therefore, if people are going to have faith in God, the message of Jesus Christ must be preached. It is impossible to believe in what you have never heard. Hearing of the Word of God ignites our faith. It is not always a one-time hearing, but it is a continuous hearing of the Word of God that feeds our faith. Whether you are a new convert or a seasoned Christian, it is imperative that your faith is continuously fed the Word of God, and that you may be strengthened on this spiritual journey.

Sources:
The Full Life Study Bible. Donald C. Stamps, gen. ed. Grand Rapids, Michigan: Zondervan Publishing Co., 1992. 1748-1749.
Henry, Matthew. *Matthew Henry's Commentary on the Whole Bible: New Modern Edition.* Vols. 1-6. Peabody, MA: Hendrickson Publishers, Inc., 2009.
Strong, James. *The New Strong's Exhaustive Concordance of the Bible.* Nashville, TN: Thomas Nelson, 2003.
Thayer, Joseph Henry. *A Greek-English Lexicon of the New Testament.* New York: American Book Company, 1889.

Say It Correctly

Esaias. eh-**SIGH**-us.
Midrash. **MIDD**-rash.

Daily Bible Readings

MONDAY
Obey God with Heart and Voice
(Deuteronomy 30:6-14)

TUESDAY
God's Salvation Announced
(Isaiah 52:1-10)

WEDNESDAY
Call on the Name of the Lord
(Joel 2:28-32)

THURSDAY
Gentiles Believe by Faith
(Galatians 3:6-14)

FRIDAY
For the Salvation of the Gentiles
(Romans 10:1-4)

SATURDAY
Regret for Not Hearing Christ's Word
(Romans 10:18-21)

SUNDAY
Salvation Is for All People
(Romans 10:5-17)

Notes

Teaching Tips

Words You Should Know

A. Substance (v. 1) *hupostasis* (Gk.)—Something basic or foundational; a concrete reality on which things can be built

B. Moved with fear (v. 7) *eulabetheis* (Gk.)—Possessing reverent regard for things commanded by God

Teacher Preparation

Unifying Principle—The Example of Heroes. People enduring life's miseries hopelessly plod along the way of life. What can enliven this emptiness of existence? Faith in God assures of hope and conviction of certainty.

A. Read the Bible Background and Devotional Reading.

B. Pray for your students and lesson clarity.

C. Read the lesson Scripture in multiple translations.

O—Open the Lesson

A. Begin the class with prayer.

B. Invite participants to share a person they look up to as a role model of faith. What difficult situation did this role model's example help them through?

C. Have the students read the Aim for Change and the In Focus story.

D. Ask students how events like those in the story weigh on their hearts and how they can view these events from a faith perspective.

P—Present the Scriptures

A. Read the Focal Verses and discuss the Background and The People, Places, and Times sections.

B. Have the class share what Scriptures stand out for them and why, with particular emphasis on today's themes.

E—Explore the Meaning

A. Use In Depth or More Light on the Text to facilitate a deeper discussion of the lesson text.

B. Pose the questions in Search the Scriptures and Discuss the Meaning.

C. Discuss the Liberating Lesson and Application for Activation sections.

N—Next Steps for Application

A. Summarize the value of perseverance in the face of unrealized hopes.

B. End class with a commitment to pray for patient faith as things work according to God's timetable rather than their own.

Worship Guide

For the Superintendent or Teacher
Theme: Meaning of Faith
Song: "Blessed Assurance"
Devotional Reading: Hebrews 11:32-40

Meaning of Faith

Bible Background • HEBREWS 11; 13:1-19
Printed Text • HEBREWS 11:1-8, 13-16 | Devotional Reading • HEBREWS 11:32-40

—————— Aim for Change ——————

By the end of this lesson, we will IDENTIFY the faith contributions of the heroes in Hebrews 11, VALUE the people in our lives who act heroically through faith, and GROW in our potential to become faith heroes.

———————— In Focus ————————

The telephone rang early in the morning. Frances reached out with her one good arm, picked up the phone, and answered it by saying, "Praise the Lord!"

"How are you today, Frances?" her prayer partner asked.

"I'm blessed," Frances replied. "I can answer to my name this morning, and my health is good." Frances then began to pray, thanking God for His mercy and goodness.

Frances always quoted the Scriptures back to God when she prayed. She was always careful to mention the names of the unsaved loved ones of the saints. Her list was extensive. Her prayer partner often wondered how Frances could remember so many people at her age. But Frances was committed to pray for each one.

Frances had lost the use of one arm and had been using a wheelchair for many years, but she could still pray. She was absolutely sure that God would save all of those for whom she prayed. Her mission was to stand in the gap for the unsaved until they found their way to the Way.

Frances lived to be 103 years old. At the time of her death, many of the people she prayed for had turned to Christ, but many more had not. Frances did not live to see her prayers fully answered, but she never doubted that God would answer them all.

In what part of your life do you need to have more faith in God's power to do His will? How do we live a life with complete faith in God?

—————— Keep in Mind ——————

"Now faith is the substance of things hoped for, the evidence of things not seen" (Hebrews 11:1, KJV).

"Faith shows the reality of what we hope for; it is the evidence of things we cannot see" (Hebrews 11:1, NLT).

Focal Verses

KJV **Hebrews 11:1** Now faith is the substance of things hoped for, the evidence of things not seen.

2 For by it the elders obtained a good report.

3 Through faith we understand that the worlds were framed by the word of God, so that things which are seen were not made of things which do appear.

4 By faith Abel offered unto God a more excellent sacrifice than Cain, by which he obtained witness that he was righteous, God testifying of his gifts: and by it he being dead yet speaketh.

5 By faith Enoch was translated that he should not see death; and was not found, because God had translated him: for before his translation he had this testimony, that he pleased God.

6 But without faith it is impossible to please him: for he that cometh to God must believe that he is, and that he is a rewarder of them that diligently seek him.

7 By faith Noah, being warned of God of things not seen as yet, moved with fear, prepared an ark to the saving of his house; by the which he condemned the world, and became heir of the righteousness which is by faith.

8 By faith Abraham, when he was called to go out into a place which he should after receive for an inheritance, obeyed; and he went out, not knowing whither he went.

13 These all died in faith, not having received the promises, but having seen them afar off, and were persuaded of them, and embraced them, and confessed that they were strangers and pilgrims on the earth.

14 For they that say such things declare plainly that they seek a country.

15 And truly, if they had been mindful of that country from whence they came out, they might have had opportunity to have returned.

NLT **Hebrews 11:1** Faith shows the reality of what we hope for; it is the evidence of things we cannot see.

2 Through their faith, the people in days of old earned a good reputation.

3 By faith we understand that the entire universe was formed at God's command, that what we now see did not come from anything that can be seen.

4 It was by faith that Abel brought a more acceptable offering to God than Cain did. Abel's offering gave evidence that he was a righteous man, and God showed his approval of his gifts. Although Abel is long dead, he still speaks to us by his example of faith.

5 It was by faith that Enoch was taken up to heaven without dying—"he disappeared, because God took him." For before he was taken up, he was known as a person who pleased God.

6 And it is impossible to please God without faith. Anyone who wants to come to him must believe that God exists and that he rewards those who sincerely seek him.

7 It was by faith that Noah built a large boat to save his family from the flood. He obeyed God, who warned him about things that had never happened before. By his faith Noah condemned the rest of the world, and he received the righteousness that comes by faith.

8 It was by faith that Abraham obeyed when God called him to leave home and go to another land that God would give him as his inheritance. He went without knowing where he was going.

13 All these people died still believing what God had promised them. They did not receive what was promised, but they saw it all from a distance and welcomed it. They agreed that they were foreigners and nomads here on earth.

14 Obviously people who say such things are looking forward to a country they can call their own.

16 But now they desire a better country, that is, an heavenly: wherefore God is not ashamed to be called their God: for he hath prepared for them a city.

15 If they had longed for the country they came from, they could have gone back.

16 But they were looking for a better place, a heavenly homeland. That is why God is not ashamed to be called their God, for he has prepared a city for them.

The People, Places, and Times

Enoch. Even though Enoch only appears in three verses in the Genesis record, much more is written of him in Jewish tradition. Ancient rabbis wrote about him in the books of 1 and 2 Enoch, wherein he prophesies about the end times. Enoch is listed in Hebrews 11 as the second hero of faith. The account in Genesis is concise: "Enoch walked with God: and he was not; for God took him" (Genesis 5:24). Enoch never tasted death; he went directly into the Lord's presence. The writer of Hebrews tells us that Enoch pleased God.

The Book of Hebrews. The authorship of Hebrews is unknown. Early church leaders believed that Paul wrote Hebrews, but almost all modern theologians and scholars reject this assertion. Some scholars have postulated that the author is Barnabas, which would explain certain theological similarities to Paul's letters.

The first audience of the book of Hebrews knew Jewish Scripture and professed faith in Christ. Centuries of Hebrew tradition were replaced with spiritual freedom based upon faith in Christ. As a result, the believers experienced the wrath of the Jewish religious establishment. The writer wanted to prevent believers from rejecting Christianity and returning to Judaism, and so emphasized the superiority of faith in Christ above even the Jewish faith.

Background

To encourage his audience in the faith, the writer of Hebrews explained the superiority of faith by examples of people who demonstrated greater faith. Through examples in biblical history, faith is revealed through assurance in God's future promises with the implications that inspire believers to persevere. Through the summary of Jewish history, the heroes of faith challenge believers to grow in faith and live in obedience to God.

In chapter 11, the writer of Hebrews uses a literary technique called anaphora, whereby he begins each account with the same Greek phrase translated, "By faith." Hebrews 11 is a literary masterpiece and a historical retrospective. The chapter should be studied for the eternal principles it teaches and read simply for the beauty of the writing.

At-A-Glance

1. Faith is Confidence and Certainty (Hebrews 11:1-3)
2. Faith Rewarded (vv. 4-5, 7-8)
3. Faith Is Necessary (v. 6)
4. Unfulfilled Hopes in Things Unseen (vv. 13-16)

In Depth

1. Faith is Confidence and Certainty (Hebrews 11:1-3)

Faith is vital for God's people. Having faith means taking God at His word and accepting what He says as true. The reality of faith is what is "hoped for" in the hearts and minds of believers. As the "evidence of things not seen," faith is the means of enduring against all opposition and the fiercest persecution. We cannot see the future nor do we know what will happen tomorrow, but our confidence is based upon the certainty of God's trustworthiness.

To encourage struggling believers to hold to the superiority of their faith in Christ, the writer refers the believers to the elders of the Old Testament, the patriarchs and heroes of Israel (v. 2). The "elders" received a "good report," which was their evidence that they would participate in God's Kingdom when it arrives in its fullness. Their actions revealed a genuine faith that brings them honor.

By faith, we believe God spoke and created the entire universe. Our faith is based upon who God is; our response should be confident and certain hope in God because He is ever present.

Do you have certain and confident faith in God's promises? What promises of God do you hold most dear?

2. Faith Rewarded (vv. 4-5, 7–8)

Abel and Enoch are the first heroes of faith. We do not hear much about them in the Genesis account. However, the writer of Hebrews makes it clear that Abel was demonstrating his faith in God with his sacrifice. Enoch's faith pleased God. At this point, the writer interjects a comment on the necessity of faith, which is discussed further below.

The third hero was Noah. Taking God at His word concerning things not yet seen, with no sign of a flood approaching, Noah built the enormous craft. If not even a single person had believed God's warning, then God might have shown mercy. However, Noah's belief shows that faith in God was not impossible even in that wicked generation. The rest of the world, therefore, were condemned by their unbelief (Hebrews 11:7).

The fourth hero was Abraham. Abraham is known as the "father of the faithful." At God's command, he left his homeland and all his relatives to journey to a new home (Genesis 12:1-4). In obedience to God, without the slightest idea of where he was going, Abraham left all that he knew. When he finally arrived at his destination, he didn't build a house. He lived in tents like a visitor in the land (Genesis 13:3-4; Hebrews 11:9).

3. Faith Is Necessary (v. 6)

Most believers desire to please God, and many attempt to please Him by their works and deeds. When our works are not done in faith, God rejects them, because without faith it is impossible to please Him. Faith is necessary to have an active relationship with God; it reveals the reality of God. Faith is necessary if you wish to walk with God.

The heroes of faith believed and obeyed regardless of the consequences. In the same way, we can believe with a willing trust and please God. Our steadfast confidence is based upon who God is—the Creator of the universe. God will recognize and reward our faith because we "diligently seek him" (Hebrews 11:6). By faith, we realize our own insufficiency and depend on God to work within us and through us. By faith we have confident trust in the continual promises of God.

Faith is the beginning of our relationship with God. What qualities of faith are necessary to continue to grow and strengthen our relationship with God?

4. Unfulfilled Hopes in Things Unseen (vv. 13-16)

A lack of faith hinders many Christians in their walk with God. The stories of these individuals should encourage us to persevere in faith, regardless of the obstacles. The faithful people of the Old Testament did not receive all that God had promised them, but they never lost hope. The focus of the heroes was never the realization of earthly promises. Instead, they looked forward to becoming heirs of righteousness (v. 7).

What gave our faithful ancestors hope even though they were "strangers and pilgrims" (v. 13)?

Search the Scriptures

1. Why is faith necessary to "understand that the worlds were framed by the word of God" (Hebrews 11:3)?

2. Who are the people commended by God because of their faith? (v. 2)

3. Why is it impossible to please God without faith? (v. 6)

Discuss the Meaning

1. Does true faith mean that God will give us whatever we ask for if we truly believe in Him? Explain your answer.

2. Tragedies and crises happen to everyone. How does faith help heal lives that have been broken by tragedy?

Liberating Lesson

Today, many are homeless or unemployed. Natural disasters destroy homes and lives. War and destruction are continually reported by the news. While positive change seems nonexistent, we must not lose hope. God is ever-present. We can rely on God for positive change as we realize our faith will be tested. Many people in our society have given up all hope of a better life for themselves. How can faith in God help to restore their hope? What part do you play in helping them acquire this faith?

Application for Activation

Although Abraham, Sarah, and the other heroes of faith were the true heirs of God's justice and promises, they lived as foreigners and strangers in the earth seeking a homeland. The Greek word for "strangers" is *xenoi* (**ZEE**-noy) and it is a part of the composite term "xenophobia" that describes a fear of strangers or people who are different. Having hope in a hopeless world and seeing opportunities where others see only defeat can make one feel like a stranger. This takes on even more materiality as we consider immigrants and refugees who attempt to live by faith and pursue a hope for a better life, but they instead are often met by lies and prejudices that attempt to limit their lives and portray them as delinquents. What can your Bible study group or church do to help immigrants and refugees in your area?

Follow the Spirit

What God wants me to do:

_____

_____

_____

_____

_____

_____

Remember Your Thoughts

Special insights I have learned:

_____

_____

_____

_____

_____

_____

More Light on the Text

Hebrews 11:1-8, 13-16

1 Now faith is the substance of things hoped for, the evidence of things not seen.

This verse is one of the most popular in Christianity, and it is extremely important for understanding the rest of the passage. It is often thought of as a definition of what faith is, but it is more like a description of what faith does. It sets the tone for the examples that follow, which demonstrate how faith operates.

The writer states that faith is the "substance" (Gk. *hypostasis*, hoo-**PO**-stah-sis) of things hoped for. This Greek word literally means "that which stands under." It is used in philosophical literature to depict the full expression of an idea or the full support of how one thinks the way they do. It also can refer to the foundation of a building. The author depicts faith as the substructure and explanation of things hoped for. Faith is the fundamental building block that allows hope to stand and have meaning.

The writer also describes faith as the *elegchos* (**EH**-leng-khos) of things that are not seen. This Greek word means more than conviction or evidence. It means scrutinized evidence that convicts. Put another way, it means the careful examination of an argument that leads to the only plausible conclusion. Faith operates in that way; it is the inscrutable, undeniable evidence of the unseen. Faith does not need to be corroborated; it is its own validation.

Things hoped for and the things unseen are supported and verified by faith. Faith must be the starting place. It is the very ground on which our hope is built, and it is the only evidence we have for what we cannot see. Even more so than faith being the foundation or the convicting evidence, the believer needs to recognize that faith is.

2 For by it the elders obtained a good report. 3 Through faith we understand that the worlds were framed by the word of God, so that things which are seen were not made of things which do appear.

Hebrews does not really follow the conventions of an ancient letter; it is actually more like a sermon. Its author is not only a writer but is also a preacher. In this verse and those that follow, the sermonic nature of this text shines clearer than anywhere else. The preacher begins a role call that moves through the history of Israel that begins at the creation. However, before the preacher begins that role they illustrate who has access to this faith.

On the one hand, the elders were commended for their faith. The Greek word *presbyteroi* (pres-**BOO**-ter-oy) describes elders and can refer both to those who are alive and to distant elders like the ancestors the preacher is about to list. "Elders" depicts those who have gone before us as models of having the faith. This probably included deceased members and older people in the preacher's congregation who were examples of having the faith. The preacher also illustrates, on the other hand, that those who are to have faith are us now. We see this by the use of the first person plural when the preacher says that by faith "we believe." Therefore, whether we are elders or not, we share the faith.

The faith that we share is better demonstrated than it is defined. One such demonstration of the faith is our understanding that the universe was put into order by the Word of God. The Greek word *aionas* (eye-**OH**-nas) is translated to "universe", which can also mean "the times." The Greek verb *katarizo* (ka-ta-**REE**-zoh) means more than formed, it means "to put in order and place." Therefore, faith manifests for believers through an understanding that all the various times of history—including the ones in which we live—were put into place by God's Word. This allows us to know that God is ultimately in control of our lives regardless of how challenging our situations may currently seem.

Many Jewish teachers believed the material universe was created according to God's invisible pattern that is exemplified in His Word or wisdom. By faith, we believe that God created everything out of nothing. With each creation, God "saw that it was good" (Genesis 1:4, 10, 12, 18, 21).

Our faith in God's ability to create via speech allows us to know that things that are seen came into existence by things that cannot be seen (i.e. God's Word). This reveals a deep truth that faith uncovers. This truth is that something that cannot be seen is ultimately in control of the world, and as believers, we recognize that God is that unseen force that organizes the world. Even more importantly, we understand that God is working in our lives even when we cannot see it. In times when this is hard to see, it is particularly relevant, because our faith should remind us that the very world we live in was brought into existence by what cannot be seen. And the One who brought it into existence is still operating on our behalves.

4 By faith Abel offered unto God a more excellent sacrifice than Cain, by which he obtained witness that he was righteous, God testifying of his gifts: and by it he being dead yet speaketh.

The preacher continues his sermon by demonstrating the faith of key figures from the beginning of Genesis. He begins with the first example of faithfulness in the Hebrew Bible, Abel. (He skipped Adam for obvious reasons.) He interprets Abel as offering a better sacrifice than his brother Cain because he offered it by faith. Abel serves as an example to assure believers that whenever they offer their gifts to God through faith, their efforts cannot be destroyed. Even though Cain killed Abel, Cain's violence did not prevent Abel's faith from continuing to speak. Even though people may not recognize the importance of a believer's

faithful sacrifice, that does not prevent the sacrifice from still being meaningful. Others' lack of appreciation certainly does not prevent the sacrifice from being effective. Even more importantly, their dismissal of the sacrifice does not prevent God from seeing and honoring it.

5 By faith Enoch was translated that he should not see death; and was not found, because God had translated him: for before his translation he had this testimony, that he pleased God. 6 But without faith it is impossible to please him: for he that cometh to God must believe that he is, and that he is a rewarder of them that diligently seek him.

The next figure that the preacher discusses is Enoch, whose life only receives 4 verses of attention in Genesis 5:21-24. Enoch was one of only two recorded biblical characters who never died (Genesis 5:24). This is how the word "translated" has been interpreted, implying that Enoch did not die, but was carried off to be with God. However, his life provoked many questions, because Genesis 5:24 states that "he was not; for God took him." The preacher in Hebrews recognizes that the reason Enoch was taken by God is that he pleased God and what ultimately pleases God is faith. The preacher so forcefully believes this truth that the sermon suggests that the opposite must also be true—non-faith displeases God. The preacher proclaims "without faith it is impossible to please [God]."

This makes sense because, as noted above, faith is the very foundation for hope and the inscrutable convicting evidence for the unseen. If one is to hope that the unseen God rewards people, then one must have faith to please God or to even encounter God. Faith makes the whole system work and without it, not only can one not please God but they do not even care whether the Organizer of Times is pleased at all. Faith is important for believers to make sense of a world that consistently attempts to crush hope and limit humans to the narrow options of what they can see.

Verse 6 contains several key points as they relate to faith: 1) the essential quality of faith (without it, it is "impossible to please him"); 2) the importance of our belief in the existence of God (we must "believe that he is"); and 3) the importance of expecting a reward from Him (we must believe that God "is a rewarder of them that diligently seek him").

The word *pistis* (Gk. **PEES**-tees) is most commonly translated "faith," but here the use of the related verb *pisteuo* (pees-**TYOU**-oh) is obscured by its translation as "to believe." "To believe" could just as easily be translated as "to have faith," because faith is belief. The object of our Christian faith is God. We are rewarded as we diligently seek and set our expectations upon Him.

7 By faith Noah, being warned of God of things not seen as yet, moved with fear, prepared an ark to the saving of his house; by the which he condemned the world, and became heir of the righteousness which is by faith.

Although Noah lived during a time of great disobedience, he heeded God's warning. Although there had never been a need for a ship the size of the ark, Noah built what God instructed him to. His entire family was saved as a result of him listening to God even though he was not able to actually see what God had said to him. In line with our discussion on verse 3, Noah's understanding that the world was ordered by God's word allowed him to recognize God's word. Noah is an example of trusting God's word even when the opposite seems true. The very salvation of our families and communities could be connected to our obedience to God's message to do something that has never been done before.

The preacher of Hebrews also says that Noah's heeding of God's warning allowed him to condemn the world. The Greek word behind "condemn" is *katakrinen* (ka-ta-**KREE**-nen) and means "to judge negatively." As Noah was building the ark, others may have judged him as radical, fanatic, or unhinged. However, his obedience to God allowed him to have the last word. Therefore, he needed to remain faithful even in a hostile environment where people could not see or understand him. His faith allowed him not only to persevere but to be able to see himself vindicated against everyone and every system that discredited him.

Noah's faith positioned him to be an heir of justice. The Greek word *dikaiosune* (dee-kai-oh-**SOO**-nay) is often translated as righteousness, but it also means justice. Noah's faith led him to heed God's voice in a world that questioned his values. Noah found favor in God's eyes and was a man of justice (Genesis 6:8, 9). In a community, nation, and world where it seemed that injustice was inescapable, Noah chose to be a representative of justice. What fueled his commitment to justice was his faith.

Noah's faith impacted how he acted in his present time, and it was also forward-looking. That is why the preacher in Hebrews refers to Noah as an heir of justice. An heir is one who has not yet received their inheritance, but they can anticipate it when their time comes. Although Noah did not know exactly when God's justice would manifest in the world, he still organized his life by faith to live justly in anticipation of God fulfilling God's commitment to him. Similarly, we are called to live by faith and pursue justice in our world. Even when it seems far away, we are to keep trusting that God will keep His word to us.

8 By faith Abraham, when he was called to go out into a place which he should after receive for an inheritance, obeyed; and he went out, not knowing whither he went.

The preacher of Hebrews then turns to the father of the faithful himself, Abraham. Here, Abraham's faith is expressed in terms of obedience and trust. Abraham answered his call, though he did not know at the time how far and how much God would call him. Even though God knew who Abraham truly was and who he would become, Abraham did not know. That did not prevent Abraham from going. He, like Noah, anticipated an inheritance even though he did not know where God was going to take him or how God was going to do what God had called him to do. His faith was not in knowing *how* God would, but his faith was in knowing *that* God would.

Like Abraham, we are called to trust God leading us even in uncertainty, not because we are sure of the destination, but because we are sure of the One who called us by name. By faith, we recognize that God knows us individually and has called us particularly.

13 These all died in faith, not having received the promises, but having seen them afar off, and were persuaded of them, and embraced them, and confessed that they were strangers and pilgrims on the earth. 14 For they that say such things declare plainly that they seek a country. 15 And truly, if they had been mindful of that country from whence they came out, they might have had opportunity to have returned. 16 But now they desire a better country, that is, an heavenly: wherefore God is not ashamed to be called their God: for he hath prepared for them a city.

The preacher of Hebrews acknowledges that faith is not rooted in receiving what is hoped for or in seeing what cannot be seen. If that were the case, then the faith of Abel, Noah, Abraham, Sarah, and others were baseless, because they died without actually seeing the fruit of their faith. Instead, the preacher of Hebrews uses immigrant and stranger imagery to portray the life of the faithful—those seeking opportunity but facing adversity. The faithful are depicted as those who choose to not focus on what they have left behind but instead concentrate on the hope that lays before them because their hope for better outweighs the risk of losing comfortable mediocrity.

They are those who are looking for a better country. This need not only apply to immigrants and refugees, but it could even apply to so-called citizens as well, who like Noah to seek justice in their nation and still look for a better country. The writer of Hebrews is attempting to stir up the congregants to recognize that this world is not our ultimate home.

The land that the examples of faith were seeking was not the Promised Land of Canaan. Nor is the land that they seek comparable to a modern Western idea of a nation-state. The land that the heroes of faith are looking for is a heavenly land—a city that God Himself has prepared for them.

The land that holds the fulfillment of our faith exists outside of the constraints of time and space and human engineering. Our faith must be completely rooted in that which we cannot see because we know by faith that the things we cannot see actually brought into existence the limited amount that we can see. The foundation of our hope cannot be limited by human systems and ideas. It has to be based in a faith that recognizes a God who put the times together through God's word, and it is that same word that continues to honor, warn, and call God's people today.

Sources:
Attridge, Harold W. *The Epistle to the Hebrews: A Commentary on the Epistle to the Hebrews.* Hermeneia; Minneapolis: Fortress Press, 1989.
Richards, Lawrence O. *The Expository Dictionary of New Testament Words.* Grand Rapids, MI: Zondervan, 1985. 463-464.

Say It Correctly

Enoch. **EE**-nock.
Xenophobia. zee-no-fo-bee-ah.

Daily Bible Readings

MONDAY
Love of Money, Root of Evil
(1 Timothy 6:6-10)

TUESDAY
Control Your Own Body
(1 Thessalonians 4:1-7)

WEDNESDAY
Abraham, Father of the Faithful
(Acts 7:2-7)

THURSDAY
Worthy Examples of the Faithful
(Hebrews 11:4-7, 17-27)

FRIDAY
Actions of Faith in Daily Life
(Hebrews 13:1-9, 17-19)

SATURDAY
Like Jesus, Offer Sacrifices to God
(Hebrews 13:10-16)

SUNDAY
The Living Actions of Faith
(Hebrews 11:1-3, 8-16)

Notes

_____

_____

_____

_____

Teaching Tips

Words You Should Know

A. Provoke (Hebrews 10:24) *paroxusmos* (Gk.)—To irritate or exasperate; to urge or stimulate

B. Reproach (v. 33) *oneidismos* (Gk.)—Insult, verbal abuse, usually in the form of public jeering or scoffing

Teacher Preparation

Unifying Principle—Keep Going. People lacking self-assurance feel overwhelmed by life's challenges. What can enable one to face life confidently? Believers in Jesus Christ, who persevere in hope and encourage others in love and good works, develop in faith.

A. Read the Bible Background and Devotional Reading.

B. Pray for your students and lesson clarity.

C. Read the lesson Scripture in multiple translations.

O—Open the Lesson

A. Begin the class with prayer.

B. Ask: How would you respond to someone who says, "I believe in Jesus, but I don't see a need for me to go to church regularly"?

C. Have the students read the Aim for Change and the In Focus story.

D. Ask students how events like those in the story weigh on their hearts and how they can view these events from a faith perspective.

P—Present the Scriptures

A. Read the Focal Verses and discuss the Background and The People, Places, and Times sections.

B. Have the class share what Scriptures stand out for them and why, with particular emphasis on today's themes.

E—Explore the Meaning

A. Use In Depth or More Light on the Text to facilitate a deeper discussion of the lesson text.

B. Pose the questions in Search the Scriptures and Discuss the Meaning.

C. Discuss the Liberating Lesson and Application for Activation sections.

N—Next Steps for Application

A. Summarize the value of a deeper and more intimate personal relationship with God through Christ.

B. End class with a commitment to pray for forgiveness for our sin and confidence that they are forgiven.

Worship Guide

For the Superintendent or Teacher
Theme: A Persevering Faith
Song: "Blessed be the Tie That Binds"
Devotional Reading: Psalm 40:1-13

A Persevering Faith

Bible Background • HEBREWS 10:19–39
Printed Text • HEBREWS 10:23–36 | Devotional Reading • PSALM 40:1–13

———————— Aim for Change ————————

By the end of this lesson, we will EXPLORE the stories of early believers who suffered for the sake of their faith, LONG for the courage to endure suffering as a result of our faithful witness, and SHARE in the suffering of Christians around the world.

———————— In Focus ————————

Anthony and Sharita had dated for one year and been friends for eight. They had had their ups and downs in their relationship. Some bad decisions from Sharita's past kept coming back to bite her, it seemed. But with prayer and heartfelt changes, they would work through the troubles as they came.

One Saturday, Anthony met with Mr. Williams, Sharita's father. Anthony said to him, "May I have your permission to ask Sharita to marry me? I love and respect your daughter and want to make her my partner for life. She is my blessing from God!"

Mr. Williams thought for a moment and smiled. "You have my permission, Anthony," he said. "Let's pray for you and Sharita's life together."

One evening as Anthony and Sharita walked through the park, Anthony knelt on one knee and proposed. Sharita was speechless. As tears ran down her cheeks, she said, "I have made too many mistakes in my life. You can't truly love me, because I have not forgiven myself. I don't deserve a life with you. I love you, but I can't marry you!"

As Sharita started to leave, Anthony said, "We all make mistakes, but God forgives us when we sincerely come to Him. I know you have a sincere heart. Otherwise, we wouldn't have made it this far. We can't let another little struggle stop us from the beautiful relationship we've been working toward."

Through faith in Christ, our sins are forgiven and we have a new life. In today's lesson, we can develop a personal relationship with Jesus by faith and enter into the presence of God.

———————— Keep in Mind ————————

"Let us hold fast the profession of our faith without wavering;
(for he is faithful that promised;)" (Hebrews 10:23, KJV).

"Let us hold tightly without wavering to the hope we affirm, for God can be trusted to keep his promise" (Hebrews 10:23, NLT).

Focal Verses

KJV **Hebrews 10:23** Let us hold fast the profession of our faith without wavering; (for he is faithful that promised;)

24 And let us consider one another to provoke unto love and to good works:

25 Not forsaking the assembling of ourselves together, as the manner of some is; but exhorting one another: and so much the more, as ye see the day approaching.

26 For if we sin wilfully after that we have received the knowledge of the truth, there remaineth no more sacrifice for sins,

27 But a certain fearful looking for of judgment and fiery indignation, which shall devour the adversaries.

28 He that despised Moses' law died without mercy under two or three witnesses:

29 Of how much sorer punishment, suppose ye, shall he be thought worthy, who hath trodden under foot the Son of God, and hath counted the blood of the covenant, wherewith he was sanctified, an unholy thing, and hath done despite unto the Spirit of grace?

30 For we know him that hath said, Vengeance belongeth unto me, I will recompense, saith the Lord. And again, The Lord shall judge his people.

31 It is a fearful thing to fall into the hands of the living God.

32 But call to remembrance the former days, in which, after ye were illuminated, ye endured a great fight of afflictions;

33 Partly, whilst ye were made a gazingstock both by reproaches and afflictions; and partly, whilst ye became companions of them that were so used.

34 For ye had compassion of me in my bonds, and took joyfully the spoiling of your goods, knowing in yourselves that ye have in heaven a better and an enduring substance.

NLT **Hebrews 10:23** Let us hold tightly without wavering to the hope we affirm, for God can be trusted to keep his promise.

24 Let us think of ways to motivate one another to acts of love and good works.

25 And let us not neglect our meeting together, as some people do, but encourage one another, especially now that the day of his return is drawing near.

26 Dear friends, if we deliberately continue sinning after we have received knowledge of the truth, there is no longer any sacrifice that will cover these sins.

27 There is only the terrible expectation of God's judgment and the raging fire that will consume his enemies.

28 For anyone who refused to obey the law of Moses was put to death without mercy on the testimony of two or three witnesses.

29 Just think how much worse the punishment will be for those who have trampled on the Son of God, and have treated the blood of the covenant, which made us holy, as if it were common and unholy, and have insulted and disdained the Holy Spirit who brings God's mercy to us.

30 For we know the one who said, "I will take revenge. I will pay them back." He also said, "The LORD will judge his own people."

31 It is a terrible thing to fall into the hands of the living God.

32 Think back on those early days when you first learned about Christ. Remember how you remained faithful even though it meant terrible suffering.

33 Sometimes you were exposed to public ridicule and were beaten, and sometimes you helped others who were suffering the same things.

35 Cast not away therefore your confidence, which hath great recompence of reward.

36 For ye have need of patience, that, after ye have done the will of God, ye might receive the promise.

34 You suffered along with those who were thrown into jail, and when all you owned was taken from you, you accepted it with joy. You knew there were better things waiting for you that will last forever.

35 So do not throw away this confident trust in the Lord. Remember the great reward it brings you!

36 Patient endurance is what you need now, so that you will continue to do God's will. Then you will receive all that he has promised.

The People, Places, and Times

Holy of Holies. It was located in the innermost sanctuary of the Temple. Separated from the other parts of the Temple by a thick curtain, the Holy of Holies was especially associated with the presence of Yahweh. In the early years of the existence of the Temple, the Holy of Holies contained the Ark of the Covenant, which represented God's presence with the people of Israel. When Jesus died on the Cross, however, the curtain separating God's presence from the world tore.

High Priest. All Temple worship was ultimately governed by the high priest. This most sacred of positions was hereditary through the line of Aaron, Moses' brother. Normally, the high priest served for life.

Background

Sacrifices were practiced from the earliest of times in the Old Testament. Animals were imperfect sacrifices that could not completely purify or atone for people's sins. The writer of Hebrews expresses the importance and superiority of Christ's priesthood to the Levitical priesthood. The Levitical high priest could only enter the Holy of Holies one day a year when he would make reconciling sacrifices for the sins of the entire nation. This was the only way the Jews knew to approach God.

The writer of Hebrews explained a new covenant promise was placed into effect when Christ died (Hebrews 9:11-12, 24-28). The new covenant frees believers from the bondage of the first covenant. God took away the Levitical sacrificial system, which was the first arrangement when He established the perfect sacrifice—Jesus Christ.

The hope of enjoying the presence of God, of approaching Him freely in an intimate relationship is the hope referred to in our first verse today. The new covenant is the promise we can trust God to keep.

At-A-Glance

1. Our Profession of Faith (Hebrews 10:23-25)
2. Knowledge of the Truth (vv. 26-27)
3. How God Will Judge His People (vv. 28-31)
4. Looking Forward Through Suffering (vv. 32-36)

In Depth

1. Our Profession of Faith (Hebrews 10:23-25)

The writer encourages believers to "hold fast the profession of our faith without wavering" (Hebrews 10:23). God reveals His promises

583

and truths through His Word; thus, we must embrace God's Word and resist temptation and opposition. He wants to reassure the believers by calling them to remember, "[God] is faithful that promised" God will do what He has promised (Hebrews 10:23).

The writer also instructs the believers to "consider" each other (v. 24). Believers must provoke or stir up the qualities of love and good works toward each other (v. 24). The writer knew believers could have an impact on one another by loving and doing good deeds for each other.

Because of the fear of persecution, some of the believers had stopped attending worship services; therefore, the writer encourages the believers to pull together to stir up loving and active faith. The fellowship of believers is a source of encouragement; it is an opportunity to share faith and grow stronger.

Think of a fellow believer close to you. How can you encourage that person?

2. Knowledge of the Truth (vv. 26-27)

The writer of Hebrews reminds the believers that if they "sin wilfully," they deliberately reject Christ (v. 26). It is a conscious rejection of God after receiving the truth and the guidance of the Holy Spirit, rather than an occasional act of sin. Believers should not willfully rebel against God's provisions after receiving and fully understanding the "knowledge of the truth," which is Christ's offer of salvation (Hebrews 10:26).

The consequences of rejecting God are "judgment and fiery indignation, which shall devour the adversaries," and there is no hope of forgiveness (Hebrews 10:27). Thus, those who reject Christ and disobey God are His adversaries. There is one certain judgment, death, and destruction, for obstinate apostates. The apostates will experience the wrath of God because there is no other help for sinners who

reject their only remedy—salvation through accepting Jesus Christ as Lord and Savior.

How would you explain verse 26 to a Christian still new in the faith?

3. How God Will Judge His People (vv. 28-31)

The Old Testament refers to the sin of idolatry that requires "two witnesses, or three witnesses ... [to] be put to death" (Deuteronomy 17:6). The judgment for idolatry was death by stoning, but there is a worse punishment for someone who rejects the word of Christ. If someone considers the "blood of the covenant ... an unholy thing," the person grieves the "Spirit of grace," which is the Holy Spirit (Hebrews 10:29). The person that rejects the Spirit of God will receive a punishment greater than physical death.

Judgment belongs to God for "the LORD shall judge his people" (Deuteronomy 32:36). There is no other sacrifice for sin except Christ's sacrifice on the Cross. Whoever rejects God's mercy will receive God's judgment. The apostate will experience an eternal punishment from God's own hands. However, believers, who have received the mercy of God through Christ, are saved, and there is nothing to fear.

Can a person lose their salvation? In light of your answer, how do you understand apostasy?

4. Looking Forward Through Suffering (vv. 32-36)

The writer then changes tone, back to the encouraging words he used in vv. 23-25. He no longer needs to scare them into compliance with God's law in the face of persecution. He already knows they can persevere, because they have been doing so already. They have undergone some of the same suffering the apostles have. They were able to do this because they were looking forward to God's reward. While it is a fearful thing to stand before God's judgment if you do not obey Him, it is a blessed thing if you do obey Him. Judgment Day for God's faithful followers, who suffer with patient endurance, will see the receipt of all God has promised.

Search the Scriptures

1. What three exhortations does the author make (Hebrews 10:23-24)?

2. What is the significance of the Old Testament quotations in verse 30?

Discuss the Meaning

1. How can we draw near and remain in the presence of God each day? How can we truly experience God's presence?

2. What is the Church's relationship with persecution today? Are Western churches really persecuted? What does this status mean for persevering in the faith?

Liberating Lesson

Faith is effective when we depend on God and rest in what Christ has done on the Cross. The writer of Hebrews urged believers to recognize the superiority of our faith and live in obedience to God each day. Through Christ, we have an eternal reward and significant privileges that we can experience through our new life in Christ.

Through Christ, we can experience God's presence and develop a relationship with Him. We can grow in faith and experience a deeper relationship with God when we trust and believe without doubts and concerns that the world presents. The world is temporary, but our life with God is eternal. Each day we must trust God and hold onto our faith and then share our faith with others. When we share our love for God, we can encourage others and introduce them to a new life through Christ.

Application for Activation

The world focuses on tangible rewards, promotions, and recognition with financial bonuses. The world encourages the pursuit of tangible endeavors and earthly wealth with retirement plans focused on life in the world. As believers, we have a purpose that is not focused on earthly rewards. Because we have accepted Christ by faith, we are friends of Christ with a purpose to share our love for Christ through faith. Consider local ministries that allow you to share your faith in God. Volunteer your time to share your love for God with people who do not know Him, or share your faith and encourage believers who are homebound or sick. Help others to remain faithful and experience the presence of God each day. Make a daily affirmation to share your faith. Finally, ask God for boldness to share your faith with others. God will give you the opportunity and bless your desire to be faithful.

Follow the Spirit

What God wants me to do:

_____

_____

_____

_____

_____

Remember Your Thoughts

Special insights I have learned:

_____

_____

_____

_____

_____

585

More Light on the Text
Hebrews 10:23-36

In Hebrews 10:23–36, the writer of Hebrews gave some stern warnings similar to the ones earlier given in chapter 6 where he spoke of those who had been enlightened and had tasted the good Word of God and the power of another world: that if it were possible they should fall away, it would be impossible to renew them.

23 Let us hold fast the profession of our faith without wavering; (for he is faithful that promised;)

Hebrews 10:23 is the second of the three commands for the people in verses 22–24: "draw near," "hold fast," and "consider." The second exhortation is to hold fast to the profession of faith. The verb translated here as "hold fast" (Gk. *katecho*, ka-**TEKH**-oh) has been previously used by the author for the readers to "hold fast" to their confidence and their glorying in hope (Hebrews 3:6) and the beginning of their confidence (3:14). Now, he wants them to retain a firm grasp on "the profession of our faith" (10:23). Christians can hold fast to their hope in this way because behind it is a God in whom they can have full confidence. God is thoroughly to be relied on. When He makes a promise, it will infallibly be kept. He has taken the initiative in making the promise, and He will fulfill His purposes in making it. He who cannot lie promises the eternal life to you that is the object of your hope. As He then is faithful who has given you this promise, hold fast the profession of your hope.

24 And let us consider one another to provoke unto love and to good works: 25 Not forsaking the assembling of ourselves together, as the manner of some is; but exhorting one another: and so much the more, as ye see the day approaching.

The third exhortation is to consider one another. This is the only place where the author uses the expression "one another" (Gk. *allelon*, al-**LAY**-lone), though it is frequently found elsewhere in the New Testament. He is speaking of a mutual activity, one in which believers encourage one another, not one where leaders direct the rest as to what they are to do. Our danger is that we become so involved in this world that we forget the other. The word "provoke" is actually a noun (Gk. *paroxusmos*, pah-rocks-ooss-**MOCE**) that is often used negatively as "irritation" or "exasperation." It is used here in a positive sense to suggest "urging" or "stimulation." The goal of this provocation is expressed in the compound "love and good works." Love is not a vague principle or emotion but is shown by the doing of good deeds. The means of stimulating one another unto love and good deeds is mutual exhortation. They are to do for one another what the author does for them (13:19), and writes this letter-sermon to accomplish (13:22).

Corporate worship is important. We must worship together with other believers. There were some among those to whom the writer of the Hebrews was writing who had abandoned the habit of meeting together. Some still today think it is possible to live the Christian life while abandoning the habit of worshiping with God's people. This should not be the case. God made us to be in community. The exhortation takes on a sense of urgency "as ye see the day approaching" (v. 25). The "day" here has eschatological overtones that derive from the Old Testament prophetic tradition that spoke of a day in which God would judge (Joel 1:15; 3:14; Amos 5:18-20), a tradition that is maintained in the New Testament (1 Corinthians 1:8; 5:5; 1 Thessalonians 5:2). The time is short. The day is approaching, the Second Coming of Christ when things as we know them will end. The early Christians lived in that expectation. So must we. In the time we have, it is our duty to do all the good we can to all the people we can in all the ways we can.

In the present day where the world and, unfortunately, the Church is characterized by rugged individualism, this verse is a stark reminder that no one is at liberty to spend all their thoughts on themselves, but we are all bound to consider our neighbors as well as brothers and sisters in Christ. The Greek word katanoeo (kah-tah-no-**EH**-oh), "let us consider" conveys the concept of careful consideration, thoughtful attention, and deep concern. It is followed by the direct object "one another," expressing the mutual reciprocity of members of the Christian community in the act of careful consideration. Only by meeting together regularly can the Church remind itself that we are indeed one body. Individuals working as one whole is a reflection of God's triune nature. This unity must be practiced. We must work at it over and over again by meeting together with fellow believers.

26 For if we sin wilfully after that we have received the knowledge of the truth, there remaineth no more sacrifice for sins, 27 But a certain fearful looking for of judgment and fiery indignation, which shall devour the adversaries.

It is clear that the writer has apostasy in mind. He is referring to people who "have received the knowledge of the truth" (Hebrews 10:26), where "truth" (Gk. *aletheia*, ah-**LAY**-thi-ah) stands for the content of Christianity as the absolute truth. Receiving the knowledge of truth means entering into the community that is defined by the true God. The people to whom the epistle was written, then, know what God has done in Christ; their acquaintance with Christian teaching is more than superficial just as Israel was well acquainted with God and His covenant. If knowing this, they revert to an attitude of

rejection—of sin—then there remains no sacrifice to cover those sins. An important word here is "wilfully" (Gk. *hekousios*, heh-koo-**SEE**-ose), which can be translated as "deliberately." It means their action is voluntary. Such people have rejected the sacrifice of Christ, and the preceding argument has shown that there is no other. The same word is used for "freewill offerings" in the Old Testament (Leviticus 23:38; Numbers 15:3). When a believer freely chooses sin, it is not a minor transgression but apostasy, a deliberate and voluntary turning away.

The sin that is freely chosen could not be considered as a minor transgression, but apostasy, a deliberate turning away. As such, this kind of sinner cannot turn back again for they are denying the basis for such return. "A certain fearful looking for of judgment" awaits such people (v. 27, KJV). The nature of this expectation (i.e. "looking for") is not defined, and the fact that the fate of these evil persons is left indefinite makes the warning all the more impressive. In Hebrews 10:27, the writer describes it as "fiery indignation," an echo of Isaiah 26:11, which is a vivid expression for the fire of judgment that is intent on devouring God's adversaries. In Hebrews 10:27, the word "adversaries" (Gk. *hupenantios*, hoo-peh-nan-**TEE**-oos) shows that the apostates were not regarded as holding a neutral position. In rejecting Him, through their own choice, they have become God's enemies.

28 He that despised Moses' law died without mercy under two or three witnesses: 29 Of how much sorer punishment, suppose ye, shall he be thought worthy, who hath trodden under foot the Son of God, and hath counted the blood of the covenant, wherewith he was sanctified, an unholy thing, and hath done despite unto the Spirit of grace?

The author now adopts the argumentation form of the lesser to the greater. Jews held the

Law of Moses to be divinely given: Anyone who rejected it rejected God's direction and was killed without compassion. There was no place for mercy. He must be executed (Deuteronomy 17:6; 19:15). The author of Hebrews invites the audience to work out for themselves what sort of worse punishment someone would deserve for rejecting the gift of God in Christ. Because Jesus is greater than Moses, it must be more severe than under the old way (Hebrews 3:1-3); the new covenant is better than the old, founded on better promises (8:6) and established by a better sacrifice (9:23).

The grievousness we experience when we "deliberately continue sinning" (10:26, NLT) is elaborated in three phrases of 10:29. First, such a person has "trodden under foot the Son of God." The verb "trodden" (Gk. *katapateo*, ka-ta-pah-**TEH**-oh) implies not only rejecting Christ but also despising Him. This is more than falling from grace; it is a mockery of the Giver of grace.

The second characterization of the apostate is that the apostate takes lightly the solemn shedding of covenant blood. That is to say, he treats the death of Jesus just like the death of any other man. The word "common" can also be understood as against the holy, and it thus comes to mean "unhallowed and unholy." This stands out all the more sharply when it is remembered that this blood has "sanctified" him. To go back on this decisive act is to deny the significance of the blood, to see it as a common thing.

The third indictment of the apostate is that he or she has done this spitefully or has "done despite unto the Spirit of grace" (v. 29). In the Greek, the writer's word for "insulted" is *enubrizo* (eh-boo-**BREED**-zo), means to reduce the honor that is due to another person. Willful sin is an insult to the Spirit, who brings the grace of God to humanity.

Verses 28–29 function together as a lesser to a greater form of argument which has been consistently used through the entire composition both for exhortation and exposition. Here he argues that those who set aside Christ's sacrifice would suffer greater punishment in comparison with those who rejected the laws of Moses who were to be killed without compassion.

The author completes the argument with a rhetorical question. The author appeals to the readers' imagination to "suppose" the kind of judgment or worse punishment one would deserve who rejects the gift of God in Christ. The willful sinner, who was previously a Christian, has treated the precious, sacred blood of Christ, which inaugurated the new covenant and by which he or she was sanctified, as something common and profane, "an unholy thing." This blood "sanctified" the individual, a reference back to Hebrews 10:10, 14. It is the height of arrogance by the sinner, an arrogance that demands nothing short of or less than a dreadful and certain penalty.

30 For we know him that hath said, Vengeance belongeth unto me, I will recompense, saith the Lord. And again, The Lord shall judge his people. 31 It is a fearful thing to fall into the hands of the living God.

The author calls God "him that hath said" words of Scripture. He is sure that God speaks to men. The author's first quotation here is from Deuteronomy 32:35. Whereas Deuteronomy speaks of God judging the enemies of Israel, the author of Hebrews applies these quotations as a warning concerning God judging His own people. Vengeance is a divine prerogative. The emphasis here is on the certainty that the Lord will act. The wrongdoer cannot hope to go unpunished because avenging wrong is in the hands of none less than God. The second quotation from Deuteronomy 32:36 leaves no doubt whatever about the Lord's intervention, for He is named and so is His activity. That a person claims to be a member of the people of God does not exempt him or her from judgment. God judges all.

"It is a fearful thing to fall into the hands of the living God" (10:31)—What a simple statement that also carries a chilling effect. "Falling into the hands" of someone means to come under his power (Judges 15:18). Two passages in the Old Testament say unequivocally that it is better to fall into "the hands of the Lord" than into the "hands of a man" (2 Samuel 4:14; 1 Chronicles 21:13). These passages provide reassurance of God's mercy. But such is not the case in this passage. Rather, falling into God's hands will be dreadful and fearsome. To fall into the hands of God is to fall under His displeasure, and He who lives forever can punish forever. How dreadful to have the displeasure of an eternal, Almighty God to rest on the soul forever! Apostates, and all the persecutors and enemies of God's cause and people, may expect the heaviest judgments of an incensed Deity; and these are not for a time but through eternity.

32 But call to remembrance the former days, in which, after ye were illuminated, ye endured a great fight of afflictions; 33 Partly, whilst ye were made a gazingstock both by reproaches and afflictions; and partly, whilst ye became companions of them that were so used. 34 For ye had compassion of me in my bonds, and took joyfully the spoiling of your goods, knowing in yourselves that ye have in heaven a better and an enduring substance.

The hearers of this letter were living in between the times: "the days of their enlightenment" and "the day of the Lord." They were to remember the "great fight of afflictions" or "the great sufferings" that they endured. The act of memory is more than a mere recollection of what they went through or recalling facts from the past. It was to remind them of the experiences that shaped their identity. Their experience in the former days are to continue

to serve as a counterpoint to the sufferings and temptations that they were currently facing, particularly the temptation of turning away and neglecting the assemblies.

The nature of the sufferings of the Hebrew Christians is spelled out more fully. They suffered public exposure to insult and persecution. "Reproach" or literally, "insult" translates the word *oneidismos*, (oh-nie-**DEES**-moce) which indicates verbal abuse, usually in the form of public jeering or scoffing. It was used to describe the treatment of Jesus as well as the early Christians. The noun *thlipsis*, (**THLEEP**-sees) used for affliction suggests physical suffering. The hearers have undergone both physical and verbal abuse in their hands of their persecutors.

In addition to their suffering, they had maintained solidarity with others who were so persecuted, and showed concern for those in prison and had experienced having their property confiscated by the authorities. In the midst of all these, the Jewish Christians maintained a positive disposition that was grounded in a certain perception of reality—an assurance of permanent possession in heaven! The possession is more than something material and ephemeral. It is the realization of God's presence through the exaltation of Christ.

35 Cast not away therefore your confidence, which hath great recompence of reward. 36 For ye have need of patience, that, after ye have done the will of God, ye might receive the promise.

The audience of the letter was given confidence or boldness in their confession of Christ. The author now urges them not to throw or "cast" it away. Those who hold fast to their confession will have a "great recompence of reward", that is, they will be "richly rewarded." There is no indication that they have already done so, but they are clearly being tempted to do so.

Given all that the readers had endured in the past, the author challenges them "cast not away" their "confidence." The Greek verb *apoballo* (ah-po-**BALL**-lo) "to throw away" can be taken in its more passive sense, as of a tree losing its leaves, or as is more likely, in the strong active sense of deliberately throwing something away, negatively in the sense of "abandoning." It is a deliberate action of tossing something aside. It is within the realm of choice. They are not to throw their confidence of boldness away because it possesses a great reward. The reward is our eternal salvation; hence it is called a "great reward."

Verse 36 provides the grounds for the preceding exhortation, and does so in counterpart fashion by pitting "patience" against "casting away." "Patience" denotes perseverance, the notion of remaining faithful to the end. Boldness has a great reward but only if they hold onto it the way they did in the past. This verse looks forward to Chapter 11 where the author lists the heroes who through their faith obtained the promises. Their faith was not simply belief, or even trust or obedience; it was all of these extended through trial by endurance. After all those heroes of faith, the writer will come to our best example: Christ. He showed us perfect biblical perseverance, and we are exhorted to fix our eyes on Him as our model.

Sources:
Allen, David L. *Hebrews, The New American Commentary* (Nashville, TN: B & H Publishing Group, 2010), 514–532.
Bruce, F.F. *The Epistle to the Hebrews, Revised: new International Commentary on the New Testament.* Grand Rapids, MI: Eerdmans. Reprint, 1988 .
Guthrie, Donald. *Tyndale New Testament Commentaries: Letter to the Hebrews.* Grand Rapids, MI: Eerdmans, 1983 216.
Holman Pocket Bible Dictionary. Nashville, TN: Holman Bible Publishers, 2004. 762-764, 773.
Johnson, Luke Timothy. *Hebrews: A Commentary.* The New Testament Library. Louisville, KY: Westminster John Knox Press, 2006 . 259.
Keener, Craig S. *The IVP Bible Background Commentary: New Testament.* Downers Grove, IL: InterVarsity Press, 1993. 647-650, 670-671.
Lane, William L. *Hebrews 9-13.* Word Biblical Commentary, Vol. 47B. Dallas, TX: Word Inc., 1991.
Life Application Study Bible, King James Version. Wheaton, IL: Tyndale House Publishers, Inc., 1997. 2154-2155, 2170-2172.
Mitchell, Alan C. *Hebrews.* Sacra Pagina, vol. 13. Collegeville, MN.: Liturgical Press, 2007, 2009.
Plummer, William S. *Commentary on the Epistle to the Hebrews.* Reprint. Grand Rapids: Baker Book House, 1980.
Radmacher, Earl D., ed. *Nelson's New Illustrated Bible Commentary: Spreading the Light of God's Word into Your Life.* Nashville, TN: Thomas Nelson Publishers, 1999. 1648-1653.

Say It Correctly

Eschatological. es-kuh-tuh-**LOJ**-ih-kuhl
Recompense. rec·om·pense
Septuagint. **SEP**-too-uh-jint
Apostasy. Ah-**PAH**-stah-see.

Daily Bible Readings

MONDAY
Save Your Life by Losing It
(Mark 8:31-37)

TUESDAY
Respond to Abusers with Blessings
(1 Peter 3:9-19)

WEDNESDAY
Be Faithful Until Death
(Revelation 2:8-11)

THURSDAY
Sanctified by Christ's Sacrifice
(Hebrews 10:1-10)

FRIDAY
The Inner Life of New Believers
(Hebrews 10:11-18)

SATURDAY
Approach God with a Pure Heart
(Hebrews 10:19-22)

SUNDAY
Act in Ways That Preserve the Faith
(Hebrews 10:23-36)

Teaching Tips

Words You Should Know

A. Perfect (1 John 4:17) *teleioo* (Gk.)—To complete or accomplish, bring to an end

B. Overcometh (5:4) *nikao* (Gk.)—To conquer, overcome, or prevail

Teacher Preparation

Unifying Principle—Perfect Love. Faced with the world's allure, people contend with its many appeals. How can one resist this unhealthy allure? Believers through faith in Jesus Christ overcome the world and its seduction with the hope of victory.

A. Read the Bible Background and Devotional Reading.

B. Pray for your students and lesson clarity.

C. Read the lesson Scripture in multiple translations.

O—Open the Lesson

A. Begin the class with prayer.

B. Ask participants to write a love letter to God, explaining how God's love dwells within and moves within them and how that love impacts them positively.

C. Have the students read the Aim for Change and the In Focus story.

D. Ask students how events like those in the story weigh on their hearts and how they can view these events from a faith perspective.

P—Present the Scriptures

A. Read the Focal Verses and discuss the Background and The People, Places, and Times sections.

B. Have the class share what Scriptures stand out for them and why, with particular emphasis on today's themes.

E—Explore the Meaning

A. Use In Depth or More Light on the Text to facilitate a deeper discussion of the lesson text.

B. Pose the questions in Search the Scriptures and Discuss the Meaning.

C. Discuss the Liberating Lesson and Application for Activation sections.

N—Next Steps for Application

A. Summarize the value of living wisely, so as not to be deceived by false teachers.

B. End class with a commitment to pray to grow in their capacity to love others as Christ has loved them.

Worship Guide

For the Superintendent or Teacher
Theme: A Conquering Faith
Song: "We Shall Overcome"
Devotional Reading: John 14:15–24

A Conquering Faith

Bible Background • 1 JOHN 4–5
Printed Text • 1 JOHN 4:2–3, 13–17; 5:4–5 | Devotional Reading • JOHN 14:15–24

Aim for Change

By the end of this lesson, we will REMEMBER the love of God described by the writer of 1 John, REFLECT on the various expressions of God's love in our lives, and RESPOND to the challenge to love others with Christ-like love.

In Focus

When Deidra got to church Sunday morning, Ricky was right in her face. He was clingy and hardly gave her space to talk to anyone else. Deidra tolerated Ricky because he was a member of her Sunday School and a fellow brother in Christ. Though Deidra appeared to be kind, inside she was fuming with anger at Ricky's inability to take what she was sure were obvious clues that she was not comfortable with his attentiveness.

Deidra began to feel guilty about being nice to Ricky and then mocking him behind his back. Deidra understood her behavior did not reflect the teachings of Christ, which meant loving our fellow brothers and sisters in the family of God. This meant she had to be honest and forthright with Ricky and stop her cruel remarks about him to others.

Deidra tried to think of how God saw Ricky. God knew that Ricky was only trying to be kind, but didn't understand social situations the way most people did. Maybe instead of shutting him down, Deidra could help Ricky learn how to read the room better.

The following Sunday, Deidra talked to Ricky and related her discomfort. She felt the resentment leave, replaced by a greater appreciation for Ricky, who graciously received her message.

How do we interact with others to show that we "dwell in love" with God? Should these interactions differ between Christians and non-Christians?

Keep in Mind

"And we have known and believed the love that God hath to us. God is love; and he that dwelleth in love dwelleth in God, and God in him." (1 John 4:16, KJV).

"We know how much God loves us, and we have put our trust in his love.
God is love, and all who live in love live in God, and God lives in them."
(1 John 4:16, NLT)

Focal Verses

KJV **1 John 4:2** Hereby know ye the Spirit of God: Every spirit that confesseth that Jesus Christ is come in the flesh is of God:

3 And every spirit that confesseth not that Jesus Christ is come in the flesh is not of God: and this is that spirit of antichrist, whereof ye have heard that it should come; and even now already is it in the world.

13 Hereby know we that we dwell in him, and he in us, because he hath given us of his Spirit.

14 And we have seen and do testify that the Father sent the Son to be the Saviour of the world.

15 Whosoever shall confess that Jesus is the Son of God, God dwelleth in him, and he in God.

16 And we have known and believed the love that God hath to us. God is love; and he that dwelleth in love dwelleth in God, and God in him.

17 Herein is our love made perfect, that we may have boldness in the day of judgment: because as he is, so are we in this world.

5:4 For whatsoever is born of God overcometh the world: and this is the victory that overcometh the world, even our faith.

5 Who is he that overcometh the world, but he that believeth that Jesus is the Son of God?

NLT **1 John 4:2** This is how we know if they have the Spirit of God: If a person claiming to be a prophet acknowledges that Jesus Christ came in a real body, that person has the Spirit of God.

3 But if someone claims to be a prophet and does not acknowledge the truth about Jesus, that person is not from God. Such a person has the spirit of the Antichrist, which you heard is coming into the world and indeed is already here.

13 And God has given us his Spirit as proof that we live in him and he in us.

14 Furthermore, we have seen with our own eyes and now testify that the Father sent his Son to be the Savior of the world.

15 All who declare that Jesus is the Son of God have God living in them, and they live in God.

16 We know how much God loves us, and we have put our trust in his love. God is love, and all who live in love live in God, and God lives in them.

17 And as we live in God, our love grows more perfect. So we will not be afraid on the day of judgment, but we can face him with confidence because we live like Jesus here in this world.

5:4 For every child of God defeats this evil world, and we achieve this victory through our faith.

5 And who can win this battle against the world? Only those who believe that Jesus is the Son of God.

The People, Places, and Times

John. The writer of 1 John is thought to be John the apostle and Gospel-writer. John, like his brother James, was a fisherman until he was called by Jesus to join the other eleven disciples. For three years, he followed and learned from Christ. John, along with Peter and James, was a part of Jesus' inner circle. In his own Gospel account, he refers to himself as the "disciple whom Jesus loved" (John 21:20). After Pentecost, John was said to have led the church in Ephesus and eventually was exiled during the reign of Domitian to the island of Patmos.

Day of Judgment. This judgment refers to the final and ultimate judgment of God. It involves the final appearance of Christ when He judges the actions of all humankind. This phrase finds its roots in the Old Testament concept of the Day of the Lord. The Hebrews believed this would be the day when God would judge the nations and vindicate His people. In the New Testament, it loses its nationalistic tone and refers to God's solemn condemnation of all evil. On that day, Christians will inherit eternal life and unbelievers the ill-fated choice of eternal damnation (hell).

Background

The letters of John are three brief epistles. This does not mean our study of them should be brief, though, for they deal with insightful and significant questions about the fundamental nature of Christian spiritual experience. The Johannine letters also provide fascinating insight into the condition of the church at the end of the first century. Heresy played a critical and deceptive role in the church. The genuine nature of a committed and obedient relationship to God through Christ is strongly and affectionately depicted and commanded.

Throughout his Gospel and epistles, John uses very simple language to relate complex theological ideas. The unity of the Trinity, the inward and outward lives of the Christian, the presence of the Antichrist and the coming of the end times are all couched in simple, repeated terms: love, light, truth, liar. In this week's passage, John describes how love is evidence of our relationship to God (1 John 4:14–21). The present assurance is so obvious that even the fear of Judgment Day is eliminated (vv. 17–18), knowing that we have already overcome the world (5:4).

At-A-Glance

1. Confident Confessions
(1 John 4:2-3, 13-14)
2. Confident Judgment (vv. 15-17)
3. Confident Victory (5:4-5)

In Depth

1. Confident Confessions (1 John 4:2–3, 13–14)

Both John's audience and we today have experienced trusting someone who betrayed or deceived them. We overcome deception with faith, that is, the right belief in Jesus, who gives the victory. John gave precautionary advice about avoiding false teachers, as many were claiming to be sent by God (vv. 1-3). Only those who were truly inspired by the Spirit of God would openly confess the crucified, resurrected Christ. John and the other apostles had witnessed and could verify that Jesus Christ was the incarnate Word (v. 14), the Messiah sent from heaven and sacrificing his life through death on the Cross. This doctrine is of the Spirit of God.

All Christians receive the Holy Spirit as living proof of God's presence in our lives. The Holy Spirit gives us power to love and confess Jesus Christ as Lord and assures that we are truly connected to our Heavenly Father and not being deceived.

Describe a time you heard of someone being misled by a false teacher. How did the experience impact those the teacher misled?

2. Confident Judgment (vv. 15–17)

Perfect love does not mean we love perfectly; rather, perfect love is the goal we always keep before us in the person of Jesus. Jesus loves flawlessly because He accepts us with all our imperfections and mistakes, and regardless of our gender, sex, race, marital, educational, economic status, physical, mental, or emotional qualities, age, or cultural background. He loves us!

Knowing we are loved by God diminishes our apprehension of Judgment Day, increases our need to see others saved and supplied us freedom to love indiscriminately and do the work God called us to do. The confidence we receive in acknowledging God's love is not arrogance. Arrogance is when we depend and boast in our own abilities. The confidence that the Bible describes is a declaration of our relationship with Jesus and evidence of the abiding Holy Spirit within us.

How do we ensure our confidence does not become arrogance that turns away rather than attracts others to Christ?

3. Confident Victory (5:4–5)

In the letter's final chapter, John turns to the interrelationship of love and righteousness. Those who are born of God do not find His commandments to be troublesome (5:3). The faith of the children of God gives them power to discover victory over the world that would obstruct the execution of commands (v. 4). That faith rests in Jesus as the Son of God (v. 5). When we believe Jesus is the Son of God, we become one with Him. This gives us the victory because He has said, "I have overcome the world" (John 16:33). This is a past tense verb, indicating the victory has already occurred.

How do we "battle against" and "overcome" the world while showing the love of God?

Search the Scriptures

1. How do we know God lives in us (1 John 4:13)?

2. What gives proof that we love God (vv. 16–17)?

Discuss the Meaning

1. Why is it important that we love one another?

2. Why do we fear judgment or punishment from God?

3. How is God's love made perfect?

Liberating Lesson

Society teaches us to love conditionally. Some people live in fear of rejection from those who claim to love them. This is not real love. One of the most remarkable attributes of God is His ability to love unconditionally and completely. No matter what we face in life, God's love is everlasting and nothing can separate us from His love! Not only do we have God's promise of love but also the promise of eternal life. With this kind of reassurance, what keeps us from loving others?

Application for Activation

The Lord has high regards for the community of believers and we should too. All we can do is learn to love and obey God's command. Pray and ask God to reveal where you can extend love to someone in the family of God. After God shows you, act! Write in a journal about how the incident impacted your life and share your experience with the class.

Follow the Spirit

What God wants me to do:

_____

_____

_____

_____

Remember Your Thoughts

Special insights I have learned:

_____

_____

_____

_____

More Light on the Text

1 John 4:2-3, 13-17; 5:4-5

2 Hereby know ye the Spirit of God: Every spirit that confesseth that Jesus Christ is come in the flesh is of God: 3 And every spirit that confesseth not that Jesus Christ is come in the flesh is not of God: and this is that spirit of antichrist, whereof ye have heard that it should come; and even now already is it in the world.

John's first epistle is full of simple either/or statements, making right doctrine absolutely clear for his audience. Those who have the Spirit of God will confess (Gk. *homologeo*, ho-mo-lo-GEH-oh) that Jesus Christ came in the flesh. Those who do not make this confession have the spirit of antichrist. The text of Christ coming in the flesh is likely a reference to false teaching from Gnostics spreading through the church at the time. They believed the physical world was completely corrupt, while the spiritual world

was completely pure. God revealing Himself to us in a body of presumably corrupt flesh, therefore, did not fit with their worldview. In order to maintain their human philosophy, they denied the orthodox doctrine of the Incarnation.

John wrote to the church several times about this kind of heresy, showing how difficult it was to root out. One reason for this is that it is almost correct. Christ Himself speaks about the world's evils (John 17:16). However, eyewitness accounts—and the very mechanism of salvation—insist on Christ having a physical, earthly body. No human philosophy should stand in our way of believing what Christ has revealed about Himself to us. We must make sure we are knowledgeable about God's Word so we can recognize false teaching and doctrines when they arise. Believers are members of the family of God who have embraced God's truth and are immersed in God's Spirit. Therefore, they have the power to triumph over the deceptions and trickery of false teachers.

It is tempting to dive into speculation about the "spirit of antichrist" and the "day of judgment" (v. 17). Since 1 John and Revelation were both written by the same apostle, it is easy to jump to discussions of the End Times in connection with these verses. However, we must simply read what the text says: "the spirit of antichrist [is] even now already … in the world" (v. 3). The antichrist here, therefore, is not precisely the Beast of John's apocalyptic vision. The word "antichrist" (Gk. *antichristos*, an-TIE-kreese-toce) is most simply translated "against Christ." The "spirit of antichrist" we see in the world is not necessarily the overt workings of the devil in the end times, but any way of life that sets itself against Christ as we understand Him from Scripture.

13 Hereby know we that we dwell in him, and he in us, because he hath given us of his

Spirit. 14 And we have seen and do testify that the Father sent the Son to be the Saviour of the world.

Two themes dominate John's exhortation in these verses: faith and love. In verse 13, John affirms that the assurance of the presence of God in the life of a Christian (cf. vv. 12, 15) is proved by the residence of the Holy Spirit in him or her. Paul also talks similarly about the Spirit being proof that we belong to God (2 Corinthians 1:22). Speaking of the Spirit this way provides a significant connection between 1 John and John's Gospel. In John's Upper Room Discourse, Jesus spoke of the Spirit (or Advocate) as one who would come to maintain a continuity and intimacy of relationship between the disciples and their Master (John 14:15-31; 15:26-27; 16:5-15). Since love is the first of the fruit produced by the Spirit (Galatians 5:2-23), John's connection of love with the Holy Spirit is obvious, in addition to the other work of the Spirit in the life of a believer.

Although no one has seen God, He has revealed Himself visibly in His Son Jesus Christ. As one of the apostolic eyewitnesses, John bears testimony to this fact (cf. 1:1–3). The Greek word *soter* (**SOH**-tare), savior or deliverer, defines both the purpose and the result of Christ's mission (cf. Matthew 1:21; John 1:29). John tells us how the Father sent the Son for this purpose and now gives us his Spirit as well. This is one of the rare places in Scripture where the Father, Son, and Spirit are each mentioned as distinct Persons of the Godhead, who are all in relationship with us and with each other.

15 Whosoever shall confess that Jesus is the Son of God, God dwelleth in him, and he in God.

John places emphasis on the test of faith in Christ as evidence of God's indwelling. The Greek word *homologeo* (ho-mo-lo-**GEH**-oh, confess) indicates that confession involves the intellectual acknowledgment of the human-divine nature of Christ and a personal acceptance of Him. If we make this profession of faith, it proves that God dwells (Gk. *meno*, **MEH**-no; to remain, live, or continue) in us and we in Him. This means that we keep intimate fellowship with Christ and allow His life-giving power to produce in us and through us. If we live in Christ and allow Him to live in us, we will produce much fruit (John 15:5). An intimate, progressive, and continuous relationship with Christ is essential to being useful servants of God. The closer we grow to Christ through study and meditation of Scripture, the more our prayers will line up with God's will. And the more our prayers line up with God's will, the more effective our prayer will be (See 1 John 5:14). Since we have this relationship, we then have the boldness and privilege to ask the Father anything (John 15:7). This relationship also gives us boldness on the day of judgment, as the epistle will soon state (v 17).

16 And we have known and believed the love that God hath to us. God is love; and he that dwelleth in love dwelleth in God, and God in him. 17 Herein is our love made perfect, that we may have boldness in the day of judgment: because as he is, so are we in this world.

John effectively connects faith with works, because to live in love is to act with divine love toward all people. Belief must find expression in behavior. Here, believing and loving are intimately joined. They are proof of God's Spirit in the believer. This is a difficult task, certainly. We may be disillusioned about the true meaning of love or we might behave lovingly toward one another without necessarily feeling love toward others. We also recognize there are different kinds of love and find it difficult to respond appropriately in relationships. John is stating that the ongoing action of God dwelling in us and us dwelling in God perfects our love. By dwelling in love and consequently in God, and by God dwelling in us, love will be made perfect (Gk. *teleioo*, teh-lay-**OH**-oh). This word refers to completion of a goal or maturity. Love will be made complete, mature, and fully accomplished in us.

The phrase "because as he is, so are we in this world" refers to God's abiding in us (v. 17). If we dwell in God and God in us, despite being in this imperfect world, we are like God, who is love. This should give us confidence on the Day of Judgment, which comes from loving as Jesus loved us. It does not mean that we will love perfectly, but that we will have evidence that we are believers, and we will have confidence that our hearts are right before God.

5:4 For whatsoever is born of God overcometh the world: and this is the victory that overcometh the world, even our faith. 5 Who is he that overcometh the world, but he that believeth that Jesus is the Son of God?

John's confidence in the believer's victory is contagious. Within two verses he uses the words "overcome" and "victory" four times (vv. 4–5). The Greek verb *nikao* (nee-**KAH**-oh) means to conquer, to overcome, or to prevail, while its related noun *nike* (**NEE**-kay) means victory or conquest. Anything that has been born of God conquers the world, but here John focuses on our faith as the victory that has already conquered the world. John uses a present tense verb to begin with because there are always obstacles to face in this world, but in talking of faith, he uses a verb that expresses certainty that our faith is complete in its victory. The way might not be full of roses, yet the Christian life is one of victory from start to finish, not a life of defeat, discouragement, or dread.

Two aspects of the believers' conquest are implied in these verses. First, Christ's victory becomes the believers' own upon their belief in the person and work of Christ, acceptance of Christ as Lord and Savior by faith and consequent union with Christ (cf. John 1:12, 16:33). Second, the abiding presence of the Holy Spirit enables the believer to live in daily victory over the flesh, the world, and the devil. In everyday experience, the Christian can constantly express thanks to God "which giveth us the victory through our Lord Jesus Christ" (from 1 Corinthians 15:57; cf. 1 John 4:4; Romans 8:37). The person who is born of God is born to win; he or she does not live like a coward or become dominated and defeated by circumstances. The born-again believer lives confidently by faith and has complete trust in God from victory to victory. God's promises are never realized by the fearful but given to those who are overcomers, conquerors through Jesus Christ (Revelation 2:7, 11, 17, 26; 3:5, 12, 21; 12:11, KJV).

Sources:
Comfort, Philip W., and Walter A Elwell. Tyndale Bible Dictionary. Wheaton, IL: Tyndale House Publishers, Inc., 2001. 719–28.
International Bible Lesson Commentary. King James Version. Colorado Springs, CO: David C. Cook Publishers, 2008.
Key Word Study Bible. New International Version. Grand Rapids, MI: Zondervan Bible Publishers, 1996. 1440–41.
Life Application Study Bible. New International Version. Wheaton, IL: Tyndale House Publishers, Inc., 1991. 1909, 2282–83.
The New Oxford Annotated Bible. New Revised Standard Version. New York: Oxford University Press, Inc., 2001. 386–87.
Rainbow Study Bible. New International Version. Grand Rapids, MI: Zondervan Bible Publishers, 1992. 1378–79.
Unger, Merrill F. The New Unger's Bible Handbook. Chicago, IL: Moody Press, 1998. 635–36.

Say It Correctly

Johannine. joe-**HAH**-nine
Antichrist. **AN**-tie-cry-st

Daily Bible Readings

MONDAY
Testing Our Love for God
(Deuteronomy 13:1-4)

TUESDAY
Love God by Keeping
His Commandments
(John 14:15-24)

WEDNESDAY
Discerning the Spirit of Truth and Error
(1 John 4:1, 4-6)

THURSDAY
Knowing God, We Can Love Others
(1 John 4:7-12)

FRIDAY
Faith Is the Victory
(1 John 5:1-3)

SATURDAY
Believers in Jesus Have Life
(1 John 5:6-12)

SUNDAY
Faith That Loves Overcomes Obstacles
(1 John 4:2-3, 13-17; 5:4-5)

Notes

_____

_____

_____

_____

Teaching Tips

Words You Should Know

A. Earnest (2 Corinthians 5:5) *arrhabon* (Gk.)—A pledge, guarantee, or down payment towards fulfilling a future promise

B. Accepted (v. 9) *euarestos* (Gk.)—Well-pleasing, good and virtuous

Teacher Preparation

Unifying Principle—Be Confident. People fear the fragility of life and the meaning of death. In weakness and death, where can any assurance be found? God gives believers in Jesus Christ an eternal, unseen place in Him that is guaranteed by the Spirit.

A. Read the Bible Background and Devotional Reading.

B. Pray for your students and lesson clarity.

C. Read the lesson Scripture in multiple translations.

O—Open the Lesson

A. Begin the class with prayer.

B. Ask: Why do most people relinquish excessive concerns about appearance as they grow older? What does having a renewed body mean to you?

C. Have the students read the Aim for Change and the In Focus story.

D. Ask students how events like those in the story weigh on their hearts and how they can view these events from a faith perspective.

P—Present the Scriptures

A. Read the Focal Verses and discuss the Background and The People, Places, and Times sections.

B. Have the class share what Scriptures stand out for them and why, with particular emphasis on today's themes.

E—Explore the Meaning

A. Use In Depth or More Light on the Text to facilitate a deeper discussion of the lesson text.

B. Pose the questions in Search the Scriptures and Discuss the Meaning.

C. Discuss the Liberating Lesson and Application for Activation sections.

N—Next Steps for Application

A. Summarize the value of knowing that some matters of faith shall remain a mystery until we meet God face-to-face.

B. End class with a commitment to pray to understand that God is a God of love, grace, and mercy, but also a God of judgment.

Worship Guide

For the Superintendent or Teacher
Theme: Hope Eternal
Song: "In The Sweet By and By"
Devotional Reading: Romans 7:14–26

Hope Eternal

Bible Background • 2 CORINTHIANS 4:16–5:10
Printed Text • 2 CORINTHIANS 4:16–5:10 | Devotional Reading • ROMANS 7:14–26

Aim for Change

By the end of this lesson, we will ACKNOWLEDGE the hope Paul, faced with death, manifested in God's eternal promise, EXPERIENCE awe in the faith of family and friends who are facing their mortality, and DEVELOP a growing trust in God's promise of eternal life through faith.

In Focus

Sharon knew that if she didn't hurry, she would be late for the funeral at the church this morning. As the lead usher, it was her responsibility to make sure the other ushers were in place, hand out funeral programs, and seat guests. Her hands were shaking as she combed out her hair. Fred, the 24-year-old son of one of the church's long-time members, had been killed in a car wreck on Saturday night. The two passengers in Fred's car were still hospitalized, both in critical condition. Fred had been thrown from the car and died at the scene. Fred came from a large family and had been a popular young man in high school and at the local community college. Although Fred's parents were faithful members, she had only seen Fred in church on Mother's Day. She had run into him several times outside of the church and had even invited him to come and visit more often. He had always laughed and teased that he was too young for that "church stuff."

Sharon had ushered at enough funerals to know that there would be a lot of crying; that part she didn't mind. It was the screaming and having to restrain guests from throwing themselves into the casket that bothered her. While Sharon understood that grief was natural, the funerals of young people were always chaotic. She wondered what Pastor would say during the eulogy; he couldn't possibly have known Fred that well. How, she wondered, would he comfort Fred's family and friends?

How do you offer comfort in the face of death? How does knowing Christ change how we understand death?

Keep in Mind

"For we know that if our earthly house of this tabernacle were dissolved, we have a building of God, an house not made with hands, eternal in the heavens"
(2 Corinthians 5:1, KJV)

"For we know that when this earthly tent we live in is taken down (that is, when we die and leave this earthly body), we will have a house in heaven, an eternal body made for us by God himself and not by human hands" (2 Corinthians 5:1, NLT)

Focal Verses

KJV **2 Corinthians 4:16** For which cause we faint not; but though our outward man perish, yet the inward man is renewed day by day.

17 For our light affliction, which is but for a moment, worketh for us a far more exceeding and eternal weight of glory;

18 While we look not at the things which are seen, but at the things which are not seen: for the things which are seen are temporal; but the things which are not seen are eternal.

5:1 For we know that if our earthly house of this tabernacle were dissolved, we have a building of God, an house not made with hands, eternal in the heavens.

2 For in this we groan, earnestly desiring to be clothed upon with our house which is from heaven:

3 If so be that being clothed we shall not be found naked.

4 For we that are in this tabernacle do groan, being burdened: not for that we would be unclothed, but clothed upon, that mortality might be swallowed up of life.

5 Now he that hath wrought us for the selfsame thing is God, who also hath given unto us the earnest of the Spirit.

6 Therefore we are always confident, knowing that, whilst we are at home in the body, we are absent from the Lord:

7 (For we walk by faith, not by sight:)

8 We are confident, I say, and willing rather to be absent from the body, and to be present with the Lord.

9 Wherefore we labour, that, whether present or absent, we may be accepted of him.

10 For we must all appear before the judgment seat of Christ; that every one may receive the things done in his body, according to that he hath done, whether it be good or bad.

NLT **2 Corinthians 4:16** That is why we never give up. Though our bodies are dying, our spirits are being renewed every day.

17 For our present troubles are small and won't last very long. Yet they produce for us a glory that vastly outweighs them and will last forever!

18 So we don't look at the troubles we can see now; rather, we fix our gaze on things that cannot be seen. For the things we see now will soon be gone, but the things we cannot see will last forever.

5:1 For we know that when this earthly tent we live in is taken down (that is, when we die and leave this earthly body), we will have a house in heaven, an eternal body made for us by God himself and not by human hands.

2 We grow weary in our present bodies, and we long to put on our heavenly bodies like new clothing.

3 For we will put on heavenly bodies; we will not be spirits without bodies.

4 While we live in these earthly bodies, we groan and sigh, but it's not that we want to die and get rid of these bodies that clothe us. Rather, we want to put on our new bodies so that these dying bodies will be swallowed up by life.

5 God himself has prepared us for this, and as a guarantee he has given us his Holy Spirit.

6 So we are always confident, even though we know that as long as we live in these bodies we are not at home with the Lord.

7 For we live by believing and not by seeing.

8 Yes, we are fully confident, and we would rather be away from these earthly bodies, for then we will be at home with the Lord.

9 So whether we are here in this body or away from this body, our goal is to please him.

10 For we must all stand before Christ to be judged. We will each receive whatever we deserve for the good or evil we have done in this earthly body.

The People, Places, and Times

Heavenly Bodies. Today, we spend so much time and money on our physical bodies while trying to ignore the fact that the aging process is an inevitable part of life. That is not to say that we shouldn't take care of our bodies by developing healthy eating habits and getting proper rest and exercise. But we must realize that the bodies we now possess are not going to function forever. Still, Christians can rejoice that one day we will receive a heavenly body that is specifically designed for heaven. Our earthly bodies are contrasted with that which is spiritual, which can exist in the heavenly realm. There is a realm for physical (natural) existence and there is another for spiritual existence. Each realm has a distinct body fashioned for it, just like each season has its own clothing.

Judgment Seat. The judgment seat was found in a palace or tent where court proceedings were held. The emperor or general would sit in this highly elevated throne-like chair to conduct trials and make pronouncements of extreme importance. Pontius Pilate and King Herod conducted business from such a seat. In the great halls, all eyes could easily find this focal point as the chair's importance was obvious.

Background

Paul founded the church at Corinth and reminded the young assembly of believers that, because he was their organizer, he had a right to speak regarding their management. The big issue rampant in the church was whether Paul was a genuine apostle. Paul asserted that he was and sent Titus to deliver that message. Titus was well received and Paul rejoiced at the happy news when he met his messenger in Macedonia.

In addition to this issue of apostolic authority, the Corinthians are wondering about how they are to deal with persecution and death. Shouldn't God protect them from these harsh realities since they are faithfully following Him? Paul turns the question on its side, saying that these harsh realities are nothing compared to the glory that awaits the Christian in heaven after death. Chapter 5 begins with Paul comparing the earthly body with the heavenly body as the difference between a tent and a building. The tent is a temporary dwelling while the building is solid. Paul hoped to be transformed into his heavenly body rather than go through the nakedness of death. The Platonists, Pythagoreans, and Gnostics during the time of Paul's writings saw the body as a prison for the soul and yearned to be rid of it. Paul saw the new body as a desirable garment which would cover the soul.

At-A-Glance

1. Light Suffering (2 Corinthians 4:16-18)
2. New Clothing (5:1–5)
3. Confident Living (vv. 6–10)

In Depth

1. Light Suffering (2 Corinthians 4:16-18)

Part of the means used by God in this transforming, renewing process is suffering (cf. 1 Peter 4:1, 13-14). Paul compared the sufferings he had experienced, severe as they were, to light and momentary troubles, pressures, and hardships. They were nothing in view of the eternal glory that would be his when he would be in Jesus' presence and would be like Him (1 Corinthians 15:49). Paul is here weighing his sufferings on God's scales. He discovers that his sufferings are light when compared to the weight of glory God has stored up for him. These verses bring wonderful assurance to the believer in times of suffering. How important it is for us to live with eternity's values in view. Life takes on new meaning when we see things through God's eyes.

Paul introduces a paradox to the unbeliever, but a precious truth to the Christian. We live by faith, not by sight; this faith enables the Christian to see things that cannot be seen (Hebrew 11:1-3). The world thinks we are crazy because we dare to believe God's Word and live according to His will. We pass up the things that people covet because our hearts are set on higher values.

How are Christians supposed to "look" at "things which are not seen"?

2. New Clothing (5:1-5)

The human body is the vehicle of expression for the soul, the inner man. It is referred to as an earthly tabernacle, a temporary tent. In this body, we "groan," indicating both physical and mental expressions. The body, wonderful though it is, has a built-in mortality factor, and will be torn down and dissolved. When it is dismantled we call it death.

In stark contrast to the temporal scene, is Paul's emphasis upon the future-our heavenly, eternal abode. In heaven, we will be at home with the Lord. Paul voiced his strong desire for this state of permanence (Philippians 1:21-23). Our heavenly or eternal body is compared to fresh, new clothing. In Paul's thought, clothes really did "make the man." The life that now is will be engulfed by the life that is real—life eternal.

How does the Spirit act as a guarantee of our new life in heaven?

3. Confident Living (vv. 6–10)

The Apostle Paul affirms that the tug toward heaven continues while we serve on earth. The brave continue to live as a testimony to the Lord. Even death is a testimony as we express confidence in what lies ahead. Death is not the worst thing that can happen to a Christian. He who created us has risen from the grave, and He will keep His promise to raise us also!

Paul also tells his readers, "to be absent from the body, and to be present with the Lord" (v. 8). We cannot live in both our temporary and our eternal, glorified bodies at the same time. Our temporary bodies are temples of the Lord (1 Corinthians 6:19) but more is yet to come. Our incompleteness urges us to desire the permanent house Jesus is preparing for us.

Paul ties it all back together. They should not fear painful trials on this earth because it's all going to be worth it when we get our heavenly bodies and God judges our perseverance. One day believers will have to stand before the judgment seat of Christ to be judged for what they have done. When God inspects us, He expects to find the fruit in our lives. In making choices, we should first ask whether God will be pleased with our choices.

Can others see Jesus Christ in you? Do you live to make a positive difference in the world?

Search the Scriptures

1. What do the afflictions that we face today actually do for us? (v. 17)

2. What are the things seen and the things which are not seen according to Paul? (v. 18)

3. What should be the aim of a believer? (5:9)

4. What will happen to a believing Christian at the judgment seat of Christ? (v. 10)

Discuss the Meaning

1. Paul says that our temporary earthly dwelling is a tent, while our permanent heavenly dwelling is a house. Where else do we see this imagery in Scripture? What implications does that have for understanding Paul here?

2. Discuss the following phrase: We are not free to live until we aren't afraid to die. How would such an idea affect our living? How can this idea be blended with an attitude of safety and caution?

Liberating Lesson

Adversities can serve a definite purpose in our lives. C.S. Lewis, in his book *The Problem with Pain*, says, "God whispers to us in our pleasures, speaks in our conscience, but shouts in our pain: it is His megaphone to rouse a deaf world."

Think of our society today. Most of the world's achievements have come through hardship and pain, including most professions, inventions, personal accomplishments, relationships, parenting, great leaders, and church ministries. Take time and talk about how pain has been a driving force even in your life. There is truth to the saying: "No pain no gain."

Application for Activation

While we still do not like pain in our lives, we must see the value that it plays. Think of someone who is going through tough times. Using the lesson today, think of ways you could encourage them. Spend time this week praying that God would give you the right words to uplift and motivate others.

Follow the Spirit

What God wants me to do:

_____

_____

_____

_____

Remember Your Thoughts

Special insights I have learned:

_____

_____

_____

_____

More Light on the Text

2 Corinthians 4:16–5:10

Paul continues to stress his courageous spirit as he begins to speak more directly about the future. He writes of present inner renewal accompanying his outer decay, and looks forward to a time without any decay, whether physical or spiritual.

16 For which cause we faint not; but though our outward man perish, yet the inward man is renewed day by day.

Beginning from this verse Paul shifts his emphasis from a defense of the suffering he incurs in his ministry to an expression of his confidence in the resurrection hope that sustains him in his suffering. Paul restates what he previously said in verse 1, "we faint not." He both summarizes the preceding section and picks up the theme of verse 1. He proceeds to distinguish the outward and inner person. The "outward man" is a whole person as seen by others or that aspect of one's humanity that is subject to various assaults and hardships of this world. The "inner man" is the unseen personality known only to God and self. The Corinthians need to understand that despite Paul's bodily weakness, his inner person is being transformed daily. He then turns to the contrast between the present and the return of Christ, between this life and the life to come.

God's mighty power is shown through human fragile vessels. Humanity that decays and the mortal labor on behalf of the Gospel is taking its toll on them. But "day by day" they are inwardly renewed. The experience of daily renewal or recycling, inspires the sure and certain hope of the resurrection life (vv. 10ff). Though the outer body may look weak, Christians are renewed by the power of God. The outer person can be equated with the sinful nature (Romans 6:6; Colossians 3:9; Ephesians 4:22). The inner person is being renewed day after day. The old wastes away but the new survives forever. The eternal weight of glory awaits a believer (cf. Romans 8:18-25). Paul connects suffering in this age and glory in the next life with Jesus. The end time is good for those who love Him (Romans 8:28). It is for us who believe to enter that glory. The purpose of God cannot be thwarted away by the present evil.

17 For our light affliction, which is but for a moment, worketh for us a far more exceeding and eternal weight of glory; 18 While we look not at the things which are seen, but at the things which are not seen: for the things which are seen are temporal; but the things which are not seen are eternal.

To substantiate what is introduced by "for which cause" in v 16, Paul explains his paradoxical affirmation with a series of startling contrasts. The life to come is a life of glory. Contrary to the position of his opponents, Paul can say that according to God's surpassing gift his present momentary suffering will be followed by eternal glory. Paul neither minimized nor glorified his sufferings. Instead he had an eternal perspective. He took his pain in stride, looking at everything in light of eternity. He fixes his gaze not upon the things that belong to this age but upon the things that belong to the coming age. As Christians, we must be careful not to base our hopes on the things we see. The unseen will endure when all else fails.

Our present troubles are real but short-lived. Trouble fades into insignificance, but eternal weight of glory awaits a believer (cf. Romans 8:18-25). Paul connects suffering in this age and the glory in the next life with Jesus. And that life is for us that believe. We, therefore, fix our eyes "not at the things which are seen, but at the things which are not seen." Christians see persecution, suffering, trouble, but look forward to the things unseen which have been prepared by God for those who love Him. So, Paul's apostleship was authenticated by God's act of power and glory. God has prepared the coming age for those who love Him. Therefore, Christians should not focus only on the present success but must fix their hope, indeed their gaze, to the glory that God has prepared for them. It is a hope based on Christ's resurrection.

5:1 For we know that if our earthly house of this tabernacle were dissolved, we have a building of God, an house not made with hands, eternal in the heavens.

In this chapter, Paul builds upon the conclusion in 4:17-18 and provides further details of his motivation for ministry. First, Paul was fully convinced of a future life that is devoid of suffering and pain. It is a life without change or death. He had an abounding hope of resurrection and heaven (5:1-8). Second, Paul was sure of future divine judgment (5:9-10). In the face of the coming judgment, he had incredible confidence, for his relation with God was already right. Third, Paul was persuaded that the reconciliation of humanity to God was God's initiative, motivated by love and manifested in and brought about by Jesus Christ.

Paul starts on a note of confidence. "We know" implies that the Corinthians knew what Paul is about to say. It indicates Paul's unwavering conviction and settled belief that the Christian will eventually be done with the frailty and suffering of their present existence. Paul does not say "we think," "we hope" or "we assume' but 'we know.' "We know" indicates the certainty of Paul's future hope, which he shares with the other apostles, the Corinthians, and all Christian believers. His courage, as he faces failing faculties and the inevitability of suffering and death, is to be found in his assurance of the unseen and the eternal (4:18), that is, in the certainty of his eternal house in heaven (5:1). What a bold statement! As Paul has previously stated (4:1-15), believers can face any trial in this life because of the hope of future resurrection.

This verse shows that at least for the first time in Paul's apostolic ministry and career, Paul reckons seriously with the possibility of his death before the return of Christ (cf. 1 Thessalonians 4:17; 1 Corinthians 15:51). This is probably because of his encounter with death spoken of earlier (1:8-11).

2 For in this we groan, earnestly desiring to be clothed upon with our house which is from heaven: 3 If so be that being clothed we shall not be found naked. 4 For we that are in this tabernacle do groan, being burdened: not for that we would be unclothed, but clothed upon, that mortality might be swallowed up of life.

Paul likens the present human body to a foldable tent that is to be replaced with a building, a clear allusion to the resurrection body that Paul mentioned previously in his previous letter to this church (1 Corinthians 15). The present tent-body that gradually ages and wears out will be taken down and folded up when we die. At the return of Christ and the resurrection of the faithful, we will receive our new bodies, and our salvation will be complete. Paul uses the image of groaning here and in his letter to the Roman church, saying that our human mortal existence is limited (Romans 8:19-20). Paul sought liberation from the imperfection of our present embodiment. He has another home in view. The believer's present existence is punctuated with suffering and pain. The present age is characterized by groaning, and believers are not exempt from the groaning of the whole created order (Romans 8:22-27). Thus, Paul says, we groan. But we do not groan as hopeless people. It is a groaning that is accompanied by a longing. It was not a longing for death. Paul's hope and groaning

were not for death. Death is not the hope of the Christian.

Many of us are not earnestly longing for heaven. Perhaps it is because we are so comfortable on earth? It is not that we should seek out affliction, but neither should we dedicate our lives to the pursuit of comfort. There is nothing wrong with earnestly desiring heaven! There is something right about being able to agree with Paul and say we groan!

5 Now he that hath wrought us for the selfsame thing is God, who also hath given unto us the earnest of the Spirit.

While Paul speaks of the transformation of the mortal body in the last part of verse 4, it is the last part of verse 5 where he indicates how the preparation takes place. God has prepared the Christian believer for transformation by giving us the Spirit as a guarantee (Gk. *arrhabon*, are-rah-**OWN**; pledge or guarantee), which is different from the final payment. How can the Spirit be God's pledge? It is clearly through His empowering the Christian's daily re-creation or renewal. In other words, what the Spirit does in the present not only prefigures but also guarantees His future completion of that work which he began (cf. Philippians 1:6). The Spirit daily renews us on earth but will fully renew us in heaven.

6 Therefore we are always confident, knowing that, whilst we are at home in the body, we are absent from the Lord: 7 (For we walk by faith, not by sight:) 8 We are confident, I say, and willing rather to be absent from the body, and to be present with the Lord.

Paul's mood and style appear to change as he begins to conclude his certainty about the future. He becomes more positive. Because of the Spirit's presence, his longing for the future encourages him in the present: Therefore we are always confident. Paul abandons the metaphors that he has previously used for the body and here he refers explicitly to the term body itself. In view is the body as the sphere of one's physical life on earth with all of its frailties (see Romans 6:12; 12:1). For Paul, a mortal body is not incompatible with life "in Christ" (2 Corinthians 5:17; Galatians 2:20).

Paul continues to use the architectural imagery of 5:1–2. The metaphors of being at home and "away from our home" are obviously related to the earlier terminology of "tent," "building," and "house." Earthly existence in the physical body means for Paul that "we are absent from the Lord." That is, although we are "in Christ" we are not yet "with Christ" (Philippians 1:23). So we walk by faith. The word translated "walk" (v. 7) is used metaphorically here to mean "conduct our total life." Paul is saying, "We conduct our lives based on faith, not by the appearance of things." While Paul (as is true of all Christians) was in the physical body, he was away from the Lord (v. 6). However, even in this life Christ lived in him, and he looked for the day when he could see the risen Lord face to face.

In verse 8, Paul talks about being away in the body and being with the Lord. This is still an idea of permanence. So you find a corollary—resident in the body is absent from the Lord, absence from the body is residence with the Lord. What did Paul understand to be involved in being at home with the Lord? It is more than location (cf. John 1:1 – 'with God'; Mark 6:3 – 'with us'). At home with the Lord depicts Christians' eternal destiny. We will be at home with the Lord means that we will not only be where He is, but also there will be a higher form of intimate relationship with Christ that we will experience.

9 Wherefore we labour, that, whether present or absent, we may be accepted of him. 10 For we must all appear before the judgment seat of Christ; that every one may receive the things done in his body, according to that he hath done, whether it be good or bad.

Unlike many who are people-pleasers, Paul considered nothing to be more important than pleasing the Lord Jesus Christ who has commissioned him. Paul's letters frequently use the adjective *euarestos* (ew-**ARE**-ess-toce) to describe human behavior that is "acceptable" or "well-pleasing" to God (see Romans 12:2; Philippians 4:18; Colossians 3:20). Pleasing Christ was the all-consuming passion of Paul's life (see v. 14) and the overall objective of his apostolic ministry. This was true whether he lived on in a vulnerable human frame or whether he died and was away from his bodily home on earth. The nature of the future, Paul's destiny of residence with the Lord (v. 8) and the necessity of appearing before him for judgment (v. 10), all motivated him to please the Lord. Although Paul is not completely devoid of the hope of being honored by the Corinthians, his proclamation of the Gospel and his entire life were devoted to pleasing the Lord, rather than winning honor from people.

That was his supreme ambition. For him, to live is Christ and to die is gain (Philippians 1:21). At the heart of Paul's desire to please the Lord is the awareness of an awaiting future judgment. While in the body we must act in such a way so that we will be pleasing to God at the judgment. We shall all be seen for what we are. All believers will be stripped of all disguises, masks, and pretensions before the judgment seat of Christ. What we do in the body has moral significance and eternal consequences. To be conformed to Christ's glorious body in the next life, we must be conformed to His image and character in this life. What a sobering thought.

Sources:

Adewuya, J. Ayodeji. *A Commentary on 1 & 2 Corinthians*. ISG 42. England: SPCK, 2009.

Belleville, Linda L. *2 Corinthians*. The IVP New Testament Commentary Series. Edited by Grant R. Osborne. Downers Grove: Inter-Varsity Press, 1996.

Bruce, F.F. *I and II Corinthians*. The New Century Bible Commentary. Edited by Matthew Black. Grand Rapids: Wm. B. Eeadmans Publishing Co., 1971.

Carver, Frank G. *2 Corinthians: A Commentary in the Wesleyan Tradition*. New Beacon Bible Commentary. Kansas City, MO: Beacon Hill Press, 2009. 168.

Comfort, Philip W., and Walter A Elwell. *Tyndale Bible Dictionary*. Wheaton, IL: Tyndale House Publishers, Inc., 2001. 719–28.

Harris, Murray J. *The Second Epistle to the Corinthians*. The New International Greek Testament Commentary. Edited by I. Howard and Hagner, Donald A. Marshall. Grand Rapids: William B. Eerdmans, 2005.

Key Word Study Bible. New International Version. Grand Rapids, MI: Zondervan Bible Publishers, 1996. 1440–41.

Life Application Study Bible. New International Version. Wheaton, IL: Tyndale House Publishers, Inc., 1991. 1909, 2282–83.

Marshall, I. Howard, A.R. Millard, J.I. Packer, and D.J. Wiseman. *The New Bible Dictionary*. Downers Grove, Illinois: InterVarsity Press, 1984. 763.

Morris, Leon. *1 Corinthians*. Tyndale New Testament Commentaries. Leicester, England: InterVarsity Press, 1995. 223.

The New Oxford Annotated Bible. New Revised Standard Version. New York: Oxford University Press, Inc., 2001. 386–87.

Rainbow Study Bible. New International Version. Grand Rapids, MI: Zondervan Bible Publishers, 1992. 1378–79.

Unger, Merrill F. *The New Unger's Bible Handbook*. Chicago, IL: Moody Press, 1998. 635–36.

Say It Correctly

Paradox. **PAIR**-uh-docks.

Platonist. **PLAY**-ton-ist.

Pythagoreans. Puh-**THAH**-gore-**EE**-ans.

Daily Bible Readings

MONDAY
From Death to Life in Christ
(1 Corinthians 15:16-23)

TUESDAY
Strengthening the Inner Being
(Ephesians 3:14-21)

WEDNESDAY
Every Deed, Good or Evil, Judges
(Ecclesiastes 12:9-14)

THURSDAY
God's Judgment of Human
Behavior Impartial
(Romans 2:4-11)

FRIDAY
Paul, Confident in the Ministry
(2 Corinthians 4:1-6)

SATURDAY
Entering the Presence of Jesus
(2 Corinthians 4:7-15)

SUNDAY
Live the Faith with Confidence
(2 Corinthians 4:16–5:10)

Notes

_____

_____

_____

_____

A

Abomination: A foul and detestable thing

Affliction: Anguish, burden, persecution, tribulation, or trouble

Angel: A messenger of God, not eternal or all-knowing; specific types include cherubim and seraphim

Ascension: Raising up in authority or physical place. Can especially refer to the event forty days after Jesus' death, burial, and Resurrection, when He returned to heaven to sit at the right hand of the Father (Acts 1:9–11)

Atone: To propitiate, satisfy the demands of an offended holy God; or reconcile to a holy God after sin

B

Baptize: To dip, immerse, or submerge

Blameless: Irreproachable, faultless, flawless

Blessedness: Happiness, joy, or prosperity, to be well spoken of by God or others

Bless the Lord: To bend the knee in praise to God

Blood of the Lamb: The blood that Jesus shed on the Cross that redeems humanity

Bowels: To ancient Middle Easterners, the place of emotion, distress, or love

C

Called by God: Appointed or commissioned to fulfill a task

Charge: Admonish, order, command

Chosen: To be approved and selected by God

Christ: The Anointed One, the expected Messiah the Jews hoped for and whom Christians believe came as Jesus of Nazareth

Commandments: God's mandates; the entire body of Laws issued by God through Moses for Israel

Conduct: Manner of living

Confess: To acknowledge or fully agree

Consider: To determine or make out

Covenant: An agreement or promise between God and humanity based on God's character, strength, and grace

Crucifixion: A method of Roman execution in which a criminal was hung on a cross

D

Decalogue: From "ten words" in Greek; the Ten Commandments

Desolation: The state of being deserted or uninhabited

Disciples: Learners, students, followers

Dominion: Rule or reign

Dwelling place: A person's refuge or home

E

El: The Hebrew word for "god" or "mighty one"

Evil: Bad, unpleasant, or displeasing things

Evil doer: A malefactor, wrongdoer, criminal, troublemaker

Evil spirits: Messengers and ministers of the devil

Exalt: To raise up to the highest degree possible

Exhortation: Giving someone motivation to change his or her behavior either by rebuke or encouragement

F

Faithfulness: Steadfastness, steadiness

Fear of the Lord: Reverence or awe of who God is, resulting in obedience to Him and abstaining from evil

G

Glory: Splendor, unparalleled honor, dignity, or distinction; praise and worship

God's bride: The Church

God's own hand: God's strength, power

Gospel: The Good News of Jesus the Messiah's arrival and presence of His kingdom

Graven image: An idol cut (often from stone, wood, or metal) and worshiped as a god

Great Tribulation: A time of great suffering that has not been experienced since the world began (Matthew 24:21, Revelation 7:14)

H

Hallowed: Consecrated, dedicated, or set apart

Hear: Listen to, yield to, or obey

Hearken: Pay attention to, give attention to

Heart: The figurative place of emotion and passion

Heathens: The Gentiles, all those who are not a part of the people of God

Holy: Anything consecrated and set aside for sacred use; set apart from sin

Honor: To revere or value

Host: An army or a vast number

I

Idolatry: The worship of anything other than God

Infidel: One who is unfaithful, unbelieving, and not to be trusted

Iniquity: Perversity, depravity, guilt, sin

J

Just: Righteous, that which is right and fair
Justice: Righteousness in government

K

Kingdom of Christ: The rule and reign of Christ as King both now and in the age to come

L

Law: Either the Mosiac Law or any human law; synonyms include commandments, ordinances, statutes, legal regulations, authoritative instructions, and teachings
Logos (LOW-gos): (Gk.) Word; the Word of God, either the Bible or Jesus

M

Manna: Food from heaven baked into a kind of bread, which God miraculously gave to the Israelites in the wilderness
Messiah: The Anointed One
Minister: A servant, an attendant, one who executes the commands of another
Mosiac Law: The law passed down by Moses from God to the Hebrew people at Mt. Sinai

O

Omnipotent: All-powerful
Omnipresent: All-present, being everywhere
Omniscient: All-knowing
Ordained: Established and founded by God; founded, fixed, or appointed

P

Parousia (par-oo-SEE-ah): (Gk.) presence, appearing; Christ's Second Coming
Peace: Wholeness, quietness, contentment, health, prosperity; more than an absence of conflict or problems, but every part of life being blessed
Pentateuch: The first five books of the Old Testament
Power: Boldness, might, or strength, especially God's
Prophets: People filled with the Spirit of God and under the authority and command of God, who pleaded His cause and urged humanity to be saved
Profit: To gain or benefit to succeed, especially in Spiritual things; to move forward or succeed in one's efforts
Prosper: Examined, tested, tried
Psalm: A piece of music or a melody, especially one dedicated to God or a god
Purity: Sinlessness, without blemish spiritually

R

Ransom: To buy back or pay a price for a person, buying their freedom
Redeem: To ransom or purchase
Refuge: A shelter from rain, storm, or danger; stronghold or fortress; a place to run to and be secure when the enemy threatens
Repent: To turn back from sin and turn to God in faith
Righteous: To be declared not guilty
Righteousness: Justness, rightness, especially God's, which He works as a gift in His people; the right way to live as opposed to a lifestyle that treats others unfairly or unjustly

S

Sabbath: From "ceasing (from work)" in Hebrew; the day set aside to worship God
Sanctuary: The holy place, either in the Tabernacle or the Temple
Salvation: Rescue, safety, or deliverance, especially from eternal punishment
Satan: A fallen angel who is opposed to God and His people
Savior: Defender, rescuer, or deliverer; a term applied to Christ as the rescuer of those who are in bondage to sin and death
Scribes: Secretaries, recorders, men skilled in the Law during Jesus' day
Selah (SEH-lah): (Heb.) A pause in singing to allow for an instrumental musical interlude or silent meditation
Septuagint: "Seventy" in Latin; the Greek translation of the Hebrew Old Testament made by 70 Jewish scholars beginning in the third century BC
Servant: A slave, subject, or worshiper
Shalom (sha-LOME): (Heb.) Peace, prosperity, blessing
Shekinah Glory: The awesome presence of the Lord; His honor, fame, and reputation
Shofar (sho-FAR): (Heb.) A ram's horn; commonly used in celebration, as well as in signaling armies or large groups of people in civil assembly
Soul: The immaterial part of a person (what leaves the body after death), or the whole being, the self, one's life
Stiffnecked: Obstinate and difficult
Strengthen: To secure, make firm
Strive: To struggle, to exert oneself
Supplication: Seeking, asking, entreating, pleading, imploring, or petitioning

T

Tabernacle: A tent; the name of the portable temple constructed by Moses and the people of Israel

Tetragrammaton: YHWH; the four consonants of God's name, as the Jews would often write it

Torah: (Heb.) Law, instrument, or direction; the first five books of the Old Testament

Transfiguration: A change or transformation. Often refers to Jesus' transformation while on the Mount of Olives with His disciples Peter, James, and John, when His face shone like the sun and His clothing was white as snow (Matthew 17:2; Mark 9:2; Luke 9:29)

Transgression: Sin, rebellion, breaking God's Law

Try: In the sense of a test, to refine or purify

Trumpet: A ram's horn or simple metal tube used in celebration as well as in signaling armies or large groups of people in civil assembly

V

Vanity (vain): A waste, a worthless thing, or simply emptiness

W

Wisdom: Prudence, an understanding of ethics

Woe: Grief or sorrow

Worship: Bow down deeply, show obedience and reverence

Wrath: Burning anger, rage

Y

Yahweh: God's name, often spelled with consonants only (see Tetragrammaton)